ISBN 978-1-332-31198-9
PIBN 10312531

1 MONTH OF
FREE
READING

at

www.ForgottenBooks.com

By purchasing this book you are eligible for one month membership to ForgottenBooks.com, giving you unlimited access to our entire collection of over 700,000 titles via our web site and mobile apps.

To claim your free month visit:
www.forgottenbooks.com/free312531

English
Français
Deutsche
Italiano
Español
Português

www.forgottenbooks.com

Mythology Photography **Fiction**
Fishing Christianity **Art** Cooking
Essays Buddhism Freemasonry
Medicine **Biology** Music **Ancient**
Egypt Evolution Carpentry Physics
Dance Geology **Mathematics** Fitness
Shakespeare **Folklore** Yoga Marketing
Confidence Immortality Biographies
Poetry **Psychology** Witchcraft
Electronics Chemistry History **Law**
Accounting **Philosophy** Anthropology
Alchemy Drama Quantum Mechanics
Atheism Sexual Health **Ancient History**
Entrepreneurship Languages Sport
Paleontology Needlework Islam
Metaphysics Investment Archaeology
Parenting Statistics Criminology
Motivational

A HISTORY

OF

THE PAPACY

DURING

THE PERIOD OF THE REFORMATION

BY

M. CREIGHTON, M.A.

LATE FELLOW OF MERTON COLLEGE, OXFORD

VOL. II.

THE COUNCIL OF BASEL—THE PAPAL RESTORATION

1418—1464

CONTENTS

OF

THE SECOND VOLUME.

———◦◦———

BOOK III.

THE COUNCIL OF BASEL.

1419–1447.

CHAPTER I.

MARTIN V. AND ITALIAN AFFAIRS.

1419–1425.

CHAPTER IV.

FIRST ATTEMPT OF EUGENIUS IV. TO DISSOLVE THE COUNCIL OF BASEL.

1431–1434.

CHAPTER V.

THE COUNCIL OF BASEL AND THE HUSSITES.

1432–1434.

CHAPTER VI.

EUGENIUS IV. AND THE COUNCIL OF BASEL.

NEGOTIATIONS WITH THE GREEKS AND THE BOHEMIANS.

1434–1436.

CONTENTS OF THE SECOND VOLUME.

CHAPTER VII.

WAR BETWEEN THE POPE AND THE COUNCIL.

1436–1438.

CHAPTER VIII.

EUGENIUS IV. IN FLORENCE.

THE UNION OF THE GREEK CHURCH.

1434–1439.

CHAPTER IX.

THE GERMAN DECLARATION OF NEUTRALITY.

ELECTION OF FELIX V.

1438–1439.

CHAPTER X.

EUGENIUS IV. AND FELIX V.

1440–1444.

BOOK IV.

THE PAPAL RESTORATION.

1444–1464.

CHAPTER I.

ÆNEAS SYLVIUS PICCOLOMINI AND THE RESTORATION OF THE OBEDIENCE OF GERMANY.

1444–1447.

CHAPTER II.

NICOLAS V. AND THE AFFAIRS OF GERMANY.

1447–1453.

CHAPTER III.

NICOLAS V. AND THE FALL OF CONSTANTINOPLE.

1453-1455.

CHAPTER IV.

NICOLAS V. AND THE REVIVAL OF LEARNING.

CHAPTER V.

CALIXTUS III.

1455–1458.

CHAPTER VI.

PIUS II. AND THE CONGRESS OF MANTUA.

1458–1460.

CHAPTER VII.

PIUS II. AND THE AFFAIRS OF NAPLES AND GERMANY.

1460–1461.

CHAPTER VIII.

PIUS II.'S RELATIONS TO FRANCE AND BOHEMIA.

1461-1464.

CHAPTER IX.

CRUSADE AND DEATH OF PIUS II.

1464.

APPENDIX.

Errata in Vol. II.

Page   9, line 14 from top, *for* 'Montefiasone' *read* 'Montefiascone'
  „   64, line 9 from bottom, *for* 'purification' *read* 'pacification
  „   107, line 10 from top, *for* 'Toh' *read* 'Tok'
  „   112, margin, *for* '1484' *read* '1434'
  „   122, margin, *for* 'January' *read* 'June'
  „   170, lines 15 and 12 from bottom, *for* 'Sicily' *read* 'Naples'
  „   174, margin, *for* 'Vienna' *read* 'Venice'
  „   196, line 9 from bottom, *for* 'Boniface XIII.' *read* 'Benedict XIII.'

BOOK III.

THE COUNCIL OF BASEL.

1419–1444.

VOL. II.

CHAPTER I.

1418–1425.

On leaving Constance Martin V. felt himself for the first time free. He had been taught by the events of the last four years that freedom was only possible for a Pope in Italy, in spite of all the temporary inconveniences which might arise from Italian politics. But much as he might desire to find himself in his native city, and revive the glories of the Papacy in its old historic seat, he could not immediately proceed to Rome. John XXIII. had abandoned Rome, and had been driven even to flee from Bologna, owing to his political helplessness and the power of his opponent Ladislas. The death of Ladislas and the abeyance of the Papacy had only plunged Italian affairs into deeper confusion, and Martin V. had to pause a while and consider how he could best return to Italy.

Through the Swiss cantons Martin made a triumphal progress, and had no reason to complain of want of respect or lack of generosity. On June 11 he reached Geneva, and in the city of the prince-bishop he stayed for three months; there he had the satisfaction of receiving the allegiance of the citizens of Avignon. He seems to have wished to display himself as much as possible, and exert the prestige of the restored Papacy to secure his position. At the end of September he moved slowly from Geneva through Savoy to Turin, and thence through Pavia to Milan, where he was received with great honour by Filippo Maria Visconti on October 12. So great was the popular curiosity to see the Pope that when he went to consecrate a new altar in the cathedral, several people were trampled to

CHAP. I.

Martin V. journeys to Italy, 1418.

Martin V. takes up his residence in Florence, February 1419.

death in the throng.[1]   At Milan Martin V. showed his desire
for the pacification of Italy by making terms between Filippo
Maria and Pandolfo Malatesta, who had seized on Brescia.[2]
There, too, he received ambassadors from the Florentines, who,
in their capacity of peacemakers, were anxious to arrange
matters so as to enable the Pope to return quietly to Rome.
They offered him a refuge in their city and also their services
as mediators.[3]   On October 19 Martin V. left Milan for Brescia,
and on October 25 he entered Mantua.   There he stayed
till the end of the year seeking for some means to make
the Papal influence a real power in Italian affairs.   At length
he resolved to accept the services of the Florentines, and set
out for their city, avoiding on his way the rebellious Bologna,
which had cast off the Papal rule.   On February 26, 1419, he
entered Florence, where he was honourably received, and took
up his abode in the monastery of Santa Maria Novella.

Fortunes of
Naples.
1414–1416.

The condition of Italy was indeed sufficiently disturbed to
need all the efforts of the Pope and of Florence to reduce it to
order and peace.   In Lombardy, Filippo Maria, Duke of Milan,
was bent on winning back the lands of his father Giangaleazzo,
which had fallen into the hands of petty tyrants.   Southern
Italy was thrown into confusion by the death of Ladislas, who
was succeeded in the kingdom of Naples by his sister Giovanna II., a woman with none of the qualities of a ruler, who used
her position solely as a means of personal gratification.   The
death of Louis of Anjou gave every hope of a peaceful reign to
the distracted Neapolitan kingdom ; but Giovanna's ungovern-
able passions soon made it a sphere of personal intrigue.   At
first the Queen, a widow of forty-seven years old, was under the
control of a lover, Pandolfello Alapo, whom she made Chamberlain and covered with her favours.   To maintain his position
against the discontented barons, Alapo formed an alliance with
Sforza, who was made Grand Constable of Naples.   But the
barons insisted that the Queen should marry, and in 1415 she
chose for her husband Jacques de Bourbon, Count of La Marche.

---

[1] See for a description of the ceremonies, Corio, *Storia di Milano*, part iv.
ch. 2.

[2] Platina, *Hist. Mantuana*, in Muratori, xx. 800.

[3] *Commissioni di Rinaldo degli Albizzi* (i. 296, &c.) gives a full account of
these negotiations.

The barons sided with the Count of La Marche, who, by their help, imprisoned Sforza, put Alapo to death, and exercised the power of King. The favour, however, which he showed to his own countrymen the French disgusted the Neapolitan nobles, and in 1416 Giovanna was able again to assert her own power. By this time she had a new favourite to direct her, Giovanni Caraccioli, who drove the King to leave Naples, and thought it wise also to find an occupation for Sforza which would keep him at a distance. For this purpose he sent him on an expedition against Braccio, who had attacked the States of the Church and had advanced against Rome.

Andrea Braccio, of the family of the Counts of Montone, was a noble Perugian who, in his youth, had been driven by party struggles to leave his native city, and had embraced the calling of a condottiere under Alberigo de Barbiano. He served on many sides in the Italian wars, and finally was in the pay of Ladislas, who played him false in an attack upon Perugia; whereon Braccio joined the side of John XXII., who left him governor of Bologna when he set out for Constance. Braccio was possessed with a desire to make himself master of his native city of Perugia, and in 1416 sold the Bolognese their liberty and hired soldiers on every side. He defeated Carlo Malatesta,[1] whom the Perugians called to their aid, and in July 1416 made himself master of the city. Soon, desirous of enlarging his territory, he advanced into the States of the Church. Todi, Rieti, and Narni soon fell before him, and he pressed on to the neighbourhood of Rome. But Braccio, to win Perugia, had drawn to his side the condottiere-general Tartaglia, who stipulated, in return for his services, that Braccio should not oppose him in attacking the dominions of Sforza. From that time Sforza conceived a deadly hatred against Braccio, and for the next few years the history of Italy is an account of the desperate rivalry of these two rival condottieri.

Rome during the abeyance of the Papacy was left in an anomalous condition. The Castle of S. Angelo, which had been taken by Ladislas, was still held by a Neapolitan governor.

Rise of Braccio.

Braccio in Rome, 1417.

---

[1] A picture by Paolo Uccelli in the National Gallery commemorates this celebrated battle, fought near Assisi on the Tiber, close to Sant' Egidio. Carlo Malatesta and his nephew were made prisoners.

John XXIII. on departing for Constance had appointed Cardinal Isolani his legate in Rome; and he was assisted, or hindered, by the presence of the Cardinal of S. Angelo, Pietro degli Stefanacci, who found Rome preferable to Constance.[1] The legate Isolani managed to retain considerable influence over the Romans, and induced them to carry on the government of the city according to the constitution established before the interference of Ladislas. But Rome was in no condition to offer resistance to Braccio when he advanced against it, and on June 9, 1417, took up his position by S. Agnese. In vain the legate tried to negotiate for his departure. Braccio harried the adjacent country, and reduced the Romans to capitulate through hunger. He had an ally in the Cardinal Stefanacci, who welcomed him on his triumphal entry on June 16 and helped him to form a new magistracy. The legate fled into the Castle of S. Angelo, and begged for help from Naples. His entreaties were heard, as Sforza was burning for revenge against Braccio, and Giovanna's new favourite, Caraccioli, was looking about for some means of getting rid of Sforza, whose manly frame might soon prove too attractive to the susceptible Queen. Braccio was engaged in besieging the Castle of S. Angelo when the arrival of Sforza on August 10 warned him of his danger. Sforza seeing how matters stood, went to Ostia, and crossed the Tiber without hindrance. When Braccio heard that he was advancing against him, he judged it unwise to risk the loss of his newly-won possessions, and on August 26 withdrew to Perugia. Sforza entered Rome in triumph with the banners of Naples and of the Church. He restored the legate Isolani to power, appointed new magistrates, and imprisoned the traitorous Cardinal of S. Angelo, who died soon afterwards.

Alliance of
Martin V.
with Gio-
vanna II.
of Naples.
1419.

Such was the condition of affairs which Martin V. had to face on his election. It was natural that his first movement should be towards alliance with Giovanna II. of Naples, seeing

---

[1] That his presence in Rome was for no good we gather from many mentions in the *Diarium Antonii Petri* (Mur. xxiv.) The following, p. 1061, may suffice : ' Statim quod supradictus Dominus Stephanus Barbarini descendit de Sanula fuit interfectus absque ulla mora, et hoc fecerunt familiares Domini Cardinalis de Sancto Angelo de mandato suo quia supradictus Stephanus ibat ad supponendum concubinam dicti Cardinalis de Sancto Angelo.' Stefano was a canon of St. Peter's.

that the Neapolitan influence seemed most powerful in Rome. He welcomed Giovanna's ambassadors and sent a cardinal to arrange matters with the Queen as early as May 1418. Giovanna agreed to restore all the possessions of the Church and make a perpetual alliance with the Pope, who was to crown her Queen of Naples. She gave a pledge of her sincerity by the usual means of enriching the Pope's relations. Martin's brother, Giordano Colonna, was made Duke of Amalfi and Venosa, his nephew Antonio was made Grand Chamberlain of Naples; and on August 21, appeared with a Bull announcing the Pope's alliance with Giovanna.[1] Antonio at first attached himself to the favourite Caraccioli; but before the end of the year Sforza was strong enough to organise a popular rising against the favourite, who was forced to leave Naples and was sent as ambassador to Martin V. at Mantua. There the surrender of the fortresses which the Neapolitans occupied in the States of the Church and the coronation of Giovanna were finally arranged. Early in 1419 a Papal Legate was sent to Naples to perform the coronation.

Thus matters stood when Martin V. took refuge in Florence. He could do nothing better than await the course of events in Naples and the results of the Florentine mediation. Return to Rome with Braccio hostile was impossible. If Braccio were to be overthrown, it could only be by the arms of Sforza; but the Pope's first steps had been to ally with Giovanna and Caraccioli, with whom Sforza was now at enmity. At Florence Martin V.'s prestige was increased by the arrival of four of Benedict XIII.'s cardinals, who were solemnly received on March 17. So far as Italy was concerned, Martin V. had nothing to fear from Peter de Luna. But the deposed Baldassare Cossa was still an object of his dread, for Braccio had threatened to espouse Cossa's cause, and might again raise him to the position of a dangerous rival. Accordingly, Martin V. was very anxious to get Cossa into his hands, and the Florentines in the interests of peace were desirous that this matter should be arranged. John XXIII., when legate of Bologna, had always been on good terms with the Florentines, and had stood in friendly relations with several of the richest citizens, amongst whom were Giovanni dei Medici and Niccolo da Uzzano, who were now ready to

Submission
of Baldas-
sare Cossa
to Martin
V. June 1,
1419.

---

[1] *Giornali Napolitani* (Mur. xxi.), p. 1080.

interfere on his behalf. They procured from Martin V. a promise that he would deal gently with his deposed predecessor, and advanced the sum of 38,500 Rhenish ducats to buy the release of Cossa from Lewis of Bavaria, in whose custody he was.[1] On his way to Florence Cossa was escorted by the Bishop of Lübeck, who was charged by Martin V. to keep a sharp eye upon him. At Parma he lodged with an old friend, who alarmed him with rumours that Martin V. meant to have him imprisoned for life at Mantua. He fled by night to Genoa, where he found protection from the Doge, Tommaso di Campo Fregoso. Friends quickly gathered round him, urging him once more to try his fortunes and assert his claims to the Papacy.[2] For a brief space there was a thrill of horror lest the miseries of the Schism should again begin. But the wise counsels of Giovanni dei Medici and his Florentine friends seem to have prevailed with Cossa; they assured him of his safety and urged him to fulfil his promise. John XXIII. no longer possessed his former vigour or felt his old confidence in himself and his fortunes. The helplessness which had overtaken him at Constance still haunted him, and though the old spirit might rekindle for a moment, it was soon chilled by doubt and hesitation. He judged it wisest to trust his friends, proceed to Florence, and submit to the mercy of Martin V. On June 14 he entered Florence, and was received with respectful pity by the entire body of the citizens. The sight of one who had fallen from a high degree kindled their sympathy, and Cossa's poor apparel and miserable look impressed more vividly the sense of his changed fortunes. On June 27, he appeared before Martin V. in full consistory, and kneeling before him made his submission. 'I alone,' he said, 'assembled the Council; I always laboured for the good of the Church; you know the truth. I come to your Holiness and rejoice as much as I can at your elevation and my own freedom.' Here his voice was broken with passion; his haughty nature could ill brook his humiliation. Martin V. received him graciously, and placed on his

---

[1] ' Documenti relativi alla liberazione della prigionia di Giovanni XXIII.,' in *Archivio Storico Italiano*, vol. iv. part i. (first series) p. 429.

[2] These details are to be found in Platina, *Vita Martini V.*; Leon.-Aretin. *Commentarii* (Mur. xix. 930); *Vita Martini V.* (Mur. iii. part ii. 863), and the note of Mansi to Raynaldus, *Annales*, No. 6 *sub anno*.

head the cardinal's hat. But Cossa did not long live under the shadow of his successor. He died in the same year on December 23, and his Florentine friends were faithful to his memory. In the stately Baptistery of Florence the Medici erected to him a splendid tomb. The recumbent figure cast in bronze was the work of Donatello, and the marble pedestal which supports it was wrought by Michelozzo. It bears the simple inscription 'Johannes quondam Papa XXIII. obiit Florentiæ.'

Martin V.'s attention was meanwhile directed to the kingdom of Naples, and he urged on Giovanna II. the duty of restoring to his obedience the States of the Church. Giovanna was not sorry to rid herself of Sforza, for she longed to recall her favourite Caraccioli. Sforza was despatched to war against Braccio, but on June 20 was defeated at Montefiasone near Viterbo. But Martin V. was enabled to detached Tartaglia from Braccio's side, and Sforza could again set an army in the field in the name of Naples and the Pope. He was not, however, supported from Naples; for Giovanna had recalled Caraccioli, and the favourite thought it better to leave Sforza to his fate. Martin V. saw that nothing was to be gained from a further alliance with Giovanna II. and Caraccioli. Moreover, the question of the Neapolitan succession was again imminent, for Giovanna was over fifty years of age, and was childless. Louis III. of Anjou had already begged Martin V. to procure from Giovanna II. a formal recognition of his claim, and Martin V. judged that the opportunity was favourable for action. Sforza was weary of the selfish policy of Caraccioli, and the Neapolitan barons resented the rule of the insolent favourite. The Florentines offered Martin V. their aid to mediate between him and Braccio. The Pope saw an opportunity of making himself the central figure in the politics of Southern Italy. At peace with Braccio and allied with Sforza, he might settle the succession to Naples in favour of Louis of Anjou, and end the Neapolitan difficulty which had so long harassed his predecessors.

In January 1420 Sforza paid Martin V. a visit in Florence, and the Pope broached his views, to which with some reluctance Sforza gave his adhesion. Scarcely had Sforza departed before Braccio at the end of February made a triumphal entry into Florence, there to celebrate his reconciliation with the Pope.

With a splendid escort of four hundred horsemen and forty
foot, with deputies from the various cities under his rule,
Braccio entered the city in grandeur that awoke the enthusiastic acclamations of the Florentines. In the middle of the
bands of horsemen, gleaming in gold and silver armour, mounted
on splendid steeds richly caparisoned, rode Braccio, clad in
purple and gold, on a steed whose trappings were of gold. He
was a man rather above the middle height, with an oval face
that seemed too full of blood, yet with a look of dignity and
power that, in spite of his limbs maimed with wounds, marked
him as a ruler of men.[1] Amid the shouts of the thronging
citizens Braccio visited the Pope, and paid him haughty reverence. After a few days spent in negotiations, an alliance was
made between Martin V. and Braccio, by which Braccio was
left in possession of Perugia, Assisi, and other towns which he
had won, on condition of reducing Bologna to obedience to the
Pope.

Martin V.'s pride was sorely hurt by the avowed preference
which the Florentines showed to the condottiere over the Pope.
The Florentine boys expressed the common feeling by a doggrel
rhyme which they sang in the streets, and which soon reached
the ears of the sensitive Pope :—

> Braccio valente
> Vince ogni gente ;
> Il Papa Martino
> Non vale un quattrino.

> Braccio the Great
> Conquers every state :
> Poor Pope Martin
> Is not worth a farthing.

He was glad to see Braccio leave Florence, and hoped that the
task of reducing Bologna would occupy him long enough to
enable Sforza to make his attack on Giovanna unimpeded by
Braccio's hostility.[2] Braccio, however, rapidly gathered his forces
and conducted matters with such skill that on July 22 the Pope's
legate took possession of Bologna.[3]

---

[1] A full account of Braccio's entering into Florence, which abounds in
interesting details, is given in Campanus, *Vita Brachii*, Mur. xix. 562.

[2] Campanus, *Vita Brachii*, Mur. xix. 566.

[3] *Chronica Novella di Bologna*, Mur. xviii. 611.

Meanwhile Sforza hastened the preparations against Giovanna II. On June 18 he suddenly raised the standard of the Duke of Anjou, and began to make war against Naples: on August 19 ten Angevin galleys made their appearance off the Neapolitan coast. Louis of Anjou eagerly caught at Martin V.'s offer of protection; he did not scruple to leave France in the hands of the English, and abandon his land of Provence to the hostile attacks of the Duke of Savoy, that he might pursue the phantom kingdom of Naples, which had proved disastrous to his father and his grandfather alike.

CHAP. I.

Sforza declares for Louis III. of Anjou. June, 1420.

Giovanna II., seeing herself thus threatened, cast about on her part also for allies. She sent an ambassador to the Pope, whose hostility was not yet declared; but the subtle Neapolitan easily saw through the Pope's equivocal answers to his demands. There was in Florence at the Papal Court an ambassador of Alfonso V. of Aragon. To him in his strait the Neapolitan turned. He reminded him that the House of Aragon had as good a claim to Naples as the House of Anjou. Giovanna II. was childless, and could dispose of her kingdom as she chose; if Alfonso succoured her in her strait, he might count upon her gratitude. This proposal was very acceptable to Alfonso V., a young and ambitious king. By the death of Martin of Sicily without children in 1409 the kingdom of Sicily had been attached to that of Aragon, and Alfonso was keenly alive to the advantage of annexing Naples also. At the time that Giovanna's offer reached him he was engaged in prosecuting against the Genoese his claims on the island of Corsica, where, after a long siege, the desperate efforts of the Genoese threatened to render his undertaking hopeless. His ambassador at Florence was endeavouring to obtain from Martin V. a recognition of Alfonso's claim to Corsica; but Alfonso V. at once saw the policy of abandoning a doubtful attempt upon a barren island for the more alluring prize of the Neapolitan kingdom. He despatched from Corsica to the relief of Giovanna II. fifteen galleys, which arrived off Naples on September 6, and Giovanna II. showed her gratitude by adopting him as her son.

Alliance of Giovanna II. with Alfonso V. of Aragon. 1420.

War was now let loose upon Naples. Alfonso and Giovanna sought to strengthen themselves by an alliance with Braccio. Martin V.'s policy had succeeded in providing occupation for all whom he had most to dread. He was now in a position

Discontent of Martin V. with the Florentines.

to take advantage of the general confusion, and amid the weakness of all parties raise once more the prestige of the Papal name. He had gained all that was to be gained from a stay in Florence, and might now with safety venture to Rome. More-over, Martin V. was not over-satisfied with the impression which he had produced on the Florentines. The common sense of the quick-witted commercial city was not taken in by high-sounding claims or magnificent ecclesiastical processions. The Florentines had shown for Braccio an admiration which they refused to Martin V. However much Martin might wrap him-self in his dignity, and affect to despise popular opinion, he yet felt that in Florence nothing succeeded like success, and that a fortunate freebooter ranked above a landless Pope. The bustling, pushing spirit of a prosperous commercial city was alien to the Papacy, which could only flourish amongst the traditions and aspirations of the past. A few days before his departure from Rome Martin V. could not refrain from showing his wounded pride to Leonardo Bruni who was present in the library of S. Maria Novella. For some time Martin V. walked gloomily up and down the room, gazing out of the window upon the garden below. At last he stopped before Leonardo, and in a voice quivering with scorn repeated the doggrel of the Florentine mob, ' Poor Pope Martin isn't worth a farthing.' Leonardo tried to appease him by saying that such trifles were not worthy of notice; but the Pope again repeated the lines in the same tone. Anxious for the fair fame of Florence, Leonardo at once undertook its defence, and pointed out to the Pope the practical advantages which he had derived from his stay—the recovery of some of the States of the Church, and especially of Bologna, the submission of John XXIII., the reconciliation with Braccio. Where else, he asked, could such advantages have been so easily obtained? The Pope's gloomy brow grew clearer before the words of the Florentine secretary.[1] Martin V. departed with goodwill from Florence; thanked its magis-trates for their kind offices, and marked his gratitude to the city by erecting the bishopric of Florence to the dignity of an archbishopric.

On September 9 Martin V. departed from Florence with due

---

[1] Leonardo, in his *Comm*, Mur. xix. 931, gives a vivid account of this curious and characteristic scene.

respect from the citizens. On September 20 he was honourably received in Siena, and used his opportunity to borrow 15,000 florins, for which he gave Spoleto as a pledge.[1] From Siena he proceeded through Viterbo to Rome, which he entered on September 28, and took up his abode by S. Maria del Popolo. Next day he was escorted to the Vatican by the city magistrates and the people, bearing lighted torches and clamorous with joy. The Romans had indeed occasion to hail any change that might restore their shattered fortunes. Everything that had happened in late years had tended to plunge them deeper and deeper in misery and ruin. The havoc wrought by the invasions of Ladislas, of Sforza, and of Braccio, the absence of the Pope, and consequent loss of traffic, the want of all authority in the Papal States, the pillage that wasted up to the walls of Rome—all these combined to reduce the city to wretchedness and desolation. Martin V. found Rome so devastated that it hardly looked like a city. Houses were in decay, churches in ruins, the streets were empty, filth and dirt were everywhere, food was so scarce and dear that men could barely keep themselves alive. Civilisation seemed almost extinct. The Romans looked like the scum of the earth.[2] Martin V. had a hard task before him to bring back order and decency into the ruined city. It was his great merit that he set himself diligently to put matters straight, and that he succeeded in reclaiming its capital for the restored Papacy. His first care was to provide for the administration of justice, and put down the robbers who infested Rome and its neighbourhood, for the purpose of pillaging the pious pilgrims who visited the tombs of the Apostles.[3] But much had to be done to repair the ravages of preceding years, and new disasters rendered the task more difficult. In November 1422 the town was overwhelmed by a flood in the Tiber, occasioned by Braccio's destruction of the wall of the Lago di Pie di Luco, the old Veline Lake. The water rose to the height of the high altar in the Pantheon, and as it subsided carried away the flocks from the fields and caused great destruction of property.

In Naples little was done worthy of the great efforts which

CHAP. I.

Martin V. takes up his abode in Rome. September 1420.

---

[1] *Annali Senesi*, Mur. xix. 428.

[2] This description, which may perhaps be rhetorical, is taken from Platina, *Vita Martini*.

[3] Infessura, *Diarium*, Mur. III. part ii. p. 1122.

were made. Alfonso's reinforcements checked the victorious career of Louis of Anjou and Sforza, till in June, 1421, Braccio brought his forces to Giovanna's aid, Alfonso himself arrived in Naples, and the Pope despatched Tartaglia to the aid of Louis. Alfonso and Braccio engaged in a fruitless siege of Acerra. Nothing serious was done, as the condottieri generals were engaged in a series of intrigues against one another. Sforza accused Tartaglia of treachery, seized him, and put him to death. Tartaglia's soldiers, indignant at the treatment of their leader, joined Braccio, who was anxious only to secure his own principality of Capua. Martin V. was weary of finding supplies, and was embarrassed by Alfonso's threats that he would again recognise Benedict XIII. Caraccioli was afraid of Alfonso's resolute character, and sowed discord between him and Giovanna: Alfonso on his part was perplexed by the Queen's doubtful attitude towards him. As everyone had his own reasons for desiring peace, the Pope's mediation was accepted for that purpose in March, 1422. Aversa and Castellamare, the only two places which Louis held, were surrendered to the Papal Legate, who soon afterwards gave them over to the Queen. Braccio and Sforza were outwardly reconciled, and Sforza joined the side of Giovanna, only with the purpose of favouring more surely the party of Louis. Louis himself withdrew to Rome, where he lived for two years at the Pope's expense, awaiting the

results of Sforza's machinations. But this peace and its reconciliations were alike hollow. The mutual suspicions of Alfonso and Giovanna II. went on increasing till in May, 1423, Alfonso determined on a decisive blow. He suddenly imprisoned Caraccioli, and made a dash to obtain the person of the Queen, who was in the Castel Capuano at Naples. The attempt to surprise the Queen failed, and Alfonso besieged the Castle. But Sforza hastened to the Queen's aid, and, though his army was smaller than Alfonso's, he gave his men fresh courage by pointing to the splendid equipments of the Aragonese; raising the battle-cry, ' Fine clothes and good horses,' [1] he led his men to the charge. His inducement proved to be sufficiently strong; he won the day, and Alfonso in his turn was besieged in the Castel Nuovo. After this failure the fortunes of Louis of Anjou began to revive. Caraccioli was ransomed from prison, and he and

---

[1] 'A li ben vestiti, a li ben a cavalli.'—*Gior. Nap.*, Mur. xix. 1088.

Sforza urged Giovanna to cancel the adoption of the ungrateful Alfonso and accept Louis as her successor. At the end of June Louis arrived in Naples, and his adoption as Giovanna's heir was formally accomplished with the Pope's sanction.

Alfonso's hopes now rested on the prompt aid of Braccio; but Braccio entered the Neapolitan kingdom through the Abruzzi, and set himself to besiege the wealthy city of Aquila that he might obtain booty for his soldiers. The defence was obstinate, and the siege slowly dragged on. In vain Alfonso besought Braccio to quit it; the stubborn condottiere refused. Meanwhile Filippo Maria Visconti, who had by this time secured his possessions in Lombardy, and had moreover made himself master of Genoa, offered help to Giovanna. He did not wish that an active king like Alfonso should establish himself in Naples and urge troublesome claims to the Genoese possessions. Alfonso was afraid lest he might lose his command of the sea before the attack of the Genoese galleys; he also received disquieting news from Aragon. Weary with waiting for Braccio, who never came, he sailed away on October 15, and revenged himself on Louis by sacking Marseilles on his homeward voyage.

The departure of Alfonso relieved Martin V. of a troublesome enemy; but his attention in this year, 1423, had to be directed to an equally troublesome matter. It was now five years since the dissolution of the Council of Constance, and the period for holding the next Council had arrived. Already in 1422 the University of Paris sent ambassadors to urge Martin V. to fulfil his promise. Among the envoys of the University was a learned Dominican, John Stoikovic, a native of Ragusa in Dalmatia, who stayed at Rome to watch Martin's proceedings and be ready for the Council as soon as it was summoned.[1] Pavia had been fixed at Constance for its place of meeting; but in his letters of summons Martin V. was careful to express his fervour in behalf of the Council by saying that if Pavia was found unsuitable, he was resolved to call it to a more convenient place rather than it should dissolve.[2] The transalpine prelates were not inspirited by this kindly assurance; they felt that a Council in an Italian city was as good as useless. Martin V.

---

[1] *Mon. Concilium*, i. 10.
[2] Letters in *Raynaldi Annales*, 1423, 1.

had taken no steps in the way of reforming the abuses of
the Church. The state of Christendom was not favourable
for a Council. In England Henry V. was dead, and the
minority of Henry VI. had already begun to open up intrigues
and jealousies. France was exhausted by its war with England.
In Germany Sigismund was engaged in war with the Hussites
in Bohemia, and had no time to spend in talk. There was
nothing to encourage men to undertake the costly journey to
Italy, where Martin V. was likely to employ them on the barren
subject of a proposed union between the Eastern and Western
Churches.

When the Council was opened, on April 24, by the four
prelates whom the Pope had nominated as presidents, it was
not largely attended.[1] Few came from beyond the Alps, and
the absence of Italians showed that the Pope's influence was
used against the Council from the beginning. Scarcely were
the opening formalities at an end when the outbreak of the
plague gave a reason for removing elsewhere, and the Council
decided to go to Siena, where, on July 2, it resumed its labours.

The first step of the Council was to organise itself according
to nations, and to determine who should have the right of
voting. All prelates, abbots, graduates of universities who
were in orders, rectors, ambassadors of kings, barons, and
universities were to be admitted freely : other ecclesiastics
were to be judged of by the nation to which they belonged. Each
nation was to have a president elected every month, who, together with chosen deputies, was to prepare the business to be
discussed by the nation according to the wishes of the majority.
While making these arrangements the Council repeatedly sent
to the Pope urging him to come to Siena, and their request
was confirmed by the city magistrates, who showed themselves
amenable to the Pope's will by granting a safe-conduct in the
terms which he demanded.

But when the safe-conduct was known at Siena, the Fathers

---

[1] John of Ragusa (*Mon. Concil.* i. 10) says : ' Præsentibus quam plurimis
episcopis, abbatibus, prælatis, doctoribus et ambassiatoribus diversarum na-
tionum.' The author of the life of Martin in Mur. iii. 2, 865, says that there
were only two Burgundian abbots, and the country had to be scoured to raise
a decent number of ecclesiastics. Perhaps both writers are exaggerating on
their own side.

saw their liberty directly menaced by it. All magistrates and officials in the Sienese territory were to take oath of allegiance to the Pope, a proceeding which left the Council entirely at the Pope's mercy. Moreover, the members of the Council were to be subject to the jurisdiction of the Pope's officers. The whole tenor of the articles of agreement was insulting to the Council, and gave manifest signs of the Pope's ill-will. In its formal language the officials of the Curia were named before the members of the Council.[1] The energy of the Council was forthwith turned to negotiate with the Sienese for a safe-conduct which would give them greater security from the Pope. Meanwhile Martin V. showed himself more decidedly hostile, and his presidents used all efforts to weaken the Conciliar party. Letters from Rome poured in to Siena; tempting promises of promotion were held out to those who showed signs of wavering.

The reforming party felt that something must be done. They settled the matter of the safe-conduct, and agreed to pass some decrees on which there could be no difference of opinion. On November 6 a session of the Council was held, which declared that the work of reform must begin from the foundation of the faith, and consequently condemned the errors of Wyclif and Hus, denounced the partisans of Peter de Luna, approved of negotiations for union with the Greek Church, and exhorted all Christian men to root out heresy wherever they found it. After this, the reforming party urged that the work left unachieved at Constance should be resumed, and the French nation put forward a memorandum sketching a plan of reform according to the lines laid down at Constance. The Curial party resolved on resistance, and the small numbers present at Siena rendered personal pressure tolerably easy. John of Ragusa, though wishing to make the Council seem as numerous as possible, can only count two cardinals and twenty-five mitred prelates, as representatives of the higher clergy,[2] at the session in November 6. The Curial party thought it best to throw the machinery of the nations into confusion. They managed to

CHAP.
I.

Contest
about safe-
conduct.
August–
November,
1423.

Intrigues
of the
Curial
party.

---

[1] 'In omnibus officiales cameræ et sequentes eamdem, *in quorum numero sunt etiam lenones et meretrices,* patribus ad concilium venientibus præponuntur,' says John of Ragusa (*Mon. Con.* i. 20).

[2] *Mon. Concil.* i. 27 : he adds : 'Cum multitudine doctorum et magistrorum et ceterorum copiosa;' but this is in a letter written to urge the Bishop of Arras to attend the Council.

cause disputed elections to the office of president both in the
French and in the Italian nation in the month of January 1424.
The Papal legates offered their services to the French to judge
in this dispute. The French answered that, on matters concerning a nation in the Council, no one, not even the Pope,
could judge, but the Council itself: they asked the presidents
to summon a congregation for the purpose. The presidents
refused, whereupon the French called the other nations together on January 10, and afterwards drew up their grievances
in the shape of a protest, which they lodged with the legates.
Meanwhile the legates were busily engaged in strengthening
their party within each nation, so as to prevent any possibility
of unanimity. While thus the nations were divided, the
legates steadily pursued the dissolution of the Council, and,
as a first step towards this, urged the appointment of deputies to fix the meeting place of the next Council. This
question in itself aroused antagonism. The French wished the
future Council to be held in France. This excited the national
jealousy of the Germans and English. The Curial party openly
avowed that they never wished to see another Council at all,
and opposed the decrees of Constance.

The re-
formers
abandoned
by the
French.
February,
1424.
There were hopes, however, of renewed concord when, on
February 12, the Archbishop of Rouen and the ambassadors of
the University of Paris arrived at Siena. They interposed to
heal the dissension among the French, and the Archbishop of
Rouen was by a compromise elected to the office of president
of the French nation. The compromise was, however, fatal.
The Archbishop of Rouen had been already won over by the
legates, and the ambassadors of the University had a greater
desire to go to Rome and seek favours for themselves than stay
at Siena and watch over the reformation of the Church. On
February 19 deputies from all the nations agreed in choosing
Basel as the meeting place for the next Council to be held in
seven years.

The dissolution of the Council was now felt to be imminent.
Only a few zealous reformers had hopes of further business, and
they were aided by the citizens of Siena, who did not see why
they should not enjoy the same luck as Constance and reap a
golden harvest for some years to come. But Martin V. knew
how to address rebellious citizens. He sternly bade them 'not

to put their sickle into another's sheaves, nor think that General Councils were held or dissolved to please them or fill their pockets.'[1] Still the Sienese were resolved to make a last attempt, and on February 20 laid the Pope's letters before the nations, and shut their gates to prevent the desertions which were thinning the Council's ranks. But the reformers were not strong enough to accept the citizens' help; the Council sent to request the gates to be opened.

Meanwhile the legates were ready to dissolve the Council, the reformers were anxious to continue their work. At last, on March 7, the legates, taking advantage of the solitude produced by the festivities of the Carnival, posted on the door of the Cathedral a decree of the dissolution of the Council, which had been secretly drawn up on February 26, and prohibited all from attempting to continue it. On the same day they hastily left Siena for Florence. Those who remained were too few to hope to accomplish anything. Thomas, Abbot of Paisley, who was a member of the French nation, published an energetic protest against the dissolution, which was joined by a few other zealous reformers. Then on March 8 they held a meeting in which they decided that, to avoid scandal to the Church, and danger to themselves on account of the nearness of the Papal power, it was better to depart quietly. The Council of Siena came rapidly to an end, and Martin V. could plead the smallness of its numbers, its seditious conduct with the Sienese burghers, and its own internal disorders, as reasons for its dissolution. Really the Council of Siena followed too soon upon that of Constance. The position of affairs had not materially changed. The Pope had not yet recovered his normal position in Italy, and those who had been at Constance were not prepared to undertake the labours of a second Council, when they had nothing to give them any hopes of success. What was impossible with the help of Sigismund was not likely to be more possible in the face of Martin V.'s determined resistance.

Dissolution of the Council of Siena. March, 1424.

Martin V. judged it wise, however, to make some promises of reform. As the Council had been too full of disturbance to admit of any progress in the matter, he promised to undertake a reform of the Curia, and nominated two cardinals as commissioners to gather evidence. The results of Martin V.'s

Reform constitution of Martin V. 1425.

---

[1] Letter in Raynaldus, 1423, § 11; also in *Mon. Concil.* i. 50.

deliberations were embodied in a constitution, published on May 16, 1424. It reads as though it were the Pope's retaliation on the attempt made at Constance to constitute the Cardinals as an official aristocracy which was to direct the Pope's actions. Martin V. provided for decorous and good living on the part of the Cardinals, forbade them to exercise the position of protectors of the interests of kings or princes at the Papal Court, or to receive money as protectors for monastic orders; they were not to appear in the streets with a larger retinue than twenty attendants; they were, if possible, to live near the churches whence they took their titles, and were to restore the dilapidated buildings and see to the proper performance of divine service. Similarly the duties of the protonotaries and abbreviators of the Papal chancery were defined and regulated. Archbishops, bishops, and abbots were ordered to keep strict residence, and hold provincial synods three times each year for the redress of abuses; all oppressive exactions on the part of ordinaries were forbidden, and propriety of life was enjoined. Finally the Pope withdrew many of his rights of reservation as a favour to the ordinaries as patrons.[1]

Martin V. considered that he had now amply fulfilled all that reformers could require at his hands, and could look around him with greater assurance. He was free for seven years from the troubles of a Council, and could turn his attention to the object which he had most at heart, the recovery of the States of the Church, which Alfonso's withdrawal from Naples had rendered a practicable measure. Fortune favoured him in this respect beyond his hopes. The desperate resistance which Aquila continued to offer to Braccio, encouraged Sforza to march to its relief. On his way there, in January 1424, finding some difficulty in crossing the river Pescara, which was swollen by the wind and tide, he rode into the water to encourage his men. Seeing one of his squires swept off his horse, Sforza hastened to his assistance; but, losing his balance in attempting to save the drowning man, he was weighed down by his heavy armour: twice his hands were seen to wave above the flood, then he disappeared. His body was swept out to sea and was never found. Thus died Sforza at the age of

---

[1] This important document is printed by Döllinger, *Beiträge zur politischen, kirchlichen und Culturgeschichte* (1863), vol. ii. p. 335.

fifty-four, one of the most notable men in Italian history. His
death tells us the secret of his power. He died in the performance of an act of chivalrous generosity to a comrade. However
tortuous he might be in political relations, to his soldiers he
was frank and genial; they loved him and knew that their lives
and fortunes were as dear to Sforza as his own.

Nor did the more accomplished Braccio long survive his sturdy
rival. In spite of the withdrawal of Sforza's troops after their
leader's death, Aquila still held out. As its possession was regarded as the key to the possession of Naples, Martin V. was
eager to raise troops for its relief. He found it as easy to
arouse the jealousy of the Duke of Milan against Braccio as
against Alfonso; and in May a joint army of Naples, Milan, and
Pope advanced to the relief of Aquila. Braccio scorned to take
advantage of his enemies as they crossed the mountain ridge
that led to the town; though their forces were superior to his
own, he preferred to meet them in the open field. An unexpected
sortie of the Aquilans threw Braccio's army into confusion.
As he rode around exhorting his men to form afresh and renew
the fight, a Perugian exile forced his way through the throng
and, with the cry, 'Down with the oppressor of his country!'
wounded Braccio in the throat. On the fall of their leader the
soldiers of Braccio gave way, and the siege of Aquila was raised,
June 2. Braccio's haughty spirit would not survive defeat;
for three days he lay without eating or speaking till he died.
Unlike Sforza, he had no grown-up son to inherit his glory.
His shattered army rapidly dispersed upon his death. His
body was carried to Rome, and was buried as that of an excommunicated man in unconsecrated ground before the Church
of S. Lorenzo.

Martin V. reaped the full benefit of Braccio's death. On
July 29 Perugia opened its gates to the Pope, and the other
cities in Braccio's dominions soon followed its example. Martin
V. found himself in undisputed possession of the Papal States.
This was a great point to have gained, and Martin V. had won
his triumph by his astute and cautious, if unscrupulous, policy.
He had not hesitated to plunge Naples into war, and had
trusted to his own acuteness to fish in troubled waters. Fortune had favoured him beyond what he could expect, and the
only further difficulty that beset him was a rising of Bologna

Martin V.
recovers
the States
of the
Church.
1424-30.

in 1429, which was put down, though not without a stubborn struggle, by Carlo Malatesta. From that time he set himself with renewed zeal and statesmanlike care to organise the restoration of law and order in the Roman territory and the rest of the Papal possessions. When we look back upon the wild confusion that he found at his accession, we must recognise in Martin V.'s pontificate traces of energy and administrative capacity which have been left unrecorded by the annals of the time.[1] The slow and steady enforcement of order and justice is passed by unnoticed, while discord and anarchy are rarely without a chronicler. It is the great merit of Martin V. that he won back from confusion, and reduced to obedience and order, the disorganised States of the Church.[2]

The policy of Martin V. was to bring under one jurisdiction separate communities, with their existing rights and privileges, and so to establish a central monarchy on which they all peaceably depended. It was the misfortune of Martin V. that his work was thrown away by the wrongheadedness of his successor, and so left no lasting results. Still, Martin V. deserves high praise as a successful statesman, though even here he displayed the spirit of a Roman noble rather than of the Head of the Church. The elevation of the Colonna family was his constant aim, and he left to his successors a conspicuous example of nepotism. His brothers and sisters were enriched at the expense of the Church, and their aggrandisement had the disastrous result that it intensified the long-standing feud between the Colonna and the Orsini, and led to a reaction upon Martin's death. So far did Martin V. identify himself with his family that, in defiance of the traditions of his office, he took up his abode in the Colonna Palace by the Church of SS. Apostoli, regarding himself as more secure amongst the retainers of his house.

The same year that saw the deaths of Sforza and Braccio freed Martin V. from another enemy. In November 1424 died Benedict XIII., worn out by extreme old age. In his retirement at Peniscola he had been powerless either for good or ill. Yet the existence of an anti-Pope was hurtful to the Papal

---

[1] Infessura: *Diarium*, Mur. III. part ii. 1112: 'Morti che furono questi rimase lo Papa senza altri impacci e mantenne nel suo tempo pace e dovizia.'

dignity, and Alfonso's hostility to Martin V., threatened to give him troublesome importance. Benedict's death might seem to end the Schism, but one of the last acts of the obstinate old man was the creation of four new cardinals. For a time his death was kept secret till Alfonso's desires were known; at length in June 1425 three of Benedict's cardinals elected a new Pope, Gil de Munion, canon of Barcelona, who took the title of Clement VIII. But schism when once it begins is contagious. Another of Benedict's cardinals,[1] a Frenchman, Jean Carrer, who was absent at the time and received no notice, elected for himself another Pope, who took the title of Benedict XIV. Martin V. was desirous of getting rid of these pretenders, and sent one of his cardinals, brother of the Count de Foix, to negotiate with Alfonso. But Alfonso refused him entrance into his kingdom, and ordered Clement VIII. to be crowned in Peniscola. Martin V. summoned Alfonso to Rome to answer for his conduct. Alfonso saw that nothing was to be gained by isolation from the rest of Europe. Time mollified his wrath at the loss of Naples, and in his hopes for the future it was better to have the Pope for his friend than for his foe. The Cardinal de Foix carried on his negotiation with wise moderation, and was helped by one of the King's counsellors, Alfonso Borgia. In the autumn of 1427 Alfonso V. received the Pope's legate, agreed to recognise Martin V., and accept his good offices to settle disputes between himself and Giovanna II. In July 1429 Munion laid aside his papal trappings, submitted to Martin V., and received the melancholy post of Bishop of Majorca. The good offices of Alfonso Borgia were warmly recognised both by Alfonso V. and Martin V., and this ending of the Schism had for its abiding consequence in the future the introduction of the Borgia family to the Papal Court, where they were destined to play an important part. The Pope of Jean Carrer was of course a ridiculous phantom, and in 1432 the Count of Armagnac ordered Carrer, who was still obstinate, to be made prisoner and handed over to Martin V.[2]

[1] See Carrer's letter to the Count of Armagnac announcing his election of Benedict XIV., in Martene, *Thesaurus*, ii. 1714. The letter is written with all possible seriousness in the most approved style.

[2] Letter in Martene, *Thesaurus*, ii. 1748.

CHAPTER II.

MARTIN V. AND THE PAPAL RESTORATION. BEGINNINGS OF EUGENIUS IV.

1425–1432.

BOOK
III.

As Martin V. felt more sure of his position in Italy, and saw the traces of the Schism disappear in the outward organisation of the Church, he was anxious also to wipe away the anti-papal legislation which in France and England had followed on the confusion caused by the schism of the Papacy.

Martin V. and France. 1420–1425.

In France Martin V. easily succeeded in overthrowing the attempt to establish the liberties of the national Church on the basis of royal edicts. Charles VI. had issued in 1418 ordinances forbidding money to be exported from the kingdom for the payment of annates or other demands of the Court of Rome, and had confirmed the ancient liberties of the Gallican Church as regarded freedom of election to ecclesiastical offices. In February 1422 he had further forbidden appeals to Rome in contempt of the ordinances. But before the end of the year Charles VI. was dead, and the confusion in France was still further increased by the English claims to the succession. The youthful Charles VII. was hard pressed, and wished to gain the Pope's support. In February 1425 he issued a decree re-establishing the Papal power, as regarded the collation to benefices and all exercise of jurisdiction, on the same footing as it had been in the days of Clement VII. and Benedict XIII.[1] The Parlement, it is true, protested and refused to register the decree. The Pope, on his part, granted an indemnity for what had been done in the past. All the reforming efforts of the University of Paris and its followers were for the time undone.

[1] *Preures des Libertés de l'Eglise Gallicane*, ch. xxii. § 19.

In England Martin V. was not so successful. In 1421 he wrote to Henry V. and exhorted him to lose no time in abolishing the prohibitions of his predecessors (the Statutes of Provisors and Præmunire) on the due exercise of the Papal rights. Next year, on the accession of King Henry VI., he wrote still more pressingly to the Council of Regency.[1] When nothing was done, he directed his anger against Henry Chichele, the Archbishop of Canterbury. Chichele in 1423 proclaimed indulgences to all who in that year made pilgrimage to Canterbury. Martin indignantly forbade this assumption of Papal rights by a subordinate; 'as the fallen angels wished to set up in the earth their seat against the Creator, so have these presumptuous men endeavoured to raise a false tabernacle of salvation against the apostolic seat and the authority of the Roman Pontiff, to whom only has God granted this power.'[2] It was long since an English archbishop had heard such language from a pope; but Chichele was not a man of sufficient courage to remonstrate. He withdrew his proclamation, and Martin V. had struck a decided blow against the independence of the English episcopate.

The restored Papacy owed a debt of gratitude to Henry of Winchester for his good offices as mediator at Constance, and immediately after his election, Martin V. nominated him Cardinal. Chichele protested against this step as likely to lead to inconveniences; and Henry V., declaring that he would rather see his uncle invested with the crown than with a cardinal's hat, forbade his acceptance of the proffered dignity. When the strong hand of Henry V. was gone, Beaufort was again nominated Cardinal on May 24, 1426, no longer from motives of gratitude, but because the Pope needed his help. In February 1427, he was further appointed Papal legate for the purpose of carrying on war against the Hussites. But the Pope still pursued his main object, and in a letter to the Bishop of Winchester denounced still more strongly the execrable statute of Præmunire by which the King of England disposed of the affairs of the Church as though himself, and not the Pope, were the divinely appointed Vicar of Christ. He bade him remember the glorious example of S. Thomas of Canterbury, who did not hesitate to offer himself as a sacrifice on behalf of the liberties

Side notes:
CHAP. II.

Martin V. reproves Archbishop Chichele. 1423.

Martin V. makes Henry Beaufort cardinal and legate, 1426-7.

---

[1] Letters in Raynaldus, *sub annis*. [2] Raynaldus, 1423, § 21.

of the Church.[1] He bade him urge the abolition of this statute on the Council, on Parliament, and on the clergy, that they may preach about it to the people ; and he asked to be informed what steps were taken in compliance with his commands. He wrote also in the same strain to the University of Oxford. Indeed, so deeply did Martin V. resent the ecclesiastical attitude of England that he said in a consistory, ' Amongst Christians no states have made ordinances contrary to the liberties of the Church save England and Venice.'[2] Martin's instincts taught him truly, and he did his utmost to blunt the edge of the weapon that a century later was to sever the connexion between the English Church and the Papacy.

Martin V.
humbles
Archbishop
Chichele.
1427–8.
Again Martin V. wrote haughtily to Chichele, bidding him and the Archbishop of York set aside the Statutes of Provisors and recognise the Papal right to dispose of benefices in England. Chichele humbly replied that he was the only person in England who was willing to broach the subject ; and it was hard that he should be specially visited by the Pope's displeasure for what he could not help. Martin V. retorted by issuing letters to suspend Chichele from his office as legate—a blow against the privileges and independence of the Archbishops of Canterbury, who since the days of Stephen Langton had been recognised as the Pope's ordinary legate (*legatus natus*) in England. Chichele so far roused himself as to appeal to a future Council against this encroachment. The Pope's letters were seized by royal authority, and the suspension did not take effect. But Chichele was a timid man, and the condition of affairs in England made him shrink from a breach with the Pope. The Lollards were suppressed but not subdued, and a strong anti-hierarchical feeling simmered amongst the people. In the distracted state of the kingdom, little help was to be gained from the royal power, and Chichele feared the consequences of an interdict. He called to his help the bishops, the University of Oxford, and several temporal lords, who addressed letters to the Pope, bearing testimony to Chichele's zeal for the

[1] Raynaldus, 1426, § 19: 'Illius gloriosissimi martyris B. Thomæ olim Cantuariensis archiepiscopi successor effectus es, qui adversus similia decertans statuta holocaustum se offerens Deo, pro libertate ecclesiastica occubuit.' The Pope stretches a point in making Thomas a martyr for his resistance to the Constitutions of Clarendon.

[2] *Commissioni di Rinaldo degli Albizzi,* ii. 443.

Church, and begging the Pope to be reconciled to him. To CHAP
Chichele's letters pleading his excuses, the Pope still answered II.
that the only excuse that he could make was active resistance
to the obnoxious statutes. At length Chichele, in 1428, appeared before the Commons, accompanied by the Archbishop of
York and other bishops, and with tears in his eyes pointed out the
dangers in which the Church and kingdom were placed by their
opposition to the Pope's demands. Parliament was unmoved
either by Martin's letters or by Chichele's half-hearted pleadings. They only petitioned the Pope to restore the Archbishop
to his favour. The King wrote in the same sense, and the
matter was allowed to drop. Martin V. might console himself
with the reflection that, if he had failed to carry his point and
abolish the hateful statutes, he had at least succeeded in hu-
miliating the English episcopate by treating them as creatures
of his own.[1]

In September 1428, Beaufort made his first appearance in Beaufort's
England since his elevation to the Cardinalate, and a protest in crusade
the King's name was issued against his exercise of any legatine Hussites.
authority within the realm. Next year the question was raised 1429.
whether Beaufort, being a cardinal, was justified in officiating
as Bishop of Winchester and prelate of the Order of the
Garter: the King's council advised Beaufort to waive his right.
Meanwhile Beaufort was allowed to gather troops for a crusade
against the Hussites. But the English statesman and the
Papal councillor came into collision; and the troops which
Beaufort had gathered for a crusade in Bohemia were turned
against France. Beaufort pleaded to the Pope the lame excuse
that he had not ventured to disobey the King's commands in
this matter; nor would the soldiers have obeyed him if he had
done so.[2] Though treacherous, the action of Beaufort was
popular. He was allowed, though a cardinal, to take his seat
at the King's council, except only when matters were under
discussion which concerned the Church of Rome. Really,
Beaufort was too much absorbed in deadly personal rivalry with
Gloucester to be of any service to the Pope in furthering
his attempt to overthrow the liberties of the English Church.

[1] The correspondence between Martin V. and Chichele is given partly in
Raynaldus, partly in Wilkins' *Concilia*, iii. 471-486.
[2] Raynaldus, 1429, 17.

BOOK
III.

Results of
Ma tin
V.'s policy
towards
England.

But the Papacy has never in its history gained so much by definite victories as it has by steady persistency. It was always prepared to take advantage of the internal weakness of any kingdom, and to advance pretensions at times when they were not likely to be resolutely disavowed. In time they might be heard of again, and when reasserted could at least claim the prestige of some antiquity. By his treatment of Archbishop Chichele, and by his grant of legatine powers to Beaufort, Martin V. exercised a more direct authority over the machinery of the English Church than had been permitted to any pope since the days of Innocent III. The Church was weak in its hold on the affections of the people, and when the kingly office was in abeyance, the Church, robbed of its protector, was too feeble to offer any serious resistance to the Papacy. Martin V. used his opportunity dexterously, and his successors had no reason to complain of the independent spirit of English bishops.

But besides being an ecclesiastic Martin V. had the sentiments of a Roman noble. He wished to restore his native city to some part of her old glory, and laboured so assiduously at the work of restoration that a grateful people hailed him as ' Father of his country.' He rebuilt the tottering portico of S. Peter's, and proceeded to adorn and repair the ruined basilicas of the city. In the church of S. John Lateran, which had been destroyed by fire in 1308, and was slowly rising from its ruins, he laid down the mosaic pavement which still exists, and built up the roof. He restored the Basilica of the SS. Apostoli. His example told upon the Cardinals, and he urged on them to undertake the care of the churches from which they took their titles.[1] His pontificate marks the beginning of an era of architectural adornment of the City of Rome.

The only part of the work of the reformation of the Church which Martin V. showed any wish to carry into effect was that concerning the Cardinals. The Papal absolutism over all bishops, which Martin V. desired to establish, aimed at the reduction of the power of the ecclesiastical aristocracy which surrounded the Pope's person, and the rules for the conduct of the Cardinals issued in 1424 were not meant to be mere waste paper. Martin V. succeeded in reducing the power of the Car-

[1] Döllinger, *Beiträge*, ii. 336.

dinals; he paid little heed to their advice, and they were so CHAP. II. afraid of him that they stammered like awkward children in his presence.[1] Sometimes he even excluded them altogether. In 1429 he retired from Rome to Ferentino before a pestilence, and forbade any of the Cardinals to follow him.

Yet all Martin V.'s injunctions could not purge the Curia from the charge of corruption. Money was necessary for the Pope, and Martin V., if he laid aside the grosser forms of extortion, still demanded money on all fair pretexts. The ambassadors at the Papal Court found it necessary for the conduct of the business to propitiate the Pope by handsome presents on the great festivals of the Church. If any business was to be done, the attention of the Pope and his officials had to be arrested by some valuable gift. Yet Martin V. showed a care in making ecclesiastical appointments which had not been seen in the Popes for the last half-century. He did not make his appointments rashly, but enquired about the capacities of the different candidates and the special needs of the districts which they aspired to serve. Even so, Martin V. was not always to be trusted. He seemed to delight in humbling bishops before him. He deposed Bishop Anselm of Augsburg simply because the civic authorities quarrelled with him. In England he conferred on a nephew of his own, aged fourteen, the rich archdeaconry of Canterbury. Yet Martin V. was never weary of uttering noble sentiments to the cardinals and those around him: no word was so often on his lips as 'justice.' He would often exclaim to his cardinals, 'Love justice, ye who judge the earth.'[2]

Court of Martin V.

In these peaceful works of internal reform and organisation Martin V. passed his last years, disturbed only by the thought that the time was drawing near for summoning the promised Council at Basel. Moreover, there was little hope of avoiding it, for the religious conflict in Bohemia had waxed so ·fierce

Death of Martin V. February 1431.

---

[1] Report of the Ambassador of the Teutonic knights in Voigt's *Stimmen aus Rom.* Raumer: *Historisches Taschenbuch*, vol. iv. 74: 'Sie dürfen wider den Papst nicht reden ausser was er gerne hört; denn der Papst hat die Cardinäle alle so unterdrückt, dass sie vor ihm nicht anders sprechen, als wie er es gerne will, und werden vor ihm redend roth und bleich.'

[2] Platina: 'Ejus sermo plenus sententiis erat. Excidebat nullum nomen tam crebro quam justitiæ nomen. Ad suos persæpe conversus his verbis utebatur, Diligite justitiam qui judicatis terram.'

that it had long been the subject of greatest interest in the politics of Europe. Army after army of the orthodox had been routed by the Bohemian heretics. Papal legates had in vain raised troops and conducted them to battle. Germany was hopelessly exhausted, and when force had failed, men looked anxiously to see if deliberation could again avail. Martin V. ordered the legate in Bohemia, Giuliano Cesarini, to convoke a Council at Basel in 1431. But he was not to see its beginning: he was suddenly struck by apoplexy, and died on February 20, 1431. He was buried in the Church of S. John Lateran, where his recumbent effigy in brass still adorns his tomb.

Character of Martin V.

Martin V. was a wise, cautious, and prudent Pope. He received the Papacy discredited and homeless: he succeeded in establishing it firmly in its old capital, recovering its lost possessions, and restoring some of its old prestige in Europe. This he did by moderation and common sense, combined with a genuine administrative capacity. He was not a brilliant man, but the times did not require brilliancy. He was not personally popular, for he did not much care for the regard or sympathy of those around him, but kept his own counsel and went his own way. He was reserved, and had great self-command. When the news of a brother's unexpected death was brought to him early one morning, he composed himself and said mass as usual. He did not care for men's good opinion, but devoted himself energetically to the details of business. He did not care to do anything splendid, so much as to do all things securely. Yet he rescued the Papacy from its fallen condition and laid the foundations for its future power. His strong-willed and arbitrary dealings with other bishops did much to break down the strength of national feeling in ecclesiastical matters which had been displayed at Constance. He was resolved to make the bishops feel their impotence before the Pope; and the political weakness of European States enabled him to go far in breaking down the machinery of the national Churches, and asserting for the Papacy a supreme control in all ecclesiastical matters. In this way he may be regarded as the founder of the theory of Papal omnipotence which is embodied in modern Ultramontanism. Yet Martin V. succeeded rather through the weakness of Europe than through his own strength. He did not awaken suspicion by large schemes, but pursued a quiet policy which was dictated by the existing needs of the Papacy, and was capable of great extension in the future. Without being a great man, he was an extremely sagacious statesman. He had none of the noble and heroic qualities which would have enabled him to set up the Papacy once more as the exponent of the religious aspirations of Europe ; but he brought it into accordance with the politics of his time and made it again powerful and respected. There were two opinions in his own days respecting the character of Martin V. Those who had waited anxiously for a thorough reformation of the Church looked sadly on Martin's shortcomings and accused him of avarice and self-seeking. Those who regarded his career as a temporal ruler, extolled him for his practical virtues, and the epitaph on his tomb called him with some truth, ' Temporum suorum felicitas,' the happiness of his times.[1] At the present day we may be permitted to combine these two opposite judgments, and may praise him for what he did while regretting that he lacked the elevation of mind necessary to enable him to seize the splendid opportunity offered him of doing more.

After the funeral of Martin V., the fourteen Cardinals who were in Rome lost no time in entering into conclave in the Church of S. Maria sopra Minerva. They were still smarting at the recollection of the hard yoke of Martin V., and their one desire was to give themselves an easy master and escape the

CHAP.
II.

Election of
Gabriel
Condul-
mier,
Eugenius
IV. March
8, 1431.

[1] These two views are expressed in the two lives in Muratori, III., part ii., 859. One says: ' Martinus vero avarissimus fuit ; miserabiliter in palatio apud sanctos Apostolos vixit.' The other says: ' Cujus quidem mors non modo populum Romanum sed universos Christi fideles magno dolore confecit.' The following stanzas from a Sapphic ode written by Gregorio Correr, great-nephew of Gregory XII., and cousin once removed of Eugenius IV., show how Martin's qualities were regarded by his friends. The ode is published from a MS. in the Museo Correr in Venice by Von Reumont, *Beiträge zur Italienischen Geschichte*, iv. 302 :—

Prodiit notis latebris latronum
Turba, securum patet iter, arces
Jam licet sacras simul et beatum
    Visere Tibrim.

Salve o sacratæ pater urbis, atque
Gentium terror, decus et Latini
Nominis, sperque ; ut maneas precamur
    Summe sacerdos.

indignities which they had so long endured. To secure this
end they had recourse to the method, which the Schism had
introduced, of drawing up rules for the conduct of the future
Pope, which every Cardinal signed before proceeding to the
election. Each promised, if he were elected Pope, to issue a
Bull within three days of his coronation, declaring that he would
reform the Roman Curia, would further the work of the approaching Council, would appoint cardinals according to the
decrees of Constance, would allow his cardinals freedom of
speech and would respect their advice, give them their accustomed revenues, abstain from seizing their goods at death, and
consult them about the disposal of the government of the Papal
States.   We see from these provisions how the Cardinals
resented the insignificance to which Martin V. had consigned
them. To reverse his treatment of themselves they were willing
to reverse his entire policy and bind the future Pope to accept
in some form the Council and the cause of ecclesiastical reform.
They entered the Conclave on March 1, and spent the next day
in drawing up this instrument for their own protection.   On
March 3 they proceeded to vote, and on the first scrutiny
Gabriel Condulmier, a Venetian, was unanimously elected.
Others had been mentioned, such as Giuliano Cesarini, the
energetic legate in Bohemia, and Antonio Casino, Bishop of
Siena.   But in their prevailing temper, the Cardinals determined that it was best to have a harmless nonentity, and all
were unanimous that Condulmier answered best to that description.

Previous
life of Con-
dulmier.   Gabriel Condulmier, who took the name of Eugenius IV.,
was a Venetian, sprung from a wealthy but not noble family.
His father died when he was young ; and Gabriel, seized with
religious enthusiasm, distributed his wealth, 20,000 ducats,
among the poor, and resolved to seek his riches in another
world.   So great was his ardour that he infected with it his
cousin, Antonio Correr, and both entered the monastery of
S. Giorgio d' Alga in Venice.   There the two friends remained
simple brothers of the order, till Antonio's uncle was unexpectedly elected Pope Gregory XII. As usual, the Papal uncle
wished to promote his nephew; but Antonio refused to leave
his monastery unless he were accompanied by his friend Condulmier.   Gregory XII. made his nephew Bishop of Bologna,

and Condulmier Bishop of Siena. He afterwards prepared the way for his own downfall by insisting on elevating both to the dignity of cardinals. But the diminution of Gregory's obedience gave them small scope for their activity; they both went to Constance and were ranked among the Cardinals of the united Church. Their long friendship was at last interrupted by jealousy. Correr could not endure his friend's elevation to the Papacy; he left him, and at the Council at Basel was one of his bitterest opponents. Martin V. appointed Condulmier to be legate in Bologna, where he showed his capacity by putting down a rebellion of the city. When elected to the Papacy at the early age of forty-seven he was regarded as a man of high religious character, without much knowledge of the world or political capacity. The Cardinals considered him to be an excellent appointment for their purpose. Tall and of a commanding figure and pleasant face, he would be admirably suited for public appearances. His reputation for piety would satisfy the reforming party; his known liberality to the poor would make him popular in Rome; his assumed lack of strong character and of personal ambition would assure to the Cardinals the freedom and consideration after which they pined. He was in no way a distinguished man, and in an age when learning was becoming more and more respected, he was singularly uncultivated. His early years were spent in the performance of formal acts of piety, and his one literary achievement was that he wrote with his own hand a breviary, which he always continued to use when he became Pope. The absence of any decided qualities in Eugenius IV. seems to have been so marked that miraculous agency was called in to explain his unexpected elevation. A story, which he himself was fond of telling in later years,[1] found ready credence. When he was a simple monk at Venice, he took his turn to act as porter at the monastery gate. One day a hermit came and was kindly welcomed by Condulmier, who accompanied him into the church and joined in his devotions. As they returned, the hermit said, 'You will be made Cardinal, and then Pope; in your pontificate you will suffer much adversity.' Then he departed, and was seen no more.

---

[1] Vespasiano says: 'Questo diceva spesso papa Eugenio *a chi lo voleva udire*.' His words seem to suggest that those around him had a horror of the story, with which they were regaled too often.

BOOK
III.

Eugenius
IV. gives
earnest of
a desire to
reform.

Eugenius IV. was faithful to his promise before election, and on the day of his coronation, March 11, confirmed the document which he had signed in conclave. He also showed signs of a desire to reform the abuses of the Papal Court. His first act was to cut off a source of exaction. The customary letters announcing his election were given for transmission to the ambassadors of the various states, instead of being sent by Papal nuncios, who expected large donations for their service.[1]

Quarrel of
Eugenius
IV. with
the Co-
lonna.

But the first steps of Eugenius IV. in the conduct of affairs showed an absence of wisdom and an unreasoning ferocity. Martin V. had been careful to secure the interests of his own relatives. His brother Lorenzo had been made Count of Alba and Celano in the Abruzzi, and his brother Giordano Duke of Amalfi and Venosa, Prince of Salerno. Both of them died before the Pope, but their places were taken by the sons of Lorenzo—Antonio, who became Prince of Salerno, Odoardo, who inherited Celano and Marsi, and Prospero, who was Cardinal at the early age of twenty-two. Martin V. had lived by the Church of SS. Apostoli in a house of moderate pretensions, as the Vatican was too ruinous for occupation; his nephews had a palace hard by. It was natural for a new Pope to look with some suspicion on the favourites of his predecessor. But at first all went well between the Colonna and Eugenius IV. The Castle of S. Angelo was given up to the Pope and a considerable amount of treasure which Martin V. had left behind him. But Eugenius IV. soon became suspicious. The towns in the Papal States grew rebellious when they felt that Martin V.'s strong hand was relaxed, and Eugenius needed money and soldiers to reduce them to obedience. He suspected that the Papal nephews had vast stores of treasure secreted, and resolved by a bold stroke to seize it for himself. Stefano Colonna, head of the Palestrina branch of the family and at variance with the elder branch, was sent to seize the Bishop of Tivoli, Martin's Vice-Chamberlain, whom he dragged ignominiously through the streets. Eugenius IV. angrily rebuked him for his unnecessary violence, and so alienated his wavering loyalty. At the same time Eugenius demanded of Antonio

---

[1] The King of Castile did not understand this, and complained of omission as a slight. Eugenius wrote to explain; see Raynaldus, 1431, No. 9.

Colonna that he should give up all the possessions in the Papal
States with which his uncle had endowed him, Genazano, Soriano,
S. Marino, and other fortresses where Eugenius imagined that
the Papal treasures lay hid. Antonio loudly declared that this
was a plot of the Orsini in their hereditary hatred of the
Colonna; he denounced the Pope as lending himself to their
schemes, and left Rome hastily to raise forces. He was soon
followed by Stefano Colonna, by the Cardinal Prospero, and the
other adherents of the family. Gathering their troops, the
Colonna attacked the possessions of the Orsini and laid waste
the country up to the walls of Rome.

Eugenius IV., like Urban VI., had been unexpectedly raised
to a position for which his narrowness and inexperience rendered
him unfit. Trusting to the general excellence of his intentions
and exulting in the plenitude of his new authority, he acted on
the first impulse, and only grew more determined when he met
with opposition.[1] He tortured the luckless Bishop of Tivoli
almost to death in his prison. He ordered the partisans of the
Colonna in Rome to be arrested, and over two hundred Roman
citizens were put to death on various charges. Stefano Colonna
advanced against Rome, seized the Porta Appia on April 23,
and fought his way through the streets as far as the Piazza
of S. Marco. But the people did not rise on his side as he had
expected; the Pope's troops were still strong enough to drive
back their assailants. Stefano Colonna could not succeed in
getting hold of the city; but he kept the Appian gate, laid waste
the Campagna, and threatened the city with famine. Eugenius
IV. retaliated by ordering the destruction of the Colonna
palaces, even that of Martin V., and the houses of their adherents, and on May 18 issued a decree depriving them of all
their possessions. The old times of savage warfare between the
Roman nobles were again brought back.

The Colonna take arms against the Pope. April 1431.

The contest might long have raged, to the destruction of
the new-born prosperity of the Roman city, had not Florence,
Venice, and Naples sent troops to aid the Pope. But the
Neapolitan forces under Caldora proved a feeble help, for they
took money from Antonio Colonna, and assumed an ambiguous
attitude. In Rome the confession of a conspiracy to seize the

Peace with the Colonna. September 1431.

[1] Billius (Mur. xix. 143) calls him: ' Sui ipsius fidentissimus quodcunque propositum cepisset.'

Castle of S. Angelo and expel the Pope was extorted from a luckless friar, and gave rise to fresh prosecutions and imprisonments. Amid these agitations Eugenius IV. was stricken by paralysis, which was put down to the results of poison administered in the interests of the Colonna. Sickness brought reflection; and the Colonnesi on their side saw that the chances of war were going against them, since Venice and Florence were determined to support Eugenius, whose help they needed against the growing power of the Duke of Milan. Accordingly, on September 22 peace was made between the Pope and Antonio Colonna, who paid 75,000 ducats and resigned the castles which he held in the Papal States. Giovanna of Naples deprived him also of his principality of Salerno. The relatives of Martin V. fell back to their former position. But Eugenius had gained by violence, disorder, bloodshed, and persecution an end which might have been reached equally well by a little patience and tact.

The disturbances in the States of the Church gradually settled down, and Eugenius in September was anxiously awaiting the coming of Sigismund to Italy for the purpose of assuming the Imperial crown. On his dealings with Sigismund depended his chance of freeing himself from the Council, which had begun to assemble at Basel, and whose proceedings were such as to cause him some anxiety.

CHAPTER III.

BOHEMIA AND THE HUSSITE WARS.

1418–1431.

THE fortunes of Sigismund had not been prosperous since his departure from Constance. The glories of the revived empire which had floated before his eyes soon began to fade away. Troubles in his ancestral states occupied all his attention, and prevented him from aspiring to be the arbiter of the affairs of Europe. His dignified position at Constance, as Protector of the Council that was to regulate the future of the Church, entailed on him nothing but disappointment. It was easy for the Council to burn Hus and to condemn his doctrines; but the Bohemian people were not convinced by either of these proceedings, and cherished a bitter feeling of Sigismund's perfidy. He had invited Hus to the Council, and then had abandoned him; he had inflicted a disgrace on their national honour which the Bohemians could never forgive. The decrees of the Council found little respect in Bohemia, and a league was formed among the Bohemian nobles to maintain freedom of preaching. The teaching of Jakubek of Mies, concerning the necessity of receiving the communion under both kinds, gave an outward symbol to the new beliefs, and the chalice became the distinctive badge of the Bohemian reformers. The Council in vain summoned Wenzel to answer for his neglect of its monitions; in vain it called on Sigismund to give effect to its decrees by force of arms. Sigismund knew the difficulties of such an attempt, and as heir to the Bohemian kingdom did not choose to draw upon himself any further hatred from the Bohemian people.

Before the election of a new Pope, the Bohemians could still denounce the arbitrary proceedings of the Council, and hope for fairer hearing in the future. But the election of Oddo Colonna, who as Papal commissioner had condemned Hus in

1411, dashed all further hopes to the ground. Martin V. accepted all that the Council had done towards the Bohemian heretics, and urged Sigismund to interpose. He threatened to proclaim a crusade against Bohemia, which would then be conquered by some faithful prince, who might not be willing to hand it over to Sigismund. The threat alarmed Sigismund, who wrote urgently to his brother Wenzel; and the indolent Wenzel, who had allowed dim notions of impossible toleration to float before his eyes, at last roused himself to see the hopelessness of his attempt neither to favour nor discourage the new movement. At the end of 1418 he ordered that all the churches in Prag should be given up to the Catholics, who hastened to return and wreak their wrath on the heretics. Two churches only were left to the Utraquists, as the reformed party was now called, from its administration of the communion under both kinds. But the multitudes began to meet in the open air, on hill-tops, which they loved to call by Biblical names, Tabor and Horeb and the like. Peacefully these assemblies met and separated; but this condition of suppressed revolt could not long continue. On July 22, 1419, Wenzel's wrath was kindled by hearing of a vast meeting of 40,000 worshippers, who had received the communion under both kinds, and had given it even to the children of their company.

These meetings at once awakened the enthusiasm of the Utraquists, and gave them confidence in their strength. On Sunday, July 30, a procession, headed by a former monk, John of Sulau, who had preached a fiery sermon to a large congregation, marched through the streets of Prag, and took possession of the church of S. Stephen, where they celebrated their own rites. Thence they proceeded to the Town Hall of the Neustadt, and clamoured that the magistrates should release some who had been made prisoners on religious grounds. The magistrates were the nominees of Wenzel to carry out his new policy; they barred the doors, and looked from the windows upon the crowd. Foremost in it stood the priest, John of Sulau, holding aloft the chalice. Some one from the windows threw a stone, and knocked it from his hands. The fury of the crowd blazed out in a moment. Headed by John Zizka, of Trocnow, a nobleman of Wenzel's court, they burst open the doors, slew the burgomaster, and flung out of the windows all who did

not succeed in making their escape. It was the beginning of
a religious war more savage and more bloody than Europe had
yet seen.

Wenzel's rage was great when he heard of these proceedings.
He threatened death to all the Hussites, and particularly the
priests. But his helplessness obliged him to listen to proposals
for reconciliation. The rebels humbled themselves, the King
appointed new magistrates. Wenzel's perplexities, however, were
soon to end; on August 16 he was struck with apoplexy, and
died with a great shout and roar as of a lion.[1] He was buried
secretly by night, for Prag was in an uproar at the news of his
death. Wenzel's faults as a ruler are obvious enough. He
was devoid of wisdom and energy; he was arbitrary and capri-
cious; he was alternately sunk in sloth, and a prey to fits of
wild fury. He had none of the qualities of a statesman; yet
with all his faults he was felt by the Bohemians to have a love
for his people, to whom he was always kindly and familiar,
and to whom in his way he strove to do justice. His own ambiguous position towards his brother Sigismund and European
politics corresponded in some measure with the ambiguous
attitude of Bohemia towards the Church, and for a time he was
no unfitting representative of the land which he ruled. Just
as events had reached the point when decision was rendered
inevitable, Wenzel's death handed over to Sigismund the responsibility of dealing with the future of Bohemia.

Sigismund did not judge it expedient to turn his attention
immediately to Bohemia. His Hungarian subjects clamoured
for his aid against the Turks, who were pressing up the Danube
valley. He was bound to help them first, and obtain their
help against Bohemia. He trusted that conciliatory measures
would disarm the Bohemian rebels, whom he would afterwards
be able to deal with at leisure. Accordingly he appointed
the widowed Queen, Sophia, as regent in Bohemia, and round
her gathered the nobles in the interests of public order. At
the head of the Government stood Cenek of Wartenberg,
who was leader of the Hussite league, and who strove to check
excesses by a policy of toleration. But men needed guarantees

---

[1] 'Cum magno clamore et rugitu quasi leonis.' Laur. de Bresina (in
Höfler, *Geschichtschreiber der Hussitischen Bewegung*, i. 341), who is the authority for the above account.

for the future. The Diet which met in September 1419, and in which the Hussites had a majority, demanded of Sigismund that he should grant full liberty for the Utraquist preaching and ceremonies, and should confer office in the State on the Tchecks only. Sigismund returned the ambiguous answer that he hoped soon to come in person, and would govern according to the old customs of his father, Charles IV. No doubt the answer was pleasant to the patriotic aspirations which their request contained ; but men significantly observed that there were no Hussites in Charles IV.'s days.

Queen Sophia was obliged to write repeatedly to Sigismund, begging him to be more explicit; but only drew from him a proclamation recommending order and quiet, and promising to examine into the Utraquist question when he arrived. Sigismund hoped to gain time till he had an army ready; he hoped to win over the Hussite nobles by a display of confidence meanwhile, and slowly gather round himself all the moderate party.

But Sigismund did not know the strength nor the political sagacity of the leaders of the extreme party, which had been slowly but surely forming itself since the death of Hus. The moderate party were men of the same views as Hus, who were faithful to an ideal of the Church, repelled the charge of heresy, and still hoped for tolerance, at least in time, for their own opinions. With men such as these Sigismund could easily deal. But the extreme party, who were called Taborites from their open-air meetings, recognised that the breach with Rome was irreparable, and were prepared to carry their opinions into all questions, religious, political, and social alike. Their position was one of open revolt against authority both in Church and State ; they rested on the assertion of the rights of the individual, and appealed to the national sentiment of the masses of the people. At the head of this party stood two men of remarkable ability, Nicolas of Hus and John Zizka, both sprung from the smaller nobility, and both trained in affairs at Wenzel's court. Of these, Nicolas had the eye of a statesman; Zizka the eloquence, the enthusiasm, and the generalship needed for a leader of men. Nicolas of Hus saw from the first the real bearing of the situation ; he saw that if the extreme party of the reformers did not prepare for the inevitable conflict they would gradually be isolated, and would be crushed by main force. Zizka set himself to the task of organising the enthusiasm of the Bohemian peasants into the stuff which would form a disciplined army. Like Cromwell in a later day, he used the seriousness that comes of deep religious convictions as the basis of a strong military organisation, against which the chivalry of Germany should break itself in vain. While Sigismund was delaying, Zizka was drilling. On October 25 he seized the Wyssehrad, a fortress on the hill commanding the Neustadt of Prag, and began a struggle to obtain entire possession of the city. But the excesses of the Taborites, and the fair promises of the Queen-regent, confirmed the party of order. Prag was not yet ready for the Taborites, and on November 11, Zizka and his troops fell back from the city.

In this state of things Sigismund advanced from Hungary into Moravia, and in December held a Diet at Brünn. Thither went Queen Sophia and the chief of the Bohemian nobles; thither, too, went the ambassadors of the city of Prag, to seek confirmation for their promised freedom of religion. Sigismund's attitude was still ambiguous; he received them graciously, did not forbid them to celebrate the communion in their own fashion in their own houses, but ordered them to keep peace in their city, submit to the royal authority, lay aside their arms, and he would treat them gently. The burghers of Prag submitted, and destroyed the fortifications which menaced the royal castle. Sigismund could view the results of his policy with satisfaction. The submission of Prag spread terror on all sides;[1] the power of Sigismund impressed men's imagination; the Catholics began to rejoice in anticipation of a speedy triumph.

From Brünn Sigismund advanced into Silesia, where he was received with loyal enthusiasm, and many of the German nobles met him at Breslau. Sigismund became convinced of his own power and importance and let drop the mask too soon. At Breslau he put down the Utraquists, enquired severely into a municipal revolt, which was insignificant compared to what had happened in Prag, caused twenty-three citizens to be executed for rebellion, and on March 17 allowed

[1] 'Timor magnus ac pavor veritati adhaerentes invasit,' says Brezina, Höfler, i. 348.

the Papal legate to proclaim a crusade against the Hussites.
The result of this false step was to lose at once the support of
the moderate party, and to alienate the national feeling of the
Bohemians. The people of Prag issued a manifesto calling all
who loved the law of Christ and their country's liberties to join
in resisting Sigismund's crusade. The nobles, headed by
Cenek of Wartenberg, denounced Sigismund as their enemy,
and not their king. The country was at once in arms, and the
pent-up fanaticism was let loose. Churches and monasteries
were destroyed on every side. No country was so rich in
splendid buildings and treasures of ecclesiastical ornament as
was Bohemia;[1] but a wave of ruthless devastation now swept
across it which has left only faint traces of the former splendour.
Again excesses awoke alarm among the moderate nobles.
Cenek of Wartenberg went back to Sigismund's side; and the
burghers of Prag saw themselves consequently in a dangerous
plight, as the two castles between which their city lay, the
Wyssehrad and the Hradschin, again declared for Sigismund.
As they could not defend their city, they again turned to
thoughts of submission, in return for an amnesty and permission
to celebrate the communion under both kinds. But Sigismund
had now advanced into Bohemia and proudly looked for a speedy
triumph. He demanded that they should lay aside their arms
and submit. This harshness was a fatal error on Sigismund's
part, as it drove the burghers of Prag into alliance with the
extreme party of Zizka.

Zizka for-
tifies
Tabor.   As yet this alliance had not been made; as yet Prag wished
to proceed on the old constitutional lines. It wished to recog-
nise the legitimate king, and obtain from him tolerance for the
new religious beliefs. If this were impossible, there was nothing
left save to throw in their lot with those who wished to create
a new constitution and a new society. Zizka had been preparing for the contest. He remorselessly pursued a policy which
would deprive the Catholics of their resources, and would
compel Bohemia to follow the course in which it had engaged.
Monasteries were everywhere pillaged and destroyed; Church
property was seized; the lands of the orthodox party were ruth-

---

[1] 'Nullum ego regnum ætate nostra in tota Europa tam frequentibus, tam
augustis, tam ornatis templis ditatum fuisse quam Bohemicum reor,' says
Æneas Sylvius, *Hist. Boh.* ch. xxxvi.

lesaly devastated. Sigismund, if he entered Bohemia, would find no resources to help him. Zizka so acted as to make the breach at once irreparable; he wished to leave no chance of conciliation, except on condition of recognising all that he had done. Moreover, he established a centre for his authority. When he failed to seize Prag as a stronghold, he sought out a spot which would form a capital for the revolution. A chance movement made him master of the town of Austi, near which were the remains of an old fortified place. Zizka's eye at once recognised its splendid military situation, lying on the top of a hill, which was formed into a peninsula by two rivers which flow round its rocky base. Zizka set to work to build up the old walls, and strengthen by art the strong natural position. The approach to the peninsula, which was only thirty feet wide, was rendered secure by a triple wall and a deep ditch. Towers and defences crowned the whole line of the wall.[1] It was not a city, but a permanent camp, which Zizka succeeded in making, and to which was given the characteristic name of Tabor. Henceforth the name of Taborites was confined to Zizka's followers.

Before the danger which threatened them with entire destruction, as Sigismund's army numbered at least 80,000 men from almost every nation in Europe, all parties in Bohemia drew together. The troops of Zizka entered Prag, and the burghers destroyed such parts of their city as were most open to attack from the Wyssehrad and the Hradschin, which were held by the Royalists. The hill of Witkow, on the north-east of the city, was still held by the Hussites, and against that Sigismund directed an attack on July 14. The attention of the enemy was distracted by assaults in different quarters, and Sigismund's soldiers pressed up the hill. But a tower, defended by twenty-six Taborites, with two women and a girl who fought like heroes, kept the troops at bay till a band of Zizka's soldiers came to their aid, and charged with such fury that the Germans fled in dismay. Sigismund learned with shame and anger the powerlessness of his great host to contend against a people actuated by national and religious zeal. Their repulse kindled in the Germans a desire for vengeance, and they massacred the Bohemian inhabitants of the neighbouring towns and

---

[1] Æn. Sylvius, *Hist. Boh.* ch. xl., gives a graphic description of Tabor, which he visited himself. ' Nos qualem vidimus descripsimus.'

villages. When the Bohemian nobles of the King's party resented this display of hatred against the entire Bohemian race, Sigismund's unwieldy army began to break up. There was again a talk of negotiation, and the people of Prag sent to Sigismund their demands, which are known as the Four Articles of Prag, and formed the charter of the Hussite creed. They asked for freedom of preaching, the communion under both kinds, the reduction of the clergy to apostolic poverty, and the severe repression of all open sins. These articles were a worthy exposition of the principles of the Reformation: the first asserted the freedom of man to search the Scriptures for himself; the second attacked one of the great outposts of sacerdotalism, the denial of the cup to the laity; the third cut at the root of the abuses of the ecclesiastical system, and the fourth claimed for Christianity the power to regenerate and regulate society. There was some semblance of discussion on these points; but there could be no agreement between those who rested on the authority of the Church and those who entirely disregarded it.

Sigismund
driven
from
Bohemia.
March
1421.
These negotiations, however, gave still further pretext for many of Sigismund's troops to leave his army. Resolving to do something, Sigismund on July 28 had himself crowned King of Bohemia, a step which gave greater appearance of legitimacy to his position. He strove to bind to his interests the Bohemian nobles by gifts of the royal domains and of the treasures of the churches. Meanwhile the Hussites besieged the Wyssehrad and succeeded in cutting off its supplies. It was reduced to extremities when Sigismund made an effort to relieve it. The chivalry of Moravia, Hungary, and Bohemia were checked in their fiery charge by the steady organisation of the Taborites, and more than four hundred of the bravest nobles were slaughtered by the flails of the peasants as they struggled in the vineyards and marsh at the bottom of the hill. Sigismund fled, and the Wyssehrad surrendered on November 1. After this, Sigismund's cause was lost, and he was regarded as the murderer of the nobles who fell in the disastrous battle of the Wyssehrad. The troops of Zizka overran Bohemia, and the Catholic inhabitants fled before them. Town after town submitted, and in March 1421 Sigismund left Bohemia in despair. He had hopelessly mismanaged affairs. He had alternated between a policy of conciliation and one of repression. He had

alienated the Bohemians through the cruelty of his German followers, and had lost the support of the Germans through his anxiety to win the Bohemian nobles. Finally, his hope of overcoming the people by the help of the native nobles had ignominiously failed and had covered Sigismund with disgrace.

The Utraquists were now masters of Bohemia, and the whole land was banded together in resistance to Catholicism and Sigismund. The nobles joined with the people, and Prag was triumphant: even the Archbishop Conrad accepted the Four Articles of Prag on April 21, 1421. The movement spread into Moravia, which joined with Bohemia in its revolution. The next step was the organisation of the newly-won freedom. A Diet held at Caslau in June accepted the Four Articles of Prag, declared Sigismund an enemy of Bohemia and unworthy of the crown, appointed a committee of twenty representatives of the different estates and parties to undertake the government of the land until it had a king, and left the organisation of religious matters to a synod of clergy which was soon to be convoked. Sigismund's ambassadors offering toleration, scarcely obtained a hearing: the offer came a year too late.

Although Bohemia was united in opposition to Sigismund and Catholicism, it was but natural that the divergencies of opinion within itself should grow wider as it felt itself more free from danger. The division between the Conservative and Radical party became more pronounced. The Conservatives, who were called Calixtins or Utraquists from their ceremonial, or Pragers from their chief seat, held by the position of Hus,— a position of orthodoxy in belief, with a reformation of ecclesiastical practice carried out according to Scripture. They altered as little as possible in the old ecclesiastical arrangements, retained the mass service with the communion under both kinds, and observed the festivals of the Church.[1] Against them were set the Radicals, the Taborites, amongst whom there were several parties. The most moderate, at the head of which stood Zizka, differed from the Pragers not so much in belief as in the determined spirit with which they were prepared to

[1] The Papal legate reported to the Council of Basel: (*Mon. Concil.* i. 141.) 'Quod in veteri Praga in omni loco ecclesiastico non alia vidit in Bohemorum ceremoniis, nisi sicut in nostris ecclesiis, excepta practica communicandi sub utraque specie.'

defend their opinions and carry them out in practice. The thorough Taborites cast aside all ecclesiastical authority and asserted the sufficiency of Scripture, for the right understanding of which the individual believer was directly illuminated by the Holy Ghost. They rejected Transubstantiation, and asserted that Christ was present in the elements only in a figurative way. Besides these were various extreme sects, who held that the Millennium had begun, that God existed only in the hearts of the believers, and the devil in the hearts of the wicked. Most notorious amongst these was the small sect of the Adamites, who took possession of a small island on the river Nezarka and gave themselves up to a life of communism which degenerated into shameless excesses. Against these extreme sectaries the Pragers and Zizka set up a standard of orthodoxy, and proceeded to measures of repression. Fifty of both sexes were burned by Zizka on the same day: they entered the flames with a smile, saying, 'To-day will we reign with Christ.' The island of the Adamites was stormed, and the entire body exterminated. Martinek Hauska, the chief teacher who opposed Transubstantiation, was burned as a heretic in Prag.

It was indeed needful that Bohemia should retain the appearance of unity if she were to succeed in maintaining her new religious freedom. Sigismund was disheartened by the failure of his first attempt, and was ready to wait and try the results of moderation. But the German electors and the Pope were by no means willing to give up Bohemia as lost. The four Rhenish Electors formed a league against the heretics: the Papal legate, Cardinal Branda, journeyed through Germany to kindle the zeal of the faithful. Sigismund was openly denounced as a favourer of heresy, and was compelled to bestir himself. It was agreed that the Electors should lead an army from Germany, and Sigismund should advance from Hungary through Moravia and unite with them. In September Germany poured an army of 200,000 men into Bohemia; but Sigismund tarried and deferred his coming. Loud accusations of treachery were brought against him by the angry princes, and disputes sprang up among them. The vast army wasted its energies in the siege of Saaz, and began gradually to disperse; the news of Zizka's advance turned it to shameful flight. It was said ironically that such was the horror which the German princes felt against the heretics, that they could not even endure to see them.[1]

When Sigismund had finished his preparations, he also in December entered Bohemia with a formidable army of 90,000 men, well armed, trained in warfare, led by Pipo of Florence, one of the most renowned generals of the age. Zizka put forth all his powers of generalship to save Bohemia from the impending danger. Zizka, who had been one-eyed for years, had lost his remaining eye at the siege of the little castle of Rabi in August. He was now entirely blind, but his blindness only gave greater clearness to his mental vision, and he could direct the movements of a campaign with greater precision than before. The very fact that he had to be dependent on others for information led him to impress more forcibly his own spirit on those around him, and so train up a school of great generals to succeed him. Under Zizka's guidance the democratic feeling of the Bohemians had been made the basis of a new military organisation which was now to try its strength against the chivalry of the Middle Ages. Strict discipline prevailed amongst Zizka's troops, and he was able to meet the dash of the feudal forces with the coolness of a trained army which could perform complicated manœuvres with unerring precision. He paid especial attention to artillery, and was the first great general to realise its importance. Moreover, he adapted the old war chariots to the purposes of defence. His line of march was protected on the flanks by waggons fastened to one another by iron chains. These waggons readily formed the fortifications of a camp or served as protection against an attack. In battle the soldiers, when repulsed, could retire behind their cover, and form again their scattered lines. The waggons were manned by the bravest troops, and their drivers were trained to form them according to letters of the alphabet; so that the Hussites, having the key, easily knew their way amongst the lines, while the enemy, if they forced their way, were lost in an inextricable labyrinth. At times the waggons, filled with heavy stones, were rolled down hill on the enemy's ranks; when once those ranks were broken, the

[1] Thomas Ebendorfer of Haselbach, quoted by Palacky, *Geschichte von Böhmen*, iii. 2, 254, from the MS. *Liber Augustalis*: ' Adeo enim eis Bohemi erant abominabiles ut non solum eos ferire sed ne quidem potuerunt eos contueri.'

waggons were rapidly driven in, and cut in two the enemy's line. It was a new kind of warfare, which spread terror and helplessness among the crusading hosts.

This new organisation was sorely tried when, on December 21, Sigismund's army advanced against Kuttenberg, and met Zizka's forces hard by its walls. The waggons of the Bohemians proved an impregnable defence, and their artillery did great execution against the Hungarians. But treachery was at work in Kuttenberg, and opened the gates to Sigismund. Next day the Bohemians found themselves shut in on all sides, and their foes prepared to reduce them by hunger. But in the darkness of the night Zizka drew his troops together, and with a charge of his waggons broke through the enemy's line and made good his retreat. Rapidly gathering reinforcements, Zizka returned to Kuttenberg on January 6, 1422, and fell suddenly upon the centre of the unsuspecting army. A panic seized the Germans; Sigismund fled ignominiously, and his example was followed by all. Zizka followed, and, aided by the wintry weather, inflicted severe losses on the invaders. More than 12,000 men are said to have perished. The second crusade against the Hussites failed even more signally than the first.

Bohemia had now beaten back both Sigismund, who came to assert his hereditary rights to the crown, and the German princes, who viewed with alarm the dismemberment of the empire. There remained the more difficult task of organising its political position. The great statesman, Nicolas of Hus, was dead, and Zizka had the talents of a general rather than a politician. His own democratic ideas were too strong for him to put himself at the head of the State, and bring about the necessary union between the Pragers and the Taborites. The Bohemian nobles and the Conservative party generally desired to take the management of affairs out of the hands of the Taborites, and re-establish a monarchy. Already they had offered the kingdom to Ladislas, King of Poland, who shrank from incurring the charge of heresy, which would hinder him in his constant warfare against the Teutonic knights in Prussia. But Witold, Grand Duke of Lithuania, a man of high political sagacity, had before his eyes the possibility of a great Slavic confederacy which would beat back all German aggression. He saw in the Hussite movement a means of bridging over the religious differences between the Latin and Greek Churches, which was an obstacle to the union of Prussia and Poland. These plans of Witold created great alarm in Germany, and many efforts were made to thwart them; but Witold took advantage of events, announced to the Pope that he wished to restore order in Bohemia, and in May 1422 sent the nephew of Ladislas of Poland, Sigismund Korybut, with an army to Prag. Prag, torn with internal dissensions, accepted Korybut as a deliverer. Zizka recognised him as ruler of the land, and Korybut showed zeal and moderation in winning over all parties to his side.

This union of Bohemia and Poland was a standing menace to Germany, and a diet held at Nürnberg in July appointed Frederick of Brandenburg to lead a new expedition into Bohemia. Frederick was keenly alive to the gravity of the situation, which indeed threatened himself in Brandenburg. He endeavoured to gather together both an army for a crusade and a permanent army of occupation, which was to be left in Bohemia. But Germany's internal weakness and constant dissensions prevented Frederick from accomplishing anything. He led a few soldiers into Bohemia, spent some time in negotiations, and then returned. Nor was Korybut's position in Bohemia a strong one. He failed in his military undertakings; his attempts at conciliation alienated the extreme Taborites; Zizka maintained an attitude of neutrality towards him. Meanwhile Martin V. was untiring in his endeavours to break down the alliance between Poland and Bohemia. He exhorted the Polish bishops to labour for that purpose. He wrote to Ladislas and Witold, pointing out the political dangers which beset them if they strayed from Catholicism.[1] Sigismund, on his part, was willing to purchase an alliance with Poland by abandoning the cause of the Teutonic Knights. The combined efforts of Martin V. and Sigismund were successful. Witold wrote to the Bohemians that his desire had been to reconcile them with the Roman Church; as they were obstinate, he was driven to abandon them to their fate. Korybut was recalled, and left Prag on December 24. The great idea of a Slavonic Empire and Church was at an end, and the future of Poland was decided

CHAP.
III.

Martin V. defeats the Polish alliance. December 1422.

[1] See his letter dated May 13, 1422, in Palacky, *Urkundliche Beiträge*, i. 199.

by its cowardice at this great crisis. Henceforth it was condemned to the isolation which it had chosen through want of foresight.

The departure of Korybut and freedom from invasion awakened amongst the Bohemians the differences which danger made them forget. The Pragers and the Taborites stood in stronger opposition to one another. The Pragers were more disposed to negotiation, and hoped that they might still find room for their opinions under the shadow of the authority of the Church. Zizka had grown more convinced of the futility of compromise, and a stern spirit of resistance took possession of him and his followers. The year 1423 is full of the records of civil war and devastation in Bohemia, and Zizka spread fire and slaughter even in the neighbouring lands of Moravia and Hungary. The year 1424 is known in Bohemian annals as ' Zizka's bloody year.' He swept like a storm over towns and villages of those who wished for compromise, and inflicted a sore defeat on the forces of the Pragers who were following on his track. The Pragers in dismay looked for a leader, and found him in Korybut, who in June 1424 returned to Prag, no longer as the deputy of Witold and the Governor of Bohemia, but as a personal adventurer at the head of the moderate party. Zizka advanced against Prag; and the capital of Bohemia, the seat of Hus and his teaching, was in danger of a terrible siege. But moderate counsels prevailed at the last moment to avert this crowning calamity. Zizka withdrew and soon after died of the plague on October 11. His followers bewailed the loss of one who was to them both leader and father; they took the name of Orphans in sign of their bereavement.

Zizka was a man of profound, even fanatical, piety, with great decision and energy, who clearly saw the issue that lay before the Bohemians if they wished to maintain their religious freedom. But he was a man of action rather than reflection. He had the qualities necessary to head a party, but not those necessary to lead a people. He could solve the problem for himself by a rigorous determination to be watchful and to persist; but his range of ideas was not large enough to enable him to form any policy which would organise the nation to keep what it had won. Amid Bohemian parties he maintained a strong position, opposed to extremes but convinced of the

hopelessness of conciliation. As a general he is almost un-
rivalled, for he knew how to train out of raw materials an in-
vincible army, and he never lost a battle. He could drive back
hosts of invaders and could maintain order within the limits of
Bohemia; but he lacked the political sense that could bind
a people together. His position became more and more a
purely personal one; his resolute character degenerated into
savagery; and his last energies were spent in trying to impress upon all his own personal convictions without any consideration of the exact issue to which they would lead. Without Zizka Bohemia would never have made good her resistance
to the Church and to Sigismund. It was his misfortune rather
than his fault that he had not also the political genius to
organise that resistance on a secure basis for the future.

By Zizka's death the party opposed to reconciliation with _{Desire of the mode-rate party for peace. 1425.}
Rome lost its chief strength. The Taborites divided into two—
the Orphans, who held by the opinions of Zizka, and were divided
from the Pragers rather on social and political than on religious
grounds—and the extreme Taborites, who denied Transubstantiation and were entirely opposed to the Church system. But
both these parties were feeble, and spent their energies in conflicts with one another. The field was open for Korybut and
the Pragers to continue negotiations for peace and reconciliation. Bohemia was growing weary of anarchy. The first fervour
of religious zeal had worn away, the first enthusiasm had been
disillusioned. Men were beginning to count the cost of their
political isolation, of the devastation of their land by foes without and quarrels within, of the ruin of their commerce.
Against this they had little to set as a counterpoise. The
exactions of feudal lords were as easy to bear as the exactions
of a plundering army; the equality which they had hoped to
find through religion was not yet attained. Though victorious
in the field, the great mass of the Bohemian people longed for
peace almost on any terms.

During the year 1425 Korybut pursued his negotiations, _{Procopius the Great defeats the Saxons at Aussig. June 1426.}
and was engaged in paving the way for reconciliation with
Rome. The people were not unwilling, but the army still
remained true to its faith. As they felt that danger was
menacing them, the Taborites again drew together, reasserted

their principles and prepared to wage war.   Besides the danger
from half-heartedness at home, two active enemies harassed the
Bohemian border.   Albert of Austria attacked Moravia, and
Frederick of Meissen, whom Sigismund had made Elector of
Saxony, was winning back Silesia.   A new leader arose to guide
the renewed vigour of the Taborites, Procopius, called the Great
to distinguish him from others of the same name.   Procopius,
like Zizka, was sprung from the lower nobility, and was a priest
at the time when he first attached himself to the party of Hus.
Without possessing the military genius of Zizka, he knew how
to manage the army which Zizka had created; and he had a
larger mind and was capable of greater plans than his predecessor.   Procopius was averse from war, and as a priest never
bore arms nor took part in the battles which he directed.   He
wished for peace, but an honourable and enduring peace, which
would guarantee to Bohemia her religious freedom.   Peace, he
saw, could only be won by arms; it was not enough to repel
the invaders, Bohemia must secure its borders by acting on the
offensive.   He led his troops up the Elbe to the siege of
Aussig.   Frederick of Saxony was absent at a Diet at Nürnberg,
but his wife Catharine called for succours and gathered an army
of 70,000 men.   The Bohemian troops, reinforced by Korybut,
amounted only to 25,000.   On June 16, 1426, was fought the
battle under the walls of Aussig.   The Bohemians entrenched
themselves behind their waggons, and the furious onslaught of
the German knights forced the first line.   But the artillery
opened on their flank; the Bohemians from their waggons
dragged the knights from their horses with long lances, and
dashed them to the ground.   The German lines were broken,
and the Bohemians rushed in and turned them to flight.   The
slaughter that ensued was terrible: 10,000 Germans were left
dead upon the field.   Procopius wished to lead his victorious
army farther, so as to teach the Germans a lesson; but the
Moderates refused to follow, and the campaign came to an end
without any other results.

Failure of
Korybut's
plans for
reconcilia-
tion. 1427.
As usual, a victory united Germany and disunited Bohemia.
Korybut pursued his schemes for union with Rome, and wrote
to Martin V. asking him to receive Bohemian envoys for this
purpose.   Martin V. expressed his willingness, provided they
would abide by the decision of the Holy See, which was, how-

ever, ready to receive information of their desires.[1] Korybut
hoped that the Pope would abandon Sigismund and recognise
himself as King of Bohemia in return for his services to the
Church. But Korybut was not yet firm enough in his position
to carry out his plan. The dissension between the Taborites
and the Pragers was not yet so profound that the Moderates as
a body were willing to submit unreservedly to Rome. Kory
but's plans were known in Prag, and a party formed itself which,
while in favour of reconciliation, stood firm by the Four Articles.
On Maundy Thursday, April 17, 1427, an eloquent and
popular priest, John Rokycana, denounced in a sermon the
treachery of Korybut. The people flew to arms, drove out the
Poles, and made Korybut a prisoner. His plans had entirely
failed, and the victory of the moderate party over him neces
sarily turned to the profit of Procopius and the Taborites.

Procopius was now ruler of Bohemia, and carried out his
policy of terrifying his opponents by destructive raids into
Austria, Lusatia, Moravia, and Silesia. Germany in alarm
again began to raise forces; and Martin V. hoped to gain greater
importance for the expedition by appointing as Papal legate
Henry Beaufort, Bishop of Winchester, whom he made Cardinal
for the purpose. Beaufort's experience of affairs and high
political position made him a fit man to interest England and
France in the cause of the Church. In July 1427 a strong
army entered Bohemia and laid siege to Mies; but the soldiers
were undisciplined and the leaders were disunited. · On the
approach of Procopius a panic seized the army, and it fled in
wild confusion to Tachau. There Henry of Winchester, who
had stayed behind in Germany, met the fugitives. He was
the only man of courage and resolution in the army. He implored them to stand and meet the foe; he unfolded the Papal
banner and even set up a crucifix to shame the fugitives.[1]
They stayed and formed in battle order, but the appearance of
the Bohemian troops again filled them with dread, and a second
time they fled in panic terror. In vain Henry of Winchester
tried to rally them. He seized the flag of the Empire, tore it

Failur
of the
Crusade of
1427.

---

[1] See letter of Martin V. to Sigismund, in Raynaldus, 1427, § 10: 'Ipsos
volebamus audire, ita scilicet, si venirent parati stare nostræ determinationi,
nobis et ecclesiæ de cætero parituri.'
[2] Andrew of Ratisbon, in Höfler, ii. 454; i. 578.

in pieces and flung them before the princes; but at last was himself driven to flee, lest he should fall into the hands of the heretics.

This disgraceful retreat did not bring men's minds nearer to peace. Martin V. urged a new expedition, and Sigismund was not sorry to see the Electors in difficulties. In Bohemia the party of peace made a vain effort to raise Prag in the name of Korybut; but the rising was put down without the help of Procopius, and Korybut was sent back to Poland in September 1427. Procopius rallied round him the entire Hussite party, and, true to his policy of extorting an honourable peace, signalised the year 1428 by destructive raids into Austria, Bavaria, Silesia, and Saxony. After each expedition he returned home and waited to see if proposals for peace were likely to be made. In April 1429 a conference was arranged between Sigismund and some of the Hussite leaders, headed by Procopius, at Pressburg, in Hungary. Sigismund proposed a truce for two years till the assembling of the Council at Basel, before which the religious differences might be laid.[1] The Hussites answered that their differences arose because the Church had departed from the example of Christ and the Apostles: the Council of Constance had shown them what they had to expect from Councils; they demanded an impartial judge between the Council and themselves, and this judge was the Holy Scripture and writings founded thereon. The proposals of Sigismund were referred to a Diet at Prag, and answer was made that the Bohemians were ready to submit their case to a Council, provided it contained representatives of the Greek and Armenian Churches, which received the Communion under both kinds, and provided it undertook to judge according to the Word of God, not the will of the Pope. Their request was equitable but impracticable. It was clearly impossible for them to submit to the decision of a Council composed entirely of their opponents; yet they could have little hope that their proposal to construct an impartial tribunal would be accepted.[2]

The negotiations came to nothing. Indeed, Sigismund was busy at the same time in summoning the forces of the Empire to

---

[1] Palacky, *Urkundliche Beiträge*, ii. 22.
[2] See ibid. ii. 50, and Andrew of Ratisbon, *Dialogus*, in Höfler, i. 582.

advance again against Bohemia. Henry of Winchester had gathered a force of 5,000 English horsemen, and in July 1429 landed in Flanders on his way to Germany. But religious considerations were driven to give way to political. The unexpected successes of Jeanne Darc, the raising of the siege of Orleans, the coronation of Charles VII. at Rheims, gave a sudden check to the English power in France. Winchester's soldiers were ordered to the relief of their countrymen; the Cardinal's influence could not persuade his men to prefer religious zeal to patriotic sentiment. The Catholics in Germany broke into a wail of lamentation when they saw the forces of the Papal legate diverted to a war with France.[1]

Germany was feeble, and Bohemia was again agitated by a struggle. The peace party in Prag had for its quarters the Old Town, and the more pronounced Hussites the New Town. The two quarters of the city were on the point of open hostility when Procopius again united Bohemia for a war of invasion. The year 1430 was terrible in the annals of Germany, for the Hussite army carried devastation into the most flourishing provinces of the Empire. They advanced along the Elbe into Saxony, and penetrated as far as Meissen; they invaded Franconia and threatened with siege the stately town of Nürnberg. Wherever they went the land was laid waste, and fire and slaughter were spread on every side.

The policy of Procopius was beginning to have its effect. The Hussite movement was the great question which attracted the attention of Europe. Hussite manifestoes were circulated in every land; the new opinions were discussed openly and in many places met with considerable sympathy.[2] The Hussites complained that their opponents attacked them without really knowing their beliefs, which were founded only on Holy Scripture; they invited all men to acquaint themselves with their opinions; they appealed to the success of their arms as a proof that God was on their side. The opinion began to prevail that,

[1] See the letters of Martin V. to Charles VII. of France, in Raynaldus, 1429, §§ 16, 17.

[2] John of Segovia (*Mon. Concil.* ii. 5) gives an account of these Hussite letters in Spain: 'Premittebant se desiderare, ut illis aperiret intellectum Deus illuminans corda eorum, narrantes quomodo jam a pluribus annis inter se et illos magna fuisset discordia, et utrinque nobiles et ignobiles multi fatui sua corpora perdidissent, &c.'

after all, argument and not arms was the proper mode of meeting heresy, particularly when arms had proved a failure. Martin V., who hated the very name of a Council,[1] was again haunted at the end of 1430 by the face of John of Ragusa, who had been negotiating with Sigismund that he should combine with the University of Paris to urge on the Pope a speedy summons of the Council to Basel. Soon after John's arrival in Rome, on the morning of November 8, the day on which Martin V. was to create three new cardinals, a document was found affixed to the door of the Papal palace which caused a great sensation in Rome.

Startling
document
in favour
of the
Council.
1430.
' Whereas it is notorious to all Christendom that since the Council of Constance, an untold number of Christians have wandered from the faith by means of the Hussites, and members are daily being lopped off from the body of the Church militant, nor is there any one of all the sons whom she begat to help or console her; now, therefore, two most serene princes direct to all Christian princes the following conclusions, approved by learned doctors both of canon and of civil law, which they have undertaken to defend in the Council to be celebrated according to the decree of Constance in March next.' Then followed the conclusions, which set forth that the Catholic faith must be preferred before man, whoever he be; that princes secular as well as ecclesiastical are bound to defend the faith; that as former heresies, the Novatian, Arian, Nestorian, and others, were extirpated by Councils, so must that of the Hussites; that every Christian under pain of mortal sin must strive for the celebration of a Council for this purpose; if popes or cardinals put hindrances in the way they must be reckoned as favourers of heresy; if the Pope does not summon the Council at the appointed time those present at it ought to withdraw from his obedience, and proceed against those who try to hinder it as against favourers of heresy. This startling document was currently supposed to be authorised by Frederick of Brandenburg, Albert of Austria, and Lewis of Brieg.[2]

Several of the Cardinals, chief of whom was Condulmier, the

---

[1] 'In immensum nomen concilii abhorrebat.'—John of Ragusa, *Mon. Con.* i. 66.

[2] It is given in Martene, *Ampl. Collectio*, viii. 48, in a letter from a Burgundian envoy; also by John of Ragusa, *Mon. Concil.* i. 65.

future pope, urged on Martin V. to comply with the prevailing wish. But Martin V. wished again to try the chance of war, and awaited the results of a diet which Sigismund had summoned to Nürnberg. On January 11, 1431, he appointed a new legate for Germany, Giuliano Cesarini, whom he had just created Cardinal. Cesarini was sprung from a poor but noble family in Rome, and his talents attracted Martin V.'s notice. He was a man of large mind, great personal holiness, and deep learning. His appearance and manner were singularly attractive, and all who came in contact with him were impressed by the genuineness and nobility of his character. If any man could succeed in awakening enthusiasm in Germany it was Cesarini.[1]

Before Cesarini's departure to Germany, Martin V. had been brought with difficulty to recognise the necessity of the assembly of the Council at Basel, and commissioned Cesarini to preside at its opening. The Bull authorising this was dated February 1, and conferred full powers on Cesarini to change the place of the Council at his will, to confirm its decrees and do all things necessary for the honour and peace of the Church. This Bull reached Cesarini at Nürnberg, shortly after the news of Martin V.'s death. The Diet of Nürnberg voted an expedition into Bohemia, and Cesarini eagerly travelled through Germany preaching the crusade. At the same time steps were taken to open the Council at Basel. On the last day of February a Burgundian abbot read before the assembled clergy of Basel the Bulls constituting the Council, and then solemnly pronounced that he was ready for conciliar business. In April, representatives of the University of Paris and a few other prelates began to arrive; but Cesarini sent to them John of Ragusa on April 30, to explain that the Bohemian expedition was the object for which he had been primarily commissioned by the Pope, and was the great means of extirpating heresy. He besought them to send envoys to help him in his dealings with the Bohemians, and meanwhile to use their best endeavours to assemble others to the Council. The envoys of the Council, at the head of whom was John of Ragusa, followed Sigismund to Eger, where he held a conference with the Hussites. The conference was only meant to divert the attention of the Bohemians, and it was

CHAP. III.

Cardinal Cesarini appointed legate in Germany. January 1431.

Beginnings of the Council of Basel. February–July 1431.

---

[1] See his character as described by Vespasiano, and Paulus Jovius in the *Elogia Virorum Illustrium.*

speedily ended by a demand on the part of the envoys that the Bohemians should submit their case unconditionally to the Council's decision. Sigismund returned to Nürnberg on May 22, and the German forces rapidly assembled. There were complaints at the legate's absence; Cesarini's zeal had led him as far as Köln, whence he hastened to Nürnberg on June 27. There he found a messenger from Eugenius IV., urging the prosecution of the Council, and bidding him, if it could be done without hindrance to the cause at heart, to leave the Bohemian expedition and proceed at once to Basel. But Cesarini's heart and soul were now in the crusade. He determined to pursue his course, and on July 3 appointed John of Palomar, an auditor of the Papal court, and John of Ragusa, to preside over the Council as his deputies in his absence.

Cesarini's
appeal to
the Bohe-
mians.
July 5.
1431.
On July 5, Cesarini addressed an appeal to the Bohemians, protesting his wish to bring peace rather than a sword. Were they not all Christians? Why should they stray from their holy mother the Church? Could a handful of men pretend to know better than all the doctors of Christendom? Let them look upon their wasted land and the miseries they had endured; he earnestly and affectionately besought them to return while it was time to the bosom of the Church. The Bohemians were not slow to answer. They asserted the truth of the Four Articles of Prag, which they were prepared to prove by Scripture. They recounted the results of the conferences at Pressburg and Eger, where they had professed themselves willing to appear before any Council which would judge according to Scripture, and would work with them in bringing about the reformation of the Church according to the Word of God. They had been told that such limitations were contrary to the dignity of a General Council, which was above all law. This they could not admit, and trusting in God's truth were prepared to resist to the utmost those who attacked them.[1]

On July 7 Cesarini left Nürnberg with Frederick of Brandenburg, who had been appointed commander of the Crusade. Cesarini had done his utmost to pacify the German princes and unite them for this expedition. He was full of hope when he set out from Nürnberg. But when he reach Weiden, where the different contingents were to meet, his hopes were rudely dis-

[1] In Martene, *Amp. Coll.* viii. 15; also *Mon. Concil.* i. 148.

pelled. Instead of soldiers he found excuses; he heard tales
of nobles needing their troops to war against one another rather
than combine in defence of the Church. 'We are many
fewer,' he wrote to Basel on July 16, 'than was said in Nürnberg, so that the leaders hesitate. Not only our victory but
even our entry into Bohemia is doubtful. We are not so few
that, if there were any courage amongst us, we need shrink
from entering Bohemia. I am very anxious and above measure
sad. For if the army retreats without doing anything, the
Christian religion in these parts is undone; such terror would
be felt by our side and their boldness would increase.'[1] However, on August 1, an army of 40,000 horse and 90,000 foot
crossed the Bohemian border, and advanced against Tachau.
Cesarini seeing it unprepared for attack urged an immediate
onslaught: he was told that the soldiers were tired with their
march, and must wait till to-morrow. In the night the inhabitants strengthened their walls and put their artillery into
position, so that a storm was hopeless. The crusading host
passed on, devastating and slaughtering with a ruthless cruelty
that was a strange contrast to the charitable utterances of
Cesarini's manifesto. But their triumph was short-lived. On
August 14 the Bohemian army advanced against them at Tauss.
Its approach was known, when it was yet some way off, by
the noise of the rolling waggons. Cesarini, with the Duke of
Saxony, ascended a hill to see the disposition of the army;
there he saw with surprise the German waggons retreating.
He sent to ask Frederick of Brandenburg the meaning of this
movement, and was told that he had ordered the waggons to
take up a secure position in the rear. But the movement was
misunderstood by the Germans. A cry was raised that some
were retreating. Panic seized the host, and in a few moments
Cesarini saw the crusaders in wild confusion making for the
Bohemian Forest in their rear. He was driven to join the fugitives, and all his efforts to rally them were vain. Procopius,
seeing the flight, charged the fugitives, seized all their waggons
and artillery, and inflicted upon them terrible slaughter. Cesarini escaped with difficulty in disguise, and had to endure the
threats and reproaches of the Germans, who accused him as the
author of all their calamities.

[1] *Mon. Concil.* i. 99.

BOOK
III.

Cesarini
arrives in
Basel. Sep-
tember 9,
1431.

Cesarini was humbled by his experience. He reproached himself for his confidence in German arms; he had now seen enough of the cowardice and feebleness of Germany. He had seen, too, the growing importance of the Hussite movement, and the force which their success was giving to the spread of their convictions throughout Germany. When he returned to Nürnberg Sigismund met him with due honour; the German princes gathered round him and protested their readiness for another campaign next year. But Cesarini answered that no other remedy remained for the check of the Hussite heresy than the Council of Basel. He besought them to do their utmost to strengthen the feeble and cheer the desponding in Germany, to exhort those whose faith was wavering to hold out in hope of succour from the Council.[1] With this advice he hastened to Basel, where he arrived on September 9. To the Council were now transferred all men's expectations of a peaceable settlement of the formidable difficulty which threatened Western Christendom.

[1] John of Segovia, in *Mon. Concil.* ii. 29.

CHAPTER IV.

FIRST ATTEMPT OF EUGENIUS IV. TO DISSOLVE THE COUNCIL OF BASEL.

1431–1434.

THE ancient city of Basel was well fitted to be the seat of a great assemblage. High above the rushing Rhine rose its stately minster on a rocky hill which seemed to brave the river's force. Round the river and the minster clusters the city. It was surrounded by a fertile plain, was easily accessible from Germany, France, and Italy, and as a free Imperial city was a place of security and dignity for the Council. To the eye of an Italian, accustomed to marbles and frescoes, the interior of the cathedral looked bald and colourless; but its painted windows and the emblazoned shields of nobles hung round the walls gave it a staid richness of its own. The Italians owned that it was a comfortable place, and that the houses of the merchants of Basel equalled those of Florence. It was well ordered by its magistrates, who administered strict justice and organised admirably the supplies of food. The citizens of Basel were devout, but little given to literature; they were luxurious and fond of wine, but were steadfast, truthful, sincere, and honest in their dealings.[1]

The Council was long in assembling. It was natural that, while the President was absent in Bohemia, few should care to undertake the journey. If the Crusade ended in a victory, it was doubtful how long the Council would sit. Cesarini's deputies, John of Palomar and John of Ragusa, opened the Council with due ceremonial on July 23. It was only sparsely at-

CHAP. IV.

Description of Basel.

Formal opening of the Council. July 23, 1431.

---

[1] This is the picture of Æneas Sylvius in a letter addressed to the Cardinal of S. Angelo, printed by Urstisius, *Epitome Historiæ Basiliensis* (1577). It was written by Æneas as an introduction to a history of the Council.

tended, and its first business was to increase its numbers, and
obtain some guarantees for its safety and freedom from the city
magistrates and from Sigismund. On August 29 came the news
of the flight of the Crusaders from Tauss. It produced a deep
impression on the assembled fathers, and convinced them of
the seriousness and importance of the work which they had
before them. They felt that the chastisement which had befallen the Church was due to her shortcomings, and that penitence and reformation alone could avert further disaster. [1]

To this feeling the arrival of Cesarini on September 9 gave
further force. Deeply impressed with the importance of the
crisis, he sent forth letters urging on prelates that they should
lose no time in coming to the Council. Only three bishops,
seven abbots, and a few doctors were assembled, as the roads
were unsafe, owing to a war between the Dukes of Austria and
Burgundy. He wrote also to the Pope to express his own convictions and the common opinion of the work which the Council might do: it might extirpate heresy, promote peace throughout Christendom, restore the Church to its pristine glory,
humble its enemies, treat of union with the Greeks, and finally
set on foot a crusade for the recovery of the Holy Land.[2] An
envoy was sent to the Pope to explain to him how matters
stood, and to urge the need of his presence at Basel. Meanwhile there were many discussions relative to the constitution
of the Council, who were to take part in it, and what was to be
the method of voting. There was a general agreement that, as
the great object of the Council was to arrange a union with the
Bohemians and the Greeks, it was desirable to admit men of
learning, that is, doctors of canon or civil law, as well as prelates. The question of the method of voting was left until the
Council became more numerous.

Invitation
sent to the
Bohe-
mians.
October 10,
1431.
The Council, moreover, lost no time in trying to bring
about its chief object. On October 10 a letter was sent to the
Bohemians, begging them to join with the Council for the promotion of unity. Perhaps God has allowed discord so long that

---

[1] John of Ragusa (*Mon. Concil.* i. 101): 'Fortius accensi ad reformationem ecclesiæ, negotia concilii multo acrius et cum majore sollicitudine et
labore cœperunt peragere et procurare, expressam Dei hanc ultionem et flagel-
lum percipientes evenire propter peccata et deformationem ecclesiæ.'

[2] The letter is given by John of Ragusa, *Mon. Concil.* i. 108.

experience might teach the evils of dissension. Christ's disciples are bound to labour for unity and peace. The desolation of Bohemia must naturally incline it to wish for peace, and where can that be obtained more surely than in a Council assembled in the Holy Ghost? At Basel everything will be done with diligence and with freedom; every one may speak, and the. Holy Ghost will lead men's hearts to the truth, if only they will have faith. The Bohemians have often complained that they could not get a free hearing: at Basel they may both speak and hear freely, and the prayers of the faithful will help both sides. The most ample safe-conduct was offered to their representatives, and the fullest appreciation given to their motives. ' Send, we beseech you, men in whom you trust that the Spirit of the Lord rests, gentle, God-fearing, humble, desirous of peace, seeking not their own, but the things of Christ, whom we pray to give to us and you and all Christian people peace on earth, and in the world to come life everlasting.'[1] This letter, which breathes profound sincerity and true Christian charity, was, no doubt, an expression of the views of Cesarini, and was most probably written by him. The greatest care was taken to make no allusion to the past, and to approach the matter entirely afresh. But it was impossible for the Bohemians to forget all that had gone before. The difficulty experienced in sending the letter to the Bohemians showed the existence of a state of things very different from what the Council wished to recognise. There was no intercourse between Bohemia and the rest of Christendom; the Bohemians were under the ban of the Council of Siena as heretics. It was finally agreed to send three copies by different ways, in hopes that one at least might arrive. One was sent to Sigismund for transmission, another to the magistrates of Nürnberg, and a third to the magistrates of Eger. All three copies arrived safely in Bohemia in the beginning of December.

This activity on the part of the Council necessarily aroused the suspicion of Eugenius IV. The zeal of Cesarini, which had been kindled by his Bohemian experiences, went far beyond the limits of Papal prudence. The Bohemian question did not seem so important at Rome as it did at Basel. A Council

Eugenius IV. orders the dissolution of the Council of Basel. November 12, 1431.

---

[1] John of Ragusa, *Mon. Concil.* i. 135; also in John of Segovia, and in Mansi, xxix. 233

which under the pressure of necessity opened negotiations with heretics, might greatly imperil the faith of the Church, and might certainly be expected to do many things contrary to the Papal headship. A democratic spirit prevailed in Basel, which had shown itself in the admission of all doctors; and the discussion about the organisation of the Council showed that it would be very slightly amenable to the influence of the Pope and the Curia. Eugenius IV. resolved, therefore, at once to rid himself of the Council. He thought it wisest to overturn it at once, before it had time to strike its roots deeper. Accordingly, on November 12, he wrote to Cesarini, empowering him to dissolve the Council at Basel and proclaim another to be held at Bologna in a year and a half. The reasons given were the small attendance of prelates at Basel, the difficulties of access owing to the war between Austria and Burgundy, the distracted state of men's minds in that quarter owing to the spread of Hussite opinions; but especially the fact that negotiations were now pending with the Greek Emperor, who had promised to come to a Council which was to unite the Greek and Latin Churches on condition that the Pope paid the expenses of his journey and held the Council in some Italian city. As it would be useless to hold two Councils at the same time, the Pope thought it better that the Fathers of Basel should reassemble at Bologna when their business was ready.

The Pope's
Bull of dis-
solution is
not ac-
cepted
by the
Council.
January
1432.
A Bull dissolving the Council on these grounds was also secretly prepared, and was signed by ten cardinals. The Council, in entire ignorance of the blow that was being aimed at it, was engaged in preparations for its first public session, which took place under the presidency of Cesarini on December 14. The Council declared itself to be duly constituted, and laid down three objects for its activity: the extirpation of heresy, the purification of Christendom, and the reformation of morals. It appointed its officials and guarded by decrees its safety and freedom. On December 23, arrived the Bishop of Parenzo, treasurer of Eugenius IV., and was honourably received; but the coldness of his manner showed the object of his mission. The Council was at once in a ferment of excitement. In a congregation on December 29, the citizens of Basel appeared in force, and protested against the dissolution. Various speakers of the Council laid before the Bishop of Parenzo four

propositions : that the urgent needs of Christendom did not allow of the dissolution of the Council ; that such a step would cause great scandal and offence to the Church ; that if this Council were dissolved or prorogued, it was idle to talk of summoning another ; that a General Council ought to proceed against all who tried to hinder it, and ought to call all Christian princes to its aid. The Bishop of Parenzo was not prepared for this firm attitude ; he found things at Basel different from his expectations. He thought it wise to temporise, and declared that if he had any Papal Bulls he would not publish them. Meanwhile he tried to induce Cesarini to dissolve the Council. Cesarini was sorely divided between his allegiance to the Pope and his sense of what was due to the welfare of Christendom. It was agreed that two envoys should be sent to the Pope, one from Cesarini and one from the Council. The Bishop of Parenzo thought it wise to flee away on January 8, 1432, leaving his Bulls with John of Prato, who attempted to publish them on January 13, but was interrupted, and his Bulls and himself were taken in custody by the Council's orders.[1]

Cesarini was deeply moved by this attitude of the Pope. To his fervent mind it was inconceivable that the head of Christendom should behave with such levity at so grave a crisis. He wrote at once to Eugenius IV. a letter, in which he expressed with the utmost frankness his bitter disappointment at the Pope's conduct, his firm conviction of the need of straightforward measures on the part of the ecclesiastical authorities to restore the shattered confidence of Christian people. He began his letter by saying that he was driven to speak freely and fearlessly by the manifest peril of the faith, the danger of the loss of obedience to the Papacy, the obloquy with which Eugenius was everywhere assailed. He recapitulated the facts concerning his own mission to Bohemia and his presidency of the Council ; detailed the hopes which he and everyone in Germany entertained of the Council's mediation. ' I was driven also to come here by observing the dissoluteness and disorder of the German clergy, by which the laity are sorely irritated against the Church—so much so, that there is reason to fear that, if the clergy do not amend their ways, the laity will attack them, as the Hussites do. If there had been no General Council, I should have

Cesarini's letter to Eugenius IV. protesting against the dissolution. January 1432.

---

[1] John of Segovia, *Mon. Con.* ii. 64.

thought it my duty as legate to summon a provincial synod for the reform of the clergy; for unless the clergy be reformed I fear that, even if the Bohemian heresy were extinguished, another would rise up in its place.' Having these opinions, he came to the Council and tried to conduct its business with diligence, thinking that such was the Pope's desire. 'I did not suppose that your holiness wished me to dissemble or act negligently; if you had bid me do so, I would have answered that you must lay that duty on another, for I have determined never to occupy the post of a dissembler.'

He then passed on to the question of the prorogation of the Council, and laid before the Pope the considerations which he would have urged if he had been in the Curia when the question was discussed. (1) The Bohemians have been summoned to the Council; its prorogation will be a flight before them on the part of the Church as disgraceful as the flight of the German army. 'By this flight we shall approve their errors and condemn the truth and justice of our own cause. Men will see in this the finger of God, and will see that the Bohemians can neither be vanquished by arms nor by argument. O luckless Christendom! O Catholic faith, abandoned by all; soldiers and priests alike desert thee; no one dares stand on thy side.' (2) This flight will lose the allegiance of wavering Catholics, amongst whom are already rife opinions contrary to the Holy See. (3) The ignominy of the flight will fall on the clergy, who will be universally attacked. (4) 'What will the world say when it hears of this? Will it not judge that the clergy is incorrigible and wishes to moulder in its abuses? So many Councils have been held in our time, but no reform has followed. Men were expecting some results from this Council; if it be dissolved they will say that we mock both God and men. The whole reproach, the whole shame and ignominy, will fall upon the Roman Curia as the cause and author of all these ills. Holy Father, may you never be the cause of such evils! At your hands will be required the blood of those that perish; about all things you will have to render a strict account at the judgment seat of God.' (5 & 6) To promote the pacification of Christendom ambassadors have been sent to make peace between England and France, between Poland and the Teutonic Knights; the dissolution of the Council will stop their valuable

labours. (7) There are disturbances in Magdeburg and Passau, CHAP.
IV.
where the people have risen against their bishops and show signs
of following the Hussites. The Council may arrange these
matters ; if it be dissolved discord will spread. (8) The Duke
of Burgundy has been asked by the Council to undertake the
part of leader against the Hussites. If the Council be dissolved,
he will be irritated against the Church, and his services will be
lost. (9) Many German nobles are preparing for another expedition into Bohemia if need be. If they are deluded by the
Pope, they will turn against the Church. 'I myself will rather
die than live ignominiously. I will go perhaps to Nürnberg and
place myself in the hands of these nobles that they may do with
me what they will, even sell me to the heretics. All men shall
know that I am innocent.' (10) The Council sent envoys to
confirm the wavering on the Bohemian borders : if the Council
be dissolved, their work will be undone and there will be a large
addition to the Hussites.

He then proceeded to answer the Pope's objections. If he
cannot conveniently come to Basel in person on account of his
health, let him send a deputation of cardinals and eminent
persons. As to the safety of the place, it is as secure as
Constance. It is said that the Pope fears lest the Council
meddle with the temporalities of the Church. It is not reasonably to be expected that an ecclesiastical assembly will act
to its own detriment. There have been many previous Councils
with no such result. 'I fear lest it happen to us as it did to
the Jews, who said, "If we let him alone, the Romans will come
and take away our place and nation." So we say, "If we
let this Council alone, the laity will come and take away our
temporalities." But by the just judgment of God the Jews lost
their place because they would not let Christ alone ; and by the just
judgment of God, if we do not let this Council alone we shall lose
our temporalities, and (God forbid) our lives and souls as well.'
Let the Pope, on the other hand, be friendly with the Council,
reform his Curia, and be ready to act for the good of the Church.
The Council is likely, if pressed to extremities, to refuse to
dissolve, and there would be the danger of a schism. He begged
to be relieved of his commission and complained of the want of
straightforwardness. If he attempted to dissolve the Council, he
would be stoned to death by the fathers ; if he were to go away,

Open hos-
tility be-
tween the
Pope and
the Coun-
cil.

the Council would be certain to appoint for itself another president.[1]

This letter is remarkable for its clear exhibition of the state of affairs in Europe at this time, and as we read it now, it is still more remarkable for the political instinct which enabled its writer to make so true a forecast of the future. It would have been well for Eugenius IV. if he had had the wisdom to appreciate its importance. It would have been well for the future of the Papacy if Cesarini's words had awakened an echo in the Court of Rome. As it was, the politicians of the Curia only smiled at the exalted enthusiasm of Cesarini, and Eugenius IV. was too narrow-minded and obstinate to reconsider the wisdom of a course of conduct which he had once adopted. He did not understand, nor did he care to understand, the sentiments of the Council. He had forgotten the current of feeling against the Papacy which had been so strong at Constance. The decrees of Constance were not among the Papal Archives; and one of the Cardinals who possessed the manuscript of Filastre was heard with astonishment by the Curia when he called attention to the decree which declared a General Council to be superior to the Pope.[2] At Basel, on the other hand, there were many copies of the acts of the Council of Constance, and it was held that the Pope could not dissolve a General Council without its own consent. The rash step of Eugenius forced the Council into an attitude of open hostility towards the Papacy, and a desperate struggle between the two powers was inevitable.

Sigismund
makes an
expedition
into Italy.
November
1431.

The first question for both parties was the attitude of Sigismund. His personal interest in the settlement of the Hussite rebellion naturally inclined him to favour in every way the assembling of the Council. In July 1431 he took the Council under his Imperial protection, and in August wrote in its interest to make peace between the Dukes of Austria and Burgundy. But Sigismund felt that the years which had elapsed since the Council of Constance had not been glorious to his reputation. He had failed ignominiously in Bohemia and had exercised little influence in Germany, where he had

---

[1] The letter is given in Æn. Syl. *Opera*, p. 64, in John of Segovia, 95, &c. and in Mansi.

[2] John of Segovia, p. 77.

quarrelled with Frederick of Brandenburg, who was the most distinguished amongst the electors. His early enthusiasm for acting with dignity the part of secular head of Christendom had been damped at Constance, and he did not care to appear at Basel without some accession to his dignity. With characteristic desire for outward show, he determined on an expedition to Italy, to assume the Imperial crown. He hoped to establish once more the Imperial claims, to check the power of Venice, who was the enemy of Hungary, and to induce the Pope to come to Basel. Yet to attain all these objects he had only a following of some 2,000 Hungarian and German knights.[1] His hopes were entirely built on the help of Filippo Maria Visconti, who was at war with Venice and Florence, and with whom Sigismund made a treaty in July. Before setting out for Italy he appointed William of Bavaria his vicegerent as Protector of the Council: then early in November he crossed the Alps, and on November 21 arrived in Milan. But the jealous and suspicious character of Filippo Maria Visconti could not bear the presence of a superior; he was afraid that Sigismund's presence might be the occasion of a rising against himself. Accordingly he gave orders that Sigismund should be honourably received in Milan; but he himself withdrew from the city and remained secluded in one of his castles. He refused to visit Sigismund, and gave the ridiculous excuse that his emotions were too strong; if he saw Sigismund he would die of joy.[2] Disappointed of his host, Sigismund could only hasten his coronation with the iron crown of Lombardy, which took place in the church of S. Ambrogio on November 25. He did not stay long in Milan, where he was treated with such suspicion, but in December passed on to Piacenza, where, on January 10, 1432, he received news of the Papal Bull dissolving the Council of Basel.

Sigismund had left Germany as the avowed Protector of the Council; but it was felt that his desire to obtain the Imperial crown gave the Pope considerable power of affixing stipulations to the coronation. In fact, Sigismund's relations with

Relations
of Sigismund to
Eugenius
IV. and the
Council.

---

[1] Poggio, *Hist. Flor. Mur.* xx. 379.

[2] Windeck, in Mencken, i. 1241 : ' Er hatte sorge dass die stat Meylon sich an dem konig fluge und er kam nye zu dem konige; er sprach und nam sich an, "Sehe er den konige, er musste von frewden sterben." Es war aber ein getewsche.'

Eugenius IV. were not fortunate for the object which he had in view. Not only was the question of the Council an obstacle to their good understanding, but Sigismund's alliance with the Duke of Milan was displeasing to Eugenius IV., who as a Venetian was on the side of his native city. When Sigismund discovered how little he could depend on Filippo Maria Visconti, his political position in Italy was sufficiently helpless. There were grave fears in Basel that he might abandon the cause of the Council as a means of reconciling himself with the Pope.

At first, however, Sigismund's attitude seemed firm enough. Immediately on hearing of the proposed dissolution of the Council he wrote to Basel, exhorting the fathers to stand firm, and saying that he had written to beg the Pope to reconsider his decision. The Council, on its side, wrote to Sigismund, affecting to disbelieve the genuineness of the Bull brought by the Bishop of Parenzo,[1] and begging Sigismund to send William of Bavaria at once to Basel. On receipt of this letter Sigismund wrote again, thanking them for their zeal, saying that he was going at once to Rome to arrange matters with the Pope, and exhorting them to persevere in their course.

Resolute
bearing
of the
Council.
1432.
Before it received the news of Sigismund's constancy the Council on January 21 issued a summons to all Christendom, begging those who were coming to the Council not to be discouraged at the rumours of its dissolution, as it was improbable that the Vicar of Christ, if well informed, would set aside the decrees of Constance, and bring ruin on the Church by dissolving the Council which was to extirpate heresy and reform abuses. Congregations were continued as usual to arrange preliminaries, and on February 3 William of Bavaria arrived in Basel, and was solemnly received as Sigismund's vicegerent. Prelates poured in to the Council, which daily became more numerous. The Dukes of Milan, Burgundy, and Savoy all wrote to express their co-operation with the Council. Cardinal Cesarini could not reconcile it with his allegiance to the Pope to continue as President of the Council in spite of the Pope's wishes, and the breach with the Papacy was made

---

[1] 'Quidam episcopus Parentinus SS. domini nostri Summi Pontificis *assertus* thesaurarius *quasdam prætensas* litteras apostolicas dissolutionis dictæ sacræ synodi, ut accepimus, attulit.'—Martene, *Amp. Coll.* viii. 53.

more notorious by the election of a new President, Philibert, Bishop of Coutances. As a farther sign of its determination the Council ordered a seal to be made for its documents. Its impress was God the Father sending down the Holy Spirit on the Pope and Emperor sitting in Council surrounded by cardinals, prelates, and doctors.[1]

On February 15 was held the second general session, in which was rehearsed the famous decree of Constance, that 'a General Council has its power immediately from Christ, and that all of every rank, even the Papal, are bound to obey it in matters pertaining to the faith, the extirpation of heresy, and the reformation of the Church in head and members.' It was decreed that the Council could not be dissolved against its will, and that all proceedings of the Pope against any of its members, or any who were coming to incorporate themselves with it, were null and void. This was the Council's answer to the Pope's Bull of dissolution. The two powers now stood in open antagonism, and each claimed the allegiance of Christendom. The movement against the Papal monarchy which had been started by the Schism found its full expression at Basel. The Council of Pisa had merely aided the Cardinals in their efforts to restore peace to the disturbed Church; the Council of Constance had been a more resolute endeavour for the same purpose of the temporal and spiritual authorities of Christendom. But the Council of Basel asserted against a legitimate Pope, who was universally recognised, the superiority of a General Council over the Papacy. It was a revolt of the ecclesiastical aristocracy against the Papal absolutism, and the fate of the revolt was a question of momentous consequences for the future of the Church.

The Council of Basel reasserts the principles of Constance. February 15, 1432.

After this declaration the Council busily sent envoys throughout Christendom, and set to work to organise itself for the transaction of business. The means for this purpose had been under discussion since September 1431, and in the plan adopted we recognise the statesmanlike capacity of Cesarini.[2]

Organisation of the Council of Basel.

---

[1] It bore the legend: ' Sigillum sacri generalis Concilii Basileensis universalem ecclesiam representantis.'—John of Segovia, p. 122.

[2] John of Segovia, 126, says that the suggestion of the deputations came from John of Ragusa, 'velut subitanea inspiratione;' considering the relations in which he stood towards Cesarini the source of the inspiration seems pretty obvious.

The fortunes of the Council of Constance showed the danger of national jealousies and political complications in an ecclesiastical synod. It was resolved at Basel to avoid the division by nations, and to work by means of four committees, which were to prepare business for the general sessions of the Council. As the objects of the Council were the suppression of heresy, the reform of the Church, and the pacification of Christendom, these objects were confided to the care of deputations of Faith, of Reformation, and of Peace, while a fourth was added for common and necessary business. The deputations were formed equally out of every nation and every rank of the hierarchy. They elected their own officers, and chose a new president every month. Every four months the deputations were dissolved and reconstituted, care being taken that a few of the old members remained. As a link between the four deputations was appointed monthly a committee of twelve, chosen equally from the four nations, who decided about the incorporation of new members with the Council, and their distribution among the deputations. They decided also the allotment of business to the several deputations, received their reports, and submitted them to a general congregation. At each election four of the old members were left to maintain the continuity of tradition; but the same men might not be reappointed twice. For the formal supervision of the Council's business was a small committee of four, one appointed by each deputation, through whom passed all the letters of the Council, which it was their duty to seal. If they were dissatisfied with the form of the contents, they remitted the letter, with a statement of their reasons, to the deputation from which it originated.

This system, which was conceived in the spirit of a liberal oligarchy, was calculated to promote freedom of discussion and to eliminate as much as possible political and national feeling. Secresy in the conduct of business was forbidden, and members of one deputation were encouraged to discuss their affairs with members of the other deputations. The deputations met three times a week, and could only undertake the business laid before them by the president. When they were agreed about a matter, it was laid before a general congregation; if three of the deputations at least were then in favour of it, it was brought before the Council in general session in the cathedral, and was finally adopted. Every precaution was taken to ensure full discussion and practical unanimity before the final settlement of any question. The organisation of the Council was as democratic as anything at that time could be.[1]

CHAP.
IV.

The first deputations were appointed on the last day of February. It was not long before cheering news reached the Council. The French clergy, in a synod held at Bourges on February 26, declared their adhesion to the objects set forth by the Council, and besought the King to send envoys to the Pope to beg him to recall his dissolution; and at the same time to send envoys to Sigismund to urge that nothing should be done by the Council against the ecclesiastical authority, lest thereby a plausible pretext for transferring the Council elsewhere be afforded to the Pope. The letters of Sigismund to the Council assured it of his fidelity; and his ambassadors to the Pope on March 17 affirmed that Sigismund's coming to Italy aimed only at a peaceful solution of the religious and political difficulties of Europe, and was prompted by no motives of personal ambition. He wished the Pope to understand that he was not prepared to win his coronation by a desertion of the Council's cause. From Bohemia also came the news that the Pragers had consented to negotiate with the Council on the basis of the Four Articles, and had desired a preliminary conference at Eger with the envoys of the Council, to which the Fathers at Basel readily assented.

Council recognised by France and Bohemia. February 1432.

Yet the success of the Council and the entreaties of Sigismund were alike unavailing to move the stubborn mind of the Pope. Envoys and letters passed between Sigismund and Eugenius IV., with the sole result of ultimately bringing the two into a position of avowed hostility. Sigismund said that no one could dissolve the Council, which had been duly summoned. Eugenius IV. answered with savage sarcasm, ' In what you write touching the celebration and continuation of the Council you have said several things contrary to the Gospel of Christ, the Holy Scripture, the sacred canons and the civil laws; although we know these assertions do not proceed from you, because you are unskilled in such matters and know better how

Sigismund and Eugenius IV.

---

[1] For the organisation of the Council see John of Segovia, 122 and 271; and Aug. Patricius in Hartzsheim, v. 788; Mansi, xxix. 377.

to fight, as you do manfully, against the Turks and elsewhere, in which pursuit, I trust, you may prosper.'[1] Sigismund must have felt keenly the sneer at his failures in the field. He fancied himself mighty with the pen and with the tongue, but even his vanity could not claim the glory of a successful general.

Sigismund
warmly
declares
for the
Council,
April 1432.

Sigismund had gone to Italy with the light-heartedness which characterised his doings. He hoped to indulge his love of display and at the same time fill his empty pockets. His coronation would give him the right of granting new privileges and would bring presents from the Jews. He was not sorry to send William of Bavaria to Basel in his stead, for he did not at first wish to commit himself too definitely to the Council's side; if the Council could restore peace in Bohemia, he was ready to support it; otherwise its action might come into collision with the Imperial pretensions. So long as Sigismund was doubtful about the Bohemian acceptance of the Council's invitation, and about the Pope's pliancy, he wished not to commit himself too far. Hence William of Bavaria had a delicate part to play at Basel, where he distinguished himself at first by care for the Council's decorum, and forbade dancing on fast days, to the indignation of the ladies of Basel.[2] But soon William had more important work to do, as Sigismund found that he needed the Council's help for his Italian projects. He had hoped, with the help of Milan, Savoy, and Ferrara, to overcome Florence and Venice, and so force the Pope to crown him. But when the Duke of Milan openly mocked him, Sigismund was driven to make a desperate effort to retrieve his ignominious position. He could not leave Italy without the Imperial crown; if he set himself to win it by submission to the Pope, Bohemia would be lost for ever. He had tried to reconcile the Pope and the Council; but Eugenius IV. scornfully refused his mediation. The only remaining course was to cast in his lot with the Council, and use it as a means to force the Pope to satisfy his demands.

---

[1] John of Segovia, 179; also Martene, *Amp. Coll.* viii. 129.

[2] They complained : ' Wäre unser Herr der König selbst hier und sein lieber Caspar (*i.e.* Schlich, the royal chancellor), sie hätten uns unsere Freude nicht verdorben; aber weil der Herzog selbst keine Freude hat und nicht zu uns gehen will, so will er sie uns auch nicht gönnen,' from a letter to Schlich in Kluckhohn, *Herzog Wilhelm von Bayern* in *Forschungen zur Deutschen Geschichte*, ii. 521, &c.

On April 1, 1432, he wrote to William begging him to keep the Council together, and not allow it to dissolve before the threats of the Papal dissolution. He advised the Council to invite the Pope and Cardinals to appear at Basel ; he even suggested that if the Council called him to its aid, its summons would afford him an honourable pretext for leaving Italy. Acting on these instructions, William prompted the Fathers at Basel to take steps to prevent Eugenius IV. from holding his Council in Bologna as he proposed to do. Accordingly, on April 29, the Council in a general session called on Eugenius IV. to revoke his Bull of dissolution, and summoned him and the Cardinals to appear at Basel within three months ; in case Eugenius could not come personally he was to send representatives.

The support of Sigismund and the obvious necessity of endeavouring to find some peaceable settlement for the Bohemian question made Europe in general acquiesce in the proceedings of the Council. No nation openly espoused the Papal side or refused to recognise the Council, which gradually increased in numbers. In the beginning of April the deputations contained in all eighty-one members ;[1] and as the hostility between the Pope and the Council became more decidedly pronounced all who were on personal grounds opposed to Eugenius IV. began to flock to Basel. Foremost amongst these was Domenico Capranica, Bishop of Fermo, who had been a favourite official of Martin V., and had been by him created Cardinal, though the creation had not been published at the time of his death. This secresy on the part of Martin V. arose from a desire to abide as closely as possible by the decrees of Constance forbidding the excessive increase of the Cardinalate. He endeavoured, however, to secure himself at the expense of his successor by binding the Cardinals to an undertaking that in case he died before the publication of such creations, they would, nevertheless, admit those so created to the Conclave. On Martin V.'s death Capranica hastened to Rome and presented himself as a member of the Conclave ; but the Cardinals were in violent reaction against Martin V. and the Colonna, and refused to admit one of their adherents. The new Pope involved Capranica in his general hatred of the Colonna party, denied him the Cardinal's hat, and showed the greatest animosity against

Domenico
Capranica
comes to
Basel to
seek confirmation
for his
Cardinalate. 1432.

[1] John of Segovia, 151.

him. Capranica for a time was driven to hide himself, and at
last set off to Basel to obtain from the Council the justice
which was refused him by the Pope.[1] On his way through Siena
he engaged as secretary a young man, aged twenty-six, Æneas
Sylvius Piccolomini, sprung from an old but impoverished
family. Æneas found the need of making his way in the
world, and eagerly embraced this opportunity of finding a
wider field for the talents which he had already begun to
display in the University of Siena. No one suspected that
this young Sienese secretary was destined to play a more important part in the history of the Council and of the Church
than any of those already at Basel, when in May Capranica
entered Basel, where he was received with distinction, and in
time received full recognition of his rank, which Eugenius IV.
afterwards confirmed.

The Bohe-
mians
agree to
send en-
voys to
Basel.
June 1432.
In Italy Eugenius IV. found that things were going against
him. In Rome the Cardinals were by no means satisfied with
the aspect of affairs and many of them secretly left the city.[2]
The efforts of Eugenius IV. to stop Sigismund's progress and
raise up enemies to him in Italy were not successful. From
Piacenza Sigismund passed to Parma and thence in May to
Lucca, where he was threatened with siege by the Florentines.
In July he advanced safely to Siena, where he fixed his abode
till he could go to Rome. In Basel the Council pursued its
course with firmness and discretion. The conference with the
Bohemians at Eger resulted in the settlement of preliminaries
about the appearance of Bohemian representatives at Basel. The
Bohemians claimed that they should be received honourably,
allowed a fair hearing, be regarded in the discussion as free from
all ecclesiastical censures, be allowed to use their own worship,
and be permitted to argue on the grounds of ' God's law, the
practice of Christ, the Apostles, and the primitive Church, as
well as Councils and doctors founded on the same true and
impartial judge.'[3] Their proposals were willingly received by

---

[1] See the life of Capranica by Baptista Poggio, in Baluze, *Miscellanea*
(Paris, 1680), iii. 266, &c.

[2] The Ambassador of the Teutonic Knights says (Voigt, *Stimmen aus Rom.;
Hist. Taschenbuch*, iv. 75): 'Ich fürchte dass ein Schisma ausbrechen und
der Hof in Rom übel stehen wird. Die Cardinäle ziehen von Rom heimlich
ohne Urlaub weg, weil man diesen einem Jeden versagt.'

[3] Articles in Martene, *Amp. Coll.* viii. 131.

the majority at Basel, and in the fourth session, on June 20, a CHAP.
IV. safe-conduct to their representatives was issued. At the same time a blow was aimed against the Pope by a decree that, if a vacancy occurred in the Papacy, the new election should be made at Basel and not elsewhere. Another and still bolder proceeding was the appointment by the Council of the Cardinal of S. Eustachio as legate for Avignon and the Venaisin, on the ground that the city was dissatisfied with the Papal governor and the Council thought it right to interfere in the interests of peace.

Eugenius IV. saw that unless he took some steps to prevent it another schism was imminent. He attempted to renew negotiations with Sigismund and sent four envoys, headed by the Archbishops of Tarento and Colocza, to Basel, where they arrived on August 14. They proposed a future Council at Avignon, Mantua, or Ferrara. It was evident that the sole object of the Papal envoys was to shake the allegiance of waverers and spread discord in the Council. To repel this insidious attempt the promoters of the Council, in its sixth session, on September 6, accused the Pope and Cardinals of contumacy, for not appearing in answer to the summons, and demanded that sentence should be passed against them. The Papal envoys were driven to demand a prolongation of the term allowed, which was granted. After this, on September 9, Cesarini again resumed the presidency of the Council, judging, it would seem, that moderation was more than ever necessary.

The Council accuses the Pope of contumacy. September 1482.

Eugenius IV. now turned his attention to Sigismund, whose position in Siena was sufficiently pitiable. Deserted by the Duke of Milan and his Italian allies, he was cut off by the Florentine forces from advancing to Rome, and was, as he himself said, caged like a wild beast within the walls of Siena.[1] It was natural that Sigismund should be anxious to catch at the Pope's help to release him from such an ignominious position. When Eugenius IV. promised to send two cardinals to confer with him, Sigismund wrote to the Council urging it to suspend its process against the Pope, until he tried the result

Sigismund uses the Council to subdue the Pope. November 1482.

---

[1] Bonincontrii Annales, Mur. xxi. 140; 'Audivi ego saepius illum dicentem quum Senis essem, "Ego ulciscar de illo perfidissimo tyranno (Filippo Maria Visconti) qui me Senis tanquam belluam collocavit."' William of Bavaria calls him 'ein betrübter verlassener armer Herr,' Kluckhohn, 562.

of negotiations, or of a personal interview. The Council was
uneasy at this, and begged Sigismund to have no dealings with
the Pope until he recognised its authority. Sigismund answered, on October 31, that such was his intention, but that
he judged it wise to see the Pope personally, and so arrange
things peaceably. The Council grew increasingly suspicious,
and Sigismund did not find that his negotiations with the Pope
were leading to any satisfactory conclusion. Again he swung
round to the Council's side,[1] which, strengthened by his support,
in its eighth session, on December 12, granted Eugenius IV.
and the Cardinals a further term of sixty days, within which
they were to give in their adhesion to the Council, or the charge
of contumacy against them would be proceeded with.

The Coun-
cil takes
Sigismund
under its
protection.
January
1433.

So far Sigismund and the Council were agreed; but their
ends were not the same. Sigismund wished only for a pacification of Bohemia and his own coronation ; so far as the Council promoted these ends it was useful to him, and he was resolved to use it to the uttermost. Accordingly, on January 22,
1433, William of Bavaria prevailed on the Council to pass a
decree taking the King under its protection. By this means
Sigismund was helped both against the Pope and the Council;
for if the Council made good its claim to elect a new Pope, it
might proceed to elect a new King of the Romans as well.
The reason of this decree was a rumour that Eugenius IV. intended to excommunicate Sigismund. The Council pronounced
all Papal proceedings against him to be null and void.

Eugenius
IV. re-
vokes his
dissolution
of the
Council.
February
1433.

Eugenius IV. at last felt himself beaten. The Council had
taken precautions against every means of attack which the Papal
authority possessed. The Pope had succeeded in driving Sigismund to espouse warmly the Council's cause, and was alarmed
to hear that he was engaged in negotiating peace with the
Florentines.[2] The arrival of the Bohemian envoys at Basel, on
January 4, gave the Council a real importance in the eyes of
Europe. The Council was conscious of its strength, and on
February 19 appointed judges to examine the process against
Eugenius IV. But Eugenius had been preparing to retreat
step by step from a position which he felt to be untenable,

[1] See his letter of November 22, in John of Segovia, 292.
[2] See Sigismund's letter to the Council, dated January 7, 1433, in Martene,
Amp. Coll. viii. 533.

and strove to discover the smallest amount of concession which would free him from his embarrassment. He sent envoys to Basel, who proposed that the Council should transfer itself to Bologna; when this was refused, they asked that it should select some place in Italy for a future Council. Next they offered that the question whether the Council should be held in Germany or Italy should be referred to a committee of twelve; finally they proposed that any city in Germany except Basel should be the seat of a new Council.[1] When the Fathers at Basel would have none of these things, Eugenius IV. at last issued a Bull announcing his willingness that the Council should be held at Basel, whither he proposed to send his legates; on March 1 he nominated four cardinals to that office.

Sigismund rejoiced at this removal of the obstacles which stood in the way of his coronation; he was anxious that the Council should accept the Pope's Bull and so do away with all hostility between himself and Eugenius IV. But the Fathers at Basel looked somewhat suspiciously on the concessions which had been wrung with such difficulty from the Pope. They observed that the Bull did not recognise the existing Council, but declared that a Council should be held by his legates. Moreover, he limited the scope of the Council to the two points of the reduction of heretics and the pacification of Christendom, omitting the reformation of the Church. It was argued that Eugenius IV. had not complied with their demand that he should withdraw his dissolution; he refused to recognise anything done at Basel before the coming of his legates.[2] Determined to affirm its authority before the arrival of the Papal legates, the Council passed a decree on April 27, renewing the decree of Constance about the celebration of General Councils at least every tenth year; asserting that the members of a Council might assemble of their own accord at the fixed period; and that a Pope who tried to impede or prorogue a Council should after four months' warning be suspended, and then after two months be deprived of office. It was decreed that the present Council could not be dissolved nor transferred without the consent of two-thirds of each deputation and the subsequent approbation

---

[1] These wearisome negotiations are told by John of Segovia, 338, &c., and are recapitulated in the Council's letter of June 16, 374.

[2] See letter of the Council, June 13, in John of Segovia, 375.

of two-thirds of a general congregation. The Cardinals were henceforth to make oath before entering the Conclave that whoever was elected Pope would obey the Constance decrees. To give all possible notoriety to these decrees, all prelates were ordered to publish them in their synods or chapters. So far as a new constitution can be secured on paper, the Council of Basel made sure for the future the new principles of Church Government on which it claimed to act. It was a transference to ecclesiastical matters of the parliamentary opposition to monarchy which was making itself felt in European politics.

When the Papal legates arrived and claimed to share with Cesarini the office of president, Cesarini answered that he was the officer of the Council and must obey their will in the matter. The Council, in a congregation on June 13, answered that they could not admit the claim of the Pope to influence their deliberations by means of his legates : not only the President, but the Pope himself, was bound to obey the Council's decrees. They were bent upon asserting most fully the supremacy of a General Council, and aimed at converting the Pope into its chief official. The concessions made by Eugenius IV. had not ended the conflict between him and the Fathers at Basel. They had rather brought more clearly to light the full opposition that had arisen between the ecclesiastical hierarchy and the Papal monarchy.

Straits of
Eugenius
IV.

But Eugenius IV. had not so much aimed at a reconciliation with the Council as a reconciliation with Sigismund. He saw that for this purpose concessions must be made to the Council ; but he hoped with Sigismund's help to reduce the Council in course of time. Sigismund's position in Italy made him eager to catch at any concession on the part of Eugenius IV. which would allow him to proceed to his coronation without abandoning the Council, from which he hoped for a settlement of his Bohemian difficulties. He received with joy the Pope's advances, and Eugenius IV. on his side felt the need of Sigismund's protection even in Rome. Five cardinals besides Capranica had already left him and joined the Council. The officials of the Curia grew doubtful in their allegiance, and began to think that their interests would be better served in Basel than in Rome. On March 11, the anniversary of the Pope's coronation, as he went from the commemoration service

he was beset by members of the Curia, who craved with tears
leave to depart,[1] and followed him with their cries to the door
of the Consistory. A few had leave given them, and all were
bent on departure.

In this state of affairs Eugenius IV. saw the wisdom of Reconcilia-
tion of
Sigismund
and
Eugenius
IV. April
7, 1488.
gratifying Sigismund in the two matters which he had at heart,
the pacification of Italy and his coronation as Emperor. There
were not many difficulties in the way of peace. Florence,
Venice, and the Duke of Milan were all equally weary of war;
and the Pope had little difficulty in inducing them to submit
their grievances to Niccolo of Este, Lord of Ferrara, who at that
time played the honourable part of mediator in Italian affairs.
By his help the preliminaries of peace were arranged at Ferrara
on April 7; and on the same day Sigismund's envoys arranged
with the Pope the preliminaries of the Imperial coronation.
Sigismund acknowledged that ' he had always held and holds'
Eugenius as the true and undoubted Pope, canonically elected;
and with all reverence, diligence, care, and labour, among all
kings and princes, all persons in the world ecclesiastical as well
as secular, venerates, protests, and acts in defence of his holiness,
and the Church of God, so long as he shall live, faithfully and
with a true heart, according to his knowledge and power, without fraud or guile, so far as with God's help he may.'[2] He
agreed also to stay at Rome for a time after his coronation, and
labour for the peace of Christendom and especially of Italy.

This alliance of the Pope and Sigismund was naturally Sigis-
mund's
coronation.
May 81,
1488.
regarded with growing suspicion at Basel. Sigismund's letters to
the Council changed in tone, and dwelt upon the evils of scandal
in the Church and the disastrous effects of a schism. On May 9
he urged the Council to treat the Papal legates with kindness,
and to abstain from anything that might lead to an open

---

[1] Report from Rome, in Königsberg Archives, printed by Voigt, *Ænea Sylvio de' Piccolomini*, i. 443: ' Et quia propter decreta Concilii multi Curtesani re-
cesserunt et fere omnes se preparant ad recedendum . . . Omnes Curtesani
de omni nacione concorditer in die Coronacionis moderni pontificis comme-
morati, dummodo papa exivit de capella majori, flexis genibus volebant petere
licenciam, sed non exauditi. Omnes pariter clamabant voce lacrimabili licenciam, licenciam, sequendo dominum nostrum usque ad locum consistorialem.
. . . Omnes habent animum recedendi, sed non audent et nec habent lucrum,
stant in tribulacionibus.'

[2] *Pacta*, in Martene, *Amp. Coll.* viii. 580.

rupture. The Council loudly exclaimed that the Pope had beguiled the King under the pretence of a coronation, and meant to keep him in Rome as a protection to himself. Sigismund, however, hastened his coronation, and on May 21 entered Rome with an escort of 600 knights and 800 foot. Riding beneath a golden canopy he was met by the city magistrates and a crowd of people. The bystanders thought that his deportment showed a just mixture of affability and dignity; his smiling face wore an expression of refinement and geniality, while his long grizzly beard lent majesty to his appearance.[1] On the steps of S. Peter's, Eugenius in pontifical robes greeted Sigismund, who kissed his foot, his hand, his face. After mass was said Sigismund took up his abode in the palace of the Cardinal of Arles, close to S. Peter's. On Whit Sunday, May 31, the coronation took place. Before the silver door of S. Peter's, Sigismund swore to observe all the constitutions made by his predecessors, as far back as Constantine, in favour of the Church. Then the Pope proceeded to the high altar and Sigismund was conducted by three Cardinals to the Church of S. John Lateran, where before the altar of S. Maurice he was consecrated canon of the Church. He returned to S. Peter's, and took his place by the side of the Pope, each seated under a tabernacle erected for the purpose. The mass was begun, and after the epistle the Pope and Sigismund advanced to the altar. The Pope set on Sigismund's head first the white mitre of a bishop, and then the golden crown; he took from the altar, and gave into his hands, the sword, the sceptre, and the golden apple of the Empire. When the mass was ended the Pope and Emperor gave one another the kiss of peace. Then Sigismund took the sword in his hand, and Eugenius, holding the crucifix, gave him his solemn benediction. When this was over they walked side by side to the church door; the Pope mounted his mule, which Sigismund led by the bridle for a few paces and then mounted his horse. Eugenius accompanied him to the bridge of S. Angelo, where Sigismund kissed his hand and he returned to the Vatican. On

[1] Poggio, in a letter to Niccolo Niccoli, in Baluze, *Miscell.* iii. 184, describes Sigismund's entrance and coronation; of himself he says: 'Aspectu perhumanus, ridenti similis, facie hilari atque liberali, barba subcana ac prolixa, ea inest in vultu comitas et majestas, ut qui illum ignorarent ipso conspectu et oris egregia specie cæterorum regem opinarentur.'

the bridge Sigismund, according to custom, exercised his new authority by dubbing a number of knights, Romans and Germans, amongst others his chancellor Caspar Schlick. The Imperial procession went through the streets to the Lateran, where Sigismund dismounted.

The days that followed were spent in formal business such as Sigismund delighted in. Letters had to be written, and all grants and diplomas given by the King of the Romans needed the Imperial confirmation, which was a source of no small profit to the Imperial chancery. It is worth noticing that after his coronation Sigismund engraved on his seal a double eagle, to mark the union of his dignities of Emperor and Roman King. From this time dates the use of the double-headed eagle as the Imperial ensign.

It soon, however, became obvious that Sigismund's coronation had affected his relations towards the Council. He was still anxious for its success in the important points of the reconciliation of the Bohemians; but he had no longer any interest in the constitutional question of the relations which ought to exist between Popes and General Councils. No doubt this question had been a useful means of bringing Eugenius IV. to acknowledge the Council; now that he had done so, and Sigismund had obtained from the Pope what he wanted, his instincts as a practical statesman taught him that in the midst of the agitation of European politics it was hopeless for a Council to continue on abstract grounds a struggle against the Pope, which could only lead to another schism. On June 4 he wrote to the Council announcing his coronation, and saying that he found in the Pope the best intentions towards furthering all the objects which the Council had at heart.[1] His envoys on their arrival at Basel found the Council preparing accusations against Eugenius, and the seven Cardinals present engaged in discussing the canonicity of his election. They had some difficulty in persuading the Council to moderation, but at last obtained on July 13 a decree which, while denouncing in no measured terms the contumacy of Eugenius IV., extended again for sixty days the period for an unreserved withdrawal of his Bull of dissolution, and for a declaration of his entire adhesion to the Council. If he did not comply within that time, the

Sigismund
mediates
between
the Pope
and the
Council.
June–
August,
1433.

---

[1] Letter in Martene, *Amp. Coll.* viii. 607.

Council would at once proceed to his suspension. Eugenius, trusting to the help of Sigismund, showed a less conciliatory spirit; for he issued a Bull withdrawing from the Council all private questions, and limiting its activity to the three points of the extirpation of heresy, the pacification of Christendom, and the reform of manners. In the same sense Sigismund's envoys on August 18 brought a message to the Council, exhorting to greater diligence in the matters of pacification and reform, for so far no fruits of its energies were apparent. He warned it against creating a schism, for after extinguishing one at Constance he would rather die than see another.[1] He begged the Fathers to suspend all proceedings against the Pope till his arrival at Basel, when he hoped to remove all difficulties between them and the Pope. The Council answered that it was the Pope and not the Council that was causing a schism; the relations of the Pope to a General Council was a matter concerning the faith and the reformation of the Church, and nothing could be done on these points till the present scandal was removed. Sigismund, in fact, was asking the Council to desist from measures which he had formerly urged. The Council naturally demanded securities for the future. Its position was undoubtedly logical, though practically unwise. Eugenius IV., to strengthen Sigismund's hands, issued a Bull on August 1 expressing, at Sigismund's request, his 'willingness and acquiescence' (*volumus et contentamur*) that the Council should be recognised as valid from its commencement. He declared that he entirely accepted the Council, and demanded that his legates should be admitted as presidents, and that all proceedings against his person and authority should be rescinded. The Fathers at Basel naturally looked closely into the language of the Bull. They were not satisfied that the validity of the Council from the beginning should merely be tolerated by the Pope. They wished for the Papal 'decree and declaration' (*decernimus et declaramus*) that it had been valid all along. Every step towards conciliation only brought into greater prominence the fact that the

---

[1] John of Segovia, 409: 'Porro quia nephandum scisma extinctum fuerat in Constanciensi Concilio, pro qua re tot tantosque labores sustinuisset, avisabat taliter fieri ne suscitaretur, quia preeligeret mori quam suis diebus scisma videre.' See also letter of August 8 in Martene, *Amp. Coll.* viii. 626.

Council claimed to be superior to the Pope, and that Eugenius was determined not to suffer any derogation from the Papal autocracy.[1]

CHAP.
IV.

In this view of Eugenius IV. Sigismund acquiesced. He wished the Council to engage in more practical business, and he dreaded as a statesman the consequences of another schism. In this he was joined by the Kings of England and France, the German Electors, and the Duke of Burgundy. All of them urged upon the Council the inexpediency of provoking a schism. Eugenius IV.'s repeated attempts at compromise at length created a feeling of sympathy in his favour. He had given way, it was urged, on the practical points at issue. The Council did not meet with much attention when it answered that he had not conceded the principle which was at stake in the conflict. The great majority were in favour of proceeding to the suspension of Eugenius IV. when the term expired; but the remonstrances of the Imperial ambassadors, and the consideration that an open breach with Sigismund would render Basel an insecure place for the Council, so far prevailed that in the session of September 11 a further term of thirty days was granted to Eugenius IV., on the understanding that within that time Sigismund would appear in Basel.

Sigismund
draws to
the Pope's
side. Au-
gust 1433.

Sigismund meanwhile at Rome had been employing his versatile mind in studying the antiquities of the city, and drinking in the enthusiasm of the Renaissance under the guidance of the famous antiquary Ciriaco of Ancona. He lived in familiar intercourse with Eugenius IV., and a story is told which illustrates the mixture of penetration and levity which marked Sigismund's character. One day he said to the Pope, 'Holy Father, there are three things in which we are alike, and three in which we are different. You sleep in the morning, I rise before daybreak; you drink water, I wine; you shun women, I pursue them. But in some things we agree: you distribute the treasures of the Church, I keep nothing for my-

Sigismund
comes to
Basel.
October
11, 1433.

---

[1] See an interesting letter of Eugenius IV. to the Doge of Venice, in Ray-naldus, 1433, 19: ' Potius enim hanc Apostolicam dignitatem et vitam insuper possuissemus quam voluissemus esse causa et initium ut Pontificalis dignitas et Apostolicæ sedis auctoritas submitteretur Concilio, contra omnes canonicas sanctiones; quod nunquam antea neque aliquis nostrorum predecessorum fecit, neque ab ullo extitit requisitum, atque in hoc ipse postmodum imperator acquievit.'

self; you have gouty hands, I gouty feet; you are bringing the Church and I the Empire to the ground.' But these days of peaceful enjoyment were disturbed by the news from Basel, where it was clear that Sigismund's presence was needed. On August 21 he left Rome, and journeyed through Perugia, Rimini, and Ferrara to Mantua. He would not go through the territories of the Duke of Milan, against whom he nourished the deepest anger. Venice took occasion of his wrath to make an alliance with him for five years, in return for which they gave the needy Emperor ten thousand ducats to pay the expenses of his journey from Rome to Germany. From Mantua Sigismund hastened to Basel, so as to reach it at the end of the term granted to the Pope. He arrived unexpectedly on October 11, having come through the Tyrol to the Lake of Constance, and thence by boat to Basel. So hasty had been his journey that he brought little baggage with him, and before entering Basel the Imperial beggar had to send to the magistrates for a pair of shoes.

The Fathers of the Council hastily assembled to show Sigismund such honour as they could. He was escorted to the Cathedral, where he took his place on the raised seat generally occupied by the cardinals, who now sat on lower benches. There he addressed the congregation, setting forth his zeal for the Council's cause, as his hasty journey testified; he asked for further delay in the proceedings against the Pope, that he might carry out successfully the work of pacification on which he was engaged. To this the Council did not at once assent, but urged that the Pope's suspension might help on Sigismund's endeavours. Murmurs were heard on all sides, and it was clear that Sigismund's authority was not omnipotent at Basel. The Council was filled with the enemies of Eugenius IV., and was convinced of its own power and importance. Sigismund reminded the Fathers that the Emperor was guardian of the temporalities of the Church. He was answered that it was also his duty to execute the decrees of the Church. He angrily asserted that neither he nor any of the kings and princes of Christendom would permit the horrors of another schism. In his vehemence he forgot his Latin, and gave *schisma* the feminine gender. It was maliciously said that he wished to show the Council how dear the matter was to his heart.[1] At last the Council, which was not really in a position to resist, reluctantly granted a prolongation of the term to Eugenius IV. for eight days.

Sigismund found it necessary to change his tactics and listen to the Council's side of the quarrel, as at Rome he had listened to the Pope. He conferred with the ambassadors and with the chiefs of the Council, and was present at a public disputation on October 16 between the president, Cesarini, and the Papal envoys. Cesarini spoke for three hours in behalf of a Council's superiority over a Pope. He argued that the Bulls of Eugenius IV. refused to admit this proposition, and that without securing the means of a reformation of the head of the Church it was useless to reform the members; as to the Pope's demand that all proceedings against himself should be revoked, there were no proceedings if only he did his duty. On behalf of Eugenius IV. the Archbishop of Spoleto urged the sufficiency and reasonableness of his proposal, to revoke his decrees against the Council if the Council would revoke its proceedings against himself. There were replies and counter-replies, but both parties were equally far from an agreement. A second prolongation of eight days to Eugenius IV. was obtained by Sigismund by a repetition of his former assertion, that he could not endure a schism. This was succeeded by a third, on which Sigismund repeated an old doggerel about the three Emperors Otto, which afforded him a pun on the eight days (*octo dies*) of the prolongation:

Otto post Otto regnabit tertius Otto.

Sigismund and the ambassadors of France united in urging the Council to give Eugenius IV. a security that no proceedings would be taken affecting his title to the Papacy. Words ran high on this proposal, and at length, on November 7, Sigismund's persistency succeeded in extorting from the Council a further term of ninety days, within which the Pope was to explain the

CHAP. IV.

Prolongation of the term granted to Eugenius IV. November 7, 1433.

---

[1] John of Segovia, p. 465, from whom this account is taken, is clearly trying to elevate a current witticism to the dignity of history when he says: 'Cum vero de scismate loquebatur, ut communiter usus est genere feminino, judicio autem presencium non generis neutri ignarus aut immemor, sed ut attenciores redderet audientes percipere, que de scismate loquebatur, cordi ejus radicitus inesse.'

BOOK
III.

Decree es-
tablishing
synodal
action
through-
out the
Church.
November
26, 1433.

ambiguities in his decrees by revoking anything which could
be construed to the ' derogation or prejudice ' of the Council.

In the interval Sigismund urged the Council to proceed with
the question of reform, a matter which had been making little
progress during the excitement of this conflict with the Pope.
The only point in which the Council had taken up reform was to
use it as a weapon against the Pope.   On July 13 a decree had
been passed abolishing reservations and provisions except in the
domain of the Holy See, and enacting that elections should be
made only by those to whom the right belonged, and that no
dues be paid for Papal confirmation.   This was merely an onslaught on the Pope's revenues, and was scarcely meant seriously.
In answer to Sigismund's exhortations the Council embodied,
in a decree on November 26, the only point on which there was
agreement, the revival of the synodal system of the Church.
The Council's scheme of reform was to extend the conciliar system to all parts of the ecclesiastical organisation.   By means of
diocesan synods the bishops were to put down heresies and
remedy scandals in their respective dioceses, and were to be
themselves restrained by provincial synods, whose activity was
to be in turn ensured by the recurrence of General Councils.
It was on all grounds easier to agree on machinery which was to
deal with questions in the future than to amend abuses in the
present.

Struggles
about pre-
cedence.

Even this measure of reform was secondary to a violent dispute which convulsed the Council concerning precedence in
seats at the sessions between the ambassadors of the Imperial
Electors and those of the Duke of Burgundy.   So keen was the
contention that it almost prevented the solemn celebration of the
Christmas services, and was only ended in July, 1434, by assign-
ing a separate bench to the representatives of the Electors
immediately below the cardinals, and arranging that the Burgundian envoys should sit next to those of kings.   This burning
question was further complicated by the claims of the envoys
of the Duke of Brittany to be as good as those of the Duke of
Burgundy; at last it was arranged that the Burgundians should
sit on the right, the Bretons on the left.

In the middle of the controversy came envoys from Eugenius IV., on January 30, 1434, announcing that he had at last
given way.   They brought a Bull revoking all previous Bulls

against the Council, acknowledging its legitimacy from its beginning, and declaring fully the Pope's adhesion to it. Great was Sigismund's joy at this triumph of his mediatorial policy. Great was the relief of all parties at Basel when, in the sixteenth session on February 3, the Council decreed that Eugenius IV. had fully satisfied their admonition and summons. It was under the pressure of necessity that Eugenius IV. had given way. His impetuous rashness had raised up enemies against him on every side. He had begun his pontificate by attacking the powerful family of the Colonna. He had plunged into Italian politics as a strong friend of Venice, and thereby had drawn upon himself the animosity of the wily Duke of Milan. With these elements of disturbance at his doors he had not hesitated to bid defiance to a Council which had the support of the whole of Christendom. Basel had become in consequence the resort of the personal and political enemies of the Pope, and on Sigismund's departure from Rome Eugenius was threatened in his own city. The Duke of Milan sent against him the condottiere Niccolo de Fortebracchio, nephew of Braccio da Montone, who on August 25, 1433, captured Ponte Molle. The Pope fled for safety to the Church of S. Lorenzo in Damaso, and in vain called for help. Fortebracchio, aided by the Colonna party, took possession of Tivoli and styled himself 'the General of the Holy Council.' Francesco Sforza, won over to the side of the Duke of Milan by the promise of the hand of his natural daughter Bianca, invaded the March of Ancona, and scornfully dated his letters 'invito Petro et Paulo,' 'against the will of Peter and Paul.' The Duke of Milan was supported by the Council,[1] which Sigismund in vain tried to interest in the pacification of Italy. The name of the Council lent a colourable pretext to all acts of aggression. Eugenius IV. found himself destitute of allies. Never had the Papacy been in a more helpless condition. No course was possible except submission.

Accordingly Eugenius IV. made his peace with the Council, and then proceeded to face his enemies at home. He detached Francesco Sforza from the side of the Duke of Milan by

CHAP.
IV.

Eugenius
IV. re-
cognises
the Coun-
cil. Janu-
ary 30,
1434.

Rising in
Rome
against
Eugenius
IV. May
29, 1434.

---

[1] John of Segovia, 532: 'Plures littere ex Ytalia particulariter destinate affirmabant, quod eciam absque ulla vi, audito quod nomine concilii habere vellet, terre et civitates marchie Anconitane reddebant se comiti Francisco.'

appointing him, on March 25, Vicar of the March of Ancona which he had overrun. Sforza willingly exchanged the dubious promises of Filippo Maria Visconti for an assured position. But the Duke of Milan sent to the aid of Fortebraccio the condottiere Niccolo Piccinino; before their superior forces Sforza was driven to retire, and the blockade of Rome was continued. The sufferings of a siege were more than the Romans cared to endure for the sake of an unpopular Pope. It was easy for the foes of Eugenius IV. to raise the people in rebellion. A crowd flocked to S. Maria in Trastevere, whither Eugenius had retired for safety, to lay their grievances before the Pope. They were referred to his nephew, the Cardinal Francesco Correr, who listened to them with haughty indifference. When they complained of the loss of their cattle, he answered that they busied themselves too much about cattle; the Venetians who had none led a much more refined and civilised life.[1] The remark might be true, but it was not consoling. The people resolved to take matters into their own hands, and on the evening of May 29 raised the old cry of ' The people and freedom ! ' stormed the Capitol, and set up once more their old republic under seven governors. Next day they demanded of the Pope that he should hand over to them the castles of S. Angelo and Ostia, give them his nephew as a hostage, and come himself to take up his abode in the palace of his predecessor by the Church of SS. Apostoli. When Eugenius refused, his nephew was dragged away by force in spite of his entreaties, and he was threatened with imprisonment. Eugenius heard that the palace by SS. Apostoli was being prepared for his custody, and he knew that there he would be the prisoner of the Council and the Duke of Milan.

Flight of
Eugenius
IV. to
Florence.
June 1484.

There was no escape except by flight, which was difficult, as his abode was closely guarded. At last a pirate of Ischia, Vitellio, who had a ship at Ostia, was prevailed upon to help the Pope in his need. His aid was secured just in time, as on the evening of June 4 the Pope was to be removed to the palace by SS. Apostoli. At midday, when everyone was taking his siesta, Eugenius and one of his attendants, disguised as Benedictine monks, escaped the vigilance of the sleepy guards, mounted a couple of mules and rode to the Tiber bank, where a

---

[1] Platina, *Vita Eugenii IV.*

small dirty boat was prepared for them. A few bishops professed
to be waiting for an audience with the Pope, so as to lull the
suspicions of his guards. But the two mules left riderless on the
bank, and the unwonted energy of the rowers, made the spectators give the alarm. The people of Trastevere gave chase
along the bank, hurling stones and shooting arrows at the boat.
The wind was contrary, the bark was crazy, the crowd of pursuers increased along both banks; Eugenius lay at the bottom of
the boat covered by a shield. When the Church of S. Paolo was
passed, and the river became broader, the fugitives hoped that
their danger was over; but the Romans ran on before, and seized
a fishing boat, which, filled with armed men, they laid across
the stream. Luckily for Eugenius his boat was commanded by
one of the pirate's crew whose courage was equal to the occasion. In vain the Romans hurled their darts, and promised him
large sums of money if he would deliver up the Pope. He
ordered his boat to charge the enemy. Their boat was old
and rotten, and they feared the encounter. The prow turned
aside and the Pope's boat shot safely past. Eugenius could
now rise from his covering of shields, and sit upright with a
sigh of thankfulness. He reached Ostia in safety and went on
board the pirate's ship. There he was joined by a few members of the Curia who had succeeded in fleeing. He sailed to
Pisa, and thence made his way to Florence, where he was
honourably received on June 23, and like his predecessor,
Martin V., took up his abode in the cloister of S. Maria Novella.[1]
There he could reflect that his inconsiderate obstinacy had endangered at Basel his spiritual supremacy, and had handed over
his temporal possessions to the condottieri of the Duke of
Milan.

[1] The flight of Eugenius is graphically described by Flavius Blondus,
Decades, iii. 6. See also the account of the Roman ambassadors to the Council
in John of Segovia, 717.

CHAPTER V.

THE COUNCIL OF BASEL AND THE HUSSITES.

1432–1434.

BOOK III.

Desire of Bohemia for peace.

IF the downfall of Eugenius IV. was due to his obstinacy, the prestige of the Council, which enabled it to reap the advantage of his weakness, was due to the hopes which were conceived of a peaceable ending of the Bohemian revolt. It was much easier for a Council than for a Pope to open negotiations with victorious heretics, and the Bohemians on their side were not averse from an honourable peace. Bohemia, with a population of four or five millions, had suffered much during its ten years' struggle against the rest of Europe. Its victories were ruinous to the conquerors; its plundering raids brought no real wealth. The commerce of Bohemia was annihilated; its lands were uncultivated; the nation was at the mercy of the Taborite army, which no longer consisted solely of the God-fearing peasants, but was recruited by adventurers from the neighbouring lands. The policy of Procopius the Great was, by striking terror, to prepare the way for peace, that so Bohemia, with its religious liberty assured, might again enter the confederacy of European States. When the Council of Basel held out hopes of peace he was ready to try what could be won; and Bohemia consented to send representatives to Basel for the purpose of discussion.

Preparations of the Council for a conference with the Bohemians. November 1432.

Accordingly the Council proceeded to prepare for its great undertaking. In November 1432 it appointed four doctors, John of Ragusa, a Slav; Giles Carlier, a Frenchman; Heinrich Kalteisen, a German; and John of Palomar, a Spaniard, to undertake the defence of the Church doctrine against the four articles of Prag. These doctors zealously studied their case with the aid of all the theologians present at Basel. As the time of the advent of the Bohemians drew near, strict orders were given to the citizens to abstain from everything that might shock the Puritanism of their expected guests.[1] Prostitutes were not to walk the streets; gambling and dancing were forbidden; the members of the Council were enjoined to maintain strict sobriety, and beware of following the example of the Pharisees of old, who taught well and lived ill. At the same time guards were set to see that the Bohemians did not spread their errors in the seat of the Council. On the part of the Bohemians seven nobles and eight priests, headed by Procopius the Great, were chosen by a Diet as their representatives at Basel. They rode with their attendants through Germany, a stately cavalcade of fifty horsemen, with a banner bearing their device of a chalice, under which was the inscription, ' Veritas omnia vincit' (Truth conquers all). In alarm lest their entry into Basel might seem like a demonstration and cause scandal, Cesarini sent to beg them to lay aside their banner. Before his messenger reached them they had taken boat at Schaffhausen, and entered Basel, quietly and unexpectedly, on the evening of January 4, 1433. The citizens flocked to gaze on them, wondering at the strange dress, the resolute faces, and fierce eyes of the men who had wrought such terrible deeds of valour.[2] They were conducted to their hotels, where several members of the Council visited them, and Cesarini sent them presents of food. On January 6, the festival of the Epiphany, they celebrated the Communion in their lodgings, and curiosity drew many to attend their services. They noticed that the Pragers used vestments and observed the customary ritual, with the sole exception that they communicated under both kinds. Procopius and the Taborites, on the other hand, used no vestments nor altar, and discarded the mass-service. After consecration of the elements they said the Lord's Prayer and communicated round a table. A sermon was preached in German, at which many Catholics were present. This scandalised Cesarini, who sent for the Bohemians, and requested them to discontinue preaching in German. They answered that many of their followers were Germans, and the sermons were for their benefit; they had the right of performing their

Arrival of the Bohemian envoys in Basel. January 4, 1433.

---

[1] John of Ragusa, *Tractatus de Reductione Bohemorum*, in *Mon. Con.* i. 258; John of Segovia, ii. 298.

[2] Æn. Sylvius, *Hist. Bohem.* ch. xlix.

services as they thought fit, and meant to use it; they invited no one to come, but they were not bound to prevent them from doing so. Cesarini sent to the magistrates of the city a request that they would prevent the people from attending their preachings. The magistrates took no measures for this end; but after a few days the crowd grew weary of the novelty, and ceased of its own accord to attend. John of Ragusa makes a sage remark, which the advocates of religious protection would do well to remember: 'Freedom and neglect succeeded where restraint and prohibition would have failed, for human frailty is always eager after what is forbidden.'[1] The Bohemians, on their side, asked to be present at the sermons preached before the Council; permission was given on condition that they entered the cathedral after the reading of the Gospel, and left when the sermon was ended, so as not to be present at any part of the mass service.

Prelim-
inaries of
the con-
ference,
January
1433.
Next day, January 7, Procopius invited John of Ragusa and others to dine; they had a general theological discussion, in which the predestinarian views of the Hussites came prominently forward. Most skilful among their controversialists was an Englishman, Peter Payne, an Oxford Lollard, who had fled to Bohemia, whom John of Ragusa found to be as slippery as a snake.[2]

On January 9 the Council ordained that Wednesdays and Fridays should be strictly kept as fast days, and prayers for union be said during the period of the negotiations with the Bohemians. A solemn procession was made for success in this arduous matter; forty-nine mitred prelates and about eight hundred other members of the Council took part in it. The Bohemians asked when and where they were to have an audience. Cesarini fixed the next day in the ordinary meeting place of congregations, the Dominican monastery. The Bohemians objected to the place as being too small and out of the way; but Cesarini was firm in refusing to depart from the usage of the Council.

[1] 'Unde factum est per neglectam licentiam, quod nullo modo factum fuisset per exactam prohibitionem, quia humana fragilitas semper nititur in vetitum.'—*Mon. Concil.* i. 259.

[2] 'Ipse Anglicus tanquam anguis lubricus quanto strictius teneri videbatur et concludi tanto citius ad impertinentes dilabebatur materias.'—*Ibid.* 260. Some information about Payne and his aliases is given in Rogers' *Loci e Libro Veritatis* of Gascoign, p. 186, &c.

On January 10 the congregation assembled, and seats were assigned to the Bohemians on two rows of benches opposite the cardinals. Cesarini opened the proceedings with a long and eloquent oration, in which, speaking in the person of the Church, he exhorted all to unity and peace, and addressed the Bohemians as sons whom their mother yearned to welcome back to her bosom. On the part of the Bohemians, John of Rokycana arose and took for his text, 'Where is He that is born King of the Jews? We have seen his star in the east, and are come to worship Him.' He said that the Bohemians were seeking after Christ, and, like their Master, had been evil spoken of; he asked the Council not to be astonished if they said strange things, for truth was often found in strange ways; he praised the primitive Church and denounced the vices of the clergy of the present day. Finally, he thanked the Council for its courtesy, and asked for a day to be fixed for a full hearing. Cesarini answered that the Council was ready at any time; after a private conference, the Bohemians fixed the next Friday, January 16.

The Bohemians brought with them to the Council the same spirit of reckless daring which had characterised them on the field of battle. Only on January 13 did they arrange finally their spokesmen, whereas the theologians of the Council had been for two months preparing their separate points. Each day the Bohemians paid visits to the cardinals and prelates; they were received as a rule with great friendliness. At first some of the Cardinals tended to be cold, if not discourteous; but Cesarini's anxious efforts to promote conciliatory conduct were in the end successful, and free social intercourse was established between the two parties. In a few days' time a cardinal discovered at least one bond of union between himself and the Bohemians; he laughingly said to Procopius, 'If the Pope had us in his power, he would hang us both.'

On January 16 the proceedings began with a ratification of the safe-conduct, and a formal verification of the powers of the Bohemian representatives. Then John of Rokycana began the controversy by a defence of the First Article of Prag, concerning the Communion under both kinds. He argued from the nature of the rite, from the words of the Gospel, the custom of the primitive Church, the decrees of the General Councils and the testimonies of the Fathers, that it was not only permissible but necessary. His speech extended over three days, and was listened to with great attention.[1] When he ended Procopius sprang to his feet—a man of middle height, of stalwart frame, with a swarthy face, large flashing eyes, and a fierce expression of countenance. He passionately exhorted them to open their ears to the Gospel truth; the Communion was a heavenly banquet, to which all were invited; let them beware lest they incurred punishment by despising it, for God could vindicate His own. The Fathers heard with amazement these expressions of a fervent conviction that right could be on the side opposed to the Church.[2] Cesarini with his wonted tact interposed to prevent an untimely outbreak of zeal on the part of the Council. He suggested that the Bohemians should first speak and then submit their arguments in writing, so that they might be fully answered on the side of the Council. This was agreed to, and the assembly dispersed.

Nicolas of Pilgram's defence of the Second Article. January 20-23.

On January 20, Nicolas of Pilgram began the defence of the Second Article of Prag—the suppression of public sins. He spoke for two days, but on the second day did not imitate the moderation of Rokycana. He attacked the vices of the clergy, their simony, their hindrance of the Word of God; he reproached them with the deaths of Hus and Jerome, whose saintly lives he defended. A murmur arose in the Council; some laughed scornfully, others gnashed their teeth; Cesarini with folded hands looked up to heaven. The speaker asked if he was to have a fair hearing according to promise. Cesarini ironically answered, 'Yes, but pause sometimes to let us clear our throats.' Nicolas went on with his speech. Afterwards Rokycana blamed him for the bitterness of his invective, and expressed a wish to speak himself on the Third Article. He was overruled by the other ambassadors, and only at the last moment was it definitely settled that Ulrich of Zynaim was to be their spokesman.[3]

Ulrich of Zynaim defends the Third Article. January 23-25.

On January 23 Ulrich began his arguments for the freedom of preaching, and also spoke for two days, urging the supremacy

[1] It is given in Martene, *Amp. Coll.* viii. 262.
[2] 'Aliaque dixit forme hujus velut Bohemi sustinerent veritatem fidei Catholicae et alii contemnerent.'—John of Segovia, 319.
[3] See Peter of Saaz, *Liber Diurnus*, in *Mon. Conc.* i. 294.

of the Word of God over the word of man, the danger of the
substitution of the one for the other, the dignity of the true
priest, and his duty to preach God's Word in spite of all endeavours to prevent him.[1] At the end of his first day's speech
Rokycana rose and said that he had heard that the Bohemians
were accused of throwing snow at a crucifix on the bridge; they
wished to deny it, and if it could be proved that any of their
attendants had done so he should be punished. Cesarini
answered that many tales were told about their doings, which,
however, the Council had resolved to endure as well as their
speeches. He wished, however, that they would restrain their
servants from going into the neighbouring villages to spread
their doctrines. He was answered that the servants only
went to get fodder for the horses, and if the curious Germans
asked them questions, such as, whether they held the Virgin
Mary to be a virgin, no great harm was done if they answered,
' Yes.' They promised, however, to see to the matter.

On January 26 Peter Payne began a three days' speech on
the temporal possessions of the clergy. He admitted that
worldly goods were not to be entirely denied them, but, in the
words of S. Paul, having food and raiment, therewith they
should be content; all superfluities should be cut off from them,
and they should in no case exercise temporal lordship.[2] When
he had finished his argument, he said that this doctrine was
commonly supposed to originate from Wyclif; he referred the
Council, however, to the writings of Richard Bishop of Armagh,
and went on to give an account of Wyclif's teaching at Oxford,
his own struggles in defence of Wyclifite opinions, and his
flight into Bohemia. When he had ended, Rokycana thanked
the Council for their patient and kindly hearing: if anything
that they had said could be proved to be erroneous, they were
willing to amend it. He asked that those who answered in the
Council's behalf should follow their example and reduce the
heads of their arguments to writing. One of the Bohemian
nobles, speaking in German, thanked William of Bavaria for his
presence at the discussion. William assured them of his protection, and promised to procure for them as free and complete

---

[1] The speech is given in Martene, *Amp. Coll.* viii. 805.
[2] The synopsis handed in to the Council is given by John of Ragusa,
p. 270.

a hearing as they wished. Cesarini then proceeded to settle the preliminaries of the Council's reply. First he asked if all the Bohemians were unanimous in their adhesion to the arguments set forth by their speakers: he was answered 'Yes.' Cesarini then commented on the various points in the Bohemian speeches which gave him hopes of reconciliation. He said that the Council was resolved not to be offended at anything which was said contrary to the orthodox belief: but if any concord was to be obtained they must have everything under discussion. Besides the Four Articles, which had been put forward, he believed there were other points in which the Bohemians differed from the Church. One of their speakers had called Wyclif 'the evangelical doctor'; with a view to discover how far they held with Wyclif he handed to them twenty-eight propositions taken from Wyclif's writings and six other questions, opposite to each of which he asked that they would write whether they held it or no. The Bohemians asked to deliberate before answering. It was the first attempt of the Council to break the ranks of the Bohemians by bringing to light the differences which existed amongst them.

Answer of
John of
Ragusa.
January
31–Febru-
ary 7.

On January 31 the reply on the part of the Council was begun. First came a sermon from a Cistercian abbot, which gave offence to the Bohemians by exhorting them to submit to the Council. Then John of Ragusa began his proof that the reception of the Communion under both kinds was not necessary and, when forbidden by the Church, was unlawful. His speech, which was a tissue of scholastic explanations of texts and types and passages from the Fathers, lasted till February 12. He angered the Bohemians by his tediousness and by the assumptions, which underlaid his speech, that they were heretics. Some stormy interruptions took place in consequence. On February 4 Procopius rose and protested against the tone adopted by the Cistercian abbot and John of Ragusa. 'We are not heretics,' he exclaimed; 'if you say that we ought to return to the Church, I answer that we have not departed from it, but hope to bring others to it, you amongst the rest.' There was a shout of laughter. 'Is the speaker going to continue rambling over impertinent matter? Does he speak in his own name or in that of the Council? If in his own, let him be stopped: we did not take the trouble to come here to listen to three or four doctors.' The Cistercian abbot and John of Ragusa both excused themselves from any intention of violating the compact under which the Bohemians had come to Basel. Rokycana asked: ' You talk of the Church: what is the Church? We know what Pope Eugenius says about you; your head does not recognise you as the Universal Church. But we care little for that and hope only for peace and concord.' Cesarini exhorted both sides to patience: he reminded the Bohemians that if they had answered the twenty-eight articles proposed to them there would be less doubt about their opinions, and it would be easier to decide what was pertinent and what was not.

On February 10 there was another outburst of feeling. John of Ragusa, in pursuing his argument respecting the authority of the Church, was examining objections that might be raised to his positions. He introduced them by such phrases as ' a heretic might object.' This enraged the Bohemians; Rokycana rose and exclaimed, ' I abhor heresy, and if anyone suspects me of heresy let him prove it.' Procopius, his eyes flashing with rage, cried out, ' We are not heretics nor has anyone proved us to be such; yet that monk has stood and called us so repeatedly. If I had known this in Bohemia I would never have come here.' John of Ragusa excused himself, saying, ' May God show no mercy to me if I had any intention of casting a slur on you.' Peter Payne ironically exclaimed, ' We are not afraid of you; even if you had been speaking for the Council your words would have had no weight.' Again Cesarini cast oil on the waters, beseeching them to take all things in good part. ' There must be altercations,' he truly said, 'before we come to an agreement; a woman when she is in travail has sorrow.' Next day the Archbishop of Lyons came to ask pardon for John of Ragusa. The Bohemians demanded that the other three speakers should be more brief and should speak in the name of the Council. During the remainder of John's address Procopius and another of the Bohemians refused to attend the conference.

It was agreed by the Council that the other three orators should speak in the Council's name, reserving, however, the right of amending or adding to what they said. Matters now went more peaceably. The speeches of Carlier, Kalteisen, and John of Palomar, which were studiously moderate, extended till February 28. Meanwhile the Bohemians, on being pressed to

Further disputations.
February 8–March 10.

answer the twenty-eight articles submitted to them, showed
signs of their dissensions by standing on the treaty of Eger.
They said that they had only been commissioned to discuss the
Four Articles of Prag, and they did not think it right to com-
plicate the business by introducing other topics.

The disputation had now come to an end; but Rokycana
claimed to be allowed to answer some of the statements of John
of Ragusa, who demanded that, in that case, he should also have
the right of further reply. It was obvious that this procedure
might go on endlessly; and Cesarini suggested that a committee
of four on each side should be nominated for private conference.
However, on March 2 Rokycana began his reply, which lasted
till March 10. When he had ended, John of Ragusa rose and
urged that the Bohemians were bound to hear him in reply.
The Bohemians announced that they would hear him if they
thought fit, but they were not bound to do so. 'We will put
you to shame throughout the world,' said John angrily, 'if you
go away without hearing our answers.' Rokycana sarcastically
said that John of Ragusa scarcely maintained the dignity of a
doctor. 'And yet,' he added, 'before we came here, we had
never heard that there was such a person in the world. Still,
I have proved that his sayings are erroneous; for is it not erroneous,' and he raised his voice with passionate earnestness, 'to
say that either man or council can change the precepts of
Christ, who said, "Heaven and earth shall pass away, but my
words shall not pass away"?'

It was clear that such war of orators was preventing rather
than furthering the union which both parties professed to seek.
William of Bavaria interposed his mediation; and the Council
deputed fifteen members, chief of whom was Cesarini, to arrange
matters in private with the fifteen Bohemian representatives.
Their meetings, which began on March 11, were opened with
prayer by Cesarini, who exerted all his persuasive eloquence
and tact to induce the Bohemians to incorporate themselves
with the Council, which would then proceed to settle the differences existing between them. The discussions on this point
were at last summed up by Peter Payne: 'You say, "Be incorporated, return, be united:" we answer, "Return with us to the
primitive Church; be united with us in the Gospel." We know
what power our voice has, so long as we are one party and you

another; what power it would have after our incorporation experience has abundantly shown.' The Bohemians began to speak
of departing; but a learned German theologian, Nicolas of Cusa,
raised the question—if the Council allowed the Bohemians the
Communion under both kinds, which they regarded as a matter
of faith, would they agree to incorporation? if so, the other
questions, which only concerned morals, might be subjected to
discussion. At first the Bohemians suspected a snare; but
William of Bavaria assured them of his sincerity. After de-
liberating, the Bohemians refused incorporation, as being beyond
the powers given them as representatives; moreover, if they
were incorporated and the Council decided against them, they
could not accept its decision. An attempt was made to advance
further by means of a smaller committee of four on each side;
but it only became obvious that nothing more could be done
in Basel, that the Bohemian representatives were not disposed
to take any decided step, and that, if the Council intended
to proceed with the negotiations, they must send envoys to
Bohemia to treat with the Diet and the people.

Meanwhile disputations continued before the Council, in
which Rokycana, Peter Payne, and Procopius showed themselves
formidable controversialists. They had been formed in a ruder
and more outspoken school than that of the theological pro-
fessors who were pitted against them. John of Ragusa especially met with no mercy. One day he was so pedantic as to
say that he did not wish to derogate from the dignity of his
university. 'How so?' asked Rokycana. 'According to the
statutes,' said John of Ragusa, 'a doctor is not bound to answer
a master; nevertheless, as it concerns the faith, I will answer
you.' 'Certainly,' was the retort; 'John of Ragusa is not better
than Christ; nor John of Rokycana worse than the devil;
yet Christ answered the devil.' Another time, when John of
Ragusa had been speaking at great length, Rokycana remarked,
'He is one of the preaching friars, and is bound to say a great
deal.' Kalteisen, in his reply to Ulrich of Zynaim, reproved him
for having said that monks were introduced by the devil. 'I
never said so,' interrupted Ulrich. Procopius rose: 'I said one
day to the President, "If bishops have succeeded to the place
of the Apostles, and priests to the place of the seventy-two
disciples, to whom except the devil have the rest succeeded?"'

There was loud laughter, amid which Rokycana called out, ' Doctor, you should make Procopius Provincial of your Order.' [1]

It was at length arranged that on April 14 the Bohemians should return to their own land, whither the Council undertook to send ten ambassadors who should treat with the Diet in Prag. Procopius wrote to inform the Bohemians of this, and urged them to assemble in numbers at the Diet on June 7, for great things might be done. On April 13 the Bohemians took farewell of the Council. Rokycana in the name of all expressed their thanks for the kindness they had received. Then Procopius rose and said that he had often wished to speak, but had never had an opportunity. He spoke earnestly about the great work before the Council, the reformation of the Church, which all men longed for with sighs and groans. He spoke of the worldliness of the clergy, the vices of the people, the intrusion into the Church of the traditions of men, the general neglect of preaching. Cesarini, on the part of the Council, recapitulated all that had been done, and begged them to continue in Bohemia the work that he trusted had been begun in Basel. He thanked Rokycana for his kindly words : turning to Procopius, he called him his personal friend and thanked him for what he had said about the reformation of the Church, which the Council would have been engaged in, if they had not been employed in conference with the Bohemians. Finally he gave them his benediction and shook them each by the hand. Rokycana also raised his hand, and in a loud voice said, ' May the Lord bless and preserve this place in peace and quiet.' Then they took their leave : as they were going, a fat Italian archbishop ran after them and with tears in his eyes shook them by the hand. On April 14 they left Basel, accompanied by the ambassadors of the Council.

The Conference at Basel was most honourable to all who were concerned in it ; it showed a spirit of straightforwardness, charity, and mutual forbearance. It was no slight matter in those days for a Council of theologians to endure to listen to the arguments of heretics already condemned by the Church. It was no small thing for the Bohemians, who were already masters in the field, to curb their high spirit to a war of words.

---

[1] These particulars are taken from the *Liber Diurnus* of Peter of Saaz, in *Mon Concil.* i., 348.

Yet, in spite of occasional outbursts, the general result of the conference at Basel was to promote a good feeling between the two parties. Free and friendly intercourse existed between the Bohemians and the leading members of the Council, chiefly owing to the exertions of Cesarini, whose nobility and generosity of character produced a deep impression on all around him. But in spite of the friendliness with which they were received, and the personal affection which in some cases they inspired, the Bohemians could not help being a little disappointed at the general results of their visit to Basel. They had been somewhat disillusioned. They came with the same moral earnestness and childlike simplicity which had marked Hus at Constance. They hoped that their words would prevail, that their arguments would convince the Council that they were not heretics, but rested on the Gospel of Christ. They were chilled by the attitude of superiority which showed itself in all the Council's proceedings, and which was the more irritating because they could not formulate it in any definitely offensive words or acts. The assumption of an infallible Church, to which all the faithful were bound to be united, was one which the Bohemians could neither deny nor accept. In Bohemia the preachers had been wont to denounce those who departed from the Gospel; in Basel they found themselves the objects of kindly reprobation because they had departed from the Church.[1] It gradually became clear that they were not likely to induce the Council to reform the Church in accordance with their principles: the utmost that would be granted was a Concordat with Bohemia which would allow it to retain some of its peculiar usages and opinions without separation from the Catholic Church. The Bohemian representatives had failed to convince the Council; it remained to be seen if the good feeling which had grown up between the two contending parties would enable the Council to extend, and the Bohemian people to accept, a sufficient measure of toleration to prevent the breach of the outward unity of the Church.

[1] Peter of Saaz gives this picture in the account of a conversation between the disputants at dinner with Cesarini: ' Dixit auditor: Augustinus dicta sua ecclesiæ judicanda commisit; similiter Hieronymus Damaso Papæ: quare vos non? forte æstimatis vos ita sapientes esse, quasi errare non possetis in fide? Et sic omnem divisionem et bellorum causam retorquebant in nostros, nostri autem e converso in eos, quia evangelio contradicerent.'—Mon. Concil. i. 320.

BOOK
III.

The Coun-
cil's envoys
go to Prag.
May 8,
1433.

The ten ambassadors of the Council, chief amongst whom were the Bishops of Coutances and Augsburg, Giles Carlier, John of Palomar, Thomas Ebendorfer of Haselbach, Canon of Vienna, John of Geilhausen, and Alexander, an Englishman, Archdeacon of Salisbury, travelled peaceably to Prag, where they were received with every show of respect and rejoicing on May 8. They spent the time till the assembling of the Diet in interchanging courtesies with the Bohemian leaders. On May 24 a Bohemian preacher, Jacob Ulk, inveighed in a sermon against the Council's envoys, and bade the people beware of Basel as of a basilisk which endeavoured to shed its venom on every side. He attempted to raise a riot, but it was put down by Procopius,[1] and the magistrates issued an edict that no one under pain of death was to offend the Council's ambassadors. On June 13 the Diet assembled, and after preliminary addresses John of Palomar submitted the Council's proposal for the incorporation of the Bohemians and the common settlement of their differences in the Council. He was answered that the Council of Constance was the origin of all the wars and troubles that had beset Bohemia; the Bohemians had always wished for peace, but they were firm in their adhesion to the Four Articles of Prag, and they wished to hear the Council's decision respecting them. John of Palomar at once answered that the Four Articles seemed to be held in different senses by different parties among the Bohemians; before he could give the Council's opinion, he wished them to be defined in writing in the sense in which they were universally believed. It was the first step towards bringing to light the dissensions of the Bohemian parties. A definition drawn up by the University of Prag was repudiated by the Taborites as containing treacherous concessions. Rokycana gave a verbal answer, and a committee of eight deputies of the Diet was appointed to confer on this point with the ambassadors of the Council. A definition was then drawn up in which the Council's side gained nothing. They saw that by this procedure they would merely drift back to the disputation which they had in Basel.

Accordingly on June 25 the Council's ambassadors took the decided step of negotiating secretly with some of the Calixtin

[1] Palacky, *Geschichte von Böhmen*, Bk. VIII. ch. iii., from Haselbach's MS., *Liber Pontificalis.*

nobles, to whom they said that the Council would most probably allow to the Bohemians the Communion under both kinds, if they would incorporate themselves for the discussion of the other points. This was received with joy by some of the nobles, amongst whom a party in favour of this course was gradually organised. The Diet enquired under what form such privilege would be granted, and a proposed form was presented by the ambassadors. The Diet in answer drew up on January 29 a form of their own, which, if the Council accepted, they were willing to unite with it. As the form contained the full acceptance of the Four Articles of Prag, the ambassadors refused to entertain it. On July 1 they again had a meeting in Rokycana's house with some of the Calixtin nobles, who agreed to moderate the form into such a shape that another Bohemian deputation might take it to Basel. In the discussion that ensued in the Diet some sharp things were said. When the Council's ambassadors begged the Bohemians to forget the past and be as they had been twenty years ago, Procopius scornfully exclaimed, 'In the same way you might argue that we ought to be as we were a thousand years ago when we were pagans.' A statement, however, was drawn up that the Bohemians agreed to unite with the Council and obey ' according to God's Word.' Three ambassadors, Mathias Landa, Procopius of Pilsen, and Martin Lupak, were appointed to take this, together with an exposition of the Four Articles, to the Council. They, with the Council's envoys, left Prag on July 11 and reached Basel on August 2, where they were received with joy.

The object of this first embassy of the Council was to survey the ground and report the position of affairs in Bohemia. On July 31 one of the envoys who was sent on before, announced to the Council that everywhere in Bohemia they had found a great desire for peace, and had been listened to by the Diet with a courtesy and decorum which the Council would do well to imitate. He urged that conciliation be tried to the utmost. The other envoys on their arrival gave a full report of their proceedings to the Council, which appointed a committee of six to be elected from each deputation who, together with the Cardinals, were to confer on future proceedings. Before this committee John of Palomar on August 13 made a secret report of the general aspect of affairs in Bohemia. He said that neither the

CHAP.
V.

Negotiations with the Diet at Prag. June–July, 1438.

John of Palomar's report to the Council. August 1438.

nobles nor the people were free, but were tyrannised over by a small but vigorous party, which feared to lose its power if any reconciliation with the Church took place; the strength of this party lay in the hatred of the Bohemians to German domination, and their willingness to carry on war to escape it. He sketched the position of the three chief sects, the Calixtins, Orphans, and Taborites; the only point on which they all agreed was the reception of the Communion under both kinds. The first party wished to obtain the use of their rite by peaceable means and desired union with the Church; the second party desired to be in the bosom of the Church, but would take up arms and fight desperately to defend what they believed to be necessary; the third party was entirely opposed to the Church, and was not to be won over by any concessions, for the confiscation of the goods of the clergy was their chief desire.[1]

Delibera-
tions at
Basel about
the Bohe-
mian ques-
tion. Au-
gust 1433.

The commission then proceeded to deliberate whether the Communion under both kinds could be conceded to the Bohemians, and what answer the Council should return to the other three articles, of which the Bohemian envoys brought a definition to the Council. The discussions lasted for a fortnight, and on August 26 an extraordinary congregation was held, which was attended by the prelates at Basel and 160 doctors, who were all bound by oath of secrecy. John of Palomar put before them, on behalf of the commission, the pressing need of settling the Bohemian question, and the desirability of making some concession for that purpose. He argued that the Church might lawfully do so, and follow the example of Paul in his dealings with the Corinthians; for he 'caught them by guile.' The Bohemian people was intractable and would not enter the fold of the Church like other Christians; they must treat it gently as one treats a mule or horse to induce it to submit to the halter. When once the Bohemians had returned to union with the Church, their experience of the miseries of a separation from it would lead them to submit to the common rites of Christendom rather than run new risks in the future. Cesarini followed in the same strain; and next day William of Bavaria, on behalf of Sigismund, urged the interest of the Emperor in securing his recognition, by means of the Council, as King of

[1] John of Segovia, *Mon. Concil.* ii. 431, and *Declaratio Gestorum in Bohemia*, in *Mon. Concil.* i. 388.

Bohemia. After three days' deliberation it was agreed to concede the reception of the Communion under both kinds, and an answer to the other three articles was framed. But the secret was still kept from the Bohemian envoys, as the Council did not wish their decision to be known too soon in Bohemia, and they were also afraid lest Eugenius IV. might interpose. On September 2 the Bohemians were dismissed with kindly words and the assurance of the despatch of four envoys from the Council to Prag. Four of the previous embassy—the Bishop of Coutances, John of Palomar, Henry Toh, and Martin Verruer—set out on September 11.

The second embassy from Basel did not meet with such a peaceable entrance into Bohemia as had the first. War had again broken out, a war in which were involved the contending interests of the Council and the Hussites. In the very middle of Bohemia there still remained a city which held fast by the cause of Catholicism and Sigismund. In the reaction which ensued after the first successes of the commencement of the Hussite movement, the strong city of Pilsen in the south-west of Bohemia had swung back to Catholicism, and from its numerous outlying fortresses had defied all efforts to reduce it. Year by year their sufferings from Hussite attacks made the inhabitants grow firmer in their resistance ; and when the Council's envoys first came as spies into the land the Bohemians keenly felt the disadvantage under which they lay in their negotiations when they could not offer a decided front to their foe. Messengers from Pilsen visited the Basel ambassadors and prayed for help from the Council. As the Bohemians began to see that all that the Council would grant them was a recognition of their exceptional position, they felt the need of absolute internal unity if they were to secure or maintain it. The Diet decreed a vigorous siege of Pilsen ; the Council's ambassadors protracted their negotiations to allow the men of Pilsen to gather in their harvest ;[1] and later the Fathers of Basel sent a contribution of money to the aid of Pilsen and used their influence to prevail on Nürnberg to do the same. On July 14 the Bohemian army began the siege of Pilsen, and in the beginning of September

Renewed
war in
Bohemia.
June 1438.

[1] John of Segovia, p. 82 : 'Quia Pilyenses, qui erant obsessi, tempore tractatuum pacis collegerant messes aliquas, qui jam præ inopia subsistere non poterant.'

the besieging host had grown to 36,000 men. The might of the Hussites was directed to secure religious unity within their land.

Pilsen was strongly defended, and the besiegers began to suffer from hunger. Foraging parties were sent to greater distances, and on September 16 a detachment of 1,400 foot and 500 horse was sent by Procopius under the command of John Pardus to harry Bavaria. As Pardus was returning laden with spoil, he was suddenly attacked by the Bavarians; his troops were almost entirely cut to pieces, and he himself with a few followers made his escape with difficulty to the camp at Pilsen. Great was the wrath of the Bohemian warriors at this disgrace to their arms. They rushed upon Pardus as a traitor, and even hurled a stool at Procopius, who tried to protect him; the stool hit Procopius on the head with such violence that the blood streamed down his face. The wrath of the chiefs was turned against him; he was imprisoned, and the man who had thrown the stool was made general in his stead. This excitement lasted only a few days. Procopius was released and restored to his former position, but his proud spirit had been deeply wounded by the sense of his powerlessness in an emergency. He refused the command and left the camp never to return.

Second em-
bassy of the
Council to
Prag.
October
1433.

This was the news which greeted the Council's envoys when they reached Eger on September 27. They feared to advance farther in the present excited condition of men's minds. The Bohemians in vain tried to discover what message they brought from the Council. The leaders of the army before Pilsen at length sent two of their number to conduct them safely to Prag, where they said that the Diet could not assemble before St. Martin's Day, November 11. The fears of the envoys were entirely dispelled by the cordial welcome which they received in Prag on their arrival, October 22. A plague was ravaging the city and the physicians vied with one another in precautions for ensuring the safety of their city's guests. The preacher Ulk still raised his voice against them; they had honey on their lips but venom in their heart, they wished to bring back Sigismund, who would cut off the people's heads for their rebellion.

The proceedings of the Diet, which opened on November 17, resolved themselves into a diplomatic contest between the

Council's envoys and the Bohemians. The Council was trying to make the smallest concessions possible, the Bohemians were anxious to get all they could. But the four envoys of Basel had the advantage in contending with an assembly like the Diet. They could gauge the effect produced by each concession; they could see when they had gone far enough to have hopes of success. Moreover, they knew definitely the limits of concession which the Council would grant, while the Bohemians were too much at variance amongst themselves to know definitely what they were prepared to accept. Accordingly, after the preliminary formalities were over, the Council's envoys began to practise economy in their concessions. John of Palomar, after a speech in which he lauded General Councils and recapitulated all that the Fathers at Basel had done to promote unity, proceeded to give the limitations under which the Council was prepared to admit three of the Articles; about the fourth, the Communion under both kinds, he said that the envoys had powers to treat if the declaration which he had made about the other three was satisfactory to the Bohemians. The Diet demanded to have the Council's decision on this also put before them. The envoys pressed to have an answer on the three Articles first. For. two days the struggle on this point continued; then the envoys asked, before speaking about the Communion, for an answer to the question whether, if an agreement could be come to on the Four Articles, the Bohemians would consent to union. John of Rokycana answered on behalf of all, ' We would consent; ' and all the Diet cried ' Yes, yes.' Only Peter Payne rose and said : ' We understand by a good end one in which we are all agreed; ' but those around him admonished him to hold his tongue, and he was not allowed to continue. Then John of Palomar read a declaration setting forth that the Communion under one kind had been introduced into the Church, partly to correct the Nestorian error that in the bread was contained only the body of Christ, and in the wine only His blood, partly to guard against irreverence and mishap in the reception of the elements: nevertheless, as the Bohemian use was to administer under both kinds, the Council was willing that they should continue to do so till the matter had been fully discussed. If they still continued in their belief, permission would be given to their priests so to administer it to those who, having reached years of discretion, asked for it. The Bohemians were dissatisfied with this. They complained that the Council said nothing which could satisfy the honour of Bohemia. They demanded that their words, that the reception under both kinds was 'useful and wholesome,' should be adopted, and that the permission be extended to children.

The Council's basis of agreement.
On November 26 an amended form was submitted to the Diet, which became the basis of an agreement. Bohemia and Moravia were to make peace with all men. The Council would accept this declaration and release them from all ecclesiastical censures. As regarded the Four Articles :—

(1) If in all other points the Bohemians and Moravians received the faith and ritual of the Universal Church, those who had the use of communicating under both kinds should continue to do so, ' with the authority of Jesus Christ and the Church his true spouse.' The question as a whole should be further discussed in the Council ; but the priests of Bohemia and Moravia should have permission to administer under both kinds to those who, being of the age of discretion, reverently demanded it, at the same time telling them that under each kind was the whole body of Christ.

(2) As regarded the correction and punishment of open sins, the Council agreed that, as far as could reasonably be done, they should be repressed according to the law of God and the institutes of the Fathers. The phrase used by the Bohemians, ' by those whose duty it was,' was too vague ; the duty did not devolve on private persons, but on those who had jurisdiction in such matters.

(3) About freedom of preaching, the Word of God ought to be freely preached by priests who were commissioned by their superiors : 'freely ' did not mean indiscriminately, for order was necessary.

(4) As regarded the temporalities of the clergy, individual priests, who were not bound by a vow of poverty, might inherit or receive gifts ; and similarly the Church might possess temporalities and exercise over them civil lordship. But the clergy ought to administer faithfully the goods of the Church according to the institutes of the Fathers ; and the goods of the Church cannot be occupied by others.

As abuses may have gathered round these last three points,

the Diet could send deputies to the Council, which intended to
proceed with the question of reform, and the envoys promised
to aid them in all possible ways.

The basis of an agreement was now prepared, and a large
party in Prag was willing to accept it. Procopius, however,
rose in the Diet and read proposals of his own, which John of
Palomar dismissed, observing that their object was concord, and
it was better to clear away difficulties than to raise them. On
November 28 the legates judged it prudent to lay before the
Diet an explanation of some points in the previous document.
The rites of the Church, which the Bohemians were to accept,
they explained to mean those rites which were commonly observed
throughout Christendom. If all the Bohemians did not at
once follow them, that would not be a hindrance to the peace;
those who dissented on any points should have a full and fair
hearing in the Council. The law of God and the practice of
Christ and the Apostles would be recognised by the Council,
according to the treaty of Eger, as the judge in all such matters.
Finally, on November 30, after a long discussion and many
verbal explanations given by the envoys, the moderate party
among the Bohemians succeeded in extorting from the Diet a
reluctant acceptance of the proposed agreement.

The success of the Council was due chiefly to the fact that
the negotiations, once begun, awakened hopes among the
moderate party in Bohemia and so widened the differences
between them and the extreme party. There was both plague
and famine in the land. More than 100,000 are said to have
died in Bohemia during the year, and men had good grounds
for feeling sadly the desolate condition of their country and
counting the cost of their prolonged resistance. Moreover, the
appearance of the Council's envoys had emboldened those who
wished for a restoration of the old state of things to lift up
their heads. There were still some adherents of Sigismund,
chief of whom was Meinhard of Neuhaus; there were still
formidable adherents of Catholicism, as the continued ill-success
of the siege of Pilsen showed. As soon as doubt and wavering
was apparent among the Hussites the party of the restoration
declared itself more openly. Further, the events of the siege
of Pilsen brought to light the disorganisation that had spread
among the army. The old religious zeal had waxed dim;

adventurers abounded in the ranks of the Lord's soldiers ; the sternness of Zizka's discipline had been relaxed, and the mutiny against Procopius bowed the spirit of the great leader and made him doubtful of the future. The Bohemian nobles were weary of the ascendency of the Taborites, whose democratic ideas they had always borne with difficulty. The country was weary of military rule ; and the party which was aiming at Sigismund's restoration determined to use the conciliatory spirit of the Diet for their own purposes. On December 1 a Bohemian noble, Ales of Riesenberg, was elected governor of the land, with a council of twelve to assist him; he took oath to promote the welfare of the people and defend the Four Articles. The moderate party, which had sought to find a constitutional king in Korybut in 1427, now succeeded in setting up a president over the Bohemian republic.[1] The peace negotiations with the Council had already led to a political reaction.

Departure
of the
Council's
envoys.
January
14, 1484.
The Compact had been agreed to, but the difficulties in the way of its full acceptance were by no means removed. The envoys demanded that, as Bohemia had agreed to a general peace, the siege of Pilsen should cease. The Bohemians demanded that the men of Pilsen should first unite with the Bohemian government, and that all Bohemians should be required by the Council to accept the Communion under both kinds. Other questions also arose. The Bohemians complained that, in treating of the temporalities of the clergy, the Council used language which seemed to accuse them of sacrilege. They demanded also that the Communion under both kinds should be declared ' useful and wholesome ' for the whole of Christendom, and that their custom of administering the Communion to infants should be recognised. The discussion on these points only led to further disagreement. The envoys had convinced themselves that a large party in Bohemia was prepared to accept peace on the terms which they had already offered. As nothing more was to be done, they asked to be told definitely whether the Compact was accepted or not; otherwise they wished to depart on January 15, 1434. The Diet answered that it would be more convenient if they went on January 14; a Bohemian envoy would be sent to Basel to announce their intentions.

[1] Palacky, *Geschichte von Böhmen*, Bk. VIII. ch. iii.

Accordingly the Council's ambassadors left Prag on January 14, and arrived in Basel on February 15.

The result of this second embassy had been to rally the moderate party in Bohemia, and break the bond that had hitherto held the Bohemians together. The envoys had laid the foundations of a league in favour of the Church. Ten of the masters of the University of Prag subscribed a statement that they were willing to stand by the Compacts and had been reconciled to the Church; even when the envoys were at Eger two nobles followed them seeking reconciliation.[1] When the ambassador of the Diet, Martin Lupak, joined them at Eger, it is not wonderful that they warned him that it was useless for him to journey to Basel if he went with fresh demands. The Council, after hearing the report of their envoys, gave Martin audience at once on February 16. He asked that the Council should order all the inhabitants of Bohemia to receive the Communion under both kinds; if all did not conform, there would be different churches and different rites, and no real peace in the land, for each party would claim to be better than the other, the terms 'catholic' and 'heretic' would again be bandied about, and there would be perpetual dissension. This was no doubt true; but the Council listened to Martin with murmurs of dissent. It was clearly impossible for them to abandon the Bohemian Catholics, and to turn the concession which they had granted to the Hussites into an order to those who had remained faithful to the Church. Still Sigismund besought them to take time over their answer and to avoid any threats. The answer was drawn up in concert with Sigismund, and on February 26 Cesarini addressed Martin Lupak, saying that the Council wondered the Bohemians did not keep their promises, as even Jews and heathens respected good faith. He besought him to urge his countrymen to fulfil the Compacts; then the Council would consider their new demands, and would do all they could consistently with the glory of God and the dignity of the Church. Martin defended his demands, and there was some altercation. At last he taunted Cesarini with

[1] 'Plures eorum conversi fuerant ad fidem eciam postquam exierint regnum: etenim se in Egra constitutis nobiles duo, qui multa dampna intulerunt in exercitu, advenerant humiliter reconciliationem petentes.'—From relation of ambassadors, in John of Segovia, p. 595.

the remark that the Church had not always wished for peace,
but had preached a crusade against Bohemia. 'Peace is now
in your hands, if you will stand by the agreement,' said
Cesarini. 'Rather it is in the hands of the Council, if they
will grant what is asked,' retorted Martin.   He refused to
receive a letter from the Council unless he were informed of
its contents, and after briefly thanking the Fathers for hearing
him, he left the congregation and departed.

Progress of
affairs in
Bohemia.

A breach seemed again imminent; but the Council knew
that it would not be with Bohemia, but only with a party in it,
which they trusted to overcome by the help of their fellow-
countrymen.   The first envoys had reported that there was a
number of irreconcilables who must be subdued by force; the
second negotiations had brought to light internal dissensions
and had founded a strong party in Bohemia in favour of union
with the Council.   Everything was done to strengthen that
party and gain the means of putting down the radicals.   On
February 8 the Council ordered a tax of 5 per cent. on ecclesiastical revenues to be levied throughout Christendom for their
needs in the matter of Bohemia.   John of Palomar was sent
to carry supplies from the Council and from Sigismund to aid
the besieged in Pilsen, where the besieging army was suffering from plague, hunger and despondency.   In Bohemia Meinhard of Neuhaus was indefatigable in carrying on the work
of the restoration.   In April a league was formed by the
barons of Bohemia and Moravia and the Old Town of Prag
for the purpose of securing peace and order in the land; all armed
bands were ordered to disperse and an amnesty was promised if
they obeyed.

Death of
Procopius
in the
battle of
Lipan.
May 30,
1434.

Procopius was roused from his retirement in the New Town
of Prag by these machinations, and once more put himself at
the head of the Taborites and the Orphans.   But the barons
had already gathered their forces.   The New Town of Prag was
summoned to enter the league, and on its refusal was stormed;
on May 6 Procopius and a few others succeeded with difficulty
in escaping.   At this news the army before Pilsen raised the
siege and retired.   Bohemia merged its minor religious differences, and prepared to settle by the sword a political question
that was bound to press some day for solution.   On one side
were the nobles ready to fight for their ancient privileges; on

the other side stood the towns as champions of democracy. On
May 30 was fought the decisive battle at Lipan. The nobles,
under the command of Borek of Militinek, a companion in arms
of Zizka, had an army of 25,000 men; against them stood
Procopius with 18,000. Both armies were entrenched behind
their waggons, and for some time fired at one another. The
Taborites had the better artillery, but their adversaries turned
this superiority to their ruin. One wing feigned to be greatly
distressed by their fire; then as if goaded to exasperation rushed
from behind its entrenchment and charged. When they thought
that the foe had exhausted their fire, they feigned to flee, and
the Taborites, thinking their ranks were broken, rushed from
their waggons in pursuit. But the seeming broken ranks
skilfully reformed and faced their pursuers, who had meanwhile been cut off from their waggons by the other wing of
the nobles' army. Shut in on every side, Procopius and his
men prepared to die like heroes. All day and night the
battle raged, till in the morning 13,000 of the warriors who
had been so long the terror of Europe lay dead on the ground.
Procopius and all the chief men of the extreme party were
among the slain. The military power of Bohemia, which had
so long defied the invader, fell because it was divided against
itself.

The fight of Lipan was a decided victory for the Council.
It is true that among the conquerors the large majority was
Hussite, and would require some management before it could
be safely penned within the fold of the Church. But the
Taborites had lost the control of affairs. The irreconcilables
were swept away, and the Council would henceforth have to
deal with men of more moderate opinions.

CHAPTER VI.

EUGENIUS IV. AND THE COUNCIL OF BASEL—NEGOTIATIONS WITH THE GREEKS AND THE BOHEMIANS.

1434–1436.

BOOK
III.

Position
of the
Council in
1434.

AT the beginning of the year 1434 the Council of Basel had reached its highest point of importance in the affairs of Christendom and of the Church. It had compelled the Pope to accept without reserve the conciliar principle for which it strove; it had gone so far in pacifying Bohemia that its final triumph seemed secure. It looked to further employment for its energies in negotiating a union between the Greek and Latin Churches. Yet the Council's success had been largely due to accidental circumstances. Eugenius IV. had been subdued, not by the Council's strength, but by his own weakness; he fell because he had so acted as to raise up a number of determined enemies, without gaining any friends in return. The Council's policy towards him was tolerated rather than approved by the European Powers; if no one helped Eugenius IV., it was because no one had anything to gain by so doing. Sigismund, whose interest was greatest in the matter, was kept on the Council's side by his personal interest in the Bohemian question; but he, with the German electors and the King of France, was resolute in resisting any steps which might lead to a schism of the Church. If the Council were to keep what it had won, it must gain new hold upon the sympathies of Christendom, which were not touched by the struggle against the Pope. Sigismund gave the fathers at Basel the advice of a statesman when he exhorted them to leave their quarrel with the Pope and busy themselves with the reform of the Church.

But to contend for abstract principles is always easy, to reform abuses is difficult. The Council found it more interesting

to war with the Pope than to labour through the obstacles
which lay in the way of a reformation of abuses by those who
benefited by them.   Each rank of the hierarchy was willing to
reform its neighbours, but had a great deal to urge in its own
defence.   In this collision of interests there was a general agreement that it was good to begin with a reform in the Papacy,
as the Pope was not at Basel to speak for himself.[1] Moreover,
the Council had grown inveterate in its hostility to the Pope.
The personal enemies of Eugenius IV. flocked to Basel, and
were not to be satisfied with anything short of his entire
humiliation.   In this they were aided by the pride of
authority which among the less responsible members of the
assembly grew in strength every day, and made them desirous
to assert in every way the superiority of the Council over the
Pope.

The first question that arose was concerning the presidency.
Eugenius IV., after his recognition by the Council, issued a Bull
nominating four Papal deputies to share that office with Cesarini.
The first decision of the Council was that they could not admit
this claim of the Pope, since it was derogatory to the dignity of
the Council, but they were willing themselves to appoint two of
the Cardinals. Again Sigismund had to interpose, and with some
difficulty prevailed on the Council to receive the Papal presidents.   They were not, however, admitted till they had bound
themselves by an oath to labour for the Council, to maintain the
decrees of Constance, to declare that even the Pope, if he refused
to obey the Council, might be punished, and to observe strict
secresy about all its proceedings.   On these terms the Papal
presidents, Cardinal Albergata, the Archbishop of Tarento, the
Bishop of Padua, and the Abbot of S. Justin of Padua, were
admitted to their office on April 26, 1434, at a solemn session
at which Sigismund in his Imperial robes was present.

The pretensions of the Council went on increasing.   On

---

[1] See the interesting chapter of John of Segovia, p. 858 :—' Experimento
quidem palparunt concilio tuno et postea interessentes circa reformationem
ecclesie quam sit velut infinita distancia inter dicere et facere, fiat reformacio
et facta est. Suave profecto est de aliorum reformacione statuum cogitare,
liberum avisare, speciosum predicare, sanctimonieque reputatur, quod facta
non sit redargucio. Sed cum venitur ad opus reformacionis, in quovis statu
sentitur, quod de justicia dicitur proverbio communi, illam desiderari ut quo-
cunque alio, neo tamen in propria fiat domo.'

BOOK
III.

Grievances
of Sigis-
mund
against the
Council.

May 2 Cardinal Lusignan, who was sent on an embassy to pacify France, received from the Council the title of *legatus a latere*, in spite of the protest of the five presidents against conferring a dignity which only the Pope could grant. Sigismund also felt aggrieved by the small heed which the Council paid to his monitions. Few German prelates were present; the large majority were French, Italians, and Spaniards. The democratic constitution of the Council prevented Sigismund from receiving the deference which was his due; he was not even consulted about the appointment of ambassadors. He felt that a slight had been offered to himself by the dealings of the Council with his enemy, the Duke of Milan. He complained bitterly of the irregular conduct of the Council in granting a commission to the Duke of Milan as its vicar, and so abetting him in his designs on the States of the Church. The Council at first denied, then defended, and finally refused to withdraw from, its connexion with the Duke of Milan. Sigismund saw with indignation that the Council adopted a policy of its own, and refused to identify its interests with his. He sadly contrasted the purely ecclesiastical organisation at Basel with the strong national spirit that had prevailed at Constance. He determined to leave a place where he had so little weight that, as he himself said, he was like a fifth wheel to a carriage, which did no good, but only impeded its progress.[1]

Proposal of
the Bishop
of Lübeck
to allow
the mar-
riage of the
clergy.

Before departing he seems to have resolved to give a stimulus to the Council. He sent the Bishop of Lübeck to the several deputations to lay before them a suggestion that the marriage of the clergy should be permitted. ' It was in vain,' he pleaded, ' that priests were deprived of wives; scarcely among a thousand could one continent priest be found. By clerical celibacy the bond of friendship between the clergy and laity was broken, and the freedom of confession was rendered suspicious. There was no fear that a married clergy would appropriate the goods of the Church for their wives and families; the permission to marry would rather bring those of the highest ranks into the clergy, and the nobles would be less desirous of secularising ecclesiastical property if it was in the hands of their relations

---

[1] John of Segovia, 663: 'Dicebat quod intendebat recedere, quia sibi videretur quod erat in concilio sicut quinta rota in curru, que de nichilo juvat sed impedit currum.'

and friends.' The fathers listened; but 'the old,' says Æneas Sylvius, 'condemned what had no charms for them. The monks, bound by a vow of chastity, grudged that secular priests should have a privilege denied to themselves.' The majority ruled that the time was not ripe for such a change; they feared that it would be too great a shock to popular prejudice. [1]

Before his departure Sigismund addressed the Council, and urged that it would be better to follow the example set at Constance, and organise themselves by nations. He wisely remarked that the reformation of the Church would be better carried out if each nation dealt with its own customs and rites.[2] Moreover, decisions arrived at by a national organisation would have greater chance of being accepted by the States so represented. He was answered that the deputations would take his suggestion under consideration. Finally, on May 19 he departed in no amiable mood from Basel, saying that he left behind him a sink of iniquity.

Departure of Sigismund. May 19, 1434.

After Sigismund's departure Cesarini besought the Council to turn its attention to the question of reformation; he said that already they were evil spoken of throughout Christendom for their delay. The basis of the questions raised at Constance was adopted, and the extirpation of simony first attracted the attention of the fathers. But there was great difficulty in keeping to the point, and little progress was made. Insignificant quarrels between prelates were referred to the Council as a court of appeal, and the Council took greater interest in such personal matters than in abstract questions of reform. The question of union between the Eastern and Western Churches was hailed with delight as a relief. This question, which had been mooted at Constance, slumbered under Martin V., but had been renewed by Eugenius IV. The Council in its struggle with the Pope thought it well to deprive him of the opportunity of increasing his importance, and at the same time to add to its own. In January 1433 it sent ambassadors to Greece to inaugurate steps for the pro-

First negotiations of the Council with the Greeks. 1432-34.

---

[1] This account is given by Æneas Sylvius, in Feal; *Pius II., a Calumniis Vindicatus*, p. 58. The matter is not mentioned by John of Segovia, who perhaps thought it beneath the dignity of his serious history.

[2] 'Præterea cum reformacio esset ex diversis consuetudinibus, existentibus variis juxta nacionum varietatem, id melius deliberari posset ab illis de nacione'—John of Segovia, 662.

posed union. In consequence of these negotiations the Greek
ambassadors arrived at Basel on July 12, 1434. They were
graciously received by the Council; and Cesarini expressed the
general wish for a conference on their differences, which he
said that discussion would probably show to be verbal rather
than real. The Greeks demanded that they should have their
expenses paid in coming to the conference, and named as the
place Ancona, or some port on the Calabrian coast, then Bologna, Milan, or some other town in Italy, next Pesth or Vienna,
and finally some place in Savoy. The Council was anxious
that the Greeks should come to Basel; but when the Greeks
declared that they had no power to assent to this, their other
conditions were accepted. Ambassadors were to go to Constantinople to urge the choice of Basel as a place for the
conference. The Greeks also demanded that Eugenius IV.
should give his assent to the Council's proposals, and envoys
were accordingly sent to lay them before him.

Negotia-
tions of
Eugenius
IV. with
the Greeks.
1433–34.
But Eugenius IV. on his side had made proposals to the
Greeks for the same purpose; and the Greeks, with their usual
shiftiness, were carrying on a double negotiation, in hopes of
making a better bargain for themselves by playing off against
one another the rival competitors for their goodwill. Eugenius IV. sent to Constantinople in July 1433 his secretary,
Cristoforo Garatoni, who proposed that a Council should be
held at Constantinople, to which the Pope should send a legate
and a number of prelates and doctors. When the Council's proposals were laid before him, Eugenius wrote on November 15,
1434, and gently warned it of the dangers that might arise from
too great precipitancy in this important matter. He mildly complained that he had not been consulted earlier. He added, however, that he was willing to assent to the simplest and speediest
plan for accomplishing the object in view. The question of the
place of conference with the Greeks was sure to open up the
dispute between the Pope and Council. The chief reason
which Eugenius IV. had given for dissolving the Council was
his belief that the Greeks would never go so far as Basel.
He was now content to wait and see how far the Council would
succeed. He already began to see in their probable failure a
means of reasserting his authority, and either transferring the
Council to Italy, as he had wished at first, or setting up against

it another Council, which from its object would have in the eyes of Europe an equal, if not a greater, prestige.

On the departure of the Greek ambassadors the Council again turned to its wearisome task of reformation, and on January 22, 1435, succeeded in issuing four decrees, limiting the penalties of interdict and excommunication to the persons or places which had incurred them by their own fault, forbidding frivolous appeals to the Church, and enforcing stricter measures to prevent the concubinage of the clergy. Offenders whose guilt was notorious were to be mulcted of the revenues for three months, and admonished under pain of deprivation to put away their concubines; fines paid to bishops for connivance at this irregularity were forbidden. The Council felt that it was at least safe in denouncing an open breach of ecclesiastical discipline, one which in those days was constantly condemned and constantly permitted.

From this peaceful work of reform the Council was soon drawn away by a letter from Eugenius IV., announcing the hopes he entertained of effecting a union with the Greeks by means of a Council at Constantinople. The letter was brought by Garatoni, who on April 5 gave the Council an account of his embassy to the Greeks, and urged in favour of the Pope's plan, that it involved little expense, and was preferable to the Greeks, who did not wish to impose on their Emperor and the aged Patriarch a journey across the sea. The Council, however, by no means took this view of the matter; it was resolved not to lose the glory of a reunion of the two churches. On May 3 an angry letter was written to the Pope, saying that a synod at Constantinople could have no claims to be a General Council, and would only raise fresh discord; such a proposal could not be entertained. Eugenius IV. gave way in outward appearance, and sent Garatoni again to Constantinople to express his readiness to accept the proposals of the Council. He was contented to bide his time. But the Council was in a feverish haste to arrange preliminaries, and in June sent envoys, amongst whom was John of Ragusa, to Constantinople for this purpose. It also began to consider means for raising money, and the sale of indulgences was suggested. This suggestion raised a storm of dissatisfaction amongst the adherents of the

Anger
with the
Pope for
his nego-
tiations
with the
Greeks,
April
1435.

Pope, and seemed to all moderate men to be a serious encroachment on the Papal prerogative.

It was not long, however, before a still more deadly blow was aimed at the Pope's authority. The reforming spirit of the Basel fathers was stirred to deal vigorously with Papal exactions. The subject of annates, which had been raised in vain at Constance, was peremptorily decided at Basel. On June 9 a decree was passed abolishing annates, and all dues on presentations, on receiving the pallium, and on all such occasions. It was declared to be simoniacal to demand or to pay them, and a pope who attempted to exact them was to be judged by a General Council. Two of the Papal presidents, the Archbishop of Tarento and the Bishop of Padua, protested against this decree, and their protest was warmly backed by the English and by many other members of the Council. There were only present at its publication four cardinals and forty-eight prelates. Cesarini only assented to it on condition that the Council should undertake no other business till it had made, by other means, a suitable provision for the Pope and Cardinals. The abolition of annates was, indeed, a startling measure of reform. It deprived the Pope at once of all means of maintaining his Curia, and to Eugenius IV., a refugee in Florence, left no source of supplies. No doubt the question of annates was one that needed reform ; but the reform ought to have been well considered and moderately introduced. As it was, the Council showed itself to be moved chiefly by a desire to deprive the Pope of means to continue his negotiations with the Greeks.

The decree abolishing annates was a renewed declaration of war against the Pope. It marked the rise into power of the extreme party in the Council—the party whose object was the entire reduction of the Papacy under a conciliar oligarchy. At the time, Eugenius was too helpless to accept the challenge. Two of his legates at Basel protested against the annates decree, and absented themselves from the business of the Council. The Council answered by instituting proceedings against them for contumacy. But the matter was stayed for the time by the arrival, on August 20, of two Papal envoys who had been sent expressly to deal with the Council on this vexed question— Antonio de San Vito, one of the auditors of the Curia, and the learned Florentine, Ambrogio Traversari, abbot of Camaldoli.

The feeling of the Italian churchmen was turning strongly in favour of Eugenius IV.; they saw in the proceedings of the Council a menace to the glory of the Papacy, which Italy was proud to call its own. Reformation, as carried out by the Council, seemed to them to be merely an attempt to overthrow the Pope, and carry off beyond the Alps the management of ecclesiastical affairs which had so long centred in Italy.[1] Traversari, who had been zealous for a reform, and had sent to Eugenius on his election a copy of St. Bernard, ' De Considera-tione,' now placed himself on the Pope's side, and went to Basel to defeat the machinations of what he considered a law-less mob.[2]

CHAP. VI.

The answers which Traversari brought from the Pope were ambiguous: he was willing that the union with the Greek Church should be conducted in the best way; when the pre-liminaries had advanced further he would be willing to consider whether the expenses had better be met by indulgences or in some other way; as to the abolition of annates he thought that the Council had acted precipitately, and wished to know how they proposed to provide for the Pope and Cardinals. There was, in this, no basis for negotiation; and Traversari in vain endeavoured to get farther instructions from Eugenius IV. He stayed three months in Basel, and was convinced that Cesarini's influence was waning, and that it was a matter of vital importance to the Pope to win him over to his side; he urged Eugenius IV. to leave no means untried for this end. Traversari was shrewd enough in surveying the situation for the future, but for the present could obtain nothing save an empty promise that the question of a provision for the Pope should be taken into immediate consideration.

Pending this consideration the Council showed its deter-mination to carry its decrees into effect. When the customary dues for the reception of the pallium were demanded by the Papal Curia from the newly elected Archbishop of Rouen, the

Steps of the Council to establish its inde-pendence of the Pope. January 1436.

---

[1] See Flavius Blondus, *Decades*, III., ch. viii. p. 527 : — ' Diximus ali-quando Basiliense concilium, per Ital'ci nominis invidiam, infestissimis animis nihil accuratius quaesivisse, ac pro viribus intentasse, quam eo pontifice per nefas omne deposito, pontificatum vel multas in partes lacerum trans Alpes traducere.'

[2] See his letters from Basel. *Ambrogii Traversari Epistolae*, ed. Mehus, p. 27, &c.

Council interposed and itself bestowed the pallium on December 11. In January 1436 it resolved to admonish the Pope to withdraw all that he had done or said against the authority of the Council, and accept fully its decrees. An embassy was nominated to carry to Eugenius IV. a form of decree which he was to issue for this purpose. The reason for this peremptory proceeding was a desire to cut away from the Pope the means of frustrating the Council's projects as regards the Greeks. Its envoys at Constantinople could not report very brilliant success in their negotiations. They could not at first even establish the basis which had been laid down at Basel in the previous year. The Greeks took exception to the wording of the decree which was submitted to them; they complained that the Council spoke of itself as the mother of all Christendom, and coupled them with the Bohemians as schismatics.[1] When the ambassadors attempted to defend the Council's wording they were met by cries, 'Either amend your decree or get you gone.'[2] They undertook that it should be changed, and one of them, Henry Menger, was sent back to Basel, where, on February [3], 1436, he reported that all other matters had been arranged with the Greeks, on condition that the decree were altered, and that a guarantee were given for the payment of their expenses to and from the conference, whether they agreed to union or no. He brought letters from the Emperor and the Patriarch, urging that the place of conference should be on the sea-coast, and that the Pope as the head of Western Christendom should be present. The envoys attributed these demands to the machinations of the Papal ambassador Garatoni.[3]

More and more irritated by this news, the Council proceeded with its plan of crushing the Pope, and on March 22 issued a decree for the full reformation of the head of the

---

[1] 'Quamobrem hujus sanctæ synodi ab initio suæ congregationis præcipua cura fuit recens illud Bohemorum antiquumque Græcorum dissidium prorsus extinguere, et eos nobiscum in eodem fidei et caritatis vinculo copulare' was the preamble of the decree of September 7, 1434. John of Segovia, 752.

[2] Letter of John of Ragusa, in Cecconi, No. LXXVII.

[3] John of Segovia, 841. 'Referebat insuper de Cristoforo Garatono Constantinopoli fecisse et dixisse quæ pro honore papæ Henricus ipse volebat præterire.' More explicitly John of Ragusa, in his relation to the Council, says (Cecconi, No. CLXXVIII.), 'Ad nihil aliud venerat nisi ut impediret directe vel indirecte hic concordata et conclusa.'

Church. It began with a reorganisation of the method of Papal election; the Cardinals on entering the Conclave were to swear that they would not recognise him whom they elected till he had sworn to summon General Councils and observe the decrees of Basel. The form of the Papal oath was specified, and it was enacted that on each anniversary of the Papal election the oath, and an exhortation to observe it, should be read to the Pope in the midst of the mass service. The number of cardinals was not to exceed twenty-six, of whom twenty-four were to be at least thirty years old, graduates in civil or canon law, or in theology, none of them related to the Pope or any living cardinal; the other two might be elected for some great need or usefulness to the Church, although they were not graduates. It was further enacted that all elections were to be freely made by the chapters, and that all reservations were to be abolished.

At the end of the month appeared the Pope's ambassadors, the Cardinals of S. Peter's and S. Croce. They brought as before evasive answers from the Pope, who urged the Council to choose a place for conference with the Greeks which would be convenient both for them and for himself; he did not approve of the plan of raising money by granting indulgences, but was willing to issue them with the approval of the Council. This was not what the Council wanted. It demanded that Eugenius IV. should recognise its right to grant indulgences. On April 14 it issued a decree granting to all who contributed to the expenses of the conference with the Greeks the plenary indulgence given to crusaders and to those who made a pilgrimage to Rome in the year of Jubilee. On May 11 an answer was given to the Pope's legates, complaining that Eugenius IV. did not act up to the Council's decrees, but raised continual difficulties; he did not join with them in their endeavours to promote union with the Greeks, but spoke of transferring the Council elsewhere; he did not accept the decree abolishing annates, except on the condition that provision was made for the Pope, although he ought to welcome gladly all efforts at reformation, and ought to consider that the question of provision in the future required great discussion in each nation; he did not recognise, as he ought to do, the supremacy of the Council which, with the presidents who represented the Pope, had full power to grant indulgences. On receiving this answer, the

CHAP.
VI.

Decree for the reform of the Pope and Cardinals. March 22, 1436.

The Council issues a decree of indulgences. April 14, 1436.

Archbishop of Tarento and the Bishop of Padua resigned their office of presidents on behalf of the Pope and left the Council. It was a declaration of open war.

Eugenius IV. on his side prepared for the contest. He drew up a long defence of his own conduct, and a statement of the wrongs which he had received from the Council since his recognition of its authority. He set forth the Council's refusal to accept the Papal presidents as the representatives of the Pope, its decrees diminishing the Papal revenues and the Papal power, interfering with the old customs of election, granting indulgences, exercising Papal prerogatives, and doing everything most likely to lead to an open schism. He commented on the turbulent procedure of the Council, its democratic organisation, its mode of voting by deputations which gave the preponderance to a numerical minority, its avowed partisanship which gave its proceedings the appearance of a conspiracy rather than of a deliberate judgment. For six years it had laboured with scanty results, and had only destroyed the prestige and respect which a General Council ought to command. He recapitulated his own proposals to the Council about the place of a conference with the Greeks, and the repulse which his ambassadors had met with. He stated his resolve to call upon all the princes of Christendom to withdraw their support from the Council, which, he significantly added, not only spoke evil of the Pope but of all princes, when once it had free course to its insolence. He promised reformation of abuses in the Curia, with the help of a Council to be summoned in some city of Italy, where the condition of his health would allow his personal presence. He called upon the princes to withdraw their ambassadors and prelates from Basel.[1]

This document of Eugenius IV. contained nothing which was likely to induce the princes of Europe to put more confidence in him, alleged no arguments which could lead them to alter their previous position so far as the Papacy was concerned. But there was much in his accusations against the Council, where the extreme party had been gradually gaining power. Cesarini was no longer listened to, and his position in Basel became daily more unsatisfactory to himself. He had earnestly striven for a settlement of the Bohemian difficulty and for the

[1] In *Raynaldi Annales*, 1436, 2, &c.

pacification of France, which had been begun at the Congress of Arras. He was desirous for reformation of the Church and so had agreed to the decree abolishing annates. But he could not forget that he was a cardinal and a Papal legate, and was opposed to the recent proceedings of the Council against the Pope.[1] Round him gathered the great body of Italian prelates, except the Milanese and the chief theologians. But the majority of the Council consisted of Frenchmen, who were led by Cardinal Louis d'Allemand, generally known as the Cardinal of Arles, a man of great learning and high character, but a violent partisan, who belonged to the Colonna faction and intrigued with the Duke of Milan. He had no hesitation in taking up an attitude of strong political hostility against Eugenius IV. The French followed him, as did the Spaniards, so long as Alfonso of Arragon was the political enemy of Eugenius IV. The Milanese and South Italians were also on his side. The English and Germans who came to the Council were animated by a desire to extend its influence, and so were opposed to the Pope.

The organisation of the Council gave the Pope a just ground for complaint. It had been decided at the beginning that the lower ranks of the clergy should have seats and votes. The Council was to be fully representative of the Church, and so was entirely democratic. All who satisfied the scrutineers, and were incorporated as members, took equal part in the proceedings. At first the dangers of this course had not shown themselves; but as the proceedings of the Council were protracted, the prelates who took a leading part in its business became fewer.[2] The constitution of the Council was shifting from week to week. Only those were permanent who had some personal interest to gain, or who were strong partisans. The enemies of Eugenius IV. clung to the Council as the justification of their

CHAP.
VI.

Results of the democratic organisation of the Council.

---

[1] From the time of the adhesion of Eugenius IV. John of Segovia tells us that Cesarini's attitude began to change: 'Ex hac die multi ex patribus manifestius animadverterunt legatum ipsum jam non fore tam ardentem pro auctoritate generalium conciliorum quo modo primum,' 606. The change was as much on the part of the opposition as of the legate: he accepted the adhesion of Eugenius and was ready to forget the past, while the enemies of Eugenius IV. had no such intention.

[2] Eugenius, in his *Apology*, Raynaldus, 1436, § 8, 9, says that there were never more than 150 prelates at Basel, and at the time he wrote scarcely 25.

past conduct as well as their hope in the future. Adventurers who had everything to gain and little to lose flocked to Basel, and cast in their lot with the Council as affording them a better chance of promotion than did the Curia. Thus the Council became more and more democratic and revolutionary in its tendencies. The prelates drew to the side of Cesarini, and found themselves more and more in a minority, opposed to a majority which was bent on the entire humiliation of the Papacy.[1]

Reaction in favour of Eugenius IV.
It was natural that the violence of the French radical party should cause a reaction in favour of the Pope. Many had been in favour of the Council against the Pope, when the Council wished for reform, which the Pope tried to check. They were shaken in their allegiance when the Council, under the name of reform, was pursuing mainly the depression of the Papal power, and the transference of its old authority into the hands of a self-elected and non-representative oligarchy. The cry was raised that the Council was in the French interest; that it simply continued the old struggle of Avignon against Rome. The friends of Eugenius IV. began to raise their heads, and attacked the Council on political grounds, so as to detach from it the princes of Christendom. Their arguments may be gathered from a letter of Ambrogio Traversari to Sigismund, in January 1436 :—'The Council of Basel has found time for nothing but the subversion of Catholic peace and the depression of the Pope. They have now been assembled for five years; and see on how wrongful a basis their business proceeds. In old days bishops, full of the fear of God, the zeal of religion, and the fervour of faith, used to settle the affairs of the Church. Now the matter is in the hands of the common herd; for scarcely out of five hundred members, as I saw with my own eyes, were there twenty bishops; the rest were either the lower orders of the clergy, or were laymen; and all consult their private feelings rather than the good of the Church. No wonder that the Council drags on for years, and produces nothing but scandal

---

[1] This complaint is universal among the writers on the Papal side, and was raised by Eugenius IV. in his *Apology*. Æneas Sylvius, himself an adventurer in Basel, says rhetorically, 'Inter episcopos, cæterosque patres conscriptos, vidimus in Basilea coquos et stabularios orbis negotia judicantes; quis horum dicta vel facta judicaverit legis habere vigorem?' *Oratio adversus Australes*, in Mansi, *Pii II. Orationes*, i. 231.

and danger of schism. The good men are lost in the ignorant
and turbulent multitude. The French, led by the Cardinal of
Arles and the Archbishop of Lyons, want to transfer the Papacy
into France. Where everyone seeks his own interest, and the
vote of a cook is as good as that of a legate or an archbishop,
it is shameless blasphemy to claim for their resolutions the
authority of the Holy Ghost. They aim only at a disruption
of the Church. They have set up a tribunal on the model of
the Papal court; they exercise jurisdiction, and draw causes
before them. They confer the pallium on archbishops, and
claim to grant indulgences. They aim at nothing less than the
perpetuation of the Council, in opposition to the Pope.'[1]

CHAP.
VI.

There was enough truth in this view of the situation to
incline the statesmen of Europe to take a more languid interest
in the proceedings of the Council. Moreover, the Council had
lost its political importance by the gradual subsidence of the
Bohemian question. The Council had done its work when it
succeeded in bringing to a head the divergence of opinion
which had always existed between Bohemian parties. The
negotiations with the Council had given strength to the party
which wished to recognise authority, and was not prepared to
break entirely with the traditions of the past. Round it
gathered the various elements of political discontent arising
from the long domination of the democratic and revolutionary
party. At the battle of Lipan the Taborites met with such a
defeat that they could no longer offer a determined resistance
to the plan for a reconciliation with Sigismund.

The Coun-
cil's success
in Bohe-
mia.

But the hopes of immediate success which the fight of Lipan
awakened in Basel were by no means realised at once. The
spirit of the Bohemian Reformation was still strong; and though
the Calixtins were, on the whole, in favour of reconciliation
with the Church, they had no intention of abandoning their
original position. The Bohemian Diet in June, 1434, proclaimed a general peace with all Utraquists, and a truce for a
year with all Catholics. It took measures for the pacification
of the land and the restoration of order. To Sigismund's
envoys, who had come to procure his recognition as King of
Bohemia, the Diet answered by appointing deputies to confer
with Sigismund at Regensburg. Thither the Council was

Negotia-
tions at
Regens-
burg.
August
1434.

[1] *Travcrsarii Epistolæ*, ed. Mehus. ii. 238.

requested by Sigismund to send its former envoys. On
August 16 its embassy, headed by Philibert, bishop of Coutances, but of which John of Palomar was the most active
member, entered Regensburg an hour after the Bohemians,
chief amongst whom were John of Rokycana, Martin Lupak,
and Meinhard of Neuhaus. As usual, Sigismund kept them
waiting, and did not arrive till August 21. Meanwhile the
Council's envoys and the Bohemians had several conferences,
which did not show that their differences were disappearing.
The Bohemians were requested to do as they had done at
previous conferences, and not attend mass in the churches.
They consented; but John of Rokycana remarked that it would
be better if the Council were to drive out of the churches evil
priests rather than faithful laymen, who only wished to receive
the Communion under both kinds. John of Palomar had to
apologise for the Council's delay in its work of reform; the
English and Spanish representatives, he said, had not yet
arrived, and everything could not be done at once.

Unsatis-
factory
results of
the nego-
tiations.
September
1434.

When negotiations began on August 22 Sigismund and the
Council's envoys found that the Bohemians were firm in their
old position. They were willing to recognise Sigismund on
condition that he restored peace in Bohemia, which could only
be done by upholding the Four Articles of Prag, and binding
all the people of Bohemia and Moravia to receive the Communion under both kinds. Sigismund appealed to the national
feelings of the Bohemians by a speech in their own tongue, in
which he recalled the connexion of his house with Bohemia.
About the questions in dispute John of Rokycana and John of
Palomar again indulged in the old arguments, till the Bohemians declared that they were sent to the Emperor, not to the
Council's envoys. They submitted their request to Sigismund
in writing, and Sigismund in writing gave answer, begging
them to stand by the Compacts of Prag. The Bohemians declared their intention of doing so, but said that the Compacts
must be understood to apply to the whole of Bohemia and Moravia. John of Palomar declared that the Council could not
compel faithful Catholics to adopt a new rite, though they were
prepared to allow it to those who desired it. The conclusion
of the conference was that the Bohemian envoys should report
to the Diet, soon to be held at Prag, the difficulties which had

arisen, and should send its answer to the Emperor and to the
Council. Matters had advanced no further than they were at
the time of accepting the Compacts. In some ways the tone of
the conference at Regensburg was less conciliatory than that of
the previous ones. One of the Bohemian envoys fell from a
window and was killed. The Council's ambassadors objected
to his burial with the rites of the Church, on the ground that
he was not received into the Church's communion. This caused
great indignation among the Bohemians, who resented this
attempt to terrorise over them. Still they submitted to the
Council's envoys a series of questions about the election of an
archbishop of Prag, and the views of the Council about the
regulation of ecclesiastical discipline in accordance with the
Compacts. Sigismund besought the Council for money to act
against Bohemia, and some of the Bohemian nobles asserted
that with money enough Bohemia could soon be reduced to
obedience. Yet Sigismund did not hesitate to express to the
Council's envoys his many grounds for grievance at the Council's
procedure. The parties in the conference at Regensburg were
at cross purposes. Sigismund, dissatisfied with the Council,
wished to make it useful for himself. The Council wished to
show Sigismund that its help was indispensable for the settlement of the Bohemian question. Bohemia wished for peace,
but on condition of retaining in matters ecclesiastical a basis
of national unity, without which it felt that peace would be
illusory. On September 3 the Conference came to an end
without arriving at any conclusion. All parties separated
mutually dissatisfied.[1]

Still these repeated negotiations strengthened the peace
party in Bohemia. Of the proceedings of the Diet held at Prag
on October 23 we know little ; but they ended in an abandon-
ment by the Bohemians of the position which they had taken
up at Regensburg. There they had maintained that, as the
people of Bohemia and Moravia were of one language and
under one rule, so ought they to be of one ritual in the most
solemn act of Christian worship. They now decided to seek a
basis of religious unity which would respect the rights of the

Proposals
of the
Bohemians
to the
Council
and to
Sigismund.
November
1484–
March
1485.

---

[1] John of Segovia, 675 : ' Itaque expedita dieta secuta minime fuerunt
que ex ipsis eventura primo autumabantur, adepcio regni Bohemie, pro qua imperator, et acceptacio firma articulorum fidei, pro qua instabat sancta synodus.'

minority, and on November 8 wrote, not to the Council, but to
the Council's envoys, proposing that in those places where the
Communion under both kinds had been accepted it should be
recognised ; in those places where the Communion under one
kind had been retained it should remain.   Mutual toleration
was to be enjoined, and an archbishop and bishops were to be
elected by the clergy, with the consent of the Diet, who were
to be subject to the Council and to the Pope in matters agreeable to the law of God, but no further, and who were to regulate the discipline of the Church in Bohemia and Moravia.[1]
It was a proposal for the organisation of the Bohemian Church
on a national basis, so as to obtain security against the danger
of a Catholic reaction.

The Council's answer to the Bohemians was, that they would
again send their former envoys to confer with them and with
the Emperor. The Bohemians, seeing that little was to be
hoped for from the Council, resolved to see if they could obtain
from Sigismund the securities which they wished. A Diet held
in Prag in March 1435 sent Sigismund its demands : the
Four Articles were to be accepted ; the Emperor, his court,
his chaplain and all State officers were to communicate under
both kinds ; complete amnesty was to be given for the past,
and a genuinely national Government was to exist for the future.[2]
The envoys who brought these demands to Sigismund enquired
if the Council's ambassadors, who were already with Sigismund
in Posen, were prepared to accept the offer made by the Diet
in the previous November; otherwise it was useless for the
Bohemians to trouble themselves further or incur more expense.
But the Council's ambassadors had come armed with secret
instructions, and refused to have their hand forced. They
answered that their mission was to the Emperor in Council of
the Bohemians assembled, and then only could they speak.

Confer-
ence at
Brünn.
July 1435.
Many preliminaries had to be arranged before the Con-
ference finally took place at Brünn.   There the Council's envoys
arrived on May 20, and were received with ringing of bells and
all manifestations of joy by the people. On June 18 came the
Bohemian representatives ; but Sigismund did not appear till
July 1. Meanwhile the Bohemians and the Council's envoys

---

[1] The letter, ascribed to Rokycana, is in *Mon. Concil.* i. 631.
[2] In *Mon. Concil.* i. 537.

had several sharp discussions. Those of the Bohemians who had been reconciled to the Church were allowed to attend the mass; but the others were forbidden to enter the churches, and were refused a chapel where they might celebrate mass after their own fashion. On June 28 some of the Bohemians, on being requested to withdraw from a church where they had come with their comrades, were so indignant that they were on the point of leaving Brünn, and were only appeased by the intervention of Albert of Austria, who had luckily arrived a few days before.

The day after Sigismund's arrival, on July 2, John of Roky- Difficulties about the interpre- tation of the Com- pacts cana brought forward three demands on the part of the Bohe- mians, that the Four Articles be accepted throughout the whole of Bohemia and Moravia; that those countries be freed from all charge of heresy, and that the Council of Basel proceed with the reformation of the Church in life, morals, and faith. He asked also for an answer to the demands sent to Eger by the Bohemian Diet in the previous November. The Council's envoys answered by justifying the procedure of the Council and blaming the Bohemians for not keeping to the Compacts but raising new difficulties. There was much disputation. The Bohemians professed their willingness to abide by the Compacts as interpreted by their demands sent to Eger; the legates answered that these demands were contrary to the Compacts themselves. Sigismund urged the legates to give way, but they refused. On July 8 the legates demanded that the Bohemians should declare their adhesion to the Compacts, as they had promised; no promise had been made by the Council about the Eger articles, otherwise it would have been fulfilled. It was clear to the Bohemians that the Council regarded the Compacts as the ultimate point of their concessions, whereas the Bohe- mians looked on them only as a starting point for further arrangements. John of Rokycana angrily answered the legates, ' We are willing to stand by the Compacts; but they cannot be fulfilled till they are completed. Much must be added to them; for instance, as regards obedience to bishops, we will not obey them if they order what is contrary to God's word. How do you ask us to fulfil our promises when you will not fulfil yours? It seems to us that you aim at nothing save to sow division amongst us, for since your coming we are worse off than before, and will take heed that it be so no longer. We ask no difficult things. We ask for an archbishop to be elected by the clergy and people or appointed by the king. We ask that causes be not transferred out of the realm. We ask that the Communion be celebrated under both kinds in those places where the use exists. These are not difficult matters; grant them and we will fulfil the Compacts. We do not ask these things through fear, or through doubt of their lawfulness; we ask them for the sake of peace and unity. If you do not grant them, the Lord be with you, for I trust He is with us.' While John of Palomar was preparing a reply, the Bohemians left the room and thenceforth conferred only with the legates through Sigismund.

Agreement of the Bohemians with Sigismund. July 6, 1435.

The Bohemian envoys had in fact begun to negotiate directly with Sigismund, who showed himself much more ready to give way than did the legates of the Council. On July 6 a proposal was made to Sigismund that he should grant in his own name what the Council refused. Under the pretext of removing difficulties and providing for some things omitted in the Compacts, Sigismund promised that benefices should not be conferred by strangers outside Bohemia and Moravia, but only by the king; that no Bohemian or Moravian should be cited or be judged outside the kingdom; that those who preferred to communicate under one kind only should, to avoid confusion, be tolerated only in those places which had always maintained the old ritual; that the archbishops and bishops should be elected by the Bohemian clergy and people. These articles Sigismund promised to uphold before the Council, the Pope, and all men.[1] The legates of the Council strongly deprecated any secret negotiations on the part of Sigismund; the Bohemians, relying on the promises they had received, showed themselves more conciliatory. On July 14 they offered to sign the Compacts with the addition of a clause, 'Saving the liberties and privileges of the kingdom and of the margraviate of Moravia.' This the legates would not accept, as it clearly carried the election of the archbishop by the people and clergy. Sigismund answered the legates privately, and besought them to consent, lest they should be the cause of a rupture, and woe to them through whom that came. When the legates again

---

[1] They are given in *Mon. Concil.* i. 662.

refused, he angrily said, 'You of the Council have granted articles to the Bohemians, and have held conferences without my knowledge, but I acquiesced. Why then will you not acquiesce for my sake in this small matter? If you wish me to lose my kingdom, I do not.' He exclaimed in German to those around him, 'Those of Basel wish to do nothing except diminish the power of the Pope and Emperor.' He showed his indignation by abruptly dismissing the legates.

CHAP.
VI.

Sigismund's anger cooled down and the clause was withdrawn. The Bohemians demanded the acceptance of various explanations of the Compacts which the legates steadily refused. At last the signing of the Compacts was again deferred because the legates would not substitute, in the article which declared 'that the goods of the Church cannot be possessed without guilt of sacrilege,' the words 'unjustly detained' (*injuste deteneri*) for 'possessed' (*usurpari*). On August 3 the Bohemians departed, and the legates undertook to lay their demands before the Council and meet them again at Prag in the end of September.

The Council's envoys dissatisfy Sigismund and the Bohemians.

The Council's envoys had acted faithfully by the letter of their instructions;[1] they had stood upon the Compacts, and had refused to make any further concessions or even admit any material explanations. The negotiations had therefore passed out of their hands into those of Sigismund. The Compacts had laid the foundations of an agreement. The Council had opened the door to concessions; and Sigismund was justified in declaring that the Council could not claim to have the sole right of interpreting the concessions so made or regulating the exact method of their application. The proceedings at Brünn led the Bohemians to think that the Council had dealt with them unfairly, and after begging them to accept the Compacts as a means to further agreement, was now bent on doing its utmost to make the Compacts illusory. The Bohemians therefore turned to Sigismund and resolved to seek first for political unity, and then to maintain their own interpretation of the Compacts by securing the organisation of a national Church according to their wishes. In this state of things the interests of the Council and of Sigismund were no longer identical. The Council wished to minimise the effect of the concessions which

The Bohemian question passes from the Council to Sigismund.

---

[1] These instructions are given in *Mon. Concil.* i. 619.

it had made—concessions which were indeed necessary, yet might form a dangerous precedent in the Church. Sigismund wished to obtain peaceable possession of Bohemia, and trusted to his own cleverness afterwards to restore orthodoxy.[1] The one thing that was rendered tolerably certain by the conference at Brünn was the recognition of Sigismund as King of Bohemia, and he was determined that the Council should not be an obstacle in the way. At the same time Sigismund was rigidly attached to the orthodox cause; but he was convinced that the reduction of Bohemia was a matter for himself rather than the Council.

Bohemia
decides to
recognise
Sigismund.
September
1435.
The proceedings with Sigismund at Brünn satisfied the peace party in Bohemia, and the Diet which met in Prag on September 21 ratified all that had been done. The submission of Bohemia to the Church and to Sigismund was finally agreed to on the strength of Sigismund's promises. A committee of two barons, two knights, three citizens, and nine priests was appointed to elect an archbishop and two suffragans. Their choice fell on John of Rokycana as archbishop, Martin Lupak and Wenzel of Hohenmaut as bishops. On December 21 the Bohemian envoys again met Sigismund and the legates of the Council at Stuhlweissenburg. The legates had heard of Rokycana's election, though it was kept a secret pending Sigismund's confirmation. They were perturbed by the understanding which seemed to exist between Sigismund and the Bohemians. They had come from Basel empowered to change the words in the Compacts as the Bohemians wished, and substitute 'unjustly detained' for 'possessed'; but before doing so they demanded that Sigismund should give them a written agreement for the strict observance of the Compacts on his part. This was really a demand that Sigismund should declare that he intended the promises which he had made to the Bohemians at Brünn to be illusory. Meinhard of Neuhaus, the chief of

---

[1] See the relation of the envoys to the Council, *Mon. Concil.* i. 669: 'Imperator nobis dixit, quod nemo putaret ipsum habere affectum ad habendum illud regnum propter se ... sed propter Deum et fidem: et quod libenter de illo faceret offertorium ad altare ut ad fidem debitam reduceretur debitumque statum.' The position of the envoys is given in p. 672: 'Cum enim ille declaraciones illorum articulorum essent non solum pro Bohemia, sed essent doctrina generalis ecclesie, et dicte declaraciones essent jam publicate per mundum, nos nuncii sacri concilii in illis verbum aliquod minime mutaremus.'

Sigismund's partisans amongst the Bohemians, was consulted on this point. He answered, 'If the Emperor publicly revoke his promises, all dealings with the Bohemians are at an end; if he revoke them secretly, it will some day be known, and then the Emperor, if he were in Bohemia, would be in great danger from the people.'[1]

Accordingly Sigismund refused to sign the document which the legates laid before him, and submitted another, which declared generally his intention of abiding by the Compacts, but which did not satisfy the legates. Sigismund referred the legates to the Bohemians, and they accordingly demanded that the Bohemians should renounce all requests which they had made contrary to the Compacts. This the Bohemians refused, and Sigismund endeavoured to lead the legates to a more conciliatory frame of mind by telling them that 'dissimulation on many points was needful with the Bohemians, that he might obtain the kingdom; when that was done, he would bring things back to their former condition.' The legates answered that their instructions from the Council were to see that the Compacts were duly executed; when this was done, the king's power would remain as it had always been; if the Bohemians wanted more than the king could grant, they could seek further favours from the Council. The question of the Emperor's agreement with the Council again raised much discussion. The Bohemians refused any responsibility in the matter. 'If there is ought between you and the legates,' they said to Sigismund, ' it is nothing to us, we neither give assent nor dissent.'[2] The agreement was at last drawn up in general terms. The legates contented themselves with Sigismund's verbal promise as to his general intentions, and a written statement that he accepted the Compacts sincerely according to their plain meaning, and would not permit that any one be compelled to communicate under both kinds nor anything else to be done in contradiction to the Compacts. Iglau was fixed by the Bohemians as a frontier town in which the final signing of the Compacts might be quietly accomplished, and the ambassadors departed on January 31, 1436, to reassemble at Iglau in the end of May.

Difficulties
with the
Council's
envoys.
December
1485.

---

[1] Carlier, *De Legationibus*, in *Mon. Concil.* i. 681.
[2] *Ibid., Mon. Concil.* i. 689.

In all these negotiations the result had been to put difficulties out of sight rather than to make any agreement. Since the conference at Prag in 1433, no nearer approach had been made by the Bohemians to the orthodoxy of the Council. They had rather strengthened themselves in a policy by which they might obtain the advantages of peace and union with the Church, and yet might retain the greatest possible measure of ecclesiastical independence. This they hoped to secure by a strong national organisation, while Sigismund trusted that once in power he would be able to direct the Catholic reaction; and the Council, after taking all possible steps to save its dignity, was reluctantly compelled to trust to Sigismund's assurance.

Signing of
the Compacts at
Iglau.
July 5,
1436.
Sigismund appeared at Iglau on June 6; but the Bohemians were on the point of departing in anger when they found that the legates had come only with powers to sign the Compacts, not to confirm the election of the Bohemian bishops. With some difficulty the Bohemians were prevailed upon to accept Sigismund's promise that he would do his utmost to obtain from the Council and the Pope a ratification of the election of the bishops whom they had chosen. At last, on July 5, the Emperor, in his robes of state, took his place on a throne in the market-place of Iglau. The Duke of Austria bore the golden apple, the Count of Cilly the sceptre, and another count the sword. Before Sigismund went the legates of the Council, and by them took their places the Bohemian envoys. The signing of the Compacts was solemnly ratified by both parties. John Walwar, a citizen of Prag, gave to the legates a copy of the Compacts duly signed and sealed, together with a promise that the Bohemians would accept peace and unity with the Church. Four Bohemian priests, previously chosen for the purpose, took oath of obedience, shaking hands with the legates and afterwards with Rokycana, to show that they held him as their archbishop. Then the legates on their part handed a copy of the Compacts to the Bohemians, admitting them to peace and unity with the Church, relieving them from all ecclesiastical censures, and ordering all men to be at peace with them and hold them clear of all reproach. Proclamation was made in Sigismund's name that next day the Bohemians should enter the Church and the Compacts be read in the Bohemian tongue.

Then the Bishop of Coutances, in a loud clear voice, began to
sing the 'Te Deum,' in which all joined with fervour. When
it was done, Sigismund and the legates entered the church for
mass; the Bohemians, raising a hymn, marched to their inn,
where they held their service. Both parties wept for joy at the
ending of their long strife.

CHAP.
VI.

The next day showed that difficulties were not at an end,
that the peace was hollow, and that the main points of disagreement still remained unsettled. In the parish church, the
Bishop of Coutances celebrated mass at the high altar, and
John of Rokycana at a side altar. The Compacts were read by
Rokycana from the pulpit in the Bohemian tongue, then he
added: 'Let those of the Bohemians who have the grace of
communicating under both kinds come to this altar.' The
legates protested to the Emperor. John of Palomar cried out:
'Master John, observe the canons; do not administer the sacraments in a church of which you are not priest."[1] Rokycana
paid no heed, but administered to seven persons. The legates
were indignant at this violation of ecclesiastical regulations,
and said: 'Yesterday you vowed canonical obedience; to-day
you break it. What is this?' Rokycana answered that he was
acting in accordance with the Compacts, and paid little heed to
the technical objection raised by the legates. Sigismund urged
the legates to grant a church, or at least an altar, where the
Bohemians might practise their own ritual. The legates, who
were irritated still more by hearing that Martin Lupak had
carried through the streets the sacrament under both kinds to
a dying man, refused their consent. The Bohemians bitterly
exclaimed that they had been deceived, and that the Compacts
were illusory. They threatened to depart at once, and it required all Sigismund's skill in the management of men to
prevail on the Bohemians to stay till they had arranged
the preliminaries about his reception as King of Bohemia.
The utmost concession that he could obtain from the legates
was, that one priest might celebrate mass after the Bohemian
ritual. They refused to commission for this purpose either
Rokycana or Martin Lupak, and accepted Wenzel of Drachow,
on condition that they should first examine him to be sure of

Dispute
between
Rokycana
and the
legates.
July 6,
1485.

---

[1] 'Non ministretis sacramenta in aliena parochia:' Thomas Eberndorf's
Diarium Mon. Concil. i. 779. See also John of Tours' *Registrum, ibid.* 8 21.

his orthodoxy. This Wenzel refused, and the Bohemians continued to celebrate their own rites in their houses, as they had done previously.

Thus the long negotiations with the Council had led to no real agreement. The signing of the Compacts was rather an expression on both sides of the desire for peace, and for the outward unity of the Church, than any settlement of the points at issue. The conception of a united Christendom had not yet been destroyed, and both parties were willing to make concessions to maintain it. But neither side abandoned their convictions, and the peace which had been proclaimed affected only the outward aspect of affairs. The Bohemians remained the victors. They had re-entered the Church on condition that they were allowed an exceptional position. It remained for them to make good the position which they had won, and use wisely and soberly the means which they had at their disposal for this purpose.

Sigismund
enters
Prag as
King of
Bohemia.
August 23,
1436.
In political matters also they saw the necessity of abandoning their attitude of revolt, and entering again the State system of Europe. They were willing to recognise Sigismund, but on condition that he ensured the Bohemian nationality against German influences. On July 20 Sigismund agreed to ratify the rights and privileges of the Bohemians, to be guided by the advice of a Bohemian Council, to uphold the University of Prag, to admit none but Bohemians to office in the land, and to grant a full amnesty for all that had happened during the revolt. On August 20 the Governor of Bohemia, Ales of Riesenburg, laid down his office in Sigismund's presence, and the Bohemian nobles swore fidelity to their king. On August 23 Sigismund entered Prag in state, and was received with joyous acclamations by the people. The pacification of Bohemia was completed. The great work which Europe had demanded of the Council was actually accomplished.

Merits of
the Coun-
cil in its
policy
towards
Bohemia.
If we consider the deserts of the Council in this matter, we see that its real importance lay in the fact that it could admit the Bohemians to a conference without injuring the prestige of the Church. A Pope could adopt no other attitude towards heretics than one of resolute resistance. A Council could invite discussion, in which each party might engage with a firm belief that it would succeed in convincing the other. The

decree for reunion with the Church arose from the exhaustion
of Bohemia and its internal dissensions ; it found that it could
no longer endure to pay the heavy price which isolation from the
rest of Europe involved on a small state.   The temper of the
Bohemians was met with admirable tact and moderation by the
Council under the influence of Cesarini.   Moral sympathy and
not intellectual agreement tended to bring the parties together.
The impulse given at first was strong enough to resist the
reaction, when both parties found that they were not likely to
convince each other.   But the religious motives tended to become secondary to political considerations.   The basis of conciliation afforded by the negotiations with Basel was used by
the peace party in Bohemia and by Sigismund to establish an
agreement between themselves.   When this had been done, the
position of the Council was limited to one of resistance to the
extension of concessions to the Bohemians.   The Council was
thenceforth a hindrance rather than a help to the unscrupulous
policy of illusory promises, which Sigismund had determined to
adopt towards Bohemia till his power was fully established.
From this time the Council lost all political significance for
the Emperor, who was no longer interested in maintaining it
against the Pope, and felt aggrieved by its treatment of himself, as well as by its democratic tendencies, which threatened
the whole State system of Europe.

CHAPTER VII.

WAR BETWEEN THE POPE AND THE COUNCIL.

1436–1438.

IF Sigismund's interest in the Council had faded away, the interest of France had equally begun to wane. At the opening of the Council, France, in her misery and distress, the legacy of the long war with England, felt a keen sympathy with one of the Council's objects, the general pacification of Christendom. The Council's zeal in this matter stirred up the Pope to emulation, and Eugenius IV. busied himself to prevent the Council from gaining any additional prestige. In 1431 Cardinal Albergata was sent by the Pope to arrange peace between England, Burgundy, and France. His negotiations were fruitless for a time; but the ill-success of the English induced them in 1435 to consent to a congress to be held at Arras. Thither went Albergata as Papal legate, and on the side of the Council was sent Cardinal Lusignan. Representatives of the chief States of Europe were present; and 9,000 strangers, amongst whom were 500 knights, thronged the streets of Arras. In the conference which began in August the rival legates vied with one another in splendour and in loftiness of pretension. But though Lusignan was of higher lineage, Albergata was the more skilful diplomat, and exercised greater influence over the negotiations. England, foreseeing the desertion of Burgundy, refused the proposed terms, and withdrew from the congress on September 6. Philip of Burgundy's scruples were skilfully combated by Albergata. Philip wished for peace, but wished also to save his honour. The legate's absolution from his oath, not to make a separate peace from England, afforded him the means of retreating from an obligation which had begun to be burdensome. On the interposition of the Church Philip laid aside his vengeance for his father's murder, and was reconciled to Charles VII. of France on September 21. The treaty was made under the joint auspices of the Pope and the Council. Both claimed the credit of this pacification. Cesarini, when the news reached Basel, said that if the Council had sat for twenty years, and had done nothing more than this, it would have done enough to satisfy all gainsayers.[1] But in spite of the Council's claims it had won less prestige in France than had Eugenius IV., and France had no further hopes of political aid from its activity.

CHAP. VII.

Thus the chief States of Europe had little to gain either from Pope or Council, and had no reason to take either side, when the struggle again broke out about the union with the Eastern Church. The letter of Eugenius IV., asking the princes of Europe to withdraw their countenance from the Council, met with no answer; but the Council had no zealous protector on whose help it could rely. The conflict that ensued was petty and ignoble.

Neutrality of Europe in the struggle between the Pope and the Council.

The policy of Eugenius IV. was to allure the Council to some Italian city where he could more easily manage to bring about its dissolution. In this he was helped by the desire of the Greeks to avoid a long journey overland, and his envoy Garatoni had continued to confirm them in their objection to go to Basel or to cross the Alps. The Council was fully alive to the Pope's project, and hoped to prevail upon the Greeks, when once their journey was begun, to give way to their wishes. But the great practical difficulty which the Council had to face was one of finance. The cost of bringing the Greeks to Basel was computed at 71,000 ducats and their maintenance, which could not be reckoned at less than 200,000 ducats.[2] Moreover it would be needful that the Western Church should not be outdone by the Eastern in the number of prelates present at the Council. At least a hundred bishops must be summoned to Basel, and it might not be an easy matter to induce them to come. The sale of indulgences had not been productive of so rich a harvest as the Council had hoped. In Constantinople the Bull was not allowed to be published, and the Greeks were by no means favourably impressed by this proof of the Council's

Financial difficulties of the Council.

[1] Martene and Durand, *Amp. Coll.* viii. 882.
[2] See *Avisamenta pro facto Graecorum*, Martene, *Amp. Coll.* viii. 895, and *Instruciones pro Oratoribus* in John of Segovia, 902.

zeal. In Europe generally it had awakened dissatisfaction; it was a sign that the reforming Council was ready to use for its own purposes the abuses which it condemned in the Pope. Altogether the Council had before it a difficult task to raise the necessary supplies and celebrate its conference with due magnificence in the face of the Pope's opposition.

Negotia-
tions for
the place
of the
conference
with the
Greeks.
May 1436.

As a preliminary step towards raising money and settling the place of the conference, envoys were sent in May 1436 to negotiate for loans in the various cities which had been mentioned. They were required to promise 70,000 ducats at once, and to undertake to make further advances if necessary. The envoys visited Milan, Venice, Florence, Siena, Buda, Vienna, Avignon, as well as France and Savoy. In August Venice offered any town in the patriarchate of Aquileia, the Duke of Milan any town in his dominions; both guaranteed the loan. Florence also offered herself. Siena was willing to receive the Council, but could not lend more than 30,000 ducats. The Duke of Austria was so impoverished by the Bohemian wars that he could not offer any money, but would welcome the Council in Vienna. The citizens of Avignon were ready to promise all that the Council wished. During the month of November the representatives of Venice, Florence, Pavia, and Avignon, harangued the Council in favour of their respective cities.[1] Venice and Florence were clearly in favour of the Pope, and so were not acceptable to the Council. In Pavia the Council would be sure enough of the Duke of Milan's hostility to the Pope, but could not feel so confident of its own freedom from his interference. If the Greeks would not come to Basel, Avignon was, in the eyes of the majority, the most eligible place.

Cesarini
joins the
Papal
party. No-
vember
1436.

But though the majority might be of this opinion, there had been growing up in the Council a strong opposition. The undisguised hostility of the extreme party to the Pope had driven moderate men to acquiesce in the pretensions of Eugenius IV., and this question of the place of conference with the Greeks was fiercely contested on both sides. Cesarini had for

---

[1] The amusingly rhetorical speech of Æneas Sylvius, acting for the Duke of Milan in behalf of Pavia, is given in Mansi, *Pii II. Orationes*, p. 5. It reads, from its careful attention to style, like a new language when compared with the other records of the Council.

some time felt that he was losing his influence over the Council, which followed the more democratic Cardinal d'Allemand. He now began to speak decidedly on the Pope's side. He argued with justice that Avignon was not specified in the agreement made with the Greeks; that the Pope's presence at the conference was necessary, if for no other reason, at least as a means of providing money; that if any help was to be given to the Greeks against the Turks, the Pope alone could summon Europe to the work; finally, he urged that if the Pope and Council were in antagonism, union with the Greeks was rendered ridiculous. On these grounds he besought the Council to choose a place which was convenient for the Pope.[1]   There were angry replies, till on November 10 Cesarini took the step of openly ranging himself on the Pope's side.   He warned the Council that henceforth they were to regard him as a Papal legate, and sent a paper to all the deputations demanding that in future no conclusions be arrived at respecting the Roman See until he had first been heard at length on the matter.[2]

But the dominant party was determined to have its own way and took measures to out-vote its opponents. It summoned the priests from the neighbourhood and flooded the Council with its own creatures.[3]   On December 5 the votes were taken, and it was found that more than two-thirds of the Council, 242 out of 355, voted at the bidding of the Cardinal d'Allemand for Basel in the first instance; failing that, Avignon, and, failing that, some place in Savoy.   Basel had been already refused by the Greeks.   The Duke of Savoy had not offered to provide money for the Council.   The vote was really given for Avignon alone.   Cesarini, in the Pope's name and in his own, protested against Avignon as not contained in the treaty made with the Greeks; if the Council refused to go to Italy, there

Choice of
Avignon
by the
Council.
December
5, 1436.

---

[1] John of Segovia, i. 913.

[2] The gradual change of opinion on the part of Cesarini may be traced in the letters of Ambrogio Traversari, 143–175. Traversari takes credit to his own arguments for producing the result.

[3] John of Palomar, in Mansi, *Supplementum*, vi. 576, says: ʻIlli qui iverant per plateas in brevibus vestibus et ad mensas dominorum ministraverant, tunc sumptis longis vestibus Deputationes intrarunt ut sic numerus vaccilium augeretur.ʼ Eugenius, in a letter to the Duke of Savoy (Cecconi, No. cxcv.) says: ʻMultitudine vocum, quas diversis artibus cotidie propter hoc negotium ad concilium venire fecerant, conati sunt eligere civitatem Avenioncusem.ʼ

remained only Buda, Vienna, and Savoy as eligible; if the
Council decided on Savoy, he would accept it as according to
the agreement; beyond this he could not go. In spite of his
written protest, the majority confirmed their vote by a decree in
favour of Avignon.

At the beginning of February 1437, the Greek ambassador,
John Dissipatus, arrived in Basel, and was surprised to find that
the Council had fixed on Avignon. He vainly pleaded that
Avignon was not included in the decree which the Greeks had
accepted, and when the Council paid no heed, he handed in
a protest on February 15. The Council requested him to
accompany their envoys to Constantinople. He refused, declaring
his intention of visiting the Pope and renewing his protest before him: if no remedy could be found, he would publish to
the world that the Council would not keep its promises. The
majority at Basel was little moved by these complaints, save so
far as they tended to strengthen the position of the minority
which was working in favour of the Pope. Through fear of
playing into their hands, a compromise was made on February
23. The Council decreed that the citizens of Avignon were
to be required to pay, within thirty days, the 70,000 ducats
which they had promised; a further term of twelve days was
allowed them to bring proof of their payment to Basel; if this
were not done in the appointed time, the Council ' could, and was
bound,' to proceed to the election of another place.[1]

The Arch-
bishop of
Taranto
organises
the Papal
party.
April 1437.
During the period of this truce arrived, on April 1, the Archbishop of Taranto, as a new Papal legate, accompanied by the
Greeks who had visited the Pope at Bologna. His arrival
gave a new turn to affairs. Cesarini was opposed, on grounds
of practical wisdom, to the proceedings of the Council rather
than decidedly in favour of the Pope; the Archbishop of
Taranto entered the lists as a violent partisan, as energetic and
as unscrupulous as was the Cardinal d'Allemand. He set to
work to organise the Papal party and to devise a policy of
resistance. Opportunity soon befriended him. As the term
allowed to Avignon to pay its money drew near its close, there was
no news of any payment. Parties in favour of the Pope and the

---

[1] 'Alioquin ex tunc ipsum sacrum concilium possit et teneatur ad
electionem alterius loci pro ycumenico concilio celebrando procedere.' The
' cedula consensus patrum ' is given by John of Segovia, 936.

Council were formed amongst the burghers, and the disunion awakened the fears of the cautious merchants, who doubted whether the Council's presence within their walls would prove a profitable investment; they proposed to defer the full payment of the money till the actual arrival of the Greeks. On this the Papal party insisted that the agreement with Avignon was forfeited, and on April 12, the day on which the term expired, Cesarini exhorted the Council to proceed to the choice. of another place. In his speech he used the words 'the authority of the Apostolic See;' there was at once a shout of indignation, as it was thought that he hinted at the dissolution of the Council. The discussion was warm, and the sitting broke up in confusion.

The position assumed by the Archbishop of Taranto was that the decree of February 23 was rigidly binding; the contingency contemplated in it had actually occurred, and the Council was bound to make a new election. Nay, if some members of the Council refused to do so, he argued, from the analogy of a capitular election, that the power of the Council devolved on those who were ready to act—a numerical minority, if acting according to the law, could override a majority which acted illegally.[1] The Papal party numbered about seventy votes, their opponents about two hundred; but the Archbishop of Taranto's policy was to create a schism in the Council and destroy the power of the majority by the prestige of the 'saner part.' Accordingly on April 17, when the deputations voted on the question of adhering to Avignon or choosing another place, the presidents in three of the deputations, being on the Papal side, refused the votes in favour of Avignon as technically incorrect, and returned the result of the voting as in favour of a new election. When the majority protested with shouts and execrations, the minority withdrew and allowed them to declare their vote in favour of Avignon. There was now a hopeless deadlock; the two parties sat separately, and the efforts of the German ambassadors and of the citizens of Basel were alike unavailing to restore concord.

[1] John of Segovia, 956: 'Continuo autem Cardinalis sancti Petri dicebat de jure fore quod in actibus communitatis, quando universitas deficit, quemlibet universitatis illius posse supplere; unde cum papa consensisset in decreto Græcorum, ad eum, quia summus pontifex, caput ecclesiæ et principale membrum, spectabat laborare ne ecclesia Latina deficeret in promissis.'

BOOK
III.

Futile
attempts at
reconcilia-
tion. April
1437.

When agreement proved to be impossible, both sides prepared to fight out their contention to the end. On April 26
the majority published its decree abiding by Avignon; the
minority published its choice of Florence or Udine, and asserted
that henceforth the power of the Council, as regarded this
question, vested in those who were willing to keep their
promise.[1] In the wild excitement that prevailed suspicions
were rife, and violence was easily provoked. On the following
Sunday, when the Cardinal of Arles proceeded to the Minster
to celebrate mass, he found the altar already occupied by the
Archbishop of Taranto, who suspected that the opportunity
might be used of publishing the decree of the majority in the
name of the Council, and who had resolved, in that case, to be
beforehand. Loud cries and altercations were heard on all sides;
only the crowded state of the cathedral, which prevented men
from raising their arms, saved the scandal of open violence.
The civic guards had to keep the peace between the combatants.
Evening brought reflection, and both parties dreaded a new
schism, and were appalled at the result which seemed likely
to follow from a Council assembled to promote the peace of
Christendom. Congregations were suspended, and for six days
the best men of both parties conferred together to see if an
agreement were possible; but all was in vain, because men
were swayed by personal passion and motives of self-interest,
and the violence of party-spirit entirely obscured the actual
subject under discussion. Everyone acted regretfully and
remorsefully, but with the feeling that he had now gone too far
to go back. The die had already been cast; the defeat of the
Council involved the ruin of everyone who had till now upheld
it; to retreat a hair's breadth meant failure. Conferences
brought to light no common grounds; matters must take their
course, and the two divisions of the Council must find by
experience which was the stronger.[2]

[1] The document is given in Cecconi, No. cxviii.: 'Cum jus et potestas
hujus sacri concilii (quoad actum istum et dependentia ab eo) apud illos
remaneat qui dicte cedule concordate et conclusioni ac determinationi hujus
sacri concilii inniti volunt, et providere ne sacrum Concilium in suis promissis deficiat,' &c.

[2] The state of feeling is vividly described in a letter of Æneas Sylvius to
Piero da Noceto, dated May 20, 1437, in Mansi, xxxi. 220, &c. A few of his
phrases are worth noting: 'Tanta inter majores vociferatio erat ut modestiores

CHAP.
VII.

Publica-
tion of
conflicting
decrees.
May 7,
1437.

On May 7, a day which many wished never to dawn, the rival parties strove in a solemn session to decree in the name of the Council their contradictory resolutions. In the early morning the Cardinal of Arles, clad in full pontificals, took possession of the altar, and the cathedral was filled with armed men. The legates arrived later, and even at the last moment both sides spoke of concord. It was proposed that, in case the Greeks would not come to Basel, the Council be held at Bologna, and the fortresses be put in the hands of two representatives of each side. Three times the Cardinals of Arles and of S. Peter's stood at the altar on the point of making peace; but they could not agree on the choice of the two who were to hold the fortresses. At twelve o'clock there were cries that it was useless to waste more time. Mass was said and the Bishop of Albienza mounted the pulpit to read the decree of the majority. The hymn 'Veni Creator,' which was the formal opening of the session, had begun; but it was silenced that again there might be negotiations for peace. All was in vain. The session opened, and the Bishop of Albienza began to read the decree. On the part of the minority the Bishop of Porto seized a secretary's table and began to read their decree surrounded by a serried band of stalwart youths. One bishop shouted against the other, and the Cardinal of Arles stormed vainly, calling for order. The decree of the minority was shorter and took less time in reading; as soon as it was finished, the Papal party commenced the 'Te Deum.' When their decree was finished, the opposite party sang the 'Te Deum.' It was a scene of wild confusion in which violent partisans might triumph, but which filled with dismay and terror all who had any care for the future of the Church. Both parties felt the gravity of the crisis; both felt powerless to avert it. With faces pale from excitement they saw a new schism declared in the Church.

Next day there was a contention about the seal of the Council, which Cesarini was found to have in his possession and at first declined to give up. But the citizens of Basel insisted that it was their duty to see that the seal was kept in its proper place. On May 14 a compromise was made. The seal

in taberna vinaria cernas bibulos.' ' Si meam petis sententiam paucissimos ex utraque parte numerarem quos credam sola moveri conscientia.' ' Apud quem sit veritas Deus noverit; ego non video neque si video scribere ausim.'

was put in custody of a commission of three, on condition that both decrees be sealed in secret; the Bull of the conciliar party was to be sent to Avignon, but not to be delivered till the money was paid by the citizens; if this was not done within thirty days the Bull was to be brought back; meanwhile the Bull of the Papal party was to remain in secret custody. Again there was peace for a while, which was broken on June 16 by the discovery that the box containing the conciliar seal had been tampered with, and the seal used by some unauthorised person. The discovery was kept secret, and the roads were watched to intercept any messengers to Italy. A man was taken bearing letters from the Archbishop of Taranto, which were produced before a general congregation. There was an outcry on both sides, one protesting against the seizure of the letters, the other against the false use of the Council's seal. Twelve judges were appointed to examine into the matter. The letters, which were partly in cipher, were read and the case against the Archbishop of Taranto was made good. He was put under arrest, and when the matter was laid before the Council on June 21, there was an unseemly brawl which ended in the use of violent means to prevent an appeal to the Pope being lodged by the Archbishop's proctor. On July 19 the Archbishop, surrounded by an armed troop, made his escape from Basel and fled to the Pope.

Eugenius
IV. fixes
the Coun-
cil in Italy.
May 30,
1437.
The majority in the Council of Basel might pass what decrees they would, but they had reckoned too much on their power over the Greeks. The Papal legates won over the Greek ambassadors and sent them to Eugenius IV. at Bologna. The Pope at once ratified the decree of the minority, fixed Florence or Udine as the seat of a future Council, and on May 30 issued a Bull to this effect. He wrote to all the princes of Christendom announcing his action. But Sigismund raised a protest against a Council being held in Italy, and the Duke of Milan strongly opposed the choice of Florence. Apparently wishing to avoid discussion for the present, Eugenius IV. prevailed on the Greeks to defer till their arrival on the Italian coast the exact choice of the place. The Greek ambassador, John Dissipatus, solemnly declared in the Emperor's name, that he recognised as the Council of Basel, to which he had formed obligations, only the party of the legates, and that

he accepted the decree of the minority as being the true decree of the Council.[1] Eugenius IV. hired at his own expense four Venetian galleys to convey the Greeks to Italy. Preparations were made with all possible speed, and on September 3 the Bishops of Digne and Porto, representing the minority of the Council, and Garatoni, now Bishop of Coron, on the part of the Pope, arrived in Constantinople. Claiming to speak in the name of the Pope and of the Council, they at once began to make preparations for the journey of the Greeks to Italy.

The assembly at Basel could not make its arrangements with Avignon quickly enough to compete on equal terms with the Pope. It had to face the usual disadvantages of a democracy when contending against a centralised power. Its hope of success with the Greeks lay in persuading them that the Council, and not the Pope, represented the Western Church, and was strong in the support of the princes of Western Europe. It determined again to proceed to the personal humiliation of Eugenius IV., and so by assailing his power to render useless his dealings with the Greeks. On July 31 the Council issued a monition to Eugenius IV., setting forth that he did not loyally accept its decrees, that he endeavoured to set at nought its labours for the reformation of the Church, that he wasted the patrimony of the Holy See, and would not work with the Council in the matter of union with the Greeks; it summoned him to appear at Basel within sixty days, personally or by proctor, to answer to these charges. This admonition was the first overt act towards a fresh schism. Sigismund and the German ambassadors strongly opposed it on that ground, and besought the Council to recall it. It was clear that the Council would meet with little support if it proceeded to extremities against the Pope. But in its existing temper it listened to the ambassadors of the King of Aragon and the Duke of Milan, the political adversaries of Eugenius IV., and paid little heed to moderate counsels. On September 26 it annulled the nomination to the cardinalate by Eugenius of the Patriarch of Alexandria, as being opposed to the decree that during the Council no cardinal should be nominated elsewhere than at Basel. It also annulled the decree of the minority on May 7,

The Council summons Eugenius IV. to Basel. July 31, 1437.

---

[1] Raynaldus, 1437, No. 13.

BOOK
III.

The Coun-
cil pro-
nounces
Eugenius
IV. con-
tumacious.
October 1,
1437.

by whatever authority it might be upheld, and took under its
own protection the Papal city of Avignon.

In vain the Council tried to win over Sigismund to its side.
Sigismund had gained by the submission of Bohemia all that
he was likely to get from the Council.   In Italian politics he
had allied himself with Venice against his foe the Duke of
Milan, and so was inclined to the Papal side.   He wrote angrily
to the Council on September 17, bidding them hold their hand
in their process against the Pope.   He reminded them that
they had found the Church united by his long labour, and were
acting in a way to cause a new schism.   They had met to reform and pacify Christendom, and were on the way to do the
very reverse; while wishing to unite the Greeks, they were engaged in dividing the Latins.   If they did not cease from their
seditious courses, he would be driven to undertake the defence
of the Pope.[1]   The Council was somewhat dismayed at this
letter; but the bolder spirits took advantage of current suspicions, and declared it to be a forgery, written in Basel, by the
same hands as had forged the Council's Bulls.[2]   Passion out-
weighed prudence, and men felt that they had gone too far to
withdraw; on October 1 the Council declared Eugenius IV.
guilty of contumacy for not appearing to plead in answer to
the charges brought against him.

Eugenius
IV. dis-
solves the
Council.
September
18, 1437.

On his side also Eugenius IV. was not idle.   He accepted
the challenge of the Council, and on September 18 issued a Bull
decreeing its dissolution.   In the Bull he set forth his desire to
work with the Council for union with the Greeks; in spite of
all he could do they chose Avignon, though such a choice was
null and void as not being included in the agreement previously made with the Greeks.   Still, in spite of the default
of Avignon to fulfil the conditions it had promised, the Council
persevered in its choice.   The legates, the great majority of
prelates, royal ambassadors, and theologians, who made up the
saner part of the Council, protested against the legality of this
choice, and chose Florence or Udine, and at the request of the
Greeks he had accepted their choice.   The turbulent spirits in

---

[1] The summary of this letter is given by Patricius, in Hartzheim, v. 819.

[2] John of Segovia, 1027: 'Non defuere qui dicerent eam fuisse nedum
immutatam sed scriptam Basilee, cognitamque fuisse manum scriptoris,
proptereaque illum ex Basilea fugisse.'

the Council, consisting of a few prelates who were animated partly by personal ambition and partly were the political tools of the King of Aragon and the Duke of Milan, gathered a crowd of the lower clergy, and under the specious name of reformation resisted the Pope, in spite of the Emperor's remonstrances. To prevent scandals and to avoid further dissension, the Pope transferred the Council from Basel to Ferrara, which he fixed as the seat of an Ecumenical Council for the purpose of union with the Greeks. He allowed the fathers to remain at Basel for thirty days to end their dealings with the Bohemians; but if the Bohemians preferred to come to Ferrara, they should there have a friendly reception and full hearing.[1]

The Council on October 12 annulled the Bull of Eugenius, on the ground of the superiority of a General Council over a Pope, and prohibited all under pain of excommunication from attending the pretended Council at Ferrara. It warned Eugenius IV. that if he did not make amends within four months he would be suspended from his office, and that the Council would proceed to his deprivation.

Both Pope and Council had now done all they could to assert their superiority over each other. The first question was which of the two contending parties should gain the adhesion of the Greeks. The Papal envoys had arrived first at Constantinople, and their offers were best adapted to the convenience of the Greeks. When on October 4 the Avignonese galleys arrived off Constantinople with the envoys of the Council, the captain of the Papal galleys was with difficulty prevented from putting out to sea to oppose their landing. The Greek Emperor was perplexed by two embassies, each brandishing contradictory decrees, and each declaring that it alone represented the Council. Each party had come with excommunications ready prepared to launch against the other. This scandalous exhibition of discord, in the face of those whom both parties wished to unite to the Church, was only prevented by the pacific counsels of John of Ragusa, who had been for three years resident envoy of the Council in Constantinople, and had not been swallowed up by the violent wave of party-feeling which had passed over Basel.[2] The Council's

---

[1] The Bull is given in full in John of Segovia, p. 1033.

[2] See his relation to the Council of Basel in Cecconi, No. clxxviii., and also Mansi, *Concil.*, xxxi. 248.

ambassadors proceeded at once to attack the claims of their
opponents to be considered as the Council. They succeeded
in reducing to great perplexity the luckless Emperor, who
wanted union with the Latin Church as the price of military
help from Western Europe, and only wished to find out to
whom or what he was to be united. The Greeks were puzzled
to decide whether the Pope would succeed in dissolving the
Council, or the Council in deposing the Pope : they could not
clearly see which side would have the political preponderance
in the West. The two parties plied the Emperor in turn with
their pleadings for a space of fifteen days. The Council had
the advantage that the Greeks were already committed to an
agreement with them. But the Papal party had diplomats
who were adroit in clearing away difficulties.[1] The Greeks
ultimately decided to go with them to Italy, and the Emperor
exhorted the Council's envoys to peace and concord, and invited
them to accompany him to Venice. They refused with cries
of rage and loud protestations, and on November 2 departed
for Basel.

Neutrality
of Sigis-
mund.
Now that the breach between Pope and Council was irreparable, and the Pope had won a diplomatic victory in his
negotiations, both parties looked to Sigismund, who, however,
refused to identify himself decidedly with either. He disapproved of the Pope's dissolution of the Council, from which he
still expected some measures of ecclesiastical reform ; on the
other hand, he disapproved of the Council's proceedings against
the Pope, which threatened a renewal of the schism.[2] Eugenius
IV. had showed his willingness to conciliate Sigismund by
allowing the Council in his Bull of dissolution to sit for thirty
days to conclude its business with Bohemia ; or, if the Bohemians wished, he was willing to receive their representatives
at Ferrara. This was important to Sigismund and to the Bohemians, as it showed that the Pope accepted all that had bee·
done in reference to the Bohemian question, and was ready . ·
adopt the Council's policy in this matter.

Sigismund had indeed reason to be content with the results

---

[1] See the relation of the Bishop of Digne to Eugenius IV. and the Council
of Ferrara, in Cecconi, No. clxxxviii.

[2] John of Segovia, 1060, gives the contents of a letter of Sigismund to
the Council, dated October 20.

which he had won. His restoration to Bohemia had been accomplished, and he had organised a policy of reaction which seemed likely to be successful. On August 23, 1436, his entry into Prag had been like a triumphal procession. He lost no time in appointing new magistrates, all of them chosen from the extremely moderate party. The legates of the Council were always by his side to maintain the claims of the Church. Bishop Philibert of Coutances began a series of aggressions on the episcopal authority in Bohemia. He asserted his right to officiate in Rokycana's church without asking his permission: he held confirmations and consecrated altars and churches in virtue of his superior office as legate of the Council. The Bohemians on their part waited for the fulfilment of Sigismund's promises, and the knights refused to surrender the lands of the Church until they were satisfied. Sigismund was bound to write to the Council, urging the recognition of Rokycana as Archbishop of Prag; but he told the legates that he trusted the Council would find some good pretext for delay. 'I have promised,' he said, 'that till he dies I will hold no other than Rokycana as archbishop; but I believe that some of the Bohemians will kill him, and then I can have another archbishop.'[1] It is clear that Sigismund knew how to manage a reaction, knew the inevitable loss of popularity which a party leader suffers if he make concessions and does not immediately gain success. Rokycana was looked upon as a traitor by the extreme party, and as a dangerous man by the moderate party. We are not surprised to find that in October rumours were rife of a conspiracy organised in Rokycana's house against the Emperor and the legates. Inquiries were made, and without being directly accused Rokycana was driven to defend himself, and then his defence was declared to be in itself suspicious.[2]

Rokycana seems to have felt his position becoming daily more insecure. On October 24 he paid his first visit to the legates to try and find out their views about the confirmation of his title of archbishop. The legates received him haughtily and talked about the restoration of various points of

---

[1] John of Tours: *Registrum, Mon. Concil.*, i. 835.
[2] John of Tours, p. 836: 'Rokssana vero longa oratione, cum non accusaretur, se excusavit et sub gravissimo anathemate de illis conventiculis; unde mirabantur multi, scientes non esse vera quæ dicebat.'

ritual which the Bohemians had cast aside. ' You talk only about trifles,' said Rokycana impatiently; ' more serious matters need your care.' ' You say truly,' exclaimed John of Palomar with passion; ' there are more serious matters : for you deceive the people and can no more give them absolution than this stick, for you have not the power of the keys seeing you have no apostolic mission.' This bold onslaught staggered Rokycana, who repeated the words of Palomar in amazement, and said that the people would be indignant at hearing them; he would consult his fellow-priests. One of his followers warned the legates that they and the Emperor were becoming unpopular through their refusal to confirm Rokycana's election as archbishop. Rokycana withdrew with a bitter feeling of helplessness.

Sigismund
and the
Council's
envoys.
November
1436.

The legates on November 8 pressed the Emperor to take further measures for the Catholic restoration. They had now been two months in Bohemia, they urged, and little had been done. The Communion was given to children, the Epistle and Gospel were read in Bohemian and not in Latin, the use of holy water and the kiss of peace was not restored, and toleration was not given to those who communicated under one kind. All this was contrary to the observance of the Compacts, and the kingdom of Bohemia was still infected with the heresy of Wyclif. Sigismund angrily answered, ' I was once a prisoner in Hungary, and save then I never was so wearied as I am now; indeed my present captivity seems likely to be longer.' He begged the legates to be patient till the meeting of the Diet. He was engaged in treating with Tabor and Königgratz, which were still opposed to him, and he needed time to overcome their resistance. Tabor agreed to submit its differences to arbitration; Königgratz was reduced by arms.

Progress
of the
Catholic
reaction
in Bohe-
mia. No-
vember
1436–June
1437.

On November 27 the legates and Rokycana came to a conference on the disputed points in the Emperor's presence. Rokycana demanded the clear and undoubted confirmation of the Compacts; the legates the re-establishment of the Catholic ritual. There were many difficulties raised and much discussion; but Rokycana found himself abandoned by the masters of the University, and opposed by the city magistrates and the nobles. He gave way unwillingly on all the points raised by the legates except the Communion of children and the reading of the Epistle and Gospel in Bohemian. On December 23 the Catholic ritual was restored in all the churches in Prag; the use of holy water and the kiss of peace was resumed, and images which had been cast down were again set up in their former places. Still Bishop Philibert abode in Prag and exercised the office of bishop. On February 11, 1437, the Empress Barbara was crowned Queen of Bohemia by Philibert, and Rokycana was not even bidden to the ceremony.

On February 13 the legates at last received from the Council the Bull of ratification of the Compacts of Iglau. Together with it came an admonition to the Emperor not to tolerate the communion of children. He was urged also to restore the Catholic ritual throughout Bohemia and to hand over to the Council Peter Payne, who maintained the Wyclifite doctrine that the substance of bread remained in the Eucharist. When the ratification was shown to Rokycana, he demanded that there should also be issued a letter to the princes of Christendom freeing Bohemia from all charge of heresy. He brought forward also the old complaint that many priests refused to give the sacrament under both kinds; he demanded that the legates should order them to do so, should enjoin the bishops to see that the clergy obeyed their command, and should request the Bishop of Olmütz himself to administer under both kinds. The legates answered that the letter clearing the Bohemians had already been issued at Iglau; for the future the Bohemians by observing the Compacts would purge themselves in the eyes of all men better than any letter could do it for them. To the other part of his request they answered that they would admonish any priest who was proved to have refused the Communion under both kinds to anyone who desired it; they could not ask the Bishop of Olmütz to administer the Communion himself, but only to appoint priests who were ready to do so. This was the utmost that Rokycana could procure, in spite of repeated renewal of his complaints.

The reaction went on with increasing strength. The rest of Bohemia followed the example of Prag and restored the Catholic ritual. Sigismund set up again in the Cathedral of Prag the old capitular foundation with all its splendour. The monks began to return to Prag; relics of the saints were again exposed for popular adoration. In this state of affairs represen-

tatives of Bohemia were summoned to Basel to discuss further
the question of the necessity or expediency of receiving the
Communion under both kinds. Sigismund, wishing to rid himself of Rokycana, urged him to go. Rokycana steadily refused, knowing that at Basel he would only meet with coldness,
and that during his absence from Prag the triumph of the reaction would be assured. On April 7, Procopius of Pilsen, in
the Emperor's presence, bade Rokycana remember that he had
been the leader in former negotiations with the Council. 'You
are experienced in the matter,' he said; ' you have no right to
refuse.' 'Procopius,' said Rokycana, forgetting where he was,
'remember how our party fared at Constance; we might fare in
like manner, for I know that I am accused and hated at Basel.'
'Think you,' said Sigismund angrily, 'that for you or for this
city I would do anything against mine honour?'[1] It was so
long since Sigismund had broken his plighted word to Hus that
he had forgotten that it was even possible for others to
remember it.

Though Rokycana stayed in Prag, he was systematically set
aside in ecclesiastical matters. On April 12 Bishop Philibert
appointed rural deans throughout Bohemia and charged them
how to carry out their duties; Rokycana was not even consulted.
The church in which Rokycana preached was given to the
Rector of the University, who was inducted by the legate.
Peter Payne was banished by Sigismund from Bohemia as a
heretic, and an opportunity against Rokycana was eagerly
looked for. This was given by a sermon preached on May 5,
about the Communion of children, in which he said that to give
up this practice would be a confession of previous error and of
present instability of purpose. ' Too many now condemn what
once they praised. But you, poor children, lament. What
have you done amiss that you should be deprived of the Communion? Who will answer for you? Who will defend you?
Now no one heeds.' Mothers lifted their voices and wept over
the wrongs of their children, and that was judged sufficient to
establish against Rokycana a charge of inciting the people to
sedition. The Diet demanded that some steps should be taken
to administer the archbishopric of Prag; and Sigismund's in
fluence with the moderate party was strong enough to obtain o:

[1] John of Tours, 860.

June 11 the election of Christiann of Prachatic to the office of Vicar of the Archbishopric. Rokycana on being asked to surrender the seal and submit to Christiann as his spiritual superior, judged it wise to flee from Prag on June 16.

The exile of Rokycana was the triumph of the moderate party, the Utraquists pure and simple, who wished for entire union with the Church, but who were still staunch in upholding the principles of a reformed Church for Bohemia. Envoys were sent off to Basel to end the work of reconciliation and settle the points which still were disputed. On August 18 the envoys, chief amongst whom were the priests John Pribram and Procopius of Pilsen, entered Basel with great magnificence. Pribram in his first speech to the Council demanded that the Communion under both kinds should be fully granted, not only in Bohemia and Moravia, but universally, seeing that it was the truth of God's law. Pribram and John of Palomar argued learnedly for many days on the subject; but Pribram felt that he met with little attention from the Council. One day he angrily met the suspicious coolness which surrounded him by declaring that the Bohemians had never been heretical, but had always remained in the unity of the faith ; if anyone said otherwise, they were ready to answer with their steel as they had done in past days.[1] When Pribram had ended his disputation, Procopius of Pilsen advocated the Communion of children with no better success.

At last, on October 20, the Bohemians submitted nine demands to the Council, which deserve mention as showing the ultimate point arrived at by these long negotiations. (1) That the Communion under both kinds be granted to Bohemia and Moravia ; (2) that the Council declare this concession to be more than a mere permission given for the purpose of avoiding further mischief; (3) that the Church of Prag be provided with an archbishop and two suffragans, who should be approved by the realm ; (4) that the Council issue letters clearing the good name of Bohemia ; (5) that in deciding whether the Communion under both kinds be of necessary precept or not, the Council adhere to the authorities mentioned in the Compact of Eger, the law

[1] 'Si quis vellet dicere contra, ipsi darent ferrea responsa, glorianter mencionando quas sibi dicebant contra eos impugnantes de celo concessas victorias.'—John of Segovia, 1066.

of God, the practice of Christ and the Apostles, general councils and doctors founded on the law of God; (6) that the Communion of children be allowed; (7) that at least the Epistle, Gospel, and Creed in the mass service be said in the vulgar tongue; (8) that the University of Prag be reformed and have some prebends and benefices attached to it; (9) that the Council proceed to the effectual reformation of the Church in head and members. Pribram besought that these be granted, especially the Gospel truth concerning the Sacrament. ' The kingdom of Bohemia is ready,' he added, ' as experience has shown, to defend and assert this even by thousands of deaths.' Great was the indignation of the Bohemians when, on November 6, Cesarini exhorted them to conform to the ritual of the universal Church as regarded the Communion of the laity under one kind only; still, he added, the Council was willing to stand by the Compacts.

Refusal of
their de-
mands
by the
Council.
Cesarini had gone too far in thus openly showing the policy of the Council to reduce the Bohemians to accept again the Catholic ritual. It required some management on the part of other members of the Council to allay their indignation. On November 24 the Council gave a formal answer to the Bohemian requests. As regarded the necessity of the Communion under both kinds the point had now been argued fully; it only remained for them to join with the Council and accept its declaration on the subject as inspired by the Holy Ghost. Their other points had either been already settled by the Compacts or were favours which might afterwards be discussed by the Council. This was of course equivalent to a refusal to grant anything beyond the bare letter of the Compacts. The Bohemian moderates saw themselves entirely deceived in their hopes of obtaining universal tolerance for their beliefs. The Council would grant nothing more than a special favour to Bohemia and Moravia to continue to use the ritual which they had adopted, until such time as it could safely be prohibited. In vain the Bohemians asked that at least they should not be sent away entirely empty-handed, lest it be a cause of fresh disturbances. They could get no better answer, and left Basel on November 29. In spite of Cesarini's remonstrance against the imprudence of such a step, the Council on December 23 issued a decree that the Communion under both kinds was not a pre-

cept of Christ, but the Church could order the method of its reception as reverence and the salvation of the faithful seemed to require. The custom of communicating under one kind only had been reasonably introduced by the Church and was to be regarded as the law, nor might it be changed without the Church's authority.

In Bohemia the disappointment of the expectations which the great mass of the people still retained caused growing irritation, and seemed likely to lead to a fresh outbreak. Moreover, Sigismund's declining health gave an occasion to the ambitious schemes of those of his own household. Sigismund had no son, but his only daughter was married to Albert of Austria; and the fondest wish of Sigismund's declining years was that Albert should succeed to all his dignities and possessions. But the Empress Barbara had already tasted the sweets of power and was unwilling to retire into obscurity. She and her relatives, the Counts of Cilly, raised up a party among the Bohemian barons with the object of elevating Ladislas of Poland to the thrones of Bohemia and Hungary, and marrying him, though still a youth, to Barbara, in her fifty-fourth year.[1] Sigismund discovered this plot and felt the danger of his position. He was seized with erysipelas, and had to submit to the amputation of his big toe. His one desire was to quit Bohemia and secure Albert's accession in Hungary. Concealing his knowledge of what was passing around him, he left Prag on November 11, borne in an open litter and dressed in the imperial robes. He was accompanied by the Empress and the Count of Cilly, and on November 21 reached Znaym, where Albert and his wife Elizabeth awaited him. There he ordered Barbara to be imprisoned, but the Count of Cilly had timely warning and escaped. At Znaym Sigismund summoned to his presence several of the chief barons of Bohemia and Hungary, and urged on them the advantages to be gained by uniting both lands

---

[1] Palacky, *Geschichte von Böhmen*. iii. pt. 3, 282, throws doubt upon this assertion of Æneas Sylvius (*Hist. Bohem.* ch. lii.), and there can be no question that Æneas has drawn a picture of Barbara which is exaggerated through his dislike to the family of Cilly. Still Windeck's account of Sigismund's last commands to his nobles makes the same assertion : ' das sie denne die kaiserynne sein frauen behilten bis das Herzog Albrechte in das königreich keme, oder sie wurden den könig von Polande nemen und in das königreich zihen,' in Mencken. I., 1278.

under one rule; he warmly recommended to their support the claims of Albert. This was his last effort. Feeling his malady grow worse, he was true to the last to that love of dramatic effect which was so strong a feature of his character. He wished to die like an emperor. Attired in the imperial robes, with his crown on his head, he heard mass on the morning of December 9. When mass was over he ordered grave clothes to be put on over the imperial vesture, and sitting on his throne awaited death, which overtook him in the evening. He was left seated for three days according to his command, 'that men might see that the lord of all the world was dead and gone.'[1] Then his corpse was carried to Grosswardein and buried in the resting-place of the Hungarian kings.

The facile pen of Æneas Sylvius gives us the following vigorous description of Sigismund:—' He was tall with bright eyes, broad forehead, pleasantly rosy cheeks, and a long thick beard. He had a large mind and formed many plans, but was changeable. He was witty in conversation, given to wine and women, and thousands of love intrigues are laid to his charge. He was prone to anger, but ready to forgive. He could not keep his money, but spent it lavishly. He made more promises than he kept, and often deceived.'[2] These words are a fair representation of the impression produced on his contemporaries by this mighty ' lord of all the world.' With all his faults, and they were many, on the whole men loved and esteemed him.

No doubt vanity was the leading feature of Sigismund's character; but it was the dignified vanity of always seeming to act worthily of his high position. He would have been ludicrous with his dramatic strut had not his geniality and keenness of wit imposed on those who came in his way, and so saved him from hopeless absurdity. It is easy to mock at Sigismund's

---

[1] Windeck, as above, ' so sollte man in stehen lassen zwen tag oder drei tage, dass alle mon in sehen möchte, dass aller der welde herre tot und gestorben were.'

[2] From a Vatican MS. published in Palacky's *Italienische Reise* (Prag, 1838), p. 113 : 'Fuit autem Sigismundus egregiæ staturæ, illustribus oculis, fronte spaciosa, genis ad gratiam rubescentibus, barba prolixa et copiosa, vasto animo, multivolus, inconstans tamen, sermone facetus, vini cupidus, in Venerem ardens, mille adulteriis criminosus, pronus ad iram, facilis ad veniam, nullius thesauri custos, prodigus dispensator; plura promisit quam servavit, finxit multa.' A portrait of Sigismund by Albert Dürer exists at Nüremburg.

undertakings, at his pretensions as compared with the results which he achieved; but it is impossible not to feel some sympathy even for the weaknesses of an Emperor who strove to realise the waning idea of the empire, and whose labours were honestly directed to the promotion of the peace and union of Christendom. Sigismund possessed in perfection all the lesser arts of sovereignty; kindly, affable, and ready in speech, he could hold his own amidst any surroundings. His schemes, however chimerical they might seem, were founded on a large sympathy with the desires and needs of Europe as a whole. He laboured for the unity of Christendom, the restoration of European peace, and the reformation of the Church. Even when he spoke of combining Europe in a crusade against the Turks, his aim, however chimerical, was proved by the result to be right. But Sigismund had not the patience nor the wisdom to begin his work from the beginning. He had not the self-restraint to husband his resources; to undertake first the small questions which concerned the kingdoms under his immediate sway, to aim only at one object at a time, and secure each step before advancing to the next. Relying on his position, he caught at every occasion of displaying his own importance, and his vanity led him to trust that he would succeed by means of empty display. Hence his plans hampered one another. He destroyed his position at the Council of Constance by a change of political attitude resulting from a futile attempt to bring about peace between England and France. He induced Bohemia to think that its religious interests were safe in his keeping, and then trusted to repress its religious movement by the help of the Council of Constance. When he had driven Bohemia to revolt, he oscillated between a policy of conciliation and one of repression till matters had passed beyond his control. He lost his command of the Council of Basel because he entered into relations with the Pope, who was bent upon its overthrow. His schemes of ecclesiastical reform slipped from his grasp, and after spending his early years in extinguishing one schism, he lived to see the beginning of another. Few men with such wise plans and such good intentions have so conspicuously failed.

The death of Sigismund removed the only man who might have averted an open outbreak between Eugenius IV. and the

BOOK
III.

Cesarini
leaves
Basel.
January 9,
1438.

Council of Basel. Both sides now proceeded to extremities.
On December 30 Eugenius IV. published a Bull declaring the
Council to be transferred from Basel to Ferrara. At Basel
Cesarini made one last attempt to bring back peace to the distracted Church. On December 20, in an eloquent speech
breathing the true spirit of Christian statesmanship, he pointed
out the evils that would follow from a schism. Farewell to all
hopes of a real union with the Greeks, of real missionary enterprise against the Mohammedans, who were the serious danger
to Christendom. He besought the Council, ere it was too late,
to recall its admonition to the Pope, provided he would recall
his translation of the Council : then let them send envoys to
meet the Greeks on their arrival in Italy and propose to them
to come to Basel, Avignon, or Savoy,—failing that, let them
frankly join with the Pope and the Greeks in the choice of a
place which would suit all parties. He offered himself as ready
to do his utmost to mediate for such a result.[1] But Cesarini
spoke to deaf ears. The control of the Council had passed
entirely into the hands of Cardinal d'Allemand, who was committed to a policy of war to the bitter end. A ponderous reply
to Cesarini was prepared by the Archbishop of Palermo, a mass
of juristic subtilties which dealt with everything except the
great point at issue.

Cesarini saw the entire disappointment of the hopes which
six years before had been so strong in his breast at the opening
of the Council. He had longed for peace and reform ; he saw
instead, discord and self-seeking. The Council, which ought
to have promoted the welfare of Christendom, had become an
engine of political attack upon the Papacy. The noble,
generous, and large-minded aims of Cesarini had long been
forgotten at Basel. The reformation which he projected had
passed into revolution, which he could no longer control nor
moderate. He shared the fate of many other reformers at
many times of the world's history. The movement which he
had awakened passed into violent hands, and the end of his
labours for peace and order was anarchy and discord. With a
sad heart he confessed his failure, and on January 9, 1438,
he left Basel amid demonstrations of respect from his opponents. At the request of the Pope and all the Cardinals, he

[1] The speech is given in full by John of Segovia, 1114.

went to Florence, where he was received with honour and lived for a time in quietness and study.

At Basel Cardinal d'Allemand was appointed president in Cesarini's stead. The Council on January 24 took the next step in its process against Eugenius IV. It decreed that, as he had not appeared to plead within the appointed time, he was thenceforth suspended from his office; meanwhile the administration of the Papacy belonged to the Council, and all acts done by Eugenius were null and void. Sixteen bishops were present at this session, of whom nine were Savoyards, six Aragonese, and one Frenchman. Of the eighteen abbots who were there, eleven were Aragonese and six were Savoyards. The Council was in fact supported only by the King of Aragon and the Dukes of Milan and Savoy. The Duke of Savoy hoped to use it for his personal aggrandisement. The King of Aragon and the Duke of Milan saw in it a means of forcing Eugenius IV. into subserviency to their political schemes in Italy. Neither of them was prepared to support the deposition of the Pope, but they wished the process against him to be a perpetual threat hanging over his head.[1] The rest of the European powers looked with disapproval, more or less strongly expressed, on the proceedings of the Council. Henry VI., of England, wrote a letter addressed to the *Congregation* (not the Council) of Basel, in which he reproved them for presuming to judge the Pope, denounced them for bringing back the times of Antichrist, and bade them desist from the process against Eugenius.[2] Charles VII., of France, wrote to the Council to stay its measures against the Pope, and wrote to the Pope to withdraw his decrees against the Council; he forbade his bishops to attend the Council of Ferrara, but allowed individuals to act as they pleased at Basel. His purpose was to regulate ecclesiastical matters in France at his own pleasure. In Germany, Sigismund's policy of mediation survived after his death; men wished to avoid a schism, but to obtain through the Council some measures of reform. The Kings of Castille and Portugal

Suspension
of Eu-
genius IV.
by the
Council.
January
24, 1438.

---

[1] Patricius, in Hartzheim, v. 824: 'Tandem post multos tractatus Philippus dux, qui suspensionem Eugenii postulaverat, nunc aperte Basileensibus ostendit, non sibi placere ulterius contra Eugenium procedi.'

[2] Patricius, in Hartzheim, v. 827.

and the Duke of Burgundy all admonished the Council to withdraw from their proceedings against Eugenius.

The quarrel of the Pope and the Council now ceased to attract the attention of Europe; it had degenerated into a squabble in which both parties were regarded with something approaching contempt. But this condition of affairs was full of danger to the future of the organisation of the Church.

CHAPTER VIII.

EUGENIUS IV. IN FLORENCE, AND THE UNION OF THE GREEK CHURCH.

1434—1439.

SINCE his flight from Rome in 1434, Eugenius IV. has merely appeared as offering such resistance as he could to the growing pretensions of the Council. During the four years that had passed from that time he had been quietly gaining strength and importance in Italy. True to her old traditions, Florence graciously received the exiled Pope; and under the shadow of her protection, Eugenius IV., like his predecessor Martin V., had been able to recruit his shattered forces and again re-establish his political position.

At first his evil genius seemed still to pursue Eugenius IV., and he played a somewhat ignominious part in Florentine affairs. The time when he arrived in Florence was a great crisis in Florentine history. The prudent conduct of Giovanni de' Medici had preserved the internal peace of Florence by carefully maintaining a balance between the aristocratic and popular parties in the city. But between his son Cosimo and his political rival Rinaldo degli Albizzi, a bitter hostility gradually grew up which could only end in the supremacy of the one or the other party. The first step was taken by Rinaldo, who, in September 1433, filled the city with his adherents; Cosimo was taken unawares, was accused of treason, cast into prison, and only by a skilful use of his money succeeded in escaping death. He went as an exile to Venice; but his partisans were strong in Florence, the city was divided, and a reaction in his favour set in. It was clear that the new magistrates who came into office on September 1, 1434, would recall him from banishment, and Rinaldo and his party were prepared to offer forcible resistance. On September 26, Florence was in a ferment, and Rinaldo degli

CHAP.
VIII.

Eugenius
IV. and
Florentine
affairs.
1434.

Albizzi, with 800 armed men, held the Palace of the Podestà and the streets which led to the Piazza. Eugenius IV. in this condition of affairs offered his services as mediator. He sent Giovanni Vitelleschi, Bishop of Recanati, to Rinaldo, who, to the surprise of everyone, was persuaded to leave his position and confer with the Pope at S. Maria Novella. It was one o'clock in the morning when he did so. What arguments the Pope may have used we do not know; but at five o'clock Rinaldo dismissed his armed men and remained peaceably with the Pope. Perhaps he was not sure of the fidelity of his adherents, and trusted that, by a show of submission, he might, with the Pope's help, obtain better terms than the doubtful chances of a conflict seemed to promise.

His enemies at once pursued the advantage thus offered to them. The Signori sent some of their number to thank the Pope for his good offices, and whatever may have been the first intention of Eugenius IV., he was soon won over to abandon Rinaldo. On October 2, the party of the Medici filled the Piazza and decreed the recall of Cosimo. Next day Rinaldo and his son were banished. The Pope attempted to console Rinaldo, and protested the uprightness of his own intentions and the pain which he felt at the failure of his mediation. 'Holy Father,' answered Rinaldo, 'I do not wonder at my ruin; I blame myself for believing that you, who have been driven out of your own country, could keep me in mine. He who trusts a priest's word is like a blind man without a guide.' Sadly Rinaldo left Florence for ever, and on October 6 Cosimo de' Medici returned in triumph amid shouts that hailed him father of his country. From that day forward for three hundred years the fortunes of Florence were identified with those of the house of Medici.

In his abode at Florence things gradually began to take a better turn for Eugenius IV. The rebellious Romans, who had proudly sent their envoys to Basel announcing that they had recovered their liberties and that the days of Brutus had returned, began to find themselves in straits. The Papal troops still held the castle of S. Angelo and bombarded the town; their commander also by a stratagem took prisoners several of the Roman leaders. The people soon turned to thoughts of peace and submission, and on October 28 Giovanni Vitelleschi, at the head of the Pope's condottieri, took possession of the city in the Pope's name and put to death the chief leaders of the rebellion. Moreover, Venice and the Pope renewed their league against the Duke of Milan, appointed Francesco Sforza as their general, and sent him against the Duke's condottiere general, Fortebracchio, who had occupied the neighbourhood of Rome. Fortebracchio was routed and slain, whereon the Duke of Milan found it advisable to come to terms. On August 10, 1435, peace was made, leaving Eugenius IV. master of the Patrimony of S. Peter and the Romagna, while Francesco Sforza obtained the lordship of the March of Ancona. The Duke of Milan also withdrew his aid from the rebellious Bologna, which on September 27 submitted to the Pope.[1] Even in Florence Eugenius IV. was not safe from the machinations of the Duke of Milan. A Roman adventurer, named Riccio, obtained the connivance of the Milanese ambassador at Florence, the Bishop of Novara, to a plot for seizing the person of Eugenius when he retired into the country before the summer heat. The city magistrates discovered the plot and Riccio was tortured and put to death. The Bishop of Novara abjectly prayed for pardon from Eugenius; and the Pope granted his life to the entreaty of Cardinal Albergata, who was just setting out as Papal legate to the Congress of Arras. Albergata took the Bishop of Novara to Basel, where he remained as one of the bitterest opponents of Eugenius IV.[2]

In another quarter the affairs of the kingdom of Naples afforded a scope for the activity of Eugenius IV. The feeble queen Giovanna II. continued to the end of her reign to be the puppet of those around her. Even her chief favourite, Caraccioli, could not retain his hold upon her changeful mind. He saw his influence fail before the intrigues of the Queen's cousin, the Duchess of Suessa, who at length succeeded in obtaining the Queen's permission to proceed against her over-weening favourite. On August 17, 1432, Caraccioli celebrated magnificently his son's marriage; in the night a message was brought to him that the Queen was dying and wished to see him. Hurriedly he rose and opened his door to a band of

Affairs of Naples 1432-5.

---

[1] *Cronica di Bologna*, Mur. xviii. 655. Blondus, *Dec.* iii. 6.

[2] Blondus, *Decades*, 493.

conspirators who rushed upon him and slew him on his bed.[1] Giovanna wept over his death and pardoned those who wrought it. His mighty tomb in the Church of San Giovanni Carbonara is worthy of a more heroic character. Three knightly figures of Strength, Skill, and Justice bear the sarcophagus on which stands Caraccioli as a warrior. The tomb is in the vast style of the old Neapolitan work; but in its execution we see the delicacy of Tuscan feeling and the hand of Florentine artists. The way is already prepared for the later flow of the Renaissance motives into the rude regions of Naples.

On Caraccioli's death Louis of Anjou prepared to return to Naples; but the imperious Duchess of Suessa preferred to exercise undivided sway over her feeble mistress. The death of Louis in November 1434 awakened the activity of Alfonso of Aragon; but Giovanna II. would not recognise him as her heir, and made a will in favour of René, Count of Provence, the younger brother of Louis of Anjou. On February 2, 1435, Giovanna II. died, at the age of 65, worn out before her time; one of the worst and most incapable of rulers that ever disgraced a throne. On her death the inevitable strife of the parties of Anjou and Aragon again broke out. René claimed the throne by Giovanna's will, Alfonso of Aragon put forward Giovanna's previous adoption of himself, and the claims of the house of Aragon. But Eugenius IV. put forth also the claims of the Papacy. The Angevin line had originally come to Sicily at the Papal summons, and had received the kingdom as a papal fief. Eugenius IV. asserted that on the failure of the direct line in Giovanna II. the kingdom of Sicily devolved to the Pope. He appointed as his legate to administer the affairs of the kingdom Giovanni Vitelleschi, who had been created Patriarch of Alexandria. Little heed was paid to the Pope's claims. Alfonso's fleet vigorously besieged Gaeta, which was garrisoned by Genoese soldiers to protect their trade during the time of warfare. Genoa, at that time under the signory of the Duke of Milan, equipped a fleet to raise the siege of Gaeta, and on August 5 a battle was fought off the isle of Ponza, in which the Genoese were completely victorious. Alfonso and his two brothers, together with the chief barons of Aragon and Sicily, were taken prisoners.

---

[1] *Giornali Napoletani*, Mur., xxi. 1695; *Tristan Caraccioli*, Mur., xxii. 35.

Italy was shaken to its very foundations by the news of this victory, of which the Duke of Milan would reap the fruit. It seemed to give him the means of making himself supreme in Italian politics. But the jealous temper of Filippo Maria Visconti looked with distrust on this signal victory which Genoa had won. His first proceeding was to humble the pride of the city by depriving it of the glory of bringing home in triumph its illustrious captives. He ordered Alfonso and the rest to be sent from Savona to Milan, and on their arrival treated them with courtesy and respect. Alfonso's adventurous and varied life had given him large views of politics and great experience of men. He recognised the gloomy and cautious spirit of Filippo Maria, who loved to form plans in secret, who trusted no one, but used his agents as checks one upon another. In the familiarity of friendly intercourse, Alfonso put before the Duke political considerations founded upon a foresight which was beyond the current conceptions of the day. 'If René of Anjou,' he argued, 'were to become King of Naples, he would do all he could to open communications with France, and for this purpose to establish the French power in Milan. If I were to become king of Naples, I should have no enemies to dread save the French; and it would be my interest to live on good terms with Milan, which could at any moment open the way to my foes. The title of king would be mine, but the authority would be yours. With me at Naples you will remain a free prince; otherwise you will be between two strong powers, an object of suspicion and jealousy to both.'[1]

The state system of Italy was already so highly organised that arguments such as these weighed with the Duke of Milan, and he determined to forego all thoughts of present glory for future safety. Instead of treating Alfonso as a captive, he entered into an alliance with him, gave him his liberty and ordered Genoa to restore his captured ships. Alfonso was sufficiently keen-sighted to perceive, and Filippo Maria was sufficiently prudent to recognise, the danger that would arise to Italian independence from the centralisation of the French monarchy and the power of the house of Austria. They devised a scheme for neutralising this danger. The idea

CHAP. VIII.

Alfonso of Aragon and Filippo Maria Visconti. 1435.

[1] Machiavelli, *Storia Fior.*, ch. v.

of a balance of power in Italy, founded on identity of interest between Milan and Naples, which was to keep Italy in peace and exclude all interference from beyond the Alps, began from this time forward to be a central point in Italian politics.

The immediate result of this policy was that Genoa, indignant at the slight thus cast upon her, revolted from Milan and joined the league of Florence, Venice, and the Pope. Eugenius IV., alarmed at the alliance between Alfonso and the Duke of Milan, withdrew his own claims on Naples and espoused the cause of René, who was a prisoner of the Duke of Burgundy, but was represented in Naples by his wife, Elizabeth of Lorraine. Neither she nor Alfonso had any resources at their command, and the war was carried on between the rival factions in the realm. We have seen that Alfonso was anxious to minimise the help which the Pope could give his rival, by supplying him with sufficient occupation in the affairs proceeding at Basel.

When Eugenius IV. had recruited his shattered fortunes by an abode of nearly two years in Florence, he left it for his own city of Bologna, on April 18, 1436. Before his departure he consecrated the stately Duomo of Florence, which had just received its crowning ornament of Brunelleschi's mighty dome, and was again ready for divine service. The city wished that the ceremonial should be befitting of its splendour. A scaffolding adorned with carpets was erected from S. Maria Novella to the Duomo, on which Eugenius IV. walked in state, the gonfaloniere of the city bearing his train.[1]

On April 22, Eugenius IV. entered Bologna with nine cardinals, and was soon followed by two others from Basel. The Papal government of Bologna had not been such as to win the affections of the people. The legate, the Bishop of Concordia, had proclaimed a general pacification, on the strength of which Antonio de' Bentivogli, after fifteen years' exile, returned to the city which he had once ruled. He had not been there three weeks when he was seized, as he left the chapel where the legate had been saying mass. He was gagged and immediately beheaded by order of the Pope's Podestà, as was also Tommaso de' Zambeccari. The only reason assigned for this treacherous

---

[1] Ammirato, bk. xxi. Machiavelli, v.

act was dread of the number of their followers.[1] The cruelty and tyranny of the Podestà made the Papal rule hateful in the city. Nor did Eugenius IV. do anything to mend this state of things. He was busied with his negotiations with the Council and with the Greeks. The only attention which he paid to the citizens of Bologna was to extort from them 30,000 ducats by holding out hopes of summoning his Council thither. When the citizens found themselves disappointed, they looked with scarce concealed discontent on the Pope's departure for Ferrara on January 23, 1438. Scarcely had he gone, when Niccolo Piccinino, the Duke of Milan's general, appeared before Bologna. On the night of May 20 the gates were opened to him by the citizens. Faenza, Imola, and Forli joined in the revolt, and the greater part of Romagna was again lost to the Pope.

This was, however, of small moment to Eugenius IV. His attention was entirely fixed on the Council of Ferrara, through which he hoped to win back all that he had lost. The union of the Greek Church was to reinstate the Papacy in its position in the eyes of Europe; the Pope was again to appear as the leader of Christendom in a great crusade for the protection of Constantinople. It is a melancholy spectacle that is offered to our view. The Eastern Empire, with its splendid traditions of past glories, has sunk to be a catspaw in the ecclesiastical squabbles of the West. The trembling Greeks are ready to disavow their religious convictions to obtain help from their Western brethren. The States of Europe are so rent by intestine struggles, or are so bent upon purely selfish ends, that they are incapable of understanding the menace to European civilisation contained in the establishment of the Turks on this side of the Bosporus. The Greeks cannot appeal to any feeling of European patriotism, or to any considerations of political wisdom. Only through the semblance of an ecclesiastical reconciliation can they hope to awaken any interest for their cause in Western Europe. At the last moment they see the Western Church itself distracted by contending parties; they engage desperately in a sacrifice of their convictions, which they half feel will avail them nothing.

The causes of the separation between the Eastern and

---

[1] *Cronica di Bologna*, Mur., xviii. 656.

BOOK
III.
Points in
dispute be-
tween the
Eastern
and
Western
Churches.

Western Churches were national rather than religious. The
beliefs and rites of the two Churches did not materially differ.
But the political development of the East and West had been
different. In the East, the Imperial autocracy had maintained and strengthened its power over the Church; in the
West, where the Teutons had weakened the fabric of the Imperial
system, the Pope, as supreme head of the Western Church, had
won an independent position for his authority. It is true that the
Greek view of Purgatory differed somewhat from that of the
Latins, that they used leavened and not unleavened bread for
the Host, that they did not adopt the addition of the words
' and from the Son ' (Filioque) to the clause of the Nicene Creed
which defines the procession of the Holy Ghost. But no vital
point was concerned in any of these differences. The real
disagreement was that the Papacy strove to assert over the
Eastern Church a supremacy which that Church was unwilling to admit. The ill-feeling created by the claim of Pope
Nicolas I. in 863, to interfere as supreme judge in the question
of the election of the Patriarch of Constantinople, simmered on
till it produced a formal rupture in 1053, when Leo IX. at
Hildebrand's suggestion excommunicated the Greek Patriarch.
Round its ecclesiastical establishment the narrow spirit of
Greek nationality centred, and the Greeks were ready in every
sphere to assert their superiority to the barbarous Latins. In
the time of their distress their pride was humbled if their
minds were not convinced. They were ready to sacrifice the
traditions of the past, which they still held firmly in their hearts,
to the pressing need for present aid. It is sad to see the feeble
representatives of an ancient civilisation lowering themselves
before the Papacy in its abasement.

On November 24, 1437, the Greek Emperor, John Palæologus, his brother, the Patriarch, and twenty-two bishops,
went on board the Papal galleys and set sail for Italy.[1] Though
the Greeks journeyed at the Pope's expense, yet the Emperor,
in his anxiety to display fitting magnificence, converted into
money the treasures of the Church. An earthquake, which oc-

[1] The account of the voyage given by Syropulus, sect. iv. ch. i.-x., is a
varied and amusing description of a journey in the Mediterranean at that
time. His impressions of Venice are also most valuable as a contribution to
an idea of the splendour of the city.

curred at the time of his departure, was looked upon as an evil
omen by the people who with heavy hearts saw the ships quit
the harbour. After many perils and discomforts on the way,
the Greeks reached Venice on February 8, 1438, and were magnificently received by the Doge, who went out to meet them in
the 'Bucentaur,' which was decked with red carpets, and awn-
ings wrought with gold embroidery, while gold lions were
standing on the prow. The rowers were clad in uniforms richly
wrought with gold, and on their caps was embroidered the image
of S. Mark. With the Doge came the Senate in twelve other
splendid ships, and there was such a multitude of boats that
the sea could scarce be seen. Amid the clang of trumpets the
Emperor was escorted to the palace of the Marquis of Ferrara,
near the Rialto, where he abode. The amazement of the
Greeks at the splendour of Venice is the most striking testimony
to the decay of their own noble city. 'Venice splendid and
great,' says Phranza, 'truly wonderful, yea most wonderful, rich,
variegated and golden, trimly built and adorned, worthy of a
thousand praises, wise, yea most wise, so that one would not be
wrong in calling it the second land of promise.'[1]

For twenty days the Greeks remained in Venice. The Doge
offered them hospitality as long as they chose, and advised them
to see whether they could get better terms from the Pope or
from the Council. There was not much difference of opinion
on this point. Three only of the Greek prelates thought it
desirable to wait; the Emperor's doubts, if he had any, were
decided by the arrival of Cardinal Cesarini, who was the representative of that 'saner part' of the Council to which the
Greeks professed to adhere. The stay of the Greeks in Venice
was not without melancholy reflections. Wherever they turned
they were reminded that the glory of Venice was in a
measure due to the spoils of Constantinople. In the rich
jewels which bedecked the colossal statue on the high altar of
S. Mark's they saw the plunder of S. Sophia's.[2]

On February 28 the Emperor set sail for Ferrara. The
Patriarch was sorely displeased at being left behind to follow in

---

[1] Phranza, *Chronicon Majus*, ii. § 185, ed. Migne.

[2] Syropulus, IV. xvi.: τοῖς μὲν κεκτημένοις καύχημα καὶ τέρψις ἐγγίγνεται, τοῖς
δὲ ἀφαιρεθεῖσιν, εἴποτε καὶ παρατύχοιεν, ἀθυμία καὶ λύπη καὶ κατήφεια, ὡς καὶ ἡμῖν
τότε συνέβη.

BOOK
III.
Arrival of
the Greeks
in Ferrara.
March 7,
1438.

a few days. The Emperor disembarked at Francolino, where he was received by the Marquis of Ferrara and Cardinal Albergata as the Pope's legate. He entered the city on March 4, riding on a magnificent black charger beneath a canopy held by his attendants. He advanced into the court-yard of the papal palace, where Eugenius IV. was seated with all his clergy. The Pope rose to greet the Emperor, who dis-mounted and advanced; Eugenius prevented him from kneel-ing and embraced him. Then he gave him his hand, which the Emperor kissed and took his seat on the Pope's left; they con-tinued some time in friendly conference. The Patriarch, who was particular to keep close to his luggage, followed grumbling, and reached Ferrara on March 7. His good humour was not increased by a message from the Emperor, telling him that the Pope expected him to kiss his foot on his reception. This the Patriarch stoutly refused to do. ' I determined,' he said, ' if the Pope were older than me to treat him as a father, if of the same age as a brother, if younger as a son.' He added that he had hoped by the Pope's aid to free his Church from the tyranny of the Emperor, and could not subject it to the Pope. The negotiations respecting this knotty question occupied the entire day. At last the Pope, for the sake of peace, consented to waive his rights, provided the reception was in private and only six of the Greek prelates were admitted at one time. On the evening of March 8, the Patriarch Joseph, an old man of venerable aspect, with white hair and a long white beard, of ·dignified bearing, and considerable experience of affairs, greeted the Pope in his palace.[1] The Pope rose and the Patriarch kissed his cheek, the inferior prelates his right hand. When the ceremony was over they were conducted to their lodgings.

Beginning
of the
Council of
Ferrara.
January
1438.

The Council had been opened at Ferrara on January 5 by the Cardinal Albergata as Papal legate. Its first decree on January 10 was to confirm the translation of the Council from Basel to Ferrara, and to annul all that had been done at Basel since the Pope's Bull of translation. On January 27, the Pope entered Ferrara escorted by the Marquis Nicolas III., of Este.

---

[1] Letter of John of Ragusa to Cesarini from Constantinople (Cecconi, *Docum.* lxxviii.) : 'Pater antiquus est, et sicut etas, canities, barba prolixa et effigies reddunt ipsum cunctis spectantibus venerabilem ; ita sensus naturalis, experientia rerum et morum compositio reddunt ipsum cunctis secum famili-ariter conversantibus mirabilem.'

He took up his abode in the palace of the Marquis; and as he
suffered grievously from gout, the citizens of Ferrara consulted
his infirmity by erecting a wooden scaffold, communicating
between the palace and the cathedral, so as to spare him the in-
convenience of mounting steps.[1] On February 8 he presided over
a congregation, and commended to its deliberation the work of
union with the Greeks, and the repression of the excesses of those
still remaining at Basel. The result of this deliberation was the
issue of a Bull on February 15, annulling the proceedings of
the Council of Basel and declaring excommunicate all who did
not quit it within thirty days. Eugenius IV. had thus done all
he could to affirm his dignity before the arrival of the Greeks.

In like manner the first point of importance with the
Greeks was to affirm their own dignity at Ferrara. The question that first called for solution was the arrangement of seats
in the Council. Cesarini suggested that the Greeks should sit
on one side of the cathedral, the Latins on the other, and the
Pope in the middle as a link between the two parties. The
Greeks bluntly answered that they needed no such link;
but if a link were thought necessary, it should be strengthened
by the addition of the Greek Emperor and Patriarch to the
Pope. Both sides fought to win prestige; but the Greeks were
not fighting on equal terms. They were the Pope's stipendiaries
in Ferrara, and the arrangement for supplying them with the
stipulated allowances went on side by side with the negotiations
about the knotty question of seats. The Pope at first proposed
to supply the Greeks with food; this they resisted, and
demanded an allowance in money. Ultimately the Pope gave
way; it was agreed that the Marquis of Ferrara should furnish them with lodgings, and the Pope give the Emperor thirty
florins a month, the Patriarch twenty-five, the prelates four, and
the other attendants three. The Greeks accepted a compromise
about seats. The Latins were to sit on one side, the Greeks on
the other. The Pope's seat was highest and was nearest the
altar; next him was a vacant seat for the Western Emperor,
opposite to which sat the Greek Emperor, and behind him the
Patriarch. When the Patriarch wished to adorn his seat with
curtains like the Papal throne he was not allowed to do so.
The Greeks murmured at this arrangement, but were obliged

_Arrange-
ments
for the
Council._

---

[1] Frizzi, *Memorie per la Storia di Ferrara*, III. 430.

to submit. The Emperor exclaimed that the Latins were not aiming at order, but were gratifying their own pride.

Before appearing at the Council the Greek Emperor insisted that it should not be merely an assembly of the prelates, but also of the kings and princes of the West. The Pope was driven to admit that some time was necessary before the princes could arrive. It was agreed that a delay of four months should take place to allow them to be duly summoned. Meanwhile a general session should be held to proclaim that the Council was to be held at Ferrara, and nowhere else.

Some time was spent in settling these matters. At last on April 9 a solemn session was held in the cathedral, 'a wonderful and awful sight,' says a Greek; 'so that the church looked like heaven.'[1] The Pope and papal retinue chaunted the psalm, 'Blessed be the Lord God of Israel.' The Patriarch was too ill to be present; but a declaration of his consent to the Council was read in his absence. Then the decree convoking all to Ferrara within four months was read in Latin and Greek, and received the formal approval of both parties. After a few thanksgivings, the synod was dismissed.

The festivities of Easter occupied some time, and the Greeks were annoyed that they could not get a church in Ferrara for the celebration of their own services. The Pope referred them to the Bishop of Ferrara, who answered that all his churches were so crowded that he could not find one large enough for their purposes. One of the Greeks said that he could not worship in the Latin churches, as they were full of saints whom he did not recognise; even the Christ bore an inscription which he did not understand; he could only make the sign of the cross and adore that.[2] The tone of mind exhibited in these remarks did not augur well for any real agreement, nor did the Emperor wish the discussions to go too far. His plan was to defer matters as long as possible, to insist upon the Council being representative of the powers of Europe, to obtain from them substantial help against the Turks, and to go back

---

[1] *Acta Græca*, in Labbe, p. 21.

[2] Syropulus, 109 : ὅταν εἰς ναὸν εἰσέλθω λατίνων οὐ προσκυνῶ τινὰ τῶν ἐκεῖσε ἁγίων, ἔτει οὔδε γνωρίζω τινά. τὸν Χριστὸν ἴσως μόνον γνωρίζω, ἀλλ' οὐδ' ἐκεῖνον προσκυνῶ διοτι οὐκ οἶδα πῶς ἐπιγράφεται, ἀλλὰ ποιῶ τὸν σταυρὸν μοῦ καὶ προσκυνῶ. τὸν σταυρὸν οὖν ὃν αὐτὸς ποιῶ προσκυνῶ καὶ οὐχ ἕτερον τὶ τῶν ἐκεῖσε θεωρουμένων μοί.

to Constantinople having made as few concessions as were possible.

The Latins, however, were anxious to make their triumph complete. They urged that it was a useless waste of time to do nothing while they waited for the appearance of the European princes. Cesarini displayed his wonted tact in inviting the Greeks to dinner, and overcoming the reserve which the Emperor wished them to maintain. He succeeded in inducing one of the most stubborn of the Greek prelates, Mark of Ephesus, to publish his views in writing, to the great wrath of the Emperor. The Papal officers were remiss in the payment of allowances, and hinted that the Pope could not continue to pay men who would do nothing. By such means the Greeks were at last driven to agree to the appointment of ten commissioners on either side, who should engage in preliminary discussions upon the points of variance. Chief among the Greeks were Mark, Bishop of Ephesus, and Bessarion, Bishop of Nicæa; the Emperor ordered that they only should conduct the discussions. On the side of the Latins Cesarini took the leading part.

The conferences began on June 4. The first question discussed was that of Purgatory, on which the real difference of opinion was not important. The Latins held that sins, not repented of during life, are purged away by purgatorial fire, which at the Day of Judgment is succeeded by everlasting fire for the reprobate. The Greeks admitted a Purgatory, but of pain and grief, not of fire, which they reserved as the means only of eternal punishment. Also the Greeks maintained that neither the punishment of the wicked nor the joy of the blessed was complete till the general resurrection, seeing that before that time neither could receive their bodies. The Latins admitted that the punishment of the wicked could not be perfect till they had received their bodies, but held that the blessed, as souls, enjoy at present perfect happiness in heaven, though on receiving their bodies their happiness would become eternal. Even the most staunch upholder of the Greek doctrines, Mark of Ephesus, was driven to admit that there was not much difference between the Greek and the Latin opinions on this question. When the discussion was ended, the Latins handed in their opinion in writing. The Greeks were timid in committing

themselves. Each wrote his opinion and submitted it to the
Emperor, who combined those of Bessarion and Mark, to the
effect that the souls of the happy departed, as souls, énjoy
perfect felicity, but when in the resurrection they receive
their bodies they will be capable of more perfect happiness
and will shine like the sun. On July 17 this statement was
submitted to the Latins. The only result of these conferences was to bring into prominence the differences existing
amongst the Greeks themselves. The narrow and bigoted spirit
of old Byzantine conservatism, expressed by the rough outspoken Mark of Ephesus, did not harmonise with the cosmopolitan feeling of the polished Platonist Bessarion, who saw the
decadence of the Greeks, and wished to bring his own ability
into a larger sphere of literary and theological activity. The
Latins learned that there were some amongst the Greeks who
would bow, and some who must be driven, to consent to union.

Then came a pause till the four months' interval had elapsed
for the fuller assembling of the Council. None of the European
princes appeared, and the delay continued. Ferrara was attacked by the plague; some of the Greeks grew terrified or
weary, and fled home. The Emperor requested the magistrates
to keep guard over the gates, and forbade any of the Greeks to
leave the city without his permission. The Emperor meanwhile
spent his time in hunting in the woods round Ferrara, and
paid no heed to the requests of the Marquis that he would spare
his preserves, which had been stocked with great difficulty.
The plague drove the Latins out of the city. Of a hundred
and fifty prelates who were present at the first session, only
five cardinals and fifty bishops remained. The Greeks escaped
the ravages of the plague, except only the household of the
Russian archbishop.

It was some time before the Pope could obtain the Emperor's consent to a second session of the Council. The Greeks
were suspicious; they were indignant at a rumour which had
been spread that they were guilty of fifty-four heresies; they
were afraid that, if they allowed the Council to proceed, they
might be outvoted. Their fears on this last point were set at
rest by an agreement that each party should vote separately.
After that they could no longer resist the Pope's entreaties
that the business of the Council should proceed.

On October 8 the second session was held in the Pope's chapel, as Eugenius was unable to move through an attack of the gout. The Greeks had previously decided among themselves the question to be discussed. The more moderate party, headed by Bessarion, who was in favour of a real union if it were possible, wished to proceed at once to the important point which divided the two Churches, the double procession of the Holy Ghost. The Nicene Creed, which had been framed to define the orthodox doctrine of the Trinity, dealt chiefly with the relation between the Father and the Son, and contented itself with the statement that 'the Holy Ghost proceeded from the Father.' The continuance of controversy in the West led to the addition of the words 'and from the Son' (Filioque), an addition which the Greeks never made. The Western Church argued that the procession of the Holy Ghost from the Father alone derogated from the dignity of the Son, who was equal with the Father in all points save only in his generation by the Father. The explanatory addition gradually became incorporated in the Creed. The greater metaphysical instinct of the Greeks led them to reject such an addition, which seemed to them dangerous, as tending to give a double origin to the Holy Ghost, and thereby to imperil the Unity in Trinity. There was no fundamental difference of opinion between the Greek and Latin fathers at first; but the genius of the Greek language admitted of finer distinctions than a Latin could comprehend. The Greeks were ready to allow that the Holy Ghost proceeded from the Father *through* the Son, not that He proceeded from the Father *and* the Son. The difference was of little moment till the resentment of the Greek Patriarch against the Papal claims to supremacy led in the ninth century to an open rupture between the two Churches, and every shadow of difference was at once brought into prominence. Tomes of learning had been amassed on either side in support of their opinions on this point, and a molehill had been piled to the height of a mountain. It was felt that this question presented the greatest difficulty in settlement. Bessarion and his followers wished to discuss it at once. Mark of Ephesus, and those who were opposed to the union, succeeded in overruling them, and proposed the more dangerous preliminary question, 'Is it permissible to make any addition to a Creed?' Six disputants were

CHAP VIII.

The question of the Procession of the Holy Ghost.

chosen on either side : Bessarion, Mark, and Isidore of Russia
were chief among the Greeks, Cardinals Cesarini and Albergata,
and Andrea, Bishop of Rhodes, among the Latins.

The arguments were long and the speeches were many on
both sides. The Fathers of Ferrara found, like the Fathers of
Basel when dealing with the Bohemians, that a disputation led
to little result. · Speech was directed against speech ; orator re-
futed orator. But amid the flow of words the central positions
of the two parties remained the same. The Latins urged
that the ' Filioque ' was an explanation of the Nicene Creed in
accordance with the belief of most of the Latin and Greek
Fathers, notably S. Basil; the Greeks urged that it was not
derived from the text of the Creed itself, but was an unauthorised addition, which gave a careless explanation of a doctrine
needing careful definition. Through October and November
the discussion rolled on. The monotony was only broken by
the arrival of ambassadors from the Duke of Burgundy, who
aroused the deepest indignation in the Greek Emperor by paying reverence to the Pope and not to himself. When they
urged that they were commissioned only to the Pope and had
letters to him alone, the Emperor was still more enraged and
threatened to leave the Council where he was subject to such
slights. He could only be appeased by the solemn and public
presentation of a letter forged by the ambassadors.[1]

The discussions were leading to no result. As a way of
escaping from a mere strife of words, Cesarini besought that
the real point of issue, the truth of the double procession of
the Holy Ghost, be taken into consideration. If they were
agreed that it was true, the addition of it to the Creed was of
small moment. The majority of the Greek prelates were loth
to enter upon a doctrinal discussion ; but the rumours of a new
Turkish attack on Constantinople made the Emperor more
desirous for succours. He assembled his prelates and said that
it was unworthy of them, after so many labours and so much
trouble, to refuse to come to the point; their refusal in the
present state of affairs would only give cause of triumph to the
Latins. In vain the Patriarch urged that it was unwise to quit

---

[1] These ludicrous proceedings are told by Syropulus, 176. The Emperor's
attendants urged him at least to receive the forged letter in his own palace,
but he insisted upon a public ceremony.

the safe position of the unlawfulness of an addition to the Creed. The Emperor succeeded in extorting from the discordant prelates a reluctant consent to the discussion of the doctrine.

The Pope meanwhile had been pressing on the Emperor the necessity of transferring the Council from Ferrara to Florence. He pleaded that at Ferrara he could get no money to fulfil his agreement with the Greeks. Niccolo Piccinino was ravaging the neighbourhood so that no revenues could reach the Papal coffers; the plague had made Ferrara an unsafe place of residence; Florence had promised a large loan to the Pope if he would again take refuge within its walls. Eugenius IV. was anxious to remove the Greeks farther from their own land, to a place where they would be more entirely dependent on himself. The Greeks murmured, but their necessities gave them little option; as the Pope's stipendiaries they were bound to go where he could best find them rations. On January 10, 1439, the last session was held at Ferrara and decreed the transference of the Council to Florence on the ground of the pestilence.

On January 16 Eugenius IV. left Ferrara for Florence; his journey was more like a flight before the troops of Piccinino than a papal progress. The sedentary Greeks were greatly wearied by the discomforts of a long journey across the Apennines in winter. The aged Patriarch especially suffered from the journey; but his vanity was gratified by the splendour of his reception in Florence, where he was met by two cardinals, and amidst a blare of trumpets and the shouts of a vast multitude he was escorted to his lodgings. Three days after, on February 16, arrived the Emperor; but a storm of rain spoiled the magnificence of his reception, and scattered the crowd which came to give him the welcome that the Florentines, better than any others, could give to a distinguished guest.

In Florence the Pope was determined to proceed more speedily with business than had been done at Ferrara. The Greek Emperor had by this time seen the actual position of affairs. He was obliged to submit to the failure of the expectations with which he had come to Italy. He had hoped to play off the Council of Basel against the Pope, and so secure good terms for himself; he found the Latins united and undisturbed by the proceedings of the fathers still remaining at Basel. He hoped that the Western princes would have assembled at the

Council, and that he could have made the question of union secondary to a project for a crusade against the Turk; he found a purely ecclesiastical assembly which he could not divert from purely theological considerations. As he could not with dignity go back to Constantinople empty-handed, and as he sorely needed succours, he saw no other course open than to accept such terms of union as could be obtained and trust afterwards to the generosity of Western Christendom. At Florence he used his influence to expedite matters, and fell in with the Pope's suggestions for this purpose.

Discussion
resumed at
Florence.
February
29, 1439.

On February 26 a meeting took place at Florence in the Pope's palace, confined to forty members on each side. It was agreed to hold public disputations three times a week for three hours at least, and also to appoint committees on each side, who might confer privately about the union. The public sessions, which began on March 2, were really a long theological duel between John of Montenegro, a famous Dominician theologian, and Mark of Ephesus. Day after day their strife went wearily on, diversified only by disputes about the authenticity of manuscripts of S. Basil against Eunomius, whose words Mark of Ephesus was convicted of quoting from a garbled manuscript.[1] The argument turned on points verbal rather than real; each side could support its own opinion more easily than prove the error of its opponent. Even Mark of Ephesus was wearied of talking, and in a long speech on March 17 fired his last shot. John of Montenegro on his part made a statement which the partisans of union among the Greeks seized as a possible basis for future negotiation. He said explicitly that the Latins

---

[1] The question here raised is of great interest as throwing light upon the condition of ancient MSS. at the time. See the accounts given in *Acta Graeca*, Labbe, xiii. 311, &c., by Andrea of Sante Croce (*ib.* 1063, &c.); by S. Antoninus, *Chronicon*, tit. xxii. ch. 13; by Bessarion in his letter to Alexius Lascaris Philanthropicus (*Opera*, ed. Migne, p. 325). Bessarion's account is very copious on the point. The text of S. Basil was ' ἀξιώματι μὲν γὰρ δευτερεύειν τοῦ Υἱοῦ, παρ' αὐτοῦ τὸ εἶναι ἔχον, καὶ παρ' αὐτοῦ λαμβάνον καὶ ἀνάγγελλον ἡμῖν, καὶ ὅλως ἐκείνης τῆς αἰτίας ἐξημμένον παραδιδῶσιν ὁ τῆς εὐσεβείας λόγος.' There were six MSS. of S. Basil *contra Eunomium* at the Council, four on parchment, of which three belonged to the Archbishop of Mitylene, one to the Latins, and two on silk belonging to the Emperor and the Patriarch. All agreed save that of the Patriarch, which Mark quoted, and in which the words καὶ ὅλως ἐκείνης τῆς αἰτίας ἐξημμένον were omitted. ' τόδε ἐν μόνον,' says Bessarion, ' τὸ τοῦ πατριάρχου δηλαδὴ, εἶχεν ἑτέρως, τινὸς περικοψάντος τὸ ῥητὸν, καὶ τὰ μὲν προσθέντος τὰ δ' ἀφελόντος.'

recognised the Father as the one cause of the Son and of the
Holy Ghost. This was the only theological point involved in
the two positions. The Emperor requested John to put his
statement in writing, and laid it before his assembled prelates.
He spoke of all his labours to bring about union, and he urged
them to accept this basis. The Greeks in truth were weary of
the controversy; they longed to return home. The Patriarch
grew feebler day by day; the Emperor grew more determined
to see some fruits of all his trouble. A passage of a letter of
S. Maximus, a Greek writer of the seventh century, was discovered by the Greeks, which agreed with the language of John
of Montenegro. 'If the Latins will accept this,' exclaimed the
partisans of the Union, 'what hinders us from agreement?' In
an assembly of the Greek prelates the Emperor's will overbore
all opposition except that of Mark and the Bishop of Heraclea.
The letter of Maximus was submitted to the Latins as the
basis for an agreement; meanwhile the public sessions were
suspended.

John of Montenegro, however, was anxious to have his
reply to the last onslaught of Mark of Ephesus. Another
session was held on March 21 to gratify the vanity of the Latins;
but the Emperor took the precaution of ordering Mark to absent
himself. When thus bereft of an adversary and listened to in
solemn silence, John of Montenegro talked himself out in two
days. An understanding had now been established between the
Pope and the Emperor; but the susceptibilities of the Greeks
were still hard to manage. Public sessions, which only awakened
vanity, were stopped. Committees composed of ardent partisans of the Union were nominated on both sides for the purpose of minimising the difficulties that still remained. Bessarion and Isidore of Russia among the Greeks strove their
utmost to overcome the rigid conservatism of their fellow-
countrymen. The Cardinals Cesarini and Capranica among the
Latins laboured assiduously to secure the Papal triumph.
Perpetual messages passed between the Pope and the Emperor.
Documents were drawn up on both sides; proposals towards
greater exactness of expression were put forward. Bessarion
argued in a learned treatise that there was no real difference
of meaning, when the Latins said that the Holy Ghost proceeded
from (ἐξ) the Son, and the Greek fathers wrote that he pro-

ceeded through (διὰ) the Son, if both agreed that there were
not two causes, but one, of the procession, and that the Father
and the Son formed one substance.

The Patriarch was lying on his death-bed. Bessarion and
his party were resolute for the Union on large grounds of
ecclesiastical statesmanship. Others of the Greeks, following
the Emperor, were convinced of its practical necessity. They
had gone so far that they could not draw back. They were
willing to seek out expressions of double meaning, which might
serve for a compromise.[1] Yet many of the Greeks held by the
stubborn Mark of Ephesus, and would not give way. The
discussion passed from being one between Greeks and Latins
to one between two parties among the Greeks. Many were
the fierce controversies, many the intrigues, great the anger of
the Emperor, before an end was visible to these troublesome
disputations. At last, on June 3, the Greeks agreed that, without departing from their ancient belief, they were ready to
admit that the Holy Ghost proceeds *from* the Father and the
Son, as one cause and one substance, proceeds *through* the Son
as the same nature and the same substance. Next day a
schedule was drawn up, of which a copy was handed to the
Emperor, the Pope, and the Patriarch: it ran: 'We agree
with you, and assent that your addition to the Creed comes
from the Fathers; we agree with it and unite with you, and say
that the Holy Ghost proceeds from the Father and the Son as
from one origin and cause.'

Matters had proceeded so far that the Emperor turned to
business, and asked the Pope what succours he would grant.
Eugenius IV. promised to supply 300 soldiers and two galleys
for the constant defence of Constantinople; in time of need,
twenty galleys for six months, or ten for a year. He also
undertook to preach a crusade and rouse the West for the defence of the Greeks. Satisfied with this promise, the Emperor
hastened to bring matters to a conclusion. Mark of Ephesus
was peremptorily ordered to hold his tongue, and he himself

---

[1] So says Mark of Ephesus (Migne, clix. p. 1076): περὶ τοῦ τρόπου τῆς ἐνώσεως
ἤρξαντο πραγματεύεσθαι, καί τινα ῥητὰ περιεργάζεσθαι δι' ὧν ἑνωθήσονται μέσην
ἐπέχ οντα χώραν καὶ δυνάμενα κατ' ἀμφοτέρας τὰς δόξας λαμβάνεσθαι.

admits that he was not unwilling to be relieved from further responsibility in the matter.[1]

But the sudden death of the Patriarch Joseph on the evening of June 10 seemed at first likely to put a stop to all further negotiations. The Greeks, bereft of their ecclesiastical head, might well urge that without his sanction all proceedings would be useless. Happily for Eugenius IV., there was found a paper subscribed by Joseph a few hours before his death, approving what seemed good to his spiritual sons, and acknowledging the supremacy of the Roman Church. The Patriarch was buried with due honours in the Church of S. Maria Novella, where the inscription on his tomb is the only memorial remaining to this day of the labours spent in uniting the Eastern and Western Churches.[2]

Fortified by the Patriarch's declaration, the Emperor urged on the completion of the work of union. The Pope submitted to the Greeks for their consideration the differences between the Churches concerning the use of unleavened bread in the Eucharist, Purgatory, the Papal Primacy, the words used in consecration. The Pope had already laid before them a statement of the views which the Latins would be ready to accept. The only question was that those who were in favour of the Union should win over the rest to accept the proffered terms. The subject of Purgatory had already been threshed out at Ferrara, and the difference was seen to be slight. A satisfactory form of agreement was soon found. It was laid down that those who died in sin went to eternal punishment, those who had been purged by penitence went to heaven and beheld the face of God, those who died in penitence before they had

CHAP.
VIII

Death of
the Patri-
arch June
10, 1439.

Discus-
sions on
minor
points.
June 1439.

---

[1] Migne, clix. p. 1088 : ἔπεσχον καὶ αὐτὸς τὴν γραφὴν ἵνα μὴ πρὸς ὀργὴν αὐτοὺς ἐρεθίσας εἰς προὖπτον ἤδη τὸν κίνδυνον ἐμαυτὸν ἐμβαλῶ.

[2] It runs—

    Ecclesiæ Antistes fueram qui magnus Eoæ
      Hic jaceo magnus religione Joseph,
    Hoc unum optaram, miro inflammatus amore,
      Unus ut Europæ cultus et una fides.
    Italiam petii, foedus percussimus unum ;
      Junctaque Romanæ est me duce Graia fides.
    Nec mora, decubui ; nunc me Florentia servat,
      Qua tunc concilium floruit urbe sacrum.
    Felix qui tanto donarer munere vivens,
      Qui morerer voti compos et ipse mei.

produced worthy fruits of penitence for their omissions and commissions went to Purgatory for purification by pains, and for them the prayers and alms of the faithful availed, as the Church ordained. The use of leavened or unleavened bread was a small point of ritual, on which the Latins could urge that their own custom of using unleavened bread was more in accordance with the facts of the institution of the Sacrament, as it was clear that at the time of the Passover Christ could only have unleavened bread. The Pope declared that, though the Latin Church used unleavened bread, the Sacrament might also be celebrated with leavened bread. The question was left open. As to the consecration of the elements, the Greeks were in the habit of using after the words of consecration a short prayer of S. Basil that the Spirit might make the bread and wine the Body and Blood of Christ. The Latins demanded that the Greeks should declare that the Sacrament was consecrated only by the words of Christ. The Greeks did not doubt the fact, but objected to the declaration as unnecessary. It was agreed that it should be made verbally, and not inserted in the Articles of Union.

Question
of the
Papal Su-
premacy.

So far all went smoothly enough; but the greatest difficulty arose about the Papal Supremacy. Up to this point the Greeks might flatter themselves that they had been making immaterial compromises or engaging in verbal explanations. Now they had to face the surrender of the independence of their Church. However true it might be that they must make some sacrifices to gain political consideration, the recognition of the Papal headship galled their pride to the quick. The Pope demanded that the Greeks should recognise him as the chief pontiff, successor of Peter, and vicar of Christ, and admit that he judged and ruled the Church as its teacher and shepherd. The Greeks requested that their own privileges should be reserved. There was a stormy discussion. At length the Greeks, on June 22, proposed to admit the Pope's Supremacy with two provisoes: (1) That the Pope should not convoke a Council without the Emperor and Patriarch, though if they were summoned and did not come, the Council might still be held; (2) That in case an appeal were made to the Pope against a Patriarch, the Pope should send commissioners to investigate and decide on the spot without summoning the Patriarch to the Council.

Next day the Pope answered roundly that he intended to keep all his prerogatives, that he had the power of summoning a Council when it was necessary, and that all Patriarchs were subject to his will. On receiving this answer the Emperor angrily said, 'See to our departure.' It seemed that the negotiations were to be broken off, and that the Greeks would not give way. But next day, June 24, being the festival of S. John Baptist, was given to religious ceremonies. The Greeks who had committed themselves to the Union, Bessarion, Isidore of Russia, and Dorotheus of Mitylene, spent the time in trying to arrange a compromise. Reflection brought greater calmness to the Emperor, and on June 26 Bessarion and his friends submitted a proposal couched in vaguer terms: 'We recognise the Pope as sovereign pontiff, vicegerent and vicar of Christ, shepherd and teacher of all Christians, ruler of the Church of God, saving the privileges and rights of the Patriarchs of the East.' This was accepted by the Pope. Nothing now remained save to draw up in a general decree the various conclusions which had been reached. For this purpose a committee of twelve was appointed, which laboured for eight days at the task.

On July 4 the decree was finished. When it was taken to the Emperor he objected to the fact that it ran in the Pope's name, in the usual style of an ecclesiastical decree, and he insisted on the addition of the words—'with the consent of the most serene Emperor and Patriarch of Constantinople.' On July 5 it was signed separately by the Latins and the Greeks. It bears the signature of one hundred and fifteen Latin prelates and abbots, and of thirty-three Greek ecclesiastics, of whom eighteen were metropolitans. A great majority of the Greeks signed it unwillingly. Syropulus tells us of many machinations which were used to win their assent. On the one hand, the declared will of the Emperor drove the compliant to submission; on the other hand, Papal largess was doled out to the needy, and social cajoleries were heaped upon the vain. Mark of Ephesus, alone of those who were at Florence, had the courage of his opinions and refused to sign. He was too considerable a person to be intimidated by the Emperor, and too stubborn a conservative to be won over by the Pope. In spite, however, of the pathetic account of Syropulus, it is difficult to feel much

CHAP.
VIII.

Acceptance
of Union by
the Greeks.
July 5,
1439.

sympathy with the reluctant Greeks. They knew, or they might
have known, when they left their home what they had to
expect. It was a question of political expediency whether or no
it was desirable in their imminent peril to abandon their
attitude of isolation, and seek a place amid the nations of
Western Christendom. If so, they must expect to make some
sacrifice of their ancient independence, to overthrow some of
the walls of partition which their conservatism had erected
between themselves and the Latin Church. An acknowledgment
of the Papal Supremacy was the necessary price for Papal aid.
It was useless to appear as beggars and demand to retain all
the privileges of independence. It was useless to advance so
far on rational calculations of expediency, and to raise objections
the moment that the actual pinch was felt by national vanity. The
wisest heads among the Greeks confessed that since the Greek
Church was no longer the centre of a vigorous national life, it
must conform in some degree to the Latin Church if the
Greeks looked for aid to the Latin nations. Moreover, the
circumstances of the time were such that the Pope was as
anxious for the Union as were the Greeks themselves. The
Latins were willing to accept vague conditions and to agree
readily to compromises. The Greeks could not complain that
they were hardly pressed in matters of detail.

On July 6 the publication of the Decrees took place in the
stately cathedral of Florence. The Greeks had at least the
satisfaction of outdoing the Latins in the splendour of their
vestments.[1] The Pope sang the mass. The Latin quire sang
hymns of praise ; but the Greeks thought their Gregorian music
barbarous and inharmonious.[2] When they had ended the Greeks
sang their hymns in turn. Cesarini read the Union Decree in
Latin and Bessarion in Greek ; then the two prelates embraced
one another as a symbol of the act in which they had engaged.
Next day the Greeks who had been spectators of the Latin
mass asked that the Pope should in like manner be present at
the celebration of their mass. They were told that the Pope
was not certain what their mass was, and would like to see it

---

[1] Vespasiano Fiorentino in his Life of Eugenius says, ' I Greci con abiti
di seta al modo Greco molto ricchi ; e la maniera degli abiti Greci pareva
assai più grave et più degna che quella de' prelati Latini.'

[2] ἡμῖν δὲ ὡς ἄσημοι ἐδοκοῦν φωναὶ ἐμμελεῖς, says Syropulus, p. 295.

performed privately before he committed himself to be present at a public ceremony. The Greeks refused to subject themselves to this supervision. The Emperor said indignantly that they had hoped to reform the Latins, but it seemed that the Latins only intended to reform them.

The Greeks were now anxious to depart, but waited to receive from the Pope five months' arrears of their allowance. The Pope tried to raise some other questions for discussion, chief of which was divorce, which the Greek Church allowed, while the Latin Church did not. He suggested that they should at once proceed to the election of a Patriarch. The Emperor refused any further discussion, and said that they would proceed to elect a Patriarch on their return, according to their own customs. The Pope requested that Mark of Ephesus should be punished for his contumacy, but this also the Emperor wisely refused. To make assurance doubly sure, the Pope demanded that five copies of the Union Decree should be signed by the original signataries, one for the Greeks, the rest to be sent to the princes of Europe. The Greeks objected that this was unnecessary; at last, however, they agreed to sign four duplicates, on the understanding that no further difficulties were to be put in the way of their departure. On July 20 the Greek prelates began to quit Florence. The Emperor remained till August 26, when he made his way to Venice, and returned to Constantinople after an absence of two years.

'Have you won a triumph over the Latins?' was the question eagerly asked of the returning prelates. 'We have made a satisfactory compromise,' was the general answer. 'We have become Azymites' (so the Latins were called by the Greeks because they used unleavened bread in the mass), 'we have become Azymites, and have betrayed our Creed,' said Mark of Ephesus, and the Greek people took his view of the matter. They were profoundly conservative, and though their leaders might see the necessity of departing from their national isolation, the people could not be induced to follow the new policy. The Greek prelates who at Florence had unwillingly accepted the Union could not stand against the popular prejudice, and by their excuses for what they had done only tended to inflame the popular wrath. Mark of Ephesus became a hero; the

prelates who had wished for the Union were treated with con-
tumely. The Emperor was powerless. The Bishop of Cyzicum,
whom he made Patriarch, was looked upon with aversion as a
traitor. When he gave the people his blessing many of them
turned away that they might not be defiled by one tainted
with the leprosy of Latinism. The Emperor, finding that he
could do nothing to abate the force of this popular feeling,
adopted an attitude of indifference. The Pope supplied for the
defence of Constantinople two galleys and 300 soldiers, as
he had promised; but no great expedition was equipped by
Europe against the Turks. The Emperor's brother, Demetrius,
despot of Epirus, who had been with him in Italy, and had
been a spectator of all that had there been done, actually ventured to raise a rebellion. He combined Turkish aid with the
fanatical feeling of the extreme Greek party against the Latins,
and for some time troubled his brother. The three Patriarchs
of Jerusalem, Antioch, and Alexandria issued in 1443 an
encyclical letter, in which they condemned the Council of
Florence as a council of robbers, and declared the Patriarch of
Constantinople a matricide and heretic.

General
results
of the
Council of
Florence.
Thus the Council of Florence was productive of no direct
fruits. The Popes did not succeed in establishing their supremacy
over the Greek Church; the Greeks got no substantial aid
from Western Christendom to enable them to drive away their
Turkish assailants. Yet the Council of Florence was not
utterly useless. The meeting of two different civilisations and
schools of thought gave a decided impulse to the literary world
of Italy, and attracted thither some of the leaders of Greek
letters. It was not long before Gemistus Pletho took up his
abode at Florence, and Bessarion became a cardinal of the
Roman Church. Greek letters found a home in the West; and
when the impending destruction at last fell upon Constantinople, the Greek exiles found a refuge prepared for them by
their fellow-countrymen.

To Eugenius IV. and to the Papacy the Council of Florence
rendered a signal service. However slight its ultimate results
might be, it was the first event since the outbreak of the
Schism which restored the ruined prestige of the Papacy.
Public opinion is naturally influenced chiefly by accomplished
facts. No one could judge of the permanence of the work, but

all were in some measure impressed by a new sense of the Papal dignity when they heard that, downcast as he was, Eugenius IV. had still succeeded in healing the schism which had so long rent asunder the Christian Church. The Pope whose name was loaded with obloquy at Basel had been accepted as supreme at Constantinople. The power which was hard pressed at Rome still had sufficient vigour to win new conquests abroad. With lofty exultation Eugenius IV. wrote to the princes of Christendom, and announced the success of his efforts. He recapitulated his labours in this holy cause, carried on in spite of many discouragements, because he knew that only in Italy, and only in the presence of the Pope, could this great result be obtained.[1] It was a home thrust which the fathers of Basel would find it hard to parry.

The Council of Florence was felt to be a triumph of Papal diplomacy. The prospect of it had drawn from Basel all men possessed of any moderation. The Italians saw in it the means of reasserting their hold on the headship of the Church, which the transalpine nations had begun to threaten. In union with the Greeks, they saw the beginning of a new epoch of crusades, in which the Papacy might again stand forth as the leader of the Latin race. The acute statesman and learned scholar, Francisco Barbaro, who was at that time Capitano of Brescia, wrote to the Archbishop of Florence at the beginning of the Council, pointing out the means to be employed. Learning and argument, he said, were useless; for the Greeks were too acute and too proud of their knowledge to be overcome by disputation. They must be treated with tact and with kindness; they must be led to see that in union lies their safety and glory. He urged the necessity of the greatest care. The union must be made to succeed; otherwise there was no chance for the Papacy, and Italian affairs would be plunged into hopeless confusion.[2] The policy recommended by Barbaro was that pursued by the Pope's advisers. Cesarini's experience at Basel

---

[1] Raynaldi, sub anno, § 9: 'Inter afflictiones et angustias multas invictam semper tenuimus patientiam, ne tantum bonum deseri pateremur: sciebamus enim rem istam per alium explicari non posse'

[2] See the letters of Barbaro in Pez, *Thesaurus*, vi. pt. 3, 172, &c. On March 1, 1438, he writes (p. 185): 'Nisi sapienter resistatur et cum Græcis rite et ordine res componantur, in magna perturbatione futura sunt omnia nisi præter expectationem hominum saluti divinitus remedium afferatur.'

had fitted him admirably for the work to be done at Florence. The Papal diplomacy won a signal triumph, and followed up its first victory by others, less conspicuous indeed, but which added strength to the Papal cause. In December 1439 the reconciliation of the Armenians to the Roman Church was announced to Europe, and Jacobites, Syrians, Chaldæans, and Maronites in succeeding years made illusory submission, which served to present a dazzling display of Papal power.

CHAPTER IX.

THE GERMAN DECLARATION OF NEUTRALITY AND THE ELECTION OF FELIX V.

1438–1439.

EUGENIUS IV. might triumph at Florence; but the fathers of Basel, weakened yet not dismayed, pursued their course with an appearance of lofty indifference. In January 1438 they suspended Eugenius IV. from his office for venturing to summon a Council to Ferrara without their assent. The logical consequence of such a step was the deposition of Eugenius, and to this Cardinal d'Allemand and his followers were ready to proceed. But, although all who had any leaning towards Eugenius, or who had any scruples about the omnipotence of the Council, had already left Basel, there still remained many who did not wish to proceed at once to extremities. Motives of statesmanship and considerations of expediency landed them in a somewhat illogical position. Through their desire to support the Council without attacking the Pope they were nicknamed at Basel 'the Greys,' as being neither black nor white.[1] This party, though it had the weakness which in ecclesiastical matters always attaches to a party that is trimming through political pressure, was still strong enough to put off for some time the deposition of Eugenius. It raised technical points, disputed each step, and gave weight to the remonstrances against a new schism which came from the princes of Europe.

Accordingly, says Æneas Sylvius, the question of procedure against Eugenius was discussed according to the Socratic method. Every possible suggestion was made, and every possible objection was raised against it. Was Eugenius to be dealt

CHAP.
IX.

Attitude of
the Council of Basel.
1438.

---

[1] Æn. Syl., *De Con. Basil.* (ed. 1700), p. 9. 'Quorum postea sectam Wilhelmus. Constantiensis Juris consultus, *Griæam* appellavit.'

with simply as a heretic, or as a relapsed heretic, or was he a heretic at all? On such points the fathers differed; but they agreed on March 24 in fulminating against the Council of Ferrara, declaring all its procedure null and void, and summoning all, under pain of excommunication, to quit it and appear at Basel within thirty days.

Declara-
tion of the
neutrality
of Ger-
many.
March 17,
1438.

It was, however, impossible that this war between the Pope and the Council could continue without exciting serious attention, on political grounds, amongst the European nations most nearly interested in the Papacy. Germany and France, about the same time, took measures to protect themselves against the dangers with which they were threatened by the impending outbreak of a schism. What Germany desired was a measure of ecclesiastical reform without the disruption of the unity of the Church. It felt no interest in the struggle of the Council against the Pope; rather the German princes looked with suspicion upon the avowed object of the Council, of exalting the ecclesiastical oligarchy at the expense of the Papacy. It bore too near a resemblance to their own policy towards the Empire, and they did not wish to be embarrassed in their own schemes by an access of independence to the bishops. Accordingly the Electors entered into correspondence with Cesarini in 1437, and lent their support to his efforts for a compromise between the Pope and the Council. When this failed, the Electors, under the guidance of Archbishop Raban of Trier, devised a plan of declaring the neutrality of Germany in the struggle between the Pope and the Council; by so doing they would neither abandon the reformation of the Church nor assist in creating a schism, but would be in a position to take advantage of any opportunity that offered. This scheme was, no doubt, suggested by the example of the withdrawal of the French allegiance from Boniface XIII., and had much to be said in its favour. The Electors had sent to obtain the assent of Sigismund when the news of his death reached them.

In March 1438 the Electors met for the purpose of choosing a new king at Frankfort, where they were beset by partisans of Eugenius IV. and of the Council. They resolved that before proceeding to a new election they would secure a basis for their new policy. In a formal document they publicly declared on March 17 that they took no part in the differences between the Pope and the Council, nor would they recognise the punishments, processes, or excommunications of either, as of any validity within the Empire. They would maintain the rights of the Church till the new king found means to restore unity; if he had not done so within six months, they would take counsel of the prelates and jurists of their land what course to adopt.[1] Next day Albert, Duke of Austria and King of Hungary, Sigismund's son-in-law, was elected king, as Sigismund had wished and planned.

CHAP. IX.

This declaration of neutrality was a new step in ecclesiastical politics, and was equally offensive to Pope and Council, both of whom were loud in asserting that in such a matter neutrality was impossible. Both hastened to do all they could to win over Albert; but Albert was not easy to win over, nor indeed was he in a position to oppose the Electors. His hold on Hungary, threatened by the Turks, was but weak, and Bohemia was insecure. His personal character was not such as to afford much opportunity for intrigue. He was upright and honest, reserved in speech, a man who thought more of action than of diplomacy. Tall, with sunburnt face and flashing eyes, he took his pleasure in hunting when he could not take it in warfare, and was content to follow the advice of those whom he thought wiser than himself.[2] Ambassadors could do nothing with him, and in July he joined the band of the Electors, and declared himself personally in favour of neutrality.

Election of Albert II. March 18, 1438.

The example of Germany was followed by France. Germany had taken up the attitude most in accordance with its views; France proceeded to do likewise. For the large questions of Church government involved in the struggle between Council and Pope, France had little care. Since their failure at Constance the theologians of the University of Paris had sunk into lethargy. France, suffering from the miseries of its long war with England, took an entirely practical view of affairs. Its object was to retain for its own uses the wealth of the

Pragmatic Sanction of Charles VII. May 1438.

---

[1] Müller, *Reichstagstheatrum*, i. 22, &c.

[2] Æneas Sylvius, in Palacky, *Italienische Reise*, 116: 'Fuit vir magnæ staturæ, venationis cupidus, in armis promptus, facere quam dicere malebat; non ipse per se cernens sed acquiescens consiliis eorum quos bonos existimavit; nigra facie, oculis terribilibus, malorum omnium hostis.'

Church, and prevent Papal interference with matters of finance. Charles VII. determined to adopt in his own kingdom such of the decrees of the Council as were for his advantage, seeing that no opposition could be made by the Pope. Accordingly a Synod was summoned at Bourges on May 1, 1438. The ambassadors of Pope and Council urged their respective causes. It was agreed that the King should write to Pope and Council to stay their hands in proceeding against one another; meanwhile, that the reformation be not lost, some of the Basel decrees should be maintained in France by royal authority. The results of the synod's deliberation were laid before the King, and on July 7 were made binding as a pragmatic sanction [1] on the French Church. The Pragmatic Sanction enacted that General Councils were to be held every ten years, and recognised the authority of the Council of Basel. The Pope was no longer to reserve any of the greater ecclesiastical appointments, but elections were to be duly made by the rightful patrons. Grants to benefices in expectancy, 'whence all agree that many evils arise,' were to cease, as well as reservations. In all cathedral churches one prebend was to be given to a theologian who had studied for ten years in a university, and who was to lecture or preach at least once a week. Benefices were to be conferred in future, one-third on graduates, two-thirds on deserving clergy. Appeals to Rome, except for important causes, were forbidden. The number of Cardinals was to be twenty-four, each of the age of thirty at least. Annates and first-fruits were no longer to be paid to the Pope, but only the necessary legal fees on institution. Regulations were made for greater reverence in the conduct of Divine service; prayers were to be said by the priest in an audible voice; mummeries in churches were forbidden, and clerical concubinage was to be punished by suspension for three months.' [2] Such were the chief reforms of its own special grievances, which

---

[1] The term Pragmatic Sanction is explained by S. Augustine, *Coll. III. cum Donatistis*: '*Pragmaticum rescriptum* quod supra *praceptum Imperiale* dicitur.' Similarly Æneas Sylvius in his *Commentaries* says: '*Pragmaticam sanctionem* quidam rescriptum principis esse dixerunt, nos melius sanctionem de causis possumus appellare   *Pragma* enim Græcè, Latinè *causam* significat ; apud Gallos autem *pragmatica sanctio* lex est quædam de negotiis ecclesiasticis '

[2] It is given in full in *Ordonnances des Rois de France de la troisième race*, xiii. 267; briefly in Martene, *Amp. Coll.* viii. 945, and in Münch.

France wished to establish. It was the first step in the
assertion of the rights of national Churches to arrange for
themselves the details of their own ecclesiastical organisation.
It went no further, however, than the amendment of existing
grievances as far as the opportunity allowed. It rested upon no
principles applicable to the well-being of Christendom. While
Germany, true to its imperial traditions, was content to hold its
hand till it discovered some means of bringing about a reformation without a schism, France entered upon a separatist policy
to secure its own interests.

The issue of both these plans depended upon the struggle
between the Pope and the Council. Charles VII. besought the
Council to suspend their proceedings against the Pope, and
received an answer that it was doing so. On July 12, at a Diet
held at Nürnberg, the Electors offered to mediate between the
Pope and Council, but were answered by the Council's envoys
that secular persons might not judge ecclesiastical matters, and
that it would be a bad precedent if Popes and Councils were
interfered with.[1] The Electors, with Albert's assent, extended
the neutrality for four months. On October 16, at a second
Diet at Nürnberg, appeared Cardinal Albergata, as the head
of a Papal embassy; but the envoys of the Council, headed by
the Patriarch of Aquileia, were received with greater marks of
distinction. Eugenius IV. never again subjected any of his
cardinals to such a slight, but chose less important and more
skilful diplomatists. The Electors again offered to mediate, on
the basis that the Councils of Ferrara and Basel should alike
be dissolved, and a new one summoned at another place. The
Basel envoys replied that they had no instructions on this matter;
they asked if the Electors accepted the decrees of the Council,
and were answered in turn that envoys should be sent to Basel
to answer this question. At Basel accordingly there was much
negotiation with the German envoys, who were joined by those
of the other princes, but the fathers resolutely opposed a translation of the Council, and rejected all proposals tending to that end.
When the third Diet met at Mainz on March 5, 1439, matters
had advanced no farther than they were at first.

The
Electors
vainly offer
to mediate
between
Pope and
Council.
July to
October
1438.

---

[1] Patricius, ch. 80 : 'Quoniam non liceret seculares principes de rebus
ecclesiasticis judicare, neque esset utile reipublicæ ut principes videantur legem
præscribere Concilio generali et Romano pontifici.'

BOOK
III.

The Diet of
Mainz pub-
lishes its
acceptance
of some of
the decrees
of Basel.
March
1489.

To Mainz Eugenius sent no envoys; but many of his adherents were there to plead his cause, chief amongst whom was
Nicolas of Cusa, a learned theologian who had been an admiring
follower of Cesarini, 'the Hercules of Eugenius' party,' as Æneas
Sylvius calls him.[1] But the Electors now wavered in their
policy of mediation, and began to turn their eyes to the
example of France. They tended towards using the opportunity for establishing the privileges of the German Church.
The Council sent again the Patriarch of Aquileia. But the
German princes had by this time seen that a reconciliation
between Pope and Council was impossible. They had an adviser of keen sagacity in the legist John of Lysura, sprung, like
Nicolas of Cusa, from a little village in the neighbourhood of
Trier.[2] He was the firm upholder, if not the originator, of the
policy of neutrality. He now advised the Electors, if nothing
were to be gained by mediation, to follow the example of
France, and secure such of the work of the Council of Basel as
satisfied them. On March 26 the Diet took the unwelcome
step of publishing its acceptance of the Basel decrees concerning the superiority of general councils, the organisation of
provincial and diocesan synods, the abolition of reservations
and expectancies, freedom of election to ecclesiastical benefices,
and the abolition of annates and other oppressive exactions of
the Curia. The Pope was not to refuse confirmation to the
election of a bishop, except for some grave reason approved by
the cardinals. Appeals to Rome until the cases had been heard
in the Bishops' courts, were, with few exceptions, forbidden.
Excommunications were not to be inflicted on a town for the
fault of a few individuals. Such were the chief provisions of
this pragmatic sanction of Germany.

Hopes of
Pope and
Council.
' The state of things which now existed in France and Ger-
many was really a reversion to the system of concordats with

---

[1] *De Concil. Basil.* p. 9: 'Hercules tamen omnium Eugenianorum Nicolaus Cusanus existimatus est, homo et priscarum literarum eruditissimus
et multarum rerum usu perdoctus, cujusque dolendum sit tam nobile ingenium
ad illa schismatis studia divertisse, ut legatione ad Græcos vigore falsi Decreti
fungeretur.' The last sentence refers to the fact that Nicolas was one of the
ambassadors sent to Constantinople in the name of the minority, who claimed
to pass their decree of May 7, 1437.

[2] About Lysura see Æn. Sylv., *De Ratisbonensi Dieta*, in Mansi, *Orationes
Pii II.*, iii. 66. At Basel he and Cusa were looked upon with equal dislike,
and there was a saying current : ' Cusa et Lysura pervertunt omnia jura.'

which the Council of Constance had ended. The rights that had then been granted by the Papacy for five years, and had afterwards proved mere illusory concessions, were now extended and secured. The strife between the Pope and the Council enabled the State in both countries to assert, under the sanction of a General Council, liberties and privileges which needed no Papal approval. Such a policy of selection was opposed equally to the ideas of the Council and of the Pope. The Council wished for adhesion to its suspension of Eugenius IV.; the Pope was not likely to acquiesce quietly in the loss of his prerogatives and of his revenues. Meanwhile, however, each was bent on using its opportunities. Eugenius IV. hoped by the brilliancy of his success at Florence to establish himself again in a position to interfere in European affairs. The Council trusted that, if it carried to extremities its proceedings against the Pope, Germany and France, after establishing reforms by virtue of its authority, would be driven to approve of a decisive step when it was once taken.

Accordingly at Basel the process against Eugenius IV. was prepared. The proctors of the Council gathered together a hundred and fifty articles against the Pope, swelling the number of charges to make the matter look more terrible,[1] though all converged to the one point, that Eugenius by dissolving the Council had made himself a schismatic and the author of a schism. It was clear that such a process might be protracted endlessly by a few determined opponents at every stage in the pleadings. The more resolute spirits, led by a Burgundian abbot Nicolas, carried the adoption of a more summary method of procedure. The Council was summoned to discuss the heresy of Eugenius and set forth the great points of Catholic doctrine which he had impugned. This discussion took place in the middle of April, and for six whole days, morning and afternoon, the dispute went on. First the theologians laid down eight conclusions ; *Discussion at Basel on the heresy of Eugenius IV. April 1439.*

(1) It is a truth of the Catholic faith that a General Council has power over a Pope or any other Christian man.

(2) It is likewise a truth that the Pope cannot by his authority dissolve, transfer, or prorogue a General Council lawfully constituted.

---

[1] Patricius, ch. 72 : 'Causidicorum more, capitibus centum et quinquaginta, ut res atrocior videretur, patribus proponunt.'

(3) Anyone who pertinaciously opposes these truths is to be accounted a heretic.

(4) Eugenius IV. opposed these truths when first he attempted by the plenitude of the Apostolic power to dissolve or transfer the Council of Basel.

(5) When admonished by the Council he withdrew his errors opposed to these truths.

(6) His second attempt at dissolution contains an inexcusable error concerning the faith.

(7) In attempting to repeat his dissolution he lapses into the errors which he revoked.

(8) By persisting in his contumacy, after admonition by the Council to recall his dissolution, and by calling a Council to Ferrara, he declares himself pertinacious.

The Archbishop of Palermo, who had formerly distinguished himself as an opponent of Eugenius IV., now at his King's bidding, counselled moderation. He argued with much acuteness that Eugenius had not contravened any article of the Creeds, nor the greater truths of Christianity, and could not be called heretical or relapsed. John of Segovia answered that the decrees of Constance were articles of faith, which it was heresy to impugn. The Bishop of Argos followed on the same side in a speech of much passion, which the Archbishop of Palermo indignantly interrupted. The Bishop of Argos called the Pope 'the minister of the Church.' 'No,' cried the Archbishop of Palermo, 'he is its master.' 'Yet,' said John of Segovia, 'his title is "servant of the servants of God."' The Archbishop of Palermo was reduced to silence.

The discussion went on; but really narrowed itself to two questions, 'Has a General Council authority over a Pope? Is this an article of faith?'[1] The disputation at last ended and the voting began. Three deputations at once voted for the conclusions of the theologians. The fourth deputation accepted the first three conclusions, but doubted about the last five; it hoped by delay to keep the whole question open. When the day came for a general congregation to be held, the Archbishops of Milan and Palermo prepared for resistance with the aid of the ambassadors of the princes. They pressed for delay, on the

[1] A summary of these arguments on the two points is given by Æneas Sylvius, *De Concil. Basil.*, p. 16-42.

ground that the princes of Europe were not sufficiently represented. When they had finished their arguments, Cardinal
d'Allemand made a splendid speech for a party leader. The
princes of Europe, he said, were well enough represented
by their prelates; the Archbishops of Milan, Palermo, and
Lyons had said all that could be said. They had complained
that the voice of the bishops was disregarded in the Council,
and that the lower clergy carried everything against them.
What Council had done so much to raise the condition of
bishops, who till now had been mere shadows with staff and mitre,
different only in dress and revenues from their clergy? The
Archbishop of Palermo had said that his opinion ought to prevail because more bishops were on his side. The order of the
Council could not be changed to suit his convenience; it had
pleased him well enough so long as he was in the majority.
Everybody knew that the prelates were only anxious to please
their princes; they confessed to God in private, to their political
superiors in public. He himself maintained that it was not the
position, but the worth, of a man that was of importance. 'I
could not set the lie of the wealthiest prelate above the truth
spoken by a simple priest. Do not, you bishops, despise your
inferiors; the first martyr was not a bishop but a deacon.' The
example of the early Church showed that Councils were not
restricted to bishops. If it were so now, they would be at the
mercy of the Italians, and there would be an end to all further
reforms. The Archbishop of Palermo pressed for delay only as a
means of wasting a favourable opportunity. He threatened
them with the anger of princes, as if the Council was to
obey princes, and not princes the Council. They must cleave to
the truth at all hazards. He ended by urging them to affirm
the first three conclusions, as a means of stopping the intrigues
of Eugenius IV., and defer for the present the remainder in
deference to the Archbishop of Palermo's request.

All listened with admiration to the dashing onslaught of
d'Allemand. But on the attempt to read the decree affirming the
three conclusions a scene of wild clamour and confusion arose,
as had happened two years before. The Patriarch of Aquileia
turned to the Archbishop of Palermo and cried out 'You don't
know the Germans; if you go on thus, you will not leave this
land with your head on your shoulders.' There was a loud cry

that the liberty of the Council was being attacked. Again the citizens of Basel had to interfere to keep the peace. The fathers were free to conduct their debates at pleasure, but a citizen guard was always present to see that arguments were not enforced by stronger than verbal means.[1]

When silence was restored, the debate was resumed for a while, till Cardinal d'Allemand again rose to put the question. The Archbishop of Palermo interposed, saying, ' You despise our entreaties, you despise the kings and princes of Europe, you despise the prelates ; but beware lest, while you despise all, yourselves be despised by all. We have the majority of prelates on our side, we form the Council. In the name of the prelates I declare that the motion must not be carried.' There was a hubbub as of a battle-field, and all was again confusion. John of Segovia was sufficiently respected by both parties to obtain a hearing while he denounced the scandal of the day's proceedings, urged the observance of the ordinary procedure of the Council, and defended the authority of the president. His speech made no impression on the Archbishop of Palermo, who declared that he and the prelates of his party constituted the Council and would not allow any decree to be published in the teeth of the protest he had just made. No one kept his seat ; the rival partisans gathered round their leaders, the Cardinal of Arles and the Archbishop of Palermo, and looked like two armies drawn up for contest. It seemed that the Archbishop's policy would prevail, that the congregation would be ended by the evening darkness without passing any vote, and thus a substantial triumph be gained for Eugenius IV. The followers of the Cardinal of Arles loudly upbraided him with his incompetency : ' Why do you sleep? Where is now your courage and your skill ? '

But the Cardinal was only waiting his time. When a slight lull prevailed he called out suddenly in a loud voice, ' I have a letter just come from France which contains wonderful, almost incredible news, which I would like to lay before you.' There was at once silence, and D'Allemand began to read some triviali-

---

[1] *Æn. Syl., De Concil. Basil.*, 60 : ' Servaverunt semper hunc morem cives, ut in omni negotio adesse curarent, quod pariturum dissensiones arbitrarentur, illud præcipue adcaventes ne qui tumultus fierent, neve aliæ quam verbales rixæ.'

ties; then the pretended letter went on to say that messengers of Eugenius IV. filled France and preached that the Pope was above the Council; they were gaining credit, and the Council ought to take measures to check them. 'Fathers,' said the Cardinal, 'the necessary measures are found in the eight propositions which you have examined, all of which, however, you do not intend at present to pass; but I declare the three first to be passed, in the name of the Father and the Son and the Holy Ghost.' Thus saying, he hastily left his seat and was followed by his triumphant partisans. He had snatched a formal victory at a time when defeat seemed imminent. He had shown that French craft was a match for Italian subtilty.

A few days afterwards arrived from Mainz the ambassadors of the Electors, from whom the opponents of the decree expected help in their resistance. But the Electors at Mainz had practically forsaken their position of mediators. They had seen the hopelessness of mediation unless supported by a general agreement of European powers. Private interests prevailed too strongly for this to be possible. Portugal and Castile were at variance. Milan and Aragon had their own ends in view in any settlement that might be made with the Pope. The attitude of France was dubious; and the Germans suspected that France aimed at getting the Council into its own hands, and reviving the French hold upon the Papacy. The Electors had no settled policy, and were content with a watchful neutrality. The German ambassadors did nothing at Basel, though an attempt was made to revive the national divisions, and procure joint action on the part of the German nation. On May 9 the German ambassadors were present, though by an accident, at a general congregation which accepted the form of decree embodying the conclusions previously passed. Again there was a stormy scene. The Archbishop of Milan denounced the Cardinal of Arles as another Catiline, surrounded by a band of ruffians. When the Cardinal of Arles began to read the decree the Archbishop of Palermo thundered forth his protest. Each side shouted down the other, to prevent their proceedings from claiming conciliar validity. The Cardinal of Arles rose to leave the room. His opponents prepared to stay and enact their protest; but a sudden cry of one who declared that he would not be untrue to his oath, and allow the Council to degenerate into a conventicle,[1] recalled all to a sense of the gravity of the situation. All felt that they were on the verge of disruption of the Council. The Cardinal resumed his seat; those who were departing were recalled. The Bishop of Albi read a protest to himself, for no one could hear him for the hubbub. The Lombards, Castilians, and Aragonese declared their adhesion to the protest, and left the congregation. The Cardinal of Arles then went on with the ordinary business, late though it was, and the form of decree was at last adopted. As the Archbishop of Palermo left the Council he turned to his followers and said with indignation, 'Twice, twice.' It was the second time that the policy of the Cardinal of Arles had been too acute for him, and had baffled his attempts at obstruction.

The decree condemning the heresies of Eugenius IV. is passed. May 16, 1439.

. For a few days the followers of the Archbishop of Palermo absented themselves from the meetings of the deputations; and on May 15 the ambassadors of the Electors feebly protested that they did not assent to any proceedings which were contrary to the conclusions of the Diet of Mainz. Next day they tried to make a compromise, but failed, as the opponents of the decree could not make up their minds what terms they were prepared to accept. A session was held on the same day, May 16, for the publication of the decree. The greater number of prelates refused to be present. None of the Aragonese bishops, none from any of the Spanish kingdoms, would attend. From Italy there was only one, and from the other kingdoms only twenty. But the Cardinal of Arles was not deterred by their absence. He had a large following of the inferior clergy, and had recourse to a strange expedient to cast greater ecclesiastical prestige over the assembly. He gathered from the churches of Basel the relics of the saints, which, borne by priests, were set in the vacant places of the bishops. When the proceedings began, the sense of the gravity of the situation moved all to tears. In the absence of opposition the decree was read peaceably, and was formally passed.

On May 22 the ambassadors of the princes appeared in a general congregation, and took part in the business, excusing themselves for their previous absence on the ground that it

---

[1] Æn. Syl., De Concil. Basil., 74. '"Absit a me," inquit Pater, "ut in vestro conventiculo maneam aut aliquid agam quod jurejurando a me præstito sit adversum."'

was not their duty as ambassadors to mix with such matters. It
was clear from such vacillating conduct on the part of their
representatives that the princes of Europe had little real interest in the struggle between Pope and Council. They had
ceased to act as moderators, and had no large views about the
need of ecclesiastical reforms. They were content to gain what
they could for their separate interests, as they understood them
at the moment, and to let the whole matter drift. They were
incapable of interposing to free the question of reform from the
meshes of personal jealousy in which it had become entangled.
So long as every power which could interfere with their own
projects was enfeebled, they were content that things should
take their own course. The only man at Basel with a settled
policy was the Cardinal of Arles; and he was no more than a
party leader, bent on using the democracy of the Council as a
means of asserting the power of the ecclesiastical oligarchy
against the Papal monarchy.

Emboldened by his first triumph, the Cardinal of Arles Deposition
of Eu-
genius IV.
decreed at
Basel.
June 25,
1439.
pursued his course. The German ambassadors still urged a
suspension of the process against the Pope. On June 13 a
solemn answer was made by the Council that the process
had now been suspended for two years in deference to the
wishes of princes. They must not take it amiss if the Council,
whose business it was to regulate the affairs of the Church,
declined to delay any longer. Faith, religion, and discipline
would be alike destroyed if one man had the power to set
himself against a General Council, and bear a tyrant's sway
over the Church; they would rather die than desert the
cause of liberty.[1] The ambassadors were silent when, on
June 23, the remaining five of the eight conclusions were
decreed by the Council, and Eugenius IV. was cited to appear
in two days and hear his sentence. The plague was at this
time raging in Basel, and very little pressure would have suf-
ficed to induce the fathers to transfer the Council elsewhere; but
there was no real agreement amongst the powers of Europe.
The session on June 25 was attended by thirty-nine bishops and
abbots, and some 300 of the lower clergy. Eugenius IV. was
summoned by the bishops, and when he did not appear was
declared contumacious. He was declared to be a notorious

[1] Cf. Patricius, ch. 91.

cause of scandal to the Church, a despiser of the decrees of the Holy Synods, a persistent heretic, and destroyer of the rights of the Church. As such he was deposed from his office; all were freed from his allegiance, and were forbidden to call him Pope any longer. The dominant party in the Council had everything to win and nothing to lose by pursuing to its end the quarrel with the Pope. In the divided state of political interests there was a chance that some of the European powers might be drawn to its side if once a decided step were taken. But it forgot, in the excitement of the conflict, that the Council's hold upon men's obedience was a moral hold, and rested upon hopes of ecclesiastical reform. When this had been sacrificed to the necessities of a party conflict, when a schism and not a reformation was the issue of the Council's activity, its authority was practically gone. It required only a little time to make this clearly manifest.

The Council, however, did not hesitate in its course. On the day of the deposition of Eugenius IV. a consultation was held about future procedure; and the opinion of John of Segovia was adopted, to defer for sixty days the election to the vacant office of Pope. The position of the Council was discouraging. The plague, which since the spring had been raging in Basel, had grown fiercer in the summer heat. Five thousand of the inhabitants are said to have fallen before its ravages. Terror prevailed on every side, and it was hard to keep the Council together. The learned jurist Pontano and the Patriarch of Aquileia, two pillars of the Council, were amongst those who fell victims to the mortality. The streets were thronged with funerals and priests bearing the sacrament to the dying. The dead were buried in pits to save the trouble of digging single graves. Æneas Sylvius was stricken by the plague, but recovered. Eight of his friends amongst the clerks of the Council died.[1]

In spite of all danger and the repeated advice of his friends

---

[1] See his account of the plague, *De Concil. Basil.*, 85, and *Commentarii*, 7. His own cure is thus described : ' Quoniam sinistrum inguen læsum erat sinistri pedis vena aperta est; tum die toto et in partem noctis prohibitus somnus; exin pulvis quidam ehibitus est, cujus materiam medicus revelare noluit; ulceri et loco læso nunc rafani viridis succi pleni incisæ portiones, nunc madidæ cretæ frusta supponebantur. Inter hæc aucta febris ingentem capitis dolorem et salutis desperationem adduxit.'

that he should flee before the pestilence, the Cardinal of Arles stood to his post, and so kept the Council together. At the beginning of October the business of the Council was resumed, and the method of the new election was discussed. The College of Cardinals was represented in Basel only by Louis d'Allemand. It was clear that 'electors must be appointed. After some discussion their number was fixed at thirty-two, but there were many opinions about the means of choosing them. At last William, Archdeacon of Metz, proposed the names of three men who should be trusted to co-opt the remaining twenty-nine. The three whose high character and impartiality were supposed to place them above suspicion were Thomas, Abbot of Dundrennan, in Scotland,[1] John of Segovia, a Castilian, and Thomas of Corcelles, Canon of Amiens. At first this plan met with great objections; but they gradually disappeared on discussion. The Germans urged that they were not represented, and it was agreed that the three should associate with themselves a German, Christian, Provost of S. Peter's in Bruma, in the diocese of Olmütz. They took an oath that they would choose fitting men who had the fear of God before their eyes, and would not reveal the names of those they chose till the time of their publication in a general Congregation.

Triumvirs appointed to nominate electors for the Papacy.

The triumvirs at once set about their business. They conferred with representative men of every nation; they did their best to acquaint themselves with the characters of those whom they had in view. Yet they displayed singular discretion in their inquiries; and when, on October 28, they met to make their election, no one knew their intentions. Next day the congregation was crowded to hear their decision. Everywhere speculation was rife. The more vain and more simple among the fathers displayed their own estimate of their deserts by appearing in fine clothes, with many attendants, ready to enter the conclave at once.[2] Suspense was prolonged because the Cardinal of Arles was late. He appeared at last with a gloomy face, and took his seat saying, 'If the triumvirs have done well, I confess that I am rather late; if

Nomination of the Electors. October 1439.

---

[1] 'Abbatem de Dunduno, Ordinis Cisterciensis, Diocœsis Candidæ Casæ' (Whithern in Galloway), Æn. Syl., De Concil. Basil., p. 89.

[2] Æn. Syl., De Concil. Basil., 91.

they have done ill, I am too soon.' He was afraid that their democratic sympathies might have outrun his own. His words were an evil omen ; everyone prepared for a dissension, which in the matter of a new election would work irreparable ruin to the Council.

The triumvirs behaved with singular prudence. First Thomas of Dundrennan, then John of Segovia, explained the principles on which they had acted. They had regarded national divisions, and had considered the representative character of those whom they chose ; goodness, nobility, and learning had been the tests which they had used. The general result of their choice was that the electors would consist of twelve bishops, including the Cardinal of Arles, which was the number of the twelve apostles, seven abbots, five theologians, nine doctors and men of learning, all in priests' orders. This announcement in some degree appeased the general dread. When the names were read, the position of the men chosen and their distribution amongst nations met with general approval. The Cardinal's brow cleared ; he praised the triumvirs for their wisdom and prudence, and the Congregation separated in contentment. On October 30, after the usual ceremonies, the electors entered the conclave in the house *Zur Brücke*.

Amadeus
VIII.,
Duke of
Savoy,
candidate
for the
Papacy.

The Cardinal of Arles was, of course, ready with a nominee for the Papal office ; naturally, he had not proceeded to extremities without making preparations for the result. If the cause of the Council was to succeed, it must again strike its roots into European politics, and must secure an influential protector. As other princes had grown cold towards the Council, the Duke of Savoy had declared himself its adherent. The greater part of the fathers now remaining at Basel were Savoyards. Amadeus VIII. had ruled over Savoy since 1391. He was a prudent man, who knew how to take advantage of his neighbours' straits, and had greatly increased the dominions and importance of Savoy, till it embraced the lands that extended from the Upper Sâone to the Mediterranean, and was bounded by Provence, Dauphiné, the Swiss Confederacy, and the Duchy of Milan. Like many others, Amadeus VIII. had drawn his profits from the necessities of Sigismund, who, in 1416, elevated Savoy to the dignity of a duchy. The Duke of Savoy refused to take any side in the internal struggles of

France or in the war between France and England, but grew rich on his neighbours' misfortunes. He married a daughter of Philip the Bold, Duke of Burgundy; his eldest daughter was married to Filippo Maria, Duke of Milan, his second was the widow of Louis of Anjou. From his wealth, his position, and his connexions, the Duke of Savoy was a man of great political influence. But the death of his eldest son caused him deep grief and unhappiness. In 1431 he retired from active life, and built himself a luxurious retreat at Ripaille, whither he withdrew with seven companions to lead a life of religious seclusion. His abode was called the Temple of S. Maurice; he and his followers wore grey cloaks, like hermits, with gold crosses round their necks, and long staffs in their hands.[1] Yet Amadeus in his seclusion took a keen interest in affairs, and, when the suspension of Eugenius IV. was decreed by the Council, sent an embassy to the Pope excusing the Council, and offering to mediate. As matters went on, his support was more openly declared, and he offered to send to Basel the prelates of his land. During the year 1439 Savoyards had largely reinforced the Council, and the scheme of electing Amadeus as the future Pope had taken definite form. Amadeus had consulted other princes on the subject, and from the Duke of Milan had received the warmest promises of support. The electors to the Papacy had been chosen equally from the nations represented at the Council— France, Italy, Germany, and Spain. But, from its geographical position, Savoy was reckoned both in France and Italy. Of the twelve bishops amongst the electors seven were Savoyards; the others were the Cardinal of Arles, two French and one Spanish bishop, and the Bishop of Basel. Without any accusation of false play in the choice of the electors, it fell out that quite half of them were either subjects of Amadeus or were bound to him by ties of gratitude.

The proceedings of the conclave were conducted with the utmost decorum.[2] At its commencement the Cardinal of Arles

---

[1] See his life by Æn. Sylvius, *De Viris Claris*; in Mansi, *Orationes*, iii. 178. Æneas saw him at Ripaille, and says: 'Vitam magis voluptuosam quam penitentialem degebat' (*Comment.* 3).

[2] Æn. Sylvius, who was clerk of the Conclave, says, 'Nihil nisi honestum vidi' (*De Viris Claris*, 180). His account of the proceedings of the Conclave, *De Concil. Basil.*, p. 100, &c. is given in great detail.

BOOK
III.
Election of
Amadeus of
Savoy.
November
5, 1439.
reminded the electors that the situation of affairs needed a rich and powerful Pope, who could defend the Council against its adversaries. On the first scrutiny of votes it was found that seventeen candidates had been nominated, of whom Amadeus had the greatest number of votes—sixteen. On the next scrutiny he had nineteen votes, and on the third twenty-one. His merits and the objections that could be raised against him were keenly but temperately discussed, and in the final scrutiny on November 5 it was found that he had received twenty-six votes, and his election to the Papacy was solemnly announced by the Cardinal of Arles.

The Council published the election throughout Christendom, and named an embassy headed by the Cardinal of Arles, with seven bishops, three abbots, and fourteen doctors, to carry to Amadeus the news of his election. Probably from want of money, the embassy did not leave Basel till December 3, when it was accompanied by envoys of the citizens and several nobles. On reaching Ripaille they were met by the nobles of Savoy. Amadeus, with his hermit comrades, advanced to meet them with the cross borne before him. Amadeus entered into negotiations in a business-like spirit, and rather surprised the ambassadors of the Council by stipulating that a change should be made in the form of the oath administered to the Pope, that he should keep his hermit's beard and his former name of Amadeus. The envoys replied that the oath must be left to the Council; they could not alter the custom of assuming a. religious name; the beard might be left for the present. Amadeus also disappointed the Council's envoys by showing an unexpected care about his future financial position. 'You have abolished annates,' he said; 'what do you expect the Pope to live on? I cannot consume my patrimony and disinherit my sons.' They were driven to promise the cautious old man a grant of firstfruits of vacant benefices.

At last matters were arranged. Amadeus accepted his election, assumed the name of Felix V., and took the oath as prescribed by the Council. Then he left his solitude in Ripaille, and went in pontifical pomp to Tonon, where, amid the ecclesiastical solemnities of Christmastide, his friends were so struck by the incongruity of his bearded face that they persuaded him to shave. On the festival of the Epiphany he took the final step of separating himself from his worldly life by declaring his eldest son Louis Duke of Savoy, and his second son Philip Count of Geneva. By the Council's advice he agreed not to fill up the offices of the Curia, lest by so doing he should hinder the reconciliation of those who held them under Eugenius IV.; as a provisional measure they were put into commission. Felix V. also submitted to the Council's demand that, in the letters announcing his election, the Pope's name should come after that of the Council. On the other hand, the Council allowed him to create new cardinals, even in contradiction to their decrees on this point. Felix named four, but only one of those, the Bishop of Lausanne, as a dutiful subject, accepted the doubtful dignity, to which small hope of revenue was attached.

CHAP. IX.

On February 26 the Council of Basel issued a decree commanding all to obey Felix V., and excommunicating those who refused. This was naturally followed by a similar decree of Eugenius IV. from Florence on March 23. Neither of these decrees was very efficacious. Eugenius IV. had strengthened himself in December by creating seventeen cardinals, Bessarion and Isidore of Russia among the Greeks, two Spaniards, four Frenchmen, one Englishman (John Kemp, Archbishop of York), one Pole, one German, one Hungarian, and five Italians. Unlike the nominees of Felix, all accepted the office except the Bishop of Krakau, who refused the offers of both Popes alike. The news of the election of Amadeus at first caused some consternation in the court of Eugenius IV.; but the sagacity of Cesarini restored their confidence. 'Be not afraid,' he said, ' for now you have conquered, since one has been elected by the Council whom flesh and blood has revealed to them, not their Heavenly Father. I was afraid lest they might elect some poor, learned and good man, whose virtues might be dangerous; as it is, they have chosen a worldling, unfit by his previous life for the office, one who has shed blood in war, has been married and has children, one who is unfit to stand by the altar of God.' [1]

Views of Eugenius IV. and his Curia.

Felix V. did not find matters easy to arrange with the Council. He stayed at Lausanne for some time, and did not comply with the repeated requests of the fathers that he would hasten to Basel No steps were taken to provide for the support

[1] Æn. Syl., *Comment.* ed. Fea. p. 79.

BOOK
III.
———
Coronation
of Felix V.
July 24,
1440.

of the Papal dignity. The letter of Felix V. nominating the Cardinal of Arles as president of the Council, was ruled to be so informal that it was not inserted in the Council's records. Questions concerning the Council's dignity in the presence of the Pope gave rise to many discussions; it was agreed that the Pope and his officials should take an oath not to impede the jurisdiction of the Council over its own members. Not till June 24, 1440, did Felix enter Basel accompanied by his two sons, an unusual escort for a Pope, and all the nobility of Savoy. On July 24 he was crowned Pope by the Cardinal of Arles, the only cardinal present. The ceremony was imposing, and more than 50,000 spectators are said to have been present. Felix V. looked venerable and dignified, and excited universal admiration by the quickness with which he had mastered the minutiæ of the mass service. No expense was spared to give grandeur to the proceedings; the tiara placed on Felix's head cost thirty thousand crowns. After this, Felix abode in Basel awaiting the adhesion of the princes of Europe.

The two Popes were now pitted one against the other; but their rivalry was unlike any that had existed in former times. Each had his pretensions, each represented a distinctive policy; but neither had any enthusiastic adherents. The politics of Europe were but little concerned with ecclesiastical matters; the different States pursued their course without much heed to the contending Popes. Germany was the least united State and had the least determined policy. To Germany both Eugenius IV. and Felix V. turned their attention; each strove to end its neutrality favourably to himself. The hopes of both parties were awakened by the death of Albert II., on October 27, 1439. He died in Hungary of dysentery, brought on by eating too much fruit when fatigued in hot weather. Albert in his short reign had not succeeded in restoring order in the Empire, in giving peace to the Church, or in protecting his ancestral kingdoms; but his noble and disinterested character, his firmness and constancy, had roused hopes in men's minds, which were suddenly extinguished by his untimely death. It became at once a question what would be the policy of the Electors during the vacancy in the Empire.

1440–1444.

THE German Electors heard at the same time the news of the death of Albert II, and of the elevation of Amadeus to the Papal dignity. They refused to receive either the envoys of Eugenius IV. or of Felix V., and renewed their declaration of neutrality. Everything urged them to hasten their election to the Empire, and on February 1, 1440, they unanimously chose Frederick, Duke of Styria, second cousin of the deceased king and head of the house of Austria. Frederick was a young man, twenty-five years of age, whose position was embarrassing and whose responsibilities in Germany were already heavy. He was guardian of the county of the Tyrol during the minority of Sigismund, son of that Frederick who had played so luckless a part at Constance. Moreover, Albert II. died without male heir, but left his wife pregnant; when she gave birth to a son, Ladislas, Frederick became guardian also of Bohemia and Hungary. At his election Frederick was held to be sagacious and upright; but he was not likely to interfere with the plans of the electoral oligarchy. Representatives of the two Popes at once beset both Electors and King. Frederick III., unlike his predecessor, was not committed definitely to the policy of neutrality, and only said that he proposed at the first Diet to confer with the Electors about the means of amending the disorders in the Church. He took no steps to hasten the summoning of a Diet, which met at Mainz a year after his election on February 2, 1441. Even then Frederick III. did not appear in person.

Meanwhile Felix V. had received the adhesion of a few of the German princes. In June, 1440, Albert of Munich recognised him, and in August Stephen of Zimmern and Zweibrücke

CHAP.
X.

Election of
Frederick
III. Feb-
ruary 1,
1440.

came to Basel with his two sons, and did him reverence. Albert of Austria, brother of Frederick III., followed, as did also Elizabeth of Hungary, widow of the late king. On the other hand Felix V. met with a decided rebuff in France, where a synod was held at Bourges to hear ambassadors of both Popes. On September 2 answer was made in the King's name that he recognised Eugenius IV., and besought his relative, ' the lord of Savoy' (as he called Felix V.), to display his wonted wisdom in aiming at peace. France had no reason to deviate from her old policy, especially as Eugenius IV. maintained the cause of René of Anjou in Naples. The Universities, especially those of Vienna, Köln, Erfurt, and Krakau, declared themselves in favour of Felix V. It was but natural that the academic ideas, from which the conciliar movement sprang, should accept the issue which followed from the application of their original principle. The Council was especially anxious to gain the adhesion of the Duke of Milan, and Felix consented to pay a large subsidy in return for his protection. But Filippo Maria Visconti merely played with the offers of Felix. He promised to send envoys, but nothing came of it. In like manner Alfonso of Aragon adopted an ambiguous attitude. Both these princes wished to play off Felix V. against Eugenius IV. in Italian affairs, but saw nothing to be gained by committing themselves too definitely.

Felix V. and the Council. 1440.
Thus Felix V. was supported by no great power, and the schism had little influence on the mind of Europe. Felix V. represented only the new-fangled ideas of the Council—ideas which had long deserted the sphere of practical utility, and so had lost their interest. Felix V. and the Council were indissolubly bound together. The Council, in electing a Pope, had taken its last step. Felix V. could not dissolve the Council against its will, and was helpless without it. Yet, in spite of their close connexion, it was difficult to regulate the relations between the two. There was at the outset a difficulty about money. The Council had elected the Duke of Savoy as a man who would spend his money in its behalf. Felix V. demanded that the Council should make due provision for its Pope and his cardinals. This could only be done by granting to Felix V. what had been taken away from Eugenius IV. The reforming Council must admit that it could not afford to carry out its

own reforms; there was no escape from this admission. On August 4 a decree was passed giving the Pope for five years a fifth, and for the succeeding five years a tenth, of the first year's revenues of all vacant benefices. It is true that the reason assigned for this special grant was to enable him to rescue from tyrants the patrimony of S. Peter. None the less it awakened opposition from the Germans in the Council, and was defended only by the fact that it was practically inoperative except in the dominions of Savoy. It brought little money; and when, on October 12, Felix V., at the instance of the Council, nominated eight cardinals, amongst whom were the Patriarch of Aquileia and John of Segovia, the question of their revenues again became pressing. On November 12 six cardinals were created to conciliate France. It was necessary to have recourse to the old system of provisions of benefices to supply them with revenues. Felix V. chafed under the restraints which the Council laid upon him, and took advantage of the absence of the Cardinal of Arles in November to preside over the Council, and pass some decrees which awoke much comment. When he asked to have the same rights granted to him over ecclesiastical benefices in Savoy as the Pope exercised in the States of the Church, the Council refused the demand.

Meanwhile Frederick III. gave no signs of his intention. This indecision, which was the result of indolence and infirmity of purpose, passed at first for statesmanlike reserve. Both parties looked to the Diet at Mainz for an opportunity of achieving a signal victory. They were disappointed to hear that the King found himself too much engaged with difficult matters in his own States to undertake in person the affairs of Germany. He sent four commissioners to Mainz, who were to hear the arguments of the rival claimants. Eugenius IV. had learned wisdom by former experience, and sent as his representatives two men skilled in affairs, but not of high dignity, Nicolas of Cusa, a deserter from the Council, who well knew the temper of Germany, and John of Carvajal, a Spaniard of great personal piety and worth, a trained official of the Papal court. The Council, on the other hand, sent its highest dignitaries, Cardinal d'Allemand and three of the new cardinals, chief of whom was John of Segovia. John claimed to appear as Papal Legate; but when he was entering with pomp the Cathedral of

Diet of
Mainz.
March
1441.

Mainz the Chapter met him, and declined to admit his legatine
authority, so that he was obliged to retire. The Diet decided to
hear him as an ambassador of the Council, but not to recognise
on either side the claims of any dignity which had been conferred since the declaration of neutrality. When the Council's
representatives tried to resist this decision, they were told by the
citizens of Mainz that their safe-conduct would be revoked
within eight days if they did not submit to the demands of the
Diet. They were driven sullenly to give way, and only the
Cardinal of Arles received the honour due to his office.

The Diet
proposes
a new
Council.
On March 24 D'Allemand appeared before the Diet, and
pleaded the cause of the Council, while his colleagues remained
sulkily at home. Next day Carvajal and Cusa answered him,
and seemed to produce considerable effect upon those present,
the Electors of Trier and Mainz, the king's commissioners, the
ambassadors of France, and a few German nobles. Stung by
the success of Cusa, John of Segovia laid aside his pride, assumed a doctor's robes, and with great clearness and cogency
restated the Council's position. He produced a vast treatise,
divided into twelve books, in which he had argued out at
length the various points raised by his speech. Carvajal and
Cusa replied. When John of Segovia wished to return to
the charge the Diet ruled that it had heard enough. It is
no wonder that it quailed before John of Segovia's treatise,[1]
especially as the matter in dispute was one in which Germany
took a political, not an ecclesiastical, interest. A paper was
circulated amongst the members of the Diet, most probably
the work of Jacob, Archbishop of Trier, urging the acceptance of whichever Pope would summon a new Council, to be
organised by nations, and would guarantee to the German
Church the reforms which it had claimed for itself. In accordance with this plan the Diet laid before the rival parties the
old proposal that a new Council should be summoned in some
neutral place with the concurrence of the kings of Europe. Six
places in Germany and six in France were submitted for choice,
and Frederick III. was to negotiate with the two Popes further
arrangements for this new Council, which was to meet on
August 1, 1442.

Both parties retired from Mainz disappointed, and beset

[1] A summary of this discussion is given by Patricius, ch. 117, 118.

Frederick with embassies. Frederick, who was rapidly showing himself to be a master of the art of doing nothing, said that he proposed to hold another Diet at Frankfort next year, when the question might be again discussed. He was not altogether satisfied with the policy adopted by the Diet. The Diet was ready to recognise the Pope who would grant to the German Church such reforms as suited the Electors; Frederick III. was desirous to recognise the Pope who was generally held to be legitimate, especially if in so doing he could further his own interests.

Pending the next Diet, the fathers at Basel composed and disseminated statements of their cause. Their proceedings otherwise were not very harmonious. There was the old difficulty about money. Felix V. complained that he incurred great expenses in sending out embassies and the like, while he received little or nothing. The Cardinals clamoured for revenues, and the officials of the Curia claimed their share of such money as came in. The Council granted to Felix a bishopric, a monastery, and one benefice in Savoy till he should recover the States of the Church. An outcry was raised against the excessive fees of the Papal Chancery; the officers answered that they only exacted the dues recognised by John XXII. Want of money led to a strict inquiry into the conduct of the financial officers of the Council; and this caused great bitterness. Felix sent the captain of his guard to imprison some who were accused of malversation. The Council loudly complained that their liberty was infringed, and called on the citizens of Basel to maintain their safe-conduct. The magistrates interfered, restored peace, and fined the Pope's captain. The Council urged on Felix V. to send embassies on all sides to set forth his cause. Felix V. answered that embassies were costly things, and as yet he had got little for his money spent on them. The Council, believing in the power of plausibility, commissioned the Archbishop of Palermo to draw up a letter to be presented to Frederick III. When he had done his work it did not satisfy them, and the facile pen of Æneas Sylvius was employed to put it into a more seductive form. The time for the Diet of Frankfort was drawing near, and Felix was prevailed to send another embassy. His cardinals at first pleaded their outraged dignity, and refused to go. Felix bade

them disregard their clothes in the interests of truth and justice. The Cardinal of Arles, the Archbishop of Palermo, and
John of Segovia accepted the office and set out in May 1442.

Eugenius IV. meanwhile had asserted his authority by decreeing, on April 26, 1441,[1] the transference of his Council from
Florence to Rome, on the ground that Rome was a fitter place
to receive the ambassadors of the Ethiopian Church, who were
conducting an illusory reconciliation with the Papacy. It was
a proud assertion of Papal superiority over Councils. An attempt was made by the more decided of the Electors to obtain
the assent of Eugenius IV. to the policy which they had put
forward at Mainz. A learned jurist, Gregory Heimburg, was
sent to Florence with the proposals of the Electors, drawn out
in the form of two bulls, one dealing with the new Council, the
other with the liberties of the German Church. Eugenius gave
no definite answer, as Heimburg brought with him no credentials. He deferred his answer to the Diet at Frankfort. But this
negotiation showed a disposition on the part of the German
princes at this time to take the matter into their own hands,
without waiting for Frederick, whose dubious attitude was probably due to a hope of winning back from the Swiss cantons
some of the Habsburg possessions, with which view he did not
choose to quarrel with Basel or with Savoy.[2]

On May 27 Frederick arrived in Frankfort with the three
ecclesiastical Electors, the Count Palatine, and the Duke of
Saxony. The Council was represented by its three Cardinals ;
Eugenius IV. by Carvajal and Cusa, as before. But they were
not permitted to air their eloquence before the King. He
decided, before entering the troubled sea of ecclesiastical disputes, to secure his position by the prestige of a coronation,
and announced his intention of going to Aachen for that purpose. In his absence commissioners would hear the arguments
of the rival envoys, that on his return he might not find them
contending. The Cardinal of Arles, as a prince of the Empire,
accompanied the King ; but at Aachen he was shut out of the

---

[1] Patricius. ch. 129, gives 1442 as the date of this translation. Mansi
in his note on Raynaldus, *sub anno* 1441, proves that the first embassy of the
Ethiopians was in 1441, and corrects the error of Patricius. The decree of
translation was signed in 1441, though Eugenius stayed in Florence till the
beginning of 1443.

[2] For these negotiations see Pückert, *Die Kurfürstliche Neutralität*, 170, &c.

cathedral by the Bishop as being excommunicated.   At Frank-
sioners for three days, and Cusa, not to be outdone, did the
same.   The weary commissioners asked that the arguments
might be reduced to writing, which was done.   On Frederick's
return, July 8, they were laid before him, and the business of
the Diet commenced.   The plan of the five Electors for recognising Eugenius was, under Frederick's influence, laid aside.
At Aachen he had signed a treaty with Zürich to help him to
recover his ancestral domains.   The Electors agreed to stand
by their King, and leave in his hands the decision of the ecclesiastical question.

The policy adopted at Frankfort did not in its contents   German
envoys sent
to the two
Popes.
differ from that previously followed.   Envoys were to be sent to
Eugenius and to Basel, urging the summons of an undoubted
Council.   But the object of this new embassy was the glorifica-
tion of the new King of the Romans.   Six places were proposed
for the Council, all in Germany, because in Germany was
greater liberty and security than in other kingdoms, where
war prevailed and scarcity was felt.   Punctilious orders were
given to the ambassadors as to the manner in which they were
to observe the neutrality.   Eugenius IV. was to be treated with
the ordinary respect due to the rank which he had held before
the declaration of neutrality.   Felix V. was not to be treated as
Pope.   Everything was done to convince both parties that they
must submit their cause to the decision of the German King.

From Frankfort Frederick III. made a kingly progress   Answer
of the
Council.
through Elsass and the Swiss Cantons, which received him
with due respect.   He was accompanied by the Cardinal of
Arles, and proposals were made to him for a marriage with Margaret, the daughter of Felix V., and widow of Louis of Anjou.
Frederick III. does not seem to have rejected the proposal.
It suited him to take no decisive steps.   He promised to visit
Basel, but demanded that first his ambassadors should be
heard, and an answer be returned by the Council, which, sorely
against its will, was driven to consider the proposal of the Diet.
After many discussions and many complaints, the Council
answered that, though they were lawfully assembled and enjoyed full security at Basel, and would run many dangers in
changing their place, still, in their desire for peace, they were

BOOK
III.
willing to agree to the King's proposal, provided the King and princes would promise obedience to all the decrees of the new Council, and also would agree to choose the place of its meeting from a list which the fathers in Basel would submit. It was clear that such reservations made their concession entirely futile.

Frederick
III. in
Basel.
November
1442.
On receiving this answer Frederick III. entered Basel on November 11, and was honourably received by the Council. He maintained, however, an attitude of strict neutrality, and visited Felix V. on the understanding that he was not to be expected to pay him reverence as Pope. The interview took place in the evening; Felix V. appeared in Papal dress, with his nine cardinals, and the cross carried before him. The Bishop of Chiemsee on Frederick's behalf explained his master's attitude, and was careful to address Felix as 'your benignity,' not 'your holiness.' Nothing was gained by the interview. Frederick was respectful, but nothing more. The marriage project did not progress, though Felix is said to have offered a dowry of 200,000 gold ducats provided he was recognised as Pope. Frederick left Basel on November 17, saying, 'Other Popes have sold the rights of the Church; Felix would buy them, could he find a seller.'[1]

Answer of
Eugenius
IV.
December
1442.
The German envoys to Eugenius IV. were referred to a commission, chief amongst whom was the canonist, John of Torquemada, who raised many technical objections to their proposals. But Eugenius IV. refused to take advantage of the technicalities of the Commission. On December 8 he gave a decided answer. He wondered at the demand for an undoubted Council, seeing that he was then holding a Council which had done great things for Christendom, and to call it doubtful was nothing less than to oppose the Catholic faith. He did not call Frederick by his title of King, but spoke only of 'the Electors and him whom they had elected.' He was willing to summon more prelates to his Council at the Lateran, and leave them to decide whether any further steps were necessary. The answers of the Pope and the Council were formally reported to the envoys of the King and some of the princes at Nürnberg on February 1, 1443. They deferred their consideration to a Diet to be held in six months; but they fixed no place for its meeting. In fact, the German Electors were rapidly falling away

[1] Æn. Sylvius, *De Dictis Alfonsi*, lib. II. 46.

from their mediatorial attitude, which had never been very genuine. No sooner had Frederick III. succeeded in checking their league in favour of Eugenius IV. than a new league was formed in behalf of Felix V. The personal and family relationships of the House of Savoy naturally began to tell upon the German princes. A man who had a dowry of 200,000 ducats at his disposal was not likely to be without friends. In December 1442 negotiations were set on foot for a marriage between the son of the Elector of Saxony and a niece of Felix V. The Archbishop of Trier was busy in the matter, and stipulated for his reward at the expense of the Church. The Archbishop of Köln was a declared adherent of the Council. These Electors were indifferent which Pope was recognised; they only bargained that the victory should be won by their help, and that they should be rewarded by an increase of their power and importance. It was hopeless to attempt to secure for Felix V. universal recognition; but it would answer their purpose if he obtained by their means a really important position.[1] A league in favour of Felix V. was definitely formed, and its success depended upon obtaining the support of Frederick III. or of the French King.

The plan dearest to Frederick III. was the recovery of the old possessions of the House of Habsburg from the Swiss Confederates. His alliance with Zürich and his march through the lands of the Cantons was regarded by Frederick III. as an important step. But the jealousy of the Confederates was easily aroused, and the quarrels which had urged Zürich to seek alliance with Frederick soon revived. Zürich was called upon to renounce her alliance with Austria, and on her refusal was attacked. The war was waged with savage determination. Zürich was overmatched in numbers but trusted to Austrian help. Frederick III. could raise no forces in his own dominions, where he had troubles on every side. The German princes refused to send troops to prosecute a private quarrel of their King. A crushing defeat on July 22, 1443, threatened Zürich with destruction, and Frederick III., in his desire for aid, turned to the French King, and begged to have the loan of some of the disbanded soldiers, who were the miserable legacy to France of the long English war. These Armagnacs, as they were called after their former leader, were a formidable element in the French king-

[1] Cf. for these negotiations, Pückert, *Die Kurfurstliche Neutralität*, p. 195, &c.

dom, and Charles VII. was willing enough to lend them to his neighbours. But he also was ready to fish in troubled waters; and the embarrassments of the Empire suggested to him that he might extend his frontier towards the Rhine. Instead of 5,000 troops, as Frederick III. demanded, he sent 30,000; instead of lending them to the Austrian general, he sent them under the command of the Dauphin. Eugenius IV. tried to use this opportunity for his own purposes. He conferred on the Dauphin the title of gonfalonier of the Church, with a salary of 15,000 florins, in hopes that he would attack Basel and disperse the Council.[1] In August 1444 the French marched through Elsass, took Mümpelgard, and, spreading devastation in their way, advanced towards Basel. In a bloody battle on the little river Birs by the cemetery of S. Jacob, not far from the walls of Basel, a body of 1,500 Confederates fought for ten hours against the overwhelming forces of the French. They were cut to pieces almost to a man; but the victory was so dearly bought that the Dauphin made no further attempts to conquer Basel, or to fight another battle against the troops of the Cantons. He made peace with the Confederates through the mediation of the fathers of the Council, and retired into Elsass, where his troops pillaged at will.[2]

Plans of
Frederick
III. meet
with no
success.

This was the state of things when, at the beginning of August 1444, Frederick III. at last arrived at Nürnberg, to be present, as he had so often promised, at a Diet which was to settle the affairs of the Church. He had during the past year sent letters to the princes of Europe, begging them to consent to a General Council, which he, following the example of the Emperors Constantine and Theodosius, proposed to summon. He received dubious answers; it was clear that such a Council was impossible. The French King,' in his answer, said that it would be better to drop the name of a Council, and bring about an assembly of secular princes; where were the princes, there was also the Church.[3] Æneas Sylvius expresses the same

---

[1] Raynaldus, *sub anno* 1444, No. 13.

[2] For this interesting episode in Swiss history see Müller, *Geschichte der Schweizerischen Eidgenossenschaft*, Bk. III. pt. ii. ch. x.; or more in detail, Barthold, in *Historisches Taschenbuch*, 1844; Tuetey, *Les Ecorcheurs*, Montbéliard, 1874.

[3] Æn. Syl., *Com.* in Fea., 84: 'Relinquendum esse concilii nomen; convenire principes bonum esse et in rebus ecclesiæ sese aperire atque com-

opinion still more forcibly : ‘I do not see any clergy who would
suffer martyrdom for one side or the other. We all have the
same faith as our rulers, and if they were to turn idolaters, we
would do so too. We would abjure not only a Pope, but Christ
Himself at their bidding. For love has waxed cold, and faith
is dead.'[1] Fortified by the proposition of the French King,
Frederick III. put off his presence at a Diet till the need had
grown urgent. He went to Nürnberg more interested about
Swiss affairs than about the position of the Church.

On August 1 Frederick III. arrived in Nürnberg, where the
Electors of Trier, Saxony and Brandenburg, awaited him, and
were soon joined by the Archbishop of Mainz. Many of the
chief German princes were also there. Frederick's first desire
was to get help from the Diet against the Swiss Confederates;
but in this he was coldly listened to, and when the news of the
battle on the Birs reached Nürnberg the King was placed in a
sorry predicament.[2] The hungry bands of France had ravaged
the possessions of the Empire, and the Dauphin was already
negotiating peace with the enemies of Austria, whom he had
been summoned to overthrow. Frederick, crimson with shame,
had to listen to reproaches which he could not answer. The
only lesson which he learned from them was not to face another
Diet, a lesson which for the next twenty-seven years he steadfastly practised. The Diet appointed the Pfalzgraf Lewis general
of the army of the Empire against ‘ the strangers from France.’
Frederick III., by his supineness, had lost his control over the
German princes. A proposition which he put forward about
ecclesiastical matters—to extend the neutrality for a year, and
proclaim a Council to meet on October 1, 1445, at Constance,
or, failing that, at Augsburg—was not accepted. The Diet
separated without coming to any joint decision. The discord
between the King and the Electors had at length become
manifest.

Moreover, at Nürnberg the Pfalzgraf Lewis had been won
over to the side of Felix V. by a marriage contract with Mar-

ponere; nihil se dubitare ubi essent principes quin illic ecclesia esset,
conventumque illorum nullum prohibere posse.'
[1] Æn. Syl., *Epistolæ*, No. 54, ed. Basel.
[2] Æn. Sylvius, who was at Nürnberg, gives an account of the news that
reached him, Ep. 87.

garet, the daughter of Felix, whom Frederick III. had refused. Four of the six Electors were now leagued together in favour of Felix. It was a question how far they would succeed. The dispute between the two Popes had passed into the region of mere political expediency and personal intrigue. The whole matter was felt to centre in Germany, and in the midst of these political intrigues the Council of Basel. sunk to insignificance. Felix V. had found that the Council was useless to him, as well as irksome. Towards the end of 1443 he quitted Basel on the ground of health, and took up his abode at Lausanne. There he might live in peace, and be rid of the expense which the Council perpetually caused him.[1] Forsaken by the Pope of its own choice, the Council became a mere shadow. Its zeal and energy had been expended to little abiding purpose. After a glorious beginning, it had gone hopelessly astray, and had lost itself in a quagmire from which there was no escape.

The hopes of Felix V. entirely rested on Germany. Eugenius IV. relied upon the revival of his prestige, as sure to tell upon Italian politics, in which the Papacy was a necessary element to maintain the balance of power. In Italy Eugenius IV. had been slowly gaining ground. In 1434 the condottiere bishop, Giovanni Vitelleschi, had taken possession of Rome in the Pope's name, and ruled it with severity. Francesco Sforza had, however, gained a firm hold of the March of Ancona. The Duke of Milan encouraged Bologna in 1438 to throw off the Papal yoke, and declare itself independent; its example was followed by Faenza, Imola, and Forlì. The condottiere general, Niccolo Piccinino, in league with the Duke of Milan, beguiled Eugenius IV. into a belief that he was going against Sforza in the March. Suddenly he showed himself in his true colours, and prepared to enrich himself at the Pope's expense. Moreover, he planned an invasion of the Florentine territory, and was supposed to have drawn to his side the Papal general,

---

[1] One of the few remaining memorials of the connexion of Felix V. with Basel is a bell in the Cathedral, which bears the following quaint inscription :—

'Te, pia Virgo, colo; tibi me dat Papa, Maria ;
Hic Felix quintus, qui germinat ut terebinthus,
Me fieri fecit ; Felix vocor: is sine væ sit :
M, cum C quater X post tot, I jungito duplex

Vitelleschi. Vitelleschi with a strong hand introduced order into Rome and the neighbourhood; he even waged war against Alfonso in Naples. He enjoyed to the full the confidence of Eugenius IV., over whom he had greater influence than anyone else, and by whom he was created cardinal in 1437. Vitelleschi was a condottiere influenced by the same ambitions as Sforza and Piccinino, and in Rome he held an independent position which tempted him to act on his own account. He was known to be bitterly hostile to Sforza, and was negotiating with Picciuino for the overthrow of their rival. When Eugenius IV. summoned to the aid of the Florentines the Pontifical forces under the leadership of Vitelleschi, the cautious Florentine magistrates were alarmed lest the understanding between the two condottieri might prove stronger than Vitelleschi's obedience to the Pope. They laid before Eugenius IV. intercepted letters of Vitelleschi to Piccinino. The favourite had many foes among the Cardinals, who succeeded in persuading the Pope that Vitelleschi was a traitor. But Eugenius IV. dared not proceed openly against a powerful general. Secret orders were sent to Antonio Redo, captain of the Castle of S. Angelo, to take him prisoner. On the morning of his departure for Tuscany Vitelleschi came to give his last orders to the commander of the Castle; suddenly the drawbridge was raised, and Vitelleschi was wounded in three places. He was made prisoner, and resigned himself to his fate. When he was told that his captivity would be brief, as the Pope would soon be convinced of his innocence, he answered, 'One who has done such deeds as mine ought either never to have been imprisoned, or can never be released.' He died on April 2, 1440, and the rumour spread that his death was due to poison, and not to his wounds.[1] At all events, the Florentines were glad to be rid of Vitelleschi, and managed to persuade the Pope to appoint as his successor a man whom they could trust, Ludovico Scarampo, who had formerly been Archbishop of Florence. In June 1440 Eugenius IV. conferred on Scarampo and his own nephew, Pietro Barbo, the dignity of cardinal.

The fall of Vitelleschi freed Florence from the fear of

---

[1] Poggio, *Hist. Flor.*, bk. vii. Platina, in *Vita Eugenii*. Bonincontrii, *Annales*, Mur. xxi. 149. Petronius, Mur. xxiv. 1123.

BOOK
III.

Peace in
North
Italy. 1441.

Piccinino, for it restored the balance between him and his rival Sforza. But the Duke of Milan was growing weary of the indecisive war which he had been waging against the League of Venice, Florence, and the Pope. Sforza and Piccinino had won all that for a time they were likely to hold. All parties wished for peace, which was concluded at Cremona in November 1441, on the usual terms that each should keep what they had won. Sforza also received in marriage the illegitimate daughter of the Duke of Milan, Bianca, whose hand had often been promised him, and often refused. Eugenius IV. alone was discontented; for Sforza was left in possession of the March of Ancona and other conquests in the States of the Church.

Alfonso
enters
Naples.
June 1442.

In Naples also the Angevin party, which Eugenius IV. supported, was gradually giving way before the energy of Alfonso. In 1442 René was driven into Naples and there was besieged. His only hope was to gain assistance from Sforza; but the Duke of Milan, jealous of his powerful son-in-law, set Piccinino to keep him in check, and Eugenius IV., who now saw in Sforza his chief enemy, was only too glad to do his part of fulminating against him.[1] Alfonso pressed the siege of Naples, which he entered on June 2, 1442. René was driven to flee from the Castel Nuovo, where the superb triumphal arch in the inner doorway still stands to commemorate the entrance of Alfonso.[2] René fled on board a Genoese galley to Florence, where he received the Pope's condolences, and afterwards betook himself to his county of Provence.

Departure
of Eu-
genius IV.
from Flor-
ence.
March
1443.

The fall of the Angevin party in Naples greatly affected the policy and position of Eugenius IV. He had little to expect from France, whose position towards the Papacy was now declared. On the other hand, he had much to gain from Alfonso, and Alfonso had shown by his dealings with the Council of Basel that his chief object was to bring the Pope to terms. By an alliance with Alfonso, Eugenius could obtain help against Sforza, and could also pave the way for a peaceful return to

---

[1] Raynaldus, 1442, 11. In this Bull of deprivation Eugenius recapitulates all his wrongs at the hands of Sforza.

[2] This splendid example of Renaissance architecture is assigned by Vasari to Giuliano da Majano, but the inscription in S. Maria Nuova on the grave of the Milanese sculptor, Pietro di Martino, claims it for him. The frieze represents Alfonso in his triumphal car followed by his Court, the city magistrates and clergy.

Rome. He had begun to feel that in a contest against a pretender the establishment of his Curia in Rome would add to his prestige. He had already decreed the adjournment of his Council from Florence to the Lateran, and it was worth while to make his hold on Rome secure. Moreover, he had gained little by his alliance with Florence and Venice ; in the peace of 1441 they had regarded only their own interests and had paid no heed to his desires. Accordingly Eugenius IV. negotiated with Alfonso to recognise him in Naples, and legitimatize his son Ferrante, on condition that Alfonso helped him against Sforza. As this was a step alienating himself from the League and from Florence, Eugenius IV. found it desirable to leave Florence on March 7, 1443. The Venetians urged the Florentines to keep him prisoner, and only on the morning of his departure did the Florentines determine to let him go.[1] Yet the final departure was courteous on both sides, and Eugenius IV. thanked the magistracy for their hospitality. He betook himself to Siena, a city hostile to Florence, and, by so doing, gave a clear indication of his change of policy.

In Siena Eugenius IV. was honourably received, and concluded his negotiations with Alfonso. He also had an interview with Piccinino, and doubtless devised with him schemes against their common enemy Sforza. On September 13 he set out for Rome, where he arrived on September 28, after an absence of eight years. The Romans received their Pope with acquiescence, but without enthusiasm. Eugenius IV. settled down quietly into his capital, and proceeded at once to open his Council in the Lateran. But the Council of the Lateran was an empty form maintained against the Council of Basel, which was now weakened by the defection of Scotland, and Castile, as well as Aragon. Eugenius IV. trusted to diplomacy to destroy the last hope of Felix V., by driving Frederick III. to abandon the German neutrality. Meanwhile in Italy he had important work to do in using his new allies as a means of recovering from Sforza his possessions in the States of the Church.

In Italy circumstances favoured the Pope's policy. The

Eugenius IV. returns to Rome. September 1443.

---

[1] Vespasiano da Bisticci, *Vita di Agnolo Acciaiuoli.* 'La mattina che si partì papa Eugenio da Firenze, era stata grandissima disputazione di lasciarlo o non lasciarlo partire ; perchè i Vineziani facevano quello che poterono che i Fiorentini lo ritenessino per forza.' See also Vespasiano's *Vita di Lionardo d'Arezzo.*

BOOK
III.

Death of
Piccinino.
October
1444.

suspicious Duke of Milan was always jealous of his powerful son-in-law, and wished to keep him in check. Alfonso of Naples was true to his agreement with the Pope, and in August 1443 marched against Sforza. He was joined by Piccinino, and their combined army is said to have numbered 24,000 men, against which Sforza could only command 8,000. Sforza resolved to act on the defensive and secure his chief cities by garrisons; but many of the leaders in whom he trusted betrayed his cause. His ruin seemed imminent, when suddenly the Duke of Milan interposed on his behalf. He wished to see his son-in-law humbled, but not destroyed, and so prevailed on Alfonso to withdraw his troops. Sforza was now a match for Piccinino, and succeeded in defeating him in battle on November 8. But Piccinino was rich in the resources of Eugenius IV., while Sforza suffered from want of money. Both sides retired into winter quarters, and as spring approached Piccinino had a superior force at his command. Again the Duke of Milan interposed, and invited Piccinino to a conference on important affairs. No sooner was Piccinino absent than Sforza hastened to seize the opportunity. He gathered together his starving troops, and told them that now was their last chance of wealth and victory. His skilful generalship outmatched Piccinino's son, who, with the Papal legate, Cardinal Capranica, was left in charge of the troops of the Church. Piccinino, already an old man, had gone to Milan with sad forebodings; he was so overwhelmed with the news of this defeat, that he died of a broken heart on October 25, 1444. He was a marvellous instance of the power of genius over adverse circumstances. Small in stature, crippled through paralysis so that he could scarcely walk, he could direct campaigns with unerring skill; though devoid of eloquence or personal gifts, he could inspire his soldiers with confidence and enthusiasm. He was impetuous and daring, and showed to the greatest advantage in adversity. But he lacked the consistent policy of Sforza, and saw, in his last days, that he had founded no lasting power. With his death his army fell in pieces, and no captain was left in Italy to match the might of Sforza.[1]

When the fortunes of war had begun to turn against the Pope, Venice and Florence joined with the Duke of Milan in urging peace, which was accepted on condition that each party

[1] See Decembrio Candido's *Vita Niccolai Piccinini*, in Muratori, vol. xx.

should retain what it held on October 18. Sforza employed the eight days that intervened between the conclusion of the peace and the date for its operation in recovering most of the cities which had been won for the Pope. Eugenius IV. only retained Ancona, Recanati, Osimo, and Fabriano, and they were to remain tributary to Sforza.[1] His first attempt against the powerful condottiere had not met with much success. Next year, however, he was again prepared to take advantage of another quarrel which had arisen between Sforza and the Duke of Milan, and war again broke out. Bologna, which had been in the hands of Piccinino, proclaimed its independence under the leadership of Annibale Bentivoglio; but the Pope and the Duke of Milan both looked with suspicion on the independence of a city which each wished to bring under his own sway. In June, 1445, a band of conspirators, supported by the Duke of Milan, assassinated Annibale Bentivoglio after a baptism where he had been invited to act as godfather to the son of their ringleader. But their plan of seizing the city failed. The people were true to the house of Bentivoglio, and slew the assassins of Annibale. Florence and Venice came to their help. There was again war in Italy with Sforza, Florence, and Venice on one side, the Pope, Naples, and Milan on the other. Again Sforza was hard pressed, and the Papal troops overran the March of Ancona. In June, 1446, Sforza made a raid in the direction of Rome, and penetrated as far as Viterbo. But the cities shut their gates against him, and he had no means of besieging them.[2] Sforza's ruin seemed certain; Jesi was the only town in the March which he held. But luckily for him the Venetians took this opportunity to attack the Duke of Milan, who, being ill provided with generals, needed the help of Sforza, whose ambition was henceforward turned to a nobler prize than the March of Ancona, which fell back peaceably into the hands of the Pope.

Thus Eugenius IV., by stubborn persistency, succeeded in repairing the mischief of his first political indiscretion, and obtained again a secure position in Italy, while the mistakes of the Council had done much to restore his ecclesiastical power, which had been so dangerously threatened. The leading theologians of the Council had been driven to quit it and range

---

[1] Simoneta, Vita Sforzæ, Muratori, xxi. 361. [2] Ibid. Mur. xxi. 377.

themselves on the side of the Pope; only John of Segovia and John of Palomar remained true to the principles with which the Council opened. It is noticeable that the great advocate of the Council's power, Nicolas of Cusa, was now the chief emissary of Eugenius IV. Cusa had been taught in the school of Deventer, and came to Basel deeply imbued with the mystic theology of the Brethren of the Common Life. His work, 'De Concordantia Catholica,'[1] written in 1433, represented the ideal of the reforming party, a united Church reformed in soul and body, in priesthood and laity, by the action of a Council which should represent on earth the eternal unity of Heaven. Cusa's work was the text-book of the Council; yet its author was disillusioned, and found his theories fade away. He quitted Basel with Cesarini, and in common with others who felt that they had been led away by their enthusiasm, laboured to restore the Papal power which once he had striven to upset. The Council of Florence gathered round the Pope an extraordinary number of learned theologians, whose efforts were now devoted to the restoration of the Papacy. Again, after the interval of a century and a half, the pens of canonists were engaged in extolling the Papal supremacy. John of Torquemada, a Spanish Dominican, whom Eugenius IV. raised to the Cardinalate, revived the doctrine of the plenitude of the Papal power, and combated the claims of a General Council to rank as superior to the Pope.[2] Now, as in other times, the immediate results of an attack upon the Papal supremacy was to gather round the Papacy a serried band of ardent supporters; if the outward sphere of the exercise of the Papal authority was limited, the theoretic basis of the authority itself was made stronger for those who still upheld it.

These labours of theologians were to bear their fruits in after times. The immediate question for Felix V. and Eugenius IV. was the attitude of Germany towards their conflicting claims. Germany was to be their battlefield, and diplomacy their arms.

---

[1] See Cusani, *Opera*, Basil, 1565, vol. ii., and Düx, *Nicolas von Cusa*, ii. 252, &c.

[2] *Summa de ecclesia et ejus auctoritate* (Venice, 1561); also *De summa potestate pontificis et generalis concilii*, in Labbe, xiii., and Mansi, xxx.

THE PAPAL RESTORATION.

1444–1464.

CHAPTER I.

ÆNEAS SYLVIUS PICCOLOMINI AND THE RESTORATION OF THE OBEDIENCE OF GERMANY.

1444–1447.

CHAP.
I.

Early life
of Æneas
Sylvius
Piccolo-
mini.
1405–1451.

THE man who played the chief part in settling the ecclesiastical affairs of Germany was Æneas Sylvius Piccolomini, whose life was closely connected with the fortunes of the Papacy in this crisis, and whose character reflects almost every tendency of the age in which he lived.

Æneas Sylvius was born at Corsignano, a village near Monte-pulciano, in the year 1405, of the noble but decayed family of the Piccolomini. He was one of a family of eighteen, of whom only two daughters besides himself reached the age of maturity. As a youth Æneas helped his father to work in the fields, and picked up such education as his native village afforded. At the age of eighteen he left home, and with scanty provision of money betook himself to the University of Siena. There he applied himself diligently to study. Mariano Sozzini taught him civil law; the preaching of S. Bernardino kindled in him for a brief space the fervour of monastic devotion. The fame of Francesco Filelfo as a lecturer in Greek literature drew him for two years to Florence.[1] At last he settled in Siena as a teacher. But Siena was soon involved in war with Florence, and the prospects of literature seemed dark, when, in 1431, Domenico Capranica, on his way to Basel, needed a secretary, and offered the post to Æneas. The journey to Basel was difficult, as North Italy was involved in war. Æneas took ship at Piombino, and was nearly shipwrecked in a storm which suddenly arose. At last he reached Genoa in safety, and travelled through Milan and

---

[1] From a letter of Filelfo, quoted by Voigt, p. 17.

over the S. Gothard to Basel, where he arrived in the spring
of 1432.

Capranica received from the Council the dignity of Cardinal; but Eugenius IV. refused him its revenues, and he could
not long afford to keep a secretary. Æneas found a new
master in Nicodemo della Scala, Bishop of Freisingen, and when
he left Basel, transferred himself to the service of the Bishop
of Novara, with whom he went to Milan, and gained an
insight into the policy of the crafty Visconti. The Bishop of
Novara was one of the Duke's confidential agents, and sent
Æneas to the camp of Niccolo Piccinino, while he himself at
Florence plotted against the life of Eugenius IV., in 1435.
When the plot was discovered, and the Bishop of Novara's life
was in danger, Æneas took refuge with Cardinal Albergata, a
man of strict monastic piety, whom Eugenius IV. sent as one
of his legates to preside over the Council of Basel. On his
journey thither Albergata visited Amadeus of Savoy in Ripaille,
and Æneas was more impressed with the luxury than with the
piety of Amadeus' retreat. From Basel Æneas accompanied
Albergata to the Congress of Arras, where he had ample opportunities of learning the political condition of France and
England. From Arras he was sent on a secret mission to the
Scottish King,[1] most probably for the purpose of instigating him
to act as a check upon England, in case the resentment of the
English King were aroused by the pacification of Arras, which
was detrimental to English interests.

The remarks on England and Scotland made by the keen-
sighted Italian are interesting, not only in themselves, but
as showing the quickening power which the new learning had
given to the faculty of observation. Men's interests were rapidly
enlarging, their curiosity was awakened, they looked on the
world as their dwelling-place, and all things human had an
attraction for their own sake. Æneas writes in the spirit of a
modern traveller, and his picture is vivid and precise. He went
to Calais, but was suspected by the English, who would neither
allow him to go on nor return. At length the interference of

---

[1] In *Pii II. Commentarii*, the reason Æneas gives is 'qui prælatum quem-
dam in regis gratiam reduceret.' In *De Viris Claris*, xxxii. he says, 'pro li-
beratione cujusdam captivi.' Campanus, *Vita Pii*, says, 'ad Regem adversus
citeriores Britannos qui paci adversabantur sollicitandum.'

the Cardinal of Winchester enabled him to set sail for London.
London struck him as the wealthiest and most populous city he
had seen. He admired the grandeur of St. Paul's Cathedral,
and in the sacristy was shown a Latin translation of Thucydides,
which, he says, dated from the ninth century.[1] He was struck by
the noble river Thames and the old London Bridge, covered with
houses, like a city in itself. He heard and recorded the legend
that the men of Strood were born with tails. But, above all
else, he was amazed by the shrine of S. Thomas at Canterbury,
covered with diamants, pearls, and carbuncles, to which nothing
less precious than silver was offered. He failed, however, in the
object of his visit, as the English Court was too suspicious of
the secretary of Cardinal Albergata to give him a safe-conduct
to Scotland. Æneas was obliged to return to Bruges; but,
determined not to be baffled, he again took ship at Sluys and
set sail for Scotland. A terrible storm drove the ship to Norway, and only after a voyage of twelve days did Æneas land at
Dunbar. He had made a vow in his peril to walk barefoot to
the nearest shrine of Our Lady. A pilgrimage of ten miles to
the shrine of Whitekirk, through the snow and ice, was the beginning of an attack of gout in the feet, from which he suffered
for the rest of his life.

Æneas describes Scotland as a cold, barren, treeless country. *Æneas's*
Its towns were unwalled; the houses were built without mortar, *description*
were roofed with turf, and had doors of ox-hide. The people *of Scot-*
were poor and rough; the men small but courageous, the women *land.*
fair and amorously disposed. The Italian was surprised at the
freedom of manners in the intercourse of the sexes. The Scots
exported hides, wool, and salt fish to Flanders; they had better
oysters than England. The Highland and the Lowland Scots
spoke a different language; and the Highlanders lived on bark
of trees. They dug a sulphurous stone out of the ground which
they used for fuel. In winter their daylight lasted scarcely
more than four hours. There was nothing the Scots heard
with greater pleasure than abuse of the English.

Æneas was well received by the Scottish King, who gave him

---

[1] *Epistolæ*, cxxvi. ed. Basil. 'Apud Angliam in sacrario nobilis ædis S.
Pauli Londiniensis vetus his oria in manus venit, ante annos sexcentos, ut
signatum erat, conscripta. . . . Auctor historiæ Thucydides Græcus annotatus
erat, quem fama celebrem clarum novimus, translatoris nullum nomen
inveni.'

fifty nobles and two horses.[1] When he had done his business, the captain of the ship, in which he had come, offered him a passage back. But Æneas had had enough experience of the North Sea, and determined to return through England. The ship set sail and was wrecked before his eyes in sight of land. The captain, who was going home to be married, and all the crew, save four, were drowned. Thankful for his providential escape, Æneas, disguised as a merchant, crossed the Tweed, and entered the wild border country. He spent a troubled night amid a throng of barbarous people who encamped, rather than lived, in the desolate plain of Northumberland. When night came on, the men departed to a tower of defence, fearing a possible raid of the Scots. They left the women, saying that the Scots would not injure them, and refused to take Æneas with them. He and his three attendants stayed amid some hundred women who huddled round the watch fire. In the night an alarm was raised that the Scots were coming. The women fled; but Æneas, fearing he might lose his way, took refuge in a stable. It was, however, a false alarm, as the approaching band turned out to be friends not foes. At dawn he set out for Newcastle, and saw the mighty tower which Cæsar had built. Here once more he was in a civilised country. At Durham he admired the tomb of the Venerable Bede. He found York a large and populous city, with a cathedral memorable throughout the world, with glass walls between slender pillars.[2] He travelled to London with one of the Justices in Eyre, who, little suspecting the real character of his companion, denounced to Æneas the wicked machinations of Cardinal Albergata at Arras. In London Æneas found that a royal order forbade any foreigner to sail

---

[1] It is curious how Æneas picked up odd scraps of information. He says: 'Cornicem novam esse, atque idcirco arborem in qua nidificaverit, regio fisco cedere.' This seems unintelligible; yet a law was passed in the first Parliament of James I., 1424, *Acts and Constitutions of Scotland*, folio v. 1556, B. 1: 'Of bigging of Ruikis in Treis, Ca., xxi. Item, forthy that mē considderis that Ruikis biggand in Kirkis, Zairdis, Orchardis, or Treis, dois greit skaith apone Cornis, It is ordanit, that thay, that sie Treis pertenis to, lat thame to big, and suffer on na wyse that thair Birdis fle away. And quhair it be taintit that thay big, and the Birdis be flowin, and the nest be fundin in the Treis at Beltane, the Treis sal be forfaltit to the King and hewin down, and v. s. to the kingis unlaw.' 'Beltane' seems to be the name of an old pagan festival which was transferred to Whitsunday.

[2] 'Sacellum lucidissimum, cujus parietes vitrei inter columnas ad medium tenerissimas colligati tenentur.'—*Com.* 5.

without the King's permission. A judicious bribe overcame the guards of the harbour. Æneas set sail from Dover, and made his way safely to Basel.

For a time Æneas remained at Basel, where he led a jovial and careless life, making himself agreeable to men of all parties, and gaining a reputation for his elegant Latinity. When the combat between Pope and Council broke out, he was driven to take a side; but he did so dispassionately, with a clear perception of the selfish motives of the various parties.[1] He first came prominently forward in an eloquent speech in favour of Pavia as a meeting place with the Greeks; by this step he hoped to win the favour of the Duke of Milan, whose character he well knew. He was thanked by the Duke, and won the favour of the Archbishop of Milan, who presented him, though a layman, to a provostship in the Church of S. Lorenzo in Milan. To hold this as a layman, and without capitular election, he needed a dispensation from the Council, which had just prohibited the Pope from similar abuses in conferring patronage. There were many who grudged the young favourite his success, and the application met with some opposition in a general congregation. But the honeyed tongue of Æneas won the day: ' You will act, fathers, as you think fit; but, if you decide in my favour, I would prefer this token of your good will without possession of the provostship to its possession by any capitular election.' After this the objectors were silenced by a shout of applause, and Æneas obtained his dispensation. When he reached Milan, he found another in possession, by the nomination of the Duke and the election of the Chapter; but Æneas won over the Duke, as he had won over the Council, and his rival was forced to give way. On his return to Basel he was nominated by the Archbishop of Milan to preach before the Council on the feast of S. Ambrose. The theologians were scandalised at this preference of a layman, but the Council enjoyed the polished rhetoric of Æneas more than the ponderous and shapeless erudition of men like John of Segovia.

Æneas was now bound to the Council by his provostship, and showed himself a keen partisan. His pen was busily employed in attacking Eugenius IV. In the Council he was a

---

[1] 'Apud quem sit veritas Deus viderit: ego non video neque, si video, scribere ausim,' he writes in May, 1437. Mansi, xxxi., 227.

BOOK
IV.

Æneas
made secre-
tary to
Felix.
1439.

person of importance, and held high positions. He was often
one of the Committee of Twelve which regulated its affairs.
He often presided over the Deputation of Faith. He went on
several embassies into Germany, and accompanied the Bishop
of Novara to Vienna in 1438, to congratulate Albert on his
accession to the throne. On his return to Basel he narrowly
escaped death from the plague; in fact, the rumour of his death
was spread, and the Duke of Milan took advantage of it to
confer his provostship of S. Lorenzo on a nominee of Eugenius
IV. The policy of the Duke had changed; he was no longer
on the side of the Council, and did not need the services of
Æneas. The Council was bound to recompense its adherent,
and conferred on Æneas a canonry in the Church of Trent.
Again Æneas found another in possession, and again he succeeded in ousting him.

Soon after this came the Papal election at Basel. So great
was the reputation of Æneas that he was urged to qualify for
the post of an elector by taking orders; the Council offered
him a dispensation to allow him to proceed on one day to the
sub-diaconate and diaconate. But Æneas had no taste for the
restrictions of clerical life, or, at least, did not consider the
inducement to be sufficient to lead him to undertake them.
He acted, however, as master of ceremonies to the Conclave,
and on the election of Amadeus was one of those deputed by
the Council to escort the new Pope to Basel. Felix V. made
Æneas one of his secretaries, and it would now seem as though
Æneas had cast in his lot for life.

Æneas
crowned
poet by
Frederick
III. June
1442.

Æneas, however, soon began to see that with the election of
Felix V. the Council had practically abdicated its position.
He did not hope for much from the wisdom or generosity of the
Council's Pope. On all sides he saw that men who had any
future before them were leaving the Council, and joining the
side of Eugenius IV. For himself such a course of conduct
was impossible. He was still a young man, and his reputation
had been entirely made in the democratic surroundings of the
Council. He had made himself remarkable in the eyes of
Eugenius IV. only by the keenness of his attacks upon the
Curia. He had no previous services to plead, no weight to
bring to Eugenius' side, no position which he could use in
Eugenius' favour. It was useless for him to desert to Eugenius,

and equally useless to stay with Felix. In this dilemma he
resolved to identify himself with the neutral policy of Germany.[1]
He took advantage of the negotiations of Felix V. to ingratiate
himself with the Bishop of Chiemsee, one of Frederick's chief
counsellors. The bishop was struck by the cleverness of the
young Italian and his capacity for writing letters. He recommended him to his master, and persuaded Frederick III. to
confer on Æneas the ridiculous honour of crowning him with
the laurel wreath as Imperial poet. We cannot guess how
Frederick was induced to revive this distinction, which had
been bestowed on Petrarch ; but Æneas was proud of the title
of 'poet,' with which he afterwards adorned his name.[2]

Æneas was offered the post of secretary at Frederick's court; Æneas
made Secre-
tary to
Frederick
III. 1442.
but he did not deem it judicious to desert abruptly the service
of Felix V. He went back to Basel, and endeavoured to
persuade Felix that he could serve his interests better at
Vienna than at Basel. He so far prevailed that, when Frederick
visited Basel in 1442, Felix reluctantly gave his consent to this
arrangement, and Æneas left Basel in Frederick's train never to
return. No sooner had Æneas changed his masters than he
changed his opinions also. Felix V. was disappointed if he
thought that the shrewd Italian would have any feeling of
loyalty towards a losing cause. Æneas tried to renew his connexion with the Duke of Milan, and win back his Milanese
provostship : he loudly proclaimed that under Frederick III.
he identified himself with the policy of neutrality.[3]

At Vienna Æneas found that he had to begin his career
afresh. He was only one amongst a crowd of hungry secretaries,
all aspirants for higher office, and all united in disliking the
Italian intruder. In the small matters of their common life
Æneas was given the lowest place at table and the worst bed ; he

[1] He says so himself in his life of the Bishop of Novara, *De Viris Claris*, v.
in Mansi, *Orationes* iii. 149 : ' Cum Felicem omnes relinquerent, nec ejus papa-
tum amplecti vellent, ego ad Fredericum Cæsarem me recepi, nec enim volui
statim de parte ad partem transire.'

[2] The diploma, dated Frankfort, July 27, 1442, is given in Chmel's
Regesta Frederici III., Anhang, xxix. : ' Nos cupientes antecessorum nostrorum
imitari vestigia, qui poetas egregios in morem triumphantium, ut accepimus,
solebant in Capitolio coronare . . . convertimus aciem mentis nostræ in
poetam eximium et præclarum Æneam Silvium,' &c.

[3] See his letter to Bishop of Milan (*Opera*, Basel ed. No. 29), dated December, 1442 ; also Nos. 30, 53,

was the object of the sarcasms of his companions. But Æneas
bore all things with equanimity, and was content to bide his
time.[1] He attached himself to the Chancellor, Kaspar Schlick,
a man whose career had many points in common with his own.

Æneas and
Kaspar
Schlick.

Kaspar Schlick was sprung from a good citizen family in
Franconia, and in 1416 entered Sigismund's chancery as a
secretary. He had little learning; but his native shrewdness
was developed by the teaching of experience, and his industry
recommended him for employment. He went on many
diplomatic missions, and followed Sigismund in his eventful
journeys through Europe. He became Sigismund's trusted
adviser and friend, not only in matters of state, but in the
many amorous intrigues in which Sigismund delighted to engage. Sigismund conferred on him riches and distinctions, and
Sigismund's successors found that Schlick's intimate knowledge
of affairs, especially of finance, rendered his services indispensable. He continued to be Chancellor under Albert II. and
Frederick III. To him Æneas first turned as to a patron,[2]
and approached him with an elaborate eulogy in Latin verse.
Schlick knew something of Æneas, for during his stay in Siena
with Sigismund he had been entertained by an aunt of Æneas,
and had acted as godfather for one of her children. He took
Æneas under his care, secured him a regular salary, gave him
a place at his own table, and counted on his assistance in
personal matters. Schlick was an ignoble politician; with
much acuteness and great capacity for affairs, he had a narrow
and sordid mind. He was greedy of small gains, and this greed
grew upon him with increasing age; in all that he did he had
some personal interest to serve. At first Æneas wished to play
the part of Horace to a second Mæcenas; but he soon learned
to change his strain, and adapt himself to the requirements of
his patron's practical nature.[3] Verses disappeared, and political
jobbery took their place. It was not long before Æneas was required to exercise his ingenuity in the Chancellor's behalf. The

---

[1] Com. 9: 'Cum statuisset malum in bono vincere auriculas declinavit, ut
iniquæ mentis asellus, cum gravius dorso subit onus.'

[2] See his letter of December 23, 1442, given by Voigt in Archiv für Kunde
Oesterreichischer Geschichts-Quellen, vol. xvi. p. 338.

[3] See his letter No. 102, written in the character of a contented man of
letters seeking only for ease and free from ambition. It ends : 'Et potissime
si tu mihi Gaspar favebis, vitæ præsidium et dulce decus meum.'

Bishop of Freising died in August 1443, and the Chancellor
wished to obtain the rich bishopric for his brother, Heinrich
Schlick, a man who had nothing but his powerful relationship
to recommend him. The chapter elected Johann Grünwalder,
one of the cardinals of Felix V., a natural son of the Duke of
Baiern-München, and called on the Council of Basel to confirm the nomination. Æneas wrote to Cardinal d'Allemand,
urging the impolicy of alienating so powerful a man as the
Chancellor.[1] The Council, however, confirmed the election of
Grünwalder, and Schlick applied to Eugenius IV., who, after
some skilful negotiations, confirmed his brother. The struggle
between the rival claimants lasted for some years ; but its immediate effect was to draw Kaspar Schlick towards the side
of Eugenius IV., and Æneas readily followed his master. After
all his services to the Council, he had neither obtained any
promotion for himself, nor could he help a friend by his
arguments.[2]

Moreover, at Vienna Æneas met Cardinal Cesarini, who had
been appointed by Eugenius IV. legate in Hungary for the
purpose of warring against the Turks. Hungarian affairs
needed rather delicate management at the Court of Vienna.
After the death of Albert II. his wife bore a son, Ladislas, of
whom Frederick III. was guardian. But the Hungarian nobles
did not think it wise to run the risks of a long minority
in such perilous times. They chose as their king Wladislaf
of Poland, and Eugenius IV. approved their choice. Frederick III. could not venture on war, and Kaspar Schlick, who
owned lands in Hungary, used his influence on the side of
peace. But it required all Cesarini's tact to reconcile the
positions of the Pope and the King. He was ready to renew
his acquaintance with Æneas, treated him as a friend, and
urged him to take the side of Eugenius IV. Æneas was
keen-sighted enough to use the opportunity. He saw at

---

[1] *Epistolæ*, No. 183.

[2] In a letter to a friend at Basel, dated October, 1443, printed by Voigt,
Kunde für Oest. Geschichts-Quellen, xvi. 345, he says : ' Fuerunt in hanc sententiam verba vestra, quæ ultimo ad me pronuntiastis Basileæ, cum diceretis
S. D. nostrum F. (Felicem) mihi absenti quam præsenti de aliquo beneficio
provisurum esse, vestrasque operas ad id spopondistis, cujus rei nullus secutus
est effectus, tametsi multis ego in rebus apud Cæsaream majestatem S. D.
nostro profuerim et dictim prosim.'

Frederick's Court the immense superiority of the diplomacy
of the Papal Curia over that of the Council. The strong character of Carvajal, the Papal envoy, produced a deep impression
on him.[1] Æneas let it be understood that he was not indisposed
to help the side of Eugenius IV. when opportunity offered.
He wrote to Carvajal, October 1440, that he assumed an attitude of judicious expectancy. 'Here stands Æneas in arms,
and he shall be my Anchises whom the consent of the universal
Church shall choose. So long as Germany, the greater part of
the Christian world, still hesitates, I am in doubt; but I am
ready to listen to the common judgment, nor in a matter of
faith do I trust myself alone.'[2] In December of the same year
he had so far advanced in his opinions as to advocate the
ending of the schism by any means; he favoured the proposal
of the King of France to summon an assembly of princes. It
matters not whether it be called a Council; so long as the
schism be done away with, the means used may be called by
any name. 'Let it be called a conventicle or a meeting; I
care not, provided it leads to peace.'[3] He wrote a clever dialogue, the 'Pentalogus,' in which he commended this plan to
Frederick III.[4] In May 1444 he had already begun to consider
how the neutrality of Germany could be brought to an end.
He wrote to Cesarini: 'The neutrality will be hard to get rid
of, because it is useful to many. There are few who seek the
truth; almost all seek their own gain. The neutrality is a
pleasing snare, because no one can be driven from a benefice,
whether he holds it justly or not, and the ordinaries confer
benefices as they please. It is a hard matter to rescue the
prey from the wolf's mouth. But, as far as I see, all Christendom follows Eugenius; only Germany is divided, and I would
gladly see it united, because I attach great weight to this
nation, for it is not led by fear, but by its own judgment and
goodwill. I shall follow the lead of the King and the Electors.'[5]

---

[1] In his *Bulla Retractationum* (ed. Helmstadt, p. 155), he gives an account of
his arguments with Cesar'ni. In a letter to D'Allemand in *Oest. Geschichl -
Quellen*, xvi. 344, he says: 'Cardinalis Aquilegiensis (the envoy of Felix V.
graviter ægrotat, neo illi tantum vires sunt quantæ Juliano Cardinali; neo
tam robustus est Aquilegiensis quam Carvajal.'

[2] *Ep.* 25. [3] Letter to Bishop of Chiemsee, *Ep.* 55.
[4] In Pez. *Thesaurus*, vol. iv. part 3, p. 736, &c. [5] *Epist.* 65.

Soon after this Æneas went to the Diet at Nürnberg, and there
saw the feebleness of Frederick III., the divisions among the
Electors, and the chance of success which lay open to enterprise. He was appointed by Frederick III. a commissioner, to
sit with others nominated by the Electors for the consideration
of ecclesiastical affairs. 'We parted in discord and division'
is the only result which the letters of Æneas chronicle.

On his way to Nürnberg Æneas passed through Passau,
where Schlick was courteously entertained by the bishop.
Æneas made himself agreeable to his host, and wrote to a
friend in Rome a pleasant sketch of Passau and its bishop.
Before sending it he requested the bishop to look it over and
correct any inaccuracies which it might contain. This delightful means of letting the bishop know that the pen of Æneas was
employed to sing his praises secured its due reward. Æneas
was presented before the end of a year to a benefice in Aspach,
in Bavaria. The bishop sent him his presentation free from
all ecclesiastical or other dues.

The character of Æneas at this time was not that of a
churchman. He had led a careless, adventurous, self-seeking
life. He had lived amongst dissolute companions and had been
as dissolute as the worst amongst them. He cannot be said to
have had any principles; he trusted to nothing but his own
cleverness, and his sole object was to make himself comfortable
wherever he was. He flattered those who were in authority; he
was willing to do anything required of him in hopes of obtaining
a suitable reward. He never lost an opportunity of ingratiating
himself with anyone, and would use any means for that purpose. His store of knowledge, his fluent pen, his subtle mind
were at the command of any promising patron. One day he
wrote to young Sigismund, Count of the Tyrol, a long and elegant letter in praise of learning, inviting him by numerous
examples to fit himself by study for his high position. A little
while after, he wrote him a love-letter to help him to overcome
the resistance of a girl who shrank from his dishonourable proposals. With characteristic levity and plausibility he even
provided the youth with excuses for his conduct. 'I know
human nature,' he says; 'he who does not love in youth loves
in old age, and makes himself ridiculous. I know too how
love kindles in youth dormant virtues; a man strives to do

what will please his mistress. Moveover, youths must not be
held too tight, but must learn the ways of the world so as to
distinguish between good and evil. I send you a letter on condition that you do not neglect literature for love; but as bees
gather honey from flowers, so do you from the blandishments of
love gather the virtues of Venus.' [1]

The private life of Æneas, as we learn plainly from his
letters, was profligate enough; but it does not seem to have
shocked men of his time, nor to have fallen below the common
standard. His irregularities were never made a reproach to
him later, nor did he take any pains to hide them from posterity.
Such as he was he would have himself known—induced perhaps
by literary vanity, more probably by a feeling that his character
would not lose in the eyes of his contemporaries by sincerity on
his part. In those days chastity was a mark of a saintly character,[2] and Æneas never professed to be a saint. His tempera-
ment was ardent, easily moved and soon satisfied. The pleasures
of the flesh had strong dominion over him. His love affairs were
many, and he did not regard constancy as a virtue. A son was
born to him in Scotland after his visit there; but the child
soon died. We know of another son, the offspring of an English
woman whom Æneas met at Strasburg when on an embassy
from Basel. In a letter to his own father he shamelessly
describes the pains that he took to overcome her virtue, and
asks his father to bring up the child. His excuses for himself
show an entire frivolity and absence of principle. 'You will
perhaps call me sinful; but I do not know what opinion you
formed of me. Certainly you did not beget a son of stone or
iron, seeing you yourself are flesh. I am not a hypocrite who
wish to seem good rather than be so. I frankly confess my
fault, that I am neither holier than David nor wiser than Solomon. It is an old and ingrained vice, and I do not know who is
free from it. But you will say that there are certain limits,
which lawful wedlock provides. There are limits to eating and
drinking; but who observes them? Who is so upright as not
to fall seven times a day? Let the hypocrite profess that he is

---

[1] *Ep.* 122.

[2] Vespasiano da Bisticci says of Cesarini with wonder: 'In prima era firma
opinione in corte di Roma, e dov' egli era stato, lui essere vergine.'

conscious of no fault. I know no merit in myself and only
divine pity gives me any hope of mercy.'

In truth Æneas took no other view of life than that of a selfish voluptuary, for whom the nobler side of things did not exist.
He gave his experiences to his friend Piero da Noceto, who was
in the chancery of Eugenius IV., and wrote to him that he
had thoughts of marrying his concubine, who had already borne
him several children. Æneas advises the step: he will know all
about his wife beforehand and will not have to endure the dis-
illusionment that often follows a honeymoon. ' I have loved
many women,' he says, 'and after winning them have grown
weary of them; if I were to marry, 1 would not unite myself to
anyone whose habits I did not know beforehand.'[1] Æneas was
the confidant of the amours of Kaspar Schlick, and took an
adventure of Schlick's with a Sienese lady as the subject for a
novel in the style of Boccaccio. This story, ' Lucretia and
Euryalus,' had great popularity and was translated into almost
every European tongue.[2]

Thus the life of Æneas at Vienna was by no means edifying, nor was it satisfactory to himself. His associates in the
Imperial Chancery were mostly younger than himself. Their
manners were rude, their enjoyments coarse, and their vices
wanting in that refinement which to a cultivated Italian gave
them half their pleasure. Æneas was never at home in Germany: he could not speak the language fluently: the country,
the climate, the people, and the manners were all distasteful
to him. He pined at times to return to Italy, and urged his
friends to deliver him from his exile in a foreign land. He
began to feel that his life was somewhat wasted; he began to
think that he ought to turn over a new leaf and enter upon a
new career. He thought of taking holy orders; but if his
cultivation did not keep him from vice, it at least prevented
him from assuming a position the duties of which he could
not with decency fulfil. ' I do not intend to spend all my
life outside Italy,' he writes in February 1444. 'As yet I
have taken care not to involve myself in holy orders. I fear
about my continency, which, though a laudable virtue, is more

---

[1] *Ep*. 45, of January 1444.
[2] It is in the letters of Æneas, No. 114, and was written in July 1444.

BOOK
IV.

Policy of
the German
Electors.
1444

easily practised in word than in deed, and befits philosophers better than poets.'[1]

While this was the frame of Æneas' mind, the proceedings of the Diet of Nürnberg gave a new direction to his energies. The Diet did nothing except confirm the current witticism that 'diets were indeed pregnant, for each carried another in its womb.' It revealed, however, to Æneas the existence of the strong party among the Electors, which had formed a league in favour of Felix V. He saw that the contest between the two Popes was becoming important in German politics. It gave the Electors an opportunity of acting without the King, and if their league in favour of Felix succeeded, the royal power would have received a serious, if not a deadly, blow. The weakness of the Electors lay in the fact that their ecclesiastical policy was not sincere. They did not venture to identify themselves with the national desire for reform, and, supported by the authority of the Council of Basel, set in order the affairs of the German Church. Their policy was oligarchical, not · popular ; they wished to strengthen their own hands against the King, not to work for what the nation desired. They looked for help, not to the national sentiment of Germany, but to the French King, and negotiated with him to support them in the old plan of demanding a new Council in a new place. But the French had just shown themselves to be the national enemies of Germany ; and Charles VII., now freed from the pressure of the English war, was no longer willing to help the Electors, but reverted to the old desire of France to have a Pope at Avignon. The negotiations between him and the Electors led to no results.[2]

Battle of
Varna.
November
1444.

This policy of the Electors naturally tended to bring the King and the Pope together. Frederick III. on his part had from the beginning inclined in favour of Eugenius IV., and events had made the friendship of Eugenius more desirable. Eugenius had so far wished to fulfil his promises to the Greeks that he proclaimed a crusade against the Turks, and sent Cesarini as his legate into Hungary. Cesarini, whose lofty character was never displayed to better advantage than when acting as the leader of a forlorn hope, stirred the courage

[1] Ep. 50.
[2] Pückert, Die Kurfürstliche Neutralität, 212, &c.

of the Hungarians, filled them with enthusiasm for the
cause of Christendom against the infidel, and awakened a
strong feeling of devotion towards Eugenius IV. In 1443
Wladislaf, the Hungarian King, compelled the Turks to sue
for peace on condition of restoring Servia and quitting the
Hungarian frontier. But next year the expectations of a combined attack upon the Turks by Venice and the Greeks led
Cesarini to urge Hungary again to war. The peace had not
been approved by the Pope, and he absolved them from all
obligations to observe it. His exhortations were obeyed, and
Wladislaf again led forth his army to join his allies on the
Hellespont. But at Varna he was startled by the news that the
Turkish Sultan Murad was advancing with 60,000 men against
his army of 20,000. Cesarini counselled a prudent policy of
defence; but Wladislaf was resolved to try the issue of a battle.
On the fatal field of Varna, November 10, 1444, the Christian
army suffered a severe defeat, and Wladislaf fell fighting.[1] The
eventful life of Cesarini found on the battle-field a noble end.[2]
Chivalrous and high-minded, he had always devoted himself
unsparingly to the loftiest and most difficult cause that was
before him. He failed in war against the Bohemians; he failed
to regulate the ecclesiastical violence of the Council of Basel;
he failed to drive the Turks from Europe. Yet his efforts were
always directed to a noble end, and the very singleness of his
own purpose made him neglect the prudence which would have
been familiar to a smaller man. Amid the self-seeking of the
age Cesarini rises almost to the proportions of a hero; he is
the only man whose character claims our entire respect and
admiration.

The news of the defeat of Varna filled Europe with consternation; but it was not without its advantages to Frederick III.
The death of Wladislaf opened the way for the settlement of

[1] See Bonfinius, *Decades*, III. ch. iv. v.; von Hammer, XI.; Dlugloss, XII.;
the letter of Æneas to Duke of Milan giving the news, dated Dec. 13, 1444,
Epist, No. 52.

[2] About the mode of Cesarini's death there were various accounts which
are epitomised by Æneas Sylvius, *Hist. Fred.* in Kollar, II. 119: 'Julianus
quoque Cardinalis in eo bello periit, de quo variam famam referunt, alii inter
prœliandum occisum, alii bello vulneratum effugisse, atque ex vulnere periisse;
constantior tamen fama est ipsum, dum fugeret, equumque potaret, ab Hun-
garis, qui et ipsi fugiebant, percussum, illustrem spiritum qui multis annis
Basiliensem conventum rexerat, emisisse.'

Hungarian affairs, and the recognition of Frederick's ward, Ladislas. To gain this end more securely, Frederick needed the help of Eugenius IV. Negotiations began to take a more intimate and personal turn in relation to the affairs of Hungary. Yet still the affairs of the Church were the subject of formal embassies, in which the old plan of a new Council was ostensibly being pursued. In November 1444 the Fathers of Basel answered this proposal by an entire refusal. They had already agreed to it in 1442, and the obstinacy of Eugenius IV. had prevented it; on him rested the blame of its failure. An envoy had next to be sent to bear a similar proposition to Eugenius IV. This was not done till the beginning of 1445, and then the person chosen was Æneas Sylvius.

Æneas at once saw that in dealings between Frederick III. and Eugenius IV. there was scope for his cleverness and his powers of intrigue. He readily started on his journey, and rejoiced to see his native land once more. At Siena his kinsfolk were alarmed at his audacity in venturing into the presence of the Pope, whom he had so often attacked and so grievously offended. They represented to him that ' Eugenius was cruel, mindful of wrongs, restrained by no conscience, no feeling of pity; he was surrounded by ministers of crime; Æneas, if he went to Rome, would never return.'[1] Æneas, no doubt, enjoyed the simplicity of these good people, and acted with dignity the part of a possible martyr to duty. He tore himself from their weeping embrace, declaring that he must either fulfil his embassy or die in the attempt,[2] and proceeded to Rome. Carvajal had already given Eugenius information of the usefulness of Æneas. He was well received by several of the cardinals for his literary or for his political merits. Amongst the officials of the Papal Curia he met several of his old friends at Basel. Before he could have an audience with the Pope it was necessary that he should be absolved from the ecclesiastical censure pronounced against the adherents of the Council. This duty was assigned to the Cardinals Landriano and Le Jeune, who afterwards introduced Æneas to the Pope's presence. Eugenius graciously allowed him to kiss not only his foot but his hand and his cheek. Æneas presented

[1] *Comm.*, ed. Fea., p. 87.　　　　[2] *Pii II. Comm.* p. 9.

his credentials, and then began to speak as a penitent on his own behalf.

CHAP.
I.

Reconcilia-
tion of
Æneas with
Eugenius .
IV.

'Holy Father, before I discharge my errand for the King, I will say a little about myself. I know that you have heard much against me; and those who have told you have spoken truly. At Basel I spoke, wrote, and did many things, I do not deny it, not with the intent of injuring you, but of benefiting the Church. I erred, but in the company of many others, men of high repute. I followed Cardinal Cesarini, the Archbishop of Palermo, the apostolic notary Pontano, men who were esteemed the eyes of the law and teachers of the truth. I will not mention the universities which gave their opinions against you. In such company who would not have erred? But when I discovered the error of the Basilians, I confess that I did not at once flee to you. I was afraid lest I should fall from one error into another. I went to the neutral camp that after mature de-liberation I might shape my course. I remained three years with the German king, and there my study of the disputes be-tween your legates and those of the Council left me no doubt that the right was on your side. Hence, when this embassy was offered me, I willingly accepted it, thinking that so I might regain your favour. Now I am in your presence, and ask your pardon because I erred in ignorance.'

Eugenius answered graciously. 'We know that you erred with many; but to one who owns his fault we cannot refuse pardon, for the Church is a loving mother. Now that you hold the truth, see that you never let it go, and by good works seek the divine grace. You live in a place where you may defend the truth and benefit the Church. We, forgetting your former injuries, will love you well if you walk well.'[1]

Thus Æneas made his peace, and entered into a tacit agreement with the Pope that if he proved himself useful his services should be rewarded. Eugenius had gained an agent in Germany on whose devotion he might rely, because it was closely bound up with self-interest. The diplomacy of the Curia had again shown its astuteness.

After this reconciliation Æneas was regarded as a person of some importance at Rome, and was well received by several of the cardinals. But there was one person who was too blunt

[1] *Pii II. Commentarii*, p. 10.

BOOK
IV.

Æneas
Sylvius in
Rome.
1445.

to disguise his contempt for this self-interested conversion. One day Æneas met Tommaso Parentucelli, who had been a companion in the service of Cardinal Albergata, but who had followed his master and had been an uncompromising opponent of the Council. He was now Bishop of Bologna, and was respected for his character and his learning. Æneas advanced to greet him with outstretched hand, but Parentucelli coldly turned away. Æneas was piqued, and afterwards adopted a similar attitude of disdain towards Parentucelli. 'How ignorant are we of the future!' he remarks afterwards, when relating this incident; 'if Æneas had known that Parentucelli would be Pope, he would have condoned all things.'[1] A reconciliation between the two was brought about by friends before Æneas left Rome; but Parentucelli was never cordial to one whose sincerity he doubted.

On the particular matter of his embassy Æneas does not seem to have done much. The party of Eugenius in Germany, headed by Schlick, saw no way of ending the neutrality except by summoning another Council. To this Eugenius was resolved not to consent, and Æneas gave him the benefit of his advice. In April he left Rome with an announcement that Eugenius would send an embassy to bring his answer to the King. His envoys, Carvajal and Parentucelli, followed close upon Æneas.

Eugenius IV. had already entered upon a policy of attacking his enemies in Germany. On January 16, 1445, he issued a Bull cutting off the lands of the Duke of Cleves from the dioceses of Köln and Münster. In this matter he acted at the request of the Dukes of Burgundy and Cleves; but in the Bull he spoke of the Archbishop of Köln as disobedient to the Roman See, and called the Bishop of Münster, 'Henry, the son of wickedness, who styles himself Bishop of Münster.' The Electors had not fared so well as they hoped in their negotiations with France. They were afraid lest the King might get the better of them by his secret dealings with Eugenius IV., and were taken aback at this hostile display on the part of Eugenius. They judged it prudent to retire from their separate position, and once more make common cause with the King. At the Diet on June 24, 1445, the neutrality of Germany was renewed for eight months,

---

[1] *Comment*, ed. Fea., p. 88.

at the end of which time the King was to summon an 'assembly
of the German Church or a national Council,' which was to be
proclaimed to the various lands depending on the Empire, including England, Scotland, and Denmark.[1] Once more the
ecclesiastical question was to be also a national question for
Germany. The Electors were willing to abandon their separate
negotiations with Felix V. on the understanding that Frederick
III. abandoned his agreement with Eugenius IV.

But Frederick III., indolent and careless as he was, saw in Negotia-
tions
between
Eugenius
IV. and
Frederick
III. 1445.
an alliance with Eugenius IV. the sole means of maintaining
himself against the formidable alliance, which threatened him,
of France with the House of Savoy and the German Princes.
If he was heedless himself, the envoys of Eugenius IV. spared
no pains to enlighten him. Schlick and Æneas Sylvius were
ever at his side, and Carvajal was busy at Vienna arranging an
alliance between the King and the Pope. 'The King hates
the neutrality,' writes Æneas Sylvius at the end of August,
'and would willingly abandon it if the princes would only concur, to which end perhaps some means may be found.'[2] In
Rome Eugenius IV. went on with his proceedings against the
Archbishop of Köln. It was known in Vienna that the Archbishop had been summoned to appear in Rome,[3] and it was
clear that further steps must follow; yet the King raised no
word of protest. He was engaged in a secret treaty with the
Pope; he was selling his neutrality, and was being bought
cheap. On September 13 Carvajal left Vienna to carry to Rome
Frederick III.'s conditions. The terms which Carvajal had
negotiated were accepted by Eugenius IV. A treaty between
Pope and King was once more firmly established, and the end
of the reform movement in Germany was rapidly approaching.

The terms on which Frederick III. sold his aid to Eugenius Terms of
the treaty
between
Pope and
King.
February
1446.
IV. are expressed in three Bulls issued in February 1446.[4] The
Pope granted to the King the right during his lifetime to
nominate to the six great bishoprics of Trent, Brixen, Chur,
Gurk, Trieste, and Piben; he granted the King and his suc-

---

[1] See Ranke, *Deutsche Geschichte*, Anhang, vol. vi. p. 8, and Pückert, *Kur-furstliche Neutralität*, 238.

[2] Voigt, in *Archiv für Oesterr. Geschichts-Quellen*, xvi. 373.

[3] See letter of Æn. Sylvius, dated September 13, carried by Carvajal to Rome, in Voigt, *Archiv.* xvi. 386.

[4] The Bulls are given in Chmel, *Materialien*, I., No. 72–74.

cessors the right to nominate for the Papal approval those who
should have visitorial powers over the monasteries of Austria ;
the King should have the right of presentation to a hundred
small benefices in Austria. Besides this, the Papacy was also
to pay the King the sum of 221,000 ducats, of which 121,000
were to be paid by Eugenius, and the rest by his successors.[1]
The indolent and short-sighted Frederick, no doubt, thought
that he had made a good bargain. He obtained a supply of
money, of which he was always in need. He got into his own
hands the chief bishoprics in his ancestral domains, and thereby
greatly strengthened his power over Austria. By the nomination of visitors of the monasteries he lessened the influence
of his enemy, the Archbishop of Salzburg, by exempting the
monasteries from his jurisdiction. By the right of presentation
to a hundred benefices he secured the means of rewarding the
hungry officials of his court. He thought only of his own personal interests ; he cared only to secure his own position in his
ancestral domains. For the rights of the Church, for his position in the Empire, he had no thought. All that can be urged
in Frederick's behalf is, that the German princes were equally
ready to abandon the German Church and make terms with
either Pope who would help them to secure their own political
power. On the other hand, Eugenius IV., though making
great concessions, was careful not to impair the rights of the
Papacy or take any irretrievable step. The Papal treasury was
exhausted; but money was well spent in regaining the adhesion of
Germany, and Eugenius IV. felt amply justified in mortgaging
for this purpose the revenues of his successors. The Pope
granted the nomination to six bishoprics, but only for Frederick's lifetime, after which the mischief, if any, might be repaired. The absolute appointment of visitors of monasteries
was not granted to Frederick and his successors in Austria,
but only the nomination of several from whom the Pope was
to select. The benefices granted to the King were not important ones; they were to be between the annual value of sixty
and forty marks, and did not include appointments to cathedral
and collegiate churches. There was nothing in all this that
materially affected the Papal position in Germany.

[1] This rests on the authority of Heimburg in a letter of 1446, given by
Dûx, *Nicolas von Cusa,* I., Beilage IV.

Moreover, Eugenius IV. was anxious that the treaty between himself and Frederick III. should be as soon as possible openly acknowledged. He promised Frederick 100,000 guilders for the expenses of his coronation. He invited him to Rome to receive the Imperial crown ; in case Frederick could not come to Rome, Eugenius, old and gouty as he was, undertook to meet him at Bologna, Padua, or Treviso. In the reunion of the Papacy and the Empire Eugenius IV. saw the final overthrow of the Council of Basel, and the restoration of the Papal monarchy.

Eugenius IV., however, did not trust only to his allurements to induce the indolent Frederick to declare himself. Knowing the feeble character of the King, he resolved to play a bold game, so as to attain his end more speedily. He had already succeeded in weakening, by his threat of ecclesiastical censures, the electoral league in favour of Felix V. As his negotiations with Frederick III. advanced, he resolved to strike a decided blow against his enemies in Germany. On February 9 he issued a Bull deposing from their sees the Archbishops of Köln and Trier, and appointing in their places Adolf of Cleves and John, Bishop of Cambray, the nephew and the natural brother of his powerful ally, the Duke of Burgundy. The German rebels were openly defied, and the allies of Eugenius IV. must range themselves decidedly on his side.

Eugenius
IV. deposes
the Electors
of Trier
and Köln.
February
1446.

If Eugenius IV. acted boldly, the Electors answered the challenge with no less promptitude. On March 21 they met at Frankfort and formed a league for mutual defence. The attack upon the electoral privileges combined the whole body in opposition to the high-handed procedure of the Pope. Undeterred by the alliance of Pope and King, the Electors united to assert the principles on which the neutrality of Germany had been founded. If the time had come when neutrality could no longer be maintained, it should at least be laid aside on the same grounds as those on which it had been asserted. The Electors again assumed the position of mediators between the rival Popes, but set forward a plan of mediation which should lead to decided results, and which should have for its object the security of the liberty of the German Church. They abandoned their scheme for the recognition of Felix V., and were willing to join with the King in recognising Eugenius IV., but

on condition that he confirmed the decrees of Constance about
the authority of General Councils, accepted the reforming decrees of Basel as they were expressed in the declaration of
neutrality, recalled all censures pronounced against neutrals,
and agreed to assemble a Council on May 1, 1447, at Constance, Worms, Mainz, or Trier. They prepared Bulls for the
Papal signature embodying these conditions: on the issue
of these Bulls they were ready to restore their obedience and
submit the formal settlement of Christendom to the future
Council.

The attitude of the Electors was at once dignified and
statesmanlike. It showed that the Bishops of Trier and Köln
possessed political capacity hitherto unsuspected. No special
mention was made of individual grievances, no direct answer
was given to the attack made by Eugenius IV. on the electoral
privileges. By accepting their terms the Pope would tacitly
recall his Bulls of deposition; if he refused to accept them, the
Electors would be free to turn to Felix V. and the Fathers of
Basel. They might summon in name a new Council; but it
would consist of the members of the Council of Basel reinforced
by Germans bound to the policy of the Electors. They resolved that envoys be sent to Frederick III. and Eugenius IV.,
and unless a satisfactory answer were obtained by September,
they would proceed further. These resolutions were the work,
in the first instance, of the four Rhenish Electors; but within
a month the Markgraf of Brandenburg and the Duke of Saxony
had also given in their adhesion. The League of the Electoral
Oligarchy, to act in despite of its nominal head, was now
fully formed.

The pro-
posals of
the Electors
laid before
Frederick
III. 1446.
Strong as was the position of the Electors, they showed
their weakness by not asserting it publicly. Their agreement
was kept secret; and the embassy sent to demand the adhesion
of Frederick III. was instructed to lay the plan only before
him and six counsellors, who were to be bound by an oath of
secrecy. Decided as was the policy of the Electors in appearance, it was founded upon no large sentiment of earnestness or patriotism. It was merely a diplomatic semblance,
and, as such, must be cloaked in diplomatic secrecy, that it
might be exchanged, should expediency require, for a more
conciliatory attitude. The envoys of the Electors were headed

by Gregory Heimburg, who hoped against hope that he might
use the opportunity of giving effect to his own reforming ideas,
and trusted that he might work through the selfishness of the
Electors towards a really national end.   Frederick III. received
through him the proposals of the Electors, by which he was
sorely embarrassed.   At his Court were Carvajal and the Bishop
of Bologna, who had just brought him the Bulls which ratified
his treaty with the Pope; but his oath of secrecy to the Electors forbade him to take counsel with them.   The separate
articles of the proposals of the Electors were discussed in the
presence of the six counsellors sworn to secrecy.   The King
was ready to accept them in principle, but made reservations on
points of detail.   The envoys were instructed not to lay before
the King the Bulls which they were to present to the Pope,
unless he fully accepted the provisions of the Electors.   Frederick, on his side, complained of this reserve as offensive to his
dignity.   'It is a new thing,' he said, 'that an agreement
should be made behind my back, and that I should be required
to accept it without a full discussion of every article.'   The ambassadors of the Electors declared that they had submitted
everything to the King.   But Frederick III. was justified in
refusing to join the Electors till they had shown him the written
proposals which they were to submit to the Pope; and they
refused to do this because they wished to keep in the background their final threat of making common cause with the
Council of Basel.[1]   The sole result of these negotiations was,
that the King proclaimed a Diet at Frankfort on September 1,
and let it be understood that he was then prepared to consider
the termination of the neutrality.

Envoys of
the Electors
in Rome.
July 1446.

In the beginning of July Heimburg and two companions
reached Rome.   Frederick III., anxious to give some hint to
Eugenius IV., told the Pope's envoys at Vienna that it would
be well if one of them returned to Rome.   Carvajal was ill of a
fever; so the Bishop of Bologna set out, and with him went
Æneas Sylvius, to whom the King confided the secret of the
Electors.   Æneas pleads, as a technical excuse for this double
dealing, that the King himself had taken no oath of secrecy,[2]

[1] For these negotiations see Pückert, *Die Kurfürstliche Neutralität*,
p. 264, &c.

[2] *Comm.* ed. Fea. p. 91.

but only his six counsellors. It is, however, probable that Æneas needed no special enlightenment, but as secretary was privy to the whole matter, aud was himself bound to secresy,[1] if not specially on that occasion, yet by the nature of his office. However that may be, he went with Thomas of Bologna, and on the way let drop enough to indicate to Thomas the advice which he ought to give to the Pope. They made such haste on their journey that the ambassadors of the Electors only entered Rome the day before them, and Thomas of Bologna was the first to have an audience of the Pope. Æneas expressly says, 'The Bishop of Bologna, though he could not know all that the ambassadors of the Electors brought with them, still guessed and opined much.'[2] ' Instructed by Æneas, he warned the Pope about the matter, and advised him to give the ambassadors a mild answer.'[3] The duplicity of Æneas was invaluable to the cause of Eugenius IV.: it averted the most pressing danger, that the Pope, by his contemptuous behaviour, should give the Electors an immediate pretext for turning to the Council of Basel.

Double dealing of Æneas Sylvius.

The presence of Æneas was also useful in another way. Frederick III. had not been asked by the Electors to send an embassy to Rome; but Æneas was there to speak in the King's name, and was called in to assist at the audience. By this means Eugenius IV. had a pretext for overlooking the fact that what was submitted to him were the demands of the Electors: he could treat them as the joint representations of the King and the Electors, and so return a vague answer. Every precaution had been taken by the Electors to put their cause clearly before the Pope. When Eugenius raised an objection to receiving an embassy from the men whom he had deposed, he was informed that the credentials of the ambassadors were signed simply with the subscription of the whole College—' The Electoral Princes of the Holy Roman Empire.'

However definitely the Electors put their propositions before the Pope, he was resolved not to give them a definite answer. When they were admitted to an audience, Æneas spoke first on behalf of the King. He recommended the ambassadors to the Pope's kindly attention, and vaguely said that

---

[1] This is the conjecture of Pückert, p. 264.
[2] *Hist. Frederici*, in Kollar, II. p. 122.　　[3] *Comm.* ed. Fea., 91.

the peace of the Church might be promoted by entertaining their proposals. Then Heimburg, in a clear, incisive, and dignified speech, set forward the objects of the Electors. There could not be a greater contrast than between Æneas and Heimburg: they may almost be taken as representatives of the German and Italian character. Heimburg was tall and of commanding presence, with flashing eyes and a genial face, honest, straightforward, eminently national in his views and policy, holding steadfastly by the object which he had in view.[1] He was the very opposite of the shifty Italian adventurer, who recognised in him a natural foe. Heimburg's speech was respectful, but uncompromising. Eugenius listened, and then, after a pause, shrewdly returned a vague answer. The deposition of the archbishops, he said, had been decreed for weighty reasons; as to the authority of General Councils, he had never refused to acknowledge it, but had only defended the dignity of the Apostolic See; as to the German Church, he did not wish to oppress it, but to act for its welfare. The proposals made to him were serious, and he must take time to consider them.

Æneas meanwhile unfolded to Eugenius the opinions of Frederick III. He advised that the archbishops should be restored, without, however, annulling their deprivation; that the Constance decree in favour of General Councils should be accepted. If this were done, the recognition of Eugenius might be accomplished; if not, there was great danger of a schism. Eugenius listened and seemed to assent. The cardinals endeavoured to discover if the ambassadors had any further instructions; but Heimburg did not consider himself justified by the Pope's attitude to lay before him the Bulls that he had brought. The ambassadors were kept for three weeks awaiting the Pope's answer, and Æneas has drawn a spiteful picture of Heimburg sweltering in the summer heat, stalking indignantly on Monte Giordano in the evening, with bare head and breast, denouncing the wickedness of Eugenius and the Curia. At length they were told that, as they had no powers to treat further, the Pope would send envoys with his answer to the Diet at Frankfort. The ambassadors left Rome without producing their Bulls. Heimburg regarded the Papal

---

[1] See Æneas' description of him, *Hist. Fred.*, in Kollar, II. p. 123.

attitude as equivalent to a refusal to entertain his proposals. Meanwhile ambassadors had been sent also to Basel, and the Council had similarly deferred its answer till the assembling of the Diet.

The results of the Diet of Frankfort would clearly be of great importance both to Germany and to the Church at large. The policy of the Electors had not received the adhesion of the King; the oligarchy had resolved to act in opposition to their head, and, if they were resolute, the deposition of Frederick III. was imminent. In this emergency Frederick entrusted his interests to the care of the Markgraf Albert of Brandenburg and Jacob of Baden, the Bishops of Augsburg and Chiemsee, Kaspar Schlick and Æneas Sylvius. At the head of this embassy stood Albert of Brandenburg, who had already shown his devotion to Frederick by taking the field against the Armagnacs, and who was bent upon overthrowing the intrigues of France with the Rhenish Electors. The representatives of the King were all convinced of the great importance of the crisis, and were not a little embarrassed to find at Frankfort no ambassadors of the Pope. The Bishop of Bologna had left Rome with Æneas Sylvius, but had been delayed at Parma by sickness, and on his recovery had gone to confer with the Duke of Burgundy about the measures to be adopted towards the deposed Archbishops of Trier and Köln. John of Carvajal and Nicolas of Cusa had come from Vienna; but they had no special instructions about the answer to be returned by the Pope to the proposals of the Electors.

In spite of the gravity of the occasion, few of the German princes or prelates were personally present at Frankfort. The four Rhenish Electors were there; but the Electors of Brandenburg and Saxony only sent representatives, as did also the majority of the bishops and nobles. From Basel came the Cardinal of Arles, bearing a decree which approved of the transference of the Council to one of the places which might be approved by the King and the Electors, and generally accepting the proposals of the Electors without making any mention of Felix V. The Electors took up a position of friendliness to the Cardinal of Arles. When, on September 14, the proceedings of the Diet began with a solemn mass, the Cardinal appeared, as was his wont, in state as a Papal legate. The royal ambassadors made

the usual protest that Germany was neutral, and could not recognise the officials of either Pope.   The Archbishop of Trier
angrily denounced their conduct; they could admit the legates
of Eugenius, the foes of the nation, and would exclude those of
the Council.   The majority agreed with him; but the citizens of
Frankfort were still loyal, and their tumultuous interference
compelled the Cardinal to lay aside the insignia of his office.

The proceedings [1] began with the reading by Heimburg of the
speech which he had made to Eugenius IV., and the written
answer of the Pope.   Heimburg further gave an account of his
embassy, and the reasons which had led him to abstain from
presenting to the Pope the Bulls which the Electors had drawn
up; the question to be discussed was, whether the Pope's
answer gave ground for further deliberation.   On the Pope's
side his envoys submitted an answer to the ' prayers of the
King and the Electors.'   Eugenius was ready to summon a
Council within a convenient time; he had never opposed the
decrees of the Council of Constance, which had been renewed
in Basel while a universal and recognised Council was sitting;
he was willing to do away with the old burdens of the German
Church provided he were indemnified for the losses which he
would thereby sustain.   About the revocation of the deprivation of the archbishops he said nothing.   The answer of
Eugenius IV. was mere mockery of his opponents.   He granted
nothing that they had asked; his concessions were merely
apparent, and he reserved to himself full power to make them
illusory.   His attitude towards the Electors was practically the
same as it had been towards the Council of Basel.

The regal and the Papal ambassadors would not have
ventured to submit such an answer if they had not seen their
way to effect a breach in the ranks of their opponents.   On
September 22 Albert of Brandenburg succeeded in inducing
the representatives of his brother the Elector, the Archbishop
of Mainz, two bishops, and one or two nobles, to agree that
they had obtained an answer from the Pope which afforded the
basis for peace in the Church, and that they would stand by

Division
amongst
the Elec-
tors.

---

[1] For the proceedings of the Diet the account given by Æneas Sylvius,
Hist. Fred., in Kollar, II. 127, &c., must be compared with the official record in
the Dresden Archives excerpted by Pückert, *Die Kurfürstliche Neutralität*,
p. 278, &c.

one another to maintain this opinion. The Archbishop of
Mainz was won over by consideration of the assistance which
he might obtain from Frederick III. and Albert of Brandenburg in the affairs of his own dominions. Æneas Sylvius is not
ashamed to own that he was the instrument of bribing four of
the Archbishop's counsellors with 2,000 florins to help in
bringing him to this decision. The adhesion of Frederick of
Brandenburg was due to the influence of his brother Albert.
The others who joined in the step had all some personal interest to serve.

Round the basis thus secured adherents rapidly began to
gather. But it was clear to the Papal envoys that they must
make some concessions, and afford their new adherents a
plausible pretext for withdrawing their support from the
Electoral League. Æneas Sylvius undertook the responsibility
of playing a dubious part. He 'squeezed the venom,' as he
puts it, out of the proposals of the Electors, and composed a
document in which the Pope undertook, if the princes of Europe
agreed, to summon a General Council within ten months of the
surrender of the neutrality, recognised the Constance decrees,
confirmed the reforming decrees of Basel till the future Council
decided otherwise, and, at the instance of the King, restored
the deposed Archbishops of Trier and Köln, on condition that
they returned to his obedience.[1] The Bishop of Bologna and
Nicolas of Cusa assented to these proposals; John of Carvajal
was dubious, and hot words passed between him and Æneas,
who was afraid lest his obstinacy or honesty might spoil all.
Æneas skilfully mixed up his relations with the Pope and with
the King, and managed to produce an impression that the
Pope had commissioned him to make this offer. The sturdy
Germans, Heimburg and Lysura, were annoyed at this activity
of the renegade Italian in their national business. 'Do you
come from Siena,' said Lysura to Æneas, 'to give laws to
Germany?' Æneas thought it wiser to return no answer.

Æneas may have exaggerated his own share in this matter;
but early in October the Royal and Papal ambassadors agreed
to submit to the Diet a project of sending a new embassy to

---

[1] The Dresden MS. has in the margin of this proposal the note: 'Nota
fallaciam, quum potius rex instare deberet ut ante omnem tractatum domini
isti restituerentur,' Pückert, 289.

Rome, to negotiate with Eugenius IV. on this basis. Their demands were to go in the form of articles, not, as before, of Bulls ready prepared.

This seemed to the majority to be a salutary compromise. The Electors of Mainz and Brandenburg considered it better than a breach with the King. The Elector of Saxony and the Pfalzgraf thought that the new proposals contained all that was important in the old. The summons of a new Council would keep matters still open; anyhow, negotiations would gain time. On October 5 the league that had been formed in favour of this compromise was openly avowed, and received many adherents. It was resolved that the articles be presented to Eugenius at Christmas; if he accepted them, the neutrality should be ended; if not, the matter should be again considered. The answer was to be brought to a Diet at Nürnberg on March 19, 1447. The Archbishops of Trier and Köln found themselves deserted by the other Electors; all they could do was to join on October 11 in a final decree that the King should try to obtain from the Pope a confirmation of the Bulls prepared by the Electors; failing that, he should obtain Bulls framed according to the articles; these were to be laid before the Electors at the next Diet, and each should be free to accept or reject them. This reservation of their individual liberty was the utmost that the oligarchical leaders now hoped to obtain for themselves. Next day the Cardinal of Arles appeared before the Electors in behalf of the Council of Basel, which had been invited to support the policy of the Electors, and had issued Bulls accordingly. He proffered the Bulls, but no one would receive them. With heavy hearts the envoys of Basel left Frankfort. On their way to Basel they were attacked and plundered; only by the speed of his horse did the Cardinal of Arles succeed in taking refuge in Strasburg. He afterwards said in Basel, ' Christ was sold for thirty pieces of silver, but Eugenius has offered sixty thousand for me.'

The league of the Electors had been overthrown at Frankfort, and with it also fell the cause of the Council of Basel. Germany was the Council's last hope, and Germany had failed. The diplomacy of the Curia had helped Frederick III. to overcome the oligarchical rising in Germany; but the Pope had won more than the King. The oligarchy might find new

grounds on which to assert its privileges against the royal
power; the conciliar movement was abandoned, and the summoning of another Council was vaguely left to the Pope's
good pleasure.   The ecclesiastical reforms, which had been
made by the Council of Basel, survived merely as a basis of
further negotiations with the Pope.   If the Papal diplomacy
had withstood the full force of the conciliar movement, it was
not likely that the last ebb of the falling tide would prevail
against it.

Proposals
of the Diet
laid before
Eugenius
IV. No-
vember
1446.
There still remained, however, for the final settlement of
the question, the assent of Eugenius IV. to the undertaking of
his ambassadors.   Even at Frankfort, Carvajal had been opposed
to all concessions; at Rome, where the gravity of the situation
in Germany and the importance of the victory won at Frankfort were not fully appreciated, there was still a chance that
the Pope's obstinacy might be the beginning of new difficulties.
But the health of Eugenius IV. was failing; he was weary of
the long struggle, and desired before the end of his days to
see peace restored to the distracted Church.   The theologians
in the Curia, headed by John of Torquemada, counselled no
concession; the politicians were in favour of accepting the
proffered terms.   Eugenius showed his desire to increase the
influence of those who were conversant with German affairs
by raising to the Cardinalate in December Carvajal and the
Bishop of Bologna.   Frederick III., the Electors, and the
princes of Germany all sent their envoys to Rome.   On behalf
of the King went Æneas Sylvius and a Bohemian knight,
Procopius of Rabstein; chief amongst the others was John
of Lysura, Vicar of the Archbishop of Mainz.   They all met
at Siena, and rode into Rome, sixty horsemen.   A mile outside
the city they were welcomed by the inferior clergy, and were
honourably conducted to their lodgings.   A difficulty was first
raised whether the Pope could receive the ambassadors of the
Archbishops of Bremen and Magdeburg, seeing that those prelates had been confirmed by the Council of Basel; but this was
overcome by a suggestion of Carvajal that they should appear
as representatives of the sees, not of their present occupants.
On the third day after their arrival an audience was given to
the German ambassadors in a secret consistory, where Eugenius
was seated with fifteen cardinals.   In a clever speech Æneas

Sylvius laid the proposals before the Pope, and such was his CHAP. I. plausibility that he managed to satisfy the Germans without offending the dignity of the Pope.[1] He touched upon the evils of ecclesiastical dissension, spoke of the importance of Germany and its desire for peace, skilfully introduced the German proposals, and besought the Pope of his clemency to grant them as the means of unity. Eugenius answered by condemning the neutrality, complained of the conduct of the deposed archbishops, and finally said that he must deliberate.

On the same day Eugenius was seized by an attack of fever, Negotiations with the Curia. which confined him to his bed. The German question was referred to a commission of cardinals, and opinion was greatly divided. Only nine cardinals were in favour of concession; the others declared that the Roman See was being sold to the Germans, and that they were being dragged by the nose like buffaloes. The German proposals were not treated as though they were meant for definite acceptance, but were regarded as the basis of further negotiation. The ambassadors were entertained and cajoled by the cardinals, while the illness of Eugenius IV. made everyone anxious to have the matter settled speedily. Little by little the articles agreed on at Frankfort were pared down: (1) As regarded the summons of a new Council, the Pope agreed to it as a favour, without issuing a Bull, which might bind his successor, but merely making a personal promise to the King and the Electors.[2] (2) Instead of the acceptance of the decrees of Constance and Basel, Eugenius agreed to recognise 'the Council of Const. nce, and its decree *Frequens* and other of its decrees, and all the other Councils representing the Catholic Church.' All mention of the Council of Basel was studiously avoided, and, by the express mention of the decree *Frequens*, the omission of the more important decree *Sacrosancta* was in a measure emphasized. (3) On the third point, the acceptance of the Pragmatic Sanction of Germany as it had been established at the declaration of the neutrality in 1439, Eugenius IV. was willing to follow the example of Martin V. in granting the concordats of Constance. He recognised the existing possessors of benefices, and agreed to send a legate to Germany, who would arrange for the liberties of the German Church in the

[1] In Mansi, *Pii II. Orationes*, i. 108.
[2] Raynaldus, *Annales*, 1447, No. 5.

future, and the proper provision to be made for the Papacy in
return. Meanwhile, the condition of the German Church was
to remain as it was, 'till an agreement had been made by our
legate, or other orders given by a Council.' The Germans, who
had at first taken the Basel decrees as the foundation of an
ecclesiastical reformation, now accepted them as a limit—a
limit, moreover, which might be narrowed. (4) In like
manner the Papal diplomacy secured for the Pope a triumph in
the matter of the deposed archbishops. Eugenius IV. was
asked to annul their deposition, if they were willing to concur
in the declaration in his favour; he agreed, when they did so
concur, to restore them to their office.

Moreover, to aid the progress of these negotiations, Æneas
Sylvius undertook, in Frederick's name, that the King would
solemnly declare, and publish throughout Germany, his recognition of Eugenius, would receive with due honour a Papal
legate, would order the city of Basel to withdraw its safe-
conduct from the Council, and, as regarded the provision
to be made for the Pope out of the ecclesiastical revenues of
Germany, would act not only as a mediator, but as an ally of
the Pope.

Illness of
Eugenius
IV.
Thus diplomacy was busily spinning its web round the bed
of the dying Pope. True till the last to his persistent character,
Eugenius IV. was resolved to see the restoration of the German
obedience before he died. The theologians might make the
best terms that they could; but Eugenius made them understand that he wished to see the end. He might well gaze
with sadness on the desolation which his unyielding spirit had
wrought in the fortunes of the Church. France was practically
independent of the Papacy; Germany was estranged; a rival
Pope diminished the prestige of the Holy See; in Italy, Bologna
was lost to the domains of the Church, and the March of
Ancona was still in the hands of Sforza. He would bequeath a
disastrous legacy to his successor; but the recovery of Germany would at least improve the position. Eugenius longed to
signalise his last days by a worthy achievement; on their side
the envoys of the German King wished their mission to succeed.
Now that a goal of some sort was in view, all were eager to
reach it. If the Pope died before matters were decided, the
powers of the envoys came to an end, for they were only com-

missioned to negotiate with Eugenius. The Germans did not wish to sacrifice the present opportunity, and see everything again reduced to doubt.

The physicians gave Eugenius ten days to live when the conclusions of the Commission of Cardinals were laid before him. The Pope was too feeble to examine them fully, much more to go through the labour of reducing them to the form of Bulls. Scrupulous and persistent to the last, he dreaded even the semblance of concession when the decisive moment came. When he finally decided to give way he devised a subterfuge to save his conscience. On February 5 he signed a secret protest setting forth that the German King and Electors had desired from him certain things 'which the necessity and utility of the Church compel us in some way to grant, that we may allure them to the unity of the Church and our obedience. We, to avoid all scandal and danger which may follow, and being unwilling to say, confirm, or grant anything contrary to the doctrine of the Fathers or prejudicial to the Holy See, since through sickness we cannot examine and weigh the concessions with that thoroughness of judgment which their gravity requires, protest that by our concessions we do not intend to derogate from the doctrine of the Fathers or the authority and privileges of the Apostolic See.'[1]

By this pitiful proceeding the dying Pope prepared to enter into engagements which his successor might repudiate. He was ready to receive the restitution of the German obedience; but the German envoys, on their side, began to hesitate. They did not, of course, know the secret protest of the Pope; but they doubted whether they ought to take a step which might divide Germany, when they had no guarantee that the successor of the death-stricken Eugenius would pursue his policy. John of Lysura, who was now as zealous for reconciliation as before he had been anxious for reform, plausibly argued that they were dealing with the Roman See, which never died; the Bulls of Eugenius would bind his successor. If they left Rome without declaring the obedience of Germany, the existing disposition of the Electors might change, and everything might again become doubtful. So long as Eugenius could stir his finger, it was enough. If they went away without accomplish-

CHAP. I.

Restoration of the German obedience. February 7, 1447.

---

[1] Raynaldus, 1447, No. 7.

ing anything they would be ridiculous. Lysura and Æneas prevailed on the other ambassadors of the King and of the Archbishop of Mainz to resolve on a restoration of obedience to Eugenius IV.

On February 7 the ambassadors were admitted into the Pope's chamber. Eugenius still could greet them with dignity, but in a feeble voice requested that the proceedings should not be long. Æneas read the declaration of obedience, and Eugenius handed him the Bulls, which he gave to the ambassadors of the Archbishop of Mainz as being the primate of Germany. The envoys of the Pfalzgraf and of Saxony excused themselves from joining in the declaration; they were not empowered to do so, but they had no doubt that their princes would give their assent in the forthcoming Diet at Nürnberg. Eugenius thanked God for the work that had been accomplished, and dismissed with his benediction the ambassadors, who were moved to tears at the sight of the dying man. A public Consistory was held immediately afterwards before the whole Curia; over a thousand men were present. Æneas spoke for the King, Lysura for the Archbishop of Mainz, the other ambassadors followed. The Vice-Chancellor in the Pope's behalf spoke words of thankfulness, and the Consistory broke up amid the joyous peals of bells with which Rome celebrated its triumph. The city blazed with bonfires; the next day was a general holiday, and was devoted to a special service of thanksgiving.

The German envoys stayed in Rome, waiting for the necessary copies of the Bulls, and anxious about the new election. Day by day Eugenius grew visibly worse, and there were signs of disturbances to follow on his death. Alfonso of Naples advanced with an army within fifteen miles of Rome. There were troubles at Viterbo, and in Rome itself the people were anxious to be rid of the severe rule of Cardinal Scarampo, the favourite of Eugenius. Amidst this universal disquiet Eugenius died hard. When the Archbishop of Florence wished to administer supreme unction the Pope refused, saying, ' I am still strong ; I know my time ; when the hour is come I will send for you.' Alfonso of Naples, on hearing this, exclaimed, ' What wonder that the Pope, who has warred against Sforza, the Colonna, myself, and all Italy, dares to fight against death also ? '

At length Eugenius felt that his last hour was approaching. CHAP.
I. Summoning the Cardinals, he addressed to them his last words. Many evils, he said, had befallen the Holy See during his pontificate, yet the ways of Providence were inscrutable, and he rejoiced, at last before he died, to see the Church reunited. 'Now, before I appear in the presence of the Great Judge, I wish to leave with you my testament. I have created you all Cardinals save one, and him I have loved as a son. I beseech you, keep the bond of peace, and let there be no divisions among you. You know what sort of a Pope the Holy See requires; elect a successor in wisdom and character superior to me. If you listen to me, you will rather elect with unanimity a moderate man than a distinguished one with discord. We have reunited the Church, but the root of discord still remains; be careful that it does not grow up afresh. That there be no dispute about my funeral, bury me simply, and lay me in a lowly place by the side of Eugenius III.' All wept as they heard him.[1] He received supreme unction, was placed in S. Peter's chair, and there died on February 23, at the age of 62. According to Vespasiano da Bisticci, he exclaimed shortly before his death: 'O Gabrielle, how much better had it been for your soul's health had you never become pope or cardinal, but died a simple monk! Poor creatures that we are, we know ourselves at last.' His body was exhibited to public view, and he was buried, according to his desire, in S. Peter's by the side of Eugenius III.

Amid the disastrous events of his pontificate, the personal character of Eugenius IV. seems to play an insignificant part. At his accession he had to face a difficult problem, which would have tried the tact and patience of the largest and wisest mind. But Eugenius was a narrow-minded monk, with no experience of the world and a large fund of obstinacy. He quarrelled with the Romans; he alarmed the politicians of Italy; he offended a strong party in the Curia, and finally proceeded to defy a Council which was supported by the moral approval of Europe. Such wisdom as Eugenius IV. ever gained, he gained in the hard school of experience. After the

Character
of Eu-
genius IV.

---

[1] This account is given by Æneas Sylvius in his letter from Rome to Frederick III., Muratori, vol. iii. pt. 2, p. 889. The other account is given by Vespasiano, *Vita de Eugenio IV.*

mistakes of the first year of his pontificate, the rest of his life
was a desperate struggle for existence. The one quality that
helped him in his misfortune was the same obstinacy as first
led him astray.[1] Where a more sensitive or a more timid man
might have been disposed for compromise Eugenius stood firm,
and in the long run won a tardy victory, not by his own skill, but
through the faults of his opponents. Time was on the side of
the representative of an old institution, and every mistake of
the Council brought strength to the Pope. Those who at first
attacked him through bitter personal animosity gradually
found that he was the symbol of a system which they did not
dare to destroy. The wisdom and skill of eminent men, which
at first enabled the Council to attack the Pope, were gradually
transferred to the Pope's service. Every mistake committed
by the Council lost it a few adherents, alarmed at the dangers
which they foresaw, or anxious for their own personal interests,
but all determined on the overthrow of that which they had
forsaken. To them Eugenius IV. was necessary; and they paid
him greater reverence through remorse for the wrongs which they
had formerly done him.[2] No man is so zealous as one who has
deliberately changed his convictions; and the success of Eugenius at the last was due to the zeal of those who had deserted
the Council. Hence Eugenius IV. was faithfully served in
his latter days, though he inspired no enthusiasm. He was
the Pope, the Italian Pope, and as such was the necessary
leader of those who wished to maintain the prestige of the
Papacy, and to keep it secure in its seat at Rome. But he
was outside the chief interests, intellectual and political, which
were moving Italy. Politically he pursued a course of his own,
and was not trusted by Venice, nor Florence, nor by the
Duke of Milan, nor by Alfonso of Naples, while in Rome
itself his rule was harsh and oppressive both to the barons and
the people. He was a man of little culture, and such ideas as
he had were framed upon his monastic training. Yet, though
he was untouched by the classical revival, he was not opposed
to it. Among his secretaries were Poggio Bracciolini, Flavio

[1] ' Fu molto capitoso e di dura testa ' is the testimony of Paolo Petrone,
Mur. xxiv. 1130.

[2] The final judgment of Æneas Sylvius was ' Alti cordis fuit, sed nullum
in eo magis vitium fuit, nisi quia sine mensura erat, et non quod potuit sed quod
voluit aggressus est,' Mur. iii. pt. 2, p. 891.

Biondo, Maffeo Vegio, Giovanni Aurispa, and Piero de Noceto.[1]
He welcomed at Rome the antiquary Ciriaco of Ancona and the
humanist George of Trebizond, and employed in his affairs the
learned Ambrogio Traversari. He pursued the plan of Martin V.
to restore the decayed buildings of Rome; and in his later
days summoned Fra Angelico to decorate the Vatican Chapel.
He also invited to Rome the great Florentine sculptor Donatello;
but his plans were interrupted by the disturbances of 1434
and his flight from the city. While at Florence he so admired
Ghiberti's magnificent gates to the Baptistery that he resolved
to decorate S. Peter's by a like work, which he entrusted to a
mediocre but eminently orthodox artist, Antonio Filarete. The
gates of Eugenius IV. still adorn the central doorway of S. Peter's,
and are a testimony of the Pope's good intentions rather than of
his artistic feelings. Large figures, stiffly and ungracefully
executed, of Christ, the Virgin, SS. Peter and Paul, fill the chief
panels; between them are small reliefs commemorating the
glories of the pontificate of Eugenius IV., the coming of the
Greeks to Ferrara, the Council of Florence, the coronation of
Sigismund, the envoys of the Oriental Churches in Rome. On the
lower panels are representations of martyrdoms of saints. The
reliefs are destitute of expression and are architecturally ineffec-
tive. The imagination of the artist has been reserved for the ara-
besque work which frames them. There every possible subject
seems to be blended in wild confusion—classical legends,
medallions of Roman emperors, illustrations of Æsop's fables,
allegories of the seasons, representations of games and sports—
all are interwoven amongst heavy wreaths of ungraceful foliage.
Eugenius IV. showed his respect for antiquity by restoring the
Pantheon, but did not scruple to carry off for his other works
the stones of the Colosseum.[2] Though personally modest and
retiring, he had all the Venetian love of public splendour;
he caused Ghiberti to design a magnificent Papal tiara, which
cost 30,000 golden ducats. Without possessing any taste of
his own, Eugenius IV. so far followed the fashion of his time
that he prepared the way for the outburst of magnificence which
Nicolas V. made part of the Papal policy.

[1] See Bonamici, *De Claris Pontificiarum litterarum Scriptoribus*.
[2] See Müntz, *Les Arts à la Cour des Papes*, i. 32, &c.

The object, however, which lay nearest the heart of Eugenius IV. was the promotion of the Franciscan Order, to which he himself had belonged. The friars held a chief place at his court, and were admitted at once to the Papal presence, where their affairs had precedence over all others, to the great indignation of the humanists. Poggio rejoiced that under the successor of Eugenius the reign of hypocrisy was at an end,[1] and friars would no longer swarm like rats in Rome. If the policy of Eugenius was to erect the friars once more into a powerful arm of the Holy See, the corrupt state of the body made such a restoration impossible. Yet Eugenius would give more attention to remodelling the rules of a religious order than to the great questions which surrounded him on every side. His notion of ecclesiastical reform was to turn monastic orders into orders of friars, and he met the demands of the Fathers of Basel by displaying great activity in this hopeless work.[2]

In person Eugenius IV. was tall, of a spare figure, and of imposing aspect. Though he drank nothing but water, he was a martyr to gout. He was attentive to all his religious duties, lived sparingly, and was liberal of alms. He slept little, and used to wake early and read devotional books. He was reserved and retiring, averse from public appearances, and so modest that in public he scarcely lifted his eyes from the ground.[3] Though stubborn and self-willed, he bore no malice, and was ready to forgive those who had attacked him. He had few intimates; but when he once gave his confidence he gave it unreservedly, and Vitelleschi and Scarampo successively directed his affairs in Italy. A man of monastic and old-fashioned piety, he was destitute of political capacity, and was more fitted to be an abbot than a pope. What might in a smaller sphere have been firmness of purpose, became narrow obstinacy in the ruler of the Universal Church. It is a proof of the firm foundation of Papacy in the political system of Europe, that it was too deeply rooted for the mismanagement of Eugenius IV., at a dangerous crisis of its history, to upset its stability.

---

[1] *Dialogus contra hypocrisim*, in *Fasciculus Rerum*; Appendix, 571.

[2] Vespasiano, *Vita di Eugenio IV.*, 'attendeva con ogni diligenza a riformare la Chiesa, e fare che i religiosi stessino a' termini loro, ed i conventuali fargli osservanti, giusto alla possa sua.'

[3] Raffaelle de Volterra, *Commentarii (Anthropologia)* xxii. : ' oculos in publico nunquam attollebat, ut a parente meo, qui eum sequebatur, accepi.'

CHAPTER II.

NICOLAS V. AND THE AFFAIRS OF GERMANY.

1447–1453.

ON the death of Eugenius IV. the troubled state of Rome made the Cardinals anxious about the future. It was of the utmost importance for the peace of the Church that the new election should be peaceable and orderly, that the new Pope should have an undoubted title; but the attitude of the Romans, who had endured with murmurs the rule of Eugenius IV., made the Cardinals dread a repetition of the tumults which had caused the Schism. The citizens of Rome held a meeting in the monastery of Araceli to draw up demands which should be submitted to the Cardinals.[1] The Cardinals in dismay urged the Archbishop of Benevento, Cardinal Agnesi, to attend the meeting and confer with the citizens. The leader of the Romans was Stefano Porcaro, a man of considerable knowledge of affairs, sprung from an old burgher's stock in Rome. Porcaro recommended himself by his capacity to Martin V., who obtained for him the post of Capitano del Popolo in Florence. There he became acquainted with many of the chief humanists, and on leaving Florence he travelled in France and Germany. By Eugenius IV. he was made Podestà of Bologna, where his reputation increased, and he won the friendship of Ambrogio Traversari,[2] who advised the Pope to employ Porcaro as mediator with the rebellious Romans in 1434. Eugenius refused all mediation, and his obstinacy was rewarded by

---

[1] Infessura, in Mur. iii. 2, 1131 ; Æn. Syl. id. 891.

[2] Our chief information about the early life of Porcaro comes from scattered notices amongst the letters of Traversari.

　　　　　　　T

success ; but it alienated Porcaro from the Papal service, and his classical studies drifted him to the republicanism of ancient Rome. In the assembly at Araceli Porcaro rose, and in a fiery speech stirred the citizens to remember their ancient liberties. They ought, at least, to have an agreement with the Pope such as even the smallest towns in the States of the Church had managed to obtain. Many agreed with him,[1] and the Archbishop of Benevento had some difficulty in reducing him to silence. The assembly broke up in confusion, and many citizens gathered round Porcaro.

Peace kept
by Alfonso
of Naples.

But the Republican party was afraid to move through fear of Alfonso of Naples, who lay at Tivoli with an army, with a view of influencing the new election. He had already sent a message to the Cardinals that he was there to secure for them a free election, and was at their commands. The Romans felt he would use any movement on their part as a pretext for seizing the city ; and it was useless to escape from the rule of the Church only to fall under that of the King of Naples. Accordingly the Republican party held its hand. The keys of the city were given to the Cardinals, who made the Grand Master of the Teutonic Knights guardian of the Capitol, and published a decree ordering the barons to leave Rome. The bands who were flocking from the country into the city were excluded, the barons unwillingly departed, and all was quiet when, on March 4, the Cardinals went into conclave in the dormitory of the cloister of S. Maria sopra Minerva.

Prepara-
tions for
the Con-
clave.

Æneas Sylvius gives a description of the preparations for the conclave. The dormitory was divided into cells for the eighteen Cardinals present; but on this occasion the partitions were of cloth, not of wood. Lots were drawn for the distribution of the cells, which each cardinal adorned with hangings according to his taste. Each entered the conclave · with his attendants, a chaplain and a cross-bearer ; each had his own food sent him every day in a wooden box, on which his arms were emblazoned. These boxes were carried through the streets in a way that made the city seem to be full of funerals ; they were accompanied by a procession of the Cardinal's household and all his dependents, who had so contracted the habit of

[1] ' Disse alcune cose utili per la nostra Repubblica,' says Infessura, Mur. iii. pt. 2, 1131.

flattery that, when their master was not there, they were fain to grovel to the box that contained his dinner.[1]

CHAP.
II.

Election of
Tommaso
Parentu-
celli, Nico-
las V.
March 6,
1447.

When the eighteen Cardinals entered the conclave it was the general expectation that their choice would fall on Prospero Colonna, the nephew of Martin V. But the old Roman proverb, ' He who goes into the conclave a Pope comes out a Cardinal,' was again proved true. Prospero Colonna was supported by the powerful Cardinals Scarampo and Le Jeune ; but the party of the Orsini were strongly opposed to an election from the house of their rivals, and many of the Cardinals thought that it would be bad policy to run the risk of kindling discord in the city. The opponents of Colonna were more anxious to prevent his election than careful who else was elected. On the first scrutiny Colonna had ten votes and Capranica eight. In the hopes of agreeing on another candidate, various names were suggested of those outside the college, such as the Archbishop of Benevento and Nicolas of Cusa. On the second scrutiny Colonna still had ten votes, but the votes of his opponents were more divided, and three were given for Thomas of Bologna. The election of Colonna now seemed secure. ' Why do we waste time,' said Cardinal Le Jeune, ' when delay is hurtful to the Church ? The city is disturbed ; King Alfonso is at the gates; the Duke of Savoy is plotting against us; Sforza is our foe. Why do we not elect a Pope ? God has sent us a gentle lamb, the Cardinal Colonna: he only needs two votes; if one be given, the other will follow.' There was a brief silence ; then Thomas of Bologna rose to give his vote for Colonna. The Cardinal of Taranto eagerly stopped him. 'Pause,' he said, ' and reflect that we are not electing a ruler of a city but of the Universal Church. Let us not be too hasty.' 'You mean that you oppose Colonna,' exclaimed Scarampo ; ' if the election were going according to your wishes, you would not speak of haste. You wish to object, not to deliberate. Tell us whom you want for Pope.' To parry this home-thrust, which was true, the Cardinal of Taranto found it necessary to mention some one definitely. 'Thomas of Bologna,' he exclaimed. ' I accept him,' said Scarampo, who was followed by Le Jeune, and

---

[1] ' Usque adeo miseros Curiales adulandi consuetudo illexit ut quum Cardi-
nalibus nequeant Cornutis assententur,' Mur. iii. 2, 892. The boxes were
called Cornuta.

soon Thomas had eleven votes in his favour. Finally, Torquemada said, ' I, too, vote for Thomas, and make him Pope ; to-day we celebrate the vigil of S. Thomas.' The others accepted the election that it might be unanimous, and Cardinal Colonna announced it to the people. The mob could not hear him, and a cry was raised that he was Pope. The Orsini roused themselves; the people, according to old custom, pillaged Colonna's house. Their mistake was lucky for themselves, as Thomas was a poor man, and they found little booty in his house afterwards. The election was a universal surprise. The Cardinal of Portugal, as he limped out of the Conclave, when asked if the Cardinals had elected a Pope, answered, ' No, God has chosen a Pope, not the Cardinals.'

Early life
of Paren-
tucelli.

Tommaso Parentucelli [1] sprang from an obscure family at Sarzana, a little town not far from Spezia, in the diocese of Lucca. His father, Bartolommeo, was a physician in Pisa or Lucca, it is not certain which. At the age of seven he lost his father, and his mother soon afterwards married again ; but she was careful to give her son a good education, and at the age of twelve sent him to school at Bologna. As he had to make his own way in the world, he went to Florence at the age of nineteen, and acted as private tutor to the sons, first of Rinaldo degli Albizzi, and afterwards of Palla Strozzi. By this means he saved in three years enough money to enable him to return to Bologna and continue his studies at the University, where he attracted the notice of the bishop of the city, Niccolo Albergata, who took him into his service. For twenty years Parentucelli continued to be at the head of Albergata's household; he looked upon the Cardinal as a second father, and served him with zeal. But he was a genuine student, and employed his leisure in theological reading. He became famous for his large and varied knowledge, his great powers of memory, and his readiness and quickness as a disputant. In Albergata's service he accompanied his master on many embassies, and obtained an insight into the politics of Europe, while at the same time, by his own reputation for learning, he

[1] The very name is uncertain. Manetti, Mur. iii. 2, 107, says : ' De nobili Parentucellorum progenie.' Two Bulls of Felix V. (Mansi, xxxi. 188, 190) call him Thomas de Calandrinis ; but Ciaconius, ii. 961, gives from Oldoinus two inscriptions from a tomb at Sarzana which call his mother Andreola de Calderinis, and an uncle J. P. Parentucelli.

made acquaintance with the chief scholars of Italy. No one
had a greater knowledge of books, and Cosimo de' Medici consulted him about the formation of the library of S. Marco.
The only luxury in which Parentucelli indulged was in books,
for which he had a student's love. He was careful to have fair
manuscripts made for his own use, and was himself famous for
his beautiful handwriting.[1]

On the death of Albergata in 1443 Parentucelli entered
the service of Cardinal Landriani, and after his death in the
same year was employed by Eugenius IV., who soon made him
Bishop of Bologna. But Bologna was in revolt against the
Pope, and Parentucelli gained such scanty revenues either from
his see or from the bounty of Eugenius IV. that he was driven
to borrow money from Cosimo de' Medici to enable him to discharge his legation in Germany. Such was Cosimo's friendship that he gave him a general letter of credit to all his cor-
respondents. The embassy in Germany led to important
results, and Eugenius IV. recognised the merits of Parentucelli
by making him Cardinal in December 1446. He had only
enjoyed his new dignity a few months before his elevation to
the Papacy. His first act was a sign of gratitude to his early
patron and friend. He took the pontifical title of Nicolas V.
in remembrance of Niccolo Albergata.

If the election of Nicolas V. was not very gratifying to any
political party, it was least objectionable to none. The Colonna,
the Orsini, Venice, the Duke of Milan, the King of France,
the King of Naples, all had hoped for an election in their own
special interest. All were disappointed; but at least they had
the satisfaction of considering that their opponents had gained
as little as themselves. No one could object to the new Pope.
He was a man of high character and tried capacity. He had
made himself friends everywhere by his learning, and had made
no enemies by his politics. Alfonso of Naples sent four ambassadors to congratulate him and be present at his coronation.
Æneas Sylvius waited on him to receive a confirmation of the
agreement which Eugenius IV. had made with Germany.
'I will not only confirm but execute it,' was the answer of
Nicolas. 'In my opinion the Roman Pontiffs have too greatly

---

[1] Vespasiano da Bisticci, himself a Florentine bookseller, speaks with admiration of the technical skill of Parentucelli as a scribe and a librarian.

extended their authority, and left the other bishops no jurisdiction.   It is a just judgment that the Council of Basel has
in turn shortened too much the hands of the Holy See.   We
intend to strengthen the bishops, and hope to maintain our
own power most surely by not usurping that of others.'[1]
These words of Nicolas V. express the entire situation of
ecclesiastical affairs.   If his policy could only have been carried
out, the future of the Church might still have been assured.
In the same sense he spoke about secular matters to his old
friend the Florentine bookseller, Vespasiano da Bisticci.   Vespasiano presented himself at a public audience, and Nicolas
bade him wait till he was done.   Then he took him into a
private room, and said, with a smile, 'Would the people of
Florence have believed that a simple priest who rang the bell
would one day become Pope to the confusion of the proud?'
Vespasiano answered that his elevation was due to his merits,
and that he now might pacify Italy.   'I pray God,' said
Nicolas, 'that He will give me grace to carry out my intention,
which is to pacify Italy, and to use in my pontificate no other
arms than those which Christ has given me, that is, His Cross.'

Embassies
of congra-
tulation
to the new
Pope.

The pacific character of the new Pope made him generally
acceptable.   After his coronation on March 18, embassies from
the various Italian States flowed into Rome, and the dexterity
and precision with which Nicolas answered their harangues increased the opinion which men already had of his capacity.   He
received the embassies in open consistory, so that those who
wished to regale themselves with a banquet of eloquence might
be fully satisfied.   Already in Italy a cultivated taste had
begun to attach great importance to the neat and decorous performance of formal duties.   Cities were anxious to have in their
service men whose speeches on public occasions could win
applause by the elegance of their style; and scholars rose to the
rank of State officials by the reputation which they gained
from these public appearances.   Under Eugenius IV. the
Papacy had not given much encouragement to this display of
eloquence; but Nicolas V., himself a scholar and the friend of
scholars, was willing to fall in with the prevalent taste.   His
public audiences were crowded with critics, and reputations
were made or unmade in a morning.   The complimentary

[1] In Mur. iii. pt. 2, 895.

harangue began to hold the same relation to the new culture of the Renaissance as had the scholastic disputation to the erudition of the Middle Ages. In this arena of eloquence Nicolas V. himself could hold his own with the best, not so much by elegance of style as by the readiness with which he could aptly reply, on the spur of the moment, to an elaborately prepared speech. The very graces of the orator who had preceded him lent a foil to the readiness of the Pope. Thus the Florentine embassy was headed by the learned Gianozzo Manetti, who spoke for an hour and a quarter. The Pope, with his hand before his face, seemed to be asleep, and one of his attendants touched his arm to wake him. But when Gianozzo had finished, Nicolas took each of his points in order, and gave a suitable answer to them all. The audience knew not which to admire most, the grace of the orator or the aptness of the Pope.[1] The cleverness of Nicolas V. soon won for him the respect of those who at first looked with disfavour on the insignificant appearance of the successor of the majestic Eugenius IV. Nicolas V. had no outward graces to commend him. He was little, with weak legs disproportionately small for his body; a face of ashen complexion brought into still greater prominence his black flashing eyes; his voice was loud and harsh; his mouth small, with heavily protruding lips.

Nicolas V., however, had more serious work in hand than the reception of ambassadors. His first care, naturally, was to secure the restoration of the German obedience. Æneas Sylvius, who had acted as cross-bearer at the Pope's coronation on March 18, set out on March 30 to carry to Frederick III. the confirmation by Nicolas V. of the engagements of his predecessor. Æneas advised the King to renew his declaration of obedience, and order all men to receive honourably the Pope's legates; so would he end the schism, conciliate the Pope, win back Hungary, and prepare the way for his coronation as Emperor. Æneas himself soon received a mark of the Pope's favour in the shape of a nomination to the vacant bishopric of Trieste. As Æneas found himself rising in the world, and his age advanced beyond the temptations of youthful passion, his objections to take Holy Orders had died away. In 1446 he resolved to live more cleanly, 'to abandon,' as he said,

---

[1] Vespasiano, *Vita di Nicola V.*

'Venus for Bacchus.' He was ordained, and 'loved nothing so
much as the priesthood.' Only through ecclesiastical preferment could he hope for any recognition of his services.
While he was at Rome there came a report of the death of the
Bishop of Trieste, and Eugenius IV. was ready to appoint
Æneas to the vacant see. The Bishop of Trieste outlived
Eugenius; but Nicolas V. carried out his predecessor's intention,
disregarding the fact that, by the compact between Eugenius
and Frederick, Trieste was one of the bishoprics granted to the
King's nomination. No difficulty, however, arose on this head,
as Frederick III., independently of the Pope, had nominated
Æneas. It is true that the Chapter of Trieste tried to
assert their rights, but were at once set aside by the King and
Pope, and Æneas won his first decided step in the way of
preferment.[1]

Congress at
Bourges.
June 1447.
As affairs stood in Germany, the King, the Archbishop of
Mainz, and the Elector of Brandenburg were ready to acknowledge Nicolas V.; the other Electors had not yet declared
themselves. Wishing to make the best terms for themselves,
they turned to the King of France, who held a congress at
Bourges in June. Jacob of Trier went there in person; the
other Electors sent representatives. England, Scotland, Burgundy, and Castile were all ready to follow the French King,
who thus asserted in the affairs of the Church the authority
which had previously belonged to the Emperor. The conclusions signed at Bourges on June 28 were a little in advance
of those accepted by Frederick III. The King of France and
the Electors were ready to acknowledge Nicolas V. if he recognised the existing condition of ecclesiastical affairs, agreed to
summon a Council on September 1, 1448, in some place to be
determined by the French King, accepted the Constance
decrees, and agreed to provide for his rival, Felix V.[2] There
was in this a pretence of standing upon the conciliar basis, and
maintaining the cause of reform more definitely than Frederick
III. had done; but it was done by an alliance with the French
King, the enemy of the German nation. It was the expression
of anarchy and self-interest rather than any care for the na-

---

[1] Pii II., *Comment.* 14.
[2] '*Advisata in facto pacis ecclesiæ*,' in D'Achery, *Spicilegium*, iii. 770.
Labbe, xiii. 1330.

tional welfare; it was merely a means of making better terms than could be obtained by joining Frederick III. The Congress then moved from Bourges to Lyons, that it might more easily negotiate with Felix V. the terms of his abdication.

Meanwhile Frederick III. summoned an assembly of the princes who had joined his party at Aschaffenburg on July 12. The Archbishop of Mainz presided, and the assembly confirmed what had been done at Rome. Frederick III. withdrew his safe-conduct from the Council of Basel, and ordered it to disperse; but no immediate heed was paid to his command. On August 21 he published in Vienna a general edict announcing his adhesion to the conclusion of the assembly at Aschaffenburg, and forbade, under the ban of the Empire, any adhesion to Felix V. or the Council of Basel.[1] The proclamation was celebrated by festivities in Vienna and by a solemn procession. But this display of joy was fictitious, and the University was only driven to take part in the procession under threat of depri-vation of its revenues and benefices.[2] The academic feeling remained till the last true to the conciliar cause.

But the Papal diplomacy steadily pursued its course. Æneas Sylvius found himself, as Bishop of Trieste, occupied in the same way as when he held the inferior office of royal secretary. He was sent to Köln to win over the archbishop, and succeeded in the object of his mission. But at Köln he found himself regarded by the University as an apostate; the sneers which had elsewhere been spoken behind his back were there expressed before his face. Æneas found it necessary to justify himself in a letter addressed to the rector of the University, and his apology is full of characteristic shrewdness.[3] He went to Basel, he said, an unfledged nestling from Siena; there he heard nothing but abuse of Eugenius, and was too inex-perienced to disbelieve what he heard. Dazzled by the eminence of the Council's leaders, he followed in their track, and his vanity led him to write against Eugenius. But God had mercy on him, and he went to Frankfort as Saul had gone to Damascus. If even Augustine had written confessions, why should not he? At Frederick's Court he first began to hear

[1] See Chmel's *Materialien*, I. 245; Raynaldus, 1447, 17.
[2] Mitterdorfer, *Hist. Univ. Viennens*, i. 161.
[3] It is given in Fea, *Pius II. a calumniis vindicatus*, p. 1.

both sides, and gradually became neutral, till the arguments of
Cesarini convinced him that he ought to leave the Council's
party. His chief reasons for doing so were: (1) The wrongful
proceedings against the Pope, who was neither heretical,
schismatic, nor a cause of scandal, and therefore ought not
justly to be deposed; (2) the nullity of the Council, which had
been translated by the Pope, did not represent the Universal
Church, and was not supported by any nation in Europe except
Savoy; (3) the Council did not trust the justice of its own
cause; was faith only to be found at Basel, as Apollo gave
oracles only at Delphi?—by refusing to go elsewhere the
Council showed disbelief in itself.

The
German
Electors
recognise
Nicolas V.
1448.
Thus Æneas justified himself, and the cause of Nicolas V.
progressed, as the Electors saw that they could gain something
from the Pope. Jacob of Trier began to make terms for himself. Dietrich of Köln used Carvajal to mediate in a troublesome
dispute between himself and the Duke of Cleve. The Pfalzgraf,
though the son-in-law of Felix V., was content with exacting a
few concessions from Frederick III., and sent his ambassador to
Rome. The Elector of Saxony obtained corresponding favours
from the King. On no side was there any real care for Church
reform; it merely served as a cry under cover of which the
Electors sought to promote their own power and their own
interests. Early in 1448 the whole of Germany had entered
the obedience of Nicolas V.

Concordat
of Vienna.
February
1448.
In accordance with the undertaking of Eugenius IV., a
legate was sent to Germany to arrange for the liberties of the
German Church in the future, and the no less important question of the provision to be made for the Pope out of its
revenues. Cardinal Carvajal was wisely chosen for this purpose, and the Concordat at Vienna on February 16, 1448, was
the work of himself and the King. It was not submitted to a
Diet, though no doubt many representatives of the Electors
and the princes were at Vienna. It would seem that the
assembly of Aschaffenburg was dexterously turned into a Diet;
and the Concordat, made in the name of the German nation, was
regarded as being a necessary consequence of that assembly.[1]

The Concordat of Vienna and the Pragmatic Sanction of

---

[1] The Concordat has been often printed, best by Koch, *Sanctio Pragmatica
Germanorum Illustrata.* Argentor. 1789, p. 210.

Bourges represent the net result of the reforming movement at Basel, and in their form, as well as their contents, go back to the system pursued at the end of the Council of Constance. The strength of the reforming party was its cry for the redress of grievances which each national Church experienced from Papal interference. Its weakness lay in the fact that it had not sufficient statesmanship to devise a means of redressing these grievances without destroying the constitution of the Church under the Papal monarchy. The Council of Constance fell in pieces before the difficulties of this task, and produced merely a temporary agreement between the Papacy and the national Churches concerning a few matters of complaint. The Council of Basel, in its desire to abolish abuses, threatened to sweep away also the basis of the Papal monarchy, and so became engaged in an irreconcilable contest with the Papacy, in which it was not supported by the public opinion of Europe. In this state of things France used the opportunity to regulate by royal authority the relations of the Gallican Church to Rome. Germany, after a vain endeavour to arbitrate as neutral between the rival Popes, fell back upon the old method of a Concordat, and aimed merely at extending the basis which had been established at Constance. The Concordat of Constance was made provisionally for five years only; the Concordat of Vienna was meant, on the Papal side, to be permanent. It was, of course, true that Eugenius IV. had agreed in February 1447 that another Council should be assembled within ten months. A year passed, and nothing was done towards summoning a Council. The Concordat of Vienna confirmed all that Eugenius IV. had granted, 'so far as they do not go against this present agreement;' it made no mention of a Council, and the promise of Eugenius IV. lapsed through non-fulfilment.

Thus Germany was contented to accept as the settlement of its grievances a private agreement between the King and the Pope. The question arranged by the Concordat of Vienna was the relations henceforth to exist between the Papacy and the German Church. It was little more than a repetition of the Concordat of Constance; but such alterations as were made were in favour of the Pope.

It dealt only with the grievances caused by Papal reservations and Papal interference with elections. It admitted the right of Papal reservation to benefices whose holders died at the Roman Court or within two days' journey from Rome, to vacancies caused by Papal deprivation or translation, to benefices vacated by the deaths of cardinals or other officials of the Curia, to offices held by any promoted by the Pope to a bishopric, monastery, or other office incompatible with residence. Moreover, Papal provisions were allowed to benefices, excepting the higher offices in cathedrals and collegiate churches, such as might fall vacant in the months of January, March, May, July, September, and November. The Concordat of Constance had given to the Pope alternate benefices. The Concordat of Vienna gave him alternate months, and it is noticeable that by this arrangement the Pope secured 184 out of the 365 days of the year.

The Papal right of confirmation of other elections was retained as before. In case the elections were canonical, the Pope was to confirm them, unless 'from some reasonable and evident cause, and with the consent of the Cardinals, the Pope thought that provision should be made for some more useful and more worthy person.' If the elections were found to be uncanonical, the Pope was to provide. The dues to the Curia, annates, first fruits, and the rest, were to be paid in two portions within two years. If the rates were thought excessive, the Pope was willing to have a revaluation; also he was ready to take into account any special circumstances which affected at any time the revenues of the office so taxed. Benefices below the annual value of twenty-four florins were to be exempt.

The Papal restoration was complete. The German Church gained nothing. The only points which showed any care for its interests were provisions that the Papal reservation should be exercised only in favour of Germans, and that the Papal months should be accepted by the Ordinaries. These advantages were, however, seeming rather than real. If so much were secured by the Papacy, it would be difficult to prevent it from overstepping these slight barriers.

No mention was made in the Concordat of the Council of Basel or of its decrees. The reforming movement had been a political failure, and the fruits of its labours were swept away by the reaction. The Council had not succeeded in accomplishing any of its objects. It had not even impressed the

Curia with a sense of the gravity of the crisis from which it had escaped. The restored Papacy was only bent on going back to its old lines, and showed no desire to lay the foundations of a gradual reform of the abuses which had exposed it to so grave a peril. The Concordat was signed at Vienna on February 18; it was confirmed at Rome on March 19, 'after careful investigation by learned canonists and eminent cardinals,' though the intervening time barely allowed it to be carried from one place to another.

The reason why Frederick III. submitted to terms, which were so manifestly in the Pope's favour, was the need which he felt of maintaining his alliance with the Pope as the only means of checking the electoral oligarchy, and preventing their further connexion with France. He had no ground for opposing the Papal power of reservation. His private agreement with Eugenius IV. allowed the Pope to confer upon him privileges which were founded on the Papal right of reservation. The assent of the Electors was gained by bribes of different kinds; the Archbishops were won over, like the King, by grants of some of the Papal reservations.[1] The Pope bought back the obedience of Germany by granting to the existing representatives of the German Church and nation some of the privileges which were restored to the Papacy. As the existing generation died out everything would again revert to the Pope.

Motives for
the acceptance of
the Concordat by
Germany.

The conclusion of the Concordat of Vienna ended the dwindling existence of the Council of Basel. On May 18 Frederick III. forbade the city of Basel, under threat of the ban of the Empire, to harbour the Council within its walls. The citizens found it necessary at last to yield, and on July 7 five hundred of them honourably escorted the remnants of the Council on their way to Lausanne, whither they transferred themselves under the protection of the French King. Charles VII. undertook the task of bringing the schism to an end, and played the same part in ecclesiastical affairs as Sigismund had done in the previous generation. Felix V. was weary of his shadowy dignity. The conciliatory temper of Nicolas V. towards him and Charles VII. made the ultimate settlement tolerably easy.[2]

---

[1] See Pückert, *Die Kürfürstliche Neutralität*, p. 321.
[2] The documents are in Martene, *Amp. Coll.* VIII. 988 &c., and Raynaldus, 1449.

The ambassadors of England and of René of Anjou took part
in the work, and Charles VII. obtained a promise from Nicolas
V. that a new Council should be held in the dominions of
France. On April 7, 1449, Felix V. laid aside his Papal office ;
but he did so in language that still asserted the principle which
he had been elected to maintain : ' In this holy synod of Lausanne, representing the Universal Church, we lay aside the
dignity and possession of the Papacy, hoping that the kings,
princes, and prelates, to whom we judge that this our communication will be acceptable, will aid the authority of General
Councils, will defend and support it ; and that the Universal
Church, for whose dignity and authority we have fought, will
by its prayers commend our humility to the chief and eternal
Shepherd.'

Dissolution
of the
Council of
Basel.
Well may the Papal chronicler remark that there is not a
sentence, scarcely a word, in this which does not merit censure.[1]
But Nicolas V. was not obstinate, like his predecessor ; provided he won the substantial point, he was not careful about
words. He had saved the Papal dignity by committing the
conduct of the negotiation to Charles VII.; Felix V. might
have his say provided he abdicated peaceably. The Council
also was allowed to save its dignity. On April 19 it elected
Nicolas V. as Pope, and on April 25 conferred by a decree on
Amadeus the office of Cardinal, which Nicolas V. had agreed
to grant him, together with the first place next to the Pope, the
position of General Vicar within the dominions that had recognised him, and the outward honours of the Papal rank. The
Council then decreed its own dissolution, and its members dispersed. True to his conciliatory policy, Nicolas V. restored
d'Allemand to his office of Cardinal, and recognised three of the
creations of Felix V. John of Segovia received from the Pope
a little bishopric in Spain, where, hidden among the hills, he
spent the rest of his days in Arabic studies, translated the
Koran into Latin, and exposed its errors.[2] D'Allemand retired to
his see of Arles, where he was famous for his personal piety and
good works, and after his death, September 16, 1450, it was
said that miracles were wrought at his tomb. So great was his
fame for sanctity that Clement VII. in 1527 pronounced him

---

[1] Raynaldus, 1449, 2.   [2] Æn. Sylv., *De Europa*, ch. 42.

worthy of the imitation of the faithful.[1]   Amadeus did not long
survive him; he died on January 7, 1451, 'more useful to the
Church by his death than by his life,' says Æneas Sylvius,[2]
though most of his contemporaries are willing to forgive his
previous misdeeds in remembrance of his renunciation.

Thus Nicolas V. had the satisfaction of seeing the schism
brought to an end, its last remnants swept away, and the
Papacy restored to a supremacy which it had not enjoyed
for nearly a century.   In Italy also Nicolas V. had the satisfaction of bringing back order into the Papal States.   He
soothed the rebellious spirit of the Romans by ordaining that
only Romans should hold magistracies and benefices within the
city, and that the imposts should be spent only for the good of
the city.[3] He soothed the barons by his mildness, and did
away with the grievances of the Colonna by allowing them to
rebuild Palestrina, on condition that it should not be fortified.
The knowledge which he had gained as Bishop of Bologna
showed him that that city could be won by a compromise.   He
was content that it should recognise the sovereignty of the
Holy See and admit a Papal legate, with certain powers of
interference; otherwise it might retain the rule of the Bentivogli and appoint its own magistrates.   The luckiest event,
however, for Nicolas V. was the death, on August 13, 1447,
of Filippo Maria Visconti, which left the affairs of Milan in
confusion, and turned elsewhere the ambition of Francesco
Sforza, who withdrew his forces from the March of Ancona, and
left the Pope in undisputed possession.

Death of
Filippo
Maria Vis-
conti. Au-
gust 1447.

Filippo Maria Visconti is a typical character of the last members of the princely families who had made themselves lords
of the cities of Italy.   He succeeded by caution, prudence,
and treachery in gathering together the broad dominions of
his father, Gian Galeazzo; but the strain which the effort
involved seems to have paralysed his faculties.   He had studied
so carefully the mode by which a principality was won, that he
had learned with fatal accuracy the ease with which it might be
lost.   His energies were entirely devoted to the security of his
own person, the suppression of possible rivals, the maintenance
of his own position.   Though engaged in many wars to avert

Character
of Filippo
Maria Vis-
conti.

---

[1] Ciaconius, ii. 843.   [2] Comment., ed. Fea., 114.
[3] Theiner, Codex Diplomaticus, III. 314.

possible danger from his own dominions, he never personally took the field, and secured himself against his generals by playing off one against another. Thus he held the balance between Sforza and Piccinino; when one seemed likely to be become too powerful his rival was pitted against him. Filippo Maria was assiduous in his attention to public matters, and regulated by minute ordinances the internal affairs of his state. He lived a lonely life in the castle of Milan and his country houses, to which he had canals constructed to convey him more secretly. He had no one around him whose character he had not tried by exposing them to temptations, while they did not suspect that he was watching. Access to him was difficult, and was only permitted after innumerable precautions. He was surrounded by spies, who were employed in checking one another. So afraid was he of assassination that he changed his bedroom two or three times in the night, and was never without a physician, whose advice he sought respecting the cause of every bodily sensation which he experienced. Yet he was a man of learning, and was especially interested in the heroes of past times and in the French romances of chivalry. He was careful in performing all religious offices, and never did anything without secret prayer. Even when he left his chamber and looked upon the sun, he uncovered his head and gave God thanks. Yet he was full of superstitions, consulted astrologers, and was terrified at a thunderstorm. He had such a horror of death that he would have no one ill within his palace, nor would he allow the death of anyone to be mentioned in his presence. Yet when his own death drew nigh he faced it with fortitude, and even hastened its approach by ordering his physician to open an old wound in his leg. His aim in life was simply to live in quietness and security, and his tortuous policy in Italy had no other object. He had a cynical contempt for mankind, and pursued none but purely selfish ends; yet he was neither cruel nor vicious, and possessed philosophic gravity and decorum.[1]

If Filippo Maria Visconti had succeeded during his lifetime in maintaining order in his dominions, he produced confusion

---

[1] The life of Filippo Maria Visconti written by Piero Candido Decembrio, in Muratori, vol. xx., is one of the most characteristic works of the early Renaissance period in Italy.

by his death. His only child was an illegitimate daughter,
Bianca, whose hand had been the bait which kept Francesco
Sforza true to her father's service, till he at last succeeded in
extorting a fulfilment of the promise so long delayed. The
rule of the Visconti was not a recognised monarchy; and no
rights of succession could pass through an illegitimate daughter.
Yet Sforza aspired to the Duchy of Milan, and his claim rested
on grounds as good as those of the other claimants. Alfonso
of Naples asserted that Filippo Maria had named him as his
successor by will; but the lordship of Milan was but the chief
magistracy of the city, and could not pass by bequest. The
Duke of Orleans, by his marriage with Valentina, sister of
Filippo Maria, claimed to represent the Visconti house; but
this was to regard Milan as a fief which passed through the
female line. Finally, Frederick III. claimed that on the extinction of the Visconti house Milan, as an Imperial fief, reverted to the Emperor; but this disregarded the fact that
Milan, though nominally subject to the Empire, had been a free
city for centuries before the Visconti made themselves its lords.
The Milanese on their part did not consider themselves as belonging to any of these claimants. They had submitted to the
rule of the great Visconti family, which had been closely connected with the past glories of their city. When that family
came to an end they decided to go back to their position of an
independent republic, and other cities in the dominions of the
Visconti followed their example.

The new republics would clearly have enough to do to hold
their own against these numerous claimants: but Venice,
always jealous of its neighbours, saw in the difficulties of Milan
its own opportunity. Engaged in war with Venice, Milan was
driven to take into its service Francesco Sforza, who, with con-
summate sagacity, used the opportunity so offered. He raised
up in Milan a party favourable to himself; he won back towns
from the Venetians, and garrisoned them with his own soldiers.
He defeated Venice so that she was driven to sue for peace;
then he suddenly changed sides, allied himself with the Venetians and advanced against Milan, which was unsuspecting and
unprepared for a siege. In vain Venice, when it was too late,
saw her mistake, made peace with Milan, and despatched an
army against Sforza. Sforza, though suffering from famine

almost as much as Milan, persisted in his blockade, and kept
the Venetian troops at bay till the Milanese, in desperation,
could endure no longer.   Then, gathering all the food he could,
he entered Milan February 26, 1450, as the saviour, rather
than the conqueror, of the people.   He arranged that supplies
should rapidly be brought into the city, and managed to present himself to the people as their benefactor.   Admiration of
his cleverness and prudence overcame all resentment of his
treachery.· His first measures were wise and conciliatory, and
promised good government for the future.   The Milanese soon
admitted that one who could plot so skilfully was likely to rule
with success.   The condottiere general, the son of the peasant
of Cotignola, took his place amongst the princes of Europe.

Jubilee of
1450.
Nicolas V. was glad to see peace again restored in North
Italy, and a power established which was strong enough to keep
in check the ambition of Venice.   He took no part in the
operations of the war.   His pursuits were those of peace.   He
was busy in organising the Papal finances, and showed his gratitude for past favours to Cosimo de' Medici by making him his
banker, a step which benefited the Papal treasury, and at the
same time increased the prestige and credit of the great banking-
house of the Medici.   Otherwise Nicolas was employed in plan-
ning the restoration of the buildings of Rome, and in increasing
the treasures of the Vatican Library.   His object was to make
Rome once more a fit residence for the Papacy, to restore its
former splendour, and make it the literary and artistic capital
of Europe.   In 1450 Nicolas V. proclaimed a year of jubilee.
The schism was at an end, and since the first jubilee of Boniface
VIII. there had not been in Rome an undisputed Pope to lend
solemnity to the pilgrimage.   Italy was peaceful, and access to
Rome was free.   Crowds of pilgrims from every land flocked to
Rome, to the number of 40,000 in one day.[1]   So great was the
crowd returning one evening from S. Peter's that more than 200
persons were killed in the crush upon the bridge of S. Angelo,
or were pushed into the water.   Nicolas took care to prevent
such an accident in the future by pulling down the houses
which narrowed the approach to the bridge, and built a memorial chapel of marble to commemorate the calamity.

The arrangements for supplying food to this great multitude

[1] Æn. Syl., *Hist. Fred.*, Kollar, II. 172.

and for keeping order were excellent, and testified to the Pope's administrative skill. The offerings that flowed into the Papal treasury were large, and gave Nicolas V. the means of carrying out still more splendidly his magnificent schemes of restoring the City of Rome—for which a new festival was in store, in the shape of an Imperial coronation. The peaceful settlement of North Italy promised Frederick III. an easy access to Rome, which he could never have won by his own arms. He was now thirty-five years old, and bethought himself of marriage, which he had never contemplated since the offer which Felix V. made him of his daughter. He sent two ambassadors to report on the ladies of royal birth who were eligible as wife of the King of the Romans, and finally fixed on Leonora, daughter of the King of Portugal and niece of Alfonso of Naples. Æneas Sylvius was sent to Naples to negotiate the marriage; and on his way thither received the news that Nicolas V. had conferred on him the bishopric of his native city of Siena. His business in Naples was successfully accomplished. Leonora, only fourteen years old, had other suitors, but she preferred Frederick III., for she rejoiced to be called Empress. ' For the title of Emperor,' says Æneas, ' was held in more esteem abroad than at home.'[1] It was agreed that Frederick should meet his bride at some port in Italy, whence they should proceed to Rome for the coronation.

When this had been arranged, Æneas visited Rome at the end of 1450, and had an opportunity of conferring another service on the Pope. There was one shadow which still hung over Nicolas V.—the shadow of a future Council, which he had promised to the French King. French ambassadors were at Rome urging the fulfilment of the promise, and Æneas supplied the Pope with a means of shelving the matter. Nicolas V. had promised to hold a Council in France, if the other princes of Europe were willing. Æneas, in a speech before the Pope and Cardinals, announced the betrothal of Frederick and his approaching coronation. He then went on to demand, in Frederick's name, a Council in Germany, as being the fittest land for such a purpose. Nicolas V. could answer the French ambassadors that the princes of Europe were not unanimous in

CHAP. II.

Negotiations for the marriage of Frederick III.

The Council in France deferred.

[1] *Hist. Fred.*, in Kollar, II. 16

consenting to a Council in France.[1] Again the cleverness of
Æneas was found useful, and the unwelcome Council was dismissed for the present.

Æneas also suggested to the Pope that it would be well if
Germany felt the influence of the religious spirit of Italy. In
the manifold productiveness of the fifteenth century in Italy,
the fervour of religious feeling had found some noble exponents.
Chief of these was Bernardino, born in 1380 of a good family
in Siena. He gave to the poor his patrimony and entered
the Franciscan Order. Bernardino was filled with an enthusiasm for moral reform, and strove to bring back the Franciscan
Order to its original purity. He followed the example of its
great founder, and, like Francis, went barefoot throughout
Italy, preaching to the crowds who in every city thronged to
hear him. Wherever he went he awakened the fervour of
devotion, which at all times can be kindled among the masses
into a transient flame. Æneas Sylvius, in his youth, was
almost stirred to become a friar by Bernardino's eloquence,
though his after-life does not show that the impression lasted
long. The Emperor Sigismund, during his stay at Siena, delighted to listen to Bernardino's preaching, though he made
little effort to give it any practical result. Bernardino preached
the simple gospel of ' Christ and Him crucified.' He attracted
the attention of the crowd by displaying a wooden tablet
emblazoned with the name of Jesus in letters of gold, and,
with loud cries and exhortations, set it before them for worship. His success raised many enemies, who besought the
Pope to silence the unseemly fanatic. But the Papacy was
wise enough to countenance every religious movement that was

---

[1] This proceeding is somewhat obscure. Æneas (*Comm.* p. 17) says :
' Concilium quod Galli petebant in Francia dissuasit.' Mansi, *Pii II. Orationes*,
pp. 140 and 152, gives two speeches of Æneas, one previously printed in Freher,
the other from a MS. at Lucca. In the first the demand is made for a
Council in Germany, in the second the matter is not mentioned. Probably
the first was what Æneas delivered ; the second was what he had prepared, and
the demand for the Council was inserted to suit the occasion. The ambassador of the Teutonic Order, quoted by Voigt, *Æn. Syl.* II. 20, mentions the
demand for the Council, and Æneas, *Oratio adversus Australes*, in Mansi, i.
234, says, ' Neque Aragonum neque Angliæ regibus neque Portagalliæ placet
in Gallia esse concilium. Ego quoque jussu Cæsaris in consistorio publico
Romæ in fine anni jubilæi hanc celebrationem concilii non sine rationalibus
causis dissuasi.'

not hostile to itself. Bernardino's teaching was examined and
approved by Martin V. and Eugenius IV. The popular devotion
found his sanctity attested by miracles. Even Æneas Sylvius
saw him dispel by his prayers a storm that threatened to
disturb his congregation. He died in 1444, and such was
his reputation for holiness that he was canonised by Nicolas V.
during the year of Jubilee.[1]

Bernardino is said to have established by his exertions more
than five hundred Franciscan monasteries in Italy. He had many
followers, chief amongst whom was Giovanni of Capistrano,
a village near Aquila. On him Bernardino's mantle fell, and
at the suggestion of Æneas Sylvius he was sent by the Pope to
evangelise Germany, and secure its allegiance to Rome. Great
was the success of Capistrano in Vienna. From twenty to
thirty thousand thronged daily to hear the preaching of the
holy friar, though he spoke in Latin, and his words had to be
translated into German by an interpreter. They revered him as
though he were an Apostle, thronged round him to touch the
hem of his garments, and brought their sick in multitudes that
he might lay his hands upon them.

Fra Giovanni Capistrano in Germany.

Capistrano's mission had, however, another object than
merely to preach to the people of Vienna and reform Franciscan houses. It was hoped that his prestige would have some
influence on Bohemia, which had not ceased to be a trouble to
the Papacy. It is true that the Catholic reaction had made
huge strides under Sigismund, and great things were hoped
from Albert II. But Albert's death left Bohemia with an infant
king, and the national feeling against German interference
revived during the minority. Rokycana returned to Prag and
resumed his office as archbishop. The nation that had raised
heroes like Zizka and Procopius the Great found in George
Podiebrad a leader who had the wisdom to unite the nobles into
a patriotic league, and pursue a policy of moderation to all parties
in Church and State alike. The religious question in Bohemia
was left more vague than ever by the dissolution of the Council
of Basel. Nothing had been said about the Compacts in the

Attitude of Bohemia.

---

[1] Æneas Sylvius gives an interesting account of him, *Hist. Fred.*, in Kollar,
II. 173. See also his life, *Acta Sanctorum*, May. vol. v. There is a modern
life by Toussaint (Regensburg, 1873), more remarkable for its tendency to
edification than for its historical value.

final agreement between the Pope and the Council. The Compacts themselves had never received Papal ratification. It suited Nicolas V. to leave the matter open, behave with moderation, and neither accept nor repudiate the Compacts, but wait till an opportunity offered for ending the exceptional position which Bohemia still claimed for itself. Meanwhile, Capistrano tried the effects of his eloquence, Cusa of his learning, and Æneas Sylvius of his cleverness.

Æneas
Sylvius in
Bohemia.
1451.
Besides the religious object of winning back the Hussites from their heresy, there was also the political motive of strengthening in Bohemia the party of Frederick III., and allowing him to proceed at leisure with his Italian journey. The Bohemians murmured against Frederick's guardianship of Ladislas, and demanded that their king should be given up to their own care. Frederick did not dare to leave his kingdom till he had taken some steps to secure quietness in Bohemia. Æneas Sylvius was sent as the head of a royal embassy to a Bohemian Diet, and we have a vivid picture drawn by his pen. He and his companions passed through Tabor, where they were hospitably received. As he entered the city gate, he saw on either side of the archway a shield: one bore the Hussite symbol of an angel holding the cup, the other a picture of the blind general Zizka. Æneas found that the old spirit still survived amid the rude dwellers in the mountain fastness. He was struck with holy horror at their disregard for ecclesiastical traditions. He had expected to find them orthodox except in the matter of the Communion under both kinds; he found them an entirely heretical and rebellious people. He left Tabor with the feelings of one who had escaped from the companionship of the ungodly, and advanced towards Prag. But the city was stricken by the plague, and the Diet adjourned to Beneschau, where Æneas discharged his mission. He besought the Diet to await peacefully the return of Frederick III. from Rome; Ladislas was yet too young to rule. The Diet was not contented with this vague assurance, and the rhetoric of Æneas could not convince them. But Æneas had better success in arranging matters with George Podiebrad, the governor of Bohemia, whom he judged to be ambitious rather than misguided. He conferred with him about the religious troubles in Bohemia; each complained that the Com-

pacts were not observed. Podiebrad demanded the recognition
of Rokycana as archbishop; Æneas asserted that it was a
breach of ecclesiastical order to compel the Pope to recognise
as archbishop anyone whom he deemed unfit.[1] No result came
from the argument; but Æneas was satisfied that he had
gauged Podiebrad's character and found him to be a harmless
man who could be easily managed. On his return Æneas again
passed through Tabor, and on this occasion the Bishop Niklas
of Pilgram, with an attendant crowd of priests and scholars,
came ready for a disputation with one who had a fame for
learning. They were all well versed in Latin, and Æneas owns
that the one good point about this perfidious race was its
love for literature. The discussion was like most theological
discussions—each side showed much learning and readiness.
The Taborites urged the scriptural nature of their doctrine;
Æneas pleaded the authority of the Church, and of the Pope
its earthly head. Yet Æneas managed to extract some humour
out of the discussion. 'Why do you extol to us the Apostolic
See?' said one of the disputants. 'We know the Pope and
his Cardinals to be slaves of avarice and gluttony, whose god
is their belly, and whose heaven is money.' The speaker was
a round fat man. Æneas gently laid his hand upon his stomach.
'Is this,' said he, 'the result of fasting and abstinence?'
There was a general laugh, and Æneas withdrew from the
dispute. Not till he reached the Catholic city of Budweis
did he breathe freely and feel as if he had emerged from the
infernal regions to the light of heaven. If Æneas had not
converted the Bohemian heretics, nor convinced the Bohemian Diet, he at least obtained so much that Frederick III.
recognised Podiebrad as Governor of Bohemia, and so procured
peace with that realm during his Roman journey.

No sooner had Æneas returned to Vienna than he was again Frederick
III. sets
out for
Italy. De-
cember
1451.
sent off to Italy to arrange for Frederick's coming, and receive
his intended bride on her landing. Frederick prepared for his
departure, and appointed regents during his absence. But when
it was known that he intended to take with him the young
Ladislas, the discontent of the barons of Austria broke out in

[1] The letter of Æneas to Carvajal (No. 130, ed. Basel) gives a full account
of the controversy and throws much light on the religious condition of
Bohemia.

revolt. Headed by Ulrich Eizinger, they formed a League, and demanded that Ladislas, their rightful king, should be given up to them. When Frederick refused, the League renounced allegiance to him, and took the government into its hands. Frederick's position was ignominious: he had no forces to send against them, and judged it better to leave Austria in revolt, and proceed with his Italian expedition. He spent Christmas at S. Veit in Carinthia, and on the last day of December, 1451, he entered Italian ground.

Even in the person of the feeble Frederick III. the glamour of the Imperial title retained some power. When it was known that he was actually coming to Italy, a certain amount of trepidation prevailed in the Italian cities. So evenly balanced was their constitutional mechanism that the slightest touch might incline it one way or another. Even Siena looked with suspicion on its bishop, Æneas Sylvius, lest he might use his influence with Frederick to seize the lordship of his native town. Much as Nicolas V. had desired an Imperial coronation at Rome, to give occasion for another festival, as well as to mark the close alliance between the Empire and the Papacy, he began to listen to the alarming hints which were poured into his ears. Frederick might plot against the peace of the Roman city; allied by his marriage with Alfonso of Naples, he might threaten the wealth of the Pope and Cardinals. If we are to believe Æneas Sylvius, it needed all his cleverness to reassure the Pope.[1]

Frederick advanced from Treviso through the Venetian territory. He did not think it wise, as Milan was in the hands of a usurper of the Imperial rights, to go to Milan to receive the iron crown of Lombardy. He was met near the Po by Borso, Marquis of Este, who received him on bended knees and escorted him to Ferrara. There Lodovico Gonzaga of Mantua came to welcome him, and Sforza's young son, Galeazzo Maria, brought a condescending invitation to Milan. From Ferrara Frederick journeyed to Bologna, where he was greeted by Cardinal Bessarion, the Papal legate. Thence he passed into Florence and saw with wonder the splendour of the city. Frederick was accompanied by his ward Ladislas, a boy of twelve, his brother

---

[1] *Hist. Fred.*, in Kollar, II. 187.

Albert, and a few bishops and smaller princes, with about
2,000 horsemen. His advent in Italy had no political significance, but was merely an antiquarian pageant.

On February 2 came the news that Leonora, with her
convoy, had arrived at Livorno. Æneas Sylvius was sent to
meet her; but the punctilious ambassador of Portugal refused
to give up his precious charge except to the Emperor himself.
Æneas, on his side, asserted the dignity of his mission. For
fifteen days they wrangled, till the matter was submitted to
Leonora, who professed herself obedient to the commands of her
future lord. She was escorted, on February 24, to Siena, where
Frederick was anxiously awaiting her. The Sienese marked
by a stone pillar the exact spot where the Emperor first embraced his bride. The elegant festivities of the Sienese charmed
Frederick as much as their scanty contribution of money displeased him. On March 1 he passed on to Viterbo, where
some unruly spirits showed their contempt for dignities, by
trying to catch with hooks the baldachin held over the Emperor, that they might make booty of the rich stuff; then
growing bolder, they made a rush for the trappings of
Frederick's horse. 'We must repel force by force,' he cried,
and, seizing a lance from an attendant, he charged the mob.
This was the beginning of an unseemly brawl, in the midst of
which Frederick entered his lodging.

On March 8 the King and his attendants came in sight of
Rome. Frederick turned to Æneas, and said prophetically:
'We are going to Rome—I seem to see you Cardinal and
future Pope.' The Cardinals and nobles of Rome advanced to
welcome Frederick, who, according to custom, passed the night
outside the walls. Nicolas V. was still perturbed at the
thoughts of his coming. Æneas went on before to assure him
of the King's goodwill. 'I prefer the error of suspicion rather
than of over-confidence,' was the Pope's answer. Next day,
Frederick and Leonora entered Rome with pomp, and were
escorted to S. Peter's, where the Pope awaited them in the
porch seated in his chair. Frederick knelt and kissed the
Pope's foot; then Nicolas rose, offered him his hand to kiss,
and kissed his cheek. The King presented a massive piece of
gold, took the accustomed oath of fidelity, and was led by the

Pope into the church.   Never before had there been such
friendly greeting between Pope and Emperor.[1]

Nicolas V. proposed to defer the coronation till March 19,
as being the anniversary of his own coronation as Pope.
Frederick acceded to the Pope's wish ; but he did not care,
meanwhile, to remain indoors at the Vatican, and scandalised
the Romans by rambling about the city before his coronation,
which was contrary to usage. He was greatly impressed by the
old buildings of Rome, as well as by the restorations on which
Nicolas V. was engaged. The Pope and the King conferred freely
within the Vatican, and their alliance was confirmed by their
mutual needs. Frederick wished the Pope to support him
against the rebellious Austrians, and compel them to submit to
his authority as guardian of the young Ladislas.   Nicholas
urged Frederick to use material weapons to bring into subjection a perfidious race which had favoured the conciliar
movement, and was yet far from showing a proper obedience to
the Papal commands. The league between Pope and Emperor
was strengthened by these conferences, and Frederick besought
the Pope to give an additional proof of his favour by conferring
on him in Rome the crown of Lombardy, which he had not
been able to receive at Monza. In spite of the protest of the
Milanese ambassadors, Nicolas V., on March 16, performed this
unprecedented act, and crowned Frederick King of the Romans,
with the crown of Aachen, which had been brought for the purpose. On the same day the marriage of Frederick and Leonora
was performed by the Pope. It was noticed that Ladislas had a
place assigned him below most of the Cardinals, and some of the
Cardinals had precedence over Frederick, who as yet only
ranked as the German King.

At length, on March 19, the Imperial coronation was performed with due pomp and ceremony. Frederick first took the
oath of obedience to the Pope, was made a canon of S. Peter's,
and, with Leonora, received the unction at the hands of the
Vice-Chancellor. The Pope said mass, and then placed in the
Emperor's hands the golden sword, the apple, and the sceptre,

---

[1] See Æn. Sylv., *Hist. Fred.* 277, *Comment.* 20, the description by Gos-
winus Mandoctes, the Papal singer, in Chmel's *Regesta*, Anhang, No. 98.
Hodæporicon in Würdtwein, *Subsida*, xii. 10 ; Columbanus de Pontremulo, in
Denis, Cod. lib. Bibl. Cæs. Vindob. i. 517.

and on his head the crown. To make the ceremony more imposing Frederick had fetched from Nürnberg the Imperial insignia of Charles the Great. Their venerable antiquity did not match the magnificent clothing of Frederick, and suggested the thought that his predecessor paid more attention to his actions than to his ornaments. The keen eye of Æneas Sylvius detected on the sword-blade the outlines of the Lion of Bohemia, which showed him that these insignia dated only from the times of Charles IV.[1] This spurious affectation of antiquity was an apt symbol of the Imperial claims and of the decrepitude of the Empire. It had grown in outward display in proportion as it had lost in real power. The Empire was but a reminiscence of the past; the Emperor was useful only as a figure in the pageant.

When the coronation was over, the Pope and the Emperor walked hand in hand to the door of S. Peter's. The Pope mounted his horse, and the Emperor held the reins for a few paces. Then he too mounted his steed, and Pope and Emperor rode together as far as the Church of S. Maria in Cosmedin. Nicolas then returned to the Vatican, and Frederick, according to ancient custom, dubbed knights on the Bridge of S. Angelo. More than three hundred received this distinction, many of them men of little worth, who excited the mockery even of Æneas Sylvius. A splendid dinner at the Lateran brought the day's festivities to an end.

When this important matter had been happily accomplished the Pope issued a series of Bulls in Frederick's favour. Some of the privileges so conferred were personal. He and a hundred persons, whom he might choose, were empowered to select their own confessor. He might have divine service performed for his benefit in a place which lay under an interdict; he might carry about with him an altar, at which a priest might say mass at any time; he and his guests might indulge in milk and eggs during times of fasting. Other rights of more importance were also conferred on Frederick, which tended to increase his power over the possessions of the Church in his own dominions. In case of need he might employ the services of unbelievers to help him in war; a provision which no doubt was meant to authorise him to use the troops of Bohemia against

[1] *Hist. Frrd.*, in Kollar, II. 292.

his Austrian subjects. To dower his daughters or for other grave necessities he might impose ' moderate taxes according to ancient custom ' on the clergy of Austria. He was empowered to imprison and confiscate the goods of all spiritual persons who had joined the rebellion against his wardship of Ladislas. He might exercise the right of visitation over all the monasteries of Austria. He received a grant of a tenth from all the clerical revenues in the Empire—a grant without precedent, as no reason of an ecclesiastical character was alleged as a colourable pretext.[1] The Pope and the Emperor were bent upon pushing to the furthest point their victory over the party of reform. The German Church was helpless before them, and they saw no reason for sparing it.

All these advantages were prospective; but Frederick made money out of his coronation by selling at once patents of nobility. Titles of Imperial Count and Doctor were sold for moderate prices. The open and shameless greed of Frederick awoke the laughter of the wits of Rome.

From Rome Frederick III. went to Naples at Alfonso's request. He was received with much magnificence; the roads were strewn with fragrant flowers, and troops of boys and girls with graceful dance and song welcomed the Emperor and his bride. Alfonso promised to help Frederick to recover Milan; but Frederick's character was not warlike, and the fulfilment of the promise was little likely to be required. During Frederick's visit to Naples Æneas Sylvius stayed at Rome to keep watch over Ladislas. He was startled by a summons, in the dead of night, to visit the Pope, who had received intelligence of a plot to carry off Ladislas. Precautions were at once taken; so suspicious was the Pope even of the Cardinals that he forbade them to invite Ladislas to hunting parties outside the city walls. Frederick on his return found Ladislas still safe. He stayed three days in Rome, and in a public consistory thanked the Pope for his magnificent reception. Æneas Sylvius delivered a speech in favour of a crusade against the Turks, and was pleased to think that his eloquence drew tears from his audience. On April 26 Frederick left Rome.

Frederick III. returned through Siena to Florence, where he received a letter from the combined Austrians, Hungarians,

---

[1] These Bulls are all quoted in Chmel's *Regesta*, pp. 282, &c.

and Moravians threatening him with war unless he gave
up Ladislas. Their deputies made a scheme for the escape of
Ladislas, and tried to enlist the Florentines on their side; but
again the plan was discovered in good time. In Florence
Frederick assumed the character of a mediator in Italian affairs.
As matters stood, Florence and Sforza were banded together
against Naples and Venice, while the Pope was neutral. Frederick urged on the Florentines peace and goodwill towards
Alfónso, and received an assurance of their peaceable intentions.
To Florence also came an ambassador from Sforza, asking
Frederick to invest him with the Duchy of Milan. Frederick
did not refuse, but demanded a yearly tribute or the surrender
of a part of the Milanese territory. Sforza, who had won his
dominions by his sword, was not prepared to barter any part of
them for a title, and the negotiations failed for the time.

At Ferrara Frederick hoped to appear as arbiter of Italian
affairs. Ambassadors from Florence, Venice, and Milan awaited
him; but those of Naples tarried, and the scheme of a Congress
came to nothing. The only display of his power which Frederick
could make was the creation of Modena and Reggio into a
duchy, and the investiture therewith of Borso of Este. On
May 21 Frederick entered Venice, and again tried to interpose
his good offices to mediate peace between Milan and the republic. 'We know that we speak with the Emperor,' was the
answer of the doge Foscari, 'and therefore we stated our intentions at first; our answer, once given, cannot be changed.'
Frederick was reminded of his powerlessness in Italy. He showed
his true character to the Venetians by wandering about privately
in ordinary attire to the shops, that he might make better bargains for the articles of luxury which Venice temptingly displayed to the needy German. On June 2 he left Venice. His
pleasant journey in Italy was at an end, and he had to prepare
to face his rebellious people, whom he had so lightly left to
their own devices.

The Roman journey of Frederick was indeed sufficiently
ignoble. 'Other emperors,' says a German chronicler, 'won
their crown by arms; Sigismund and Frederick seemed to have
begged it.'[1] 'He had neither sense nor wisdom,' says the
gentle Archbishop of Florence, ' but all men saw the greed with

---

[1] Mathias Döring, in Mencken, III. 18.

which he looked for presents, and the joy with which he received them.'[1] Poggio judged him to be only a doll of an emperor, before whom it was useless to make a speech, as he would neither understand it nor pay for it.[2] Frederick was looked upon as a mere figure in an antiquated ceremony, and his personal qualities were not such as to win any respect from the cultivated Italians. The sole result of his expedition was to show clearly the selfish nature of the alliance between Pope and Emperor. Nicolas V. was bent only on identifying the Papacy with the glories of Italian culture, and asserting Italian supremacy over the ruder peoples of Germany. Frederick III. had no higher object than to extend his power over his ancestral dominions, and retain his influence over the kingdoms of Ladislas. The clear vision of real statesmanship was wanting to both. The danger from the Turkish inroads was a real question on which Europe might have been united. Union, however, is only possible under trustworthy leaders. The restored Papacy had done nothing to redress the grievances of which Germany complained; the Emperor, who trusted to the Pope's help to maintain his position in Germany, was no fitting exponent of the national feeling.

Rebellion against Frederick III. 1452.
When Frederick returned he found Austria under Eizinger, Hungary under Hunnyadi, even Bohemia under Podiebrad, and the chief nobles of Moravia banded together against him. They demanded that their king, Ladislas, should be admitted to reign over his ancestral kingdoms; but this was only a demand for their own freedom from Frederick's control. No sooner had Frederick left Rome than an embassy from his rebellious subjects appeared to plead their cause before the Pope. The answer of Nicolas was that they must obey the Emperor. They requested that the excommunication, which had been threatened against their disobedience, should be withdrawn. 'This is a temporal, not a spiritual matter,' said one of them; ' it is not in your province.' Nicolas angrily answered that all causes were subject to the judgment of the Apostolic See; the Austrians must either obey, or they would be excommunicated. The envoys hastily left Rome, and scarcely thought themselves safe till they were out of Italy. They brought back news that

---

[1] S. Antonini, *Chronicon*, III. xxii. ch. 12.
[2] Poggio, letter 80 in *Spicilegium Romanum*, x.

the Pope was altogether on Frederick's side, and was opposed
to the national cause.[1] On April 4 Nicolas issued a threat
of excommunication against Eizinger and his followers,[2] and
wrote to Hunnyadi and Podiebrad, charging them to give the
Austrians no help.

Frederick III., at the end of June, boldly entered Neustadt,
and tried to gather around him his partisans. He trusted to
the effects of the Pope's letter, which he sent for publication
on all sides. But the Bishop of Salzburg would not allow it to
be published; the Canons of Passau mocked at it; the Viennese
threw the bearer of it into prison, and the theologians of the
University drew up a formal protest, in which they appealed
from an ill-instructed Pope to one better instructed, or to a
General Council. They asserted that Nicolas V. had usurped the
place of Felix V., and professed themselves ready to join with the
French to procure a future Council.

Frederick III. was soon besieged in Neustadt, and had no
stomach for the fight. When he saw that his adversaries paid
no heed to the Pope, he turned to more pacific counsels.
Æneas Sylvius plausibly urged that, after all, Ladislas could
not be kept in wardship for ever. Frederick was driven
to hold a conference with Eizinger on September 2, and submit to conditions which the Markgraf of Baden and the
bishops negotiated. He agreed to hand over Ladislas to the
Count of Cilly, on condition that the Austrian troops were
withdrawn; the other matters in dispute were to be decided
in a Diet to be held at Vienna. On September 4 Ladislas was
given up to the Count of Cilly, who, in spite of the previous understanding that nothing was to be done till the meeting of
the Diet, took the youth to Vienna, where he was received
with triumph. The Bohemians negotiated with him that, before
acknowledging him for their king, he should ratify the Compacts and accept the nomination of Rokycana as archbishop.

The Diet was fixed for November 12, but it was not till
after Christmas that Frederick sent his three envoys, headed
by Æneas Sylvius. At Vienna were the Dukes Lewis and
Otto of Bavaria, William of Saxony, Albert of Austria, Charles
of Baden, and Albert of Brandenburg, with representatives of
other princes, and deputies from Hungary, Bohemia, and

[1] Æn. Sylv., *Hist. Fred.*, in Kollar, II. 340.   [2] Raynaldus, 1452, 7.

Moravia. Albert of Brandenburg insisted that a dispute between himself and the city of Nürnberg, which had been long
pending, should first be settled. He refused to accept any
decision but the Emperor's, and drew the princes after him to
Neustadt. The Diet seemed likely to break up at once, as the
Imperial envoys were driven to follow Albert. In vain
Frederick endeavoured to put off the decision : Albert was
violent, and would not be refused. While Frederick was
taking counsel with Cusa, the Pope's legate, Æneas, and the
Bishop of Eichstadt, Albert burst into the room, and rated
Æneas and the rest, exclaiming loudly that he cared neither
for Emperor nor Pope. Æneas sadly remarks that princes,
being brought up amongst their inferiors, rarely know how to
behave towards their equals, but lose their temper and behave
with violence.[1] The Emperor was driven to hear the case.
Gregory Heimburg, on behalf of the citizens of Nürnberg,
spoke with warmth and justice of the wrong that would be
done, if princes closely allied with Albert sat to judge a cause
in which he was a party. The Emperor was in a sore strait.
He did not wish to alienate the cities by assenting to a
notoriously partial judgment against Nürnberg ; but he was
powerless to withstand Albert and his confederates. He bade
one of his counsellors collect the opinions of the princes ;
Albert took him by the coat and thrust him to the door, saying,
' Are you a prince, that you mix with princes ? ' Frederick
did not even venture to raise his voice against this act of insolence. Still the pleading of Heimburg seems to have produced some impression, and Æneas managed to have the final
decision of the case deferred to inquire into a technical point
which Heimburg had raised. Albert was left in possession of
the castles which he had seized, and the Emperor was spared
the shame which would otherwise have fallen upon him.

This preliminary scene gave the Imperial envoys no hopes
of any help from the German princes in the proceedings of the
Diet at Vienna. The Austrians, who felt that they were
masters of the situation as against the feeble Emperor, did not
much wish for any settlement of the matters in dispute. They

[1] ' Hoc est principum commune vitium ; nutriti namque inter minores,
qui cuncta laudare solent quæ dicuntur ab eis, cum ad extraneos sibique
pares veniunt, furunt atque insaniunt ubi se reprehensos intelligunt.'—*Hist.
Fred.* 417.

urged that the time fixed for the Diet was now past, and that their agreement had consequently lapsed. They raised every kind of difficulty, and negotiations proceeded slowly. In the course of these proceedings Æneas Sylvius delivered his most effective speech 'Against the Austrians,'[1] in which he defended the conduct of the Emperor in his wardship of Ladislas, justified the interference of the Pope, and defended the Papal power against the attacks of the Viennese University. 'The Austrians,' he said, 'exclaim with haughty mien, "What have we to do with the Pope? Let him say his masses, we will handle arms; if he lays his commands on us we will appeal." The Waldensian heretics, the Saracens themselves, could not say more.' He proceeded to examine the grounds of an appeal to a future Council. The decrees of Constance recognise, as questions to be submitted to a Council, the case as of heresy, schism, or grievous scandal caused by the Pope to the Universal Church; such 'grievous scandal' meant some change made by a Pope in ecclesiastical usage, such as allowing priests to marry, pronouncing judgment of death, or alteration of ritual against the wish of the community of the faithful. Æneas had forgotten much that he had urged at Basel; he had nothing to say against simony, oppression of the Church, or refusal to accept the conciliar principle. He scoffed at the Councils of Constance and Basel—they were tumultuous and disorderly. 'I saw at Basel cooks and grooms sitting side by side with bishops. Who would give their doings the force of law?'— 'But the Austrians appeal from an uninstructed to an instructed Pope. What a wonderful thing is wisdom! What a splendid procedure they suggest! The person of the Pope is divided into him from whom an appeal is made and him to whom it is made! Such a scheme might suit Plato's ideal State, but could be found nowhere else. They add to this an appeal to a future Council, which, they say, is due according to the Constance decrees within ten years of the dissolution of that of Basel. I am afraid it will be twenty or a hundred years before a Council is held; since its summons depends on the judgment of the Pope as to its opportuneness. If they expect one from the Savoyards' (so he calls the party of Basel), 'it is absurd for them to talk of Councils every ten years, when the

---

[1] In Mansi, *Pii II. Orationes*, i. 184, &c.

last sat for nearly twenty. Would that the times were favourable to a Council, as the Pope wishes; it would soon dispel
the folly of these dreams. But they appeal to the Universal
Church, *i.e.* the congregation of all faithful people, high and low,
men and women, clergy and lay. In early days, when the
believers were few, such an assembly was possible; now it is
impossible that it should come together, or appoint a judge
to settle any cause. It were as wise to appeal to the judgment
of the Last Great Day.'

The arguments of Æneas represent the position of the
restored Papacy; and it cannot be denied that the scorn of
Æneas was rightly exercised upon the unwieldy mechanism of
the conciliar system, whose logical claims could scarcely be put
fittingly into action. For his immediate purpose, the speech
of Æneas produced no result. The princes sided with the
Austrians in refusing to open for discussion the general question
of their relations to Frederick. The only points that the Diet
would consider were those referring to details. It was taken
for granted that Frederick's wardship had actually come to an
end. The question for decision was the claims that arose in
consequence. Frederick had to submit his accounts, and the
points which the princes were prepared to settle were, how
much he had spent, and how much was due. Austrian castles
had been pledged by the Emperor: who was to be held
responsible for redeeming them? There was much discussion,
but at last the princes agreed on what they considered fair conditions. The Imperial envoys refused to accept them; whereon
the princes again went to Frederick at Neustadt. Albert of
Brandenburg told the Emperor that he would get nothing more:
he must accept these conditions or prepare for war. The
princes then departed, and left Frederick to his fate. Frederick
was obliged to give way; even then the conditions were not
signed by his opponents, as the Count of Cilly, who was now
master of Ladislas, preferred to keep the matter open.

Thus Frederick's league with the Pope had not been able
to save him from the direst humiliation. At the beginning of
April 1453, the Emperor, who had been received with such
pomp in Rome, was left master only of his own lands of
Carinthia and Styria. His influence over Austria, Bohemia,
Hungary, and Moravia was gone, and he was powerless in

Germany. The Papacy, having allied itself with the Empire, shared its humiliation. The threat of excommunication had been openly defied, and Ladislas was willing to negotiate with the French King for the summons of a Council. At Frederick's request the Pope recalled his admonition to the Austrians,[1] Germany had not been subdued by the first exercise which the Pope made of his newly-restored power.

[1] Voigt, *Ænea Sylvio de' Piccolomini*, II. 88, from unpublished letters of Æneas at Vienna.

CHAPTER III.

NICOLAS V. AND THE FALL OF CONSTANTINOPLE.

1453–1455.

BOOK
IV.

Nicolas V.
and the
Romans.

IF Nicolas V. was humiliated at Vienna, he was about the same time profoundly afflicted by occurrences at Rome. He was sincere in his wish to promote peace in Italy; he was most desirous to gain the affection of the Roman people, whom he enriched by the jubilee and gratified by the imposing ceremony of an Imperial coronation. Above all, he had shown his desire to associate the city of Rome with the glories of the revived Papacy by the magnificence of the public works in which he was engaged. Others might have grievances to allege: surely the Roman citizens had no reason to look upon the Pope in any other light than a splendid benefactor. Yet, at the beginning of 1453, Nicolas V. learned to his amazement that a dangerous plot against his personal safety was formed within the walls of Rome.

Plot of
Stefano
Porcaro.
January
1453.

The revival of classical learning in Italy had developed a tendency towards republicanism; and though the movement of the Roman citizens had been checked by the neighbourhood of the King of Naples at the time of the election of Nicolas V., the spirit that had then inspired it still survived. Nicolas V. had not thought it wise to take any severe measures to assure the Papal Government. He trusted to his own good intentions to overcome the opposition that had been threatened. The republican ringleader, Stefano Porcaro, was sent into honourable exile, as Podestà of Anagni. But when his period of office expired, Porcaro returned to Rome to play the part of demagogue. Taking advantage of a tumult that arose at the carnival, he again raised the cry of ' Liberty ' amongst the excited crowd. Nicolas V. thought it better to remove such a firebrand from Rome, and Porcaro was exiled to Bologna, where he enjoyed perfect freedom on condition that he showed himself every day to the Legate, Cardinal Bessarion. But Porcaro's dreams had possessed his imagination too deeply to be dispelled by any show of clemency, and the desire to appear as the liberator of his country become more and more rooted in his mind. From Bologna he managed to contrive a plot against the Pope, and to assure himself of many confederates. His nephew, Sciarra Porcaro, gathered together a band of three hundred armed men, who were to be the chief agents in the rising. Their scheme was to take advantage of the solemnity of the Festival of the Epiphany, and while the Pope and Cardinals were at mass in S. Peter's, set fire to the Papal stables, and, in the confusion, seize the Pope and his brother, who was captain of the Castle of S. Angelo. While one band seized the Castle, another, at the same time, was to occupy the Capitol. The booty of the Pope and Cardinals, which they estimated at 700,000 ducats, would give them means to carry out their plan of abolishing the Papal rule and securing a Roman Republic. The aspirations of Petrarch, the dreams of Rienzi, were at last to be realised.

When all was ready, Porcaro left Bologna on the night of December 26, 1452, and four days after reached Rome, where he hid himself in the house of a kinsman. The conspirators were summoned to a banquet, in the midst of which Porcaro appeared, clad in a dress of gold brocade, and incited them to their great enterprise. Delay was fatal to the success of his plan. Messengers came from Bessarion bringing the news of Porcaro's flight from Bologna. The armed men of his nephew caused suspicion by an encounter with the police. Some of the conspirators gave information to the Senator and Cardinal Capranica. Porcaro's house was watched by night, and the presence of the conspirators was detected. On the morning of January 4, the Senator, with fifty soldiers, surrounded the house. Sciarra Porcaro, with four comrades, cut his way through the soldiers and escaped from Rome. Stefano's courage deserted him; he did not dare to follow his nephew, but abandoned his confederates, and, through a back door, made his escape to the house of a sister. Meanwhile, the Papal Vice-Chamberlain addressed the people in the Capitol, accused Porcaro of sedition and ingratitude, pronounced the ban

against him, and offered a reward to any who should deliver
him up, alive or dead. His sister's house was no safe place of
hiding, and by her advice he went with a friend by night to beg
a refuge from the generosity of Cardinal Orsini. His friend,
who went first to plead his cause, was made prisoner; when
he did not return, Porcaro fled to the house of another sister,
where he was followed. His sister hid him in a box, and tried
to avoid detection by seating herself on the lid; but it was in
vain. His hiding-place was discovered; he was carried off to the
Castle of S. Angelo, and after a summary trial was beheaded
on the morning of January 9. He died bravely, and his last
words were: 'People, to-day dies the liberator of your country.'[1]
On the same day nine others followed him to the gallows.
Nicolas V. sent throughout Italy to discover those who had
escaped, and Sciarra Porcaro was put to death at Città di Castello
before the end of the month. If Nicolas had been gentle at
first, he showed himself relentless in his fright. One culprit's
life was granted to the entreaties of the Cardinal of Metz; but
next day Nicolas withdrew his promise, and the prisoner was
put to death.[2]

Judgments
on Porcaro.

The Pope and the Curia were alike filled with alarm at the
discovery of this determined scheme. They did not know
how far it represented any plan concerted with the other powers
of Italy. Naples, Florence, Milan, and Venice all might have
some share in this desperate attempt to overthrow the Papacy and
seize its revenues. Nicolas was full of suspicion, and fell into
cruelty which was alien from his character. It was a bitter
blow to him that enemies should rise up against him in his
own city. The plot of Porcaro permanently disturbed his
peace of mind. He grew morose and suspicious, denied access
to his presence, and placed guards around his person. Porcaro's plot revealed to him the incompatibility of the Papal
rule with the aspirations after freedom which the Romans
nourished. The judgments of contemporaries differed as they
fixed their eye on the glories of the Papacy or of the Roman
city. 'Porcaro,' says the Roman Infessura, 'was a worthy man
who loved his country, and sacrificed his life because, when
banished without cause from the city, he wished to free her

[1] Infessura, in Mur. iii. 2, 1135.
[2] Letter to Florence of January 16, in Tommasini, *Documenti relativi a
Stefano Porcari*, 45.

from slavery.' On the other hand, the men of letters whom the CHAP.
III. Pope's liberality had gathered to Rome cannot find language strong enough to express their horror at the monstrosity of Porcaro's plan, which seemed to them to be a rising of barbarism against culture, of Roman ruffians against the scholars who graced their city by their presence.[1] Both judgments contain some truth; but the difference which underlies them is still irreconcilable. Rome had many advantages conferred upon it as the seat of the Papal power, the capital of Christendom; it had in the Pope a munificent lord, and shared the benefits of his greatness. But it had to pay the price of isolation from the political life of Italy. There were always those who felt that they were citizens in the first place and churchmen afterwards, and who aspired to recover for their city the political independence of which the Papal rule deprived it.

Nicolas V. was enfeebled in health by the pains of gout as well as by his disappointments. A still heavier blow fell on Capture of
Constan-
tinople by
the Turks.
May 1453. him when the news reached Rome that on May 29 Mahomet II. had made himself master of Constantinople. It might seem that no one, who had noticed the rapid advance of the Turks, could doubt that the fall of Constantinople was imminent; yet Western Europe was entirely unprepared for such an event. Men looked round with shame and alarm when it actually took place. They felt shame that nothing had been done to save from the unbelievers the relics of an ancient and venerable civilisation; they felt alarm when the bulwark was removed which had so long stood between Europe and the Eastern tribes. It was natural that they should ask themselves what had been done by the heads of Christendom, the Pope and the Emperor, to avert this calamity. It was natural that Nicolas V. should feel that the glories of his pontificate had been obscured by the mishap that in his days such a disaster had occurred. It was true that the Greeks had not maintained the union of the Churches which had been ratified at Florence. It was true that Nicolas had urged upon them the necessity of so doing as a first step towards obtaining help from Europe. It was true that the fanaticism of the Greeks refused to seek for help on the condition of submitting to the Azymites.

---

[1] Comp. Infessura, 1134, with Alberti, Mur. xxv. 313, and Peter de Godis, *Dialogon*, ed. Perlbach.

BOOK
IV.
Still the fact remained that Constantinople had fallen, and the Turks had gained a foothold in Europe.

Help given
by Nicolas
V. to the
Greeks.
Yet Nicolas V. had not been entirely neglectful. In answer to the entreaties of Constantine Palæologos, he had sent Cardinal Isidore of Russia to commemorate the reconciliation of the two Churches. In December 1452 a solemn service was held in S. Sophia, and amid the muttered execrations of the Greeks the formality of a religious agreement was again performed. Nicolas prepared to send succours to his ally, and twenty-nine galleys were equipped for the purpose; but Mahomet II. began the siege of the doomed city unexpectedly, and pressed it with appalling vigour. The Papal vessels arrived off Eubœa two days after the fall of Constantinople, and through some mishap were captured unawares by the Turks.[1] Cardinal Isidore with difficulty escaped in disguise, and made his way back to his own land, while the Greek Emperor Constantine Palæologos fell boldly fighting against the invader.

Effects of
the news on
European
sentiment.
If Nicolas V. could plead that he had been willing to do what he could to avert this catastrophe, no such plea could be urged by the Emperor, who, says a German chronicler, ‘sat idly at home planting his garden and catching birds.’[2] Yet Frederick III. wept to hear the news, and wrote to the Pope urging him to rouse Europe to a crusade. Everywhere a wail of sorrow was raised. Not only was the sentiment of Europe outraged by the fall of Constantinople and the forcible entrance of a new religion into the domains of Christendom, but commercial communications with the East were checked, and there was an uneasy feeling of dread how far the Turkish power might push its borders in Europe. Moreover, the blow affected not only the political, but also the literary sentiment of Europe. Greece, which was the home of Thucydides and Aristotle—Greece, to whose literature men were turning with growing delight and admiration, was abandoned in her last hour by those who owed her so deep a debt of gratitude. The literary treasures of Constantinople were dispersed, and no man could say how great had been the loss. ‘How many names of mighty men will perish,’ exclaims Æneas Sylvius in a letter to the Pope. ‘It

[1] Æn. Syl., *Epist.* 155, ed. Basel.
[2] Matthias Döring, in Mencken, iii. 18.

is a second death to Homer and to Plato. The fount of the Muses is stopped.'[1]

In the same letter Æneas goes on to depict truly enough the change which the fall of Constantinople had wrought in the historical position of the Papacy of Nicolas V. 'Historians of the Roman Pontiffs, when they reach your time, will write: "Nicolas V., a Tuscan, was Pope for so many years. He recovered the patrimony of the Church from the hands of tyrants; he gave union to the divided Church; he canonised Bernardino of Siena; he built the Vatican and splendidly restored S. Peter's; he celebrated the Jubilee, and crowned Frederick III." All this will be glorious to your fame, but will be obscured by the doleful addition: "In his time Constantinople was taken and plundered (or, it may be, burnt and razed) by the Turks." So your fame will suffer without any fault of yours. For, though you laboured with all your might to aid the unhappy city, yet you could not persuade the princes of Christendom to join in a common enterprise in defence of the faith. They said that the danger was not so great as was reported, that the Greeks exaggerated and trumped up stories to help them in begging for money. Your Holiness did what you could, and no blame can justly attach to you. Yet the ignorance of posterity will blame you when it hears that in your time Constantinople was lost.'

Nor was Æneas solitary in his utterances. Isidore of Russia, Bessarion, the Archbishop of Mitylene, and many others wrote in the same strain. There was no lack of writing either then or for many years later. But even without admonition from others the course of the Pope was clear. He must make amends for the past by putting himself at the head of Europe; and it was lucky for the Papacy to have a cry which might once more gather Christendom around it. On September 29 Nicolas issued a summons to a crusade, in which, after denouncing Mahomet II. as the dragon of the Apocalypse, he called on all Christian princes, in virtue of their baptismal vow, to take up arms against the Turks. He declared remission of sins to all who, for six months from the 1st of February next, persevered in the work of the crusade or sent a soldier in their stead; he dedicated to the service of the crusade all the revenues which came to the Apostolic See, or to the Curia, from benefices of

CHAP.
III.

Effects on
Nicolas V.

Nicolas V.
proclaims
a crusade.
September
1453.

---

[1] *Epist.* 162, ed. Basel; the letter is dated July 12, 1453.

any kind; he exacted from all the clergy a tithe of their ecclesiastical revenues, and proclaimed universal peace, that all
might devote themselves to this holy purpose.[1]

The Pope's words and promises were weighty enough; but
there were grave difficulties in giving them any practical effect.
The state of Europe was by no means peaceful, nor were men's
minds turned in the direction of a crusade. The old ideal of
Christendom had grown antiquated; the Emperor was a poor
representative of united Europe. The Holy Roman Empire
had been the symbol of a central organisation which was to
keep in order the anarchic tendencies of feudalism. But feudalism, which was founded upon actual facts, had prevailed over
a system which rested only upon an idea; and the anarchy
caused by feudalism had made national monarchies a necessity.
The fifteenth century was the period when national monarchies
were engaged in making good their position against feudalism.
In France Charles VII. was asserting the power of the
restored monarchy against the mighty Duke of Burgundy.
England was intent on the desperate struggle of parties which
ended in the Wars of the Roses. The Spanish kingdoms,
jealous of one another, could urge their crusade against the
Mussulman at home as a reason for not going abroad. In
Germany each prince was engaged in consolidating his own dominions, and the feebleness of the Emperor made him more keen
to use the opportunity offered. Poland was at enmity with
the Teutonic Knights. Hungary and Bohemia were bent on
maintaining their nationality against their German king. It
was difficult to combine for united action this chaos of contending interests.

It was natural for the Pope to begin at home, and first to
pacify Italy, an object which at his accession he had generally
professed, but which on reflection he deferred till a more
convenient season. He was anxious, above all things, to be at
peace himself, to maintain tranquillity in the States of the
Church, and to gratify his passion for restoring the buildings of
Rome. He saw that he would be most powerful when the rest
of Italy was weak, and that the States of the Church would be
most secure when there were other objects for the ambition of

---

[1] Raynaldus, 1453, 9.

the Italian powers.[1] Even now the same motives weighed with him, and he was only half-hearted in his attempts to heal the breaches of Italy, where Alfonso of Naples, in alliance with Venice, still contested the duchy of Milan with Sforza, who was helped by Florence. He summoned ambassadors of these States to Rome, but in the discussions that arose was so careful to please everybody, and commit himself to nothing, that his sincerity was suspected,[2] and after some months of conference the ambassadors left Rome without arriving at any conclusions. To the shame of Nicolas V., the work which he had been too half-hearted to undertake was accomplished by an Augustinian monk, Fra Simonetto of Camerino,[3] who secretly negotiated peace between Sforza and Venice. The peace was published at Lodi on April 9, 1454, and in the following August Florence also accepted it. When matters had gone so far, the Pope sent Cardinal Capranica to exhort Alfonso of Naples to join it also. After some difficulty Alfonso, on January 26, 1455, agreed to the pacification of Lodi, excepting only Genoa from its provisions, and a solemn peace for twenty-five years was established amongst all the Italian powers.

Meanwhile efforts were being made under the auspices of the feeble Frederick III. for a demonstration of unanimity on the part of the powers of Europe. At the end of December 1453, the Bishop of Pavia, as Papal legate, arrived at Neustadt, and the Emperor issued invitations for a European Congress to be held at Regensburg on April 23, 1454. He promised to be present in person unless hindered by some serious business. But as the time drew nigh Frederick discovered that there were hindrances enough to keep him at home. He had no money; he was afraid lest Austria or Hungary might attack his domains if he left them unprotected ; he did not wish to face the Electors, lest under the cover of

---

[1] Manetti, *Vita Nicolai V.*, in Mur. iii. pt. 2, 913 : ' Bella enim inter predictos totius præne Italiæ principes ecclesiæ suæ pacem, concordiam vero illorum versa vice bellum ecclesiæ, non solum verisimilibus conjecturis sed certis et expressis argumentis et experientia quoque, rerum magistra, intelligebat.'

[2] Manetti : 'Cum tepide in hoc pacis tractatu, ne dicam frigide, sese gereret.'

[3] 'Hominem haud magnæ doctrinæ sed fidei plenum,' says Simoneta, *Vita Fr. Sfortiæ*, Muratori, xxi. 666.

reforms in the Empire they should still more diminish the
Imperial power. 'It is hard,' he said to his counsellors, who
urged him to go, 'it is hard to take care of the common good
at one's own cost. I do not see anyone who will study the
benefit of others more than his own.'[1] So Frederick resolved to
stay at home, and send in his stead an embassy, of which Æneas
Sylvius was a member. He nominated also as his representatives such of the Electors and princes as he thought friendly
to himself, amongst others Lewis of Bavaria, whom Æneas on
his way met at Burghausen on the Inn. When Æneas gave
him the Emperor's commission, Lewis answered that, though
sensible of the compliment, he feared that his own youth and
inexperience rendered him unfit for the task; he would probably
send representatives to Regensburg. While he spoke the dogs
were barking, and a band of huntsmen were impatiently
waiting for the Duke and cursing the Imperial envoys for
causing a delay. Lewis graciously invited the envoys to follow the hunt, and when they declined rode off with his friends.
This was not the spirit of a crusader, and it was but a sample
of the attitude of the German princes towards the great
question which they professed to consider seriously.

At the period fixed for the Congress only the Imperial
presidents and the Papal legate had arrived. Cardinal Cusa,
one of those who had been appointed by Frederick III., advanced to the neighbourhood of Regensburg, and then wrote
to his colleagues to know if he should come any farther, and to
ask who would pay his expenses. When this was the zeal
displayed by a prince of the Church, we cannot wonder that
the secular princes did not bestir themselves more eagerly. From
Italy no one came except the Papal legate, the Bishop of Pavia.
Venice sent ambassadors, but they only entered Germany after
the Congress was over. Florence and Lucca excused themselves as being engaged with other matters. Borso, the newly-
made Duke of Modena, was not sure enough of the peace of
Lodi to think of anything save Italian complications. Siena
did not receive the summons in time to attend to it. The
letter to Lodovico of Mantua had been by mistake addressed
to his brother Carlo. The other Italian States sent neither
excuses nor representatives. The summons addressed to

[1] Æn. Syl. *De Ratisponensi Dieta*, in Mansi, *Orationes*, iii. 9.

the Kings of France, England, Scotland, Hungary, Poland, and Denmark had been of the nature of a brotherly invitation; but none of them were inclined to show complaisance to the feeble Emperor. Charles VII. of France did not wish to seem to act in concert with Frederick. He wrote to the Pope, and said that he was willing to take up arms if the German princes on their part agreed to do so. Christian of Denmark wrote to express his sorrow that the shortness of notice and an expedition in which he was engaged against Norway prevented him from sending ambassadors, but he was willing to do what he could when the time for action arrived.[1] The Kings of England and Scotland paid no heed. Ladislas of Hungary and Bohemia was expected, but never came. Casimir of Poland alone sent representatives; but they came to complain of the Teutonic Knights.

It was no wonder that the foreign powers showed little zeal when Frederick himself stayed at home, and only three of the Electors sent ambassadors. Everyone was suspicious, and there was no real union. Frederick had urged the Pope to join with him in issuing a summons to the German princes; but Nicolas V. was afraid to give any countenance to the Congress, lest it might be turned into a Council. The remembrance of Basel was still too vivid for the Pope to run any risk of its revival.[2]

As the presidents sat at Regensburg, somewhat embarrassed how to proceed, a rumour reached them, which at first seemed like a dream, that the Duke of Burgundy was on his way and had reached Constance. When it was known that he had actually arrived at Ulm, they wrote to Frederick begging him to come in person and welcome one who was as powerful as a king. In truth, Philip of Burgundy, who, besides Burgundy and Franche Comté, ruled over the rich lands between the Somme and the Meuse, was one of the most powerful princes in Christendom, and was a thorn in the side of the French King. He was by birth connected with the crusading movement; for his father was taken prisoner by the Turks at the battle of Nicopolis where Sigismund was defeated. He was now the heir of his

Crusading zeal of the Duke of Burgundy.

---

[1] His letter is in Æneas Sylvius, *Op.* ed. Basel, p. 658.

[2] Æn. Syl. *De Ratisponensi Dieta*, 4: ' Ea res Apostolicæ Sedi non placuit; quia fortasse latere dolos sub ea vocatione Nicolaus timuit; nihil est enim in alto sedenti tutum. Magni conventus magnos motus pariunt: inimica est novitatum summa potestas; spes mutationis enutrit miseros.'

father's policy, and had just succeeded in reducing under
his sway the independence of the Flemish cities.   Rich and
magnificent, he put the French King to shame, and was the
ideal of European chivalry.   It was a gross and fantastic
chivalry, much given to tournaments and festivals of every
sort, yet not without its culture, as the paintings of John van
Eyck still witness.   Philip's proceedings in defence of Christendom are characteristic of the man and of the time.   When he
received the Pope's letter proclaiming a crusade, he held high
festival at Lille—a festival adorned with all the sumptuous
grandeur of Flemish pageantry.   After a banquet, in which
figured a pasty containing twenty-eight men playing on musical
instruments, an elephant was led into the hall by a Saracen
giant.   On its back was a tower, in which sat a captive nun,
representing the Church, who wept and implored succour.
Two lovely maidens advanced with a live pheasant, and the
Duke, laying his hand upon it, swore on the pheasant that he
would drive out the Turk from Europe.   His guests followed
his example, and a splendid ball was the appropriate exploit
which immediately followed.[1]

The news of Philip's approach to Regensburg caused the
utmost excitement.   Everywhere he was received with honour,
and rumour was rife with the causes of his coming.   Some
said that he wished to win over the Germans, and was ambitious of the Imperial crown ; others that he hoped to prevail
on the Emperor to erect Brabant, Holland, and Zeeland into a
kingdom, that he might bear a royal title.   Anyhow, his
coming brought prestige to the Congress.   It impelled the
Cardinal of S. Peter's to hasten to Regensburg without waiting
to have the question of his expenses further settled.   Lewis of
Bavaria left his hunting, and went to meet Philip; he sent
also four envoys to Regensburg, but declined to act personally
as one of the Emperor's representatives.

The presidents now thought that it was time to open the Congress.   The Bishop of Gurk excused the Emperor's absence,
and inveighed against the Turks.   Then Cardinal Cusa pointed
out that the Greeks had drawn their ruin upon their own heads
by their stubbornness in rejecting union with the Holy See.

[1] This vow of the Pheasant is described by Olivier de la Marche, who himself personated the Church in the pageant.

The Papal legate spoke a few words.   Next the ambassadors of
the Teutonic Knights inveighed against the King of Poland,
and the session ended in a wrangle. The next session was spent
in a strife about precedence between the Polish envoys and those
of the Electors.

On May 9 Philip of Burgundy and Lewis of Bavaria entered Arrival of
the Duke of
Burgundy
at Regens-
burg. May
9, 1454.
Regensburg with pomp.   The Imperial presidents offered to
hold their sessions in Philip's house if that would suit his convenience.   Philip modestly declined; and it was agreed that
the congress should sit in the Town Hall.   Indeed, the proposal would hardly have suited the Duke's habits: for Æneas
tells us that he rose at noon, did a little business, dined, had a
nap, took some athletic exercise, supped till late at night, and
finished his day with music and dancing.   Such a man was
not likely to sit very long over tedious deliberations.   But
before the business of the crusade was undertaken, the German
princes declared their intentions.   John of Lysura, the confidential adviser of the Archbishop of Trier, suggested that the
Germans should meet separately at the house of Lewis of
Bavaria. There he proposed that they should consider what
strength they had to lead against the Turks.   The Imperial
representatives saw in this a means of exposing the poverty of
the Emperor, and refused to enter upon the subject.   Then
Lysura spoke warmly of the distracted state of Germany, and
its need of internal reform before it embarked on enterprises
abroad; he insisted that the Emperor ought to meet the
Electors, and deliberate on German affairs before he put forward a scheme for a crusade.   The Imperial envoys admitted
the truth of Lysura's complaints, but urged the primary importance of the crusade : if it were to be deferred till Germany
was reorganised, it would have long to wait.

The arrival of the Markgraf of Brandenburg increased the
number of princes, but brought an ally of the Teutonic Knights
against Poland, and threatened to divert the Congress from the
question of the crusade.   At length, however, the public proceedings were resumed.   Æneas Sylvius spoke against the
Turks, and urged immediate action.   Silence followed his
speech, which, being in Latin, was probably understood by
few, and was translated into German by the Bishop of Gurk.
Then Cardinal Cusa gave an account of Constantinople, and of

the Turks, from his personal knowledge; his speech was similarly translated into German by John of Lysura. The Bishop of Pavia spoke also, and the assembled princes separated to deliberate. Next day the Imperial envoys were asked to state the Emperor's proposals. This they did in writing, and demanded that by April 1455, an army sufficient to over-whelm the Turks should be in readiness to serve for three years. They suggested that throughout Germany every sixty men should furnish one horseman and two foot duly equipped for the field; in this way an army of 200,000 men would be raised. Besides this, the cities were to provide all necessary ammunition and means of transport. The Pope, Naples, Venice, and the other maritime cities of Italy should prepare a fleet, while the land army, joined by the Bohemians and Hungarians, was to cross the Danube. A peace for five years was to be proclaimed throughout Germany, beginning from next Christmas; whoever violated it should be under the ban of the Empire. To make further arrangements, another Diet was to meet on September 29 at Nürnberg, if the Emperor could come there; if he could not, at Frankfort.

It was a splendid scheme; but schemes on paper are not costly, and Frederick III. was willing to be magnificent where no expense was involved. The Germans listened, but urged their own business. John of Lysura clung to his scheme of a reform-ation of the Empire. Albert of Brandenburg was busy with his quarrel against Poland. The Congress might have sat long had not the Duke of Burgundy grown impatient: his health suffered at Regensburg and he was anxious to get away. Ac-cordingly it was agreed that an answer should be given to the Emperor's proposals. Albert of Brandenburg spoke on behalf of the Germans. He faintly praised the Emperor's zeal, but deferred all criticism of his scheme till the forthcoming Diet, when there would be a fuller assembly and fuller information. Nothing, however, could be done till Germany was at peace, and for this purpose the Emperor must meet the princes and fully discuss with them the state of affairs. After this lukewarm speech, which dealt rather with the affairs of Germany than the affairs of Christendom, the Bishop of Toul, in the name of the Duke of Burgundy, declared his master's zeal for the crusade, and his willinness to take part in any expedition which might be agreed upon by the Emperor or any other Christian princes. CHAP. III. Then Æneas Sylvius, and afterwards the Bishop of Pavia, thanked the Duke of Burgundy and Albert of Brandenburg for their zeal, and the Congress separated at the end of May, with every outward appearance of satisfaction and hope.

Yet this empty talk deceived no one. Æneas Sylvius wrote to a friend in Italy [1] on June 5, in the following strain: 'My wishes differ from my hopes: I cannot persuade myself of any good result. You ask, Why? I answer, Why should I hope? Christendom has no head whom all will obey. Neither Pope nor Emperor receives what is his due. There is no reverence, no obedience. We look on Pope and Emperor alike as names in a story or heads in a picture. Each state has its own king; there are as many princes as there are houses. How will you persuade this multitude of rulers to take up arms? Suppose they do, who is to be leader? How is discipline to be maintained? How is the army to be fed? Who can understand the different tongues? Who will reconcile the English with the French, Genoa with Naples, the Germans with the Bohemians and Hungarians? If you lead a small army against the Turks, you will be defeated; if you lead a large one, there will be confusion. Thus there are difficulties on every side.'

Having such opinions, Æneas was desirous to escape further disappointment and leave the uncongenial land of Germany for his native country. He had gained all that he could from his sojourn at the Imperial court. Frederick's position had now sunk so low as to be desperate, and important affairs no longer centred round him. Frederick, however, refused to part with Æneas just then; he was determined not to go in person to the Diet, but to send again Æneas and the Bishop of Gurk. Among the princes he nominated as his representatives the Markgrafs of Brandenburg and Baden. The Pope contented himself with again nominating as his legate the Bishop of Pavia. The Diet of Frankfort filled the month of October 1454, and in its outward forms resembled that of Regensburg. Æneas showed more than his wonted eloquence, and spoke for two hours; the Bishop of Toul asserted the zeal of the Duke of Burgundy, and the Bishop of Pavia, in the name of the Pope, tried to inflame the ardour of Christendom. The demand for a crusade had

Opinion of Æneas Sylvius about the Congress.

Diet of Frankfort. October 1454.

---

[1] Letter to Leonardus de Benevolentibus, *Epistolæ* 127, ed. Basel.

already become more serious, as was seen by the presence of ambassadors from Hungary, who loudly called for help, and declared that if it were not given they would be driven to make peace with the Turks to protect their own frontier. With a view to awaken more enthusiasm Fra Capistrano came and preached at Frankfort. The people heard him gladly; but the diplomats of the Congress were unmoved. Of the German princes there were present the Markgrafs of Brandenburg and Baden, and the Archbishops of Trier and Mainz. But they were all bent on their own schemes. Albert of Brandenburg, who was regarded as friendly to the Emperor, was the most conspicuous man among the German princes, and urged the reform of the Empire as a means of obtaining a wider sphere for his energy. Against him was secretly formed a party, at the head of which was the Pfalzgraf Frederick, but its moving spirit was Jacob of Trier. This party won over Albert of Austria, the Emperor's brother, by holding out hopes of the deposition of Frederick and his own election in his stead. On the deposition of the Emperor would follow the summons of a new Council and the revival of the cry for ecclesiastical reform. Thus in Germany the princes were agreed that internal reform must precede any undertaking abroad; but they were not united in their conception of reform, and under the name of reform were pursuing private ends and separate intrigues.[1]

Coldness of the Diet towards the crusade.
In this state of things the Emperor's ambassadors had to listen to nothing save complaints. When the time came for a definite promise, they were told that the crusade was merely a pretext used by the Pope and the Emperor to extort money; they would find that Germany would give them neither money nor soldiers. The zeal of the Burgundians was turned into ridicule; the Hungarians were bidden to defend their own kingdom, and not try to involve Germany in their calamities. It required all the diplomacy of the Imperial and Papal party to avert an absolute refusal of supplies for a crusade.[2] It was only through the influence of Albert of Brandenburg that a decent semblance of zeal for the cause of Europe was expressed. It was agreed that an army of 10,000 horse and 30,000 foot be sent by Germany to the aid of the Hungarians, on condition that the Pope equip in Italy a fleet of twenty-five galleys to

[1] See Droyssen, *Geschichte Preussens Politik*, ii. 116 (ed. 1868).
[2] *Pii II. Comm.* p. 23.

attack the Turks in Greece. This undertaking was made the more readily because of the belief that the conditions would never be fulfilled. 'The princes say,' writes Capistrano to the Pope, 'Why should we spend our zeal, our goods, the bread of our children, when the Pope consumes in building towers the revenues of S. Peter, which ought to be devoted to the defence of the Christian faith?'

The Diet might arrive at its own conclusions; but Jacob of Trier was secretly pursuing his course. As it was clear that the Emperor would not come to meet the princes, it was resolved that the princes should go to him. Another Diet was proclaimed to be held at Neustadt on February 2, 1455, ostensibly for the purpose of arranging for the levy of the German forces, really for the purpose of bringing pressure to bear on the Emperor so as to strengthen the power of the princes. Jacob of Trier had skilfully drafted a scheme for the reform of the Empire, which was accepted by the Archbishops of Köln and Mainz. It proposed that the Emperor should confer with the Electors about the pacification of the Empire, for which was needed a reorganisation of judicature and finance. Moreover, the Emperor should be required to urge on the Pope the summons of a new Council, in accordance with the provisions of the decrees of Constance, and the Papal undertaking at the time of the restoration of the German obedience. It was a fair-sounding scheme; but even while he penned it Jacob of Trier let it be seen that it was only meant to be a pretence. He recommended his proposal on the ground that 'when the Pope sees us anxious to have a Council, he will be more willing to please us, and will pay more heed to the requests made by us to the Curia in matters which he now refuses. Likewise the Emperor, when he sees that we wish to stir him up, will be more willing to please us and follow our advice in all matters.'[1] The plan was to bring pressure to bear both on the Emperor and the Pope, so as to establish still more surely the independence of the German princes, and win from both sides all the concessions which they wished. To make their plan stronger, Albert of Austria was to be used as a rival to Frederick;

---

[1] This document, entitled 'Abschiedt zwischen geistlichen Churfürsten, mit was Mittel das Röm. Reich wieder aufzubringen wäre, und wie man im künfftigen Concilio reden solle,' is printed in Ranke, *Deutsche Geschichte*, vi. 10.

BOOK
IV.

and the threat of a Council was to be a means of separating the interests of the Pope from those of the Emperor.

Diet of
Neustadt.
February
1455.

Such were the schemes of Jacob of Trier, when, in February 1455, he arrived at Neustadt. He was the only Elector present ; but four others sent representatives, who were under Jacob's orders. Ladislas of Hungary came to Vienna ; but refused to advance to Neustadt, as he had no desire to meet his former guardian. Æneas Sylvius invited Fra Capistrano to bring his eloquence to Neustadt. He promised him good sport. 'Our amphitheatre will be established, and there will be Circensian games grander than those of Julius Cæsar or Cnæus Pompeius. I do not know whether there will be foreign beasts or only those of Germany : but Germany has wild beasts of many kinds, and perhaps Bohemia will send the Beast of the Apocalypse. If our sport be only moderate, you will have a bag well filled with every kind of game, slain by the sword that proceeds from your mouth. If your valour comes victorious out of the amphitheatre, we will have an army against our foes abroad, when our enemies at home have been dispersed.'[1] Æneas could jest even on the most serious matters, and Fra Capistrano was not so simple a devotee that he could not understand the subtleties of the higher politics.

Fruitless
proceed-
ings of the
Diet.

Albert of Brandenburg and Charles of Baden were the only other German princes who appeared. The Bishop of Toul again came from Burgundy, and the Bishop of Pavia again represented the Pope. The only foreign power who sent an envoy was the King of Naples. On February 26 the proceedings began with a wrangle about precedence of seats between Jacob of Trier and the Neapolitan ambassadors. Then Æneas and the Bishop of Pavia spoke about the crusade : but neither of them had any assurance to offer of the Pope's activity. The Bishop of Pavia had not visited Rome during the interval between the Diets, and had no fresh instructions to communicate. The Neapolitan envoys declared that their King would be ready in May to sail against the Turks, if Germany sent its army for a land expedition at the same time. The Bishop of Toul again asserted the zeal of the Duke of Burgundy. Jacob of Trier declared that the Electors were ready to do all that befitted good Christians.

---

[1] Æn. Sylv. *Epist.* 403, ed. Barel.

After these empty words Jacob of Trier pressed upon the
Emperor his scheme of reform. He spoke in the name of all
the Electors; and the representatives of the princes and Imperial
cities were all on his side. Moreover, Jacob was in constant
communication with Ladislas of Bohemia and Hungary, whose
presence at Vienna was a perpetual threat to the Emperor.
The Hungarian envoys pleaded for help from Germany; and
the luckless Emperor sat helpless to answer. It seemed almost
impossible for him to extricate himself with decency from the
difficulties that beset him on every side. If he gave way to
the Electors, the scanty remnants of his power were gone; if
he refused, the Diet would not vote troops for the crusade,
and the Emperor would be rendered ludicrous in the eyes of
Christendom. From this perplexity he and his counsellors
were delivered by the news of the death of Nicolas V., which
reached Neustadt on April 12. As this news threw into un-
certainty the possibility of an expedition from Italy, it was
useless to determine on a German expedition. The Pope's
death also opened up other plans to Jacob of Trier and his confederates. It was agreed to put off till next spring the levy
of troops for the aid of Hungary, and meanwhile to proclaim
throughout the Empire peace for two years. With this lame
conclusion the Diet came to an end, to the Emperor's great
relief.

CHAP.
III.

Proposals
for reform
of the
Empire.

Nicolas V. had been greatly affected by the capture of Constantinople, and by the new responsibilities which were consequently thrown upon his shoulders. The character of a
statesman and a warrior, summoning Europe to a mighty
enterprise, was not within the conceptions which Nicolas V. had
set before himself. He regarded it as a cruel misfortune to his
future fame that he should have to undertake a position for
which he had in no way fitted himself. He had not the energy
to reconstruct his plans; he was half-hearted in the conduct of
the crusading movement, yet he keenly felt the ignoble position
in which he was actually placed. He had dreamed of leaving a
great reputation as the restorer of Rome, the patron of men of
letters, the inaugurator of a new era, in which the Papacy at the
head of European culture quietly reasserted its old prestige
over the minds of men. This was not yet to be; and Nicolas,
disappointed and enfeebled by the gout, grew daily more infirm.

Death-bed
of Nicolas
V. March
1455.

When he felt that his end was approaching he wished to justify his policy, and claim due recognition of his merits before he quitted the stage of life.[1] He gathered the Cardinals round his bedside the day before his death, and addressed to them his last testament. First he spoke of the mercies of God as shown in the sacraments, and of his hope of a heavenly kingdom. Then he proceeded to defend himself for his expenditure of money in buildings in Rome, on which point the Cardinals listened with the most profound interest. Only the learned, he said, could understand the grounds of the Papal authority: the unlearned needed the testimony of their eyes, the sight of the magnificent memorials which embodied the history of Papal greatness. The buildings of Rome were the means of securing the devotion of Christendom, on which the Papal power rested. They were also the means of procuring for the Pope safety and peace at home. The records of the past, even the events of the pontificate of Eugenius IV., showed how needful were precautions for the personal safety of the Pope. 'Wherefore,' said the dying Pope, 'I have built fortresses at Gualdo, Fabriano, Assisi, Castellana, Narni, Orvieto, Spoleto, Viterbo, and other places: I have repaired and fortified the walls of Rome; I have restored the forty stations of the Cross, and the Basilicas founded by Gregory the Great: I have made this palace of the Vatican, and the adjacent Basilica of S. Peter, with the streets leading to it, fit for the use and dignity of the Holy See and the Curia.' He recalled the glories of his pontificate—the ending of the schism, the celebration of the Jubilee, the coronation of Frederick, his efforts for a crusade, the pacification of Italy. 'The towns in the States of the Church,' he continued, 'that were in ruins and in debt, I have restored to prosperity, and have adorned with pearls and precious stones, with buildings, books, tapestries, gold and silver vessels for the use of the churches. All this I have done, not by simony, by avarice, nor by parsimony—for I have been most liberal in gifts to learned men, in buying and transcribing manuscripts—but by God's blessing of peace and tranquillity in my days. The Roman Church, thus wealthy and thus

---

[1] This is Manetti's metaphor; *Vita Nicolai*, Mur. iii. pt. 2, 945 : 'Tanquam absoluta quædam totius comœdiæ perfectio reliquis prioribus tam laudabilibus et tam celebratis operationibus suis non injuria correspondisse et consonasse videatur.'

ˉpeaceful I leave to you, beseeching you to pray for God's grace that you may preserve and extend it.'[1] When he had ended his exhortation he dismissed the Cardinals with his benediction, and next day, March 24, he died.

The last words of Nicolas V. sufficiently show the character of his pontificate. Himself a scholar and a man of letters, he strove to mould the Papacy into the shape of his own individual predilections, which indeed fitted well enough with the aspirations of Italy in his day. Thoroughly Italian, he aimed at adapting the Papacy to the best ideal of Italy. He did not try to become powerful by arms or statesmanship, but rather withdrew from the current of Italian politics. In the midst of storm and strife, which raged in North and South Italy, the States of the Church were to be the abodes of peace, in which was to be realised the splendour of taste and learning which was the dream of Italian princes. Rome was to sum up all that was best in Italian life, and was to transmit it to the rest of Christendom. Revered in Italy as the capital of Italian thought, Rome was to be a missionary of culture to Europe, and so was to disarm suspicion and regain prestige. It was not exactly a Christian ideal that Nicolas V. set before himself. But the more religious aspirations of the time ran in the direction of ecclesiastical reform; and after the proceedings at Basel it was not judicious for a Pope to interfere with that matter at the present. Nicolas V. saw that reform was needed; but reform was too dangerous. If the Papacy could not venture on reform, the next best thing was to identify itself with art and learning. To the demand of Germany for reformation Nicolas V. answered by offering culture. His policy was so far wise that it enabled the Papacy to exist for sixty years before the antagonism broke out into open rebellion.

In personal character Nicolas V. was a student, with a student's irritability and vanity as well as a student's high-mindedness. He loved magnificence and outward splendour, and demanded the utmost decorum from those around him. To his household he was a kind master, but impatient, hard to satisfy, and of a sharp tongue. He was easily angered, but soon repented. He was straightforward and outspoken, and

---

[1] This speech is in Manetti's Life, p. 945.

required that everyone else should be the same; he was re-
morseless to anyone who equivocated or expressed himself
clumsily. He was staunch to his friends, though they all had
to bear his anger. He did not pay attention to his health,
but studied at all hours of the day and night, was irregular in
his meals, and was too much given to the use of wine as a
stimulant to his energies. Æneas Sylvius puts down as his
greatest fault, 'he trusted too much in himself, and wished
to do everything by himself; he thought that nothing was done
well unless he were engaged in it.'[1]

[1] *Commentarii*, ed. Fea., 109.

CHAPTER IV.

NICOLAS V. AND THE REVIVAL OF LEARNING.

THE great glory of Nicolas V. was the splendour of the
artistic revival, which he knew how to foster and direct.
The restoration of the city of Rome had already occupied the
attention of Martin V. and Eugenius IV. But Martin V. had to
discharge the inglorious though useful work of arresting the
decay of the buildings of Rome and making necessary repairs;
Eugenius IV. had neither opportunity nor money to proceed far
with architectural works. Still they did so much that Nicolas V.
found the way prepared for great schemes of embellishing the
city, and with unerring taste and judgment entered zealously
upon the task. His successors, Julius II. and Leo X., have left
their mark more decidedly in the form of great monumental
works; Nicolas V. left his impress on the city as a whole. He
wished not to associate his name with some particular work, but
to transform the whole city according to a connected plan. He
represents the simplicity, the sincerity, the freshness of the
early Renaissance, when it was an impulse and not a study.

So Nicolas V. was not content with one task only. His
keen eye glanced over the whole field, his taste penetrated
to the smallest details, and his practical sagacity kept pace
with his architectural zeal. Besides building the Vatican
palace and the basilica of S. Peter's, he restored the walls of
Rome, and erected fortresses throughout the Papal States.
Besides adapting the Borgo to be the residence of the Curia, he
proposed to make straight the crooked streets of Rome, to
widen the entrances to the piazzas, and connect them with one
another by colonnades such as made civic life more commodious
in Bologna or Padua. Nor was his care confined to the adornment of Rome only; he built at Civita Castellana, at Orvieto,
and other places in the Papal States palaces fit for the
residence of the Pope or his vicar. Whatever he did he did

CHAP.
IV.

Architec-
tural plans
of Nicolas
V.

The adorn-
ment of
Rome.

thoroughly; if he built a chapel, he provided for every kind of ornament down to the illumination of the missal for the altar.

The schemes of Nicolas V. seem beyond the power of one man to achieve; but if his pontificate, instead of lasting eight years, had lasted for sixteen, his restless energy might have seen his plans far advanced towards completion. As it was, he began great works to which his successors gave a final shape. To carry out his designs he gathered round him a band of noble artists. Chief amongst his architects were the Florentines Bernardo Gamberelli, known as Rosellino,[1] Antonio di Francesco, and the famous Leo Battista Alberti. As painters he had Fra Angelico, whose frescoes of the lives of S. Stephen and S. Laurance still adorn the Capella di S. Lorenzo in the Vatican, Benozzo Gozzoli and Andrea Castegno, from Florence; and from Perugia, Benedetto Bonfiglio, the master of Pietro Perugino. There were decorators, jewellers, workers in painted glass, in intarsia, and in embroidery. The city swarmed with an army of artisans, employed by the magnificent Pope to convert Rome into a strong and splendid city, of which the crowning glory was to be the Papal quarter beyond the Tiber, with its mighty palace and church, which were to be the wonder of the world. Blocks of travertine were quarried at Tivoli, and brought by water down the Anio, or dragged by oxen to the city. Nor did Nicolas V. spare the antiquities of Rome to minister to his new glories. The Colosseum was used as a quarry, and some of the smaller temples disappeared. The Renaissance was to Nicolas V. a new birth, sprung from his own magnificence and identified with his glory. Rome was to be the city of the Popes, not of the Emperors.

When Nicolas V. died he had rebuilt the walls of Rome, strengthened, from Alberti's plans, the Castle of S. Angelo, fortified the chief towns in the Papal States, restored the churches of SS. Apostoli, S. Celso, S. Stefano Rotondo, and S. Maria Maggiore, rebuilt a great part of the Capitol, reorganised the water supply of Rome, and begun the fountain of Trevi. Besides all this, he had commenced from the foundation the rebuilding of the basilica of S. Peter, and had begun the choir. In the Vatican palace he had finished the chapel of

---

[1] See Vasari's life of Bernardo Rosellino, and Müntz, *Les Arts à la Cour des Papes*, i. 80.

S. Lorenzo, and had built and splendidly decorated many chambers round the Cortile del Belvedere, where he began the library. He might sigh that he could not finish all that he had undertaken ; but he succeeded in marking out a plan which his successors carried out, the plan of erecting a mighty symbol of the Papal power, which should to all time appeal to the imagination, and kindle the enthusiastic admiration of Christendom.

This architectural revival of Nicolas V. rested upon a new conception which had gradually been changing the thought of Europe. Literature can only be concerned with expressing and arranging the ideas which are actually moving the minds of men. At the downfall of the Roman Empire the old classical culture had to give way before the necessities of the struggle against the barbarians, and Christianity formed the common ground on which Roman and barbarian ideas could be assimilated in a new form. Christian literature was first engaged with the expression of Christian truth and the task of ecclesiastical organisation. The work that occupied thinking men in the early Middle Ages was the reconstruction of society on a Christian basis. Their labour found its expression in the conception of the Empire and the Papacy, a conception which the genius of Gregory VII. impressed upon the imagination of Europe, and the Crusades gave a practical exhibition of its force. It was natural that during a period of reconstruction there was little thought of style ; the builder, not the artist, was needed for an edifice in which strength, not ornament, was required. To this the literature of classical antiquity could contribute nothing : it was known by some, perhaps by many, but there was no place for it in the world's work.

Decay of literature in the Middle Ages.

As soon, however, as Christendom was organised there was a possibility for the individual to find his own place in the new structure; there was room for the organisation of individual thought, for expression of individual feeling. While society was struggling to assert itself against anarchy, the individual had no place. When the lines of social organisation had once been traced the individual, having gained a foothold, could survey his lodging. Classical literature, which had been hitherto of little value, became precious as a model, both of individual feeling and of the means of giving it expression. Italy was naturally the first country to lead the

Revival of the classical spirit in Italy.

BOOK
IV.

way to this new literature. She was conscious of her antiquity, while other European nations were only awakening to the consciousness of their youth. While the Teutons turned for literary inspiration to nature and to the legendary heroes of their early days, Italy turned to classical antiquity, to the memorials that surrounded her on every side. Her early literature was reflective and displayed the workings of the individual soul. Teutonic literature was national, and aimed at expressing the rude aspirations of the present in the forms of a legendary past.

Dante.

So it was that Dante summed up the first period of Italian literature, and gave an artistic form to the aspirations of Christian culture. To him classical antiquity and Christianity went hand in hand. Virgil led him in his soul's pilgrimage to a spiritual emancipation which was the combined result of philosophic thought, the experience of life, and the guidance of heavenly illumination. To the large spirit of Christian culture, in which faith and reason were combined, and to which the mediæval ideal of a cosmopolitan Christendom was still a reality, Dante gave an ultimate expression. It was the ideal of Gregory VII. transformed by all the knowledge, all the sentiment, and all the reflection which the individual could acquire for himself.

Revival of
learning.

But this ideal of Christendom was not to be realised. Dante, though he knew it not, lived through the period of the fall of Empire and Papacy alike. With the Pope at Avignon and the Empire in anarchy it was no longer possible for the individual life to attach its aspirations to what was manifestly powerless. The individual was more and more driven to consider himself and the workings of his own mind. Dante had used his own personality as a symbol of universal man. Petrarch did not advance beyond the expression of phases of feeling. But the study of phases of feeling led to a larger conception of the variety of individual life, a conception which animates with reality the pages of Boccaccio. This distinctly human and individual literature brought with it a quickened sense of beauty, an appreciation of form, a desire for a more perfect style. When once this feeling was awakened the study of classical antiquity assumed a new importance : only through it could men attain to clear ideas, accurate expressions, beautiful forms. To discover these the Italian mind devoted itself with passionate enthusiasm to the revival of classical antiquity, the CHAP.
IV. study of its records, the imitation of its modes of thought. Instead of striving to reconstruct the decaying ideal of a united Christendom, Italy devoted itself to the development of the individual life; instead of labouring for the reform of the Church, Italy was busy with the acquisition of literary and artistic style.

Hence it was that Italy played so small a part in the great *Teutonic* movement of the fifteenth century for the reformation of the *and Italian spirit.* Church. France and Germany laboured at Constance and Basel for the ending of the schism and the reorganisation of Christendom in accordance with the consciences of men. Italy had passed beyond the sphere of the scholastic formulæ which were in the mouths of conciliar theologians. She was inventing a new method, and had little interest in questions which concerned merely external organisation. While the Fathers of Constance looked upon Hus as a rebel who would rend asunder the unity of Christendom, the cultivated Italian, Poggio, admired his originality and compared him with the great men of old time. While theologians were engaged in determining by appeals to Christian antiquity the authority of General Councils, Poggio was ransacking the adjacent monasteries in search of manuscripts of classical authors. The breach had begun between the Italian and the Teutonic spirit. The Italians were bent upon securing for the individual emancipation from outward systems by means of culture; the Teutons wished to adapt the system of Christendom to the requirements of the awakening individual. The Renaissance and the Reformation began to pursue different courses.

The Papacy, as having its seat in Italy, could not remain *The* unaffected by the national impulse. Though Florence was the *Papacy and the* centre of the early Renaissance, its influence quickly spread, *revival of* and students of classical antiquity were rapidly attached to *learning.* every Italian court. Manuscripts were collected, academies were formed, and public business was transacted with strict attention to the best models. The Papacy could not lag behind the prevailing fashion. Already, under Innocent VII., Leonardo Bruni and Poggio Bracciolini were attached to the Papal Curia as secretaries. The Greek scholar, Emmanuel Chrysoloras, was employed by John XXIII., and followed him to Constance, where he died. Martin V. was too busy with other matters to pay much heed to literature; but under Eugenius IV. the Italian humanists found that their own interests were closely bound up with the Papacy. The struggle between the Pope and the Council of Basel brought into prominence the growing antagonism between the Italian and the Teutonic spirit, between the Renaissance and the Reformation. The opposition of the Council to the Pope was resented as an attempt to rob Italy of part of its old prestige. The new learning was animated on its side by a missionary spirit; its mission was to carry thoughout Europe a new culture, and the Papacy was one of its means. Though Eugenius IV. was in no way associated in character with the Italian spirit of culture, yet the humanists gathered round him, and Poggio, Aurispa, Vegio, Biondo, and Perotti were numbered amongst his secretaries.

Literature under Nicolas V.
Nicolas V. was genuinely Italian, and was himself thoroughly penetrated with the spirit of the new learning. Before he became Pope he had been a great collector of manuscripts, which he delighted to transcribe with his own hand. He had arranged the library of S. Marco for Cosimo de' Medici, and was eager to eclipse it at Rome. If the Papacy by its magnificence were to assert its power over Christendom, it must stand at the head of the mission of Italian culture. So Nicolas V. declared himself the patron of all men of learning, and they were not slow in gathering round him. Rome had produced few scholars of its own; but Nicolas V. was bent on making it a home of learning. He eagerly gathered manuscripts from every side, and employed a whole host of transcribers and translators within the Vatican, while his agents traversed Greece, Germany, and even Britain in search of hidden treasures. Even the fall of Constantinople could not be regarded as entirely a misfortune, for it brought to Italy the literary wealth of Greece. 'Greece has not fallen,' said Filelfo, 'but seems to have migrated to Italy, which in old days bore the name of Magna Græcia.' [1] When Nicolas V. died he left behind him a library of five thousand volumes, an enormous collection for the days before printing.[2] When in 1450 the Jubilee brought with it a pestilence, occasioned by the crowded state of the city, and Nicolas fled before the plague to Fabriano, he took with him

---

[1] Philelphi, *Epistolæ* xiii. 1.
[2] Manetti, in Muratori, iii. part 2, 926.

his host of transcribers, of whom he demanded as much zeal as he himself displayed. 'You were the slave of Nicolas,' says Æneas Sylvius to his friend Piero da Noceto, ' and had no fixed time for eating or sleeping ; you could not converse with your friends or go into the light of day, but were hidden in murky air, in dust, in heat, and in unpleasant smells.'[1] The Pope's passion was well known, and the world's tribute flowed to Rome in the shape of manuscripts. For these literary treasures Nicolas V. rebuilt the Vatican library, and appointed as its librarian Giovanni Tortelli, of Arezzo, the author of a grammatical work, ' De Orthographia Dictionum a Græcis tractarum.'

Chief amongst the Pope's assistants in his formation of a library was the good Florentine bookseller, Vespasiano da Bisticci, whose love and respect for his patron may be read in his own simple language.[2] From Florence also Nicolas V. invited his more famous biographer, Gianozzo Manetti, whom he made a Papal secretary, and also conferred on him a pension of six hundred ducats. Manetti, a small man with a large head, who enjoyed robust health, was a rigorous student, and had generally spent five hours in reading before the greater part of his fellow-men had risen from bed. He was of great repute in his native city of Florence, and was a leading statesman, employed in many important embassies, where his eloquence always gained him a ready hearing. He obtained leave from the Florentines to transfer himself to the Pope's service, and was engaged by Nicolas V., with characteristic impetuosity, on the two mighty works of writing an Apology for Christianity against Jews and Heathens, and translating into Latin the Old and New Testaments. Manetti had so far advanced in his task at the death of Nicolas V. that he had written ten books against the Jews, and had translated the Psalms, the four Gospels, the Epistles, and the Revelation.[3] Manetti's life of his patron is the chief record of the greatness

Vespasiano da Bisticci and Gianozzo Manetti.

---

[1] Æn. Syl. *Epistolæ*, 188.

[2] There is no more interesting work, nor one which throws a more intimate light on the history of Italy in the fifteenth century, than Vespasiano's *Vite di Uomini Illustri*, originally published by Mai in *Spicilegium Romanum*, vol. i., afterwards by Bartoli (Florence, 1859).

[3] See Naldus, *Vita Manetti*, Muratori, xx. 529. There is at the end a list of all Manetti's writings.

of the schemes of Nicolas V., which Manetti chronicled with
enthusiasm, though his style is pompous and his panegyric
laboured.

Nicolas V. found in the Curia an old acquaintance, the
literary veteran Poggio Bracciolini, who in the days of Boniface IX. took service in the Papal Chancery, and soon associated with himself his friend Leonardo Bruni. He went to
Constance with John XXIII., and on his fall betook himself
to the occupation of searching for manuscripts in the neighbouring monasteries, while he surveyed the proceedings of the
Council with quiet contempt. Poggio was a true explorer
and warmed with his task; he rescued from the dust and dirt
of oblivion Quintilian, several orations of Cicero, Ammianus
Marcellinus, Lucretius, and many other works. His zeal
carried him to Langres, to Köln, and ultimately to England,
where, however, he found scanty patronage in the turbulent
times of Henry VI. Many were his endeavours to send ex-
plorers to Sweden in search of the lost books of Livy. Long
were his negotiations to obtain from the monastery of Fulda
the complete manuscript of the 'Annals' of Tacitus, which he
edited in 1429. Under Eugenius IV. he did not find himself amid
congenial surroundings; and he hailed with delight the accession
to the Papacy of his friend Tommaso of Sarzana, to whom he
had dedicated in 1449 a Dialogue on the 'Unhappiness of
Princes.' It was a species of composition then much in vogue,
consisting of moral reflections illustrated by historical examples,
founded on the model of Cicero's 'Dialogues.' Following upon
the same lines, Poggio went on to write and dedicate 'to the
same man, though not under the same name,' his most interesting work, a Dialogue on the 'Vicissitudes of Fortune.'
Poggio represents himself as reposing with a friend on the
Capitol after an inspection of the ruins of Rome. He mo-
ralises on the scanty remnants of her ancient grandeur, and in
so doing gives the completest description we possess of the
appearance of the city at that time. From this he goes on to
quote great instances of the instability of fortune, which leads
him to survey the changes of Europe from 1377 to the end of
Martin V. The pontificate of Eugenius IV. illustrates his
theme so pointedly, that a whole book is devoted to it. Then
the writer takes a sudden leap, and tells us the travels of a

Venetian, Niccolo Conti, who had told him the story of his
adventures during a residence of twenty-five years in Persia
and India. The whole work is a store of curious and interesting
information, given with much sprightliness of style and keenness
of observation.[1] Poggio hailed Nicolas V. as a second Mæcenas,
and expressed his joy at the downfall of the monkish favourites
of Eugenius IV. by a stinging ' Dialogue against Hypocrisy,' in
which he held up to ridicule the affected piety of self-seeking
monks, and gathered a number of scandalous stories of their
frauds and tricks practised in the name of religion.[2] Poggio
himself made no pretence at the concealment of his own life
and character, but published soon after his ' Facetiæ,' or jest-
book, a collection of good stories which he and his friends in
the Papal Chancery used to tell for one another's amusement in
their leisure moments. We are not surprised that men who indulged in such frankness as these stories betoken, found even
the restraint of the neighbourhood of a monk's frock burdensome to their overflowing and unseemly wit. Poggio's pen,
like that of many of his contemporaries, was ready not only
to copy the finer forms of classical expression, but also
the licentiousness of paganism and the fertility of vituperation
which marked the decadence of classical literature. To please
Nicolas V., Poggio composed a philippic against Amadeus of
Savoy, and called to his aid all the wealth of Ciceronian invective to overwhelm the anti-Pope and the Council of Basel. He
was, however, employed on more serious works of scholarship
and translated Xenophon's ' Cyropedia,' and at the request of
Nicolas V., the ' History of Diodorus Siculus.'[3]

These scholars of the Papal Court were by no means free
from literary jealousies and rivalries. Factions and disputes
were rife amongst them, as was natural when each had to
preserve a reputation for preeminence in his own subject.
Chief amongst the Greek scholars whom Nicolas V. welcomed
in Rome was George of Trapezus, who translated for him
many of the works of the Greek fathers, Eusebius of Cæsarea,
Chrysostom, Gregory of Nazianzum, and Basil. But the revival

CHAP.
IV.

George of
Trapezus
and Bes-
sarion.

[1] Poggio, *De Varietate Fortunæ*, was not published in its completeness till
1723, by the Abate Oliva, at Paris.
[2] *Dialogus contra Hypocrisim* is published in the Appendix to *Fasciculus
Rerum Expetendarum et Fugiendarum*, 570, &c.
[3] Printed Bononiæ, 1472.

of Greek literature led to a deep interest in Greek philosophy, and Gemistos Plethon established at Florence a school of devoted students of Plato, who was almost a new discovery to the thought of the time. The doctrines of Aristotle and Plato were eagerly discussed; and Cardinal Bessarion, at the request of Nicolas V., translated Aristotle's 'Metaphysics,' while Theodore Gaza translated the 'History of Animals,' and Theophrastus's 'History of Plants.' George of Trapezus thought it due to his own importance to attack a work of Bessarion, which maintained the Platonic view that nature acts with design, which is the stamp of the Divine Intelligence. Bessarion answered him, and the controversy created great interest. George of Trapezus, in an evil moment, undertook to translate Plato's 'Laws,' which he did with great rapidity. Bessarion criticised his translation, a task of some moment, as George professed to give a specimen of Plato's teaching; he convicted him of 259 errors, and concluded that his translation had almost as many mistakes as it had words.[1] George certainly cannot have been an accurate translator, as Æneas Sylvius says, that in one of his translations from Aristotle he found Cicero mentioned.[2] Nicolas V. felt his belief shattered; he withdrew his patronage from George, who in 1453 retired to Naples, where he was received by King Alfonso. He was an irritable man and took his revenge by general railing. Amongst other things he asserted that Poggio's translations had been made by his assistance; that the merits were his, and the mistakes were Poggio's.[3]

Lorenzo
Valla.

No doubt Poggio would have answered this aspersion on his scholarship; but probably it never came to his ears, as in 1453 he was appointed to the honourable office of Chancellor of his native city of Florence, where he took up his abode after spending fifty years in the Papal service. Moreover, he was engaged in a literary controversy with an opponent more formidable than George of Trapezus—the learned Lorenzo Valla. If Poggio is the most celebrated literary man of the Early

[1] This controversy is to be found in Bessarion's treatises, *De Natura et Arte*, and *In Calumniatorem Platonis*.

[2] *Epistolæ*, 95.

[3] 'Quotidianis laboribus meis . . . . vel vertisse illum vel pervertisse,' in a letter of George, quoted by Georgius, *Vita Nicolai V.* 177.

Renaissance, Valla is undoubtedly the man of the keenest mind. Poggio might boast of a more limpid style, but Valla was the sounder scholar. Poggio founded himself on Cicero, Valla preferred Quintilian. Valla's 'Elegantiæ' is a comprehensive attempt to deal with Latin grammar in a scientific spirit, and it was this that gave him a pre-eminence over men like Poggio, who were merely literary Latinists. Valla was born in Piacenza, but was educated in Rome under the care of Leonardo Bruni till he reached the age of twenty-four. Then he taught at Piacenza and Pavia, till he betook himself to Alfonso of Naples, at the time when he was bitterly opposed to Eugenius IV. The hate of a Roman against priestly domination joined with a desire to strike a blow in his patron's behalf. Valla turned his keen critical spirit, which had been trained in the methods of scientific inquiry, to an examination of the grounds on which rested the story of the donation of Constantine of the patrimony of S. Peter to Pope Sylvester. In his work, 'On the Donation of Constantine,'[1] he set forth vividly the historical aspect of such an event; he imagined Constantine wishing to make such an alienation of the territory of the Empire; he pictured the remonstrance of the Senate, the humble deprecation of the Pope. He examined the nature of the evidence for this donation, and mocked at the claims of tradition to be credited when contemporary records were silent. 'If anyone among the Greeks, the Hebrews, or the Barbarians were to say that such a thing were handed down by tradition, would you not ask for the author's name or the production of a record?' He criticised the wording of the forged decree (no difficult task), and showed its gross inconsistency with the facts and forms of the time at which it professed to be framed. He ended with a savage attack on the iniquities of the Papal Government, and exhorted all Christian princes to deprive the Pope of his usurped power, and so take away his means of disturbing the peace of Europe by interference in temporal affairs.

Nor was this Valla's only onslaught upon orthodox belief; he ventured to call in question the tradition that the Apostles' Creed was the joint composition of the Twelve, who met in solemn conference and each contributed a clause. This brought

---

[1] It is printed in Valla's works, and in *Fasciculus Rerum*, i. 132.

him into collision with the friars, and he was threatened with
the Inquisition; but Alfonso interposed on his behalf, and
Alfonso's reconciliation with Eugenius IV. carried Valla's
reconciliation with it. Valla had no fanatical hatred to the
Papacy, and was willing to own that his attack had been of
the nature of a literary exercise. He wrote an apology to
Eugenius IV., who did not, however, admit him to his favour;
but Nicolas V. cared little for monastic orthodoxy, and was not
prevented by Valla's free thinking from summoning to his
court so eminent a scholar. For him Valla translated
Thucydides; and so pleased was the Pope with his translation
that he presented him with five hundred ducats, and begged
him to translate Herodotus also, a task which Valla began
but did not finish.

Quarrel of
Poggio
and Valla.
The keen critical spirit of Valla made him haughty and
supercilious to his literary compeers; and meekness was in no
sense their crowning virtue. As ill-luck would have it, one of
Valla's pupils at Rome had a copy of Poggio's 'Letters,' in the
margin of which he had written criticisms on the style, pointing out and amending what he conceived to be barbarisms.
The book fell into the hands of Poggio, who was filled with
wrath at this attempt to improve perfection. He at once concluded that the criticisms proceeded from Valla, and adopted
his usual mode of chastising the offender. He wrote, in the
most approved Ciceronian style, a violent invective against
Valla, in which he defended himself against Valla's supposed
criticism, scourged his arrogance and vanity, and impeached
his orthodoxy. Valla replied by an 'Antidote to Poggio,' which
he addressed to Nicolas V. Not content with repelling
Poggio's attacks or discussing his literary character, he cast
aspersions upon his private life. Poggio retorted by opening
the flood-gates of abuse on Valla. Every scandalous story was
raked up, every possible villany was laid to his charge; nay,
even a picture was drawn of the final judgment of the Great
Day, and Valla was remorselessly condemned to perdition.
Replies and counter-replies followed, and the contest between
these two eminent scholars was carried on by clothing the
lowest scurrility with classical language. The actual question
in dispute disappeared: the wrath alone remained. Rhetorical exercises in declamatory abuse were poured forth in

rapid succession. What fills us with surprise is the fact that Nicolas V. did not use his influence to stop this unseemly exhibition. He received the dedication of Valla's 'Antidote;' and, though other men of letters, who were by no means squeamish, remonstrated with the angry combatants, Nicolas V. did not interfere. It would seem that an interest in style had already overpowered, even in the head of Christendom, any feeling of decorum, not to say morality, as regarded the subject-matter. Love for the forms of classical antiquity was already strong enough to override the spirit of Christianity. The criticisms of Valla on popular religion awakened no anxiety in the heart of Nicolas V. for the stability of ecclesiastical tradition; the low scurrility of Poggio excited no care for Christian morality. An antagonism had begun which was to widen hereafter and produce disastrous results on the future of the Papacy.

The man who interposed his good offices to stop this fray between Poggio and Valla was Francesco Filelfo, the most adventurous and most reprobate of the literary men of the time. A native of Tolentino in the march of Ancona, Filelfo sought his fortune on every side. First he taught in Venice; then in 1420 went as secretary to an embassy to Constantinople. There he studied Greek under John Chrysolaras, whose daughter he married. He won the favour of the Greek Emperor, went as envoy to Murad II., and afterwards to Hungary, and returned to Venice in 1427 with a treasure of Greek manuscripts. As Venice would not pay him enough, he went to Bologna, and thence to Florence. He was a savage literary gladiator, openly seeking his fortune and restrained by no moral principles. His overweening vanity offended his literary contemporaries, whom he attacked in shameless satires. He and Poggio had a fierce war of words, and he raised up enemies on every side. At last he attacked even Cosimo de' Medici, and found it necessary to flee to Siena, thence to Bologna, and afterwards to Milan. In 1453 he passed through Rome on his way to Naples; Nicolas V. summoned him to his presence, presented him with five hundred ducats, and made him one of his secretaries. He read with pleasure Filelfo's satires, and urged him to undertake a translation of the Iliad and Odyssey; for this task he offered to give him a house in Rome, an estate in the country,

and to pay him ten thousand golden ducats. The death of
Nicolas V. prevented the bargain from being completed.

Many other scholars of less fame worked for Nicolas V.
Niccolo Perotti translated Polybius; Guarino of Verona the
geography of Strabo; Piero Candido Decembrio, who had been
the chief scholar in the service of Giovanni Maria Visconti,
took refuge in Rome from the disturbances that followed his
patron's death, and translated Appian for the Pope. Nor was
it only in the sphere of Latin and Greek scholarship that
Rome became the capital of literature. The sight of the
monuments of Rome aroused an interest in an exact study
of its past topography. Poggio looked on the ruins of
Rome with the eye of a literary man who found in them food
for his imagination. His contemporary, Flavio Biondo, a native of Forlì, who was made a Papal secretary by Eugenius
IV., may be regarded as the founder of serious archæology.
His work, 'Roma Instaurata,' which was finished just before the
death of Eugenius IV., is a careful topographical description of
the city of Rome and an attempt to restore its ancient monuments. When we consider the materials which Biondo had at
his command, we are struck with the sense of order and
accuracy which was growing up among the Italian scholars.
The work of Biondo may be formless—it cannot be said that
archæology has yet advanced very far in style—but it is a
careful and scholarly piece of work, such as had never been
attempted before. His concluding words are an expression of
the ideal of Nicolas V. After surveying the classical monuments of Rome he pauses. 'Not,' he says, 'that we despise
the Rome of our own day, or think that its glories came to an
end with its legions, consuls, and senate. Rome still exercises
her sway over the world, not by arms and bloodshed, but by
the power of religion. The Pope is still a perpetual dictator,
the cardinals a senate; the world still brings its tribute to
Rome, still flocks to see its holy relics and its sacred places.'
Though Biondo himself did not proceed to describe the Christian antiquities of Rome, he warmly appreciated them; and his
contemporary, Maffeo Vegio of Lodi, also a Papal secretary,
wrote a careful account of the antiquities of the Basilica of
S. Peter's.

Such were a few of the scholars whom Nicolas V. gathered

round him. Their names are now almost forgotten, though
in their own day they received a respect which has rarely
fallen to the lot of literary men. Their works repose undisturbed in libraries; their fame, of which they were so careful,
has vanished; they are remembered merely as literary curi-
osities. Yet we owe some debt of gratitude to those who
cleared the way for European culture. They were not men
of creative genius; their merits are scientific rather than
literary. They rescued from destruction the treasures of
antiquity, and prepared the way for a proper understanding of
them. Their method was crude; their knowledge was imperfect;
their attention to rhetorical forms ludicrously exaggerated.
Yet they laid the foundation of classical philology, of the
science of grammar, of intelligent criticism, of clear expression.
They stood at the opening of a new era, and their labours only
furnished the foundation for the labours of others. One generation of scholars succeeds another, and the past are soon forgotten,
however great may have been their services to a better understanding of the classical spirit, however great may have been
the impulse which that heightened knowledge gave to the
thought of Europe.

We have spoken only of a few of the most famous scholars
who gathered round Nicolas V. They are but samples of their
kind, as the court of Nicolas V. was but a brilliant sample of
the literary and artistic movement that was pervading the
whole of Italy. Of this movement Florence was its home; and
Cosimo de' Medici had seen the wisdom of identifying his power
with all that was most eminently Florentine in the aspirations of
his native city. He set the example of a literary patronage,
which was splendidly followed by Nicolas V., and scarcely less so
by Alfonso of Naples, who made himself more Italian than the
Italians, and became the ideal of a cultivated prince. He was
never tired of reading classical authors, and had them read
to him even at his meals. He was cured of an illness by hearing
Quintus Curtius' 'Life of Alexander the Great,' and received
from the Venetians a bone of Livy with all the reverence
due to the relic of a saint. He and Nicolas V. carried on
an honourable rivalry, which should do most for learning;
and their example spread rapidly throughout the congenial soil

of Italy. Almost every court had its literary circle, and literary interests held a prominent place in Italian politics of the
ensuing time.

Amid these now forgotten scholars stood Nicolas V.
Though not himself a man of letters, he was for that very
reason better fitted to play the part of patron. He was
not merely a collector of books, but was also an intelligent
director of the studies of others. When we consider all that
he did, we may well be amazed at the greatness of his plans
and the energy with which he prosecuted them. The trans-
formation of Rome into the undisputed capital of Europe, the
attainment for the Papacy of an overpowering prestige which
was to enthral men's minds—these apparently chimerical objects
were pursued with unerring precision and untiring labour. Nothing was overlooked in the great plan of Nicolas V. : every part
of the work was pressed on at the same time, and every part of
the work was regulated by the personal judgment of the Pope.
Fortresses and libraries, churches and palaces, were alike
rising under the Pope's supervision ; the fine arts, the literature
and science of the time, all were welcomed to Rome, and found
by the Pope's care a congenial sphere. We cannot render too
much praise to the thoroughness with which Nicolas V. conceived and executed the plan which he had formed. But the
plan was in itself a dream of almost superhuman magnificence,
and Nicolas V. expected too much when he hoped that the
world's commotions would stand still and respect the charming
leisure of the Papacy. The fall of Constantinople dispelled the
pacific vision · of the Renaissance, and brought back the
mediæval dream of a crusade. Before Christendom could be
rearranged under the peaceful sway of literature and theology
going hand in hand, the enemies of her faith and of her civilisation had stormed the bulwark that had stood for twelve
centuries, and were threatening her with a new invasion.

CHAPTER V.

CALIXTUS III.

1455-1458.

CHAP.
V.

Election
of Alfonso
Borgia,
Calixtus
III. April
8, 1455.

AFTER the funeral of Nicolas V. fifteen of the twenty Cardinals entered the Conclave. They were greatly divided in opinion, and, in fact, had no clear policy to which they were desirous to commit themselves. The first scrutinies led to no result, and the Cardinals conferred privately with one another. At first Capranica seemed to be the favourite, being commended by his learning, his high character, and his political ability. But Capranica was a Roman and a friend of the Colonna; as such he was opposed by the party of the Orsini. He was therefore passed by in favour of Bessarion, who had no enemies and enjoyed a high reputation for learning. His election would have given a worthy successor to the policy of Nicolas V., and would also have shown the zeal of the Cardinals for the crusade. In Bessarion they would have chosen a Pope sprung from the Greek nation and keenly sympathising with his conquered countrymen. For a night it seemed that Bessarion would be elected; but the morning brought reflection. He was an alien and a neophyte, a stranger to Italy and to the traditions of the Papacy. 'Shall we go to Greece,' said Alain of Avignon, 'for a head of the Latin Church? Bessarion has not yet shaved his beard, and shall we set him over us?' There was a sudden revulsion of feeling. The Cardinals, weary with the debate, suddenly made a compromise, and an old Spanish cardinal, Alfonso Borgia, was elected by accession on April 8. Borgia was seventy-seven years old, and owed his election to his age. As the Cardinals could not agree, they made a colourless election of one who by his speedy death would soon create another vacancy.

Alfonso Borgia was a native of Xativa in Valencia, who had

BOOK
IV.

*Early life
of Cardinal
Borgia.*

distinguished himself in his youth at the University of Lerida.
There he attracted the attention of his countryman, Benedict
XIII., who conferred on him a canonry, and Alfonso of Aragon
took him as his secretary.   He did good service to the
Papacy in winning for Martin V. the allegiance of Spain, and
in negotiating the renunciation of the Spanish anti-Pope,
Clement VIII.   In recognition of these services Martin V.
conferred on him the bishopric of Valentia.   When the Council
of Basel began its sessions Alfonso chose Borgia as his representative.   Borgia refused the office, but visited Eugenius IV.
at Florence, and showed great skill in negotiating peace between Alfonso and the Pope.   In return Eugenius IV. in
1444 raised him to the Cardinalate, and by his wisdom and
moderation Cardinal Borgia deservedly held a high place in the
Curia.   When the Conclave could not agree on a successor to
Nicolas V., Borgia was an excellent person for the purposes of
a compromise.   His learning was profound, his character
blameless, his political capacity stood high.   His election
was gratifying to Alfonso of Naples.   As a Spaniard, he bore
an hereditary hatred to the Turks, which would make him a
fitting representative of the crusading movement.[1]

*Riot at his
corona-
tion.*

On April 20 Alfonso Borgia was crowned Pope, and took the
title of Calixtus III.   The solemnity was disturbed by a riot
arising from a quarrel between one of the followers of Count
Averso of Anguillara and one of the Orsini.   Napoleone Orsini
raised his war-cry; 3,000 men-at-arms gathered round him,
prepared to storm the Lateran and drag the Count of Anguillara from the Pope's presence.   Only the intervention of
Cardinal Latino Orsini could appease his brother's wrath and
persuade him not to mar the festivities with bloodshed.   The
turbulent Roman barons began at once to reckon on the feebleness of the aged Pope.

*Crusading
zeal of
Calixtus
III.*

In spite of his years Calixtus soon showed that he was
filled with a devouring zeal for prosecuting the war against the
Turks.   He solemnly committed to writing his inflexible determination.[2]   'I, Pope Calixtus, vow to Almighty God and the
Holy Trinity that by war, maledictions, interdicts, excommunications, and all other means in my power, I will pursue the Turks,

[1] See Platina, *Vita Calixti III.*
[2] See Infessura, Muratori, iii. pt. 2, 1136.

the most cruel foes of the Christian name.' With this object in view Calixtus IV. sent legates to every country to quicken the zeal of Christendom. The buildings which Nicolas V. had begun were neglected; his swarms of workmen were dismissed; men of letters found themselves little regarded in the new court where severe simplicity reigned, and the old Pope rarely left his chamber. The revenues of the Papacy were no longer devoted to the erection of splendid buildings and the encouragement of letters; they were used for the equipment of the Papal fleet, and the peaceful city was full of warlike preparation.

The hopes of a European crusade were fixed on Germany; but the proceedings of the Diet of Neustadt were scarcely such as to inspire much confidence. The death of Nicolas V. and the election of a new Pope gave an opportunity to the Electors to urge upon the Emperor their grievances against the Papacy. Jacob of Trier exclaimed that now was the time to vindicate the liberty of the German Church, which was treated as the Pope's handmaid; before Calixtus III. was recognised, the observance of the Concordat made by Eugenius IV. should be rigorously exacted, and the grievances of the German Church should be reformed. Æneas Sylvius confirmed the troubled Emperor, who had his own grievances, because the private agreement made by Eugenius IV. had not been more strictly observed than the published Concordat. It was vain, said Æneas, for a prince to please the people, seeing that the multitude was always inconstant, and it was dangerous to give it the rein. On the other hand, the interests of the Pope and Emperor were identical, and a new Pope only gave a new opportunity for receiving favours. After a little hesitation Æneas prevailed, and he, with the jurist John Hagenbach, was sent to Rome to offer to Calixtus III. the obedience of Germany, and to lay before him the Emperor's demands.[1]

Æneas and his colleague did not reach Rome till August 10, when they asked for a private audience to lay Frederick's requests before the Pope. Calixtus III. stood in a more independent position towards the Emperor than his two predecessors. Eugenius IV. had bought back the obedience of Germany by secret concessions and a promise of money.

[1] *Pii II. Commentarii*, 25.

Nicolas V. had been privy to this transaction, and felt himself
bound by it; he had paid his share of the money promised to
Frederick, but 25,000 ducats were still due.[1] Calixtus had
had no part in the negotiations with Frederick, and knew
how hopeless it was to satisfy the feeble and needy Emperor.
He refused to consider his requests until he had received the
obedience of Germany. Æneas Sylvius, who was anxious to
reach the Cardinalate, had no objection to use his position of
Imperial envoy as a means of showing his readiness to please
the Pope. He professed to be confounded at this demand of
the Pope; but to avoid scandal he gave way to it. He proffered
the obedience of Germany in a public consistory, and made a
speech, in which was no mention of the Emperor's demands,
or of the stricter observance of the Concordat. This speech
was merely a string of compliments to the Pope and the Emperor and declamation about war against the Turk.[2] When,
after this, the ambassadors returned, in several private audiences,
to the matters entrusted to them by the Emperor, they could
only appear as petitioners, not as negotiators. Calixtus roundly
declared that he had no money to pay the 25,000 ducats which
Frederick claimed; his other requests for a share in the tenths
to be raised for the crusade, and for the right of nomination
to vacant bishoprics, were deferred for further consideration.
Cardinal Carvajal should be sent to satisfy the Emperor so far
as was consistent with the rights of the Church.[3] Frederick III. was no longer the necessary ally of the Pope: his
cause was now so far identified with that of the Pope that he
could not desert the Papacy, and he was too unimportant in
Germany to be of much service. Æneas Sylvius felt that he
had now done all he could for the Papacy in Germany; his
connexion with the Emperor could be of no further profit
to him. He had brought to Rome letters from Frederick III.,
and also from Ladislas of Hungary, recommending him
for the Cardinalate. This honour had been long in coming.
Nicolas V. had almost promised it; but the outspoken and

[1] Letter of Gregory Heimburg, dated 1466, in Düx, *Nicolas von Cusa* I.
Beilage iv.
[2] In Mansi, *Pii II. Orationes*, i. 336.
[3] These details are given in Voigt, *Æneas Sylvius Piccolomini*, ii. 160,
from MS. letter of Æneas at Vienna.

fiery Nicolas had never liked the subtle, shifty Sienese, and
Æneas had been passed over. He now stayed in Rome in the
hopes that Calixtus, as everyone expected, would create him
Cardinal in the coming Advent.

But the expectations of Æneas were for a time doomed to
disappointment. A consistory was held for the creation of
cardinals, and congratulations were brought to Æneas, who
lay bedridden with the gout. The congratulations, however,
were premature. The sitting of the consistory was long and
stormy; when it broke up the Cardinals were pledged to
secresy. Calixtus III. went back to the policy of Martin V.,
and wished to elevate his family at the expense of the Church.
He proposed as the new cardinals two of his nephews, Rodrigo
Lançol and Juan Luis de Mila, both young men little over
twenty years of age, remarkable for nothing except their
personal strength and vigour. Together with them he nominated a third youth, Don Jayme, son of the Infante Pedro of
Portugal. The Cardinals protested loudly against this creation
of two nephews; they pointed out the scandal that was likely
to arise. For a time the Pope paused; he did not venture to
publish the creation till September, when most of the Cardinals
had left Rome to avoid the heat. The Cardinals murmured,
but were helpless against the stubborn old man.

The desire to aggrandise his nephews was the only object
which shared with the war against the Turks the interest of
Calixtus III. Legates and preaching friars swarmed throughout Europe. Calixtus had no belief in Congresses; he issued
himself a proclamation of war, imposed a tax on all the
clergy throughout Christendom, and fixed March 1, 1456, as
the day on which a combined fleet and army was to set forth
against the Turks. He appointed special priests to say mass
daily in behalf of the holy war; he ordered processions to be
made for its success; at midday each church bell was to be
rung to summon the faithful to prayer, and they who said three
Aves and Paternosters for victory against the Turk earned an
indulgence for three years. All that was possible was done to
kindle the zeal and gather the contributions of Christendom.

The princes, however, did not show the same zeal as the
Pope. They made high-sounding promises and professions,
and were ready enough to receive the money collected in

their realms; but this was all. Alfonso of Naples equipped a fleet, but sent it against Genoa instead of the Turks. The Duke of Burgundy was content with the renown he had already won as a crusader, and was busy in watching the French King. Charles VII. of France at first refused to allow the Pope's Bulls to be published; he was too busily engaged in watching England and Burgundy to have any care for foreign enterprises. At length Cardinal Alain of Avignon prevailed upon him to sanction the collection of tenths from the French clergy; but the money was spent in building galleys at Avignon, which were afterwards used against Naples. Germany, England, and the Spanish kingdoms did nothing; the Italian powers were too cautious to take any decided steps. Nowhere did the Papal summons meet with any real response.

In spite of the lukewarmness of Europe the Pope was not disheartened. From his sick chamber he urged the building of his galleys along the Ripa Grande. To obtain money he took the treasures of art which Nicolas V. had lavished on the Roman churches; he even stripped the splendid bindings off the books which Nicolas V. had stored in the Vatican library. One day his eye fell on a salt-cellar of richly-chased gold work upon his table: 'Take it away,' he cried, 'take it for the Turkish war; an earthenware salt-cellar is enough for me.' [1] The result of these efforts was that in May 1456 a fleet of some sixteen galleys was anchored at Ostia. Calixtus appointed as his admiral Cardinal Scarampo, and bade him sail at once against the Turks. Sorely against his will, Scarampo was driven to undertake this hopeless task. His position was indeed pitiable. Under Eugenius IV. he had been the general of the Papal forces, and had ruled Rome at his will; under Nicolas V. his power came to an end, and he indulged himself in ease and luxury. With a new Pope a new field was opened for his ambition, and he had been foremost in promoting the election of Calixtus III., believing that the old man would be a flexible instrument in his hands. But Calixtus fell under the power of his stalwart nephews, who looked with suspicion on Scarampo, and so poisoned the Pope's mind against him that he was forbidden to approach the Vatican. In this strait Scarampo made a bid for a renewal of favour by professing the

---

[1] Letter of Gabrielle of Verona to Capistrano, in Wadding, vi. 185.

greatest zeal for the Turkish war. Calixtus was mollified, and hoped that Scarampo would devote his own wealth to this purpose; the nephews were not sorry for an excuse for removing him from Rome, and he was appointed admiral of the fleet. In vain Scarampo tried to evade this unpleasant duty; in vain he urged that thirty galleys at least were needful before anything could be done. The obstinate and fiery Pope ordered him to set out at once, and threatened him with a judicial inquiry into his past conduct if he refused. Scarampo set sail and won back a few unimportant islands in the Ægean which had been captured by the Turks. He carried succours to the knights of Rhodes, and might pride himself on a few trivial successes. But his forces were inadequate to any serious undertaking, and Scarampo was neither a hero nor an enthusiast who cared to risk his life in a rash attempt. His only desire was to cruise about and make a decent show of activity. So far as he gave the islands a notion that they were being aided, he filled them with false security and unfounded hopes, which only tended to make them less self-reliant.

The only country which urged war successfully against the Turks was Hungary, which was bravely fighting for its national existence. There Fra Capistrano showed the power of religious zeal to stir a nation to a deep consciousness of the principles at stake. There also Cardinal Carvajal, as Papal legate, brought wisdom as well as devotion to aid the cause of patriotism. Carvajal had gone in 1455 to aid the crusading movement, and to reconcile the Emperor with his former ward, Ladislas. The reconciliation Carvajal soon found to be hopeless; he turned his attention to the more important business of national defence, and helped the brave Governor of Hungary, John Hunyadi, who was resolved to withstand the Turkish onslaught. In April 1456, came the news that the Sultan with a host of 150,000 was advancing along the Danube valley to the siege of Belgrad. Hunyadi gathered such troops as he could and hastened to the relief of the threatened city. He besought Carvajal to remain in Buda, and gather forces to send to his support. King Ladislas, who was in Buda, went out hunting one morning with the Count of Cilly, but thought it more prudent not to return to such dangerous quarters, and made off to

Siege of
Belgrad
by the
Turks.
April
1456.

[1] See Cribelli, *De Expeditione in Turcos*, Muratori, xxiii. 57.

Vienna. The nobles and the King were alike afraid; the two churchmen, Carvajal and Capistrano, alone assisted the national hero.

Repulse of
the Turks.
When Hunyadi arrived the siege of Belgrad had already been carried on for some fourteen days, and the walls of the city were terribly shaken; but the sight of Hunyadi and Capistrano with their forces gave the defenders new courage. On the evening of July 21, Mahomet II. gave the signal for a storm. All the night and all the next day the battle raged desperately. Hunyadi and Capistrano stood on the top of a tower and surveyed the fight. Capistrano, with uplifted hands, bore the banner of the cross and a picture of S. Bernardino; from time to time shouted aloud the name of 'Jesus.' Hunyadi, with a soldier's eye, saw where help was needed, and rushed to aid the waverers till the fight was restored. More than once the infidels forced their way into the town, and were repelled by the valour of Hunyadi. At last an unexpected sally was made by a troop of Capistrano's crusaders; the Janissaries were preparing to attack them in the flank, when Hunyadi charged furiously to their aid, and the voice of Capistrano succeeded in rallying them. The Janissaries amazed at the onslaught fled to their tents; the Sultan, who had been slightly wounded by an arrow, gave the signal for retreat, and Belgrad was saved.[1]

Death of
Hunyadi
and Capis-
trano.
1456.
There was a cry of triumph throughout Europe at the news, and Calixtus naturally expected that this success would rouse men's minds, and fire the lagging princes of Europe for the holy cause. But after the first glow of enthusiasm no one was moved to any decided action. In Hungary itself the heroes of Belgrad passed away, and it was doubtful who would take their place. A month after his victory, on August 11, John Hunyadi died of the plague. When he felt that death was approaching and preparations were being made to administer to him the Eucharist, he exclaimed. 'It is not fitting that the Lord should be brought to visit the servant.' He rose from his bed and prepared to seek the

---

[1] The account of the battle of Belgrad is rendered obscure by the desire of many friars to elevate Capistrano into a second Joshua. Wadding, vol. vi., has an account by Giovanni da Tagliacozzo, and another by Nicola da Faro, both of which are full of Capistrano. See also Thurocz in Schwandtner, *Scriptores*, i. ch. 55. Æn. Sylv , *Hist. Bohem*. ch. 65. *Hist. Frod*. in Kollar, ii. 460. *Comment*. 327.

nearest church; his strength failed him, and he had to be carried. He confessed his sins, received the Eucharist, and died in the hands of the priests.[1] Capistrano was not long in following him; he died of fever on October 23, 1456.[2]

The death of Hunyadi might fill the Hungarians with woe, but it was a source of relief to King Ladislas, and more especially to his guardian the Count of Cilly. Now that the mighty Vaivod was removed, the Count of Cilly hoped that he would be supreme over the young King and would assert over Hungary the royal power, freed from the trammels which Hunyadi had imposed. Ladislas and the Count of Cilly returned to Hungary, and even went to Belgrad to see the battle-field whose glory they had so basely refused to share. There one morning while the King was at mass the Hungarian nobles, led by Ladislas Corvinus, Hunyadi's son, fell upon the Count of Cilly and slew him. The King for some time dissembled his wrath, and the sons of Hunyadi accompanied him unsuspiciously to Buda, where they were seized, and Ladislas Corvinus was publicly beheaded as a traitor. The King himself did not long enjoy his triumph; on November 23, 1457, he died suddenly in Prag, whither he had gone to prepare for his marriage with Margaret of France.

The question of the Hungarian succession added to the confusion in Germany, where things were already sufficiently confounded. The electoral party was still aiming at its own objects as against the feeble Emperor, and the death of Jacob, Archbishop of Trier, in May 1456, altered the state of parties and introduced a new subject of discord. The Pfalzgraf now stood at the head of the opposition, and both parties struggled to obtain the vacant archbishopric. John of Baden and Rupert of the Pfalz were the candidates; but the power of the Pope was sufficiently strong to secure the victory for John of Baden, son of the Markgraf Jacob, who was the Emperor's friend. The opposition now consisted of the Pfalzgraf and the Archbishops of Mainz and Köln. The collection of the tenths imposed by the Pope gave an occasion to raise again the old

Marginal notes:

Death of Ladislas of Hungary. November 1457.

Schemes of the Electoral opposition against Frederick III. 1456.

---

[1] Æn. Sylv., *Hist. Fred.*, p. 465.

[2] The letter of Giovanni da Tagliacozzo, in Wadding, vi. no. 85, is so animated by a desire to procure the canonisation of Capistrano that it passes into the fabulous.

grievances of the German Church and to recur to the old policy of reform. The victory of Belgrad gave an opportunity of attacking the indolence of the Emperor, and the Electors sent Frederick III. an invitation to be present at a Diet to be held in Nürnberg on November 30, 1456, to consider the war against the Turk; if he did not come, the Electors would take such steps as they thought best.

It was noticeable that this Diet, which was forbidden by the Emperor, was attended by a Papal legate. It would seem that the Electoral opposition counted on having the Pope on their side, if only they joined in war against the Turk and laid aside their anti-Papal measures. However that might be, the question of the private interests of the Electors overrode both the Turkish war and the reform of the Church. The discussions were purely political, and the Diet adjourned till March 1457, when it again met at Frankfort, and again adjourned. Meanwhile, Albert of Brandenburg succeeded in forming a strong party in the Emperor's favour, and the opposition was driven to fall back. When baffled in its political objects it bethought itself of the question of Church reform. The Papacy was threatened with what it dreaded even more than a General Council—the establishment of a Pragmatic Sanction for Germany.

Æneas
Sylvius
made Car-
dinal.
December
1456.
Proceedings were begun in secresy by the Electors; but, as usual, information early reached the Curia, and preparations were made to resist the attempt. To Æneas Sylvius was left the organisation of the defence. Æneas had at length attained to the goal of his ambition. On December 18, 1456, the Pope had created him Cardinal with five others. It would seem that the College, steadfast in its opposition to the Pope and his nephews, resisted as long as it could this new creation. ' No cardinals,' writes Æneas to one of the newly-created dignitaries,[1] ' ever entered the College with greater difficulty than we; for rust had so spread over the hinges (cardines), that the door could not turn and open. Calixtus used battering rams and every kind of instrument to force it.' Æneas wrote at once to Frederick III. to thank him for his good offices. ' All men shall know,' he said, 'that I am a German rather than an Italian cardinal.'[2] He soon proceeded to show the sense in

[1] To the Cardinal of Pavia, *Ep.* 195.   [2] *Ep.* 189.

which he meant that promise, by using all his skill to baffle
the aspirations of Germany for freedom from ecclesiastical
oppression.

About the grievances of Germany there was no doubt; but
there was little earnestness in the means taken to have them
redressed. The cry for reform was raised by the Electors when
they had something to gain from the Pope: it gradually died
away when a sop was thrown to the personal interests of the
leaders of the movement. The proceedings were insincere
even on the part of those who saw most forcibly the evils. The
present leader of the movement was the Archbishop of Mainz;
and his Chancellor, Martin Mayr, sounded the note of war
in a letter to Æneas Sylvius, in which, after congratulating him
on his cardinalate, he put forth a powerful indictment of the
Papal dealings with Germany.[1] The Pope, he said, observed
neither the decrees of Constance nor Basel, nor the agreements
of his predecessors, but set at nought the German nation.
Elections to bishoprics were arbitrarily annulled, and reservations of every kind were made in favour of cardinals and
Papal secretaries. 'You yourself,' proceeded Mayr, 'have a
general reservation of benefices to the value of 2,000 ducats
yearly in the provinces of Mainz, Trier, and Köln, an unprecedented and unheard-of grant.'[2] Grants of expectancies were
habitually given, annates were rigorously exacted, nor was the
Pope content simply with the sum that was due. Bishoprics
were given not to the most worthy, but to the man who offered
most. Indulgences were granted; Turkish tenths were imposed without the consent of the bishops, and the money went
to the Pope. Cases that ought to be decided by the bishops
were transferred to the Papal Court. In every way the German
nation, once so glorious, was treated as a handmaid by the
Pope. For years she had groaned over her slavery; her nobles
thought that the time was come for her to assert her freedom.

Martin
Mayr
attacks the
Papal
policy in
Germany.

---

[1] This letter is given in the Basel edit. of 1571 of *Æneæ Sylvii Opera*,
p. 1035.

[2] Æneas excuses himself for this in a letter to the Dean of Worms (*Ep.*
356), dated July 22, 1457: 'Nos quidem supra xxiv. annos in Alamania ser-
vivimus et semper honorem illius nationis pro virili nostra promovimus, et
nunc ad Cardinalatum quamvis insufficientes vocati id conamur quod illi nationi
utile decorumque esse putamus. . . . Quibus in rebus non sumus arbitrati
Germaniæ nationi futurum odiosum si beneficia in ea pro duobus millibus
ducatorum in annuis reditibus obtineremus.'

The letter reads as though it were genuinely meant; but Æneas in his answer shows that he, at all events, had read between the lines.[1] In answering Mayr he asserted the Papal supremacy, rejected the decrees of Basel, agreed that the Concordat should be observed, and suggested that if the Electors had any grievances on this point, they should at once send envoys to the Pope, who would be willing to grant redress. As regarded the Papal interference with elections, it was exercised in the way of judicial intervention, the need for which was caused by the ambition and greed of contending claimants, not by Papal rapacity. If money were paid to officers of the Curia, that was not the Pope's doing, but was caused by the ambition of the claimants, who were willing to do anything which might further their cause. Men were not all angels at Rome any more than in Germany; they took money when it was offered, but the Pope in his chamber decided according to justice. The Pope's officials might be extortionate, and the Pope greatly wished to check them; but he himself received nothing save what was due. Everyone makes a grievance of parting with money, and always will do so. The complaint of the Bohemians against the Germans was the same as that of the Germans against the Papacy—that their money is taken out of the land. Yet Germany, from its connexion with the Papacy, had steadily grown in wealth and importance, and, in spite of its complaints, was richer than at any previous time. Æneas found it hard that Mayr complained of the provision made in his favour; he had lived and laboured in Germany so long that he did not think he was regarded as a stranger. However, he thanked Mayr for his personal offer to help him in realising his provision, and would be glad to know of any eligible benefices that might fall vacant. From the last sentence we see that Mayr in another letter had drawn a distinction between the German grievances and his own personal feelings; though theoretically he might regard his friend as an abuse, he was practically ready to help him.

Æneas showed that he interpreted this letter of Martin Mayr to mean that the Archbishop of Mainz had some con-

---

[1] The dates of these letters are perplexing. The letter of Mayr, in all editions, bears the date of August 31, 1457: the answer of Æneas is dated August 8, 1457. There must be an error in the date of one of them.

ditions to propose to the Pope. He was not wrong in his
conjecture, for early in September came a secretary of the
Archbishop, who was empowered to negotiate, through Æneas
Sylvius, for an alliance with Calixtus III.; the Archbishop of
Mainz was ready to desert to the Pope's side if he received the
right of confirmation of episcopal elections throughout Germany. Æneas answered in a letter to Mayr with a decided
refusal, cleverly couched in courteous yet stinging language.
He was glad to hear that the Archbishop no longer joined
with the malignants against the Pope, but regretted to hear
that he had been ill advised to ask for a right inherent in the
Papacy, which none of his predecessors had enjoyed. No
understanding was necessary between Christ's vicegerent and
his subjects—all were bound to obey. He was sure that the
modesty of the Archbishop had been improperly represented
by this request, which he, for his part, could not venture to
lay before a Pope so blameless, so wise, and so upright as
was Calixtus III.[1]

Æneas might answer Mayr conclusively; yet the danger was
threatening, and all the diplomatic power of Æneas was set at
work to avert it.   He assured the Archbishop of Mainz that the
Pope was ready to grant all his smaller requests; he assured
Mayr of his strong personal friendship, and of his desire to
serve him in all ways. He wrote to Frederick III. in the name
of Calixtus III. to supply him with an answer to the murmurs
against the Papacy. He wrote to the King of Hungary, to the
German Archbishops, to remind them of their duties to the
Papacy. He stirred up the Cardinals Cusa and Carvajal to
exert all their influence in Germany. Above all he wrote
most confidentially to his former friends, the jurists and
secretaries who occupied important posts at the different
German Courts; Peter Knorr, the councillor of Albert of Brandenburg; Heinrich Leubing, Procopius of Rabstein, Heinrich
Senftleben, and John Lysura, to whom he sent a cipher that
communications might be carried on with greater secrecy.[2]
Moreover, a new envoy was sent into Germany, a skilful
theologian and diplomatist, Lorenzo Rovarella, who was laden
with Bulls to the Emperor and the Electors. Æneas gave him

*Papal
measures
against the
German
opposition.*

[1] Letter of September 20, 1457, n). 338, ed. Basel.
[2] *Ep.* 349, 320, ed. Basel.

instructions[1] to warn the Archbishops of Magdeburg, Trier, Riga and Salzburg to abstain from joining in any measures against the Pope. He was to urge the Duke of Bavaria to use his influence with the Pfalzgraf in the same direction; and as soon as possible was to proceed from the Emperor's Court to the Rhenish provinces, which were the seat of the anti-Papal movement. The princes were reminded that capitular elections were rarely in favour of junior members of princely families, and that only through the Papal intervention could these meet with their due rewards. The bishops were asked to consider that any blow aimed at the Papal dignity would eventually be disastrous to all episcopal authority as well. It was frankly admitted that there were abuses in the Papal Curia which the Pope desired to remedy. The German princes were asked to send their complaints to Rome, and trust to the Pope's judgment. A judicious mixture of cajolery and fair promises was applied to soothe the discontent of Germany.

Moreover, Æneas Sylvius took up his pen in defence of the Papacy, and expanded his letter to Mayr into a tractate ' On the Condition of Germany.'[2] He represented the Concordat as depending on the goodwill of the Pope, and expressed the Pope's desire for a reform of all abuses which could be shown to attach to the proceedings of the Curia. He discussed the complaints of the Germans with sophistical skill. He condemned generally the abuses complained of, denied their existence, and then plausibly accounted for a few exceptional cases. Grants in expectancy, he said, have never been made by the Pope, except at the earnest request of princes, and solely for the purpose of raising money for war against the Turk. Capitular elections have never been annulled except on legal grounds, though he admitted that some legal ground had been discovered to annul every election brought before the Curia during the past two years. As to the complaints about indulgences, he said, pertinently enough, that the Papacy only offered indulgences to the faithful who showed their zeal for their religion by contributing to the expenses of the Turkish war. It was a free gift on their

---

[1] *Ep.* 344.

[2] ' De ritu, situ, conditione et moribus Germaniæ ' in the Basel ed. *Æneæ Sylvii Opera*, 1571, p. 1035, dated in a Viennese MS. February 1, 1458. Voigt, *Archir für Kunde Oesterreich. Geschichtsquellen*, xvi. 420.

part; why should it be laid as an exaction to the Pope's
charge? Germany had received from Rome more than she
had given. Her complaint that money went from her to Rome
was an old grievance, as old as human nature itself, and was
never likely to disappear.

The pleadings of Æneas and the diplomacy of Rovarella
had the effect in Germany of staying any definite proceedings
for a time; and in German politics to pause was to lose the
day. If for a brief space a strong party of the princes was united
for a common object, it needed only a few months for some
change to occur in the position of affairs which led to a new
combination. The death of Ladislas of Hungary in November
1457 caused great excitement in Germany. The dominions
of Austria, Hungary, and Bohemia were left in dispute, and
most of the German princes were interested in the settlement.
It is true that a Diet met at Frankfort in June 1458, and
agreed to send an embassy to the Pope; but this was felt to
be a mere empty form. The Papacy gained its object of
putting off the enactment of a Pragmatic Sanction for Germany, and the death of Calixtus III. in September removed him
from further threats.

All these disturbances in Germany promised little for the
favourite design of Calixtus III.—a great expedition against
the Turks. Nothing was done for this object. Scarampo still
cruised about the Ægean islands with the Papal fleet, and
Scanderbeg in Albania showed how strong national feeling
could supply courage to a handful of men contending against an
invading host; but Europe did nothing. Calixtus III. grew
daily more indignant at the remissness of Alfonso of Naples,
his former friend, in whose service he had entered Italy. His
friendship rapidly turned to hostility when Alfonso sent his
fleet against Genoa instead of joining with Scarampo. He opposed
Alfonso's Italian policy, and strove to prevent the alliance with
Milan by which Alfonso wished to secure the succession of his
son to the Neapolitan kingdom. Alfonso had no child born in
lawful wedlock; but his illegitimate son, Ferrante, had been
legitimatised and recognised as successor to the Neapolitan
kingdom by Eugenius IV. and Nicolas V. In spite of this, on
Alfonso's death, on June 27, 1458, the impetuous Pope threatened to plunge Italy into war by refusing to acknowledge
Ferrante, and claiming Naples as a fief of the Holy See.

It was not only anger at Alfonso's remissness to help in the
Turkish war that prompted Calixtus III. to this step. The
only object, which shared with crusading zeal the Pope's interest,
was the enrichment of his nephews; and for this the vacancy of
the Neapolitan throne gave an opening which he hastened to
use. Besides the two nephews who had been elevated to the
cardinalate was a third, Don Pedro Luis de Lançol, on whom
Calixtus III. was desirous to heap every worldly distinction.
He made him Gonfalonier of the Church and Prefect of Rome;
he committed to his hands all the castles in the neighbourhood of the city. He conferred on him also the Duchy of
Spoleto, in spite of the protest of Capranica, who made himself
the mouthpiece of the discontent of the Cardinals. Calixtus
tried to rid himself of Capranica by sending him on distant
embassies; when this failed he threatened to imprison him.[1]
There was nothing that Calixtus would not do for his nephews,
whom he identified still further with himself by bestowing on
them his own family name and arms of Borgia. These three
vigorous young men were all-powerful with the Pope, and the
cardinals who maintained an independent footing were either
sent on distant embassies or compelled to leave the city.
Carvajal and Cusa were at a safe distance in Germany;
Scarampo, against his will, was sent to sea; Cardinal Orsini in
vain tried to resist, and was driven to quit Rome. The other
cardinals of any importance, Estouteville, head of the French
party, Piero Barbo, the nephew of Eugenius IV., even Prospero
Colonna, thought it wise to be on good terms with the
Borgia. Æneas Sylvius was too much accustomed to be on
the winning side to find any difficulty in making friends with
the powerful. With his wonted amiability he was ready to
help Cardinal Borgia in his desire to enrich himself with Church
preferment. He acted as his agent and informed him of eligible
vacancies during his absence. 'I keep an eye on benefices,' he
writes on April 1, 1457, 'and will take care of you and myself.
But we are deceived by false rumours. He whose death was
reported from Nürnberg was here a few days ago, and dined
with me. The Bishop of Toul, also, who was said to have died
at Neustadt, has returned safe and sound to Burgundy. I will,

---

[1] Poggio's *Vita Cardinalis Firmani*, in Baluze, *Miscell.* iii. 290.

however, be watchful for any vacancy; but you have the best
proctor in his Holiness.' [1]

Thus watchful and thus supported, the Borgia ruled Rome
and filled the city with their creatures. Dependents of their
house flocked from Spain to share the booty, and their party
was known by the name of 'the Catalans.' All the offices of
the city were put in the hands of these strangers, who connived at robbery and murder by the members of their own
faction. One day Capranica was asked for alms on the bridge
of S. Angelo by a beggar, who pleaded that he had escaped
from the Catalans. 'You are better off than I am,' answered
the Cardinal, 'for you have escaped, while I am still in their
hands.' [2]

The death of Alfonso offered Calixtus III. an opportunity of
exalting his nephew Pedro still higher. By claiming the kingdom of Naples he might at least get hold of some portion
which might be made into a fief for Pedro's benefit. On July 31
he conferred on him the Vicariate of Benevento and Terracina.

It was not, however, to be expected that Ferrante would
flee before the Papal threats. He summoned a meeting of
the Neapolitan nobles, who accepted him as their king; he
appealed from the Pope to a future Council, and prepared to
defend himself against an attack. He claimed only the kingdom of Naples; on Alfonso's death without lawful issue Aragon
and Sicily passed to his brother John of Navarre. Even without the Pope's interference there were other claimants of the
throne of Naples. John of Anjou revived the claims of his
house; and Charles of Biana, son of John of Navarre, was prepared to maintain his right of legitimate succession to Alfonso.
Calixtus III. might disturb the peace of Southern Italy; but he
was by no means strong enough to secure his own success.
His policy could only lead to the introduction of foreign
invaders, and was in consequence strongly opposed by the far-
seeing Duke of Milan, whom Calixtus III. vainly tried to win
over to his side. Sforza answered, that the settlement made
under the auspices of Nicolas V. had met with the approval of
all the Italian Powers, and he for his part would fight in

Opposition
of Calixtus
III. to the
succession
of Ferrante
of Naples.
June 1458.

---

[1] *Ep.* 257.

[2] This story is told both by Vespasiano, *Vita del Cardinale Capranica*, and
by Poggio, in Baluze, *Miscell.* iii. 290.

defence of Ferrante, rather than see the concord of Italy disturbed.[1]

This answer of Sforza was a bitter disappointment to the
old Pope. But the end of his plans was approaching. He was
seized with a fever, and it was clear that his end was drawing
near. The Orsini began to take up arms against the hated
Catalans. The nephew Pedro grew more fearful for himself as
he saw his uncle on his deathbed. He judged it better to beat
a prudent retreat while there was yet time. He sold the castle
of S. Angelo to the Cardinals for 20,000 ducats, and on
August 5 left the city with his Catalan friends. The Orsini
occupied the gates and watched the roads to prevent his
escape; only by the friendly aid of Cardinal Barbo did he
manage to flee, in the darkness of the night. Barbo led him
to the Tiber, where he took boat and made his way to Civita
Vecchia.[2] Next day, Aug. 6, Calixtus III. died. The Orsini at
once plundered the houses of the Catalans and all that bore the
arms of the Borgia. Calixtus was buried with little respect
in the vault of S. Peter's, and was followed to the grave only
by four priests.

The pontificate of Calixtus III. was a violent reaction
against the policy of Nicolas V. The energy of Nicolas V. and
the greatness of his schemes had naturally caused some dismay
among the Cardinals, who heard the murmurs of Germany and
feared the results of localising the Papacy too exclusively in
Rome. Under the influence of this feeling they elected a
stranger, whose advanced age was a guarantee that his pontificate would only be a temporary breathing space, in which
they might recover from the impetuosity of Nicolas V. But the
reaction of Calixtus III. was too violent and too complete. He
not only checked the works of his predecessor; he allowed them to
fall into decay. Had he continued in any degree the buildings
of his predecessor, the schemes of Nicolas V. might have been
slowly realised in the future side by side with other objects of
Papal interest. But the entire suspension of the works by
Calixtus III. was fatal. The scheme of the Renaissance, instead
of advancing to gradual completion, was laid aside to be superseded by the more splendid, though less thorough, plan of

---

[1] Simoneta, *Vita Sfortiæ*, in Mur. xxi. 686.
[2] Cannesio, *Vita Pauli II.*, in Mur. iii. pt. 2, 1003.

a later age. Rome, that might have borne the impress of the calm strength and simplicity of Nicolas V. and Alberti, is stamped with the more passionate magnificence of Julius II. and Bramante. No institution, least of all an institution like the Papacy, admits of a sudden change of policy, or can without loss direct its energies entirely into a different channel. While we may admire the zeal of Calixtus III. for a crusade against the Turks, we must regret that it was so exclusive as to sacrifice with impatience all the labours of Nicolas V.

Even Calixtus III. did not entirely abandon some care for the architecture of Rome; but his wilfulness is shown in the works which he did, no less than in those which he left undone. He restored the Church and the palace of SS. Quattro Coronati, because from the Church he took his title as Cardinal, and the palace had served as his residence. He restored also the Church of S. Calixtus, in honour of his Papal name; and the Church of S. Sebastiano Fuori, because it was situated over the Catacombs of S. Calixtus. Besides these, he did some repairs to the Church of S. Prisca, and began a new ceiling in S. Maria Maggiore. The few painters who remained in Rome in the days of Calixtus III. were employed for the purpose of painting standards to be borne against the Turks.[1]

If Calixtus III. was thus inconsiderate and narrow-minded in despising the work of his predecessor, the same qualities stood in the way of his success in the object which was foremost to himself. It must always be an honour to the Papacy that, in a great crisis of European affairs, it asserted the importance of a policy which was for the interest of Europe as a whole. Calixtus III. and his successor deserve, as statesmen, credit which can be given to no others of the politicians of the time. The Papacy, by summoning Christendom to defend the ancient limits of Christian civilisation against the assaults of heathenism, was worthily discharging the chief secular duty of its office. Of the zeal and earnestness of Calixtus III. there was no question; but the lethargy of Europe prevented him accomplishing much. Moreover, the zeal of Calixtus was displayed by passionate impetuosity, which disregarded the means in its desire to reach the end. All that Bulls, exhortations, and indulgences could do, Calixtus did; but he trusted merely

[1] See Münts, *Les Arts à la Cour des Papes*, i. 196, &c.

to words, and took no means to remedy the evils which kept Europe suspicious and divided and prevented the possibility of combination for a common object. He did not try to win the confidence of Germany by wise measures of ecclesiastical reform, which might have formed the beginning of a political reorganisation. He did not even in Italy strive to maintain the pacific spirit which he found. Under the influence of his greedy nephews the Papacy again threatened to be a centre of territorial aggression.

Character of Calixtus III.

The impetuosity of youth has passed into a common phrase. The history of the Papacy gives many examples of the no less dangerous impetuosity of old age. Men of decided opinions, who come to power late in life, expend on accomplishing their cherished desires the accumulated passion of a lifetime. Inflexible, overbearing, inconsiderate, Calixtus III. pursued his own plans, and seemed to form no part of the life around him. He brooked no contradiction; he saw no one who was not prepared to re-echo his opinions; he had no care of anything outside the circle which he had marked for himself. The vow which he made on his election was one of the ornaments of his chamber;[1] it was ever before his eyes and ever in his thoughts. He left at his death 150,000 ducats, which he had stored up for the Turkish war.

Personally Calixtus III. was a man of rigid piety and of simple life. He was largely charitable and attentive to all religious duties. Little could be said against him save that he was obstinate and irritable; yet he inspired little affection and accomplished little. His weakness left more permanent results than did his strength. The ardour of his zeal for Christendom is forgotten; the evil deeds of his nephew Rodrigo and his race have made the name of Borgia a byword, and Calixtus III. is remembered as the founder of a race whose actions marked the Papacy with irretrievable disgrace.

[1] Müntz (*Les Arts à la Cour des Papes*, i. 213) gives from the Roman Archives an inventory of the furniture of the rooms occupied by Calixtus III. in the Vatican. Amongst them we find 'Item votum domini Calisti in una carta magna.'

CHAPTER VI.

PIUS II. AND THE CONGRESS OF MANTUA.

1458–1460.

ON August 10 the eighteen Cardinals who were in Rome en- CHAP. VI.
tered the Conclave in the Vatican Palace. The first day was
spent in preliminaries. The next day was devoted to framing The Con-clave.
the solemn agreement, which since the death of Martin V. had August
been subscribed by all the Cardinals before a Papal election. 11–18, 1458.
It contained the chief points to which the College wished to
bind the future Pope, and so expressed the desire of the electors
to limit, while there was yet time, the absolute power of the
infallible ruler whom they were about to set over the Church.
On the present occasion the points insisted on were, the prosecution of the Turkish war, respect for the wishes of the Cardinals in new creations, proper provision for the Cardinals,
due consultation of the College in all important matters, care
for the States of the Church, and such like matters.[1] On
the third day the first scrutiny was taken, and it was found
that Cardinals Piccolomini and Calandrini had each received five
votes, while no other candidate received more than three. The
first scrutiny, however, was generally of little consequence, and
merely served as a means of opening private discussions among
the Cardinals. It soon appeared that the French Cardinal
Estouteville, by his wealth and magnificence, had gained a
considerable following, and could count with certainty on six
votes. A little private consultation showed that the real issue
was the election of Estouteville or an Italian. Estouteville had
many arguments to use in his own favour. 'Will you take
Æneas,' he said, ' who is both gouty and poor? How can one
who is poor and infirm govern the Church? Perhaps he will
transfer the Papacy to his beloved Germany, or introduce his
heathenish poetry into the statutes of the Church. Calandrini

---

[1] In Raynaldus, 1458, no. 5.

is incapable even of governing himself. I am an older cardinal than they; of the royal race of France, rich, and with
many friends; my election will vacate many benefices which
will be divided among you.' The adherents of Estouteville
met in secresy [1] and bound themselves to secure his election.
They counted on eleven votes, and regarded the election as
won; already Estouteville had promised them the due rewards
of their zeal in his cause.

But at midnight Calandrini visited the cell of Piccolomini.
'To-morrow,' he said, 'Estouteville will be elected. I counsel
you to rise and offer him your vote so as to win his favour. I
know from my experience of Calixtus III. how ill it is to have
the Pope for one's enemy.' Æneas answered that it was against
his conscience to do so; he could not vote for one whom he
considered unworthy. But Æneas was disturbed in his mind,
and early in the morning visited Cardinal Borgia, to see if he
was pledged. Borgia said that he did not wish to be on the
losing side, and had received from Estouteville a document
promising to confirm him in the office of Vice-Chancellor, which
he had held under Calixtus III. 'Are you not rash in trusting
to the promise of an enemy to your nation?' said Æneas. 'Do
you not know that the Chancery is also promised to the Cardinal of Avignon? which promise is the new Pope most likely
to keep?' Next Æneas sought Cardinal Castiglione and asked
him if he had promised his vote to Estouteville. Castiglione
made a like answer; he did not wish to stand alone, since the
affair was as good as settled. Æneas recalled the miseries of
the Schism, the dangers of a French Papacy, and the disgrace
which it would bring on Italy: had they escaped the Catalans
only to fall before the French? Æneas next met Cardinal
Barbo, who was equally anxious that some decisive step should
be taken to defeat the schemes of Estouteville's party. Barbo
was one of those who had entertained hopes of his own election; he determined to lay them aside, and try to gain a
majority for the best candidate of an Italian party. He invited the Italian Cardinals to assemble in the cell of the Cardinal of Genoa, and six answered his summons. He laid

[1] Æn. Syl., in Meuschen, *Ceremonialia*, 'in latrinis;' but this was in
mediæval times a spacious hall, with only a row of cells at one side for its
ostensible purpose.

before them the condition of affairs, appealed to their national
sentiment, exhorted them to lay aside all personal feelings,
and proposed Piccolomini as their candidate. All agreed except Æneas, who modestly declared himself unworthy of the
honour.

Soon after this the public proceedings of the Conclave began
with the mass, which was followed by a scrutiny. Estouteville, pale with excitement, was one of the three cardinals
whose office it was to guard the chalice, while the rest advanced
in order and dropped into it their votes. As Æneas approached
the altar, Estouteville whispered, 'Æneas, I commend myself
to you.' 'Do you commend yourself to a poor creature like
me?' answered Æneas, as he dropped his vote. Then the
chalice was emptied on a table and the scrutineers read out the
votes: when this had been done, Estouteville announced that
Æneas had eight votes. 'Count again,' said Æneas, and Estouteville was obliged to confess that he had made a mistake; and
Æneas had nine votes, and he himself had six. It was clear
that, with nine votes out of eighteen, Æneas had won the day;
only three votes were wanting, and the Cardinals remained
seated to try the method of accession. 'All sat,' says Æneas,
'pale and silent, as though rapt by the Holy Ghost. No one
spoke or opened his mouth, or moved any part of his body
save his eyes, which rolled from place to place. The silence
was wonderful as all waited, the inferiors expecting their superiors to begin.'[1] At last Borgia arose and said, 'I accede to
the Cardinal of Siena.' The conversation of Æneas about the
Vice-Chancellorship had no doubt shown Borgia which way his
interest lay. Æneas had now ten votes, and in a desperate
attempt to prevent the election being made that day, Isidore
of Russia and Torquemada rose and left the Conclave. No one
followed, and they soon returned. Then Cardinal Tebaldo rose
and said, 'I also accede to the Cardinal of Siena.' One vote
only was wanting, which Prospero Colonna rose to give. Estouteville and Bessarion upbraided him for his desertion of their
cause, and seizing his arms tried to lead him from the Conclave; but Colonna loudly called out, 'I also accede to the
Cardinal of Siena and make him Pope.' The deed was done;
the intrigues were at an end. In a moment the Cardinals were

Election
of Æneas
Sylvius
Piccolo-
mini, Pope
Pius II.
August 19,
1458.

---

[1] *Pii II. Commentarii*, p. 30.

prostrate at the feet of the new Pope. Then they resumed their seats, and formally confirmed the election.

Bessarion, in the name of the adherents of Estouteville, addressed Æneas. ' We are pleased with your election, which we doubt not comes from God ; we think you worthy of the office and always held you so. Our only reason for not voting for you was your bodily infirmity : we thought that your gouty feet might be a hindrance to that activity which the perils from the Turks might require. It was this that led us to prefer the Cardinal of Rouen. Had you been strong in body there was no one whom we would have chosen before you. But the will of God is now our will.' ' You have a better opinion of us,' answered Æneas, ' than we have of ourselves; for you only find us defective in the feet, we feel our imperfections to be more widely spread. We are conscious of innumerable failings which might have excluded us from this office ; we are conscious of no merits to justify our election. We would judge ourselves entirely unworthy, did we not know that the voice of two-thirds of the Sacred College is the voice of God, which we may not disobey. We approve your conduct in following your conscience and judging us insufficient. You will all be equally acceptable to us; for we ascribe our election, not to one or another, but to the whole College, and so to God Himself, from whom comes every good and perfect gift.'

Æneas then put off his robes and assumed the white tunic of the Pope. He was asked what name he would bear, and with a Virgilian reminiscence of ' Pius Æneas,' answered ' Pius.' Then he swore to observe the agreement entered into by the Cardinals at the beginning of the Conclave. He was led to the altar, and there received the reverence of the Cardinals. Then the election was announced to the people from a window. The attendants of the Conclave plundered the cell of the newly-elected Pope, and the mob outside rushed to pillage his house, which they did with such completeness that they tore even the marble from the walls. Unfortunately he was one of the poorest cardinals ; but part of the mob professed to mistake the cry of ' Il Sanese ' for ' Il Genovese,' and plundered the house of Cardinal Flisco as well.

Coronation
of Pius II.
September
3, 1458.

The election of Cardinal Piccolomini was popular with the Romans : the citizens laid aside their arms, with which they

were provided in case of a tumult, and went to S. Peter's.
Pius II. was placed on the high altar, and received the adoration
of the cardinals, the clergy, and the people. At nightfall the
magistrates of the city came on horseback, bearing blazing
torches, to pay their respects to the new Pope. On Sept. 3
he was crowned in S. Peter's, and rode in solemn procession
to the Lateran, where he experienced the unruliness of the
Roman mob, who, according to old custom, seized the horse
and trappings of the Pope. So eager were they for their booty
that they made a rush too soon. Swords were drawn in the
fight for the plunder, and the crippled Pope was in danger of
his life in the confusion. He was, however, happily saved
from hurt, and entertained the cardinals, the foreign ambassadors, and chief citizens at a banquet.

The election of Pius II. gave general satisfaction in Italy, Feelings of
where the new Pope was well known to most of the princes Pius II.
on his
and republics. His reputation for learning and his diplomatic election.
ability made everyone look upon him with respect. The
French, however, felt aggrieved at the rejection of Estouteville, and the opponents of the Emperor in Germany looked
with suspicion on one whose cleverness they knew too well.
To Pius II. himself his elevation was a source of mingled joy
and fear. True, he was ambitious, vain, desirous of glory;
true, he had schemed and plotted for his own advancement,
and had made success the great object of his life. But when
success came at last, he shrank from the responsibilities of
which he well knew the extent. He was no inexperienced
enthusiast who might dream that he had the future in his
hands. Though only fifty-three years old, Pius II. was already
old in body, racked by the gout, suffering from gravel, afflicted
by the beginnings of asthma. He knew full well how useless
it was in the existing condition of Europe to hope for any
great opportunities which he might use to leave his mark
upon the world. He had reached the height of his ambition,
and saw nothing but difficulties before him. When in the
first moments after his election his friends thronged round him
with joyful congratulations, he burst into tears. 'You may
rejoice,' he said, 'because you think not of the toils and the
dangers. Now must I show to others what I have so often

demanded from them.'[1] During all the festivities of his accession his face was careworn and melancholy.

When Pius II. reviewed the condition of Europe he had no
hesitation in deciding that the chief object of his policy must
be the same as that of his predecessor, the prosecution of war
against the Turk. What Calixtus III. had urged with the
unreflecting fanaticism of a recluse, Pius II. would press with
the wisdom of a statesman. Already Pius II. had identified
himself with the cause of the crusade ; his speeches, his
writings, had advocated it ; his knowledge of European politics
convinced him of its absolute necessity. But he saw that,
to ensure success, the crusade must be undertaken by the
whole of Christendom, and Christendom must be united for
this purpose by wise management on the part of the Pope.
Accordingly Pius II. determined to proceed with stately deliberation, and put the project on its proper footing. He lost
no time in laying before the Cardinals a plan for a general
conference of the princes of Europe, to be held under the
Pope's presidency. But the Cardinals were half-hearted; the
majority of them were content to stay in Rome and enjoy
themselves, and shrank from the trouble of a serious undertaking. They raised difficulties about the place of the proposed conference; the princes of Europe could not well be
summoned to Rome; there was a danger, if an assembly were
held in France or Germany, that it might turn into a Council,
whose very name was hateful. Pius II. pointed out that the
state of his health gave him an excuse for refusing to cross
the Alps, while he was ready to show his zeal by going to some
place in North Italy, so as to meet the European representatives half way: he proposed Udine or Mantua as suitable
places for the Congress. The Cardinals reluctantly consented ;
and Pius II. hastened to publish his resolution to an assembly
of ambassadors and prelates in S. Peter's. There were present
eleven cardinals, three archbishops, twenty-nine bishops, and
the ambassadors of Castile, Denmark, Portugal, Naples, Burgundy, Milan, Modena, Venice, Florence, Siena, and Lucca.
To them Pius II. announced his plan ; though an old man and
infirm, he would brave the dangers of crossing the Apennines
to confer with the princes of Europe on the step to be taken

---

[1] Campanus, *Vita Pii II.*, Mur. iii. pt. 2, p. 974.

to avert the ruin of Christendom: he asked for their opinion and advice. For a time there was silence. Then Bessarion begged the ambassadors to speak. One after another they praised the zeal of the Pope, and asserted the good intentions of their several states. Pius II. was pleased with these expressions of assent, and invited all to a public consistory to be held in three days' time, on October 13. There a solemn summons to a Congress to be held on June 1, 1459, was read to the assembly,[1] and a few days afterwards Pius II. sent letters to the various kings of Christendom, urging their presence at this great undertaking.

But before he could proceed to a Congress, Pius II. had a political question to settle nearer home. Calixtus III. had refused to recognise the succession of Ferrante in Naples, and had claimed the kingdom as a fief of the Holy See. He had not conferred it on any claimant, and any scheme that he might have had of establishing his nephew in Naples was at once overthrown by his death. An envoy of Ferrante had been sent to the Cardinals during the vacancy; Pius II. found the Neapolitan question pressing for his decision. Nor was the question one which could be decided easily on general grounds. The condottiere general, Jacopo Piccinino, had occupied in Ferrante's name Assisi, Gualdo, and Nocera. The States of the Church were in confusion, and in many cities Pius II. had to buy off the Catalan governors, and assert his rule with difficulty. The presence of Piccinino was a continual menace.

Moreover, the general lines of the Papal policy towards Naples had been somewhat obscured by the predecessors of Pius II. The Papacy had, on the whole, favoured the Angevin party. Eugenius IV. had been the constant opponent of Alfonso, and Nicolas V. had only recognised him for the sake of peace. The question which Calixtus III. had opened was full of difficulty. Pius II. might well doubt the wisdom of supporting in Naples the line of Anjou, and introducing into the neighbourhood of the Papacy the influence of the country of the Pragmatic Sanction. Pius II. himself had known and liked the scholarly Alfonso, and his own sympathies were probably on the side of Ferrante. But the French party was strong among the Cardinals, and the envoys of the

---

[1] It is given by Cribelli in Mur. xxiii. 70.

French King laid before the Pope the impolicy of offending a
prince so powerful as their master. As the Archbishop of
Marseilles pleaded in this strain, Pius II. suddenly asked him
if René of Anjou were ready to drive out Piccinino from the
States of the Church. The Archbishop was driven to answer
'No.' 'Then what are we to expect from one who cannot help
us in our straits?' said the Pope. 'We need a king in Naples
who can protect both himself and us.'

Pius II.
recognises
Ferrante
as king.
October
1458.

So Pius II. proceeded to make the best bargain he could
with Ferrante. When Ferrante wished to negotiate, the
Pope roundly answered that he was no merchant to barter with.
On October 17 an agreement was made that Pius II. should
free Ferrante from all ecclesiastical censures, and invest him
with the kingdom of Naples, 'without prejudice to another's
right.' The Pope did not venture to decide entirely against
the Angevin claims, but merely recognised Ferrante as the
actual king. Ferrante undertook to pay the Pope a yearly
tribute, and recall Piccinino from the States of the Church
within a month. Benevento, which had been granted as a
personal fief to Alfonso, was restored to the Church; but Terracina, which was held in the same way, was to be retained by
Ferrante for ten years. The French cardinals still opposed
the agreement, and refused to sign the Bull in which it was
embodied. Piccinino was driven to leave the States of the
Church, and Pius II. sent Cardinal Orsini to crown Ferrante in
Naples.

Departure
of Pius II.
for the
Congress
of Mantua.
January
1459.

When peace had thus been restored to some extent at home,
Pius II. proceeded with the preparations for his departure to
the Congress. The Romans were ill pleased to see the Pope
leave his city. Some exclaimed that he was going to take the
Papacy to Germany; others declared that he would go no
farther than Siena, and there would devote himself to the
adornment of his native land. All joined in lamenting the loss
which the city would sustain from the departure of the Curia.
They deprecated the danger to which the Pope was about to
expose his life, and foretold that his departure would be the
signal for disturbances in the Papal States. To allay their
anxiety Pius II. left some cardinals and officials of the Curia
behind him, that Rome might not be entirely deprived of its
glory; he appointed the Cardinal Nicolas of Cusa Vicar during

his absence. He decreed that if he died away from Rome, the
election of his successor should still take place in that city after
a due delay for the return of the absent cardinals. He granted
their ancient privileges to the cities in the Papal States, and
remitted their tribute for three years. Finally he summoned
the Roman barons, and administered to them an oath that
they would keep the peace during his absence. As a token of
his zeal for the crusading cause, he founded a new military
order, the order of S. Mary of Bethlehem. But the day for
military orders was gone, and this revival existed only in name.
After these precautions he set out from Rome on January 22,
1459, accompanied by six cardinals—Calandrini, Borgia, Alain,
Estouteville, Barbo, and Colonna.

The journey of Pius II. was like a triumphal progress. It
was long since a Pope had been seen by any of the dwellers in
the Papal States. Throngs of people welcomed him wherever
he went with shouts of rejoicing and expressions of goodwill,
which afforded sincere enjoyment to Pius II. who fully appreciated the dignity of his office.

At Narni the crowd thronged round his horse, and strove to
carry off the baldachino held over his head. Swords were
drawn in the struggle, and Pius II. thought it wiser in the
future to be carried in a litter, so as to avoid such unseemly
brawls. At Spoleto he was entertained for four days by his
sister Catarina. Thence he passed through Assisi to Perugia,
where he stayed three weeks.[1] He was loth to pass by his
native place, and leave Siena unvisited ; but there was a
conflict between the Pope and the government of Siena,
where the popular party were in the ascendent, and had
driven out the nobles. They had tried to pacify the Pope
by admitting the Piccolomini to office, but Pius II. demanded the restitution of the nobles. The popular party gave
way a little at the Pope's pressure, and relaxed the rigour of
their proscription, but they regarded the Papal visit with undisguised suspicion. From Perugia Pius II. crossed the lake
Trasimene, and entered the Sienese territory at Chiusi. He
turned aside to visit his native place, Corsignano, a little town
perched among the hills, which he had left as a poor boy and
now entered as the head of Christendom. He experienced the

Pius II. visits Cor- signano. February 1459.

---

[1] Campanus, in Mur. iii. pt. 2, p. 975.

same sad feelings that attend everyone who revisits the haunts of his youth. His father and mother were dead; those whom he had known were mostly confined to bed through sickness; faces which he remembered flushed with the pride of youth were unrecognisable in the deformity of old age.[1] Here, in the little church, the Pope celebrated mass on February 22, the festival of S. Peter's installation. He resolved to honour his native place by elevating it to a bishopric under the name of Pienza. He ordered workmen to be collected to build there a cathedral and a bishop's palace.

After a sojourn of three days Pius II. left Corsignano for Siena. There he stayed nearly two months, and strove to propitiate the people by presenting the city with the golden rose on Palm Sunday. At last he brought before the magistrates his political object, and urged on them the restoration of the excluded nobles. After some opposition they agreed to admit them to a quarter of some offices and an eighth of others. Pius II. was not satisfied with such a small concession, but thanked them for what they had done, and said that he hoped on his way back to hear that they had granted more. At Siena Pius II. received the first ambassadors from the powers beyond Italy, who sent to offer their obedience to the new Pope. There came representatives of the Kings of Castile, Aragon, Portugal, and Matthias Corvinus, the new King of Hungary. All were received with due state, and were answered by Pius with his wonted eloquence. The Imperial ambassadors were at Florence, and when they heard that the envoys of Matthias Corvinus had been received by the Pope, raised difficulties about presenting themselves, as Frederick III. still urged his own claims on Hungary and refused to recognise Matthias. But Pius II. had himself given the Imperial envoys an example not to be too careful about their master's dignity in dealing with the Papacy. They were readily mollified by the assurance of the Pope that in such formal matters he only dealt with the existing state of things, and treated as king him who held the kingdom. They came to Siena, and gave to Pius II. the obedience of the Emperor. Pius II., on his part, could not

---

[1] *Pii II. Comment.* 44: ' Major pars æqualium e vita excesserat, et qui adhuc superabant, gravati senio morbisque domi detinebantur; et hi qui sese exhibebant mutati vultibus vix agnosci poterant, exhausti viribus et deformes.'

do less than confirm to the Emperor the provisions of the
secret agreement which he himself had negotiated, and for
which the German obedience had been sold to Eugenius IV.

To Siena came also the envoys of George Podiebrad, who
had been elected King of Bohemia, and their coming brought
before Pius II. the chief difficulty which he had to face. Podiebrad, as governor of Bohemia under Ladislas, had pursued with
firmness and sagacity a successful policy in uniting Bohemia
and bringing back order into the distracted country. He was,
above all things, a statesman who appreciated the exact bear-
ings of the situation. He saw that Bohemia must be united
on a basis which would allow the various factions to live peaceably together, and would also free the country from its
isolation from the rest of Christendom. He aimed at bringing
about this union on the basis of moderate utraquism. He
overthrew the fanatical Taborites, and reduced their stronghold.
He wished to be on good terms with the Papacy; but he knew
that Bohemia would not be content with less than a faithful
observance of the Compacts made with the Council of Basel,
and the recognition of Rokycana as Archbishop of Prag. But
the Compacts had been wrung out of the Council by necessity,
and the restored Papacy had no idea of frankly accepting
them. They were in its eyes a temporary compromise to be
withdrawn as soon as possible. If Podiebrad hoped to draw
the Papacy to toleration, the Papacy hoped to bring back
Bohemia to submission. Cusa, Carvajal, Capistrano, and Æneas
Sylvius had tried all that diplomatic skill and religious enthusiasm could do, and all had failed against the resolute
determination of the Bohemians. Rokycana was still unrecog-
nised, the Compacts were still treated as temporary provisions,
while Bohemia under Podiebrad was again organising itself
into the strongest kingdom in Eastern Europe.

Policy of
George
Podiebrad
King of
Bohemia.

So long as Ladislas lived the Papacy had hopes that his
influence might grow with years. But on his death the election
of Podiebrad to the Bohemian crown made the Bohemian question important both to the Papacy and to Germany. To
Germany it meant the destruction of German influence in
Bohemia, and the rise of a power which might become the
arbiter in the affairs of Germany itself. Podiebrad, conscious
of the difficulties in his way, desired a legitimate position as

Recog-
nition of
George by
Calixtus
III. 1458.

King of Bohemia, accepted by Utraquists and Catholics alike.
Hence he shrank from receiving the crown at the hands of
Rokycana, and wished for recognition by the Pope. Calixtus
III., in his crusading zeal, was willing to put great confidence
in one who could put an army in the field to war against the
Turk. Podiebrad led the Pope to suppose that he would make
greater concessions than he intended. He applied to Carvajal,
the Papal legate in Hungary, to send two bishops for his coronation. The request could not well be refused; nor could
Carvajal expect from Podiebrad an open abjuration, which
would have alienated his people. He charged the bishops,
however, not to crown him before he had sworn to root out
heresy and establish the Catholic faith in Bohemia. King
George managed to have the oath couched in general terms,
without any direct mention of the Compacts or of the utraquist
faith. He swore secretly before the bishops to bring back his
people from their errors to the faith and worship of the
Catholic Church. Then he was crowned on May 7, 1458.

Carvajal and Calixtus III. recognised in George a true,
though secret, friend of the Church, and believed in his sincerity and good intentions. George wrote to Calixtus proffering his aid against the Turks, and Calixtus in reply addressed
him not only as king, but as his dear son. The letter of
Calixtus was spread far and wide by George, and cut away the
ground from those who would have opposed him as a heretic.
The German and Catholic provinces of Silesia, Lusatia, and
Moravia, which were ready to rebel, returned to their obedience.
When it was too late the eyes of Calixtus III. were opened, and
he died with the knowledge that he had been deceived.[1]

In this condition Pius II. found the Bohemian question.
He was not, like Calixtus III., without experience of Bohemia
or of George. He knew that the King's oath was not meant
by him to signify a withdrawal from the Compacts; but he
knew that an open quarrel with Bohemia would hinder his plan
of a Congress, and he hoped through the Congress to put the
Papacy in a position which would enable it to deal with
Bohemia in the future. He judged it best to affect to look on
George's oath as a promise of complete submission. He sent
him a summons to the Congress, and gave him the title of

[1] *Cardinalis Papiensis Commentarii*, p. 430.

king; but sent the summons through the Emperor, saying that
Bohemia was a fief of the Empire, and that the Pope recognised
as king whoever the Emperor recognised. Frederick III.,
embarrassed by Hungary and Austria, began to look on George
as a possible ally. He admitted him to a conference near
Vienna in September 1458, and so gave him moral support.
As Pius had intended, the Emperor sent on the summons
to George, who at once published it. The Silesian League,
which still opposed George's accession, began slowly to melt
away before this proof of his success. Breslau, animated by
Catholic zeal, still held out, and sent envoys to Pius II. at
Siena, complaining of his recognition of George, as harmful
to Catholicism. Thither came also the ambassadors of George,
professing the obedience of their master to the Pope. Pius II.
was sorely embarrassed. He could not receive the obedience
of a King who had not yet disavowed his heresy: he could not
refuse his support to those who were resisting him in the name
of the Catholic faith. Accordingly, he attempted a compromise. In a secret consistory he received the personal
obedience of George, but declined to give him the rank of a
king till he had made public profession of Catholicism. The
envoys of Breslau he praised for their zeal, and promised to
find a remedy for their grievances; he hoped that George
would show himself true to his oath to the Papacy, and prove
himself a Christian king; otherwise he would have to take
other measures. For a time the Pope's answer satisfied both
parties. George used this period of truce to increase his
prestige in Germany. In April he held a conference at Eger,
to settle territorial disputes about the possessions of Bohemia,
Brandenburg, and Saxony; by his conciliatory policy he
gained recognition at the hands of his German neighbours,
and also entered into a perpetual peace and alliance with
Saxony and Brandenburg. On July 30 Frederick III. met
George at Brünn, and in return for promises of help against
Matthias of Hungary, conferred on him the Imperial investiture of the Bohemian kingdom. The policy of George had so
far succeeded in establishing his power on a legitimate basis.
It remained for Pius II. to see if his Congress could exercise
any influence on the restoration of Catholicism in Bohemia.

After a stay of nearly two months in Siena Pius II. set out

BOOK
IV.

Pius II. at
Florence
and
Bologna.
April–May
1459.

on April 23 for Florence, whither he was escorted by the young Galeazzo, son of Francesco Sforza, of Milan, as well as by several vassals of the Church. In Florence, where he stayed for eight days in the cloister of S. Maria Novella, the Pope received all honour and magnificent tokens of respect. But Cosimo de' Medici kept his bed on the plea of sickness, and the visit of Pius II. had no political fruit. From Florence he passed to Bologna, the rebellious vassal city of the Church. It is true Bologna was not in open rebellion : she admitted a Papal legate, but allowed him no authority, for the power was exercised by Xanto de' Bentivogli, supported by a council of sixteen.[1] The rulers of Bologna doubted whether to admit the Pope within their walls. On the one hand, if he passed by the city, such a mark of displeasure might ·encourage the Bolognese exiles to renew their attempts at revolution ; on the other hand, the presence of the Pope within the walls might encourage a rising of the popular party. At last it was decided to invite the Pope to Bologna, but to summon a large body of cavalry from Milan to keep the city in order during his stay. Pius II. was obliged to accept these conditions ; but the Milanese leaders took an oath of fidelity to the Pope, and the whole body was put under the command of Galeazzo Sforza. The entry of Pius II. into Bologna through lines of armed men was different from the peaceful procession which he had hitherto enjoyed. Bologna was sullen and suspicious. The orator who welcomed the Pope gave offence to the rulers by the way in which he spoke of the condition of the city. He was exiled for his outspokenness, and was restored only on the entreaties of Pius II.[2]

Pius II. was glad to leave the uncongenial city for Ferrara, where Borso of Este received him with open arms. Borso had many demands to make from the Pope ; he wished for the title of Duke of Ferrara and the remission of his yearly tribute to the Papacy for the fief which he held. Though Pius II. refused to go so far, yet he gave Borso many proofs of his friendliness, and his stay in Ferrara was one unceasing festivity.

[1] ' Legatum admisit qui verius ligatus appellari potuit,' says Pius, *Comm.* 55.

[2] Campanus, *Vita Pii II.*, Mur. iii. pt. 2, p. 976.

When Pius II. first announced his Congress, he mentioned as the place for its assembling Udine or Mantua. Udine was in the Venetian territory; and the Venetians, who had made a treaty with the Turks for commercial purposes, did not think it wise to lend their cities for a hostile demonstration against their ally. It had been, therefore, settled that the Congress was to meet at Mantua. Thither Pius II. travelled by boat up the Po; he was welcomed by the Marquis Ludovico Gonzaga, and entered the city, on May 27, in solemn procession. First came his attendants and three of the cardinals; then twelve white horses without riders, with gold reins and saddles. After these were borne by three mounted nobles the three banners, of the Cross, the Church, and the Piccolomini. Then followed a rich baldachino, behind which walked the clergy of Mantua in their robes. Next were the royal ambassadors, then the officials of the Curia, preceded by a golden cross and followed by a white horse bearing the Eucharist in a gold box, under a silken canopy surrounded by lighted candles. Then came Galeazzo Sforza and Ludovico Gonzaga, followed by the cardinals. After them the Pope, clad in full pontifical attire and blazing with jewels, was borne in his litter by nobles, and was followed by a crowd of prelates. At the entry of the gate Gonzaga dismounted, and presented to the Pope the keys of the city. Then the procession moved over carpets strewn with flowers to the cathedral. Next day Bianca, the wife of Sforza, with her four sons and her daughter Ippolita, visited the Pope. It is characteristic of the education of the age that the youthful Ippolita addressed the Pope in a Latin speech, which excited general admiration, and received from him an appropriate answer.[1]

So far all things had smiled on Pius II. He had enjoyed to the full the pleasures of pomp and pageantry, and had received all the satisfaction that fair speeches and ready promises could give. He was now anxious to reap the fruits of his journey in the results of the Congress. With laudable punctuality he arrived in Mantua three days before the appointed time, June 1; but he found no one there to meet him. The ambassadors who had been sent to him at Siena were not empowered to represent their masters at the Congress. On June 1 a service

CHAP.
VI.

Pius II.
arrives at
Mantua.
May 27,
1459.

Pius II.
waits at
Mantua.
June 1459.

[1] They are given by Mansi, *Pii II. Orationes*, ii. 192.

was held in the cathedral, after which the Pope addressed the
prelates.   He lamented the lukewarmness of Christendom, and
his own disappointment.   He asked them to pray that God
would give men greater zeal for His cause.   He would stay in
Mantua till he had found what were the intentions of the
princes: if they came, the Congress would proceed, if not, he
would go back home and bear the lot which Heaven assigned.
They were brave words; and those who had heard them thought
that they befitted the occasion.   But as Pius II. remained
in Mantua week after week, the patience of the Cardinals
became exhausted and they longed to return to the pleasures
of Rome.   Mantua, they murmured, was marshy and unhealthy;
did the Pope mean to destroy them by pestilence in that
stifling spot, where the wine was poor, the food scarce, and
nothing could be heard save the croaking of the frogs?   'You
have satisfied your honour,' they pleaded to Pius.   ' No one
imagines that you alone can conquer the Turks.   The princes
of Europe pay no heed to us: let us go home.'   Bessarion and
Torquemada were the only cardinals who held by the Pope.
Scarampo, who had left his fleet to come to Mantua, withdrew
to Venice, where he openly ridiculed the Congress.

But Pius II. hoped too much from the Congress to give it
up so readily.   Not only was he in earnest about the crusade,
but he wished the Congress to give a practical overthrow to the
Conciliar movement.   At Constance the hierarchy under the
presidency of the Emperor had decided the affairs of the
Church; Pius II. desired to establish a precedent of the princes
of Europe under the presidency of the Pope deciding the
affairs of Christendom.   If even partial success should follow
such an attempt, it would be the completion of the Papal
restoration, the assertion of the Papal supremacy over the
nationalities of Europe.   Pius II. hoped that the Papacy
would show its superiority over the fruitless Diets of Germany, and would establish its authority, high above the Empire,
as the undisputed centre of the state-system of Christendom.

Arrival of
envoys of
the despot
of Morea.
The first envoys who came to Mantua were sent by Thomas,
the despot of the Morea, a brother of the last Greek Emperor,
Constantine Palæologus.   Thomas and his brother Demetrius
had maintained themselves in the Morea on condition of paying
tribute to the Sultan.   But they quarrelled with one another;

the Turks advanced against them; they were incapable either
of fighting or paying tribute. The envoys of Thomas brought
as a present to the Pope sixteen Turkish captives, and with
the boastfulness of his race, represented himself as victorious;
he did not want much help; with a handful of Italians he
would clear the Morea of Turks. His request was discussed
by the Cardinals, and at the earnest instance of Bessarion,
against the better judgment of the Pope, it was resolved to send
him three hundred men. They were rapidly equipped, and
received the Pope's benediction before they departed for Ancona.
Of course their services were of no real use, and they were
little better than freebooters.

CHAP.
VI.

There was no lack of envoys clamouring for aid, though
those who could offer aid were wanting. From Bosnia, Albania,
Epirus, Illyria, Cyprus, Rhodes, and Lesbos, came messengers
demanding help. At last came three ambassadors from the
Emperor—the Bishop of Trieste, Heinrich Senftleben, and
Johann Hinderbach, who had been fellow-secretaries with Æneas
in the Emperor's Chancery: they were men of no standing to
represent the Emperor in a matter concerning the interests of
Christendom. Pius II. sent them back with a severe letter of
remonstrance; he did not recognise them as ambassadors, and
urged the Emperor to come himself, or send men of rank
and position. Letter followed upon letter; but the Emperor
tarried and the other German princes followed his example. At
last at the end of August, the envoys of the Duke of Burgundy,
—his nephew, John of Cleves, and Jean de Croy—drew near.
The Pope wished that they should be received outside the walls
by the Cardinals; but the Cardinals answered that they were the
equals of kings, and ought not to pay honour to a duke. Pius
II. urged that all appearance of arrogance should be avoided,
and finally the Cardinals Orsini and Colonna offered to go as
a deputation from the Sacred College. The Burgundians were
honourably received, and on the day after their arrival were
welcomed by the Pope in a public consistory. The Bishop of
Arras made a speech excusing the Duke of Burgundy's absence
on the ground of age. Pius II. replied in praise of the Duke's
zeal. But when these ceremonies were over, and the Pope
wished to turn to business, the Duke of Cleves brought forward
a private question of his own. He had taken under his protec-

Arrival
of the
Imperial
and Bur-
gundian
envoys.
August
1459.

tion the town of Soest, which had rebelled against the Archbishop of Köln. The case had long been before the Papacy,
and Pius II. had issued an admonition to Soest to return to its
rightful allegiance. The Duke of Cleves demanded that this
admonition should be recalled, and refused to treat of the business of the Congress till the Pope had complied with his request.
Pius II. was in a strait: he could not abandon the possessions of
the Church; he did not wish to draw down failure on the Congress. He adopted a dubious policy of delay. 'The Roman
Pontiffs,' he says, 'have been accustomed, where justice cannot
be done without public scandal, to dissemble till a convenient
season. Nor do the lawgivers forbid such a course; for the
greater evil must always be obviated.'[1] So Pius II. withdrew
his admonition to Soest, to satisfy the Duke of Cleves, and
promised the representatives of the Archbishop of Köln that
he would renew it as soon as affairs allowed.

Nego-
tiations
with the
Burgun-
dians.

After this the Pope tried to bring the Burgundian envoys
to business; but it soon became evident that the crusading
zeal of their master had cooled. Their instructions simply
empowered them to hear the Pope's views and report them
to the Duke of Burgundy. They added that the Duke considered an expedition against the Turks to be a matter that
would tax the energies of united Christendom; in its present
discordant state a crusade was hopeless. Pius II. in reply
pointed out the peril to Europe if the Turks were to become
masters of Hungary. The pacification of Europe was no doubt
desirable; but it would take some time to wipe out the hostilities of years. Meanwhile Hungary was in extremities.
Though Europe was troubled, yet if every nation contributed
equally to the crusade, the balance of power would be left
unaltered. No vast expedition was needed; fifty or sixty
thousand men would be as many as could be fed and maintained in the field, and would be enough to keep the Turk in
check. Surely that was not much to ask from Europe. So
pleaded the Pope. Many conferences and many arguments
were needed before the Burgundian envoys at length promised
that the Duke would send into Hungary 2,000 knights and
4,000 foot, and would maintain them so long as the Christian

[1] *Commentarii*, p. 68.

army remained in the field. When this was settled the Duke CHAP.
VI. of Cleves prepared to go. In vain Pius II. strove to keep him at Mantua. He and his colleague departed, leaving a few of the humbler members of the embassy behind. Again Pius II. and his Cardinals were left alone; again the murmurs of the Curia waxed loud against the useless sojourn in Mantua.

In the middle of September came Francesco Sforza, Duke of Milan, who again was welcomed by the Cardinals. Again was held a public Consistory, and Francesco Filelfo, the celebrated scholar, delivered a long and eloquent speech in behalf of Sforza. The change of human affairs had brought about that the young Sienese lad, who had once scraped together money to go to Florence and attend the lectures of the famous Filelfo, now sat on the Papal throne and received the elegant adulation of his former teacher. Pius II. listened and applauded; in his reply he called Filelfo the 'Attic Muse,' and extolled Sforza as a model of Christendom. But Sforza had his own political ends to serve. He wished to agree with the Pope on an Italian policy, which for the next thirty years gave Italy peace such as she had not enjoyed for centuries. He proposed to the Pope a league in defence of the throne of Ferrante in Naples. Sforza saw clearly enough that the success of the House of Anjou in Naples would make French interest predominant in Italy, and would bring upon Milan the claims of the House of Orleans. If Naples, Milan, and the Papacy were united, the danger of French intervention might be averted.[1] Moreover, Sforza wanted the aid of the Pope to procure for him from the Emperor the investiture of the Duchy of Milan.

Arrival of
the Duke
of Milan.
September
1459.

The coming of Sforza had at least the effect that it induced most of the Italian powers to send their envoys to Mantua; if the Congress did not become of great importance to Europe, it was at least a great conference of the Powers of Italy. It is true that Borso of Modena would not forgive the Pope for his refusal to make him Duke of Ferrara; he preferred his own amusements to the dull work of the Congress. But Florence, Siena, Lucca, Bologna, and Genoa sent envoys, as

Arrival of
Italian
envoys.

---

[1] See Simoneta, *Vita Sfortiæ*, Mur. xxi. 690.

did Ferrante of Naples. An embassy came also from Casimir, King of Poland, and tardily from the Duke of Savoy. Even Venice, which had refused to give offence to the Turks, sent two envoys when the news of Sforza's arrival was received.

At last Pius II. might claim that something which might be called a Congress was assembled at Mantua. There was no time to wait any longer, as Sforza was already anxious to depart. So on September 26 the Congress was opened by a solemn service in the cathedral, after which the cardinals and envoys assembled before the Pope. Then Pius II. delivered a speech, which was regarded as a masterpiece of oratory. Copies were circulated throughout Europe; and if an appreciation of eloquence had borne any practical fruit, the Turk would soon have been driven back into Asia. For three hours the rounded periods of Pius II. rolled on; and, though he was affected by a cough, his excitement freed him during his speech from that troublesome enemy of rhetorical effect.[1] After an invocation of divine assistance Pius II. put forth the causes of war, the losses which Islam had inflicted on Christendom, both in the remote past and in more recent days. Even though the present might be endured, the worst had not yet been reached. The Turks were still pressing on, and if Hungary fell before them there was no further barrier for Europe. 'But alas, Christians prefer to war against one another rather than against the Turks. The beating of a bailiff, even of a slave, is enough to draw kings into war; against the Turks, who blaspheme our God, destroy our churches, and strive to destroy the whole Christian name, no one dares take up arms.' Then he turned to his second point, the chances of success. The Turks had conquered only degenerate peoples, and were themselves an easy prey to the superior strength of Europeans, as the exploits of Hunyadi and Scanderbeg might show. Moreover, God was on the Christian side, for Islam denied the divinity of Christ. Here Pius II. lowered the level of his rhetoric by turning aside to display his learning; he gave a summary of the arguments by which Christ's divinity was maintained. But he skilfully used this as the ground for an impassioned appeal to his hearers;

---

[1] *Pii II. Comm.* p. 82 : 'Quamvis tussi per eos dies laborasset gravissime divina tamen ope adjutus inter orandum neque tussivit unquam neque vel minimum ostendit impedimentum.'

he besought them to show the sincerity of their faith, the depth of their reverence for their divine Redeemer, by driving from Christendom the Turks who blasphemed His name. Then Pius II. proceeded to his third point, the rewards which the war would bring. First there were kingdoms, booty, glory, all in abundance that usually stirred men to war. Besides this was the sure promise of the heavenly kingdom, and the plenary indulgence of sins which he had granted to all crusaders. How short was life in comparison with eternity! How full were the joys of Paradise, where they would see God, and His angels, and all the company of the blessed, and would understand all things! 'Our soul freed from the chain of the body will, not as Plato says, *recover*, but, as Aristotle and our own doctors teach, *attain* to the knowledge of all things. It is a prospect which once stirred men to martyrdom. But we do not ask you to undergo the martyr's tortures; heaven is promised you at a lesser price. Fight bravely for the law of God, and you will gain "what eye never saw nor ear heard." O fools and slow to believe the promises of Scripture! Would that there were here to-day Godfrey or Baldwin, Eustace, Hugh the Great, Bohemund, Tancred, and the rest who in days gone by won back Jerusalem! They would not have suffered us to speak so long, but rising from their seats, as once they did before our predecessor Urban II., they would have cried with ready voice, "Deus lo vult, Deus lo vult"!'

'You silently await the end of our speech, nor seem to be moved by our exhortations. Perhaps there are among you those who think, "This Pope says much why we should go to war and expose ourselves to the enemy's swords. Such is the way of priests; they bind on others heavy burdens which themselves will not touch with their finger." Think not so of us. No one was ever more ready than ourselves. We came here, weak as you see, risking our life, and the States of the Church. Our expenses have greatly increased, our revenues diminished. We do not speak boastfully, we only regret that it is not in our power to do more. O if our youthful strength still remained, you should not go to the field without us. We would go before your standard, bearing the cross; we would hurl Christ's banner amidst the foe, and would count ourselves happy to die for Jesus's sake. Even now, if you think fit, we will not hesitate to vow to the war our pining body and our weary soul. We shall deem it noble to be borne in our litter through the camp, the battle, the midst of the foe. Decide as you think best. Our person, our resources, we place at your disposal; whatever weight you lay upon our shoulders we will bear.'[1]

Proceedings of the Congress.
When the Pope had ended, Bessarion spoke on behalf of the Cardinals. Not to be outdone by Pius II., he also addressed the assembly for three hours. If Pius II. showed his learning by a defence of the divinity of Christ, Bessarion made a display of scholarship by citing historical instances of those who had died for their country. He was at first tedious; but when he described the capture of Constantinople he grew eloquent, and when he spoke of the actual condition of the Turkish resources, which he estimated at 70,000 men, he was listened to with more attention.[2] When he had ended, the envoys present praised the Pope's speech and extolled his zeal. Sforza spoke in Italian, with 'a soldier's eloquence,' says the Pope. Last of all the Hungarian envoys addressed the assembly, and loudly complained of the Emperor's interference in Hungarian affairs, thus adding to their trouble when the Turk was at their gates. The Imperial envoy, the Bishop of Trieste, had not a word to say. Pius II. himself had to defend his former master by saying that this was not the place for general political discussion; he knew that both the Emperor and the King of Hungary were just and upright, and he had sent a legate to heal their quarrels.

Proposals of Pius II.
The Congress contented itself with decreeing war against the Turks in general terms, and Pius II. saw that this was all that he could expect the Congress to do. Next day he summoned the envoys to a conference in his palace for the discussion of ways and means. He put before them the questions— were the Turks to be attacked by land, or sea, or both? What soldiers were necessary, and how they were to be obtained?

[1] In Mansi, *Pii II. Orationes*, ii. 9, &c.
[2] M. Vast (*Le Cardinal Bessarion*, Paris, 1878) gives a summary of this speech from a MS. in the Bibliothèque Nationale at Paris, p. 238. In spite of M. Vast's admiration for his hero, he seems to have been somewhat dull, and was regarded as the standing bore on the Eastern question—excellent but tedious.

Sforza rose and gave his opinion as a soldier. The Turks should be attacked by land and sea; soldiers should be furnished by Hungary and the neighbouring lands, as being best acquainted with the tactics to be employed in fighting the Turks; Italy and the rest of Christendom should furnish money. The Venetians agreed, and added that thirty galleys and eight barks would suffice to cause a diversion on the shores of Greece and the Hellespont, while 40,000 horsemen and 20,000 foot would be enough for war by land. Gismondo Malatesta, Lord of Rimini, seeing an opportunity of booty for himself, advocated that the war should be carried on by Italian forces. Pius II. observed significantly, that Italian generals did not care to fight outside Italy, and in this war there was little to gain except for their souls. Other countries offered troops, but would not offer money; their offer must be accepted or nothing would be got from them. The Turkish troops numbered about 200,000, of whom the only real soldiers, the Janissaries, were 40,000: to face them 50,000 European troops would suffice, and thirty galleys would also be required. To raise money he proposed that the clergy should pay a tenth, the laity a thirtieth of their revenues for three years, and the Jews a twentieth of all their possessions. The assembly approved the decree in general; but when the Pope proposed that all should sign it, there was much hesitation. Florence and Venice especially hung back. The Venetians at length declared that they would sign it if double the number of ships were provided, and they were paid for supplying them, and received all the conquests made by the crusaders. Matters began to wear a doubtful aspect when Pius II. attempted to turn general promises into definite undertakings. Sforza had done his duty by joining the Congress, and left Mantua for Milan.

Pius II. professed himself satisfied with the results which *Disappointment of the Pope.* he obtained, and strove in public to maintain a semblance of contentment. His real feelings, however, are expressed in a letter to Carvajal, written on November 5. 'We do not find, to confess the truth, such zeal in the minds of Christians as we hoped. We find few who have a greater care for public matters than for their own interests. Yet we have shown how false is that calumny so long cast against the Holy See; we have proved that no one is to be accused except themselves. We seem, however, to have disposed affairs in Italy for God's service, since the princes and potentates have entered into obligations confirmed by their own signatures. But we hear that Genoa is sending a fleet to urge the French claims in Naples, and we fear that we shall lose not only help from those engaged in war, but that all the rest will be drawn into the struggle. Unless God help us, the first fruits of our labour will be lost in the calamities of Christian people.'[1]

Arrival of French envoys. November 16, 1459.

In truth everything depended for Pius II. on the attitude assumed by France, whose ambassadors were announced as on their way to Mantua. They had halted at Lyons on receiving the news of the reception given to the Burgundians, and doubted whether it became the national dignity that they should advance farther. One of their number, the Bishop of Chartres, went on beforehand. He had a private end to serve ; for having been appointed Bishop according to the Pragmatic Sanction, he had not been confirmed by the Pope. Pius II. readily gave him his confirmation, and the Bishop returned to his colleagues, but never went back to Mantua. The French embassy was joined by the envoys of René of Anjou, and of the Duke of Brittany. At last on November 16 they entered Mantua. France was represented by the Archbishop of Tours and the Bishop of Paris ; René by the Bishop of Marseilles ; and the Duke of Brittany by the Bishop of S. Malo. Genoa also sent an embassy, and soon after arrived from the Emperor envoys more worthy to represent him—Charles of Baden and the Bishops of Eichstädt and Trent.

Reception of the French envoys.

It was the general expectation that the French envoys would at the outset challenge the Pope's proceedings in regard to the Neapolitan kingdom, and would refuse obedience or threaten a General Council. Some anxiety was felt when they were admitted before the consistory on November 21. The Bishop of Paris spoke for two hours in praise of the French King and his anxiety about the Neapolitan question. He said little about the Turks, less about any aid in a crusade. Finally, he offered to the Pope the obedience of the French Church as that of a son to a father ; he said this pointedly to exclude any notion of dependence as on a master.[2] The obe-

[1] Raynaldus, 1459, No. 78.
[2] Pii II. Comm. p. 88 : ' Filialem obedientiam appellavit, ut serrilem excluderet.'

dience of René and of Genoa was afterwards tendered by their
envoys. Pius II. in his answer dwelt on the dignity of the
Apostolic See, established by God, and not by councils or decrees,
above all kingdoms and peoples. Twice he repeated this, with
increased emphasis, and then passed on to say that he wished
to receive with all favour 'his dear son in Christ, René, the
illustrious King of Sicily,' but would answer more privately
his demands.[1] Both sides were satisfied with the result of
their first interview. The Pope was content that, after all their
threats, the French had at least submitted formally to his
obedience. The French flattered themselves that the Pope had
recognised the power of the French King, and was willing to
obey his will.

But these proceedings were merely formal; the real struggle
began when the French envoys came to lay before the Pope
their complaints about his Neapolitan policy. They were
resolved to show no diplomatic reserve, and brought with them
to the audience all the envoys who were present at Mantua.
The Bailly of Rouen spoke in praise of France, 'the nation of
the Lilies,' as he persisted in calling it. He dwelt on the
services rendered by France to the Papacy and on its connexion
with Naples; he complained that Alfonso had seized Naples by
force, not by right; that Pius had acted wrongly in recognising
Ferrante his bastard son, which even Calixtus III., though an
Aragonese, had not ventured to do. He demanded that Pius
should recall all that he had done for Ferrante, should invest
King René, and help his forces to gain the kingdom; should
recognise the French party in Genoa, and revoke all ecclesiastical censures against the city. The friends of France listened to the trenchant orator, and raised their crests in triumph:
they thought the Pope would not venture to reply. Pius answered, that what he had done regarding Naples had been done
with the advice of the Cardinals, whom he must consult before
saying more. So saying he dismissed the assembly.

Next day Pius II. was attacked by a cramp in the stomach,
and a violent cough which confined him for some days to his
bed. The French declared that this was a pretence to cover
his confusion and escape from answering their attack. Perhaps
the Pope made the most of his illness to gain time to prepare

[1] His clever speech is given in Mansi, *Pii II. Orationes*, ii. 31, &c.

his answer, and render its delivery more effective. 'Though I should die in the middle of my speech, I will answer them,' he said, and summoned all the ambassadors to a public audience. He dragged himself from his sick bed, and, with pale face and trembling limbs, seated himself on his throne. At first he could scarcely speak for weakness and excitement; soon gathering strength, he spoke for three hours, and his effort had such a beneficial effect that it entirely freed him from his cramp. In his speech the Pope complained of the charges brought against him by the French. He spoke of the glories of their nation in language which outdid even their own orator. He set forth their services to the Holy See and the benefits which they had in turn received. Then he traced the history of the Neapolitan succession under his immediate predecessors. 'We did not exclude the French, we found them excluded,' he said; 'we found Ferrante in possession of the kingdom, and recognised the actual state of things. If the French had been nearer we would have preferred them. We could not disturb the peace of Italy for those who were at a distance. In recognising Ferrante we reserved the rights of the House of Anjou. The case is still open for our decision.' He urged the need of peace in Christendom and war against the Turks. Finally, as the French had spoken of the gratitude due to France from the Holy See, the Pope turned to the Pragmatic Sanction by which the power of the Pope in France had been reduced to such limits as pleased the Parlement of Paris. He admitted the good intentions of the French King, but warned him that by his present course he was imperilling the souls of his people.[1] The French ambassadors expressed their wish to answer some things that the Pope had said, as being contrary to the honour of their King. Pius II. replied that he was willing to hear them when, and as often as, they chose, and so retired. The Curia thronged round him with joy. 'Never,' said they, 'within the memory of our fathers have words been spoken so worthy of a Pope as those about the Pragmatic Sanction.' Pius II. had won an oratorical triumph, and had given another proof that it was impossible to get the better of him in discussion. Next day the French appeared before him in

private, in the presence only of eight Cardinals. The time for
public displays, they felt, was past. There was some more discussion about the Pragmatic Sanction, and the envoys in their
private capacity made their peace with the Pope. But this
political wrangle had driven into the background the question
of the crusade. When Pius II. asked them what help he
might expect from France, he was answered that France could
do nothing till she was at peace with England. The Pope proposed that France and England should contribute an equal
number of soldiers, so as to leave the balance unaltered: if
they could not send troops, they might give money. The
French said that they had no powers for any such undertaking,
but assented to the Pope's proposal for a conference to arrange
peace with England.

England was too much involved in internal conflicts to pay
much heed to the request of Pius that it should send envoys to
Mantua. Henry VI. had nominated an embassy, at the head
of which was the Earl of Worcester, but it never set out for
Mantua. Two priests arrived on the King's behalf, proffering
the Pope the obedience of England and bringing his excuses.
Their credentials bore the usual endorsement, 'Teste Rege;'
and we are surprised to find Pius II. so ignorant of the forms
used in England that he thought that the King, bereft of
all officials, had been compelled to act as his own witness in
default of others.[1] To England, however, was sent as Papal
legate, to make peace, the Bishop of Terni, who fell into the
hands of the Earl of Warwick, identified himself with the cause
of the House of York, excommunicated the Lancastrians, and
gathered for himself large sums of money from the English
Church. When the Pope heard of this he recalled his legate,
degraded him from his priestly office, and confined him in a
monastery for the rest of his life.[2] However, no efforts of a
Papal legate could have given peace to England or obtained
from her aid for a crusade. France was offended by the
Pope's dealings with Naples, and was more anxious to assert

*England
and the
Congress.*

---

[1] 'In litteris mandati non fuerunt de more, aut testes nominati, aut sub-
scripti tabelliones; sed adnotata erat regis manu hujuscemodi subscriptio,
Henricus teste me ipso: et sigillum regni appensum. Contempsit Pontifex
derisitque tanti regis tam vilem legationem.'—*Pii II. Comm.* 88.

[2] *Pii II. Comm.* 277; *Cardinalis Papiensis Epistolæ,* 162.

the claims of René than to attack the Turks. England and
France alike were useless for any help to the Pope in his great
endeavour.

Negotia-
tions with
the Ger-
mans.

It only remained for Pius II. to see what promises he could
get from Germany. There were in Mantua the ambassadors of
the Emperor and of many German princes; chief amongst
them was the old opponent of Æneas Sylvius, Gregory Heimburg, who represented Albert of Austria. Pius II. called them
together, and wished to obtain a common understanding. The
Imperial envoys were ready to accept his proposals; but those
of the princes, led by Heimburg, refused. Heimburg was convinced that the Pope's proposal of levying a tenth and granting
indulgences was merely a scheme for enriching himself and his
Imperial ally. He would agree to no general proposal; and
Pius II. had to deal with each embassy separately. By means
of private negotiations the Pope at length contrived to obtain a
renewal of the promise made at the Diets of Frankfort and
Neustadt to equip 10,000 horse and 32,000 foot. To arrange
for general peace, and settle all preliminaries, a Diet was to be
held at Nürnberg, and another in the Emperor's dominions,
to make peace between him and Matthias of Hungary; the
Pope was to send a legate to both. Pius II. was compelled to
accept the sterile procedure of a Diet, the futility of which he
knew so well, and which Calixtus III. had endeavoured to
escape without success. He appointed as his legate Bessarion,
probably because he was the only cardinal whose zeal would
induce him to undertake the thankless office. Moreover,
Pius II. attempted to give the agreement greater definiteness
by appointing Frederick general of the crusading army, and
empowering him, if he could not lead it himself, to nominate a
prince in his stead.

Arrival
of Sigis-
mund of
Austria.

While these negotiations were in progress Sigismund of
Austria arrived in Mantua on November 10, with a brilliant
train of 400 knights. He was honourably received, and Heimburg, in a public audience, spoke in Sigismund's behalf. He
recounted the glories of the House of Austria and the virtues
of Sigismund; he dwelt on the acquaintance that had existed
in earlier days between Sigismund when a boy and Æneas
Sylvius, the Imperial secretary. Æneas had indeed written for
Sigismund love-letters, which were not edifying; and Heimburg,

embittered by resentment against the Pope, mockingly recalled the past, which Pius II. would fain have forgotten. The
culture of Sigismund, he said, had been greatly formed by the
delightful love-letters which his Holiness had transplanted from
Italy to Germany.[1] Pius II. had to sit with a conviction that
he was being laughed at, unable with any dignity to reply.

In truth neither Sigismund nor his orator Heimburg were
friendly disposed towards the Papacy. Sigismund had on his
hands an ecclesiastical quarrel which was destined to give
Pius II. a great deal of trouble, and whch dated ten years back.
In 1450 Nicolas V. conferred on Nicolas of Cusa, whom he had
just made Cardinal, the Bishopric of Brixen. Cusa was a poor
man and needed the means of supporting his new dignity; but
the provision of Nicolas V., made without waiting for a capitular election, was in direct contravention to the Concordat,
and was also an infringement of the agreement made with
Frederick III., as Brixen was one of the bishoprics to which
the Emperor was allowed to appoint during his lifetime. The
Chapter of Brixen made their election, and turned to Sigismund, as Count of the Tyrol, to help them to maintain their
rights; but the Pope and the Emperor were too strong for
them. Sigismund did not judge it expedient to prolong the
contest, and Cusa was unwillingly admitted as Bishop of Brixen
in 1451. Cusa was for a time employed as Papal legate, in
selling to the Germans the benefits of the year of Jubilee without
giving them the trouble of going to Rome, and in stirring up
the crusading spirit. He was not in earnest with either of
these tasks, and returned as soon as he could to his own diocese,
which he proposed to make a model to the rest of Germany.

Quarrel of
Sigismund
of Austria
and Car-
dinal Cusa.
1451-1457.

---

[1] Pius, in his *Commentaries*, p. 90, gives his account of the matter : ' Inter
cætera dixerat Gregorius Sigismundum Pii, cum in minoribus ageret, fuisse
discipulum, qui suas epistolas avide legisset, quarum volumen apud se haberet,
et aliquæ illarum Sigismondo essent scriptæ ; quod verum inveniet, si quis
epistolas sæculares legerit quas Pius nondum sacris initiatus scripsit.' The
remark is apologetic, and the letter addressed to Sigismund about his mistress
(No. 122, ed. 1551) is not one which a Pope would care to be reminded of. Voigt
(*Æneas Sylvius*, iii. 100) quotes from a Munich MS. of Heimburg's speech : ' Quæ
(noticia) simul cum ætate crevit adaucta feliciter fomentum subministrantibus
litteris illis *oratoriis* quas ipsa S. V. persona ab Ytalis traduxit in Germanos .
. . . Dixi, pater beatissime, firmamentum contracte noticie (et) amoris accensi
præstitisse litteras illas *oratorias*, &c.' He suggests that *oratorius* makes no
sense, and is probably a mistake for *amatorias* ; there seems much probability
in this correction.

Cusa was a man of learning—not the learning of the
Renaissance, but the technical theology of the schoolmen.   Of
humble extraction, he had nothing save his talents on which to
rely.   He had been a follower of Cesarini at Basel, had abandoned with the other moderates the Council's cause, and had
made his reputation by his learned writings in favour of the
Papacy.   He was an able but narrow-minded man, whose bent
was to abstractions and technicalities rather than to zeal or
statesmanship.   He did not abandon the reforming ideas he had
held at Basel, but transferred them from one field to another.
He had striven to reform the Church in its head ; he was equally
bent on reforming it in some of its members.   A movement
such as that expressed at Basel could not entirely die out ; but
it was easily diverted to trivialities.   If the entire Church
system could not be reformed, there was at least one part of it
to which a mechanical rule might be applied.   If the ecclesiastical organisation was not to be revised, it might at least be more
tightly strung and reduced to greater uniformity.   There was
a decided feeling that the monastic orders ought to be brought
back to a straiter observance of their original rule.   It was
a cry which afforded some satisfaction to the technical mind of
a man like Cusa, who could point to success in this sphere as
the proper beginning of a conservative reformation within the
Church itself.

So Cusa began a strict visitation of the monasteries within
his diocese.   If his visitation had only aimed at restoring neglected observances and ceremonies in the cloisters, it would at
least have been harmless.   But a rigid visitation of monasteries,
in the face of a strong opposition, raised many legal questions
concerning the Bishop's visitatorial power.   It was hard to
define the limits of the spiritualities and the temporalities of
the monasteries.   It was difficult to determine what were the
powers of the Bishop as visitor, and what were the rights of the
Count of the Tyrol as protector of the temporalities of foundations within his dominions.   The Benedictine nuns of Sonnenburg in the Pusterthal resisted the Bishop and appealed to Sigismund as protector of their monastery.   Sigismund was loth to
quarrel with Cusa, who laid the nuns under an interdict.   He
mediated with the Cardinal ; but the Sonnenburg difficulty embittered the feelings of both parties and broadened into other and

more important issues. Cusa turned the formal acuteness of his mind to determine the exact rights of the Bishopric of Brixen. He established to his own satisfaction that the protectorship over monastic foundations, exercised by the Counts of the Tyrol, was granted to them by the Bishop of Brixen, together with lands, for which they were vassals to the see. The Bishop of Brixen was a prince of the Empire, and the Emperor was in things temporal the protector of the see ; the rights of the Counts of the Tyrol depended only on a grant from their Bishop. Sigismund naturally asserted that the Bishopric of Brixen was under the Counts of the Tyrol, to whom belonged the protectorate with all its rights, however much the formal investiture had been conferred on the Counts by the Bishops. The angry feelings on both sides waxed high ; but Cusa had only the weapons of interdict and excommunication. As he was extremely unpopular through his harshness, the national sentiment was all on the side of Sigismund, and the excommunications were little heeded.

Attempts were made to bring about a peace, and Sigismund invited Cusa to an interview at Wilten in 1457. Whether Cusa lost his nerve, or whether he deliberately chose to set up a plea for further proceedings, cannot be determined. But he fled from Wilten, declaring that his life was in danger, though the evidence which he could afterwards produce for his terror was very slight. Still Cusa had the ear of the Curia, and Calixtus III. laid Sigismund under an interdict till he had satisfied Cusa of his freedom and personal security. Sigismund, prompted by Gregory Heimburg, appealed to a better-informed Pope, but offered full security to Cusa, and declared himself ready to withdraw his appeal if friendly overtures were made. Cusa was inflexible, proceeded with the interdict, and showed his willingness to use forcible means. He forbade the peasants who held under the Sonnenburg nuns to pay their dues to the rebellious abbess. The convent employed a band of forty men to collect them ; whereupon a captain in Cusa's pay fell upon this luckless band and cut it to pieces.

Open breach between Cusa and Sigismund. 1457

Thus matters stood when Calixtus III. died, and both the combatants turned with expectation to his successor. Cusa had been an old friend of Æneas, and hastened to Rome to lay his case before him. Sigismund had been a pupil of Æneas

Pius II. mediates between Cusa and Sigismund. November 1459.

when he was at Frederick's Court. Pius II. was in all things desirous of peace, and would fain have mediated in the quarrel. On setting out for Mantua he left Cardinal Cusa as his representative in Rome; but Cusa was afterwards summoned to Mantua, that the Pope might try to settle matters between him and Sigismund. It was for this purpose that Sigismund had come. Pius II. offered his services as a mediator ; he did not decide as a judge. In the presence of the Cardinals and of the Imperial ambassadors, he listened to the complaints of both parties. He had no desire to favour one rather than the other, and at last patched up a temporary reconciliation, on the understanding that the legal question of the relations between the Bishop and the Count was to be decided by a process within two years, and the other points in dispute were to be arranged between the two parties at a Diet to be held in Trent. Thus nothing was definitely decided, and Sigismund departed from Mantua in indignation on November 29.[1] Pius II. had no feeling against Sigismund as to the points in dispute ; but he had seen enough to know that, under Heimburg's advice, Sigismund was ready to prosecute his cause in a manner most offensive to the Papacy. The appeal to a future Council was a relic of the state of things which Pius II. hoped to obliterate for ever; it was a revolutionary memory which must never be again awakened in Germany. Pius II. was ready to wait for a while and see if Sigismund would pursue a more respectful course ; if not, he must at least cut the ground from under his feet before he pressed him further.

The Bull 'Execrabilis.' January 18, 1460.

If one object of Pius II. was to wage war against the Turk, the other was to wipe out of the ecclesiastical system all traces of the conciliar movement. The two objects were, moreover, closely connected. The Neapolitan question threatened to bring the Papacy into collision with France, and France might use its old engine of a Council. If Germany were to be useful for the crusade, if the Papal decrees for taming Germany were to be effective, the Diets must be prevented from throwing hindrances in the way by raising untoward questions of the

---

[1] The details of this long struggle are to be found in Jäger, *Der Streit des Cardinals Nicolas von Cusa mit dem Herzoge Sigmund von Oesterreich als Grafen von Tirol.* Innsbruch, 1861. Jäger has also published a register of the whole matter in *Archiv für österreichischer Geschichtsquellen,* Bde. vi. vii.

rights of the German Church, clamouring for further reform and appealing to future Councils. The example of Sigismund, the machinations of Heimburg, must be checked from doing further mischief; the power of the restored Papacy must be fully asserted in the person of one who had devoted the best energies of his life to the cause of that restoration. It was pardonable that Pius II. should wish to put the crown to his life's work. If the Congress of Mantua had not been successful in raising the prestige of the Papacy, and showing Europe the unwonted sight of a Pope directing the activity of Christendom, it might at least be made memorable as the occasion of a firm assertion of the Papal authority. Pius II., after Sigismund's departure, unfolded his scheme to the Cardinals and prelates assembled in Mantua, who all gave their cordial assent. A Papal Constitution was accordingly drawn up and published on January 18, 1460, known, from its first words, as 'Execrabilis et priscis inauditus temporibus.' In it the Pope condemns, as an 'execrable abuse, unheard of in former times,' any appeal to a future Council. It is ridiculous to appeal to what does not exist and whose future existence is indeterminate. Such a custom is only a means of escaping just judgment, a cloak for iniquity, and a destruction of all discipline. All such appeals are declared invalid; anyone who makes them is declared *ipso facto* excommunicated, together with all who frame or witness any document containing them.[1] The Bull was a master-stroke on the part of one who well knew the dangers against which he had to contend. If Bulls could have established the Papal authority, Pius II. would have known how to frame them. His precaution was wise; but it failed of effect. Both René of Anjou and Sigismund of the Tyrol lodged appeals in spite of the Papal denunciation. Yet the Bull of Pius II., though not immediately successful, worked its way into the ecclesiastical system and became one of the pillars on which the Papal authority rested.

Only one other prince visited Mantua, Albert of Brandenburg, whom Pius II. greeted warmly as 'the German Achilles.' He made the usual protestations of zeal against the Turks, and received from the Pope, on the Festival of the Epiphany, a consecrated sword. But Albert had his own ends to serve; it

Dissolution of the Congress. January 19, 1460.

---

[1] *Pii. II. Com.* p. 90. Raynaldus, 1460, 10.

suited his position in Germany to be on good terms with Emperor and Pope. When Albert had gone there was nothing
more to do at Mantua. On January 14 Pius II. declared war
against the Turks, and promised indulgences to all who took
part in it. He issued, also, decrees imposing a subsidy of a
tenth on the clergy and a thirtieth on the laity, especially in
Italy. Then on January 19, after a speech in which he magnified
the offers of help which had been made, Pius II. enumerated his
expectations. It was not all that he had hoped for, yet it was
a fair show.[1] The ambassadors present solemnly renewed their
promises. Then Pius II. knelt before the altar and chanted
some appropriate psalms. The Congress was over, and next
day the Pope left Mantua after a sojourn of eight months.

Results of
the Con-
gress of
Mantua.
The Congress of Mantua could not be called a success, yet
Pius II. could urge, with some show of truth, that it could not
be called an entire failure. It was true that the Papacy had not
gathered round itself the enthusiasm of Christendom, and had
not drawn the powers of Europe from their national jealousies to
common action for the common weal. But at least the Congress had
shown the sincerity of the Pope's intentions, and had freed him
from blame. Pius II. had not disguised from himself the difficulties which beset the politics of Europe ; he had hoped that
a little enthusiasm might sweep some of them away. He had
forgotten that the restored Papacy was scarcely in a position to
appeal to the enthusiasm of Europe. He had forgotten his own
antecedents, but others had not. He had been too closely connected with the questionable intrigues which brought about the
Papal restoration to stand high in the estimation of Europe.
The shifty diplomat was not likely to be trusted however cleverly
he talked about common interests. The appeal of Pius II.
awoke no general response.

Yet the Congress of Mantua had its results. If it had not
succeeded in raising Europe above its particular interests, it at
least brought those interests clearly to light. Pius II. was able
to gauge the attitude of France towards Naples ; he saw that
Germany centred round the new power of Bohemia, and was
able to consider how far he could cope with the Bohemian king ;

[1] ' Fatemur non omnia facta sunt quæ putavimus, sed neque omnia præter-
missa : neque maxima neque minima sunt quæ Christiani principes promisere,'
was the judgment of Pius II. *Orationes,* Mansi, ii. 79.

he saw in Sigismund of the Tyrol the strength of the remnants of the German neutrality. Above all things, the Congress of Mantua established the system of Italian politics, and gave the Pope a commanding influence. Pius II. saw that his interests lay in opposite directions. As an Italian power he could not satisfy France; as head of the Church he could not satisfy Bohemia or pacify Sigismund. With the greatest desire for peace at home and war against the Turk, he saw the probability of the failure of his crusade before the threats of war at home. To pacify Europe he was asked to sacrifice Italy and the Church. It would need all his cleverness to avoid this dilemma. In preparation for the difficulties which he foresaw, he strengthened the Papal armoury by the Bull ' Execrabilis.'

CHAPTER VII.

PIUS II. AND THE AFFAIRS OF NAPLES AND GERMANY.

1460-1461.

BOOK
IV.

Civil war
in Naples.

BEFORE Pius II. left Mantua war had broken out in Naples, and events soon made it necessary for the Pope to decide what part he was prepared to play. Alfonso had won the kingdom of Naples by his own sword, and ruled it with magnificence. His strong hand and statesmanlike wisdom had kept in subjection the barons, who had grown in power and turbulence during the long period of conflict to which the kingdom had become habituated. They had accepted Ferrante at first, but soon raised their heads in conspiracy against him; for civil war increased their power and suited their interests. They had been so long accustomed to play off one claimant against another that they hastened to seize the opportunity which was now offered to their spirit of lawlessness. The withdrawal of Piccinino from the States of the Church had alienated from Ferrante's side that powerful condottiere general. Headed by the Prince of Taranto, the Neapolitan barons plotted against Ferrante, and invited René to prosecute his claims on Naples.

Jean of
Anjou in
Naples.
October
1459.

René himself had had enough of Neapolitan warfare, and preferred to lead an artist's life in Provence. But his son Jean assumed the title of Duke of Calabria, and received promises of help from the King of France, and from Genoa, which was then under French influence. Moreover, Jean took possession of twenty-four galleys, which had been built out of the proceeds of the Turkish tithe levied on France by Calixtus III., and which then lay at Marseilles. On October 4, 1459, Jean set sail from Genoa, and appeared before Naples. He landed at Castellamare, and the barons of Naples one by one flocked to his standard. Ferrante was confounded at this almost universal treachery and scarcely knew where to turn. Only the coming of the winter saved him from disaster; he shut himself up in Naples, and summoned Pius II. and Sforza to his aid. The first object of their endeavour was to prevent the Angevin party from receiving the aid of Jacopo Piccinino, who on withdrawing sulkily from the States of the Church had sought to enrich himself at the expense of Gismondo Malatesta, Lord of Rimini. Gismondo was a strange mixture of an unscrupulous condottiere and a munificent patron of art and letters. He adorned Rimini, held a splendid court, and cast longing eyes on the dominions of his neighbour Federigo da Montefeltro, Duke of Urbino. Federigo and Piccinino made common cause against him, and at Mantua he had called on the Pope to mediate. Pius II. was in too great need of soldiers to refuse his favour even to one who, like Gismondo, openly avowed his contempt for all religion and lived in defiance of all law. Pius mediated between Gismondo and his enemies, but sold his mediation at a good price. He took into his hands, as security for a payment of 60,000 ducats due from Gismondo to the King of Naples, Sinigaglia and Fano, which he afterwards conferred on his favourite nephew. Piccinino, by this mediation of the Pope, saw himself a second time robbed of his prey and was more indignant than before against Pius II. and Ferrante. The first object of Pius II. and Sforza was to prevent Piccinino from making his way from Cesena, where he was posted, to Naples. They trusted to Federigo of Urbino; while Piccinino was aided by Malatesta, and secretly by Borso of Este.

When Pius II. left Mantua he retraced his steps to Ferrara, where Borso perfidiously offered to treat with Piccinino in his behalf; but Pius II. was not deluded by this offer. He pursued his way to Florence, where he conferred with Cosimo de' Medici about the condition of Italy, and urged on him the prudence of supporting Ferrante for the purpose of excluding the French from Italy. Florence had always been on the Angevin side in Naples, and Cosimo was not convinced. Nor did Pius II. succeed in inducing the wary Florentines to accept his decree of a tax for the crusade; he might perhaps be permitted to tax the clergy, but the laity demurred. On January 31, Pius II. entered Siena, where he took up his abode for some time.

The archbishopric of the city had just become vacant, and
Pius II. conferred it on his nephew Francesco de' Todeschini, a
youth of the age of twenty-three.

Creation of
Cardinals.
March
1460.
When the period in the Lenten season arrived at which
creations of Cardinals were usually made, Pius II. announced
his intention of exercising his power. On March 5, he summoned the Cardinals to a Consistory; they agreed to the creation of five new Cardinals, on condition that only one should
be a nephew.[1] 'You will not,' said Pius II., 'refuse a sixth
whom I will name as above all controversy.' The Cardinals
pressed that he should be named before they consented. Pius
refused, and ultimately had his own way. He named Alessandro Oliva, General of the Augustinian Order, a man renowned for piety and theological learning. The others were
the Bishops of Reati and Spoleto, men whom Pius II. needed
for the government of the States of the Church; the nephew
Francesco, Archbishop of Siena, Niccolo di Fortiguerra, a relation
of Pius II.'s mother, and Burchard, Provost of Salzburg, whose
nomination was not announced till other Transalpine Cardinals
were created. Pius II. was of opinion that he had deserved
well of Italy for creating five Italian cardinals. He was also
proud of the fact of having created two of his own relatives in
the same Consistory. It must be admitted that his two relatives both proved themselves worthy men. Fortiguerra was
the chief adviser of the Pope in military matters, and the
nephew Francesco was himself raised to a brief tenure of the
Papacy in 1503.

Troubles in
Naples.
The ecclesiastical festivities consequent on this creation
were disturbed by the news that Piccinino had succeeded in
eluding Federigo of Urbino and the Papal Legate, who were
watching him, and by forced marches had made his way along
the coast into the Abruzzi. Men said that both Federigo and
the Pope had connived at his escape, being glad to see their
own territories free from the risk of a protracted war.[2] The
arrival of Piccinino was a new terror to Ferrante; but Pius

---

[1] 'Ea lege adjecta ut nepos unus esset,' says Pius II., *Com.* 98. He seems
to wish to represent that the Cardinals desired one nephew, as he says (99),
'negavit se promoturum fuisse [nepotem] nisi cardinales multis precibus id
exegissent.'

[2] Simoneta, in Mur. xxi. 709 : ' Quod sibi quisque timeret ne bellum in sua
finitimorumque ditione renovatum diutius quam vellent duceretur.'

II. sent him reinforcements under his condottiere general Simonetto.

While awaiting news from Naples Pius II. lingered in Siena, which he loved so well, under pretext of his health. It would seem that, after his long life of wandering and exile, Pius returned with deep satisfaction to the scenes of his youth, where only he could be genuinely happy and content with the simple enjoyments of country life, which are always dear to a man of real culture. Pius feasted his eyes on the lovely landscape which from the hills of Siena lay open to his view, in all the freshness of fine spring weather. He made his health a reason for indulging his taste for country life by expeditions to Macereto and Petrioli in the neighbourhood. The language of Pius II. is interesting as showing his manysidedness, his keen susceptibility to the pleasures of the eye. 'The pleasant springtime had begun; and round Siena all the valleys smiled in their dress of leafage and of flowers, and the crops were rising luxuriant in the fields. The view from Siena was inexpressibly charming; hills of a merciful height, planted with fruit trees and vines, or ploughed for corn, overhang pleasant valleys, green with crops and grass, or watered with a constant stream. There are, moreover, many woods, resonant with the sweet song of birds, and every height is crowned by magnificent country houses of the citizens. On one side are splendid monasteries peopled with holy men, on the other the castellated houses of. the burghers. The Pope passed with joy through this country, and found the baths equally delightful, lying in a valley about ten miles from the city. The land is watered by the river Mersa, which is full of eels, sweet in flavour though small. The valley at its entrance is cultivated, and full of castles and villas, but grows wilder as it approaches the baths, where it is shut in by a stone bridge of massive workmanship, and by cliffs covered thick with trees. The hills which circle the valley on the right are clad with evergreen ilex, on the left by oaks and ash trees. Round the baths are small lodginghouses. Here the Pope stayed a month, and though he bathed twice a day, never neglected public business. Two hours before sunset he would go out into the meadows by the riverside, and in the greenest spot received embassies and petitions. The countrywomen came daily, bringing flowers and

Dissolute
life of
Cardinal
Borgia.

strewing them in the way by which the Pope went to the bath,
content with the reward of kissing his foot.' [1]

While leading this simple life at Petrioli the Pope was
scandalised by hearing of the dissolute life of Cardinal Borgia,
who already showed the qualities which were to render him
infamous as Alexander VI. A story reached the Pope that an
entertainment given by Borgia was the talk of Siena. The
Cardinal had invited some Sienese ladies to a garden, from
which their fathers, husbands, and brothers were carefully excluded; for five hours the Cardinal and his attendants had
engaged in dances of questionable decorum.[2] Pius II. wrote
him a letter of severe yet friendly remonstrance. 'If we were
to say only that this conduct displeases us, we should be wrong.
It displeases us more than we can say; for the clerical order and
our ministry is brought into disrepute, and we seem to have
been enriched and magnified, not for righteousness of life, but
for an occasion to licentiousness. Hence the contempt of
kings, hence the daily scoffs of the laity, hence blame on our
own life when we wish to blame others. The Vicar of Christ,
who is believed to permit such things, falls into the same
contempt. Remember your various offices and dignities. We
leave it for yourself to judge if it befits your station to toy with
girls, to pelt them with fruits, to hand to her you favour the
cup which you have sipped, to look with delight on every kind
of pleasure, and to shut out husbands that you may do this
with greater freedom. Think of the scandal you bring on us
and on your uncle, Calixtus III. If you excuse yourself on the
ground of youth, you are old enough ' (Borgia was twenty-nine)
' to understand the responsibility of your position. A cardinal
ought to be irreproachable, an example of conduct, good not
only for the souls but for the eyes of all men. We are indignant if princes do not obey us; but we bring their blows upon
ourselves by making vile the authority of the Church. Let
your prudence, therefore, check this vain conduct; if it occurs
again, we shall be driven to show that it is against our will, and
our rebuke must needs put you to open shame. We have
always loved you, and regarded you as a model of gravity and

----

[1] *Pii II. Comment.* 101.

[2] 'Saltatum est, ut accepimus, cum omni licentia; nullis illecebris
amatoriis parsum.'—Raynaldus, 1460, No. 31.

decorum: it is for you to re-establish our good opinion. Your
age, which gives hopes of reformation, is the cause why we
admonish you as a father.'

On his return to Siena in June Pius II. soon had graver
matter of disquietude than the delinquencies of Cardinal Borgia.
News reached him that on July 7 Ferrante of Naples had been
repulsed in an attempt to storm the city of Sarno, into which
Jean of Anjou and the Prince of Taranto had retired; the
Pope's general, Simonetto, had been killed, and many horses
and men had fallen into the enemies' hands.   Stirred to
activity by the news, Piccinino, in the Abruzzi, attacked and
defeated, after a stubborn battle, Alessandro Sforza and
Federigo of Urbino. These battles, according to the custom
of Italian warfare, were neither bloody nor decisive.   The
Prince of Taranto would not let Jean of Anjou pursue his
victory by an attack on Naples, but led him into Campania,
where he spent the summer in sieges of insignificant places.
Still, the loss of these battles required additional men and
money from Sforza and the Pope, and for a moment Pius II.
began to waver.   The French party in the Curia did not
hesitate to show its joy at the Angevin successes; it even went
so far as to light bonfires in Siena and insult members of the
Pope's household. But Sforza was well versed in Italian warfare, and knew that the ultimate success lay with him who
held out longest.   He was more than ever convinced that his
own security lay in keeping the French out of Italy, and he
managed to inspire the Pope with greater confidence.[1] So Pius
II. put on a bold front to the Angevin envoys, who requested
him to recognise René, or, at least, declare himself neutral.   He
took his stand on the peace of Lodi, declared that he was only
recognising the existing state of affairs, expressed his willingness to decide the question of right if René submitted it to his
legal cognisance, and complained of René for disturbing by
violence the peace which was so necessary for a crusade.
Finally, he warned René against persisting in an appeal to a
future Council, lest he incurred the penalties of the decree

[1] Pius, in his *Comm.* 106, represents himself as heroic and patriotic in this
extremity; but Simoneta (Mur. xxi. 713) calls him 'exterritum auxiliique
incertum,' and Pius wrote to Federigo of Urbino bidding him not risk another
battle, 'quod status noster facile pati posset.' Raynaldus, 1460, N o. 63.

recently issued at Mantua.[1] Pius II., however, used Ferrante's distress as a means of obtaining grants for his own family. The town of Castiglione della Pescaia and the island of Giglio were given to Andrea, the Pope's nephew—not, as the Pope explains, for his own good, but for the good of the country, whose coast could now be made secure.[2]

The pleasant sojourn of Pius II. at Siena was brought to an end by bad news from Rome, where the Pope's absence was the signal for disorder. Cardinal Cusa, who had been left in charge of the city, soon left Rome for Mantua, and thence went to Brixen. The Sienese senator, whom Pius had put in office, was not strong enough to rule the turbulent city. The spirit which had been kindled by Stefano Porcaro still burned in the hearts of some of the Roman youth, but showed itself in a desire for license rather than for liberty. A band of three hundred youths, many of respectable families, enrolled themselves under Tiburzio and Valeriano, the two sons of Angelo de' Maso, who had been executed for his share in Porcaro's plot. They levied blackmail on the citizens, committed outrages with impunity, and filled the city with alarm. The governor, afraid of a rebellion if he called the citizens to arms, judged it prudent to withdraw from his palace in the Campo dei Fiori to the more secure shelter of the Vatican. This open show of incompetence emboldened the rioters, till at last one of them, who went by the appropriate nickname of Inamorato, seized and carried off a girl on her way to her wedding. The magistrates, driven to action, imprisoned Inamorato; his comrades captured one of the senator's household in return, and entrenched themselves in the Pantheon, where they obtained supplies by raids on the neighbouring houses, till at last, after nine days, the magistrates, fearing the end of such confusion, negotiated an exchange of prisoners, and Inamorato went free. The rioters in the city were supported by the barons of the Campagna, the Colonna, the Savelli, and Everso of Anguillara. The governor was afraid that, if he took strong measures against Roman citizens, he would not be supported by the citizens themselves, and might give occasion to an invasion from without. The Pope's nephew, Antonio, on his way to Naples,

[1] In Mansi, *Orationes,* ii. 158. Mansi wrongly dates it 1462.
[2] *Comm.* 108.

made an attempt to capture some of the rioters, but they re- treated into the palace of Cardinal Capranica, and Antonio was afraid to commence a siege. Tiburzio ruled Rome as a king, and did as he chose in all things. At last the chief citizens warned him that they could no longer endure this anarchy, and begged him to depart peaceably from the city. Tiburzio graciously consented, knowing that he could return when he pleased. He was escorted to the gates by the magistrates, as though he were some mighty prince, and the people thronged to witness his departure. Soon after this a band of rioters broke into the nunnery of S. Agnese, violated the nuns, and plundered the sacred vessels.

Pius II. was not to be moved from his pleasant quarters in Siena by these disorders so long as they only affected the citizens of Rome. It became a different thing when they threatened to imperil the States of the Church. Piccinino thought the opportunity favourable for an inroad into the Roman territory, and marched to Rieti; he was joined by the Colonna and Savelli, and plundered far and wide. At the same time a messenger between the Colonna and the Prince of Taranto was seized in Rome, and confessed that he was nego- tiating a scheme for seizing Rome in the interests of Jean of Anjou, the Roman barons, and Tiburzio. Pius II. wrote for help in great agitation to Francesco Sforza, who testily ex- claimed that his alliance with the Pope gave him more trouble than all his enemies.[1] However, he wrote to the Pope exhort- ing him to return to Rome, and all would still be well.

On September 10 Pius II. left Siena with tears at the thought that he might never revisit it. He journeyed over Orvieto to Viterbo, where envoys from Rome greeted him. The Pope, in his reply, dwelt on his unwillingness to leave Rome, and his regret that his health had prevented him from returning sooner; he grieved over the disturbances during his absence, and praised the Romans for their loyalty. ' What city,' he continued, ' is freer than Rome? You pay no taxes, you sell your wine and corn at what price you choose, you fill the most honourable magistracies, and your houses bring you in good rents. Who also is your ruler? Is it count or marquis, duke, king, or emperor? Greater still is he whom you obey—

---

[1] Simoneta, p. 717.

the Roman Pontiff, successor of S. Peter, Vicar of Jesus Christ, whose feet all men desire to kiss. You show your wisdom in reverencing such a lord ; for he enriches you and brings you the world's wealth ; you feed the Roman Curia, and it feeds you and brings you gold from every land.' They were fine words, but poor comfort for the absence of government from which Rome during the last year had been suffering.

As Piccinino was threatening Rome, many of the Cardinals counselled that they should go no farther ; but Pius II. proceeded, though he found scanty preparations made for his entertainment, and could only get rustic fare. When the governor and senator advanced to meet him, they found the Pope reclining beside a well, and trying by an early dinner to eke out the scanty supper of the previous night. Six miles from Rome he was greeted by the Conservators with a band of Roman youths, who had come to carry his litter. Many advised him to beware of these youths, who had belonged to the Tiburtian band. ' I will walk on the asp and the basilisk,' said Pius II. with a smile, ' and will trample on the lion and dragon.' The rebels carried him safely, and on October 7 Pius II. entered his capital.

Suppression of
the Roman
revolt.
October 31,
1460.
The conspirators still continued their plots ; but their rashness proved their ruin. One of them, Bonanno Specchio, entered the city secretly, and was there joined by Valeriano and others. An informer warned the Pope, and an ambush was laid for them in the Colosseum, where Bonanno was taken prisoner, though Valeriano and the others escaped. Tiburzio heard of this at Palombaria, a castle of the Savelli, near Tivoli, where he had his head-quarters. Thinking that his brother also was a prisoner, he hurried to Rome to the rescue with a band of only fourteen men. He raised the cry of ' Liberty,' and called on the citizens to rise. ' It is too late,' was the general answer. The Papal body-guard advanced against the rebels, who fled outside the city and hid in the brushwood. They were hunted by dogs, and were trapped like pheasants among the grass.[1] Tiburzio, with his hands tied behind his back, was led into the city, surrounded by a crowd, who mocked the king, the tribune, the restorer of ancient liberty. Tiburzio only

---

[1] ' Obvolutis sub herba capitibus in morem fasaniarum avium comperti per pedes abstracti sunt.'—*Pii II. Comment.* 119.

asked for speedy death, and the Pope interfered to prevent him
from being tortured. On October 31 Tiburzio, Bonanno, and
six others were hanged in the Capitol. In the following March
eleven others of his confederates shared the same fate.

The Roman plot thus ended in entire failure; but Pius II.
was helpless to reduce the rebellious barons or free himself
from Piccinino at Rieti. He had brought with him to Rome
only a small band of horsemen, and had no troops save those
in Naples. He wrote in distress to Sforza, even to Florence,
for aid;[1] but Florence saw no reason to interfere, and Sforza
was not sorry to give his troublesome ally a lesson, as Pius II.
had just given another instance of his readiness to take advantage of Ferrante. Terracina, which Pius II. had granted to
Ferrante for ten years, had been taken by the Angevins; but
the people unwillingly endured the French yoke, and called
for the protection of the Papal troops. The Pope's nephew,
Antonio, became master of the city; and the Pope, instead of
restoring it to Ferrante, conferred it on Antonio, to the great
wrath of Ferrante and the Duke of Milan. Still they could not
entirely abandon their ally; and during the winter the troops
of Sforza and Federigo of Urbino, feebly aided by Antonio
Piccolomini, forced Piccinino to quit the Papal States, and
reduced the Savelli to submit. Pius II., like most of his successors, trusted not so much to any definite organisation or
government to keep peace and order in his own dominions, as
to foreign help rendered on grounds of political necessity. He
spent the winter in restoring order in Rome, haranguing the
Romans on the advantage of the Papal Government, and receiving complaints against Gismondo Malatesta, which be appointed
Cardinal Cusa as his commissioner to investigate.

In the spring of 1461 Ferrante showed great activity in
recovering the castles near Naples, and some. of the barons who
had joined the Angevin side began to return to his allegiance.
These signs of a reaction in his favour made him more anxious
to hold his party together. He promised the Pope to confer
on the nephew Antonio the hand of his illegitimate daughter
Maria and the Duchy of Amalfi. Antonio at the head of
the Papal forces went to justify these promises in the field,
but was not very successful. The decision of the Neapolitan

Rising of
Genoa
against the
French.
March
1461.

---

[1] Raynaldus, 1460, No. 70, 71.

war was suddenly transferred from Naples to Genoa, where an attack of the exiled party of the Adorni and Fregosi on March 10 succeeded in raising the city on their side and drove the French into the citadel. Charles VII. of France at once sent reinforcements to their succour, and René of Anjou set out himself for Genoa. But the Genoese, supported by Sforza, fell upon the French troops and nearly annihilated them. René, unfortunate as ever, had to withdraw hastily to Marseilles. The French garrison in the castle was driven to surrender. Genoa was again free from French influence; the Angevin party in Naples saw itself cut off from supplies, and deprived of its chief support. In Naples itself nothing of moment was done, save that the brave Albanian leader, Scanderbeg, brought to the aid of Ferrante a troop of 800 horse, who distinguished themselves by a few plundering raids, and then departed to the worthier task of defending their own land against the Turk.

Pius II. meanwhile saw his home troubles disappearing. Rome was quiet; Piccinino had gone; the rebellious barons were reduced; his nephew Antonio was prospering in Naples. In June 1461 the Pope gratified his love for Siena and his desire to exercise his oratory by canonising Catharine of Siena, the Bull of whose canonisation he tells us that he dictated himself. Anxious to escape the summer heat in Rome, he departed early in July for Tivoli, under the escort of Federigo of Urbino, with ten squadrons of horse. 'The Pope was pleased with the flash of arms, the trappings of men and horses, as the sun gleamed on shields, breast-plates, nodding plumes, and forests of lances. The youths galloped on all sides, and made their horses move in circles; they brandished their swords, levelled their spears, and engaged in mimic contests. Federigo, who was a well-read man, asked the Pope if the great heroes of antiquity had been armed like men of our day. The Pope answered that in Homer and Virgil mention was made of every arm now in use, and many that were used no longer. So they fell talking about the Trojan war, which Federigo wished to make little of; while the Pope asserted that it must have been great to leave such a memory behind. Then they talked about Asia Minor, and were not quite agreed about its boundaries. So the Pope afterwards used a little leisure at Tivoli to write a description of Asia Minor from Ptolemy, Strabo, Pliny, Q. Curtius, Solinus, and Pomponius Mela, and other ancient writers.'[1] So ready was Pius II. to receive pleasure from outward impressions, so active was his mind to turn with unabated freshness to a new topic of interest. In Tivoli Pius II. began the rebuilding of the citadel, so as to have a strong fortress of defence for the Papal territory, and busied himself in the reorganisation of the monastery, from which he ejected the Conventuals and established Observants in their stead.

CHAP. VII.

Eighteen months had now passed since the end of the Congress of Mantua, and nothing had been done in the matter of a crusade. The Neapolitan war had absorbed all the forces of the Pope and all the military resources of Italy; nor was Germany more free from political complications. Bessarion, in spite of the infirmities of age, hastened from Mantua in the winter storms to be present at the Diet of Nürnberg on March 2, 1460. Few princes appeared, and they paid no heed to Bessarion; for attention was all directed to the war which was imminent between Albert of Brandenburg, the friend of the Pope and Emperor, and Lewis of Bavaria, the leader of the opposition to the Emperor. Soon the war broke out and ended in the rapid discomfiture of Albert, who was obliged to surrender all that his opponent claimed. The Emperor suffered by this defeat of his chief partisan, and became more powerless than ever. Bessarion sorrowfully went to Vienna to hold there the second Diet, which had been resolved at Mantua. Not till the middle of September did the Diet meet; and then none of the princes appeared in person. In vain Bessarion reminded their representatives of the promises made at Mantua; in vain he asked them to agree to the levying of a tenth in Germany. They answered with many protestations of zeal, but said that they had no powers to do anything definite. The Germans were lukewarm, and Bessarion was not the man to conciliate them. In vain he employed his eloquence; his words seemed only to be twice-told tales.[2] The only means that Pius II. could devise for kindling the zeal of Germany was to offer the title of general of the crusading army to the Pfalzgraf Frederick, the military leader of the

Fruitless Diets in Germany. 1460-1461.

[1] *Pii II. Com.* 136.
[2] *Ibid.* 126: 'Verba ejus quasi fabulas exceperunt.'

BOOK
IV.

Further
quarrel of
Cusa and
Sigismund
of Austria.
1460.

dominant party.   Frederick refused the proffered honour, and
Bessarion, early in 1461, left Germany, vexed and dispirited.

Yet the Pope was not entirely free from blame for the
dissensions of Germany. There, as in Italy, the requirements
of ecclesiastical politics were a disturbing cause. Pius II.
could not unreservedly put himself at the head of a united
Christendom, because the needs of the Papal policy led him to
take a part in creating internal dissensions. The quarrel between Cardinal Cusa and Sigismund of the Tyrol had only been
patched up at Mantua, and broke out afresh immediately upon
Cusa's departure to his bishopric. Neither party had any confidence in the legal termination of their disputes. Hostilities
were carried on by both alike. At length Sigismund determined on making a bold stroke. In April 1460 Cusa was at
Bruneck negotiating with Sigismund, displaying his usual
obstinacy, and threatening to betake himself again to the Pope.
Sigismund sent him a formal defiance, as did also most of the
vassals of the Church of Brixen. Gathering his forces, Sigismund closed round Bruneck, and Cusa found himself a prisoner
in his hands. He granted all that Sigismund demanded, with
the intention of protesting that it was extorted by violence.
As soon as he could escape he fled to the Pope at Siena and
clamoured for aid. Pius II. would willingly have escaped
a conflict; but he could not overlook violence offered to a cardinal, and behind Sigismund stood the hated Gregory Heimburg, the representative of the German opposition to the
Papacy. The Pope issued an admonition to Sigismund, in which
he declared that his criminality was proved by its notoriety,
and had involved him in the penalty of excommunication : he
was willing, however, to hear him personally, and summoned
him to a Consistory to be held on August 4. Sigismund in
reply assumed that the Pope was ignorant of Cusa's encroach-
ments on the rights of the Count of the Tyrol, which had made
his capture at Bruneck a necessary step. He detailed his
grievances, and appealed to a better-instructed Pope. Sigismund's attitude was conciliatory, but decided ; he stood on the
ground of the conciliar movement against the arbitrary action
of an individual Pope, and by so doing interposed a technical
objection against the validity of the coming sentence, while he
still left the dispute open to friendly settlement.

But Cusa would be satisfied with nothing but unconditional submission to his demands, and the Pope was determined to do away with every trace of the conciliar heresy. The Emperor also was glad to see Sigismund in trouble, as he had shown himself a dangerous neighbour. Accordingly, when August 4 arrived, and Dr. Blumenau, as Sigismund's proctor, handed in the appeal, the Pope's wrath broke out against him. He was seized and imprisoned as a heretic for drawing up and presenting an appeal contrary to the bull 'Execrabilis.' Blumenau escaped, and fled in terror across the Alps to his master. On August 8 the Pope declared that the penalty of excommunication had been incurred by Sigismund, all who had joined with him in defying Cusa, all who had been hostile to Cusa, and especially the inhabitants of Bruneck. He followed this by declaring the dominions of Sigismund under an interdict, and took the see of Brixen under the Papal protection till its bishop could return.

CHAP. VII.

Pius II. threatens Sigismund with ex- communi- cation. August 1460.

Sigismund was prepared for this, and knew that excommuni- cation and interdict had little force when directed against an entire people. The men of the Tyrol gathered round their Count, and so long as they stood by him he had little to fear. On August 13 Heimburg drew up for Sigismund a second appeal, in which he said that, as all human judgment might err, the remedy of appeals had been devised by our forefathers as a help for the oppressed. As the Pope's conduct showed that his ears were closed to justice, it was useless to appeal to him when better instructed: 'We appeal, therefore, to a future Pope, who may revise the doings of his predecessor; further, to a General Council, to be held in accordance with the decrees of Constance and Basel. Nor is this appeal a subterfuge, as we do not wish to avoid the course of natural justice. As the Pope has rendered himself notoriously suspected, we will accept any impartial judge whom he may name; we do not refuse his sentence as president of a General Council. If this be denied us, we appeal further to the whole people of our Saviour Jesus Christ; we appeal to all who love justice and favour in- nocency. If this be denied us, we call God to witness that it is not our fault that justice is not done, and that we are oppressed.'[1] This spirited document was meant for general

Sigis- mund's protest against the Pope. August 1460.

---

[1] This remarkable document is given in Goldast, *Monarchia*, ii. 1587, and in Freher, *Rerum Germanicarum Scriptores* (ed. Struvius), ii. 201.

publication; it was addressed directly to the public opinion of
Christendom, and was fixed on the church doors even of Florence
and Siena.

A war of writings now began. Pius justified himself and
denounced Sigismund in letters addressed to all Christian people.
Cusa attacked the life and character of Sigismund. Heimburg,
in moderate language, but with many cutting references to the
early life of the Pope, detailed the grievances of his master.
So indignant was the Pope against Heimburg that he did not
scruple to write to the magistrates of Nürnberg and Würzburg,
ordering them to seize Heimburg's goods which were in their
cities, and bidding them no longer harbour one whom he called
' a child of the devil, the father of lies.'[1] Not content with
this, the Pope called on all the powers of Germany to seize
Heimburg, wherever he might be, and hand him over to the
judgment of the Church.

Heimburg's reply breathed the scornful honesty which
characterised his entire life. He is a noticeable figure in the
history of these times as the representative of German as
opposed to Italian culture, as the determined opponent of the
subtilty by which Æneas Sylvius had won back Germany for
the Papacy, as the resolute supporter of ecclesiastical reform for
his country. The personal antipathy of the two men lent a
zest to the struggle between Heimburg and the Pope; and
Heimburg never forgot in the Vicar of Christ the shifty secretary
of Frederick IV. The dignity of the Pope would not allow him
to answer Heimburg's personal thrusts; but he keenly felt that
the laugh was turned against him by Heimburg's dexterous
references to his past career. The answer of Heimburg to the
Pope's proceedings against himself is the most powerful statement of the position of the German reformers in that day.

He begins by complaining that the Pope has condemned
him unheard, unsummoned, by his own arbitrary power. He
has given no grounds, except that Christ set S. Peter as ruler
over His Church, and therefore that rebellion against the
successor of S. Peter is heresy. But Christ gave command-
ment to all the Apostles to teach all nations; and the successors

[1] ' Quidam ex patre diabolo mendaciorum natus, Gregorius de Heimburg,'
in Goldast, *Monarchia*, ii. 1591; also in Ebendorffer, ' Chronicon Austriacum,'
in Pez. *Rer. Aust. Scriptores*, ii. 930, where also is Heimburg's answer.

of the Apostles as a body are General Councils which ought, from time to time, to revise the actions of the Pope and correct his errors. The superstition which Pius II. is trying to set up, that the Pope is greater than a Council, must be overthrown. The Pope appeals to the Congress of Mantua in support of his decree; but that Congress was not a Council, but an assembly of ambassadors. The decree was made by the Pope and Cardinals simply that they might pillage Germany under the pretext of a crusade, and might not be hindered by any threat of a Council. ' A Council, the fostering mother of liberty, the Pope shudders at as though it were an offspring of unlawful passion ; by a monstrous decree he condemned it before its birth, and by his condemnation justified. His prohibition showed his fear; his condemnation has given life to what was almost obscured by long silence. He would have been more prudent if he had imitated Solon, who, when asked why he had enacted no special penalty against parricide, answered, " Lest by forbidding I might suggest." Wherefore, prelates of Germany, hold to this point of the Council as the strongest fortress of your freedom. If the Pope succeed in carrying it, he will tax you at his pleasure, will take your money for a crusade, and send it to Ferrante of Naples. For the Pope is fond of bastards ; for that reason he calls Heimburg " a child of the devil," because he was born in lawful wedlock. He calls Heimburg also greedy, turbulent, lying. If he strove with blessings, he would be answered; as he strives with curses, he must find another to reply. I am not such a one. My goods are less than my deserts ; I have done more work than I have received pay ; I have always loved liberty more than flattery. These are no signs of greed. Let the Pope consider his own past and the life he once led.

' I leave these personal matters and go back to the Pope's decree. If the whole body of the Apostles was above Peter, a Council is above the Pope. If an appeal can be made to the Pope during a vacancy, it can be made to a Council which is not summoned ; for the power of the Church, like the Church itself, never dies. By forbidding such an appeal the Pope treats us like slaves, and wishes to take for his own pleasures all that we and our ancestors have gained by our honest labour. The Pope calls me a chatterer—the Pope, who is himself more talkative than a magpie. I own I have given some attention to the windiness

of words, but I have never for that neglected the study of civil
and canon law; the Pope has never even smelt at them, but
has contented himself with sheer verbosity.　I profess myself a
member of the lawyer tribe; the Pope is one of those who think
that everything can be managed by the force and artifice of a
rhetorician.　If the Pope excommunicates me for talking, who
deserves the penalty more than himself, who has no merit save
wordiness?　The Pope declares me guilty of treason; he is
using a flynet to catch an eagle.[1]　He calls me a heretic because
I say a Council is above the Pope; I call him a heretic because
he says that the Pope is above a Council.　He orders my goods
to be confiscated; I trust that I live amongst those who count
my services as of more value than any gain they could expect
from my possessions.　He says that they who seize my goods
will do a service to the Catholic Church; such a statement
would be ridiculous if we had not seen at Mantua the Pope's
folly when he, with a flow of words, praised adultery and
illegitimacy.

'So much for the Pope's charges.　Yet all men may appeal
from an inferior to a superior tribunal.　Like the woman who
appealed from Philip drunk to Philip sober, I appeal from the
Pope angry to the Pope appeased, from the topical orator to the
same man when his fit of wind is over, when he has sent away the
Muses and has turned to the canon law.　In the second place,
I appeal to him, if he will bind himself to judge according to
the decision of a good man.　In the third place, I appeal to any
man above suspicion to whom the Pope may choose to delegate
the matter.　In the fourth place, I submit myself to the judgment of the Pope, if he will remove all cause for suspicion.
Finally, if the Pope contemn all these, nothing remains save to
appeal to the Universal Church, as men of old appealed from
the Senate to the Roman people.　Let not the Pope object
that the Church is not assembled; that is not my fault, but his.'

Contro-
versy with
Heimburg.
This answer of Heimburg's was largely circulated throughout Europe, and Pius II. keenly felt its bitter sarcasm.　By
his attack on Heimburg the Pope had made a serious mistake:
he had given a private person an opportunity of making an

---

[1] Heimburg makes a pun here which is untranslatable: 'Irretiat ipse
Reatinos suos, aut eos, quos servili metu constrictos habet; mecum erit (Deo-
duce) libertas Diogenis et Catonis.'

onslaught on personal grounds upon the Papacy. So long as
Heimburg was writing in Sigismund's name, he could only
speak on general grounds of ecclesiastical grievances.   By attempting to crush a private person, Pius II. exposed himself to
the indignity of a private attack, which it was beneath his lofty
position to answer or even to recognise.   One of his friends in
the Curia, Teodoro de' Lelli, Bishop of Feltre, answered in the
Pope's behalf, and asserted in the strongest terms the principles
of the restored Papacy—the necessity of a Papal monarchy over
the Church, the divine institution of the rights of S. Peter and
his successors.   He paid back the sneers of Heimburg with the
contemptuous vituperation which the language of ecclesiastical
controversy has always bestowed on one who can be branded
with the name of heretic.[1]   This only gave Heimburg an opportunity of returning to the charge.   'Like a Molossian hound,'
he said, 'I will track my prey even through the snow.'   He
scoffed at Lelli as the Pope's stalking-horse, content to put his
vanities into shape and bear blows on his behalf. The Pope
himself will do nothing.   'If you were to put before him the
library of Ptolemy, you would not call him away from his care
for Corsignano and the Piccolomini.   But if your other follies,
Lelli, turn out as well as this, you will get your reward, and
your crown will soon be red with a Cardinal's hat.'   He hit
Cusa, calling him 'a hard and rigid man, stern, ungenial, in-
exorable, vehement in stirring up others, keen in discovering
those who can help him or hurt his adversary, with no wisdom
to help himself, and no restraint over his passion.'   He next
considered the proceedings of the Congress of Mantua, whither
he went himself to test the Pope's sincerity.   'I laid before
him and the Cardinals obvious considerations of the difficulties
in the way of a crusade.   I urged that it must be a decided
success, or it would do more harm than good.   I showed that
agreement amongst the soldiers was necessary for success, and
pleaded that the establishment of peace between the Emperor
and the King of Hungary was the first step to be taken.   I
spoke to the dead ; I told my story to the deaf.   All the juice
of the Jubilee was exhausted, and the Pope and Cardinals were

[1] The pamphlet of Lelli and Heimburg's answer are given in Goldast,
Monarchia, 1595, and in Freher, ii. 228. The greater part of both is taken up
with technical arguments for and against the Papal supremacy.

seeking something on which to fasten like leeches. You, Cardinal Cusa, answered my arguments for prudence by saying,
"Let us lay all this aside, and put our trust only in God,"—
which was the same as saying that rashness and not wisdom
ought to direct affairs. This is the heresy of Gregory Heimburg,—his constancy in resisting the Pope's avarice, his persistency in giving wise advice. This is his sacrilege,—his plea for
liberty, his support of the oppressed, his defence of General
Councils, which the Mantuan decree aimed at overthrowing.
This is his treason,—he disturbed the Papal plot for taming
Germany.' The defence of Lelli had only given Heimburg a
chance of going further in his attack upon the whole policy of
the Pope.

Pius II. no doubt had been led by Cusa to think that a little
determination on his part would raise the Tyrol in rebellion
against Sigismund, and would bring upon him many foreign foes.
The Pope was careful in his interdicts to save all the rights of
the House of Austria: neither the Emperor nor his brother
Albert was to be injured, and might if they chose seize the
Tyrol for themselves. But no one stirred against Sigismund.
The Pope vainly tried to incite the Swiss; but they preferred
to use the opportunity to make a peace which satisfied their
own interests. The Pope appealed on all sides for someone to
punish Sigismund; but even his ally the Duke of Milan refused
to move, and would not allow the excommunication to be
published in his dominions. In this state of things Pius II.
felt himself bound at least to do something; and, by way of
opening up a new stage in the proceedings, which might pos-
sibly lead to new negotiations, he issued on January 23, 1461, a
citation to Sigismund and his associates to appear within sixty
days and answer to a charge of heresy. The citation called
Sigismund 'a principal limb of Satan,' declared him suspected
of the heresy which is above all other heresies, of not believing
the article of the Creed, 'I believe in one Holy Catholic and
Apostolic Church,' seeing that he refused to heed the censures
of the Pope, who was the head of that Church.[1] Probably the
Pope thought that by transferring the matter to a doctrinal
ground he might open a way to reconciliation.

But Sigismund and Heimburg remained true to their policy

[1] In Freher, ii. 191.

of appeal, and answered by renewing it. The Pope summoned Sigismund for despising his censures—he did not recognise the validity of those censures. The Pope summoned Sigismund's adherents to Rome, more than 100,000 men ; who was to nurse the children and look after the country in their absence ? Did he wish to drive a whole people into banishment ? What had rustics to do with disputes about the Creed, which was the business of theologians ? Sigismund believed in the Church of the Apostles' Creed and of the Nicene Creed ; but the Creed did not ask him to believe in the Church in the same way as he believed in the persons of the Trinity. He could not say anything about the obedience required by the Pope and Cusa, lest he should be called to worship a creature instead of the Creator.[1] He renewed his appeal to a future Council, which the Pope, contrary to the decrees of Constance, was striving to bind and fetter. The Pope took no notice of this appeal, but in the greater excommunication, issued on Maundy Thursday, Sigismund and Heimburg appeared in the same class as Wicliffites, Pirates, and Saracens.

As the next step in the controversy, Cardinal Cusa wrote an anonymous pamphlet, with the object of separating Sigismund from Heimburg. He besought Sigismund to return to the Christian faith and shake off the man who had so long misled him. Heimburg retorted, and at once exposed his anonymous foe. ' Crab, Cusa, Nicolas,' he began, playing on Cusa's family name of Krebs, ' who call yourself Cardinal of Brixen, why do you not come openly into the lists ? ' In this strain he answered Cusa's statements one by one, and repeated his own arguments.[2] It was clear that Heimburg was a dangerous controversialist, and that he and Sigismund stood firm in their position.

Nor was the quarrel with Sigismund the only one in which Pius II. was engaged in Germany. In 1459 the Archbishop of Mainz died, and there were two candidates for the vacant office, Diether of Isenburg and Adolf of Nassau ; each had three votes in the Chapter, and the seventh vote, which decided the election, was said to have been secured by bribery in favour of Diether. When

CHAP. VII.

Further appeal of Sigismund.

Strife about the Archbishopric of Mainz. 1459–61.

---

[1] ' Jam satis respondimus nos credere unam sanctam Catholicam et Apostolicam Ecclesiam; non autem in illam, ne latriam soli Deo debitam creaturæ et facturæ impendamus.'—Freher, 195. He draws a difference between ' Credo in ecclesiam ' and ' Credo ecclesiam.'

[2] In Goldast, *Monarchia*, ii. 1624. Freher, ii. 255.

the representative of Diether sought the pallium from the Pope
in Mantua, Pius II. wished to use the opportunity. First he
required that Diether should assent to the levy of a Turkish tithe
in Germany; then he summoned him to appear at Mantua.
Diether sent his excuses and a proctor to arrange about the
payment of annates, which were negotiated by bonds drawn on the
bankers of the Curia. These obligations he afterwards repudiated,
alleging that his proctor had been induced to promise more than
the ordinary payment. He refused to go to Rome when summoned, brought his complaints before the Diet, spoke of a
future Council, and welcomed Heimburg at his court. His object clearly was to frighten the Curia and escape the payment
of the money which had been promised on his behalf. The
judges of the Papal Camera pronounced an excommunication
against Diether for not paying his debts. Diether replied
that he had offered to pay all that his predecessors had paid ;
if that was refused, he appealed to a future Council.

Scheme
for the de-
position
of Frede-
rick III.
1460-1461.
The differences with Sigismund of the Tyrol and with the
Archbishop of Mainz were troublesome enough in themselves;
but they began to wear a more serious aspect in the light of
the movement in German politics, which agitated the end of
the year 1460. It became clear that King George of Bohemia
was scheming to depose Frederick and obtain the Imperial
crown. Already the plan of setting aside the feeble Frederick
had often been mooted ; the defeat of Frederick's chief ally, the
Markgraf of Brandenburg, and the power of the Bohemian king,
gave a new impulse to the wish to have a reorganisation of
Germany under a competent head. In Church matters George
of Bohemia purposed to work for the summons of a Council, and
sent Heimburg to secure the co-operation of Charles VII. of
France. Secretly a scheme was formed between George of Bohemia and the Pfalzgraf; the Archbishop of Mainz was only
too willing to join in anything that would overthrow the Emperor and the Pope. The Archbishop of Trier and the Elector
of Saxony were both related to the Emperor, and could hardly
be won over, unless the Markgraf of Brandenburg set them an
example. A Diet at Nürnberg, March 1461, called on the
Emperor to reform the empire and war against the Turk; it
invited him to appear personally at a Diet in Frankfort in June,
when the conspirators hoped to proceed to a new election.

The Emperor and the Pope were now genuinely alarmed. Pius II. wrote letters to all the German princes, defending his action in the matter of the Turkish tithe. The Emperor began to negotiate peace with Hungary, and forbade the meeting of the Diet at Frankfort. The citizens of Frankfort sided with the Emperor and closed their gates against the princes. Instead of a Diet in Frankfort an assembly was held at Mainz, at which the only Electors present were the Pfalzgraf and Diether of Mainz. The Pope sent representatives, and Heimburg came to plead the wrongs of Sigismund of the Tyrol. The discussions turned almost entirely on ecclesiastical matters; but Diether was only seeking his own interest, and was easily won over to withdraw his appeal to a Council and submit himself to the Pope's indulgence. Still he did not trust the Pope, nor could the Pope trust him. Pius II. was secretly engaged in taking measures to overthrow Diether, and his emissaries were busy at Mainz. The assembly separated without any definite conclusion. Matters in Germany advanced into a new stage by the outbreak of a war between the Emperor and his brother Albert of Austria, who, in August 1461, advanced with his forces against Vienna.

CHAP. VII.

Alarm of Pope and Emperor.

It was of great importance to cause a diversion in Germany, and Pius II. was ready to do so by attacking Diether of Mainz. He had sent John of Flassland, Dean of Basel, as a confidential agent to Mainz, and John had succeeded in raising a party against Diether. It was agreed that the Pope should depose Diether, and set up in his stead Adolf of Nassau, whom the Archbishop of Trier, the Markgraf of Baden, the Count of Wirtemberg, and others, promised to support. Secretly John collected evidence against Diether and bore it back to Pius II. in his summer retreat at Tivoli. There, with equal secresy, Pius II. laid the evidence before the five Cardinals who were with him. They agreed that the charges against Diether were matters of notoriety, and that a regular process against him was unnecessary. On August 21 Pius II. issued a Bull deposing Diether;[1] at the same time Adolf was appointed, by a Papal provision, archbishop in his stead. Armed with these docu-

Deposition of Diether of Mainz. August. 1461.

---

[1] The matter is told by Pius II., *Comment.* 143, &c., and in his Bull, Raynaldus, 1461, 21. Diether's side is given by Bodman in *Rheinischen Archiv,* iv. 7, &c.

ments, John of Flassland hurried back to Mainz. Adolf gathered
his friends around him, took Diether by surprise, and was en-
throned on October 2. Diether made his escape, called on the
Pfalzgraf for help, and renewed his appeal to a future Council.
Both sides gathered their forces round them and prepared for
war.

Thus, in the middle of 1461 Pius II. saw in Germany also
his crusading policy rendered useless by the conflict between a
large policy of European interest and a policy of small expediency. The Pope might preach a crusade, might exhort Europe
to peace, but the question was, Where was peace to begin?
The Pope did not see his way to set an example of patience.
He could not afford to let himself be smitten on one cheek
without resistance, for he was afraid lest he should be smitten
also on the other. So far from pacifying Germany, he was a
cause of dissension: in Mainz and in the Tyrol alike there was
warfare in the name of the Holy See. We cannot wonder that
the princes of Germany were equally jealous of their own rights,
and were more eager to use every opportunity of asserting their
own interests than to promote the well-being of Christendom.
Germany was distracted by intrigues and divided into parties.
The war of Albert of Austria against the Emperor attracted all
its attention.

CHAPTER VIII.

PIUS II. AND HIS RELATIONS TO FRANCE AND BOHEMIA.

1461-1464.

If Pius II. found nothing but disappointment and trouble in Germany, he had more cheering prospects in France. Charles VII. died on July 22, 1461, and from his successor, Louis XI., the Papacy expected great things. The Dauphin Louis had been on bad terms with his father, had fled from France, and, for the last five years of his father's life, had been a refugee in the Court of the Duke of Burgundy. As an outcast and a dependent Louis thought it wise to make friends where he could. He had entered into friendly relations with the Pope, whose aid might stand him in good stead if any attempt were made to set him aside from the succession. On the death of Charles VII. Louis returned in haste to France, and was surprised to find that he met with no opposition. But Pius II. did not forget the promises made by the exile, and on August 20 sent Jean Geoffroy, Bishop of Arras, as his legate to France to urge the abolition of the Pragmatic Sanction.

It was natural that the Papacy should hate the Pragmatic Sanction with a bitter hatred. It was the standing memorial of the conciliar movement, and kept alive in Europe its principles and its endeavours. Moreover, it was a memorial of national opposition to the theory of the Universal Church: it expressed the claim of a temporal ruler to arrange at his pleasure the affairs of the Church within his realms. So long as France retained the Pragmatic Sanction she gave an example to which other countries might appeal, and was a standing threat to the Papal power. So long as the Pragmatic Sanction remained unrepealed, the restored Papacy could not claim to have entirely re-established its authority. The position of France was founded on the decrees of Constance and Basel, and

CHAP. VIII.

Accession of Louis XI. in France. July 1461.

The Papacy and the Pragmatic Sanction.

France was bound to sympathise with any movement which had for its object the assertion of the supremacy of a Council over the Pope.

Not only was the theory of the Pragmatic Sanction opposed to the principles of the Papal monarchy, but its working was still more prejudicial to the Papal interests. Grants of benefices in expectancy were entirely lost to the Pope, and reservations were only allowed to the smaller posts. Annates were not paid, and appeals to Rome were only made in important matters. The power of raising money in France was largely forbidden to the Pope, and the Curia saw an important source of revenue removed from its grasp. It was not to be expected that the Papacy should endure without a struggle this diminution of its authority. Eugenius IV. protested against the Pragmatic Sanction, and refused to recognise it. Nicolas V. trusted to the growth of the Papal prestige to overcome the opposition of France. Calixtus III. raised the question more decidedly by sending Cardinal Alain of Avignon as legatus a latere to raise Turkish tithes in France. Charles VII., however, would not let him exercise his functions except by his permission, and made him execute a document that he would do nothing contrary to the royal pleasure, or against the liberties of the Gallican Church as secured by the Pragmatic Sanction.[1] The King granted leave to collect tithes from the clergy, on the condition that the money was spent in building galleys at Avignon. He was true to the national principle that French gold was not to be taken to Rome, and he probably had even then formed the plan of using the galleys against Genoa or Naples when occasion suited. Yet many of the French clergy, headed by the University of Paris, protested against this Papal taxation and appealed to a future Council. Calixtus III. angrily bade his legate proceed to Paris, rebuke the insolence of the University, and demand the revocation of the appeal.[2] The King had to interpose and settle the difference by a declaration that he had granted the Pope a tithe from reasons of public expediency; though this had been done without the formal assent of the clergy, the King did not thereby intend to derogate from the liberties of the Gallican Church.[3]

---

[1] *Preuves des Libertés de l'Eglise Gallicaine*, ed. 1651, 496.
[2] Raynaldus, 1457, No. 55.   [3] *Preuves des Libertés* (ed. 1651), 566.

Charles VII. was firm in his adhesion to the Pragmatic Sanction; and the attack upon it made by Pius II. at Mantua awakened the determined resistance of the French, who regarded it as a political manœuvre of the Pope to justify his support of Ferrante of Naples. When Pius II. issued his Bull 'Execrabilis' France at once accepted the challenge. A Master of the University, Jean Dauvet, as proctor for the King, registered a formal protest that nothing in the Bull should deprive the King of his right to press for the summoning of a Council according to the Constance decrees; if the Pope were to inflict any ecclesiastical censures in France, the King would call on a future Council to judge between him and the Pope; if the Pope refused to summon a Council, the King would instigate the princes of Europe to summon it themselves.[1] Pius II. judged it prudent to take no notice of this protest; but he did not cease in his letters to Charles VII. to urge upon him gently and persuasively the abolition of the Pragmatic Sanction.[2]

It must not be supposed that the Pragmatic Sanction was an unmixed good to the Gallican Church. The Papal supremacy had been accepted by the Church throughout Europe because it set up a barrier against royal and aristocratic oppression. As the Papal sovereignty grew more and more exacting, churchmen were willing to rid themselves of its taxation, which seemed to outweigh the advantages of its protection. The Pragmatic Sanction of Bourges adopted so much of the reforming decrees of Basel as seemed to suit the national needs, and gave them validity for France by a royal decree. Thus the French Church was exempt from the technicalities of the canon law: the decree itself could be explained by royal judges, and left no loophole for Papal interference. Its provisions sounded fair; but they did not in practice come up to all they promised. It enacted that elections to ecclesiastical benefices should be free according to the canons: but this was subject to many exceptions in practice. First, there was the royal right of the *regale*, by which the King enjoyed the revenues of vacant benefices and the disposal of them during vacancies. If disputes arose about the election, as only

---

[1] See letter in Raynaldus, 1460, 46, &c.
[2] *Preuves*, 229.

too often happened, the King had as great an interest in pro-
longing the vacancy so as to enjoy the revenues, as had the Curia
in protracting the appeal that it might receive larger fees.
Besides, the nobles used their rights of nomination in such a
way as to override the Chapters.   Moreover, the Pragmatic
Sanction assigned to graduates of the Universities a third of
all vacancies, on the ground of encouraging learning.   The
Universities were not slow to claim their privilege, and were
skilful in extending its limits.   The jurisdiction in ecclesiastical
matters was exercised by the Parlement and the University of
Paris; and these bodies did not show themselves more disinterested or more expeditious than the Curia had been.   It is
doubtful whether the Gallican Church was more free from practical abuses under the Pragmatic Sanction than it had been
under the Papal rule;[1] but it made all the difference that at
least the oppressors were men of the same nation as the
oppressed, that French gold stayed in the kingdom, and did
not flow to Rome, where it might be used against the interests
of France.   There was no murmuring within France itself; the
French clergy were all willing to stand by the Pragmatic, and
the Pope had no opportunity afforded from within to justify
his interference.

Views of
Pius II.
about the
Pragmatic
Sanction.
Still the position of France was anomalous, and there was
some excuse for the view taken of it by Pius II. 'The prelates
of France,' he says, 'who thought that they would be made free
by the Pragmatic Sanction, were reduced to the most entire
slavery and became the creatures of the laity.   They were
compelled to answer in all causes before the Parlement, to
confer benefices at the will of the King, or other princes or
nobles, and to ordain unfit persons.   They were bidden to
pardon men whom they condemned for their misdeeds, and
to absolve excommunicated persons without satisfaction.   No
power was left them of inflicting ecclesiastical censures.   Whoever brought into France letters from the Pope which were
adverse to the Pragmatic, was liable to the punishment of
death.   Cognisance of episcopal causes, of metropolitan
churches, of marriages, of heresy, was taken by the Parlement.
Such was the presumption of the laity that even the most
holy body of Christ, borne in procession for the veneration of

[1] See Du Clercq, *Mémoires*, Bk. IV. ch. iv. and xxiv.

the people, or being carried to the sick, was bidden to stand still by the mighty hand of the King. Bishops and other prelates, venerable priests, were hurried to the public prisons ; estates belonging to the Church, and the goods of clergy, were seized on slight grounds by a decree of a secular judge. The Pragmatic Sanction gave rise to much impiety, sacrilege, heresy, and indecorum, which were either ordered or permitted by the ungrateful King.' [1]

The accession of Louis XI. opened up an alluring prospect to Pius II., who had already negotiated with him for the abolition of the Pragmatic. So bitterly was Louis XI. opposed to his father, that the reversal of his father's policy had in itself a charm for his mind. On his visit to his father's grave he allowed the Bishop of Terni, who had so grossly misconducted himself as Papal legate in England, to pronounce an absolution over his father's ashes, as though he had died excommunicated for his adhesion to the Pragmatic. The Bishop of Arras was sent by Pius II. to take advantage of this favourable state of mind of the King; and his zeal was spurred by the understanding that a cardinal's hat was to be the reward of his success. Louis XI. dismissed his father's ministers, and looked coldly on the Parlement and the University by whose aid the Pragmatic Sanction had so long been maintained. His policy was to maintain the royal power in its existing privileges, by the help of the Pope, rather than by the help of the constitution of the realm. It was the task of the Bishop of Arras to negotiate skilfully the details of such an arrangement.

While awaiting the results of this negotiation Pius II. spent the autumn in making an excursion from Tivoli to Subiaco, to visit the mighty monasteries that clustered round the cave of the great S. Benedict. As usual, he enjoyed a leisurely journey by the side of the Anio, and was pleased with the simple homage of the rustics. He would dine by a spring of water, with a crowd of peasants at a respectful distance. When he resumed his journey the peasants plunged into the water to fish, following the Pope in his course. When a fish was caught a loud shout called the Pope's attention to the fact, and the trout were given as a friendly offering to the Pope's

---

[1] *Pii II. Commentarii*, 160.

attendants.[1] From Subiaco Pius II. paid a visit to Palestrina, and on October 6 returned to Rome.

Soon after his return Pius II. was reminded of his crusading scheme, which the current of events had thrust into the background. The luckless Queen Charlotte of Cyprus came to demand help against the Turks. The island of Cyprus had been handed over by Richard I. of England to the House of Lusignan, under whose feeble and profligate rule it had been a medley of Greek and Latin civilisation. It was further distracted by being a field for the commercial rivalry of Venice and Genoa, and was a helpless prey to Egyptian pirates. Queen Charlotte in 1459 had married Louis, son of the Duke of Savoy; but her bastard brother, John, fled to Egypt, offered his homage to the Sultan, and, with the help of an Egyptian fleet, overran Cyprus, shut up Louis in the castle of Cerina, and drove Charlotte to seek for help in Western Europe. She was received at Ostia with royal honours. The Pope was favourably impressed with the Queen, a handsome woman of twenty, with merry eyes, a pleasant address, and stately carriage, who spoke in Greek manner like a torrent, but dressed in French fashion.[2] She poured out her griefs to the Pope, who magnanimously promised that he would never desert her, but pointed out that her misfortunes were due to the lukewarmness of Savoy at the Congress of Mantua. All that he could do was to provide her with means to go to Savoy and plead with her father-in-law. She went to Savoy, but with no result; she could only return to Venice, and thence make her way back to Rhodes.

Louis XI.
abolishes
the Prag-
matic
Sanction.
November
1461.

Meanwhile the Bishop of Arras was rapidly advancing the Pope's interests in France. Pius II. knew well how the national opposition in Germany had been overcome by a secret understanding to the mutual advantage of the King and the Pope, and he practised the same plan in France. The Bishop of Arras promised Louis XI. that the Pope would send a legate to France, who would dispose of benefices at the King's pleasure. Pius II. himself wrote to the King, commending his independent spirit, and urging him to abolish the Pragmatic without taking counsel with any. 'You are wise,' he said, 'and show yourself a great king, who are not ruled, but rule; for he is the best prince who knows and does what is right by himself, as we trust is the case

[1] *Pii II. Comment.* 167.   [2] *Ibid.* 179.

with you.' He adds significantly, ' If your prelates and the University desire anything from us, let them use your mediation; for if any Pope was ever well disposed to France, we certainly will be found the chief to honour and love your race and nation, nor will we ever oppose your honourable requests.'[1] Pius II. meant to imply that the King would find a close alliance with the Papacy to be the best way of making the French clergy dependent on himself. Louis XI. kissed the Pope's letter, and ordered it to be placed in a gold box amongst his treasures. On November 27, 1461, he wrote to the Pope announcing the abolition of the Pragmatic Sanction, and sent the letter to the Parlement to be registered as a royal ordinance.

Thus Louis XI., by the plenitude of the royal power, swept away the bulwark of the liberties of the Gallican Church, and Pius II. wept with joy to receive the news. Louis XI. had abolished the obnoxious decree without making any conditions; but he expected his reward, and it was a question for the Pope how he could best meet his views. With characteristic astuteness Pius II. used the opportunity first of all for his own advantage. He longed to use his power in the creation of Cardinals, and now laid before the College the necessity of pleasing the French King by creating some French Cardinals; the Ultramontanes had been omitted in the last creation, and their claims ought to be considered. The Cardinals, who were reluctant to see the College increased, were driven unwillingly to consent. Pius II. seized his opportunity, and having secured a majority by private interviews, proposed six creations in a Consistory on Dec. 18. The Cardinals sat in silence and looked at one another. Pius II. at once declared his creations, and the publication was made on the same day, though the Pope was suffering so severely from an attack of the gout that he had to entrust the ceremony to Cardinal Bessarion. The Cardinals created at the request of the French King were the Bishop of Arras, and Louis d'Albret, a prince of the blood royal. Besides these were Don Jayme de Cardona, a relative of the King of Aragon; Francesco Gonzaga, son of the Marquis of Mantua, a youth of seventeen; Bartolommeo Rovarella, Bishop of Ravenna, an old official, of great experience in the affairs of the Curia; and Jacopo Ammannati, Bishop of

---

[1] *Ep.* 887 (ed. Basel), dated October 26, 1461.

Pavia, the special favourite of Pius II., the only one of the new creations who was a scholar and a man of culture. Pius II. could now plume himself that he had done great things for Louis XI., who 'had obtained two cardinals from one litter,' as the Pope put it. He also sent him, on Christmas Day, a consecrated sword, with an inscription: ' Let your right hand, Louis, draw me against the furious Turks, and I will be the avenger of the blood of the Greeks. The Empire of Mahomet will fall, and again will the renowned valour of the French, with you for leader, reach to heaven.'[1] This was very pretty, no doubt; but Louis XI. wished for something more substantial. He had been led to suppose that the Pope, in return for the abolition of the Pragmatic, would withdraw from his alliance with Ferrante of Naples, and would even espouse the Angevin side. Pius II. had behaved as though he were wavering in this matter. His ally, Francesco Sforza, had been seriously ill of a fever during the summer, and Sforza's death would have entirely changed the aspect of affairs. Pius II. held himself ready for any contingency ; he intimated to Louis XI. that he was weary .of the trouble of the Neapolitan war, and thought it better to rule the States of the Church in quietness.[2] But when the abolition of the Pragmatic Sanction was completed, when Sforza's recovery was assured, and above all the marriage of his nephew Antonio to Maria, the illegitimate daughter of Ferrante, solemnised, Pius II. began to be more resolute, and bethought himself that his honour would not allow him to abandon Ferrante.

Pius II. was disappointed to find that the new Cardinal of Arras, so soon as he had gained all that the Pope had to give, transferred his services to the King's side, and became an ardent negotiator in favour of the Angevin claims. He besought the Pope to ensure the favour of Louis XI. by withdrawing from the Neapolitan war. He offered, on the King's behalf, that Ferrante should have Sardinia with the title of

---

[1] *Pii II. Commentarii*, 184 :—

> ' Exerat in Turcas tua me Ludovice furentes
> Dextera; Graiorum sanguinis ultor ero.
> Corruet imperium Maumetis, et inclyta rursus
> Gallorum virtus te petet astra duce.'

[2] Simoneta, *Vita Sfortiæ*, in Muratori, xxi. 731 ; he says of Pius II. : ' Ut erat ingenio astuto callidoque.'

king, and the lands of the Prince of Taranto, and that the
Pope's nephew, Antonio, should have a portion of Calabria;
otherwise Louis XI. would ally with Venice and pour his troops
into Milan, so that the Pope would be left single-handed.   On
March 13, 1462, a French embassy, headed by the Cardinals of
Arras and Coutances, entered Rome to announce the abolition
of the Pragmatic, and to receive the Pope's answer about
Naples.   In a public Consistory the Cardinal of Arras presented
the royal letters abolishing the Pragmatic, spoke much in
praise of Louis, and said that so soon as Naples was secured for
the Angevin dynasty, and Genoa had again submitted to
France, Louis was ready to send 40,000 horse and 30,000 foot
against the Turks, drive them from Europe, penetrate into
Syria, and recover the Holy Sepulchre.   Pius II. was wearied
with the pompous and mendacious speech, and anxiously
awaited its end.[1]   He answered with equally high-sounding
praises of Louis XI. and of his predecessors on the French
throne; about Naples he briefly said that he would speak
privately.[2]   He placed the red hat on the Cardinal's head, and
proclaimed a general holiday for three days.   Rome blazed with
bonfires for joy at the Papal triumph in winning back the unconditional allegiance of France.

When the festivities were over the French ambassadors
returned to the Pope, who offered to negotiate a truce, or to
withdraw his troops, provided the Neapolitan question were
referred to a judicial decision of the Curia.   This was all that
the Pope would promise; and the embassy returned with loud
complaints of the Papal ingratitude.   If, in France, the abolition of the Pragmatic had been hateful at first, it now seemed
a positive indignity.   The story was current that Pius II., on
receiving the news, had waved his cap and cried out, 'Guerra,
guerra' (war, war), meaning that the increased revenues now
secured to him would enable him to carry on more vigorously
the Neapolitan war.   Pius wrote to Louis XI. to contradict this
story, and it was even judged wise that Cardinal Ammannati
should write in the name of the College and disclaim it.[3]   Louis

---

[1] *Comment.* 187 : 'Ampullosa miscens verba et aperta mendacia pro veris
affirmans . . . expectatum et diu desideratum finem fecit.'

[2] Mansi, *Pii II. Orationes,* ii. 103.

[3] *Cardinalis Papiensis Epistolæ,* 18.

XI. wrote angrily to the Pope to this purport :[1] 'I thought to win your kindness by benefits. I abolished the Pragmatic Sanction ; I gave you my free obedience ; I promised help against the Turks ; I gave a stern answer to innovators who talked about a Council ; I could be persuaded to nothing that was contrary to your dignity. Who would not have thought that this would have softened your harshness ? But the reverse has happened. You seek to drive from his kingdom my own flesh and blood. What am I to do if kindness will not win your unquiet spirit ? Shall I try the opposite way ? No, it is not my will to persecute the Vicar of Christ. I will pursue the way I have begun, though there is none of my counsellors who does not advise me otherwise. Perhaps some day you will repent.'

This letter was followed by the Seneschal of Toulouse, a man who knew neither Latin nor Italian, and delivered through an interpreter a message that if the Pope did not change his ways, he had orders from the King to bid the French prelates leave the Curia. At first this caused some alarm ; but Pius II. was shrewd enough to know that it was a mere threat. He answered that the French prelates might go if they chose ; they made a pretence, but did not go. Louis XI. felt that he had been out-manœuvred by the Pope ; embassies passed between them fruitlessly, and the national feeling in France only grew more strong against the Papacy.

Pius II. and George of Bohemia.

If Pius II. could flatter himself that he had succeeded in sweeping away from France the memorials of the Council of Basel, he was obliged to confess that he had been deceived in his hopes of obtaining a like result in Bohemia. George Podiebrad had lulled the Pope into a false security while he needed time to secure himself on the Bohemian throne, and by the Pope's help had made a truce for three years with the Catholics of Breslau. But the men of Breslau were not so confiding as the Pope, and watched George with suspicion. When at last George began to intrigue for the Imperial crown, Pius II. was driven to admit that his policy was opposed to the Papacy. As a claimant for the empire George was the leader of the anti-papal party, the upholder of a Council, the ally of Diether of

[1] We only have the letter given by Pius II., *Comm.* 207, who says, ' dictavit ad Pontificem *in hunc modum* epistolam.'

Mainz. The failure of George's scheme weakened his position: he had abandoned his attitude as mediator in the disputes of Germany; he had thrown off the mask, and had shown himself to be opposed to Pope and Emperor; he had alienated somewhat his Bohemian subjects, who suspected that in these schemes of higher policy their national interests might be betrayed. Pius II. began to listen more heedfully to the reports that came from Breslau. He pressed for the embassy which was to declare at Rome the obedience of Bohemia, according to the promise which George, before his coronation, had made to the Pope. At length the embassy, which had been so long delayed, arrived in Rome on March 10, two days before the arrival of the French embassy which was to announce the abrogation of the Pragmatic Sanction.

The coincidence seemed auspicious for the Papal success; but Pius II. was soon driven to admit that Bohemia was different from France. The Bohemian embassy was headed by Procopius of Rabstein, a Catholic, an old friend of Pius II., who had been his colleague in the chancery of Frederick III., and Sdenek Kostka of Postupic, an Utraquist baron who stood high in the King's confidence; with them was Wenzel Coranda, burgomaster of Prag. Pius II. adopted his usual plan of endeavouring to discover in a private interview the commission of the envoys, before he admitted them to a public audience.[1] On March 13 he summoned Procopius and Kostka, who said that they were sent to offer to the Pope the obedience of the Bohemian King ' as was customary and as his predecessors had offered it.' The Pope answered that the realm of Bohemia did not stand like other realms in the unity of the Church; the King had promised at his coronation to bring back his people from the error of their ways; before his obedience could be accepted he must take oath to do so. The envoys answered that they could only do what they were commissioned to do. The question was referred to a committee of Cardinals, chief of whom were Carvajal, Cusa, and Bessarion. There were many conferences and a repetition of the arguments that had been used at Basel; but the Bohemians remained firm to their position, that by accepting the Compacts they remained in the unity and obedience of the Church, and

Bohemian envoys in Rome. March 1462.

---

[1] The account of this embassy is given in a relation of Wenzel Coranda, which has been followed by Palacky, *Geschichte von Böhmen*, iv. pt. 2, 215, &c.

that they stood by the Compacts. On March 21 a public audience was given. Kostka, after making excuses for the delay of the embassy in appearing at Rome, professed the obedience of his King. 'You only offer the obedience of the King,' said the Pope, 'not of the kingdom.' Procopius whispered to Kostka, 'What shall we do? I will offer the obedience of my party, of which I am sure; do you the same on behalf of yours.' 'Speak in the name of all,' answered Kostka; 'what the King does all will accept.' Then Procopius repeated the declaration of obedience in the name of the King and the realm. 'If you have anything else to say,' said the Pope, 'say on.' Then Wenzel Coranda, with the loud voice and rapid speech which the Pope had so often heard from the Bohemians at Basel, set forth the origin of the Hussite movement, the troubles in Bohemia, the peace negotiations at Basel, and the Compacts; by holding fast to them King George had given peace to Bohemia; that peace was endangered by the open and secret attempts made in Bohemia and outside it, to do away with the Compacts; the Bohemians were called heretics and schismatics. He besought the Pope to free Bohemia from all suspicion, to give it peace and enable it to turn its energies against the Turks, by confirming the Compacts so that there should be no misunderstanding in the future. The Pope answered in a long speech which gave a history of Bohemia, showed how prosperous it had been while it remained Catholic, complained that the Compacts, which were a conditional indulgence granted by the Council of Basel, had been so violated in every way by the Bohemians, that they had ceased to be binding. Finally, he declared that the demand made of him was impossible, for it was contrary to the unity of the Church; yet he would consult further with the Cardinals.

More conferences were held and more arguments were advanced on both sides. Carvajal pointed out the weakness of the Bohemian position. They declared that only the recognition of the Compacts could give Bohemia peace; yet peace was impossible so long as there were two different rituals. The aim of the Utraquists was the abolition of the Catholic ritual and the union of Bohemia under their own views. As the Compacts would never bring peace, he urged that it was better to drop them. Kostka was not a disputant; but he was for that reason all the better fitted for his office. He answered that, if the King were to attempt anything against the Compacts, the Hussites would rise and a more bloody war than had been seen before would devastate Bohemia; he trusted that the Pope would listen to the request that had been made; if not, Bohemia must maintain itself in the future as it had done in the past. It was clear that nothing could come of controversy, and on March 31 the Pope gave his answer to the envoys. He spoke words of warning about the obedience which had been offered on the King's behalf: ' We praise the King, who seeks the door of the Lord, which is the Apostolic seat, to which are entrusted the keys of the kingdom of heaven. The King is wise in seeking the true door, the true pasture, the true shepherd; ourselves, though undeserving, he honours as the Vicar of Christ. In virtue of that obedience just offered we bid him remove all novelties from his kingdom; obedience is shown not in words but in deeds.' [1] Then the Pope turned to the request that he would confirm the Compacts. He repeated the familiar arguments used at Basel against the Communion under both kinds. The Compacts gave an indulgence in Bohemia and Moravia to those who united with the Church; they promised that the Council would give power to certain priests to administer the rite under both kinds to those who desired it in Bohemia. It did not appear that the Council had ever empowered any priests to do so, nor that Bohemia had returned to the unity of the Church. No argument in favour of their request could be founded on the Compacts themselves. If he was asked to grant them by his apostolic power, it would be impossible for him to grant what his predecessors had refused, what would scandalise Christendom, give offence to other nations and be harmful to themselves. ' As Christ said to the sons of Zebedee, so say I to you, "Ye know not what ye ask." We are the stewards of the mysteries of God; it is for us to feed the sheep and guide the flock of the Lord in the way of safety. Not all understand what is for their good.'

When the Pope had ended, his Procurator-fiscal rose and read a public protestation, ' that our most holy Lord the Pope has extinguished and destroyed the Compacts granted by the Council of Basel to the Bohemians, and has said that the Communion under both kinds is nowise necessary to salvation, nor

---

[1] *Pii II. Orationes*, ii. 93.

BOOK
IV.

will he hold the obedience made to be real obedience, until the King, uprooting and extirpating all errors, has brought the kingdom of Bohemia to union with the Roman Church, and has conformed himself and his kingdom in all things and through all things to the Roman Church.'[1]

Bohemian policy of Pius II.

There was now no doubt of the Pope's meaning. Next day the Bohemian envoys took leave of the Pope, who received them in his garden and gave them his blessing. He bade them tell the King that he was willing to do all he could for Bohemia consistently with his honour and that of his office. Let the King himself communicate under one kind only, and the people would follow the example of a prince whom they loved. If he remained obstinate the Church would have to try other methods; it was better to have the glory of restoring his land to the union of the Church than to suffer compulsion. The Bohemians asked that someone should accompany them to carry the Pope's instructions to the King. The Pope commissioned for this purpose Fantinus, a Dalmatian priest, who had for two years acted as King George's proctor at Rome. He was a Catholic who had discharged his mission with good faith in the King's intentions. The Pope, who had been suspicious of him at first, was now secure of his integrity; and the nomination of the King's own proctor seemed a conciliatory measure. On April 3 the Bohemians left Rome. Pius II. had taken a decided step, and had forced George to declare himself. The Bohemian King had to consider whether he would face the difficulties of a breach with the Pope and with his Catholic subjects and neighbours, or whether he would abandon the Utraquists. Pius II. awaited his opportunity in either case.

Reception of the head of S. Andrew in Rome. April 11, 1462.

From the troublesome task of receiving refractory embassies Pius II. turned gladly to the more congenial occupation of organising an impressive display of ecclesiastical ceremonial. A holy relic, the head of the Apostle S. Andrew, had been carried away from Patras by the despot Thomas Palæologus that it might be saved from the Turks; and Pius II. offered it a secure refuge in Rome. It was received at Ancona by Cardinal Oliva and safely conveyed to Narni. Now that times were peaceable, Pius II. prepared for its reception at Rome. Three

[1] In Palacky, *Urkundliche Beiträge*, in *Fontes Rerum Austriacum*, vol. xx. p. 269.

cardinals were sent to bring it from Narni, and on Palm Sunday, April 11, carried their precious burden to Ponte Molle, where on the following day the Pope went out to meet it. The weather was wet and stormy, but Pius II. tells us with great satisfaction that the rain ceased during the time of the procession. A lofty stage was erected in the meadows by the Ponte Molle, large enough to contain all the clergy in Rome, and in the middle was an altar. The Pope and prelates advanced carrying palms in their hands. As the Pope mounted the platform on one side, Bessarion and two cardinals advanced on the other side bearing the reliquary. The Pope received it with reverence, placed it on the altar, and kneeling, with pale face and tremulous voice broken by tears, poured forth a prayer of welcome. The people who thronged around wept tears of devout joy, and when the Pope, rising, exposed the relic to their gaze, the 'Te Deum' burst from their lips. Then was sung a hymn in Sapphic verse specially composed by the Bishop of Ancona.[1] Then the Pope bore the relic to the city and deposited it on the altar of S. Maria del Popolo, where he himself passed the night.

The ceremony of the next day seemed likely to be spoiled by the rain, which fell with violence during the night; but the prayers of the sightseers prevailed, and in the morning the sun shone again.[2] Still the streets were covered with mud, and the Cardinals expressed a desire to take part in the procession on horseback. The Pope would not allow the effect to be

---

[1] It ended—

> 'Da Pio vitam, rogitamus omnes;
> Solus in Turcos animo perenni
> Ausus Alpinos superare montes
>   Arma vocavit;
> Et caput præbet proprium libenter,
> Nomen ut Christi veneretur orbis;
> Et viam nostræ videat salutis
>   Perfidus hostis.'

               Pii II. Commentarii, 196.

[2] Pius II. tells us that the distich rushed into his mind:—

> 'Nocte pluit tota, redeunt spectacula mane,
> Divisum imperium cum Jove Cæsar habet.'

Campanus adapted it to the requirements of piety:—

> 'Nocte pluit tota, redierunt tempora nostra;
> Nox fuit acta hostis, lux erit ista Dei.'

               Pii II. Comm. 197.

marred by this incongruity ; he ordered all who could to walk;
those who were too old or feeble might go to S. Peter's and
there welcome the procession on its arrival. ' It was a great
sight,' he tells us, ' full of devotion, to see old men going on
foot through the slippery streets, carrying palms in their hands,
with mitres on their hoary heads, their eyes fixed on the ground,
intent on prayer: many nurtured in luxury who could scarce
endure to go a hundred yards on horseback, on that day easily
accomplished two miles on foot, through the mud and wet,
carrying the weight of their priestly attire.' The Pope's eye
was keen to see how some of the more corpulent managed to
carry the burden of their flesh. ' It was love,' he exclaims,
' that bore the weight ; nothing is difficult to one who loves.'
Pius II. was delighted with the devotional effect produced upon
the people ; he estimated that more than 30,000 wax candles
were burned during the procession. The whole city was decorated, and boys dressed as angels sang hymns along the way.
At last the Pope reached S. Peter's. Bessarion delivered an
address, and Pius II. followed with a few words : he gave his
benediction, and indulgences were announced in his name. So
pleased was the Pope with the success of his festival, that he
gave notice that on Easter Sunday he would celebrate mass in
S. Peter's, and would again display the head of S. Andrew. It
was four years since the Romans had seen a Pope say mass.
So crippled was Pius II. with the gout that means had to be
devised by which he might perform the office half-seated.

But ecclesiastical ceremonies could not satisfy the restless-
ness of the Pope. He longed for the delights of country life and
for greater freedom ; and on the pretext that his health required
him to take baths, he set out in May for Viterbo. There he
was carried into the fields in the fresh hours of early morning
' to catch the breeze and admire the green crops, and the flax
in flower which imitated the hues of heaven, and filled beholders
with delight.' In Viterbo also Pius II. resolved to try the effect
of a splendid ecclesiastical ceremonial in celebration of Corpus
Christi Day. He caused to be erected a tent adorned with
splendid hangings and tapestries ; from this tent to the Cathedral each cardinal undertook the decoration of a portion of
the way. The Arras tapestries of the French Cardinals provoked great admiration. The Cardinal of S. Sisto contributed

a representation of the Last Supper. Carvajal set forth a dragon surrounded by a herd of horrible demons ; as the Pope passed by, S. Michael descended and cut off the dragon's head, and all the demons fell headlong, barking as they fell. Bessarion had a band of quiring angels. But Cardinal Borgia outdid all others in splendour. He erected a large tent covering the road with purple trappings ; as the Pope approached, two angels advanced and knelt in reverence to the Host which the Pope carried ; then turning towards the tent they sang, ' Lift up your heads, O ye gates, and King Pius, Lord of the world, will come in.' Five kings and a band of armed men tried to prevent the entrance, crying out, ' Who is the King Pius ? ' ' The lord strong and mighty,' replied the angels ; the curtain fell, the kings and their troops knelt before the Pope and sang songs in his honour, to the accompaniment of a band of musicians. A wild man of the woods led in chains a lion, and strove with him from time to time, as a symbol of the Pope's might. Next Cardinal Forteguerra showed his taste in the decoration of the chief piazza, which he roofed in with star-spangled cloth ; on twelve columns sat twelve angels, who sang in alternate verses ; in the middle of the piazza was a representation of the Holy Sepulchre, with the sleeping soldiers and the angels keeping watch around. An angel descended by a rope and sang in honour of the Resurrection. A gun was fired ; the soldiers woke and rubbed their eyes ; the tomb opened, one bearing the banner of the Resurrection stepped out, and in Italian verse announced to the crowd that their salvation had been won. In the piazza before the Cathedral, Cardinal Milo had fitted up a representation of heaven ; on the housetops were stars and angels and God in glory, while below was the tomb of the Virgin. Mass was said in the Cathedral, and the Pope blessed the people. As he left the Church, the tomb of the Virgin opened, and a lady stepped out who was borne by angels to the housetops, dropping her girdle on the way. Then she was received into heaven amid the joy and songs of the angels.[1] The Pope was so satisfied with all he saw that day, that he

---

[1] I give the realistic description in the words of the Pope himself : ' Cui occurrens Filius, idemque Pater et Dominus in fronte osculatus matrem, et oblatam æterno Patri, ad dexteram suam collocavit. Tum canere cælestium spirituum agmina.'—*Com.* 210.

says, 'Those who beheld these wonders thought that they had
doubtless entered the realms above, and said that they had seen
while alive in the flesh the presentation of their heavenly
country.'

The restless spirit of Pius II. was not long content to
remain at Viterbo. Taking occasion of an alarm of plague, he
withdrew to Bolsena, and thence gradually made his way towards
his native Corsignano, which had probably been his destination
when he first left Rome. He wished to see the buildings with
which he had adorned the little town. He strove still further
to convert it into a memorial of himself by changing its
name Corsignano into Pienza, and elevating it to the dignity of
a bishopric. From Pienza Pius II. went to the baths of Petrioli
and thence to Todi : he did not return to Rome till December 18.

Humilia-
tion of
Sigismondo
Malatesta.
October
1463. Meanwhile success attended the Papal policy in Italy. On
August 18 Ferrante of Naples won a decided victory over Picci-
nino and Jean of Anjou at Troja. The effect of his success
was to shake the confidence of the Angevin barons and incline
them to sue privately for peace. In September the powerful
Prince of Taranto abandoned the cause of Jean ; and in
October a French embassy came to propose a truce to the Pope.
Pius II. objected to include in it Gismondo Malatesta, an excommunicated heretic; and the negotiations were broken off. The
Pope had no wish to make peace with Malatesta, who now
seemed entirely in his hands. He had in the summer invaded
the lands of the Pope's nephew, Antonio Piccolomini, but had
been surprised by Federigo of Urbino, while attempting to
withdraw from Sinigaglia which he had seized, and had been
entirely defeated on August 12. His troops were scattered ; his
castles fell before Federigo; he was driven to seek the good
offices of Venice to escape entire destruction. In October 1463
he had to accept the Pope's terms. His proctors publicly ab-
jured in his name the heresies with which he was charged, and
the Pope freed him from the ban on condition that he fasted
every Friday on bread and water. He was left only in possession of Rimini and the territory a few miles round. The power
of the Malatesta was humbled, and Pius II. could plume himself on having won a signal success. But it was a small thing
that a Pope who wished to hurl Europe against the Infidel

should triumph in overthrowing, after four years of warfare, one
Italian baron.

In Germany Pius II. was not so successful. Since 1461
that unhappy country had been plunged in war and confusion.
Frederick III. was attacked by his brother Albert of Austria,
and peace was only made by the interposition of the Bohemian
King. The opposing parties in the Empire had broken out
into open war. On one side was the Pfalzgraf and Lewis of
Bavaria, on the other Albert of Brandenburg and Charles of
Baden, the Emperor's friends. With this the struggle about
the Archbishopric of Mainz was naturally connected, and the
claims of Diether were supported by the party opposed to the
Emperor. On July 2, 1462, the Emperor's friends were
entirely defeated. Frederick III. was afraid of an attack from
his brother Albert and was helpless; nor could the Pope do
more than utter mild expostulations in behalf of peace.

This state of affairs in Germany reacted speedily on Bohemia, where Pius II. had hoped by his resolute demeanour to
strike terror into George, compel him to abandon the Compacts and reduce Bohemia to obedience to Rome. George was
not in Prag on the arrival of the Pope's envoys. When he received from Fantinus the Pope's demands that he should publish
through Bohemia the Papal sentence, should himself and his
family receive the Communion under one kind only, and should
dismiss all heretical priests, he did not give an immediate
answer, but referred the matter to a Diet which was to meet
in Prag on August 9. No doubt the part which the King then
resolved to play was largely determined by the weakness of the
Pope's friends in Germany.

The Diet met on August 12 in large numbers. Catholics
and Utraquists alike were doubtful about the King's attitude;
there was great uneasiness and great excitement. The King
took his seat, with the Queen on his right hand, and briefly
opened the proceedings. By their advice, he said, he had sent
an embassy to Rome in confident expectation of securing
thereby the peace of the realm: what obstacles had hindered
this result he knew not. He asked the envoys to give their
own account of what had befallen them, that common counsel
might be taken about the future. Procopius and Kostka gave
a plain and truthful statement of the facts. Then George

rose and said, ' We wonder what the Pope means: perhaps he
wishes to plunge again into discord this kingdom which was
united by the Compacts. How can he annul and take away
what the Holy Council of Basel, which is more than he, and
what his predecessor Eugenius, granted us ? If every Pope is to
abolish what his predecessor granted, who will feel justice
secure? We are accused by the Pope of not fulfilling the
oath made at our coronation. We will read the oath.' Then
he read it in Bohemian, and continued : ' You hear that we
swore to do away with all heresy from our realm. Assuredly
we have no love for heretics. But to do as the Pope wishes
and make the reception of the Communion under both kinds
a heresy was never our intention ; for it is founded on Christ's
gospels, and on the institution of the primitive Church, and,
moreover, was granted to us by the Council of Basel as a privilege for our devotion and virtue. The Pope says we swore to
put this away. By no means ; but know for certain that as
we were born and bred in this Communion, and in it were
raised to the royal dignity, we promise to uphold it and live
and die in its defence. So too our queen, our children, and all
who wish to do us pleasure, will live as we do in this matter.
Nor do we think that there is any other way for the salvation
of our souls than to die in this faith, and use the Commu nion
under both kinds according to the Saviour's institution.'

The King hoped to produce an impression by this unexpected firmness, and he succeeded. The majority of the Diet
burst into tears. George determined to use his opportunity :
he ordered the confirmations of the Compacts of Sigismund,
Albert, and Ladislas to be read, and finally the Compacts
themselves. Then he arose: ' I ask you all severally,' he said,
' if anyone, whoever he be, wishes to defy and defame us and
our kingdom on account of the Compacts, will you lend us your
aid ? ' The Utraquists, after a brief conference, deputed Kostka
to answer. ' Sire,' he said, ' we hear with pleasure that you, your
queen, and your children, are with us in the faith, and we
give you thanks without measure ; we promise sev erally to aid
you with our goods and with our persons in upholding the
Compacts.' The King turned to the Catholics, who were in a
minority in the Diet: ' Say openly what you will do.' The
Bishops of Breslau and Olmütz were present amongst others.

After a short conference amongst themselves, Sdenek of Stern-
berg answered: 'Sire, you know that hitherto we have had
nothing to do with the Compacts; but as we were born and
have lived in the union and obedience of the Roman Church,
so we wish to live and die. As you say that you must hold
to the faith in which you were born, we argue that we must
equally hold to ours. As to your request for help, you never
asked our counsel, as is customary; as you have decided to
maintain the Compacts, you will have the help of those by
whose counsel you made your decision. We promise to do all
that is according to justice for your honour and that of the
kingdom.' The King, who had apparently expected that the
Catholics would have been impressed by the scene which they
had witnessed, was dissatisfied with this answer, and pressed
for something more explicit. It was, however, now late; and
the Catholics demanded an adjournment, which the King at
last granted, saying that next day they would hear Fantinus as
the Pope's nuncio; 'as my proctor,' he added, 'I have some
complaints against him.'

Fantinus was warned that the King was much displeased
at him for his conduct as royal proctor at Rome; but he was
resolved to discharge faithfully his mission from the Pope.
When he appeared before the Diet he seemed to the Catholics
'like a lamb among wolves;' and it was noticed that he had no
special place assigned to him, but stood among the rest. He
spoke in Latin, and his words were translated into Bohemian by
an interpreter. He began by demanding the rights of an ambassador to speak freely according to the law of nations. When this
was granted, he proceeded to attack the Compacts, denounced
as heretical the Communion under both kinds, asserted the
Papal power and defended the Pope's action in annulling the
Compacts. He insisted that the interpretation of George's
oath was a matter for the superior, not the inferior; for him
who received, not for him who gave the promise; for the Pope,
not for the King. George angrily interrupted him. 'In all
and everything we have kept our oath as our conscience
teaches us. If the Pope or anyone wished us to interpret
it against our conscience, we would give him full satisfaction and support ourselves as best we could. We doubt not
that we keep our oath as truly as the Pope or anyone else.'

Fantinus resumed his speech undaunted. He went on to say that, if he had believed that the King wished to act as protector of the Compacts and of the Communion under both kinds, he would never have acted as his proctor ; he publicly renounced that office, and in the Pope's name declared the suspension from the priesthood of all clergy who upheld the Compacts ; he warned the King that he ran great risks in opposing the Pope's will. The King briefly said : ‘My lords, you have elected me your King and protector; you have the power of electing a lord, and you must stand by him.’ In private his anger blazed forth ; he bitterly complained of the indignities which Fantinus and the Pope heaped on him, and declared that he would be avenged. ‘You know,’ he added, ‘that on the Apostolic seat have sat many renegades and wicked men ; it is not the seat of holiness, but of pestilence. The holy seat is the union of all faithful people, and that is not Rome.’ [1]

If King George had hoped by his sudden display of firmness to kindle the enthusiasm of the Hussites, so that it should carry away the Catholics or fill them with terror, the boldness of Fantinus upset his plans. The grandeur of the King on the first day was overshadowed by the determined bravery of Fantinus on the second. The Catholic party at once plucked up courage and prepared for the contest, which began next day, when the King ordered Fantinus to be imprisoned for treacherous dealings as royal proctor, and also deprived Procopius of Rabstein of his office as Chancellor. The Bishops of Breslau and Olmütz at once fled from Prag, and it was clear that George's hopes of a peaceable settlement of Bohemia had failed. Fantinus was kept in prison for a short time, and Pius II. tells us that George visited him and said, ‘I can scarce restrain myself from strangling you with my own hands.’ ‘I expected a common executioner,’ said Fantinus, ‘but if a king puts his hands to the work I shall die more honourably ; but you will grudge me the glory.’ The mediation of Lewis of Bavaria persuaded George at length that it was unwise to imprison the Papal nuncio. In October Fantinus was released

---

[1] The account of this Diet, given by Pius II., *Comment.* 237, has clearly been elaborated from the two reports given by Palacky, *Urkundliche Beiträge zur Geschichte Georg's von Podiebrad*, p. 272, &c.

and returned to Rome, where Pius II. rewarded his services with a bishopric.[1]

If George had not succeeded in winning all the nobles to his side, he hoped that he might be more fortunate with the clergy. He ordered the administrator of the Arch-bishopric of Prag to summon all the clergy to an assembly on September 16, to hear what he intended for the good of peace. There came 714 clergy, of whom about 200 were Catholics. The Catholics assembled by themselves, and agreed who was to be their spokesman and what he should answer. Then they formed in procession, three abreast, and advanced to the royal presence, where the Utraquists under Rokycana were already assembled. The King spoke: ' We always seek the peace of our kingdom; but you priests quarrel amongst yourselves, accuse one another of heresy, refuse sepulture to the dead, exclude the living from the churches; you pollute your priest-hood by consorting with light women, play at dice, and commit many other disorders. Unless you change your manners we will proceed against you, as you have no spiritual judge. We bid you, however, observe faithfully the Compacts granted for the peace of the realm by the Council of Basel to our pre-decessors. If anyone does otherwise he will provoke our anger.' The Catholics listened in silence: after a short de-liberation they made answer: 'We thank your Majesty for the peace which we enjoy, and pray that it may long continue. We do not deny that ill deeds are done by the clergy; in such a multitude there must be some who are evil. Yet we do not know who they are: if you would point them out they should be punished, for we still have authority amongst ourselves. As to the Compacts, we answer as did your nobles. We never wanted them; we do not want them; the Roman See never granted them, but the Council of Basel gave them as an indul-gence. Whether or no those to whom the indulgence was given use it as it was granted, God must judge. The peace which you say the Compacts have brought we gladly accept: that they bring any aid in gaining our salvation we do not see. We feel sure that your Majesty will not hinder the Church of Prag in her ceremonies, and will not impose on us any other ritual than

---

[1] *Pii II. Comment.* 241.

that handed down to our ancestors by the Apostolic See—which
is the gate of heaven.'

King George angrily declared that he was no heretic : he
had never resisted the Apostolic See, but he would not abandon
the Communion under both kinds : he must obey God rather
than the Pope. He produced an intercepted letter from a
Catholic priest, in which he was denounced as a heretic : he
bitterly complained of such conduct. Next day the assembly
met again ; but George did not succeed in obtaining from the
Catholic clergy more than he had obtained from the Catholic
nobles. Yet he still strove to keep his position as a mediator.
Rokycana brought before him a complaint against one of the
clergy. ' You wish that everyone should obey you,' was the
King's answer, ' while you obey no one.' The assembly was
dismissed in peace. George did not attempt to interfere with
the Catholic services. In spite of the breach with the Papacy,
men said that the peace of Bohemia had never been more
secure.[1] Pius II. was ready to proceed to extremities : on
October 8 he issued a letter to the men of Breslau, releasing
them from their allegiance to George, ' as he had not returned
to the bosom of the Church, but held in his kingdom doctrines
that had been condemned.' The Pope was ready to plunge
Bohemia into another civil war ; George trusted that events
might still be too powerful for Pius II., and might drive him to
leave the Bohemian question alone, if not formally to ratify
the Compacts.

Position of
George as
regards
Germany.
The Bohemian King was soon able to claim the mediation
of the Emperor. Austria was a prey to plundering bands of
soldiers, whom Frederick III. was helpless to repress. The
people of Vienna rose in rebellion against their incompetent
prince. They solemnly defied him on October 5, called in his
brother Albert, and besieged Frederick in the citadel. George
of Bohemia went to the Emperor's aid. ' As an Elector
of the Empire,' he said, ' he felt himself bound to support his
lord.' By his means peace was made between the two brothers.
Albert was to govern Austria for eight years, and Frederick was
to be allowed to depart in safety. He left Vienna ignominiously

---

[1] Palacky, *Urkundliche Beiträge*, 281. *Zeitungen aus Prag*, October 5 :
' Die Slesier . . . habin vorstanden, das sie in besserm fride nye gewesin sein
denn itzunder.'

and withdrew to Neustadt; but it was understood that he was to repay his Bohemian ally by interceding on his behalf with the Pope. Though Pius II. was determined to continue his policy of opposition to the Compacts in Bohemia, he judged it wise to hold his hand for a time. He could not attack the King who held in his hands the peace of Germany.

Other struggles and other heresies claimed the Pope's attention. It was as difficult to keep the peace between the monastic orders as between the Catholics and Utraquists in Bohemia. Contests as fierce raged within the bosom of the Church as those which distracted it from without; and the heresies of Bohemia were not the only ones which the Pope was called upon to decide. The reaction that produced the Papal restoration intensified also a movement within the Franciscan Order for the revival of the old rule of S. Francis in all its pristine simplicity. The Minorites of the Observance, as they called themselves, denounced as renegades their brethren who were content to dwell in settled abodes and hold the property which the piety of their predecessors had won. The strife waxed bitter between the Observantists and Conventuals; and each party strove to gain the favour of the Pope. Eugenius IV., whose highest ideal was a monastic reformation, naturally favoured the Observantists, and hoped to make of them a bulwark of the Papal power. He gave them the privilege of electing a Vicar of their own, exempt from the authority of the General of the Order, and conferred on them other favours, which put them in a position of superiority over the Conventuals. Nicolas V. had no interest in these disputes, and to promote peace withdrew some of the special favours which had most irritated the Conventuals. This brought upon him the remonstrances—even the wrath—of the great leader of the Observantists, Fra Giovanni Capistrano; but Nicolas V. was not the man to be moved from his determination by clamour. It was now the turn of the Conventuals to act on the aggressive. They demanded that the Observantists should either renounce their separate Vicar, or should leave the Franciscan Order altogether, and call themselves 'Brethren of the Bull,' or 'The Privileged.' Calixtus III. in vain strove to make peace. Peace was impossible; but as Calixtus saw that the Observantists were useful for his purpose by preaching a crusade and gather-

ing Turkish tithes, he resolved to support them. Yet his Bull
wore the appearance of a compromise. All Franciscans were to
obey the General of the Order, and the Vicars of the Observantists were to attend the chapters; they were to submit to
the General three names, from whom he should choose one to
be Chief Vicar of the Observantists; this Vicar was to have over
the Observantists all the authority of the General.[1] The compromise only awoke new questions about the right of the Observantists to vote at the election of a General, to whom they did
not owe obedience. Pius II. revoked the Bull of Calixtus III., and
restored that of Eugenius IV. The alternations of the Papal
policy were admirably adapted to keep alive the spirit of
rivalry which they professed to heal.

Dispute
about the
worship
due to the
Blood of
Christ.
Under Pius II. the conflict entered upon a new stage.
Pius II. favoured the Observantists, because he needed them
for his crusading projects; and they, no doubt, thought that
the opportunity was favourable for gaining still higher privileges for themselves. One of their oldest and most respected
members, Fra Giacomo della Marca, took occasion, in preaching
at Brescia on Easter Sunday, 1462, to assert that 'the Blood of
Christ shed on the ground during the Passion was not an
object of worship, since it was separated from the Divine
Person.' It was an old question of dispute whether the Blood of
Christ so shed had lost, or not, 'the hypostatic union of the Logos.'
By raising the question at Brescia, the seat of the Dominican
Inquisitor, Fra Giacomo threw down the gauntlet, and showed
his wish to provoke a trial of strength. The Inquisitor
accepted the challenge, condemned the opinion as heretical,
and ordered Fra Giacomo to recant. But Giacomo appeared
in the pulpit, and after recounting his long services to the
Church during his career of forty years as a preacher, proceeded
to confirm his opinion by citing authorities. This was the
beginning of a furious strife; the people were divided between
the two parties, and the hatred of rival theologians was let
loose in all its fanaticism. The Bishop of Brescia in vain interposed. The matter was referred to the Pope, who proclaimed
a truce, and summoned both sides to a disputation at Rome.
Three eminent theologians appeared for either party; and the
dispute began before the Pope and Cardinals on Christmas

[1] Wadding, *Annales Minorum*, vi. 304.

Day 1462. For three whole days they argued, the Dominicans maintaining that the Blood of Christ, inasmuch as it returned to His body, never lost the hypostatic union; while the Minorites asserted that during the three days ·of the Passion this union ceased. Pius II. has preserved in his 'Commentaries'[1] a long record of the arguments; but he felt little real interest in the matter, and regarded the disputants with amusement. To him theological disputation seemed a form of athletic exercise, not merely mentally but physically. 'It was a pleasant and agreeable thing,' he says, 'to hear the fine intellects of learned men contend with one another, and to see now one, now another, shoot ahead. They strove, as was fitting before the Pope's majesty, with modesty and fear; but so sharp was the contest that, though it was the middle of winter and the world was stiff with frost, the disputants were bathed with sweat; such was their zeal for victory.' When all had been heard, the Pope conferred with the Cardinals for several days. The majority were on the side of the Dominicans; and Pius II. agreed with the majority. But he determined not to publish his decision, 'lest the crowd of Minorites, whose help was necessary in preaching against the Turks, should be offended.' He contented himself with accepting from the Dominicans, and entering in the Papal archives, a copy of a decision in their favour on this subject given by Pope Clement VI. in 1351. The Friars were contented not to have their doctrine condemned; and this momentous discussion was allowed to rest for a few years in peace.

Visit of Pius II. to Ostia. May 1468.

Pius II. had now established the custom of taking excursions for pleasure from Rome, and in May 1463 accepted an invitation from Cardinal Estouteville to pay him a visit at Ostia. Pius II. went, as a modern traveller would do, to inspect the antiquities and enjoy the natural beauties of the place. His enjoyment was slightly marred by a terrible storm of wind and rain, which rose suddenly in the night and wrought considerable havoc. As the Bishop's palace was not large enough to accommodate all the Cardinals and their attendants who had accompanied the Pope, many of them were sleeping in tents. The tents were blown away, and the occupants, in their attempts to gain shelter in the darkness of the

[1] Pages 279-292.

night, suffered many misadventures. Even in the palace the Pope was afraid that the roof might fall, and was being wrapped up that he might sit outside in the rain rather than run the risk indoors, when the wind ceased, 'as though fearing to incommode the Pope,' Pius complacently observes.[1]

After his return from Ostia Pius II. did not stay long in Rome. He again set out for an excursion to Albano; thence he went to Castel Gandolfo, rejoicing in the beauties of the Alban Lake; and finally to Rocca di Papa. As he journeyed along the Appian Road he was grieved to see the tombs being used as quarries for neighbouring buildings, and gave orders that they should be taken under the protection of the Pope. He returned to Rome for Whit Sunday, but at the end of June, complaining of the heat, departed to Tivoli, where he remained till the middle of September.

Piccinino deserts the Angevin cause in Naples. August 1463.

The summer of 1463 saw the end of several of the Pope's little contests. It was decisive for the Neopolitan war, which, since the battle of Troja, had lingered on while the Angevin barons were avowedly seeking to find what were the best terms they could make for themselves. Jean of Anjou discovered that he had been from the beginning the tool of the Neapolitan barons, headed by the Prince of Taranto. When the Prince of Taranto found that he was no longer profitable, he did not scruple to abandon his cause. The condottiere Piccinino was Jean's only support, and Piccinino was also preparing to desert him. In August 1463 Alessandro Sforza offered battle to Piccinino, which Piccinino did not find it convenient to accept. He came instead into Sforza's camp to talk matters over. His arguments, as given by Pius II., are extremely characteristic of the general condition of Italian politics. 'Why,' said he, ' do you wish to conquer me? It is I who bring you glory, riches, pleasure—all that you enjoy. Because I took up arms and overthrew the peace of Italy, you who were lying idle at home, were called to the field. Will you do any good by taking me prisoner? Who wants peace? No one, save priests and merchants, the Roman Curia, and the traders of Venice and Florence. Peace in Italy brings them all they want, and leaves us nothing to scrape together. In peace we are despised and sent to the plough; in war we become mighty,

[1] *Comment.*, p. 304.

and may follow the example of Francesco Sforza, who has
raised himself to a dukedom. Our policy is to refuse to
conquer, and prolong the war, the end of which is the end of
our gains.' Many of the captains agreed with Piccinino; but
Alessandro Sforza answered: 'Do not fear. Italy will never be
free from war till she is under one rule, and that is a far
distant prospect. Let us finish this war and betake ourselves
to a greater. You need not boast, Piccinino, as if you only kept
war on foot. Had not the Pope and the Duke of Milan sent
us against you, you would have finished this war long ago in
favour of the French, an unworthy undertaking for an Italian,
for one who had borne arms for Aragon and for the Church.'
Piccinino replied: 'I was driven to fight for the French because
no one else wanted me. Bred in arms, I could not leave the field.
I would rather have declared war against my own father than
have disbanded my troops. I served the French because they
gave me pay. Now I am free, and willing to negotiate with
you if you will give me worthy terms.' It was agreed that
Piccinino should be made Ferrante's commander-in-chief, with
a salary of 90,000 ducats, and should keep his conquests in the
Abruzzi. Ferrante and Pius II. in vain protested against these
terms; the military leaders were agreed, and all others had to
submit.[1] Piccinino changed sides, and Jean of Anjou retired
to Ischia, awaiting ships and men from France, which never
came. In April 1464 he left Ischia and returned to France.
Ferrante was now undisputed master of Naples; but he had
learned how little confidence he could place in his barons, and
waited quietly his opportunity to reduce their power. To the
very last Pius II. kept his hold on Naples, and tried still further
to enrich his nephews. The county of Celano, whose young
Count had joined the Angevin party, was overrun by the Pope's
troops in the name of the Church; Pius II. succeeded in handing it over to Antonio Piccolomini. The Neapolitan policy of
Pius II., no doubt, was sound as regarded Italian affairs: the
success of Ferrante secured the peace of Italy so long as he
lived. But the part which the Pope played had been a perpetual
hindrance to his good understanding with France, and its most
immediate result had been to make a good provision for two
of the Pope's nephews.

[1] The account of this is given by Pius II., *Comment.* 819-21.

Anger of
Louis XI.
at the
Pope's
Neapolitan
policy.

This turn of affairs in Naples filled up the measure of the French King's wrath against the Pope.　He had abolished the Pragmatic Sanction partly out of caprice, partly with an expectation of receiving an adequate reward.　He was now conscious that he had acted contrary to his own interests and that he had been beguiled by the Pope.　He wrote to Pius II. a letter, 'unworthy of his dignity' as Pius II. plaintively remarks, 'and as though he were the Pope's superior, condemned his doings and gave him rules of life.' [1]　Unfortunately we have only the Pope's account of the contents of this letter; but that describes them as sufficiently severe.　The Pope's policy was submitted to a damaging criticism : he had disturbed Naples, had ruined the Church of Mainz, had excommunicated the Pfalzgraf and Sigismund of Austria, had accused the Bohemian King of heresy—in short, would allow no one to live in peace ; it would be much better if he would turn his attention to the Turks.　At the same time Louis XI. wrote also to the Cardinals asking if they could inform him what the Pope's intentions really were.　Pius II. has not told us what the French party said in the Consistory when these letters were laid before them; but he felt that he was put on his trial before the College, and found it necessary to justify himself.　The Cardinals affected to wonder at the tone of the letters and to doubt that they were really what the King had intended.　Pius II. did not answer in writing, but proposed that he should send one envoy and the Cardinals another, with instructions to excuse the Pope, to appease the King, and urge on him, as the supreme remedy for all differences of opinion, that he should wage war against the Turk.[2]

The envoys were, however, unable either to stem the torrent of the royal displeasure or to gain from France any help for the crusade.　Louis XI. showed that he did not intend to leave the Pope much room for interference in France.　A strife had been for some time raging between the Bishop of Nantes and the Duke of Brittany, in which the Bishop had called on the Pope for aid.　Louis XI. suddenly interfered in the matter, declared that Duke and Bishop were alike vassals of the crown of France, took prisoner the Pope's legate who was on his way to Brittany, and deprived him of his letters on the ground

[1] *Comm.* 323.　　　　　　　　[2] *Comm.* 343.

that in a dispute concerning a fief of the French crown he and not the Pope was the judge. Pius II. calls this 'a tyrannical and lying statement;'[1] it was indeed an assertion of feudal rights for which Duke and Bishop were as little prepared as was the Pope. Not content with this, Louis XI. deprived Cardinal Alain of Avignon of his temporalities for having advised the sending of the nuncio; he treated similarly two bishops, nephews of Alain, and even threatened Cardinal Estouteville. In vain the Pope expostulated. 'Who' he bitterly exclaims, 'could persuade a king who takes his greed for law and listens only to those who tickle his ears?'

As soon as it was seen that Louis XI. was willing to oppose the Pope the Gallican party at once revived. The Parlement and the University laid their grievances before the King, and the clergy who had felt the weight of the exactions of the Curia were ready to accept relief at the King's hands. A series of royal ordinances were issued which took back almost all that had been granted to the Papacy by the abolition of the Pragmatic. 'The King,' says Pius II. sadly, 'did not show himself so religious by the abolition of the Pragmatic Sanction as he showed himself sacrilegious by issuing such decrees.'[2] The first of these ordinances, dated February 17, 1463, set aside a Constitution of the Pope which took into the Papal Camera the goods of deceased prelates, together with half the benefices which they held in commendam. When the Papal officials tried to avoid this edict by threats of excommunication against those who refused to pay, a second edict was issued in June 1464, forbidding all such exactions and punishing by confiscation of goods and banishment from the kingdom all collectors who strove to levy them.[3] Another edict (May 1463) maintained the royal right of disposing of benefices during vacancies, as against those who came provided with Papal reservations and the like.[4] All cases concerning such matters were declared to be under the cognisance of the Parlement; in case of Papal censures being directed against this ordinance the Proctorgeneral was ordered to appeal to a future Council.[5] In June

Royal
ordinances
restore the
provisions
of the
Pragmatic
Sanction.
1468–1464.

---

[1] *Comm.* 330.   [2] *Comment.* 324.
[3] The edicts are given in *Preuves des Libertés*, 467–70.
[4] 'Ordonnance' in *Preuves*, 800.
[5] Letter to Parlement, *Preuves*, 705.

1464 another ordinance declared the sole right of the royal
courts to determine causes concerning the claims of the
crown; those who appealed to the Curia against them were
banished from the kingdom; ecclesiastics who aided in such
appeals were declared incapable of holding benefices in France.[1]
To protect the Parlement against Papal interference it was
declared that its officials were responsible to no court outside
the boundaries of Paris. When Pius II. regarded all these
edicts he might well feel that if he had deluded Louis XI. into
the abolition of the Pragmatic Sanction by false hopes, Louis XI.
showed himself capable of retaliating. The extinction of the
Pragmatic proved illusory in its turn, and the place of the
legislation which had been abolished was rapidly filled up by a
new series of laws still more markedly anti-papal in their spirit.

Germany in 1463 seemed tending towards peace. After
the rescue of Frederick by George of Bohemia, Adolf of Nassau
had surprised Mainz by night, had driven out Diether and
his adherents, set parts of the town in flames, and ruined for
his own quarrel the prosperity of his cathedral city. It was a
happy stroke and did much to restore the balance of parties in
Germany. Negotiation was again possible; the Pfalzgraf became reconciled with Albert of Brandenburg. Diether, after
many conferences, agreed to renounce the Archbishopric of Mainz
in return for a portion of its lands, over which he was to exercise ecclesiastical jurisdiction; Adolf succeeded to the title, the
debts and the ruins of the greatest see in Germany. The death
of Albert of Austria in December 1463 paved the way also for a
reconciliation between Frederick and Sigismund of the Tyrol,
who renounced his claims in Austria, on the understanding that
Frederick was to reconcile him with the Pope. Pius II. and
Cusa were weary of their long struggle; Sigismund made submission and was absolved in the beginning of 1464. The Pope
might claim that he had vindicated the dignity of the Papacy;
but assuredly he had lost more than he had gained in the long
duel with Heimburg. Before the final agreement about the
disputes concerning Brixen was made, Pius II. and Cusa were
both dead, and Heimburg had sought a refuge in the Court of
the Bohemian King.

Pius II. was a skilful diplomat, and no doubt expected great

[1] *Preuves*, 703.

results from the energy which he had displayed on so many sides. Yet, after all, the general aspect of affairs remained much the same as it had been at the end of the Congress of Mantua. France was still hostile to the Papacy; Bohemia was still unsubdued. It is true that Naples had been won for Ferrante, Gismondo Malatesta had been overthrown, Pienza had been beautified, and the Pope's nephews had been well provided for. On the other hand, Mainz had been well nigh ruined, Heimburg had dealt many crushing blows at the Pope's prestige, the Papacy had become more closely involved in the party struggles of Germany, and the German opposition had become more purely political.

CHAPTER IX.

CRUSADE AND DEATH OF PIUS II.

1464.

Attitude
of Pius II.
towards
the cru-
sade.

SINCE the end of the Congress of Mantua little has been heard
about the war against the Turks; yet we should wrong Pius II.
if we did not admit the sincerity of his desire for a crusade. But
he had not the fanaticism of Calixtus III. to drive him to do
something, however inadequate it might be, nor had he the
resoluteness of a great statesman to pursue constantly one
supreme end. His early training had made him ready to catch
at advantages as they offered themselves. He did not try to
mould European affairs into accordance with his own plans; but
he strove to make the Papal power prevail along the whole line
of its pretensions, and trusted in the long run to have his way.
While animated by a desire for the general interests of Christendom, he could not rise above the particular interests of the
Papacy. He failed to impress his contemporaries with his
sincerity; even had he done so, he seems to have felt it doubtful whether he could win them to united action.

Opinion of
Europe.

Pius II. must have felt that the action of his predecessors had not been such as to inspire Europe with much confidence. Nicolas V. had gathered Turkish tithes, which he had
spent on the adornment of Rome. Calixtus III. had squan-
dered his treasure in insignificant expeditions, which showed
no sense of the work in which he was engaged. Pius II. might
have expected that his protestations at Mantua would be subjected to the calm criticism of observers. His leisurely and
magnificent progress to the Congress seemed a needless waste
of money: his share in the Neapolitan war was opposed to his
expressed desire for universal peace. Italy hesitated to grant
him the supplies which he demanded. Europe saw in the Congress of Mantua a series of negotiations on matters which

concerned the Papal interests. When Pius sojourned at ease in his beloved Siena, men said that the whole matter was merely an excuse to enable the Pope to leave Rome and enjoy a visit to his native place. Few thought that the Pope was in earnest, or that his future action would go beyond eloquent protestations from time to time.

We have seen enough of the Pope's activity to feel that there was some justification for those who judged that he had not the cause of a crusade so deeply at heart as to forego for its sake any advantage to himself. He did not even interfere decidedly in such matters as might have furthered it. Hungary had long been the bulwark of Christendom against the Turk, and bravely had John Hunyadi defended it. On John's death the Hungarian nobles took as their king his young son Matthias Corvinus, in the hopes that they would find him a powerless ruler under whom they might pursue their own interests. When the young Matthias displayed the same resolute disposition as his father, they began to pay more heed to the claims on Hungary of the Emperor Frederick, whom in February 1459 the discontented party solemnly elected as their king. Here was a matter which clearly demanded the Pope's intervention as a mediator. The internal peace of Hungary was of vital importance to Christendom, was of prime necessity if the Turk was to be held at bay. But Pius II. saw the political difficulties in the way of quarrelling with the Emperor; the interests of Christendom could not outweigh in his mind the advantages to be gained by the Curia through its Imperial ally. Pius II. could not bring himself to act with decision: he received the obedience of Matthias and called him king on the principle, which he wished to be allowed to apply to Naples, of recognising things as they were. Beyond this he assumed an attitude of impartial neutrality, and kindly offered to judge the rival claims if they were submitted to his decision. Whatever other steps might be taken with advantage, there could be no doubt of the need of supplying Matthias with money to enable him to war against the Turks. Pius II. had much good advice to give and many expressions of sympathy; but all the urgency of Carvajal, who was legate in Hungary, could not obtain supplies that were of any purpose.

Still Pius II. had undertaken the cause of the crusade, and

however much he might pursue more immediate objects, he did not entirely forget it. Some of the things that befell him as advocate for the Christian cause are ludicrous enough. A Franciscan Friar, Ludovico of Bologna, had gone to the East in the days of Calixtus III. and brought back reports of Christians in Persia who were ready to submit to the Pope, and join an alliance against the Sultan. Soon after the return of Pius II. to Rome from the Congress of Mantua, Fra Ludovico appeared, bringing with him envoys from potentates of the East, the Emperor of Trapezus, the King of Persia, the King of Mesopotamia, the Duke of Greater Iberia, and the Lord of Armenia Minor. They had come through Scythia over the Don and the Danube, through Hungary to Germany, where they had been welcomed by the Emperor; thence they had passed through Venice to Rome. They were received with honour as royal ambassadors, and had quarters and food assigned to them,—which was indeed necessary, as some could eat as much as twenty pounds of meat a day. When admitted to an audience they set forth, through Fra Ludovico as interpreter, that their kings had heard from him of the Congress of Mantua, and were willing to attack the Turks in Asia, while the Christians attacked them in Europe; for this purpose they would raise an army of 120,000 men; they begged the Pope to make Ludovico Patriarch of the Eastern Christians. The Pope assented to their request, and offered to pay the expenses of their journey to the Courts of France and Burgundy, on whose co-operation the proceedings in Europe mainly depended. They were coldly listened to in France and Burgundy; but no doubt they passed the time pleasantly. Meanwhile the Pope began to suspect Fra Ludovico, and on his return to Rome threatened to imprison him for having styled himself Patriarch on his travels, without having received consecration. He was, however, allowed to depart for his companions' sake. At Venice he prevailed on some unwary bishops to ordain him priest and patriarch. When Pius II. heard this, he wrote to the Patriarch of Venice to imprison the impostor; but Ludovico was warned by the Doge, and made his escape. It was a cruel imposture, and was by no means the only one of which the Pope had to complain.[1]

---

[1] Pius II. tells us about this embassy in *Comm.* 127. Cornelius Zantfliet, *Chronicum* in Martene and Durand, *Amp. Coll.* v. 502, gives an account of it in Germany, and Du Clercq, Bk. IV. ch. xxvii., in Burgundy.

Still more extraordinary than this pretended embassy is the
fact that Pius II. actually attempted to convert the Sultan by his eloquence. As rhetoric was the only contribution to a
crusade which the Pope saw his way towards making, he seems
to have resolved to try its effect to the uttermost. It is a strong testimony to the tolerant spirit of the Turks that stories were rife of the Sultan's willingness to listen to Christian teaching. It is no less characteristic of the temper of the early Renaissance that Pius II. should have thought that all subjects admitted of reasonable discussion. He wrote a long letter to the Sultan pointing out the advantages that would follow from his acceptance of Christianity. Already the spread of the Turkish arms had led Cardinal Cusa to write an elaborate examination of the Koran, from which Pius II. borrowed many of his theological arguments. His letter dwelt first upon the horrors of war, and his desire to avert them; he does not hate the Sultan, though his foe, but rather wishes him well. The conquest of Europe is not like that of Asia; it is impossible to the Turkish forces; yet Mahomet may obtain all the glory that he wishes without bloodshed, by means simply of the little water needed for baptism. If he accepted that, the Pope would recognise him as Emperor of Asia and of Greece; what he now possessed by violence would become lawfully his : by this means, and by this only, might the golden age be brought back to the world. The Sultan might object that the Turks would refuse to follow him if he abandoned his religion. The Pope reassured him by the examples of Clovis and Constantine. How great is the glory that he might so attain! All literature, Latin, Greek, and Barbarian alike, would extol his name. More than this, he would gain the heavenly promise, and would be able to add to the virtues of a philosopher the three theological virtues of faith, hope, and charity, without which no man can be perfect. The Pope then unfolded to him the Christian scheme and discussed the points in which it differs from the Koran ; he expatiated on the superiority of the law of Christ over that of Mahomet, and again exhorted the Sultan to consult his own interests, both here and hereafter, by accepting Christian baptism.[1]

The letter forms a bulky pamphlet, and is written with

---

[1] In Raynaldus, 1461, 44, &c. *Pii II. Epistolæ* (ed. Basil), No. 396. There is no date given to this letter, but perhaps it may be assigned to the end of 1461.

great spirit and clearness: it abounds in historical allusions and quotations from classical poets and philosophers. It is to be regretted that we have no answer from the Sultan, nor do we read that any was returned. Still the Pope's letter was widely read in Europe, and produced a great effect on the imagination of Christendom. From this time forward forgeries of a similar correspondence formed part of the vast store of literature which gathered round the Turkish war.

While Europe was engaged in quarrelling, and the Pope was busy writing, the Turks pursued their conquests. The Morea fell into their hands, as did Rhodes, Cyprus, Lesbos, and the chief islands of the Ægean; Scanderbeg, in Albania, was driven to make peace, and Bosnia fell before the Turks' arms. Pius II. was stirred to action, and in March 1462 he summoned six Cardinals to a private meeting, and to them unfolded his schemes. 'You think, perhaps, my brothers,' he said, 'as all the world does, that we think nought of the general interest, because since our departure from Mantua we have made no preparations, and uttered no words about the crusade, though day by day the foe presses nearer. We have, indeed, been silent and have done nothing; but it was through lack of power, not through lack of will. We have often thought what could be done for Christendom. We have passed many sleepless nights, tossing from side to side, and were ashamed of our inaction. Our bosom swelled, our old blood boiled. To proclaim war by ourselves is useless, for the Holy See cannot, with its own resources, wage a war against the Turk; we need the help of the princes of Christendom. We considered all possible means to obtain this, but none seemed fitting. If we think of a Congress, the experience of Mantua shows that it is vain. If we send legates, they are mocked. If we impose tithes on the clergy, an appeal is made to a future Council. If we promulgate indulgences, we are accused of avarice; everyone thinks that it is done to scrape up money; no one believes our words. Like bankrupt merchants we have lost all credit. Whatever we do is construed for the worse; everyone measures our character by his own. We turn our mind's eye everywhere and find nothing firm. Meditating day and night, we have hit upon one remedy, perhaps the only one, certainly the most efficacious.' Then the Pope went on to unfold his scheme.

Philip of Burgundy had vowed to go on the crusade if some other prince did so; he was bound by a solemn oath, which he would not venture to set aside. Old as he was, the Pope would offer to set out himself; Philip could not refuse to accompany one who was both Pope and King,—one who was greater than King or Emperor. If Burgundy set out, France would, for very shame, send some forces, and so would the other powers of Europe. It was, however, useless to propose this till Venice would provide a fleet. Venice must first be sounded, then France and Burgundy. When they agreed, the Pope would proclaim a European truce for five years, call on the clergy for subsidies, under pain of excommunication, and by indulgences raise money from the laity. ' The noise of our plan,' he added, ' will come like a crash of thunder, and rouse the minds of the faithful to the defence of their religion.' [1]

The Cardinals heard the Pope's plan with amazement, and asked for some days to deliberate. All the difficulties that they could raise were foreseen and answered by the Pope. They at length pronounced the scheme worthy of the Vicar of Christ, and Pius II. wrote at once to the Doge of Venice binding him to secresy for the present. The Bishop of Ferrara was at the same time sent to Louis XI. of France. But Louis was not on such terms with the Pope as to look on his proposals with a friendly eye. He regarded them as a blind to draw his attention from the affairs of Naples; and the only answer that he would vouchsafe was, that he purposed sending an envoy to the Pope who would treat about Naples and the crusade together. Meanwhile, he added, he had on hand the business of restoring to his throne Henry VI. of England, which he hoped to do within a year. 'I will give you four years more for that,' said the legate, as he took his leave.[2]

On arriving at Brussels the Bishop of Ferrara found Philip of Burgundy dangerously ill of a fever. Philip had shown great lukewarmness at Mantua, and had been busied since then in attempting to consolidate the Burgundian dominions by obtaining from the Emperor the title of King, and so reviving the old middle kingdom of Lotharingia. But illness awoke again the old man's zeal for the holy cause. The Bishop of Ferrara was admitted to an audience of the Duke, who was in

---

[1] *Pii II. Commentarii*, 189-91.   [2] *Comment.* 221.

bed. When he heard the Pope's letter he exclaimed, 'I thought that the fever would conquer and would carry me off; but you have brought me health by your message. Death seemed to me hard, because I would leave my father's captivity unavenged on the Turks. Now I will live to avenge my father and benefit Christendom.' He began at once to arrange details with his counsellors, and promised to send an envoy to the Pope in October.¹ Difficulties, however, arose with France. Louis XI. summoned the Duke of Burgundy as his vassal to aid in an expedition against England, and a rebellion of the Liègois against their Bishop occupied the Duke's attention. As he recovered his health, the crusade was again forgotten, and a Papal nuncio, sent in the spring of 1463 to remind the Duke of his promises, found him engaged in festivals, dances, and sports. His counsellors were all opposed to the crusade as both chimerical and dangerous, and they threw all possible hindrances in the way of its accomplishment. Suddenly the Duke took ill and became unconscious; his life was for a time despaired of; but he recovered, and with his recovery his good intentions returned. The Papal envoy was dismissed with a new promise that representatives of Burgundy would be at Rome on August 15.

Increase
of the
Papal
revenues
by the dis-
covery of
alum at
Tolfa.

Perhaps an additional stimulus was given to the determination of Pius II. by a discovery which materially increased the Papal revenues. An Italian merchant who had been driven from Constantinople by the Turks, and who had experience of the alum works of Asia Minor, discovered alum in the barren hills of Tolfa, not far from Cività Vecchia. At first Pius II. was incredulous; but the discoverer brought workmen from Genoa and established the truth of his surmise. The alum was speedily worked, and proved to be of excellent quality. In April 1463 Pius II. informed all the faithful of the compassion of Heaven in depriving the unbelievers of the revenues which they obtained from Christians by the sale of alum, which the Holy See was now prepared to supply; he warned them no longer to buy from the Turks.² The alum mines of Tolfa were, indeed, as profitable to the Pope as was the year of jubilee, and are said to have yielded a revenue of 100,000 ducats.

¹ *Comment.* 231.
² Bull in Raynaldus, 1463, No. 84. See also *Pii II. Com.* 185.

The first practical step towards opposing the Turks was the establishment of peace between Frederick III. and Matthias of Hungary, a task which the Pope took earnestly in hand in the spring of 1463. It required two Papal legates to arrange the terms; but at làst peace was made in July. Matthias was recognised as king, on condition of paying the Emperor 80,000 ducats and submitting to a rectification of frontier; in case Matthias died childless, Hungary was to go to the Emperor's second son. When Hungary was thus freed from internal troubles, Matthias found no further difficulty in making an alliance with Venice, which had always shown more readiness to help Hungary than had the Pope. Venice was by this time thoroughly alarmed at the losses which the progress of the Turk was inflicting on her commerce, and on September 12 signed an alliance with Hungary for war against the Turks. Meanwhile the Burgundian envoys found Pius II. at Tivoli, and brought him the assurance of their master's zeal. The Pope set out for Rome, where he arrived on September 9, ready to welcome the Italian envoys whom he had summoned to consultation. The Congress at Rome was not so full as had been the Congress of Mantua; but it was more in earnest. The Bishop of Tournay, on the part of the Duke of Burgundy, promised 6,000 men in the spring; the Duke himself would lead them if his health allowed. Pius II. then asked the Italian envoys for money, according to the Mantuan decree; but all, save Venice, declared that they had no powers for the purpose, and must consult their States. The Florentine envoy privately approached the Pope and warned him that this war would be for the sole benefit of Venice, which, if the Turks were overcome, would turn its hand to the subjugation of Italy; it would be wise to leave the Venetians and the Turks to weaken one another. Pius II. rejected this policy as shortsighted and unworthy of a Christian people, and the envoy referred the Pope's opinion to the Florentine Government.

While awaiting the return of the Italian envoys, Pius II. judged it well to arrange matters with the Cardinals. He knew that his plan was opposed by the French party in the College, and was not popular with those who preferred a quiet life at Rome to a dangerous expedition abroad. Calling a Consistory, the Pope addressed the Cardinals. For six years, he

said, he had sat on the Papal seat, and the policy which by the
advice of the Cardinals he had initiated at Mantua was yet
unfulfilled: he had been most desirous to carry it out, but
troubles at home prevented him. 'We were bound either to
give up Rome or fight against the French, who, despising our
commands, contrary to all law occupied the kingdom of Naples
and attacked our vassals. We fought for Christ when we
defended Ferrante ; we warred against the Turks when we smote
the lands of Malatesta. At last victory has crowned the Papal
arms, and Italy is at peace; at last the time has come for
action. "But what," it will be asked, "can you do in war: an
old man, a priest, a martyr to a thousand ailments ? What use
are the Cardinals in a camp? They spent their youth in
pleasure ; will you starve their old age with war ? Better stay
at home with your Cardinals, and send your fleet and your
money to the Hungarians." It would be sound advice if we had
any money ; but our treasury is exhausted. Our revenues never
exceed 300,000 ducats, and half of that sum is required for the
necessary expenses of the Papal rule. The Turkish war would
need 1,000,000 ducats yearly for three years at least. You
will say : "If so much is required for the war, what hopes have
you of obtaining it before you start ?" We answer : "The war is
necessary: if we do not undertake it we should be deservedly
infamous." Money is hard to raise, for the people do not trust
us. They say that we live in pleasure, amass money, follow our
ambition, have fatter mules and better horses than other folk,
make broad the hems of our garments, walk through the
city with cheeks puffed out beneath a red hat, keep dogs for
hunting, give much to actors and parasites, nothing for the
defence of the faith. These charges are not altogether false ;
there are many among the Cardinals and other members of the
Curia of whom this is true. There is too much pride and
luxury in the Curia ; so that when we speak the truth to the
people we are so hated that we are not heard. What, then, is
to be done ? Abstinence, chastity, zeal for the faith, religious
fervour, the desire for martyrdom, these made the Roman Church
pre-eminent over the world. We must imitate our predecessors
and show that we are willing to sacrifice our lives for the pre-
servation of the flock committed to our charge. Our purpose is
to go to war against the Turks, and invite the princes of

Christendom to follow. Perchance when they see their master, the Vicar of Jesus Christ, though old and sick, advancing to the war, they will feel ashamed to stay at home. If this way does not rouse Christians to arms, we know no other. We know that we are going to meet certain death, but that does not deter us. We commit all to God, and will die happy if we end our days in His service.

'You, too, who advised us to begin the war against the Turks, cannot remain at home at ease. The members must follow their head; and what we do is done of necessity. We do not go to fight; but will imitate Moses, who, when Israel fought against Amalek, prayed on the mountain. We will stand on our ship's prow, or on some hilltop, and having before our eyes the holy Eucharist, will ask from Jesus Christ safety and victory for our soldiers in the battle.[1] God will not despise a contrite heart. You will be with us, and will join your prayers with ours; the old only will be left behind.' Then the Pope explained that he would leave in Rome two legates, one for temporal and the other for spiritual affairs, and would make provisions for the discharge of the ordinary business of the Curia. The nephew Antonio, with 3,000 horse and 2,000 foot, would provide for the safety of the States of the Church.[1]

The Pope's voice was often broken by tears, in which the Cardinals also joined. When called upon to give their opinions, no one save the Cardinal of Arras spoke very decidedly against the scheme. Though the French party was opposed to it, even Estouteville did not raise any insuperable objections. Cardinal Erolo, though he was one of the six whom the Pope had first consulted, raised some objections, 'to show himself cleverer than anyone else,' says the Pope. The objections were, however, overcome, except in the case of the Cardinal of Arras, who left Rome and returned to France.

The Italian envoys soon returned with their answers to the Pope's request for money. Ferrante of Naples, the Duke of Milan, the Marquis of Modena, the Marquis of Mantua, the cities of Bologna and Lucca, all assented. Some states, however, held aloof. Genoa was too busy with her own factions

---

[1] In *Pii II. Comm.* 336, &c.; but the Pope there omits the severer part of the accusations against the clergy which are in Mansi, *Pii II. Orationes*, ii. 168.

to pay any heed to general matters; the Duke of Savoy and the Marquis of Monteferrate also sent no representatives. The Florentines refused to take any part till they had had time to withdraw their merchants from Constantinople. The Sienese, to the indignation of the Pope, pleaded poverty, and offered the paltry sum of 3,000 ducats, which they afterwards increased to 10,000. Pius II. wrote most pressingly to the Duke of Milan, urging him to come in person and assume the command of the Papal forces. The letter of the Pope was a masterpiece of persuasive eloquence; the answer of the Duke was similarly a masterpiece of courteous prevarication. He deplored the woes of Christendom, professed his firm resolve to war against the Turk, his confidence in the Pope, and his desire to do everything that he required; but he added that his health was not yet restored, that the time allowed for preparation was not quite adequate, that the undertaking was difficult and needed careful measures.[1] The Pope understood that he was not coming in person, and soon learned that 3,000 men was all the contingent which he proposed to send.

On October 22 was held a public consistory in which was read the Pope's Bull proclaiming a crusade. Pius II. recounted all his efforts for the holy cause, proclaimed his zeal, combated objections, called on all to help, and promised indulgences to those who either came in person or contributed their substance.[2] The Bull took two hours to read, and the Pope was gratified with the effect which it produced. 'The sweetness of the composition, the novelty of the thing itself, and the readiness of the Pope offering his life for his sheep, drew tears from many bystanders.'[3] The Bishop of Tournay, on behalf of the Burgundians, warmly thanked the Pope for his zeal. But the Romans were touched by no sentimental enthusiasm for the weal of Christendom; they only saw that the Pope was going to leave Rome, and they feared that the hope of their gains was gone. Pius II. answered their loud murmurs by the assurance that the officials of the Curia would be left behind.

[1] The Pope's letter is in Mansi, *Orationes*, iii. 103; Sforza's answer in *Pii II. Epistolæ* (ed. Basel), 393.

[2] The Bull 'Ezechielis prophetæ' is No. 412 in *Pii II. Epistolæ* (ed. Basel).

[3] *Pii II. Comment.* 344.

Then, racked with gout, till he could scarce restrain himself from showing his anguish, he was carried to his bed.

CHAP.
IX.

Alliance of
Pius II.
with
Venice and
Hungary.

A few days before Pius II. had signed an alliance with Venice and Hungary, by which they bound themselves to carry on the war for three years if necessary, and no one of the contracting powers was to withdraw without the rest. The Pope promised that, on the arrival of Philip of Burgundy in Italy, he would set out with him for Greece. Hungary and Venice were already engaged in warring against the Turk. Matthias invaded Bosnia with some success, and the Venetians sent a fleet to the Morea which rose against the Turkish yoke : Lemnos and several islands fell into the hands of the Venetians. Cardinal Bessarion was sent by the Pope to Venice, and enjoyed a success such as had never yet befallen him. He was received in state by the Doge on the 'Bucentaur,' and preached the crusade to a people already convinced. A box was placed in the Piazza to receive the contributions of the faithful, and was soon found to contain 700,000 ducats. Pius II. wrote to the Doge, Cristoforo Moro, urging him to come in person to the war, and join the Pope and Philip of Burgundy ; if he appeared in ducal array on board the 'Bucentaur,' not Greece only but Asia and all the East would be terrified. 'We shall be three old men,' he says, 'and God rejoices in trinity. Our trinity will be aided by the Trinity of Heaven, and our foes will be trampled under our feet.'[1] The Great Council of Venice voted almost unanimously that the Doge should go ; when the Doge, a few days afterwards, tried to excuse himself on the ground of age and incapacity before the Collegio, he was told by one of the Council, 'If your highness will not go of goodwill, we will make you go by force, since the honour and welfare of this land is dearer to us than your person.' The Doge answered that if the land wished it he was content.[2] Before the end of the year news came that the Turks had forced the wall which guarded the entrance to the Peloponnesus, and had driven out the Venetians. This news did not affect the zeal of Venice, which prepared at once to send out reinforcements; but it gave Philip of Burgundy an opportunity to write to the Pope

---

[1] Malipiero, *Annali Veneti*, in *Archivo Storico Italiano* (prima serie), vol. vii. pt. i. p. 18.

[2] Sanudo in Muratori, xxii. 1174.

and urge a delay in the expedition to enable Venice to recover
her strength. Pius II. refused to accede to this request;[1] he
had written, he said, throughout Europe, and must not now
delay. In truth, the Pope's legates were busy in almost every
land: everywhere they were received with enthusiasm by the
people, everywhere they received from the princes fair words
enough, but no definite promises of help.[2]

It soon became obvious that the political intrigues of
Europe were throwing hindrances in the way even of the
accomplishment of such promises as the Pope had received.
First of all, Italy received a shock which deeply stirred men's
minds, by the news that Louis XI. of France had made an
alliance with the Duke of Milan, and had invested him with
Genoa and Savona. We have seen that Florence looked with
jealous eyes on the crusading project as likely to increase the
power of Venice; she entered into a close alliance with Milan
for their mutual protection, and did her utmost to reconcile
Francesco Sforza with Louis XI. of France.[3] Louis XI. was
embarrassed with the possession of Savona, in which the
French garrison was entirely useless since the loss of Genoa
to the French. He was not indisposed to rid himself of
an incumbrance, and in doing so to gain an ally in North
Italy. The Neapolitan war had taught him the power of
Sforza, and Louis XI. had a genuine admiration for a man
whose success had been so brilliant. In February 1464 Savona
was given up to the Milanese, and the Italian Powers were
astonished by a notification from Louis XI. that he had made
over to the Duke of Milan his rights over Genoa.

This news filled Italy with alarm. It was clearly a blow
aimed by Florence and Milan against Venice. The Duke of
Modena feared this increase of the power of Milan; Lucca and
Siena were afraid of the designs of Florence; Ferrante of
Naples thought himself betrayed to the French by his former
ally. Sforza tried to restore confidence by protesting that he
had entered into no engagements which could disturb the
peace of Italy; by taking Genoa into his power he had re-

---

[1] Raynaldus, 1464, 4, &c.
[2] See Book XIII. of *Pii II. Commentarii*, published by Voigt, *Æneas
Sylvius*, ii. 360, &c., from the hitherto unedited MS.
[3] See Buser, *Die Beziehungen der Medicaer zu Frankreich*, p. 101, &c.

moved the only ground for French interference in Italian affairs. The Archbishop of Genoa, Paolo Fregoso, who was at the head of the government of the city, clamoured for help against Sforza; but Pius II. advised him to submit rather than hinder the war against the Turks. The archbishop fled, and Sforza advanced against the city. It was at all events clear that neither Milan nor Genoa would send any forces to the crusade.

From Burgundy also the Pope received doubtful news. Duke Philip was not on good terms with his son Charles, who had left his court and gone to Holland. If Philip went to the Turkish war, Charles would naturally be regent during his absence, and this prospect was very distasteful to a strong party headed by the powerful family of the Croy. They strove to increase the feud between the Duke and his son so as to keep Philip at home. Philip, however, was resolute. Charles returned, and was reconciled to his father. Next the Croy represented to the Duke the dangers which might befall his land if he departed before the war between France and England was at an end; they besought him to remain, at least till a truce was arranged. Louis XI. joined his entreaties to the same purpose; if a truce were made with England France could join in the Crusade with Burgundy. The Duke wavered, and asked the Pope to defer the expedition for the purpose of this pacification. Pius II. knew that delay meant entire failure, and refused. Then the Croy managed to bring about an interview between Louis XI. and the Duke at Lille in February 1464. Louis XI. repeated his desire that the Duke should stay till France was at peace with England: neither Venice nor the Pope was ready; in a year's time he would send 10,000 men to the Turkish war. When the Duke pleaded his promise, Louis XI. ordered him as his vassal to remain at home, and handed him a written injunction to obey. The Duke gave way, and announced to his people the King's commands: next year he would himself go against the Turk; meanwhile, not to disappoint the Pope, he would send his illegitimate son, the Bastard of Burgundy, with 2,000 men. The tower, says Pius II., fell at last before the repeated strokes of the battering-ram, and the Croy triumphed.[1]

[1] *Pii II. Commentarii*, Book XIII., in Voigt, ii. 369, &c.

Pius II. had left Rome in February to recruit his health at
the baths of Petrioli, and stayed at Siena during the month of
March.   On Thursday in Holy Week, the day on which excommunications were published, the Pope anathematised all heretics
and all, even kings, who strove to hinder the crusade.   The
anathema was aimed at those who were shaking the constancy
of the Duke of Burgundy ; but Pius II. soon found that it had
been delivered too late.   On Good Friday, March 30, he received the letter of the Duke of Burgundy, ' worthy,' he says,
' of being read on the day of the Lord's Passion.'   Yet Pius II.
was not entirely unprepared for the blow ; he had already consulted with eight Cardinals, who were present, what course he
should adopt in case Philip refused to go.   They were unanimous in their opinion that, though the Pope was in that case
released from his engagement, he should solemnly renew it.
This was also his opinion ; and he communicated his resolution
as a decree to the absent Cardinals, who murmured at his
obstinacy.

Pius II. was resolute in his determination in spite of all
hindrances.   Yet we cannot assign this resolution solely to
zeal for the good of Christendom ; there was mixed with it
also a motive of utility for the interests of the Papacy.   There
was still a power in Europe which stood opposed to the Pope,
and whose activity threatened danger.   George of Bohemia
was a formidable foe, and had devised a scheme which might
lead to serious results if it were not baffled.   Pius II. had
brought to an issue the question of the relations between
Bohemia and the Holy See.   George must either alienate the
majority of his people by submitting to the Pope's demands,
or must expose himself, by refusing, to the hostility of a determined minority who looked for help outside Bohemia.   The aim of
George was to pacify Bohemia on the basis of toleration offered
by the Compacts, and weld it into a powerful kingdom.   The
Pope was keenly alive to the danger which might ensue if
a power at variance with the authority of the Church became
predominant in Germany.   Pius II. and George were equally
convinced of the magnitude of the issue at stake.   Each was
equally resolute and equally far-seeing ; but the Pope had the
advantage of being able to choose his time for the attack.
George met it by attempting to inaugurate a new policy in

European affairs. He had first hoped to cope with the Papacy by possessing himself of the Empire; when that failed, he stayed the Pope's hand by binding the Emperor to his cause by conferring benefits upon him. This could only be a temporary check; he tried to find a permanent one in the establishment of a confederation of European States against the Papal aggression. According to his scheme the States of Christendom were to take back again into their hands the supremacy in matters temporal and spiritual which they had been content to delegate to the Emperor and the Pope; a Council of European States was to regulate the international relations of Christendom.

The agent of George in this matter was Anton Marini, a knight of Grenoble, who in August 1462 proposed to Venice a league between France, Bohemia, Poland, Hungary, Burgundy, and Saxony, for war against the Turk. Venice replied that notwithstanding Marini's arguments the Pope's co-operation was necessary; for the presence of the head of Christendom was of great weight in such a plan.[1] Louis XI., in his anger against the Pope, listened to Marini's proposals, and sent him back to Venice with an expression of his readiness to join such a league. Venice, now engaged in war against the Turks, was ready to accept help from any side; and the league of the Pope with Venice and Hungary was no doubt hastened by a desire to cut away the ground from Marini's feet. The crusade of the Pope was in part an appeal to the sympathies of Europe to defeat the machinations of the Bohemian King. He could not shrink from it without giving a dangerous handle to his foe. In March 1464 Marini was at the Court of Hungary, offering Matthias a league against the Turks and a Council of European Powers to promote the peace and welfare of Christendom; in June he was at the Court of Louis XI. In the face of such activity Pius II. could not retreat from his engagement.

George's plan for a parliament of European princes.

Pius II., however, though determined to proceed on his expedition, had neither the physical vigour nor the qualities requisite for the organisation of such a scheme. Money came in slowly from Italy, and the Burgundian envoys at Rome saw little to impress them with a sense of military stir; they reported

Preparations for the crusade.

[1] Palacky, *Urkundliche Beitrage*, p. 290.

that it was the poorest preparation they had ever seen, and that two galleys only were ready.[1] The Pope vaguely trusted that soldiers would flock from different parts of Europe, prepared to serve for at least six months at their own expense, and that the Venetians would give them convoys. The crusade was preached with zeal throughout Europe by the friars; but they were scarcely to be trusted to arrange in an intelligible shape definite instructions to the crusaders. Many flocked to Venice before the time, and met only with scoffs when they had not money to pay their passage. The clear-sighted Venetians did not want enthusiasm but capacity on the part of those engaged in the enterprise. Their cruelty was published throughout Europe; but wiser heads thought that they had exercised a justifiable discretion.[2] Many crusaders returned with disappointed hopes: many died of hunger and pestilence; many came to Rome or Ancona, and found no signs of preparation.

Pius II. returned to Rome early in May to prepare for his departure. Before going he aimed a blow at George of Bohemia, whom in a Consistory on June 16 he cited to appear in Rome within 180 days to answer to the many charges against him. Pacific as he might now feel towards other Powers, Pius II. could make no truce with Bohemia. The beginning of his crusade was to him an earnest of his triumph over the heretical king. The time had come to lay the axe to the root of the tree that had threatened to overshadow the Holy See with its branches.

Departure
of Pius II.
on his
crusade.
June 18,
1464.
On June 18 he took the cross in S. Peter's, and after repeating his conviction of the necessity of his undertaking and deploring the hindrances which it had suffered, he prayed before the high altar and then set out in his litter accompanied by all the prelates. At Ponte Molle he took leave of them, and attended by the Cardinal of Pavia, the Bishops of Torcello, Tiferno, and Camertino, his secretary Goro Lolli, and his nephew Andrea, embarked on a barge on the Tiber. This method of

---

[1] Chastellain, ed. Buchon, part iii. ch. xxi.: 'Selon leur rapport c'estoit la plus povre disposition qu'ils veirent oncques; et n'avoit en tout le monde, pour celle heure, que deux gallées.'

[2] Chastellain, ch. xx.: 'Les Venétiens, qui sages gens sont et cler voians, firent mieux de véer le passage à tel monde de gens inutiles que de leur ouvrir; car ne soufit point en tel cas d'avoir les gens, més il convient avoir le sens et le povoir pour faire effect.'

conveyance was chosen to spare the Pope the fatigue of a land journey; he was already suffering from a slight fever, but forbade his physicians to mention it. The first night was spent by the Pope on the barge, as he was too weary to quit it. Navigation was difficult up the stream, and on the second night he had only advanced to Fiano. On the third day the Pope was grievously distressed by an accident which befell one of the rowers who fell into the river and was drowned before his eyes. Pius II. lay silent and with tears prayed for his soul. Cardinal Carvajal came to him from Rome with the news that a crowd of crusaders were assembled at Ancona vainly seeking for means of transport; the authorities of the city were afraid of a tumult and besought the Pope to take means to prevent it. Pius II. besought Carvajal in spite of his seventy years to undertake this difficult task, and the brave old man, already broken by his many labours, answered, 'My motto is, Go and I go : I cannot refuse to Christ's service the end of my life.' Next morning he set off for Ancona.

The Pope proceeded up the Tiber as far as Otricoli, whence he was carried in a litter by easy stages to Spoleto. There the Cardinal of Pavia was seized with a fever and had to be left behind. Already the Pope was distressed by the sight of crusaders returning from Ancona; to hide from his eyes this melancholy sight, the physicians pretended that the wind was injurious to him and closed the curtains of his litter. Slowly he proceeded under the blazing heat of an Italian summer through Foligno, Assissi, and Fabriano, across the Apennines to Loreto; there he offered a golden cup and bowl to the Virgin, whose cottage had been borne by angels from Bethlehem to its resting place on a hill by the Adriatic. Finally on July 18 he entered Ancona and took up his abode in the Bishop's palace, on the hill by the church of S. Ciriaco.

The first question was how to deal with the crowd of crusaders who disturbed the peace of the citizens of Ancona. Pius II. had only asked for such as would serve for six months at their own cost; he found a miserable herd expecting him to supply them with pay and food. As this was impossible, the Pope rewarded their zeal by a plenary indulgence; and they sold their arms as a means of obtaining money to take them to their homes. Those who could afford to do so remained in expecta-

tion of the Venetian ships which were to give them transport.
Day by day they waited; but the ships delayed. At last the
crusaders graduall dispersed, so that when the ships came
in sight there were no soldiers to embark. The Pope meanwhile lay helpless and saw his hopes fade away. Messengers moreover arrived from Ragusa that the Turkish army had
advanced to the siege and demanded the immediate surrender
of its vessels. Pius II. called Carvajal to counsel. 'What
must be done,' he asked, ' if Ragusa is besieged?' ' I will go
to-night,' answered the intrepid old man, ' with the two galleys
that are in the harbour and will either break the siege or give
spirit to the disconsolate citizens.' 'What hinders me from
sailing with you?' said the Pope, 'the knowledge of my presence will either drive away the Turks or will incite Christendom
to follow with help.' Cardinal Ammannati, who had recovered
from his fever and had followed the Pope; cried out against this
plan. 'I miserable,' he says, 'savouring of the flesh rather
than of the spirit, dissuaded him, not because I did not think
that what he proposed would succeed, but because I saw that to
his body wasted with fever the voyage would bring the end.'
Yet the Pope remained firm in his intentions; and preparations
were being made, when in four days the news was brought that
the Turks had retired from Ragusa.

Death of
Pius II.
August 14,
1464.
Pius II. was rapidly sinking; the fever raged fiercely and the
burning heat of the weather denied him any relief. The physicians said that he had but a few days to live, when at last on the
morning of August 12 the Venetian fleet was seen in the offing.
The Pope roused himself and ordered his galleys to advance to
meet them. He was carried with difficulty to the window of
his chamber whence he could see the stately entry of the fleet
into the harbour. Next day he was too ill to receive a visit
from the Doge. The day after was the eve of the Assumption
of the Virgin, when it was customary for the Pope to appear at
Vespers. He could not go, but sent the Cardinals and afterwards summoned them to his bed. He told them that his last
hour was at hand; he died in the faith of Christ and committed
to their hands the work which he had begun. He admonished
them to behave worthily of their high calling, and asked forgive-
ness if he had offended them in aught. Finally, he commended
to their good offices his household and his relatives. The Car-

dinals wept, and Bessarion as their spokesman said a few farewell words and begged for his blessing. All kissed his hand in
tears, and he blessed them saying : ' May the God of pity pardon
you and confirm a right spirit within you ! ' Then he received
the sacrament, and arranged to receive it again next morning
from the hands of Cardinal Ammannati in special honour of the
Virgin. But as the sun went down Pius II. also began to sink.
He received supreme unction and was left alone with Cardinal
Ammannati, Goro Lolli, and his nephew Andrea. He talked a
little with Ammannati and again commended his nephews to his
care. Ammannati asked him if he wished to be buried at Rome.
' Who will take care of that ? ' he answered with tears. When
Ammannati undertook to do so he seemed relieved. Again he
beckoned Ammannati to his bedside. ' Pray for me, my son,' he
said, ' for I am a sinner.' Then after a pause he added, ' Bid
my brethren continue this holy expedition and help it all you
can ; woe to you if you desert God's work.' Ammannati could not
speak for tears ; the Pope put his arm round his neck, and
said, ' Do good, my son, and pray to God for me.' They were
the last words he spoke. He listened to the prayers that were
being read till his spirit passed away.[1]

Next day the corpse of Pius II. was borne into the Cathedral, and the funeral mass was said. Then the Cardinals
assembled in the palace, and the Doge of Venice in a long
speech bewailed the Pope's death, praised his zeal, and
besought the Cardinals to elect a worthy successor. The
Cardinals decided to show their good intentions by giving over
to the Doge the Papal galleys which lay in the harbour, on
condition that they should be restored to the new Pope if he
purposed undertaking the expedition in person. The money
which Pius II. left behind, 48,000 ducats, was sent by them to
Matthias of Hungary. Next day, August 16, the Doge sailed back
to Venice, and the crusade of Pius II. was at an end. The body
of the Pope was taken to Rome, and buried in S. Peter's, in
the chapel of S. Andrea ; thence it was transferred, when

[1] The account of the last hours of Pius II. is given by Cardinal Ammannati,
Commentarii, 357-62, also in his letters, Nos. 41-57. Campanus adds a few
details, but Ammannati was an eyewitness and Campanus only knew by
hearsay. I have only followed him for a few of the more personal remarks of
Pius II. which Ammannati might think it desirable to omit.

S. Peter's was restored by Paul V. in 1614, to the Church of
S. Andrea della Valle, where a monument was erected in his
honour.

Pius II. was lucky in the moment of his death. He left
behind him the touching memory of an old man who died in
the attempt to do his duty. When the princes of Europe were
heedless of the welfare of Christendom, the dying Pope pain-
fully dragged his feeble body to martyrdom for the common
weal. It was well that he died when he did; for his expedition
had no elements of success, and was already doomed to failure.
He died before its failure had become too manifest, before an
inevitable retreat exposed to ridicule the Papal prestige. He
died in time to bequeath to Christendom the memory of the
greatness of his undertaking, unblurred by any feeling of its
hopelessness. The feeling of his contemporaries is shown by a
coin struck in his honour, which bore the impress of a pelican
feeding its young with its own blood; underneath was the
inscription—

Ales ut hæc cordis pavi de sanguine natos.
Like this bird I feed my children with my heart's blood.[1]

Yet even at the last there were many who were incredulous of
the Pope's intentions. It was the doom of Pius II., even on his
deathbed, to be distrusted by those who could not forget his
previous career, who sought in all he did for some motive of
self-interest or vain display. The Venetians did not think
that he was in earnest. The Doge, on his arrival at Ancona,
regarded the Pope's illness as a feint, and sent his own
physician to see if it was real. He was of opinion that his
arrival was a disappointment to the Pope, who never intended
to go on the expedition, and hoped to escape by throwing the
blame on Venice.[2] Filelfo was still more ill-natured. He
declared that Pius II. had gone to Ancona to seize the citadel,
and hand over the town to his nephew Andrea; then he intended to sail to Ragusa and await quietly the result of the
Hungarian arms; if they were defeated he would at once
retreat, if they succeeded he would go to Constantinople and

[1] Vannti, *Numismata Pontificum Romanorum*, p. 21.
[2] Malipiero, p. 29: 'El Papa sentì gran dolor, perchè ghe despiaseva andar
in persona, e ghe despiaseva anche mancar della promessa.

seize it for a Piccolomini.[1] The Milanese envoy did not
credit the Pope with any loftier pretensions; he reported to
Sforza that, if Pius II. had lived, he meant to sail to Brindisi and
stay there during the winter, return to Rome in the spring,
and throw the blame of failure on the lukewarmness of the
princes of Christendom.[2] A Brescian chronicler imputes to
him another design : he went to Ancona without any intention
of proceeding farther, simply in consequence of a secret understanding with Florence and Milan for the purpose of seizing
Ancona, and handing it over to the Florentine republic.[3] Italy
was so accustomed to look upon Pius II. as an astute diplomatist
that she could not credit him with purely disinterested
motives.

It is the fate of a character like Pius II. to lend itself to
different interpretations, and to remain enigmatical. One who
has changed his opinions is always liable to the charge of insin-
cerity, which comes with double force when a policy of easy
pliancy raises him to a lofty position. Such a judgment, however, is generally crude, and misses the real elements of
character. The distinguishing feature of Pius II. was his
readiness to learn from events. He equipped himself with
the panoply of the new learning, and went forth as a knight-
errant in quest of adventures. He had no prepossessions, no
prejudices, no definite opinions. His object was to make the
most of life, to learn from its experience, to win what it had to
give, to reap its successes, to adapt himself to its requirements.
Æneas Sylvius was not an adventurer in the sense that he
intended to prey upon the world; he was an explorer who
set out bravely upon the stormy sea of life, resolved to make
his voyage as prosperous as might be. He was ready to run
before the wind, to make for any haven which he could reach
with sails flying. His skill consisted in seeing how the wind
was likely to blow, and steering his course accordingly. He
cannot claim the praise of high resolve, of steady purpose, of
great design, or laborious achievement. He was not a man to
mould the world; but he frankly offered himself for the world
to mould. He was not heroic; but he was not base. He

---

[1] Letter of Filelfo to Paul II., September 15, 1464.
[2] Simoneta, in Mur. xxi. 764.
[3] Cristoforo da Soldo, *ib.* p. 900.

cannot fairly be accused of self-seeking, for self was in him the product of the exigencies amongst which his lot was cast. He was content to do the thing which needed to be done, and to reap the fruits of his foresight in being the first to perceive its necessity.

Many, we might say the majority, of politicians have little better claims to respect than Pius II.; but no man who rose to such distinction has left behind him so complete a record of his career. It is hard that Pius II. should be treated with contempt because he was a man of letters as well as a man of action, because he has frankly told us his impressions of events as they arose. We know his inconsistencies chiefly from his own confessions, while for those who have been more reserved about themselves we are at liberty to frame an imaginary consistency. The very frankness of Pius II. is a proof of his sincerity: he did not wish to make himself out to be nobler than he was. The record of his soul's progress might contain pages which he wished to forget; but he left all to the judgment of posterity, with the consciousness that in the end the verdict formed on the fullest knowledge would be the truest and most lenient. He who fixes his attention upon a few passages of the life of Pius II. tends to judge him with severity; he who follows him through his whole career forgives him much, and recognises a steady growth in greatness and nobility. Weakness and strength are strangely blended; vanity and littleness mix with high purpose and far-reaching plans; but before the eyes of Pius II. there floated fitfully a loftier ideal of Christendom than was visible to any of his contemporaries, and juster views than he was enabled to express in action.

Pius II.'s
Bull of
Retracta-
tion.
April
1463.

It was the fate of Pius II. to reap the fruit of his early inconsistencies. In 1440, while secretary of Felix V., he wrote some dialogues in favour of the conciliar system, which he sent to the University of Köln.[1] During his Pontificate, a quarrel arose between the burghers of Liège and their bishop; the bishop was upheld by the Pope, the burghers applied to the University of Köln, which used the authority of Æneas Sylvius for an appeal to a better instructed Pope. This drew from Pius II. a Bull addressed to the University, dated April 26,

---

[1] They are printed in Kollar, *Analecta Vindobonensia*, ii. 685.

1463, in which he gives his own defence of his early life.[1] He erred, he says, 'but what mortal does not err? Who is wise save the good; who is good save God alone? We walked in darkness; we erred not to ourselves alone, but drew others with us; as blind leaders of the blind, we fell with them into the ditch. Our writings may have deceived many, whose blood if God require at our hands, we can only answer that as men we · sinned, and our hope is placed in God's mercy only. Some would rather die than confess their error. Some go on in their error, that they may keep the reputation of constancy, and act with pride, wishing to seem gods rather than men, as did Hus and Jerome, who were burned at Constance. We are men, and confess that as men we sinned; not, however, like Arius and Nestorius, who deliberately chose the way that was condemned; we sinned like Paul, and ignorantly persecuted the Church and the Holy See. We are ashamed of our error, we repent of our writings and our deeds; but we did more hurt by writing than by deeds. What are we to do? The word once written and sent forth speeds on irrevocable; our writings are not now in our power, they have fallen into many hands and are generally read. Would that they were in obscurity, lest they cause scandal in the future, lest men say, "He who wrote this sat at length in S. Peter's seat." We fear lest the words of Æneas be counted those of Pius.'

To avoid this, the Pope goes on to say, he will imitate the example of S. Augustine, and make full confession of his shortcomings. He professes his belief in the commission given by Christ to S. Peter, in the supremacy of S. Peter's successors over the Universal Church. 'If you find anything contrary to this doctrine either in our Dialogues, or in our Letters, or in our other works (for we wrote much in our youth), cast it forth and contemn it. Follow what we now say: believe the old man rather than the youth; esteem not the layman higher than the Pope; reject Æneas, accept Pius; the Gentile name was given us by our parents at our birth, the Christian name we took on our Pontificate. Perhaps some may say that our

---

[1] He had done so previously, in 1447, in a letter to the Rector of the University of Köln; see supra p. 281-2. Fea's *Pius II. a calumniis vindicatus*, gives the completest version of this Bull, 'In minoribus agentes;' Raynaldus, 1463, 114, &c., gives extracts.

opinion came to us with the Papacy, that our views were changed by our dignity. It was not so ; far otherwise.'

Pius II. goes on to plead his youth and inexperience when first he went to Basel. Great names supported the Council, and he heard nothing save abuse of Eugenius IV. The Pope himself at last recognised the Council, and when he attempted to transfer it the claims of the Council were zealously put forward. 'We taught, therefore, what we heard, and after some years, thinking we were somebody, we exclaimed with Juvenal—

> Semper ego auditor tantum, nunquamne reponam ? [1]

We were ashamed always to be a pupil ; we began to talk, and occupy the teacher's place ; we wrote letters and pamphlets, and, like all poets, loved our own children and were pleased with the applause they won. When Cesarini and others left Basel, we believed that they acted through fear of losing their temporalities ; as we had none to lose, we boldly stayed, and on the deposition of Eugenius IV. accepted Felix as the true Vicar of Christ. But when Frederick, the future Emperor, came to Basel and refused to treat Felix as Pope, then first we began to think it possible that we were in error. As we would not willingly err, we accepted his invitation to join his household, and went over to the neutral side that we might learn the truth. At the Court of Frederick we discovered the falsity of much that had been said against Eugenius. In the Diets of Germany we heard both sides, and the darkness at last fell from our eyes ; we recognised our error, we went to Rome, cast off the doctrines of Basel, submitted to Eugenius, and were reconciled to the Roman Church. Not till after that did we assume the priesthood. Such was our conversion, in which Thomas of Sarzana, afterwards Pope Nicolas V., had the chief share.'

Character
of Pius II.
Pius II. is frank enough in his confession, and probably believed that he was actually frank. He might phrase it as he chose, but men credited him solely with a capacity for floating with the stream. His keen susceptibility to outward circumstances and impressions was the secret of his greatness, and was at the same time the source of his weakness. It brought

[1] Still shall I hear and never quit the score ?

him to the highest earthly dignity; but it robbed him of the
strength to secure the lasting fame that his great gifts might
otherwise have deserved. He aspired as Pope to be the leader
of Christendom; but he had not the moral position to inspire
the confidence necessary for this task. His equivocal past rose
up against him at every turn, and the mental habits of his
early life prevented him from rising to the greatness after which
he longed. He could not resist the temptation of grasping the
advantage which he saw to be immediately attainable. Though
he saw clearly and declared resolutely that the expulsion of the
Turks from Europe was the first duty of Christendom, he had
not sufficient self-restraint to devote himself with singleness
of purpose to the task which he recognised as supreme. The
conquest of the States of the Church, the aggrandisement of
the Piccolomini, the restoration of the Papal prestige, the
abolition of the last spark of the conciliar spirit—these he pursued when a tempting opportunity offered, and did not trust
that if he was faithful to his first great duty, all else would
follow unsought. To him and to Nicolas V. alike culture gave
largeness of mind and set a lofty imaginative ideal. But in
Nicolas V. the ideal subordinated to itself the strong practical
sense which he possessed : he swept away all obstacles from his
path, and devoted himself with unceasing energy to the one
object that he had in view. In Pius II. practical capacity was
led away into any field which offered a tempting opportunity for
its display; the imaginative ideal remained imaginative to the
last. Pius II.'s energies were expended on a number of small
matters in which success was possible at the time, but little
result remained for the future. He grew conscious that fame
was slipping away from his grasp, and rallied his dying force to
give a faint expression to the aspirations which he really felt,
but was not strong enough to turn to shape.

Those who saw Pius II. close at hand were impressed by his
geniality, his mental quickness, and his unceasing energy in
spite of bodily infirmities. Platina has left us a finished picture
of the master whom he respected above all others whom he
served. 'Pius II.,' he says, ' was a man of undoubted courage
and remarkable foresight, born not for ease and idleness, but
for conversance with great affairs. He so apportioned his
time that he could not be accused of slothfulness. He rose

with the dawn, and after divine service at once engaged in public business. Then he was carried through the gardens for a little relaxation before breakfast. He was moderate in his use of food, and did not care for delicacies: he was very sparing of wine, which he drank greatly diluted. After breakfast he would talk for half an hour with his attendants, then enter his chamber for rest and devotion: after that he would read or write as long as his public duties permitted. After dinner he did the same, and read or dictated till late at night, lying in his bed; he never slept more than five or six hours. In appearance he was below middle height, slender in his youth, but gaining flesh in old age. His eyes were cheerful, but kindled easily with anger; his head was prematurely bald. His face was pallid, and fell with the slightest sign of illness.[1] He was attacked almost every month by stone; he suffered from gout, so that he had almost lost the use of his legs; he was also troubled by a cough. So severe were his sufferings that often there seemed nothing but his voice to tell you that he was alive. He had such command over himself that, while racked with stone, he would continue a speech without giving any sign of his pain except by biting his lips. He could endure toil, hunger, thirst, and heat. He was always easy of access, sparing of words, and unwilling to refuse a petition. He was quick to anger, but quick to repress it. He readily pardoned insolence unless it injured the Apostolic seat, whose dignity he steadfastly upheld. Towards his household he was kind and genial: those who erred through ignorance or sloth he admonished with fatherly affection. He never put down those who spoke against him, for he wished all to speak freely in a free state. When someone complained one day of being maligned, 'You will find plenty who abuse me, too,' said the Pope, ' if you go into the Campo dei Fiori.' He had no love for luxury, saying that books were his sapphires and chrysoliths. He did not care for grandeur at table, but preferred to picnic by a fountain or in a wood. When he was in the country he never dined indoors, save in winter, or when the weather was wet. One day a shepherd gave him a wooden cup full of milk, and his attendants smiled to see how dirty it was. ' It is cleaner,'

---

[1] I have introduced a few more particular details given by Campano, *Vita Pii II.*

he said, 'than the cup of Artaxerxes: he who is thirsty does not
need a glass.' He loved the country, and inquired about everything he saw, connecting the history with the place, and ex-
pounding it to them around him.

'He was a man true, upright, open, without deceit or simu-
lation. He was a devout and sincere Christian, frequent in
confession and communion. He despised dreams, portents, and
prodigies, and showed no sign of timidity. He was neither
elated in prosperity nor depressed by adversity. 'Misfortune,'
he used to say, 'could be cured by wisdom, if it were applied in
time.' He was a master of proverbs, of which the following
may be quoted:—

The nature of God can be better grasped by believing than by
disputing.

Christianity, even if it were not approved by miracles, ought to be
received for its own worth (*honestate*).

A miser cannot be satisfied with money, nor a wise man with
knowledge.

He who knows most is most persecuted by doubt.

Serious matters are settled by arms, not by laws.

A cultivated man submits his own house to his city, his city to
his country, his country to the world, and the world to God.

As rivers flow to the sea, so vices flow to courts.

A king who trusts no one is useless, and he is no better who
believes all.

He who rules many ought to be ruled by many.

Fit men should be given to dignities, not dignities to men.[1]

Bad physicians kill the body, unskilful priests the soul.

Their virtues enriched the clergy, their vices make them poor.

For weighty causes marriage was taken from the priests, for
weightier it ought to be restored.

He who spoils his son nourishes an enemy.

A miser pleases men in nothing save his death.

These appreciative remarks of Platina show us that the
personality of Pius II. was deeply attractive to his associates.
But the character which Platina has sketched is that of a
cultivated man of letters, not of a statesman or a theologian.
It is, indeed, as a man of letters that Pius II. has the deepest
claims on our attention. He is one of the earliest representatives of the man of letters pure and simple; he is, perhaps, the

[1] 'Dignitatibus *viros* dandos, non dignitates *hominibus*.'

only man of letters who has been equally eminent in literature
and in statesmanship.　His capacity for affairs developed out
of his literary instinct; the keen eye and the ready apprehension,
which he gained from the study of the world around him, were
the means by which he won his way to high position.　When
first he came to Basel, fresh from his university career, he had
a young man's gift for writing verses, which he exercised in
Ovidean love poems and Horatian epistles.　He wrote a long
poem, which he called ' Nymphiplexis,' in honour of the mistress
of his Sienese friend Mariano de' Sozini, and rejoiced that it
was more than two thousand lines in length.[1]　It has not come
down to us; but Campano pronounced it to be flowing rather
than correct in versification.　Æneas prided himself on his
poetry, and gladly received from Frederick III. the laureate's
crown.　But he soon had the practical sense to see that Latin
verse would not do much for him, and his attendance at the
Council stimulated him to seek the reputation of an orator.
The example of Cesarini fired his emulation.　Night after
night he spent in study, while his comrade, Piero da Noceto,
who shared his room, would laugh and say, ' Why thus exhaust
yourself, Æneas?　Fortune favours the unlearned as much as the
learned.'[2]　Still Æneas studied, and seized the first opportunity
to air his eloquence; but it is noticeable that he spoke in
behalf of a hopeless proposal to transfer the Council to Pavia.
He spoke merely to win the applause of the Fathers and to
gain the good graces of the Duke of Milan.　His oratory was
artificial, and lacked depth of purpose and sincerity.　Æneas
was never sufficiently in earnest to be a great speaker, nor was
he a sufficiently polished master of words to satisfy the cultivated
taste of the Italians.[3]　But the Fathers of Basel were wearied
with the formless utterances of scholastic disputants, which
might be logical in reasoning but were wearisome to hear.
The neat, flowing, and ornate style of Æneas pleased them, and
he established his reputation as an orator.

---

[1] *Epist.* 35 (ed. Basel): 'Absolvi libellum versuum ultra duo milia
quem appellavi Nymphiplexim de laudibus Baptistæ tuæ.'　Campanus calls it
'Niraphiloticum versu magis facili et expedito quam accurato.'

[2] Æneas recalls this twelve years after in a letter of 1456.　*Ep.* 188 (ed.
Basel).

[3] So Campano judges: 'Sententiis quam verbis illustriores; copia mira
et ad magnitudinem rerum excrescente.'

The chief quality of the mind of Æneas was a ready receptivity of outward impressions, which prompted him to narrative writing. He seems to have designed a history of the Council of Basel, and wrote a description of the city which was to serve as an introduction.[1] If his work had been carried out, he would have given us a precious memorial of the actual life at Basel, and of the intrigues in the Council; what knowledge we have on these points comes from his letters.[2] Probably, however, Æneas felt that such a work would lead him into questions of controversy, in which he had no keen personal interest. He did not, therefore, write the history of the Council as a whole; but in 1440, when he was secretary of Felix V., he wrote three books of Commentaries on the Council of Basel, which dealt only with the circumstances leading to the deposition of Eugenius IV. and the election of Felix V. The work was really a pamphlet in defence of his master Felix; only here and there do we find the vivid touches of personal interest attaching to its pages, which otherwise merely cast the cover of an historical narrative over the learned arguments adduced by theologians in the Council's favour. The preface is ingeniously adapted to beguile the reader, unawares, into a controversial pamphlet, and with an affected artlessness to beg promotion for the writer. 'It is my misfortune,' says Æneas, ' to waste my energies on writing history when I ought to spend them in providing for my old age. My friends say to me, "What are you doing, Æneas? Are you not ashamed, at your age, of having no money? Do you not know that a man should be stalwart at twenty, cautious at thirty, rich at forty? He who has passed that limit will try in vain." I acknowledge the truth of this; time after time I have put aside poets and historians, but like a moth round a candle I flutter back to my ruin. Since fate wills it, so let it be. The poor as well as the rich can live till death calls him. Poverty is wretched in old age, but it is the more wretched to those who have no taste for literature. I will enjoy what heaven sends, content, in the words of Horace—

> Nec turpem senectam
> Degere nec cithara carentem.'

---

[1] It is given in Urstisius, *Epitome historiæ Basileæ.*

[2] Especially that of May 21, 1437, to Piero da Noceto, in Mansi, xxxi. 220.

In this graceful way Æneas announced that he was serving
Felix in hopes of preferment; nor was the form of historical
writing the only one which he was prepared to use for this purpose. He followed the example of Poggio in reviving the
Ciceronian dialogue. The occasion of this production was a
decision given by the University of Köln to some questions submitted to them by their Archbishop concerning the controversy
between Eugenius and Felix. The University set forth their
views in three propositions, which asserted the supremacy of
general councils, condemned the German neutrality, and said
that the Church was synodically assembled at Basel, if the
Council had not been lawfully translated. The saving clause was,
as Æneas calls it, ' the sting at the end of the serpent's tail;'
and Æneas generously offered the University of Köln to remove
its venom. His interest really lay in stating the commonplace arguments in favour of the Council with taste and grace.
For this purpose he wrote his pamphlet in a series of dialogues.
He and his co-secretary, Martin Lefranc, a Frenchman, are
returning from a day's ramble outside Basel, delighted with
their holiday, expatiating on the blessings of a country life,
and expanding the Virgilian idylls into very tolerable Latin
prose. Another couple draws near them, Nicolas of Cusa and a
Novarese legist, Stefano da Caccia, also in earnest converse.
Æneas and his friend retire behind the bushes and listen to
their disputation. The literary skill of the dialogue consists in
the alternation of the two pairs of interlocutors. When the
scholastic arguments of Cusa and his friend may be supposed
to have wearied the reader, Æneas gives a little relief by
discussions on classical archæology, literature, history. When
quotations from Fathers and decrees of Councils have palled,
quotations from Virgil and Latin historians succeed. This
reaches a climax when Cusa and Caccia pause at vespers to say
their hours. Æneas and Martin agree that literary discussion is
more profitable than the repetition of canonical hours, which
may be a useful solace in the cloister, but is a weariness to men
of learning. The two pairs at length show themselves to one
another. Cusa, who had maintained the cause of Eugenius,
confesses himself vanquished, and goes back to Basel to sup
with Lefranc. Æneas also invites himself on the ground that
he is so poor he has nothing in his house. We are tempted to

think that the dialogues of Æneas, like the propositions which
he combats, were meant to carry their point in their tail.[1]

At Vienna Æneas had increased reason to use his pen for
the purpose of gaining fame. He turned again to light and
frivolous subjects, wrote love poems, epigrams, epitaphs, whatever he thought would be read and admired. He wrote a Latin
comedy in the style of Terence, called ' Chrisis,' and a Latin
novel in the style of Boccaccio, ' Lucretia and Euryalus,' which
was the most famous of his works, and had still greater circu-
lation after its author became Pope. It was not a book which
the Pope could read without shame, and Pius II. apologised for
having written it. It contained, he said, two things—an in-
delicate story and an edifying moral; all read the first, but few
heeded the last.[2] They might indeed be forgiven for overlooking it, as it is by no means obvious; Æneas wrote his tale
without any desire for edification, merely to please Kaspar
Schlick, whose amours it most probably describes. In matters
ecclesiastical he signalised his position as a neutral by writing a
treatise, the ' Pentalogus,' in which he put the arguments for
neutrality as cogently as before he had advocated the cause of
the Council.[3] He wrote treatises on all subjects—on the favourite
theme of ' The Miseries of a Court Life,' on ' Education ' for
the young Ladislas of Hungary, on ' The Nature and Care of
Horses.' Nothing came amiss to the pen of Æneas; but the
subjects in which he was most interested were history and
geography, and it is his great merit that he saw the close connexion between these two studies. To him curiosity supplied
the spur as well as the method; to observe and to inquire
were the first steps, and he was then content to arrange
his knowledge as he obtained it. He is the Herodotus of
the fifteenth century, without the simplicity and dignity of
his forerunner; too much concerned himself in what he relates
to be entirely trusted, yet with the same quickness of apprehension, the same vividness, and the same profound belief in
the mighty movement of human affairs. His first account of
the events at Basel was rather a polemical pamphlet than an
historical work. But when the fate of the Council was decided,

---

[1] These dialogues are given by Kollar, *Analecta Vindobon.* ii. 691.
[2] *Epistolæ*, No. 395.
[3] In Pez, *Thesaurus Anecdotorum*, t. iv part iii. 650.

Æneas in a second book set forth his new opinions, displayed
the mischievous activity of the conciliar movement, and traced
with precise brevity the steps in its rise and fall.[1] He followed
this by a collection of short biographical sketches of illustrious
contemporaries.[2] In 1452 he began a history of Frederick III.,
which he continued up to the time when he left Germany.[3] On
his return to Italy he undertook to write for Alfonso of Naples a
history of Bohemia, which he carried to the death of Ladislas.
The picturesqueness of the Hussite wars attracted the fancy of
Æneas, and he described them in his best Livian style. In
1458, while suffering from an attack of the gout, he was asked
by a bookseller to revise a sketch of universal history and carry
it down to his own times. This led Æneas to put together the
contents of his commonplace book in the form of a book
'about the condition of Europe,' which is a mixture of geography and history, with little attention to style and no proportion in the events related. This was the beginning of a
'Universal History and Geography' which he projected, and
of which when Pope he found time to write the part dealing
with Asia. He redacted also for popular use the 'Decades' of
Flavius Blondus, so far as the accession to the Papal throne of
John XXIII.

Apology
for his
devotion to
literature.
In the preface to the 'Asia' Pius II. apologises for the fact
that a Pope should have any time to devote to literature.
'There will be malign interpreters of our work who will say that
we rob Christendom of our time and devote ourselves to what is
useless. We answer that our writings ought to be read before
they are blamed. If elegance of style has no charms for the
reader, he will still find much useful information. Our time has
not been taken from our duties; but we have robbed our old age
of its rest that we might hand down to posterity all that we
know to be memorable. We have given to writing the hours due
to sleep. Some will say that we might have spent our vigils
better. We know that many of our predecessors made better
use of their leisure; but ours is not unfruitfully employed, for
knowledge begets prudence, and prudence is the leader of life.'

[1] This is published by Fea, *Pius II. a calumniis vindicatus.* Rome, 1822.
[2] *De Viris Claris,* as appendix to Mansi, *Orationes,* iii. 144; more fully, *De
Viris Illustribus,* in the publications of the Literary Society in Stuttgart, 1843.
[3] The fullest edition is in Kollar, *Analecta Vindobon.* ii.

The Pope's critics might have been strengthened in their opinion, had they known that he was also engaged in writing a history of his own pontificate. The Commentaries of Pius II. is his most important literary work, and contains a full account of all the events in which he was engaged. Platina in his Life of Pius II. mentioned the existence of these Commentaries; but they were not published till 1584, by Francesco Bandini de' Piccolomini, Archbishop of Siena, who possessed a manuscript which had been copied by a German priest, Johannes Gobellinus. Archbishop Piccolomini assigned to the copyist the honour of being the author. The Commentaries of Pius II. were published under the name of Gobellinus, and have .continued to be quoted by his name. Campano, however, in a letter to Cardinal Piccolomini, tells us that Pius II. wrote Commentaries, and handed over to him for correction the results of his hurried dictation ;[1] he pronounces that they need no other hand to increase their dignity, and are the despair of those who would wish to imitate them. Campano, however, divided them into twelve books, and probably made a few additions and alterations. Platina mentions the beginning of a thirteenth book which Gobellinus did not include in his manuscript.[2]

In his Commentaries we have the best literary work of Æneas. The study of history was to him the source of instruction in life, the basis for the formation of his character. He looked upon events with reference to their results in the future, and his actions were regulated by a strong sense of historical proportion. Similarly, the present was to him always the product of the past, and he shaped his motives by reference to historical antecedents. It was probably this historical point of view which made him engage in so many schemes, because he felt that, when once affairs were in movement, the skilful statesman might be able to reap some permanent advantage. He was not willing to let slip any opportunity which might afford an opening for his political dexterity. Had he been less of a student, had his mind been less fertile, he might have concentrated his energies more successfully on one supreme object.

We have made sufficient use of the writings of Pius II. to

---

[1] *Campani Opera* (ed. Rome, 1495), Epistol. i. 1.

[2] The thirteenth book is published by Voigt in the appendix to vol. ii. of his *Ænea Sylvio de' Piccolomini.*

illustrate his vividness of pictorial power, his insight into
character, his statesmanlike analysis of political motives. But
Pius II. is not content only to record matters in which he was
himself engaged. His Commentaries are full of digressions
about European affairs generally. He never mentions anything
without fully investigating its causes; he never sees a town
which he does not describe with reference to its past. Pius II.
is the first writer who attempted to represent the present as
it would look to posterity; who consciously applied a scientific
conception of history to the explanation and arrangement of
passing events.

In illustration of this genuine historical insight the judgment of Pius II. on the life of Jeanne Darc may be quoted.
Pius II. tells the story with commendable accuracy, and then
sums up: 'Thus died Joan, a wondrous and stupendous maid,
who restored the fallen and almost ruined kingdom of France,
and inflicted many serious disasters on the English. Making
herself a leader of men, she preserved her modesty unharmed
amid troops of soldiers, and nothing unseemly was ever heard
about her. Whether her work were of God or of man I
should find it difficult to affirm. Some think that when the
French nobles were at variance, and one could not endure the
leadership of another, the successes of the English drove one,
who was wiser than the rest, to devise a scheme by which they
might be induced to submit to the leadership of a maid who
asserted that she was sent by Heaven; in this way the conduct
of the war was entrusted to her, and a supreme command was
assured. This, at all events, is most certain, that it was a maid
by whose leadership the siege of Orleans was raised, by whose
arms the territory between Bourges and Paris was conquered, by
whose advice Rheims was recovered and the coronation there
performed, by whose onslaught Talbot was routed and his army
slain, by whose boldness the gate of Paris was burnt, by whose
care and zeal the fortunes of France were secured. It is a
worthy matter to hand down to memory, although posterity
may lend it admiration rather than belief.'[1] We seem to be
reading the words of a modern critic who stands on a basis of
assured fact, and though suggesting a rationalistic explanation of

[1] *Comment.* 157-8.

what is almost incredible, still prefers to keep a suspended
judgment.

In spite of his literary gifts, Æneas Sylvius did not enjoy a
great reputation in Italy; nor was he famous before his elevation to the cardinalate.   Italian men of letters were very exclusive, and reigned within their own circles, absorbed in their own
labours and their own jealousies: one who lived in Germany
was regarded as outside the pale of culture.   When Æneas became Cardinal many were ready to flatter him; but Æneas knew
the trick of flattery too well to be deceived.   In truth he had
left Italy too young to be a finished scholar; he knew scarcely
anything of Greek, and he was by nature a man of action rather
than a student.   He could not in respect of knowledge compete
with the professed scholars of Italy, Guarino, Filelfo, and the
like.   Moreover, as a stylist he was imperfect and lacking in
finish.   His residence in Germany had infected his Latinity with
barbarisms,[1] and in Italy Latinity was nothing if it was not
strictly classical.

Thus Pius II., though the most eminent man of letters of
his age, and one who deserves a high position amongst literary
men of all times, was not regarded as a member of the literary
clique which prevailed in Italy.   He was not a profound
scholar, he was not an elegant stylist; his penetration, his ready
sympathies, his knowledge of human nature, his largeness of
view were qualities which the literature of his time regarded as
of little moment.   Pius II., on his side, was not concerned to
gain the applause of the famous scholars of his own day.   No
doubt he would have welcomed it, if it had been genuinely
given; but he did not choose to beg the homage of a crowd of
literary sycophants.   He had too great a sense of his personal
worth to accept flattery which was prompted only by an expectation of future favours.   He had too keen a knowledge of
men to confound genuine merit with a capacity for writing
eulogy.   He was too confident in himself to trust to the praises
of others rather than his own record of his own actions, to commend him to the consideration of posterity.   Hence the great
literary Pope proved to be but a poor patron.   The hopes of
the humanists, which had risen high on the accession of Pius II.

---

[1] ' De verborum delectu non nihil illi Germania detraxerat, coacto sæpe
apud barbaros cultiora negligere,' says Campano.

to the pontificate, were rudely dashed. An army of copyists
was not re-established in Rome; there was no zeal for the collection of manuscripts, no orders for translations or com-
pilations, no glad acceptance of dedications or of complimentary
verses. Not that Pius II. was heedless of such things; but he
could do all that he wanted for himself, or with the assistance
of a few trusted friends. He did not wish, like Nicolas V., to
found his fame on the patronage of literature and art; he did
not wish to narrow the sphere of his activity. The reputation
of a man of letters he was sure to gain by his own writings;
it was necessary for him to emphasise his practical energy rather
than his care for literature, if his fame was to acquire its due
proportion.

His un-
popularity
with the
humanists.
Great was the disappointment of the humanists when the
sad truth dawned upon them. For a time they hoped by
perseverance to overcome the Pope and convince him of their
usefulness. The older generation—Poggio, Guarino, Manetti,
Valla—had almost died out when Pius II. ascended the Papal
throne. Filelfo was the one literary veteran who remained,
and he resolutely pursued the siege of the Pope's goodwill.
Pius II. treated him with courtesy rather than with honour,
received his letters and compositions, listened to his speeches
with good humour rather than with gratitude, and made him
presents which were marks of recognition rather than of favour.
It soon became known that the Pope behaved as a critic and
not as a patron, that he pulled to pieces the poems presented
to him, and that his motto was, 'poets and orators ought
to be supreme, or they are nothing.' He professed his contempt for mediocrity, and cared only for such compositions as
were really excellent. He did not value the fashionable style
of oratory in Italy, but declared that a needless use of words
showed the indolence of the speaker.[1] Sentiments more shocking
to the views of the humanists of the fifteenth century could not
have been expressed. We are not surprised that his biographer
adds to his account of Pius II., 'he incurred great odium.'

An epigram of the Pope's, which he made during his sojourn
at Mantua, was rapidly spread through literary circles, and
excited the wildest wrath. Ammannati, who was then the
Pope's secretary, tells us how the epigram arose, and gives us a

[1] Campano, *Vita Pii*, in Mur. iii pt. 2, 986.

faithful picture of the Pope's amusements.[1] One day at Mantua, while weary with affairs, Pius II. took his usual relaxation of a ramble in the country. With Ammannati and three other of his friends, he took boat on the Mincio to visit a monastery about three miles distant. To beguile the journey, his secretary read aloud some of the congratulatory poems which had been addressed to the new Pope at his accession, and had been laid aside till a convenient season offered when they might be read. The sound of verses soon kindled the poetic flame, and impromptus began to fly about the company. Presently was read a poem by Campano, which said that gifts ought not to be given to those who asked, but to those who did not ask, and then insinuated that, as he had not asked, he ought to receive. On this the Pope produced the following repartee:

> Munera, Campane, si non sunt danda petenti,
> Jure tuos surda currimus aure preces.
>
> To your request you've made our duty plain,
> Since he who asks ought nothing to obtain.

As all the poems asked for something, the Pope at last said with a smile, 'I will give you something for your poets,' and then made the epigram:

> Discite pro numeris numeros sperare poetæ,
> Mutare est animus carmina non emere.
>
> Take, poets, for your verses, verse again;
> My purpose is to mend, not buy your strain.

Ammannati capped this by another:

> Discite pro numeris nummos tractare poetæ,
> Expectata dabit munera nulla Pius.
>
> Learn, poets, to turn from your verses to gain,
> From the bounty of Pius you nought will obtain.

But Pius II. had had his joke, and altered Ammannati's epigram into—

> Discite pro numeris nummos sperare poetæ,
> Expectata dabit munera magna Pius.
>
> Hope, poets, hope on, from your verses for gain,
> From the bounty of Pius you much will obtain.

At the same time he granted the petitions of the needy bards.

---

[1] *Cardinalis Papiensis Epistolæ*, 49.

This is Ammannati's account of the jocular way in which the epigram of Pius II. was thrown off; but

> Mutare est animus carmina non emere

was passed on from mouth to mouth in literary circles, and awoke the profoundest wrath. A stinging repartee was also current, which was attributed to Filelfo, but which Filelfo himself assigned to Angelo Pontano.[1] It ran:

> Si tibi pro numeris numeros fortuna dedisset,
> Non esset capiti tanta corona tuo.

> Verse for your verse if fate had given to you,
> The Papal crown had never decked your brow.

Pius II. was decidedly unpopular amongst the humanists. Filelfo, after long hoping against hope, at last attacked the Pope in an anonymous invective,[2] which assigned to him the practice of every classic vice. After the death of Pius II. the tongue of Filelfo was still more loosened. He wrote a poem of triumph on the death of Pius II., and set to work to blacken his memory. At first the friends of Pius were indignant at such scurrility, and used their influence to keep Filelfo from the good graces of the new Pope; but Filelfo managed to play upon the vanity of Cardinal Ammannati by offering him his literary homage. Ammannati demanded a faint retractation of the calumnies against Pius, and then extended the hand of friendship to Filelfo. So venal was the praise of the humanists, so interested the judgments which they offered to hand down to posterity. It was an additional testimony of the penetration and profound practical sense of Pius II. that he disregarded their windy homage, and estimated at its due value their influence over posterity. No man could be more desirous of glory than Pius II.; but he was shrewd enough to see that glory would be won by his own acts and by his own writings more surely than by the inflated eulogies of hired pedants. As was natural for a man of wide culture, Pius II. had a keen sense of reality, and was not deceived by a display of the apparatus of learning, and by the false glitter of laborious style. He was a foe to pedantry and ostentation; he knew that mere

---

[1] *Filelfi Epistolæ*, xxvi. 1. quoted by Voigt, *Æneas Sylvius*, iii. 628.
[2] We know of this from the defence of Girolamo Agliotti, *Opuscul.* ii. 346, &c.

verbiage had no genuine vitality. In this, as in most other
points of his character, Pius II. stands a little way outside the
common current of his age. Himself a humanist, he saw the
shallowness of many of the prevalent literary tricks. He strove
to estimate at its real value everything by which he was surrounded. He was a critic of his own life as well as that of
others; he knew the worth of the fashions which he followed,
of the opinions which he heard and expressed; he could use all
things, but would not surrender himself to any. CHAP.
IX.

But though Pius II. refused to form a literary court and
surround himself with humanists, dependent on his bounty,
he had a small circle of scholars whom he chose as his intimates. The private life of Pius II. was singularly simple.
When occasion offered, his sense of decorum and his cultivated
taste led him to display a becoming magnificence. He was
careful to do all that beseemed a Pope; but he was not prepared
to sink his personality entirely in his office. His Papal duties
were thoroughly performed; but he reserved to himself the
right of using his leisure in literary pursuits. He gave audience
daily, and read and signed all documents presented to him;
but he would not bind himself to do it always at Rome in the
Vatican. If his taste so chose, those who needed him might
find him beneath the chestnut trees of Petrioli, or by the side
of a fountain at Tivoli. A magnificent court, the constant
presence of a band of literary flatterers—such things would have
been intolerable to him. Pius II. was a genuine man, and
would not lay aside his natural tastes. He needed a few trusty
friends with whom he could unbend freely. Warm-hearted
and affectionate, he wished to feel the contact of a few congenial minds, chosen not because they were distinguished or
might be useful, but because they were personally attractive to
his character and tastes. Simple life
of Pius II.

It was this strong personality that led him to seek the promotion of his nephews, and made him feel such a strong interest
in men of Sienese extraction. His two secretaries, to whom he
dictated his writings, Goro Lolli and Agostino de' Patrizzi, were
both Sienese. Francesco de' Patrizzi also, who was chancellor
of the Sienese republic, and was obliged for political reasons to
quit his country, received from Pius II. the rich bishopric of
Gaeta. The chief friend, however, of Pius II. was Jacopo Cardinal
Amman-
nati.

Ammannati, a man of lowly origin, born near Peschia, in the Lucchese territory, who had gone to Rome to seek his fortune as a scholar in the palmy days of Nicolas V. Calixtus III. made him one of his secretaries, and Pius II. found in him a literary nursling. He made him Bishop of Pavia and Cardinal; he adopted him into the family of the Piccolomini, and procured for him the citizenship of Siena. Ammannati took the Pope as his model both in character and in literary composition. He continued the Commentaries of Pius II. for the five years following his death, and adopted the same style and method. During all the pontificate of Pius II. Ammannati enjoyed his full confidence, and at the last closed his eyes in death. He was a true friend, and did not abuse the Pope's confidence to enrich himself. He was acute rather than profound, a man of letters of the same type as Pius II., without his practical capacity or his loftiness of aim. He did not aspire to be a statesman, and his attempts at ambition did not rise higher than vanity. He had the same delight in life as Pius II.; but in him it took the shape of an excessive devotion to the pleasures of the chase. He was an excellent and amiable man, but not a strong one, a sympathetic companion rather than a counsellor to Pius II.[1]

Campano.
The other distinguished literary friend of Pius II. was Gianantonio Campano. He was the son of a peasant in Campania, and his surname is merely taken from the province in which he was born. At the age of three he lost his father, and soon afterwards his mother; under the guardianship of his aunt he was sent into the fields as a shepherd boy. His precocious intelligence induced a neighbouring priest to take him as a domestic servant, and give him some instruction in his leisure hours. Soon he advanced far enough to act as tutor to the sons of a noble in Naples. Here he attended the lectures of Lorenzo Valla, and in six years of persistent study gained a large fund of knowledge. From Naples he betook himself to Perugia, where at the age of twenty he began to teach and soon acquired a considerable reputation. In Perugia he stayed for some time, wrote love poems of a questionable sort, and made speeches when speeches were needed. On the accession of

[1] There is a notice of him by Jacopus Volterranus prefixed to his *Commentaries* (ed. 1614), but his character appears sufficiently from his letters.

Pius II. he went with the Perugian embassy to congratulate the new Pope. He seems to have felt that the Curia was his sphere, for he followed Pius II. to Mantua, ingratiated himself with Ammannati, then with the Pope, and was soon rewarded by the Bishopric of Croton, which was afterwards exchanged for the richer see of Teramo.[1]

Campano was a sort of buffoon whose sallies amused the Pope. He was a genuine peasant, and carried his character in his appearance. Short, thick-set, and clumsy, with an enormous paunch, he had a large face with a turned-up nose and broad spreading nostrils. His small, keen, twinkling eyes were deep set under a bushy and projecting brow. He was, as he tells us himself, covered all over with hair like a wild boar. It was clear that Pius II. was not considering abstract decorum when he bestowed on such a man a bishopric.[2] He needed Campano to amuse him with his ready geniality and his power of good-humoured satire; moreover, the pen of Campano was always at the Pope's command for an epigram, an inscription, or whatever was needed. He was a master of a clear, flowing, incisive style, who won reputation as a historian by his Life of Bracchio, and as an essayist by a composition against ingratitude. When Pius II. wished to unbend himself in private, the refinement of Ammannati and the sturdy joviality of Campano gave him the social elements which he required.

As in literature, so also in art, Pius II. possessed too genuine a taste to indulge in indiscriminate patronage, and his strong individuality impelled him to seek a field where he might leave a record entirely his own. Pius II. was catholic in his taste, and did not merely follow the prevailing fashion. Though a lover of antique art, he did not shut his eyes to the great artistic revival which was going on in Italy. He saw that art and literature went hand in hand. 'After Petrarch,' he writes, 'literature emerged. After Giotto rose a band of painters, and

Pius II. and art.

---

[1] There is a life of Campano by Michael Fernus prefixed to his works, of which there are two editions, Rome, 1495, and Venice, 1502; see also Paulus Jovius, *Elogia.*

[2] Campano was at least not vain; he describes himself, *Ep.* iii. 47: 'Quid in Campano? Totas noctes stertit; videas medio in thoro hominem nudum feris omnibus horridiorem quas sylvæ alunt: pedes uncos: curvas et hirsutas manus; nares platas et patentes, et subductam frontem; turgidum jam novis ferculis et inflatum ventrem; membra brevia, teretia, corpulenta.'

now we see both arts at their height.'[1] He did not, like most
of his contemporaries, draw all his artistic ideas from classical
antiquity; but he admired the paintings of Giotto at Assissi,
and boldly declared that the sculptors of the façade of the
Cathedral at Orvieto were no way inferior to Phidias and
Praxiteles.[2] Nor was his admiration confined to Italian work
only; he could appreciate the beauties of London, the splendour
of York Minster, and the magnificence of the Sebalduskirche
Nürnberg.[3]

His build-
ings in
Rome and
Siena.
With these wide sympathies Pius II. was as little likely to
make his pontificate an epoch of architectural splendour as of
literary activity. He collected manuscripts, but with discretion; he built, but it was in moderation. He respected the
great schemes of Nicolas, without being carried away by them,
and was content to contribute his share towards the projected
splendours of the Vatican and S. Peter's. He built a tower at
the entrance of the Vatican palace and adorned several of its
rooms. He restored the terrace which led to S. Peter's and
ornamented it with colossal statues of S. Peter and S. Paul,
while inside he erected a chapel of S. Andrew. But it was not
Rome which stood first in the affections of Pius II.; in the
'loggia del Papa' and the Piccolomini palace at Siena we find
more enduring records of his architectural taste.

Buildings
in Pienza.
The abiding memorial, however, of Pius II. is his birthplace, Corsignano, which he indissolubly associated with himself
by giving it his name and elevating it to the seat of a bishopric
under the title of Pienza. The little town lies high upon a
spur of the volcanic hills that form the Sienese territory. It
looks upon the old Etruscan seat of Radicofani and the lofty
heights of Monte Cetona and Monte Amiata. There Pius II.
erected the full equipment of buildings necessary to give
grandeur to an Italian city. On one side of a spacious piazza
lies the Cathedral; over against it the Palazzo Pubblico, a
younger sister of the stately Palazzo dei Signori at Florence;
the other sides of the piazza are enclosed by the Archbishop's
palace and the palace of the Piccolomini. The architect of
these buildings was Bernardo of Florence, most probably Bernardo Rosellino.[4] Yet in the building of the Cathedral Pius II.

[1] *Epistolæ*, 119.   [2] *Comment.* 111.   [3] *De Ritu Germaniæ*, 1054.
[4] Vasari puts down these works to Francesco di Giorgio; but Pius II., in

would not place himself entirely at the disposal of an Italian architect. He remembered some features that had struck him in the churches of Germany, and ordered that the aisles should be of the same height as the nave, while in the arrangement of the five chapels into which the apse is divided, we trace still further the influence of the German Gothic. The building is impressive through its simplicity and elegance, but unfortunately has suffered through the crumbling of the tufo on which it is built, which offered from the first great difficulties in the way of laying a foundation.

The façade is divided into three equal parts, with three square-headed doorways, separated from one another by massive pilasters, flanked by pillars, which are continued to the second tier of the building, and there are symmetrically formed into an arcade. Above this rises a triangular architrave, in the centre of which is a lunette, containing the Papal arms, with the crossed keys above. The Piccolomini palace is an exquisite specimen of the domestic architecture of which Siena contains so many examples; but its great feature is the second courtyard, which leads into a garden, descending with terraces along the precipitous hill-side. Here the Pope has emphasised his love of nature as part of the accompaniments of cultivated life —the two lower storeys of the house on this side are broken by arcades of delicate and graceful architecture, which extend along the whole length of the building, and afford a glorious prospect over the Etruscan hills.

The care of Pius II. extended also to the details of his building. Two massive fountains still adorn his palace, and the cathedral is full of records of his taste. The choir books are enriched by illuminations; the sacristy contains a cope, which is a marvel of embroidery, adorned with the history of David and Solomon, on a ground wrought with birds and flowers. He also gave a series of tapestries to hang round the piazza on days of great festivals, a pastoral staff, a pax, a chalice, a mitre set with enamels, and a head of S. Andrew in gold. Nowhere can more characteristic specimens of the varied works of the early

the *Commentarii*, 235, calls him ' Bernardus natione Florentinus,' and Rumohr, *Italienische Forschungen*, ii. 182, identifies him with Bernardo Rosellino, though others have identified him with Bernardo di Lorenzo. See Münts, *Les Arts à la Cour des Papes*, i. 233.

Renaissance be seen than at Pienza, which, from its remote situation, has many times escaped the spoiler's hand.

Pius II. hoped to make Pienza a considerable town; it still remains a village with about nine hundred inhabitants. The Cathedral is sinking in its foundations; the Piccolomini palace is scarce better than a desolate ruin. The Pope's scheme to give importance to his birthplace has proved a failure; the individuality that resolved to leave its mark upon the world has been baffled by the laws that regulate man's affairs. This is but a symbol of all that Pius II. did. He coped successfully with the world in his own day, but his plans were founded on his individual powers or caprices, not on a large sympathy with the needs and aspirations of mankind. Yet still Pius II. has the reward that ever attaches to the strong work of a genuine man. At Rome one building superseded another, and the traces of each man's energy have to be reconstructed in detail. Few may visit Pienza; but those who do so are at once brought into close communication with the mind of Pius II., which there speaks without contradiction from others. So with the rest of the achievements of Pius II. They did not leave any decisive mark upon the world's history; but they were founded on a higher and nobler conception of Christendom and of the Papal mission than prevailed for the next century.

General results of the pontificate of Pius II.

We have lingered over Pius II. partly because the records of his pontificate are so full that they serve to illustrate much that was common to all popes, partly because Pius II. is a character most illustrative of the changes that were slowly passing over Europe in his day. In him the modern and the mediæval spirit meet and mingle. His life covers a great epoch in the history of the Church, the epoch in which reformation from within was pronounced impossible. His skill did much to sweep away from the ecclesiastical system all traces of the abortive attempt, and to make good the position of the Papal monarchy against the threatened revolution. He further strove to set the Papacy once more in the forefront of European politics, and although he was not entirely successful, yet he did not entirely fail. He left the question still open, and it depended on his successors to determine the future direction of the Papal policy.

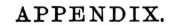

APPENDIX.

APPENDIX

APPENDIX.

—◦◦—

1. *Lives of Martin V.*

MURATORI, iii. pt. ii. 857–88, prints two lives of Martin V., from
MSS. in the Vatican. The first is short and annalistic, opposed to
Martin V. on the grounds of his avarice and nepotism, written under
the influence of the reaction of the Curia which set in after Martin's
death. Even this hostile writer is bound to confess 'suo tempore tenuit stratas et vias publicas securas; quod non fuit auditum
a ducentis annis et circa.' The second life is fuller, and is eulogistic;
it is in general accurate, but is the work of one who thinks little of
the conciliar movement, and rejoices over the dissolution of the
Council of Siena as averting the danger of another schism. This
last life was known to PLATINA, who has taken it as the basis of his
life of Martin V., incorporating other information.

2. *Florentine Authorities.*

For the relations of Martin V. with Florence we have information from POGGIO, *Hist. Florentina* in MURATORI, xx. 322, and
LEONARDO BRUNI, *Commentarii* in MURATORI, xix. 630. As both of
these were in the confidence of the Pope, their information is valuable. Still more important are the *Commissioni di Rinaldo degli
Albizzi*, edited by Cesare Guasti (Florence, 1867). Rinaldo was a
celebrated Florentine statesman, born in 1370, and engaged in the
business of the Republic from 1399 to 1434, when he went into exile
before the power of Cosimo dei Medici. Rinaldo went in 1418 as
ambassador of Florence to Martin V., whom he met at Pavia, and in
his *Commissioni* (i. 294) we have an account of the negotiations
which brought the Pope to Florence. Again, in 1421, Rinaldo was
ambassador at Rome to make peace in Naples (i. 312). In 1424 he
was again sent to Rome to win over Martin V. to side with Florence

against the Duke of Milan (ii. 85, &c.). In 1425 Rinaldo again returned to Rome for the same purpose (ii. 320). From Rinaldo's complaints of Martin's long delays in answering we see the Pope's caution and diplomatic skill. The *Commissioni* of Rinaldo generally are full of incidental remarks on the Pope's policy, and chronicle the rumours which from time to time prevailed. They show us that Martin V. commanded the respect of the politicians of Italy.

For the period of Martin V. the *Chronicon Domini Antonini Archipræsulis Florentini* becomes valuable. S. ANTONINUS was the son of a Florentine notary, who entered the Dominican order in that city at the age of 16, about the year 1405. He was celebrated for his theological learning as well as for the sanctity of his life, and his *Summa Theologiæ* was a work of considerable repute. He distinguished himself as a theologian in the Council of Florence, and in 1445 Eugenius IV. made him Archbishop of that city, where he was much venerated till his death in 1459. In 1523 he was canonised. He wrote a universal chronicle, compiled with the carefulness of a theologian rather than with the insight of a historian. His chronicle was continued till the time of his death. Though it is deficient in critical spirit, is destitute of style and abounds in inaccuracies, it still contains valuable information on many points of detail which cannot be found elsewhere. For the early period of Martin V. he has borrowed largely from Leonardo Bruni, and becomes more valuable as he approaches matters of which he was contemporary.

3. *Bracchio and Sforza.*

For the history of these condottieri generals we have two lives which relate their exploits at length. MURATORI, xix. 435, prints *Vita Bracchii Perusini*, by JOANNES ANTONIUS CAMPANUS, the friend of Pius II. and Bishop of Croton. Unfortunately the life of Bracchio is written chiefly as an exercise of style, and though it relates the actual facts of Bracchio's exploits, the information that it contains has to be stripped of turgid laudation, and the real meaning of events has to be supplied from other sources. Similarly we have a life of Sforza by LEODORISIO CRIVELLI in MURATORI, xix. 628. Crivelli was a member of a noble Milanese family, and intended to write a history of Francesco Sforza, to which this account of his father was to serve as a preface; the work, however, was not continued beyond 1424. There is another work of Crivelli in Muratori, xxiii. 21, *De Expeditione Pii II. in Turcas*, written when Crivelli was a Papal secretary, an office on which he entered in 1458. Some writers have wished to make out that these works are by two different authors of the same name; but the reasons which induce them to do so seem inadequate (*see* Tiraboschi). Though we know little of Crivelli we are justified in assuming that he was amply acquainted with affairs. His life of Sforza is, like that of Campanus, of the nature of a panegyric, but is more modest and restrained.

---

4. *Naples.*

For the general history of Naples we have the authorities referred to in Appendix to vol. i. The *Annales Bonincontrii Miniatensis* in MURATORI, xxi., are also useful. Lorenzo Bonincontri was born at S. Miniato in 1410; but his father was obliged to go into exile in 1431, in consequence of an appeal to the Emperor Sigismund to save S. Miniato from the tyranny of Florence. Bonincontri, after many wanderings, settled at Naples under the protection of King Alfonso. He was celebrated as an astrologer, a poet and a scholar, and wrote works on astrology as well as poems. He was a friend of learned men, amongst others of Marsilio Ficino. He began a history of Naples, which did not go beyond the year 1436, *i.e.*, did not reach the period with which he himself was personally familiar. Muratori has printed his *Annales* from 1366 to 1458. They are brief, but to the point—a pithy summary of facts with few judgments; his narrative, though not vivid, is correct and careful.

---

5. *The Council of Siena.*

Till recently very little was known about the Council; what was known was principally gathered from casual mentions by the various chroniclers previously mentioned, the letters in RAYNALDUS sub anno, and a few documents in MANSI, vol. xxviii.

Valuable as a more vivid picture of the relation of an Italian city towards the Papacy and towards a Council is the brief chronicle of FRANCESCO DI TOMMASEO in MURATORI, xx. 23. It is one of a series of Sienese chronicles. The writer tells how the Sienese regarded the Council and were discontented at losing the prospects of a rich harvest from its dissolution.

The chief authority, however, for the Council of Siena is JOHN STOJKOVIC of Ragusa, who was himself present as a representative of the University of Paris, both at Rome before the Council, at Pavia, and at Siena. He afterwards went to the Council of Basel, and wrote *Initium et Prosecutio Basiliensis Concilii*, edited by Palacky, in vol. i. of *Monumenta Conciliorum Generalium Seculi XV.* (Vienna, 1857). Pages 1–65 of this work are occupied with an account of the Council of Siena, which I have mostly followed, though it differs in many particulars from the accounts of the chroniclers mentioned above.

They wrote in view of the ignominious collapse of the Council, which
no one really wanted; to John of Ragusa it was a necessary link
between the decree *Frequens* and the Council of Basel. His account
is detailed, and is by an ecclesiastical eye-witness; the other mentions are only those of outsiders, who looked solely on the political
aspect of the matter. As regards the numbers present at Siena,
John seems to exaggerate as much as the others seem to minimise.

6. *France and England.*

The documents relating to Martin V. and France are to be found
in *Preuves des Libertés de l'Eglise Gallicane*, ch. xxii. Martin V.'s
correspondence with Chichele and Beaufort is in RAYNALDUS, *Annales
Ecclesiastici*, and WILKINS, *Concilia*, vol. iii. 471, &c. Additional
documents are to be found in DUCK'S *Life of Chichele* (1617), and
SPENCER'S *Life of Chichele* (1783).

7. *Rome.*

The letters of the celebrated scholar POGGIO BRACCIOLINI, edited
by TONELLI (Florence, 1832), give us some idea of the atmosphere
of the Curia under Martin V. Poggio was a Papal secretary, and
though it is disappointing that his letters say so little about actual
events, still they give us an idea of the extortion that prevailed.
See especially the letter to the secretary of the Bishop of Winchester,
Tonelli, ii. 18. A still more vivid picture of the Court of Martin V. is
to be found in the letters of the ambassadors of the Order of the Teutonic
Knights, who watched over the interests of the Order at Rome. Extracts from these letters, which are in the Archives of Königsberg, are
given by J. VOIGT, *Stimmen aus Rom über den päpstlichen Hof im
fünfzehnten Jahrhundert* in VON RAUMER'S *Historisches Taschenbuch*,
vol. iv., 1833. These letters are written in a plain, business-like
spirit, which treats bribes to the Pope as a necessary and natural
source of expense. The following may serve as a specimen :—' Der
Papst thut dieses nur darum mit so grosser Verfolgung und Übermuth,
weil er uns zu zwingen meint, ihm 10 bis 12,000 Gulden zu zuweisen,
was wir doch, ob Gott will, nimmer thun wollen, denn er ist so gierig,
übermüthig und drückend gegen diejenigen, über die er Macht zu
haben meint, als nur jemals ein Papst gewesen ist' (p. 170).

Concerning the relations of Martin V. with his family, information is to be found in COPPI'S *Memorie Colonnesi* (Rome, 1855), and
VAN REUMONT, *Beiträge zur Italienischen Geschichte*, vol. v.

MURATORI, xxiv. 1106, prints the *Mesticanza di Paolo di Liello
Petrone de lo Rione di Ponte*, a diary written by a Roman citizen;

some of the MS. is lost, but the part which remains covers the period between 1433 and 1446 ; it is the work of an eye-witness who was keen and observant.

8. *Death of Benedict XIII., and End of the Schism.*

The death of Benedict XIII. is assigned by RAYNALDUS to the year 1423, on the ground of his condemnation in the Council of Siena as " damnatæ memoriæ ; " also Martin V.'s letter to Alfonso, announcing the transfer of the Council from Pavia to Siena, begins : ' Per litteras crebras et nuntios habetur quod Petrus de Luna ab hac luce subtractus est ' (Raynaldus, 1423, § 9). But Mansi, in his note to Raynaldus, points out that a French Cardinal of Benedict XIII.'s obedience, Jean Carrer, in a letter to the Count of Armagnac gives the following circumstantial account of the death of Benedict XIII. and the election of his successor :—' Novembris die xvii. anni Domini MCCCCXXIV. sanctæ memoriæ dominus Benedictus XIII. Papa verus incipiens infirmari eodem mense die xxvii. quatuor cardinales . . . creavit ; quibus creatis die penultima ejusdem mensis inter septimam et octavam horam in Domino expiravit ' (MARTENE, *Thesaurus*, ii. 1731). This letter was written in 1429, protesting against the action of the Cardinals who elected Gil Munoz. The writer says that he was not present himself, and received no notice of Benedict XIII.'s death from the Cardinals who were present, nor did he hear of it till the following June, when he was informed by the Count of Armagnac. If this were so in his case, we need not wonder that rumours of Benedict XIII.'s death had prevailed previously, and that Martin V. believed him to be dead in 1423. Contelorius, in CIACONIUS, *Vitæ Paparum*, ii. 744 ; *Vita Dahæ* says :— ' Extat Martini V. Diploma datum quinto Idus Octobris Anno X. Pontificatus (1427) in quo narratur Benedictum mense Septembri die ante obitum anno 1424 in Paniscola de novo enunciasse nonnullos Cardinales ;' from which it would appear that Martin V. afterwards learned the truth.

The documents relating to the end of the schism are in MARTENE, *Thesaurus Novus Anecdotorum*, ii.

9. *The Hussite Wars.*

The difficulty that I have found in this chapter has been to give a condensed account of the affairs in Bohemia, selecting only such points as are necessary for an understanding of the problem which faced the Council of Basel. I regret that many picturesque details had to be omitted ; but I am not dealing primarily with the history of Bohemia. This subject has received much attention in the present century.

The current accounts till a few years ago were taken from German and Catholic sources. The fluent pen of ÆNEAS SYLVIUS in his *Historia Bohemica* produced an admirably interesting account of Bohemian affairs, which he had many opportunities of personally studying at Basel, Vienna, and afterwards in Bohemia itself. The artistic rendering of Æneas was mainly followed by succeeding writers, such as COCHLÆUS and DUBRAVIUS, whose writings were incorporated by LENFANT in his *Histoire de la Guerre des Hussites et du Concile de Bâle*. The present century, however, has seen the opening out of the historical records of Bohemia itself, chiefly through the labours of Palacky, Höfler, and more recently Tomek. PALACKY's *Würdigung der alten böhmischen Geschichtschreiber* (1830) was the beginning of studies the results of which are expressed in the ten volumes of his *Geschichte von Böhmen*. As I do not know the Tcheck language, I have followed Palacky in all points in which he draws from the Bohemian writers in that tongue. Many Latin documents dealing with the beginning of the religious movement in Bohemia are contained in PALACKY, *Documenta Magistrum Joh. Hus. illustrantia*, which reaches to the year 1418. The period from 1418 to 1436 is illustrated by the documents contained in PALACKY, *Urkundliche Beiträge zur Geschichte des Hussitenkriegs* (1873). A number of annals and chronicles are published by HÖFLER, *Geschichtschreiber der Hussitischen Bewegung* (1856–1866), and Höfler's preface contains much valuable criticism.

The most interesting among the Bohemian chronicles is LAURENTIUS OF BREZOVA, HÖFLER, i. 321, &c., whose chronicle is of the utmost importance for the years 1419–1423, where it unfortunately ends. This is the period of the outbreak of the religious war, and Brezova enables us to judge of the feeling of the Bohemian people. He was at the Court of Wenzel and was an eye-witness of affairs in Prag; he is a strong Utraquist, but is decidedly opposed to the Taborites. On the Catholic side we have a more lengthy chronicle by BARTOSCHEK OF DRAHONICZ, in DOBNER, *Monumenta Historica*, i. 130, &c.; it extends from 1419 to 1443, and though without style or proportion, it is valuable for military history. Bartoscheck was a royalist baron and soldier. The same period is also illustrated by the *Tractatus de Longævo Schismate* of the Abbot LUDOLF OF SAGAN, edited by LOSERTH (Vienna, 1880). PALACKY in his *Italienische Reise* had already called attention to this work, which has little new to say, but is important as giving the impressions of a contemporary from the strong Catholic point of view. The work begins with the election of Urban VI., and goes down to the year 1423. On the other hand, we have the *Chronicon Taboritarum* of NICOLAS OF PELHRSCHIMOW, in HÖFLER, ii. 475, &c., which deals, chiefly from a theological point of view, with the disputes between the Taborites and the theologians of Prag; it extends to the year 1444. It may suffice to have indicated these four works as illustrating the different sides of contemporary opinion.

Amongst German writers WINDECK in MENCKEN, i. 1073, shows us the opinion which Sigismund and his circle entertained of the Hussites and their doings. So, too, does ANDREAS RATISBONENSIS, an Augustinian canon of S. Magnus at Regensburg, who devoted himself to historical writing, stimulated, it would seem, by the Council of Constance. He entered the Augustinian order in 1410, and his writings extended to the period of 1439. His works dealing with the Hussites have been published by HÖFLER; they are *De Expeditionibus in Bohemia contra Hussitas hereticos* (HÖFLER, ii. 406, &c.), which embraces the period from 1418 to 1429, and the DIALOGUS (HÖFLER, i. 565) between *Ratio* and *Animus*, in which the theological as well as the political significance of the Hussite movement is discussed. These writings of Andreas give us the general feeling of the orthodox party in Germany. Andreas writes from the clerical point of view and is indignant at the lukewarmness of the princes; in a *Sermo secrete editus* (HÖFLER, ii. 416), dated 1422, he makes a violent attack on Sigismund, whom he accuses as a deceiver and beguiler of the Church, spending its wealth in profligate living and heeding not its distress.

Further examination of the writings of this period may be found in PALACKY's *Würdigung* and HÖFLER's preface. For modern works on Bohemia PALACKY's *Geschichte von Böhmen* supersedes all others. ASCHBACH's *Geschichte Kaiser Sigmunds* tells the tale from a German point of view; but the most accurate examination of the period of warfare against the Hussites is that of BEZOLD, *König Sigmund und die Reichskriege gegen die Husiten*, 3 vols., Munich, 1872-7. For the general aspect of the Hussite movement in its religious and political character, BEZOLD's *Zur Geschichte des Husitenthums* (Munich, 1874) is excellent. A more popular book dealing with the entire subject is DENIS, *Huss et la Guerre des Hussites*, Paris, 1878.

---

10. *Eugenius IV.*

1. Lives of Eugenius IV. :—

The life in MURATORI, vol. iii., part 2, 868, is slight and unimportant save for the Pope's dealings with the Colonna at the beginning of his pontificate. On this point we gather much additional information from the diary of STEFANO INFESSURA in MURATORI, iii., part 2, 1123. Infessura's career is not known; but in 1478 he was praetor in Horta, and afterwards secretary of the Senate. His diary begins in 1295, and is very fragmentary; it is written partly in Latin and partly in Italian. It grows more connected as it approaches

his own time, but has some information, not given elsewhere, of the
events of the years 1431 and 1434.

The life of Eugenius IV. by PLATINA can scarcely be ranked as an
authority, though it has some value as a compilation made while
events were still fresh; but there is little in Platina that we do not
find more fully elsewhere, save again the episode of the Colonna
rising.

More valuable is the life by VESPASIANO DA BISTICCI, in his most
interesting book *Vite di Uomini Illustri*, first published by MAI, in
the *Spicilegium Romanum*, vol. i. Vespasiano was a Florentine bookseller, born about 1420, and who lived certainly till 1493. He had
to do with the formation of many great libraries, especially those of
S. Marco at Florence, of Nicolas V., and of the Duke of Urbino. In
his position as copyist of manuscripts he was intimate with almost
all the chief patrons of learning in the fifteenth century. He writes
with great simplicity, and is a biographer rather than a historian;
but his book is full of interesting traits of the men of his time, and
no work gives such a vivid impression of the greatness of the early
Renaissance movement. About Eugenius IV., he chiefly informs us
of his stay at Florence and his zeal for the reformation of the
neighbouring monasteries. He had no personal knowledge of Eugenius IV., but regards him primarily as the patron of Nicolas V.
His judgment of Eugenius IV. is expressed in the words which he
puts into the mouth of the dying Pope—' O Gabriello, quanto sarebbe
suto meglio per la salute dell' anima tua, che tu non fussi mai suto
nè papa, nè cardinale, ma fussiti morto nella tua religione.'

Other authorities, who have been previously mentioned, are S.
ANTONINUS, whom Eugenius made Archbishop of Florence; BONICON-
TRIUS in MURATORI, xxi.; POGGIO, *Historia Florentina* in MURATORI,
xx.; BILLIUS and LEONARDO BRUNI, in MURATORI, xix. The ecclesiastical ceremonies during the stay of Eugenius IV. in Florence are
chronicled in an anonymous *Istorie di Firenze*, in MURATORI, xix.
949.

2. The *Vita Cardinalis Firmani*, by BATTISTA POGGIO, son of the
famous Poggio Braccioli, in BALUZE *Miscellanea*, iii. 266, is mainly an
exercise of style, and was dedicated to Cardinal Ammannati as such.
Still it contains some materials for the beginning of the pontificate of
Eugenius IV.

The letters of POGGIO BRACCIOLINI, who was in the service of
Eugenius IV. till his flight to Florence, give us notices of what was
passing at Rome. In a letter written just after the election of
Eugenius IV. (TONELLI, iv. 20), he says: ' Deus autem effecit ut
Pontificem habeamus quem cupiebamus, eum scilicet qui præteritorum
errorum reformationi vacaturus videatur suscepturusque publicam
orbis curam, si ei per aliorum molestias liceret. . . . Id me con-
solatur nos habere Pontificem bene cordatum et qui non terreatur

inanibus minis aut vagis rumoribus.' More important still is the
Dialogue *De Varietatibus Fortunæ* (Paris, 1723), a work owing its
origin to the sight of the ruins of Rome, containing a most valuable
description of the city in his day, and full of picturesque details of contemporary history. It was written in 1447, just after the death of
Eugeneus IV. The sight of the ruins of Rome leads the writer to
moralise on the mutability of fortune, of which he produces many
historical examples. Finally, he settles on the pontificate of
Eugenius IV., as amply illustrating his theme, and Book III. of the
Dialogue is devoted to a sketch of the troubles of Eugenius. 'Cum
pace uti posset, bello se implicuit minime necessario,' is his comment
(p. 87) on the attempt made by the Pope on the Colonna.

Still more important for the history of Italy during the first ten
years of Eugenius IV. are the *Decades Historiarum* of FLAVIUS
BLONDUS (Basel, 1569). Flavio Biondo was a native of Forlì,
born in 1388, and died in 1463. He was a diligent student of
antiquity, and went to seek his fortune at the Papal court early in
the pontificate of Eugenius IV.; he served as secretary to Eugenius
and his three successors. His labours in elucidating the antiquities
of Italy are amply shown in his great works, *Roma Restaurata* and
Italia Illustrata. His *Decades* mark an important epoch in historical
writing. Beginning with the invasion of Alaric, Biondo traces the
history of Italy up to his own times : his work was cut short by his
death, and extends only to the date 1440. He divided it into decades,
after the example of Livy. His work is excellent in arrangement,
in largeness of view, and in diligent research. He writes like a true
student seeking for light in dark places. We are, however, concerned only with the period of Eugenius IV., whose flight from
Rome in 1434 he describes with masterly vividness. Of the entire
history of Italy during this period he gives a careful sketch. Biondo
shows us the passion for knowledge of the humanists before their
attention had been devoted primarily to style. But the desire for
style had begun to prevail before his death ; Pius II. made an
epitome of the *Decades* so as to make them more popular, and speaks
of Biondo's book as 'opus laboriosum et utile, verum expolitore
emendatoreque dignum' (*Com.* xi.)

3. Sigismund in Italy.

Besides the general authorities above quoted and those which
especially deal with Sigismund, such as WINDECK, we have some
special sources of information. The learned Sienese, PIETRO ROSSI,
in his Chronicle in MURATORI, xx. 40, &c., gives a detailed account
of Sigismund's sojourn in Siena. To this period of Sigismund's
history is to be referred the famous novel of ÆNEAS SYLVIUS, *Lucretiæ
et Euryali Amores*, which is founded upon a love story of Kaspar
Schlick, Sigismund's chancellor. Schlick supplied Æneas with the
outlines, which he worked up into a tale, and contributed the details

of Sienese life with which it is coloured. A description of Sigismund's coronation is given by POGGIO in a letter to Niccoli in
BALUZE, *Miscellanea*, iii. 183 (ed. Luca). From the German side
the fullest account, except that of Windeck, is given by CORNELIUS
ZANTFLIET in his *Chronicon*, in MARTÈNE and DURAND, *Amplissima
Collectio*, vol. v. Zantfliet was a monk of S. Jacob at Liège: his
chronicle extends to the year 1461, when he probably died. We do
not know the sources from which he gained his information; but
concerning Sigismund in Italy, he seems to have had especially
accurate accounts, and gives details which are not to be found'elsewhere.

For Sigismund's relations with the Council during this period we
have several of his letters in MANSI, xxix., in MARTÈNE, *Amplissima
Collectio*, vol. viii., also in JOHN OF SEGOVIA. Much interesting
information is given by KLUCKHOHN in an article on *Herzog
Wilhelm III. von Bayern* in *Forschungen zur Deutschen Geschichte*,
vol. ii. (1862), 521. The article contains the results of the writer's
research into the letters of William of Bavaria, who represented
Sigismund at Basel, addressed partly to Sigismund, partly to his own
brother in Bavaria. They are preserved in the Reichs Archiv at
Munich.

4. For Italian politics at the end of the pontificate of Eugenius IV. we have the remarkable Life of Filippo Maria Visconti,
by PIERO DECEMBRIO CANDIDO, in MURATORI, xx. 986, &c. Piero's
father was secretary to Giovanni Maria Visconti, and he himself was
born in 1399. He was a famous scholar, and served first the Duke of
Milan, afterwards Nicolas V., and finally Alfonso of Naples. His Life
of Filippo Maria is one of the most notable biographies of the period,
and shows the power of delineating character, and the careful appreciation of individuality, which existed amongst the early humanists.
We are tempted sometimes to think that Piero has exaggerated
slight traits in his desire to produce a finished picture of a typical
Italian despot. His Life of Francesco Sforza in MURATORI, xx. 1024,
is more brief, and as 't treats of a living personage is more guarded;
but the description of Sforza's entering into Milan is vivid and
powerful.

More important for the life of Francesco Sforza is *Res gestæ
Francisi Sfortiæ*, by GIOVANNI SIMONETA, in MURATORI, xxi. 179.
Simoneta was Sforza's secretary, and from the year 1444 to his death
in 1466 was constantly in his service. He conducted many negotiations for his master, and State papers passed through his hands, so
that he is an authority of the highest importance for the relations
between Sforza and the Popes.

For the war between Sforza and Venice we have also *Commentarii
Jacobi Piccinini* of PIERO PORCELLIO, in MURATORI, xx. 69, &c., continued in MURATORI, xxv. 1, &c. Porcellio was the envoy of Alfonso

of Naples to Venice, and during the interregnum after the death of Filippo Maria Visconti he was in the camp of Piccinino and informed Alfonso of events as they passed. He afterwards reduced his impressions to a definite form in his Commentaries, which cover the years 1451–1453. Porcellio writes a somewhat inflated panegyric on his hero, and has not much real historical insight. More valuable is the *Vita di Niccolo Piccinino*, by PIERO DECEMBICO CANDIDO, in MURATORI, xx. 1051; it was written as a funeral oration on Niccolo's death in 1444, and gives a brief sketch of his life and exploits in a laudatory strain.

A modern work which gathers much information about the condottieri of Italy is RICOTTI, *Storia delle Compagnie di Ventura in Italia* (1845).

A work which covers much of the history of the Papal States is *Cronica de' Principali Fatti d'Italia dal anno* 1417 *al* 1468, by NICCOLO DELLA TUCCIA, edited by Orioli, Rome, 1852. Tuccia was a merchant of Viterbo, born in 1400, who wrote also a chronicle of Viterbo, besides this general record of Italian affairs. For the pontificates of Eugenius IV. and Nicolas V. his sketch is full and accurate; for the later period he becomes more annalistic.

---

11. *The Council of Basel.*

The Acts of the Council, and a number of documents relating to it, are given in MANSI, *Consilia*, vols. xxix.–xxxi. For this period Mansi's collection is particularly rich. The greater part of vol. viii. of MARTÈNE and DURAND, *Amplissima Collectio*, is also devoted to letters and documents dealing with this subject. The Acts of the Council of Basel were largely circulated, and the Council produced its own historiographer in John of Segovia, whose vast collection of documents remained at Basel. It was used by AUGUSTINUS PATRICIUS, a canon of Siena, who, in 1480, wrote a *Summa Concilii Basiliensis* at the request of Cardinal Piccolomini. He says about the MS. of John of Segovia: 'Hos quidem codices ipsi Basileæ vidimus, magna diligentia ut Sibyllarum libros a civibus servatos; quorum exemplum a Reverendissimo Domino Cardinali Sancti Marci, rerum ecclesiasticarum diligentissimo perscrutatore, nuper habuimus.' He cannot, however, have had a transcript of all John of Segovia's MS., but at best an abstract. He had, however, other sources of information: 'Habui et primam hujus synodi partem collectam a piæ memoriæ Dominico Cardinale Firmano qui tamdiu Concilio interfuit, quamdiu mansit concordia cum Eugenio Pontifice.' Besides this use of Capranica's papers by Patricius, they were also used by MICHAEL CATALANUS, *De Vita et Scriptis Dominici Capranicæ*, Firmi, 1793. The use of these authorities gave the work of Patricius great weight; it is published in SCHANNAT and HARTZHEIM, *Concilia Germaniæ*, vol. v. 774, &c.

But the work of Patricius has been thrown into the shade by the publication of JOHN OF SEGOVIA'S *Gesta sacrosanctæ synodi generalis Basiliensis* in *Monumenta Conciliorum generalium sæculi decimi quinti*, vol. ii. (Vienna, 1873.) Unfortunately only the first part of this vast collection has yet appeared; but it covers the most interesting part of the Council's activity, up to the departure of Cesarini at the end of 1437. John of Segovia, as his name shows, was a Spaniard, a learned canonist, one of the first who came to the Council, and one of the last who left it. His history contains the decrees and many of the letters of the Council, which his position enabled him easily to procure. He was one of the leading members of the assembly, thoroughly convinced of the rightfulness of the Council's position, and a firm adherent of the conciliar principle. He was, however, a wise and moderate man, averse from extreme measures, and dragged against his will to follow the lead of the Cardinal d'Allemand. He was one of the Cardinals of Felix V., and after the dissolution of the Council returned quietly to a small bishopric in Spain, to which Nicolas V. appointed him. His work is devoid of style, and is the production of a canonist rather than a historian, but it is a careful collection of documents and an accurate statement of facts. We can only regret the absence of picturesque details, and the exclusively theological nature of the judgments which it contains. John of Segovia is only interested in tracing the development of the conciliar principle, which he does in an abstract manner. Yet his work remains as the most complete account of the Council's activity as a whole.

What is wanting in John of Segovia is partly supplied by ÆNEAS SYLVIUS PICCOLOMINI, who projected an entire history of the Council, of which we have only the beginning in a letter describing Basel, printed at the end of URSTISIUS, *Historiæ Basiliensis Epitome*. We possess, however, two works of his concerning the Council—(1.) *Commentarii de Gestis Basiliensis Concilii*, which is printed in all the editions of his works. This is, however, a fragment; it begins with the Diet of Nürnberg in 1438, and reaches to the election of Felix V. in 1439; it was probably written soon after the events it describes. It has a strong theological aspect, and gives at length the arguments of the Council in favour of its final proceedings against the Pope. As an appendix is a letter of Æneas to John of Segovia, describing the coronation of Felix V. (2.) More important is his second work, *De Rebus Basiliæ Gestis Commentarius*, dedicated to Cardinal Carvajal, written probably in 1451, when the Council of Basel was a thing of the past. In this Æneas writes as a historian and gives a philosophical survey of the causes of the conciliar movement and its failure. He looks at the Council in the light of his own after-experiences, and so takes a clear and decided view of its revolutionary character and its unfounded pretensions. The great merit of the book is its clear and incisive judgments of character. The step from John of Segovia to Æneas Sylvius is from the mediæval to the modern world. The one deals with abstract ideas, the other with definite personalities; one is obscure and involved in style, the other writes with epigrammatic terseness in every sentence. This interesting work is only to be found in FEA, *Pius II. a calumniis vindicatus*, Rome, 1822.

Another work of Æneas Sylvius, in defence of the Council of Basel, is the *Libellus Dialogorum de generalis Concilii authoritate et Gestis Basiliensium* in KOLLAR, *Analecta Vindobonensia*, ii. 685. These dialogues are written in the style of Cicero's Tusculans, and are a masterpiece of elegant style in dressing up the arguments in favour of the conciliar principles in an attractive manner, and enlivening the tedium by appropriate digressions. They show Æneas bidding for the Council's favour by his power of fine writing. He is dazzling the theologians by showing them what a scholar can do.

The letters of Æneas Sylvius, written from Basel, contain incidental notices of the Council, especially one of May 20, 1437, in MANSI, xxxi. 220.

The history of the beginning of the Council of Basel, and of its relation with the Councils of Constance and Siena, is given by JOHN OF RAGUSA, *Initium et Prosecutio Basiliensis Concilii* in *Mon. Conciliorum*, i. 1, &c. It extends only to October 1431, the period in which John represented Cesarini.

If John of Segovia writes from the conciliar point of view, and Æneas Sylvius somewhat as an indifferentist, we have the Italian opinion in the letters of AMBROGIO TRAVERSARI, the learned general of the Camaldulensians, who was the envoy of Eugenius IV. to Basel in 1435, and afterwards to Sigismund in 1436. These letters have been edited by MEHUS (1759), whose Life of Traversari is a mine of information about the literary history of the time. The letters of Traversari to Eugenius IV., to Sigismund, and to Cesarini are especially valuable. It was largely owing to Traversari's arguments and to his mediation that Cesarini was reconciled to the Pope, and his letters enable us to see the motives which weighed with Italian Churchmen. They show the general feeling of the Council, and give many details about its chief members. Traversari was also an active member of the Council of Florence, and tells us much about the Greeks, especially Bessarion. He died soon after the end of the Council of Florence in October, 1439. VESPASIANO DA BISTICCI has written a short life of him.

For Cesarini we have, besides other authorities, a most attractive life by VESPASIANO DA BISTICCI, which gives us a clear picture of his gentleness and tact as well as his sterling worth. The eulogium of POGGIO pronounced on Cesarini's death also contains some information about him.

Other details about the Council are to be found in the *Formicarius* of JOHANNES NIDER, a Dominican prior of Basel, who was employed in the negotiations with the Bohemians, and died in 1438. The *Formicarius* is a parable of the Christian life founded on the example of the ant; it gives many details of the religious life of the time, with incidental references to passing events.

12. *The Council of Basel and the Hussites.*

The labours of Herr Palacky and the munificence of the Austrian Government have made public a series of relations which enable us to follow in detail the proceedings of the Council with the Bohemians. These interesting works are printed in vol. i. of the *Monumenta Conciliorum sæculi decemiquinti*, and are written by members of the Council who took a leading part in the events which they record.

(1.) JOHN STOJCOVIK OF RAGUSA has already been mentioned as an envoy of the University of Paris to urge the assembling of the Council, and as acting as Cesarini's representative at the opening. We have seen him taking a chief part in the disputation with the Bohemians at Basel in 1433. In 1435 he was sent by the Council to Constantinople to arrange matters with the Greeks; this proved a difficult task, and he remained at Constantinople till the beginning of 1438. In the same year he was sent to confer with the new King of the Romans, Albert of Austria, whom he found at the siege of Tabor. He entered the service of Felix V., and was by him made Cardinal, under the title of S. Sixtus, and died in 1444. He was staunch in his allegiance to the Council, but by an error he has been confounded with another John, ' ἀνὴρ φιλόσοφος τῶν Λατίνων,' ' provincialis Lombardiæ,' who was a disputant against Mark of Ephesus in the Council of Florence. It is impossible that John of Ragusa should have quitted Basel for Florence and have again returned to Basel. Echard, *Scriptores ordinis Prædicatorum*, identifies the orator at Florence with John of Montenegro, provincial of the Dominicans in Tuscany. The *Tractatus quomodo Bohemi reducti sunt ad unitatem ecclesiæ*, in *Mon. Concil.* i. 1358, begins with the first negotiations of the Council with the Bohemians at the end of 1431, and gives all the documents relating to the preliminaries, and an account of the Conference till the end of February 1433, when it abruptly ends. The relation of John of Ragusa to the Council concerning his Greek embassy is printed by CECCONI, *Studi Storici*, No. clxxviii.

(2.) Still more important is the *Liber Diurnus* of PETER OF SAAZ, *Mon. Concil.* i. 289. Peter of Saaz was one of the Hussite representatives, and his journal covers the period of the presence of the Hussites in Basel in 1433. Besides its historical value, it throws much light on the feelings and opinions of the different sections of the Bohemians.

(3.) GILES CARLIER, dean of Cambray, one of the scholars of Gerson and D'Ailly at the University of Paris, went to the Council of Basel as the representative of his bishop. He was a famous theologian, and was one of the four disputants chosen by the Council to answer the Bohemians. He was one of the envoys who accompanied the Bohemians to Prag in April 1433; he was also sent to Regensburg to meet Sigismund and the Bohemians in August 1434, and again to the Diet of Brünn in 1435. Soon after this he saw the troubles impending over the Council, and judged it wisest to return to his Cathedral of Cambray early in 1436. His *Liber de Legationibus Concilii Basiliensis pro reductione Bohemorum*, in *Mon. Concil.* 361, gives an account of the three embassies in which he was engaged, as well as the second embassy to Prag in September 1433, in which he did not take part.

(4.) THOMAS EBERNDORFER OF HASELBACH was a leading member of the University of Vienna, who came to Basel as the University's representative in 1432 and stayed there till 1435, when he was bound to return, because he had taken an oath to the University that he would never consent to grant the Hussites the Communion under both kinds. He was, however, present, at Sigismund's request, at the Diet of Iglau in 1436. His *Diarium* in *Mon. Concil.* i. 703, &c., covers the period from 1433 to 1436, and is especially valuable for the Diet of Iglau. Eberndorfer took part in several of the diets held later on, and laboured to make peace between the Council and Eugenius IV. He was at first an adherent of the Council, but would not follow it in its bitter antagonism to the Pope. He was afterwards engaged in the stormy politics of Austria till his death in 1464. Eberndorfer was a considerable writer of history. His *Chronicon Austriacum*, in PEZ, *Scriptores Rerum Austriacarum*, ii. 689, is useful for the period of his own lifetime, though it is put together in the form of scattered notes rather than a consecutive history. He also wrote a *Liber Augustalis*, or history of the Emperors, and a *Chronicon Pontificum Romanorum*, which have not been printed; but Palacky, in his *Geschichte von Böhmen*, has made use of the MSS. and quotes passages from them.

(5.) The *Registrum* of JOHN OF TOURS in *Mon. Concil.* i. 782, reaches to the departure of Rokycana from Prag in June 1437. Of John we know little save that he was a notary who accompanied the Council's envoys to Bohemia.

13. *The Councils of Ferrara and Florence.*

The preliminary negotiations between the Greeks, the Pope, and the Council, tedious and unimportant as they may seem, are yet a most interesting record of diplomacy. Thanks to the diligence of a Florentine canon, CECCONI, *Studi Storici sul Concilio di Firenze,* Florence, 1869, we can study them at length. He has brought together and arranged the documents already printed, and has supplemented them largely from the Florentine and Vatican archives.

For the proceedings of the Council we have—

(1.) On the Latin side, the Acts of the Council first compiled from the Vatican archives in 1638, by Orazio Giustiniani, the Vatican librarian, and published in MANSI, *Concilia,* xxxi., and LABBE, *Concilia,* xiii. 825, &c. The important part of Giustiniani's collection is by ANDREA DE S. CROCE, a Roman, and pontifical advocate, whose work is thrown into the form of a dialogue between himself and Ludovico Pontano, a form which is not conducive to clearness of expression in a record of the sittings of a deliberative assembly.

(2.) On the side of the Greeks, who were in favour of the union, we have what is known as the *Acta Græca,* in MANSI and LABBE, as above. It is the work of a Greek who was present and who was well acquainted with everything that passed. It is principally engaged with an account of the disputes in the Council, and is evidently written from notes made at the time. It has no writer's name appended to it; but all critics are agreed that it must be the work either of Dorotheus, Archbishop of Mitylene, or of Bessarion. The evidence is purely internal, and the arguments on either side are put forward by Fromman, *Kritische Beiträge zur Geschichte der Florentiner Kircheneinigung,* 69, &c., who argues for Dorotheus, and by Vast, *Cardinal Bessarion,* Appendix I. I incline to think that Vast has made out a strong case in favour of Bessarion's authorship.

(3.) SYLVESTER SYROPULUS was a Greek ecclesiastic, who, under the title of μέγας ἐκκλησιάρχης καὶ δικαιοφύλαξ, went in attendance on the Patriarch Joseph. He wrote a history of the proceedings of the Greeks, to which he applies the title of 'Απομνημονεύματα. His work was first published from a MS. in Paris by Robert Creyghton, chaplain to Charles II., in 1660. It was issued under the title *Vera Historia Unionis non veræ;* but the Latin translation which accompanies it is by no means to be trusted. The work of Syropulus is most interesting; for he tells us not so much the sessions of the Council as the private doings of its members, the dissensions among the Greeks, the persistency of Bessarion, and the pressure used by the Emperor. Syropulus signed the decree of the Council in favour of union, unwillingly, but afterwards repented, and wrote his History as a kind of retractation.

The theological points raised by the Council of Florence are many and interesting, and I have been reluctantly compelled to pass them by. The historical importance of the union entirely dwarfed its theological aspect, and it was the result of necessity, not of conviction. The whole aspect of the relations between the Eastern and Western Churches is drawn out with care and impartiality by PICHLER, *Geschichte der Kirchlichen Trennung zwischen dem Orient und Occident*, Munich, 1864. From the Papal point of view the history of the Council has been fairly set forth by HEFELE, *Concilien Geschichte*; from the point of view of the Greek Church by an anonymous Russian writer (Professor Gorski in Moscow), whose work has been translated into English, *History of the Council of Florence*, by BASIL POPOFF, edited by NEALE (London, 1861); and finally a German Protestant has dealt critically with the authorities, FROMMAN, *Kritische Beiträge zur Geschichte der Florentiner Kircheneinigung* (Halle, 1872). The real question in dispute is whether Syropulus or the *Acta Græca* is to be regarded as the record of what happened. There were clearly two parties amongst the Greeks from the beginning, and these two authorities express their different views. As a matter of history, it is not difficult to combine them; as a theological question affecting the proceedings of a general Council, there are greater difficulties. Added to the other difficulties in the way of arriving at the exact facts, we must remember that the Greeks and Latins knew little of one another's language, which must have hindered an understanding on small points of discussion.

Even concerning the Union-decree itself many curious questions have arisen. Syropulus tells us that there were five original copies, signed by the Greeks; but the Protosyncellus Gregorius signed only the first on July 5, and refused to sign the others, which were submitted on July 20. The Pope was anxious to have several copies of the decree to circulate as widely as possible. Many more than five were current. BRÉQUIGNY, in vol. xliii. of *Mémoires de l'Academie de Belles Lettres de Paris* (1786), mentions ten copies, but none of them was the original. VESPASIANO DA BISTICCI, in his *Life of Cesarini*, says that Cesarini was entrusted with the superintendence of the decree; wishing to keep the original at Florence in the Palazzo dei Signori, he consequently only gave copies to others. This original decree, with the signature of Gregorius, in the box in which Cesarini put it, is preserved in the Laurentian Library of Florence; it has been published by MILANESI in *Archivio Storico Italiano*, vol. vi. Nuova Serie (1857), p. 219.

The account of the reception of the union by the Greeks is given by GEORGE PHRANTZES, *Chronicon Majus*, bk. ii., in MIGNE'S *Patrologia*, clvi.

14. *The Ecclesiastical Policy of France and Germany.*

The Pragmatic Sanction of Bourges is given in full in the *Ordon-nances des Rois des France de la troisième Race,* vol. xiii. 267. Many documents concerning it are in PINSON, *Caroli Septemi Pragmatica Sanctio* (Paris, 1666); also *Traitez des Droits et Libertez de l'Eglise Gallicane.*

For German affairs the documents are to be found in MÜLLER'S *Reichstagstheatrum unter Keyser Friedrich V.* (1713); KOCH, *Sanctio Pragmatica Germanorum* (1789); MÜNCH'S *Sammlung aller ältern und neuern Konkordate*; LEIBNITZ, *Mantissa Codicis Juris Gentium diplomatici*; WÜRDTWEIN, *Subsidia Diplomatica*, viii. ix.; BRAUN, *Notitia Historica,* vol. vi.

Besides these are the documents more immediately relating to Frederick III., in CHMEL'S *Materialien zur österreichischen Geschichte*; CHMEL'S *Regesten des Friedrich III.*; CHMEL, *Zur Kritik der österreichischen Geschichte* (1850–51); CHMEL'S *Literarische Reise* (1851). CHMEL has also written *Geschichte Kaiser Friedrich IV.*, which unfortunately reaches only to the year 1452.

We have need to hold fast by all the documentary evidence which we can obtain in order to check the narrative of ÆNEAS SYLVIUS, who is an excellent representative of the dangerous facility of a man of letters writing the history of things in which he himself took part. Valuable as are the writings of Æneas, we have always to allow for the strong personal element which they contain. No doubt Æneas tells us how things looked to him ; but it is necessary to look beyond his narrative for the forces which were at work. The accounts of Æneas are to be found in his Commentaries in FEA, and his other Commentaries edited by GOBELINUS, in his *Historia Frederici,* of which the only complete edition is that of KOLLAR, *Analecta Vindo-bonensia,* ii. 2, &c., and in his letters, the chronological arrangement of which has been determined by VOIGT, in *Archiv für Kunde öster-reichischer Geschichts-Quellen,* xvi. 323, where some are given that have not been previously published. There is a valuable criticism by BAYER, *Die Historia Frederici III. Imperatoris des Æneas Silvio di Piccolomini* (Prag, 1872).

The work, however, which guides us through the complications of German ecclesiastical policy in this period is PÜCKERT, *Die Kur-fürstliche Neutralität während des Basler Concils* (Leipzig, 1858). Pückert has used as his material the papers in the Dresden archives, consisting of instructions to ambassadors, correspondence, and drafts of negotiations, drawn up during the period of the prevalence of the oligarchical policy, between 1438 and 1448. He has disregarded Æneas Sylvius, and gives us the diplomacy without the picturesque details.

For a more general view of this period, DROYSSEN'S *Geschichte Preussens Politik*, vols. i. and ii., is excellent.

---

15. *Nicolas V.*

(1.) For Nicolas V. we are lucky in possessing the Life written by GIANOZZO MANETTI in MURATORI, iii. pt. ii. 907. Manetti, as the Pope's secretary, who was employed in literary work, had ample opportunities of seeing and estimating the activity of the Pope, which he celebrates in a tone of ardent eulogy. Yet Manetti is given to bombast, and strives to lend an air of miraculous greatness to his subject. The value of Manetti's Life is not so much political as literary and artistic. He gives accurate details of the buildings contemplated and erected by Nicolas V., of his work in gathering MSS., of the treasures of every sort which he collected. For this reason his book is a storehouse of information for the architectural and artistic history of the early Renaissance. The 'Testamentum Nicolai V.,' which forms the third book of his Life, can hardly be regarded as strictly historical. No doubt Nicolas V. addressed his cardinals, and no doubt he said something of the sort which Manetti attributes to him; but we are not to take this *testamentum* as a literal account of the Pope's last words. ' Hæc et alia quædam hujus modi *memoriter* peroravit,' says Manetti. His speech is to be regarded as a speech of Thucydides—it graphically expresses the tendencies and aims of the life of Nicolas V., but it is not to be taken as his own view of himself.

The Life of PLATINA is a tolerable compendium of events, but is marked by no special merit.

The Life by VESPASIANO DA BISTICCI is one of Vespasiano's best and happiest. He knew Nicolas V. as a book collector in his days of poverty, and the sympathy of a common taste connected the two men. Vespasiano's account of his interview with Nicolas V. after his accession to the Pontificate is a piece of life-like description.

Besides these we have a valuable authority for Nicolas V. in GEORGIO, *Vita Nicolai Quinti* (Rome, 1742). Georgio was chaplain to Pope Benedict XIV., and had access to the Vatican archives, which he used in compiling his work.

For the early life of Nicolas V. we have much information in ÆNEAS SYLVIUS PICCOLOMINI, *Commentarius*, ed. FEA. The circumstances of the death of Eugenius IV. and the election of Nicolas V. are related at length by Æneas in a *relatio* to Frederick III., printed by MURATORI, iii. pt. ii. 878, &c.

(2) For German affairs we have ÆNEAS SYLVIUS, *Vita Frederici III.*, with the same authorities to check it as have been mentioned before. Interesting, however, are the brief remarks of MATTHIAS DÖRING, the continuator of the chronicle of Engelhus, in

MENCKEN, *Rerum Germanicarum Scriptores*, iii. 1, &c. Döring was a Franciscan professor of theology at Erfurt and minister of Kiritz in Saxony; his share of the continuation of Engelhus seems to extend from 1420–1464. He is chiefly concerned with the affairs of Saxony and Brandenburg; but his pronounced personality makes him speak out, and his opinions on matters of ecclesiastical as well as general politics show us the tone of independent German feeling. Thus of the year of jubilee he says, 'Magnus populus Romam visitavit propter spem vanam absolucionis sine restitucione injuste detentorum et ablatorum.' He calls Frederick 'Rex Romanorum, verius Judæorum.' Of his conduct towards the crusade he says, 'In his omnibus Imperator Fredericus Australis sedit in domo, plantans ortos et capiens aviculas ignavus.' These are but samples of the flashes of suppressed scorn which illumine Döring's pages.

For the activity of Fra Capistrano in Hungary we have several letters of his and of his followers in WADDING, *Annales Fratrum Minorum*, vol. vi., especially the letters of Giovanni da Tagliacozzo and Nicola de Fara, who tell of Capistrano's death; but they magnify his acts with a view to his canonisation.

For Frederick III.'s coronation ÆNEAS SYLVIUS' *Historia Frederici* is almost a journal of events. We have also *Desponsatio et Coronatio Frederici Imperatoris tertii*, by NICOLAS LANCKMAN VON FALKENSTEIN, one of Frederick's envoys to Portugal, who accompanied Leonora, and gives a diary of the diplomatic and ceremonial proceedings in which he was engaged. It is printed in PEZ, *Rerum Austriacarum Scriptores*, ii. 572, &c. CHMEL, *Regesta Fredrici III.*, i. Anhang, publishes a *Descriptio introitus Im. Frederici III.* by GOSWIN MANDOCTES, who calls himself 'cantor in capella papæ,' and was an eyewitness.

Further materials for German affairs are given by ÆNEAS SYLVIUS, *Oratio adversus Australes*, in MANSI, *Pii II. Orationes*, i. 184. Mansi also publishes a work of Æneas Sylvius, *De Ratisbonensi Dieta*, iii. 1, &c. The crusading zeal of the Duke of Burgundy is narrated by MATTHIEU DE COUSSY (ed. Buchon), the excellent continuator of Monstrelet.

(3). The conspiracy of Stefano Porcaro is an interesting episode in the history of the city of Rome, and as such excited considerable attention. The authorities are INFESSURA, *Diarium*, in MURATORI, iii. pt. ii. 1134, who gives a brief account of affairs as he had gathered them; he is full of the Roman spirit, and calls Porcaro 'uomo di bene ed amatore della sua patria.' More important is the account by the great architect, LEO BATTISTA ALBERTI, *De Conjuratione Porcaria*, in MURATORI, xxv. 293. Alberti, as an aristocrat and a friend of Nicolas V., regards with horror this attempt against the Pope, and has no interest in the Roman side of the question. An interesting work has recently been published by PERLBACH, *Petri de Godis,*

Dyalogon de Conjuratione Porcaria (1879). Piero de Godi was a native of Vicenza, apparently a curial, as his Dialogue, written at the time, is full of admiration of the Pope and detestation of Porcaro. It contains much information about Roman affairs. Still more important is TOMMASINI, *Documenti relativi a Stefano Porcari* (Rome, 1879), who publishes a letter from a Florentine resident in Rome, which was clearly the basis of the account given by MACHIAVELLI in his *Storia Fiorentina*, and is a plain account given by an observer of events. Tommasini also publishes *Conformatio Curie Romane loquentis edita per Joseph B.* (probably Giuseppe Bripio, a learned Milanese in the employment of Nicolas V.). This is a poem celebrating the deliverance of Nicolas V.; its importance has already been noticed by Ranke, *Die Römische Päpste*, Anhang i., but it is now published entire, and enables us to compare the views of another writer with those of Manetti on the greatness of the works of Nicolas V.

---

16. *Calixtus III.*

It was natural that a man like Calixtus III., succeeding one like Nicolas V., should meet with small affection from men of letters. After the copious materials for Nicolas V. we have little about Calixtus III. His Life, by PLATINA, is short and almost contemptuous, yet does full justice to the excellent intentions of the Pope, and his blameless private life, save as regards nepotism. The Life of Capranica, by POGGIO, in Baluze, *Miscellanea*, iii. 263, gives us some information of the feeling of the Cardinals. We have also the letters of ÆNEAS SYLVIUS, and the mention in his *Commentaries*, ed. GOBELINUS. For Germany the authorities remain the same. For the crusading projects of Calixtus III. we have the documents in WADDING, vi., and many mentions in SANUDO, *Vite dei Duchi di Venezia*, in MURATORI, xxii. 1158, &c.; also documents in THEINER, *Monumenta Hungariam sacram illustrantia*, vol. ii.; and in D'ACHERY, *Spicilegium*, iii. A somewhat inflated account is given by LEODORISUS CRUVELLI, *De Expeditione Pii II. in Turcas*, in MURATORI, xxiii. 21, &c.

Pius II.

For the Pontificate of Pius II. we are exceptionally well supplied with materials, of which the most important are the *Commentarii Pii II.*, which are supplemented by the *Cardinalis Papiensis Commentarii* in the Frankfort edition of 1614. Ammannati begins his Commentaries with the Crusade of Pius II., and so takes up the story where Pius ceases. Besides these we have *Vita Pii II.*, by his friend CAMPANO, in MURATORI, iii. part ii. 969; and also his Life

by his secretary, PLATINA. Campano writes in the humanistic
strain, somewhat as a discreet panegyrist of one whom he feels to be
unpopular with his readers. Platina, on the other hand,.looks back
upon the days of Pius II. as golden in comparison with those of
Paul II., and writes with genuine affection and respect. It is
customary to speak in terms of high praise of the biography of Campano; but I find it laboured, and though it contains many intimate
details, yet it has little real power of characterisation and is badly
put together. The Life by Platina, on the other hand, is by far his best
work, and though to some extent founded upon Campanus, it is full
of individual appreciation of an extremely attractive man.

Besides these Lives, the letters of AMMANNATI, following the *Commentarii* in the Frankfort edition of 1614, as well as the letters of
CAMPANO, and FILELFO, tell us much of Pius II. in his personal and
literary character.

For Italian affairs under Pius II. we have, as of special value,
SIMONETA, *De Rebus gestis Francisci Sfortiæ*, in Muratori, xxi.
Simoneta's account of the relations of Sforza and the Pope regarding
Neapolitan affairs gives us Sforza's view, while Pius II. in his Commentaries tells his own. It is interesting to compare the two, and
the comparison affords material for appreciating Pius II.'s estimate of
his own doings. For the Neapolitan wars we have JOVIANUS PON-
TANUS, *De Bello Neapolitano*. Pontano was a literary favourite of
Ferrante, and was present with him in several expeditions during
the campaign. Pontano was a highly gifted-man, a poet, an as-
tronomer, and a philosopher, as well as a historian; but his chief
claim to glory will not rest on his historical merits. His book aims
at imitating Livy, and is neither good for military nor political history,
but confuses, in an attempt after the graces of style, the accounts
even of things which he himself saw. COSTANZO has used Pontano,
and supplemented him from other sources.

For a brief account of Pius II. in relation to Siena we have
Fragmentum Historiæ Senensis, by FRANCESCO TOMMASIO, in MURATORI,
xx. 55. For the wars of Federigo of Montefeltro, and Piccinino
we have the *Chronicon Eugubinum* of GUERNIER DE BERNI, in
MURATORI, xxi. 923. This chronicle deals with events, as seen at
Gubbio, from 1350 to 1472. Berni served under Federigo, and
dedicates his book to him; his avowed object is to contrast the
miserable state of Gubbio from internal dissensions in former times
with the happiness and glory which it enjoys under the rule of the
Montefeltri. Federigo of Urbino has two historians, who date from
the middle of the sixteenth century—GIROLAMO MUZIO and BERNAR-
DINO BALDI, who both used documents preserved at Urbino. The
only English book that deals with any thoroughness with Italian
history of the period which I have traversed is DENISTOUN's *History
of the Duke of Urbino* (1851).

There are many incidental mentions in SANUDO, *Vite de' Duchi di Venezia*, in MURATORI, xxii., a work founded on a knowledge of Venetian documents. Still more important are the *Annali Veneti* of DOMENICO MALIPIERO, published in vol. vii. of the first series of the *Archivio Storico Italiano*. These annals cover the period from 1457 to 1500, and are written with the care which distinguishes the Venetian writers of this and the following century. Malipiero was born in 1428 and died in 1515; he took part in the conduct of Venetian affairs, and had access to documents which he has incorporated in his work. The Annali are divided into two parts, 'Delle Guerre coi Turchi,' and 'Delle Guerre d'Italia.' The first part enables us to judge of the crusading schemes of Pius II.

For the proceedings of the Congress of Mantua we have a brief narrative from NICOLAS PETIT, a French ambassador, in D'ACHERY, *Spicilegium*, vol. ii. 806, where are also some other documents relating to the Congress. Other accounts of the Congress and the subsequent proceedings of the Duke of Burgundy in relation to the crusade are given by the two excellent Burgundian contemporary chroniclers, MATTHIEU DE COUSSY and JACQUES DU CLERCQ (ed. Buchon). They also tell us much of the dealings of Pius II. with Louis XI. The documents relating to the Pragmatic Sanction are to be found in *Preuves des Libertés de l'Eglise Gallicane*.

For Pius II. and Germany we have the authorities already mentioned for Frederick III., with a number of other sources of information about points of detail. For the strife of Nicolas of Cusa and Sigismund of the Tyrol we have the results of a diligent investigation amongst the archives of the bishopric of Brixen, preserved at Innsbruck, in a lengthy work by JÄGER, *Der Streit des Cardinals Nicolaus von Cusa mit dem Herzoge Sigmund von Osterreich als Grafen von Tirol* (Innsbruck, 1866.) The interesting controversy with Heimburg is given in GOLDAST, *Monarchia*, ii. 1587, &c., and in FREHER, *Germanicarum Rerum Scriptores*, ii. 120, &c. A work which deals with Heimburg in detail is BROCKHAUS, *Gregor von Heimburg*, Leipzig, 1861, which has, however, the qualities of a biography rather than a history. For the dealings of Pius II. with the Archbishopric of Mainz we have a narrative by a citizen of Mainz, *Nachricht von der Unterjochung der Stadt Mainz*, published by BODMANN, in vols. iv. and v. of the *Rheinisches Archiv* (1811.)

For Bohemian affairs we have important sources of information in PALACKY, *Urkundliche Beiträge zur Geschichte Böhmens in Zeitalter Georg's von Podrebrad*, forming vol. xx. of *Fontes Rerum Austriacarum*. Most valuable is the *Historia Wratislaviensis* of PETER ESCHENLOER, edited by MARKGRAF, in vol. vii. of *Scriptores Rerum Silesiacarum*. Eschenloer was a native of Nürnberg, who came as town clerk to Breslau in 1455, and died in 1481. His history extends from 1457 to 1471, but after the year 1468 becomes annalistic, as though his interest were gone. About the relation of the Latin version of Eschenloer to a German version published by KUNISCH in 1827 I must refer to Markgraf's preface and LORENZ, *Deutschland's Geschichtsquellen*, ii. 234. As a supplement to Eschenloer, MARKGRAF has also published *Politische Correspondenz Breslau's*, 1454–1463, vol. viii. of *Scriptores Rerum Silesiacarum*. It contains several reports and letters of Fantinus, the Papal envoy in Bohemia. The entire period of the Catholic reaction in Bohemia is largely illustrated by KLOSE, *Documentirte Geschichte und Beschreibung von Breslau* (1780), of which vol. iii. is full of valuable information respecting the attitude of the Catholics towards King George. For this period of Bohemian history, besides PALACKY's *Geschichte Böhmens*, we have an excellent work by JORDAN, *Das Königthum Georg's von Podebrad*, Leipzig, 1861, which treats especially of the ecclesiastical side of George's political position.

For the whole period comprised by the Life of Pius II., I am under great obligations to VOIGT, *Ænea Silvio de' Piccolomini als Papst Pius der Zweite, und sein Zeitalter*, Berlin, 1856–63.

INDEX.

END OF THE SECOND VOLUME.